VINTNER'S CHOICE

Hilde Gabriel Lee

1⊛

Ten Speed Press

Ten Speed Press
Post Office Box 7123
Berkeley, California 94707

First Edition

Cover and interior designed by Fifth Street Design, Berkeley, California

Interior illustrations by Pamela Poole

Typography by Fifth Street Design, Berkeley, California

Library of Congress Cataloging-in-Publication Data

Lee, Hilde Gabriel
Vintner's Choice.

Includes index.
1.   Wine and wine making — California.
2.   Cookery (Wine)   I. Title.
TP557.L44   1986   641.2'2'09794   86-6037

ISBN 0-89815-173-2

Manufactured in the United States of America

86   87   88   89   90   —   5   4   3   2   1

Table of Contents

Preface

After several years of visiting wineries and tasting wines throughout California, my husband and I found ourselves returning time after time to the small family wineries. Not only did we find them charming in themselves, but we found ourselves appreciating their wines, frequently handcrafted the old fashioned way. We are not and do not pretend to be wine connoisseurs, but over the years we have enjoyed the wines of these family wineries and appreciated their comments about food so much that we wanted to share our experience with others.

What better way to experience an adventure in good food and fine wines than to share the recipes of the vintners who produce fine quality wines and to learn something about these individuals. They express their individuality through their wines. In this book I have focused on the stories of the small family vintners of California and on their family recipes.

I found that people who have a palate for premium wines and can produce them also have an appreciation for good food as a complement to wine. They have interesting recipes to share, and the career paths that lead them to become vintners make for fascinating stories. The result of this premise and research is this book.

I consider myself a writer about food and wine and am neither a connoisseur of wines nor an expert on food — although I have 30 years of cooking and food writing experience. (My culinary training was from an excellent teacher — my grandmother, who was one of the foremost caterers in Germany.) In my writing, I try to bring information to the public without letting my own prejudices interfere, for that is the job of the food and wine critic.

For many years I wrote a food column in a newspaper in Virginia and Tennessee, where I grew up after emigrating from Germany. The experience of writing the column gave me an insight into the food preferences of the people of a local area. It also made me sensitive to how precious an individual recipe can be, not only to the cook of the family, but to all members. I also became fascinated with how creative family cooks can be, and with people themselves. It was these same fascinations that were rekindled as I came to know the family vintners of California, hence the inspiration for this book.

Vintner's Choice originally started only as a book of recipes from family wineries of California. It soon evolved to include their histories as well. The two, I felt, naturally went together. I discovered years ago that one cannot fully appreciate family recipes without also wanting to become acquainted with the people who contribute them. In developing the stories of the vintners, I found myself expanding the scope of the book a second time. The personal stories needed a context, causing me to explore the general history of the wine industry of California. Hence, a third segment of the book was born.

My criteria for selecting the 126 wineries who graciously participated in the book were fourfold. First and foremost, I wanted to focus on the small winery where the vintner was still actively involved in both the vineyard and the winery operation. For my purposes, this limited the size of the winery to those with production under 50,000 cases per year. The second criterion focused on the basic cookbook purpose of the book. The recipes provided by the vintners and their families had to fit in with the overall scheme of recipes I had in mind — duplicate and previously published recipes were eliminated. Third, I, along with my husband, had to have visited the winery, met with and interviewed the vintner and enjoyed his or her wines. Finally, there had to be an interesting story to tell concerning the vintner, his family, and the vineyard and winery.

I found that the wine industry is full of fascinating people all of whom have interesting stories. Unfortunately, I was unable to include all of the wineries who did contribute their recipes and their time. To them I apologize and express my hope that there will be another opportunity in the future to promote their accomplishments. There is an old saying in the South where I grew up: "I've never meet a nicer bunch of people." And that certainly applies to all members of the vintner families.

Many of the terms used in the wine industry are foreign to most of us. Therefore, I have included a glossary of terms, at least those terms used within this book, for the convenience of the reader. I have interviewed all of the vintners in this book and have seen them working in all phases of their winemaking activities. I have watched the punching down of the caps of their fermenting red wines; have interviewed vintners while they were filtering and blending various lots of wines; have had them show me how to riddle a bottle of champagne; tried to obtain a recipe while they operated a bottling line; and — best of all — attended their celebrations.

In the months that my husband and I visited the vintners we were treated most graciously and, on occasion, became part of their extended family. Words cannot express my thanks to all of the vintners who so graciously gave of their precious time to tell us about how they make wine, why they do it and what prompted them to become vintners. I also want to acknowledge the help given by the vintners' wives in developing the recipes. In my mind, they are the spirit that keeps the vintner family working as a unit.

My deep appreciation also goes to my husband, Allan, who so tirelessly gave of his time, energy and patience to help make this book informative. His research and draft material on the historical aspect and the trends of the wine industry provided invaluable additions to the book. He has also been a guiding spirit in my writing because of his many years of experience as a management consultant and business researcher.

It has been a great pleasure working with Pamela Poole, whose artistic drawings enhance the pages of this book. I want to express special thanks also to Mike Hamilton, whose advice and encouragement have been of great help, and to my editor, George Young, a special thanks for his patience.

May *Vintner's Choice* provide you not only with a great choice of recipes, but with a source of new and "choice" acquaintances among the fascinating individuals who make up the world of wine.

Hilde Gabriel Lee
June 1986

Introduction to Vintners

Grape growing and wine making is the common interest and bond that links this fascinating group of people, all from very different backgrounds. The small family vintners are, for the most part, full-time operators of their vineyards and wineries.

The backgrounds of family vintners runs the gamut. They include college professors, pilots, engineers, accountants, real estate entrepreneurs, people involved in the media, deep sea demolition experts, doctors, farmers, graphic artists, administrators, and a host of others. For example, Warren Winiarski, of Stag's Leap Wine Cellars, gave up teaching political science at the University of Chicago and apprenticed himself to the Robert Mondavi Winery so he could learn all facets of becoming a vintner before starting his own winery. David Coleman, of Adler Fels, was an industrial designer designing wine labels when he decided that he could make just as good a product as the wineries that were his clients. Almost every one of the vintners in this book has a fascinating background and unique reason for their career changes.

In the 1970s, when most of the family wineries included in this book were founded, there were basically three reasons for establishing a winery besides the universal desire to live in the country and have the more relaxed lifestyle that accompanies that atmosphere.

The first of these stems from a burning desire to make wine. Among the stories contained in this book, one can identify a group of vintners who, for one reason or another, took up home winemaking as a hobby. Frequently it was because their wives gave them a home winemaking kit. They joined or formed a club or association in which their amateur products were judged as successful. With the encouragement of friends and family they decided to produce their own wines on a commercial basis.

It usually took them several years of not only saving for that great day when they became full-fledged vintners, but also there was usually a lengthy search for vineyard property. A majority of these aspiring commercial winemakers not only wanted to make wine, but they knew exactly the type and varietal they wanted to produce. In those cases, the search for vineyard land with the appropriate climatic

and soil conditions was more difficult. Most of them had limited capital and therefore sought out hillside or mountainous property which was a little less expensive than prime land in the major wine growing valleys. As it turned out, mountainside conditions can frequently produce exceptionally fine wines.

The second group of new 1970s vintners described in this book started as grape growers. Many of this group had not even intended to grow grapes, but acquired a piece of property which would eventually be their retirement home. In the process of obtaining the property in the country, they found that the soil and climate were conducive to grape growing. Often times the surrounding area, or the land itself, had a history of viticulture. In several cases, there was an existing vineyard, or the remains of one, on the property. In any event, they became totally involved in grape growing. Even before they were able to retire they had acquired another career.

In the late 1970s, economic conditions were such that there was a glut of grapes on the market. The growers were producing more grapes than the major wineries — who purchased the crops — could use. The price of grapes went down. This situation coincided with the consumer preference for white wines instead of the bigger and heavier reds. Consequently, the growers of the reds not only budded

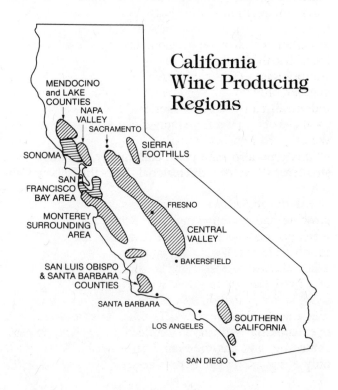

California Wine Producing Regions

MENDOCINO and LAKE COUNTIES
NAPA VALLEY
SACRAMENTO
SONOMA
SIERRA FOOTHILLS
SAN FRANCISCO BAY AREA
MONTEREY SURROUNDING AREA
FRESNO
CENTRAL VALLEY
SAN LUIS OBISPO & SANTA BARBARA COUNTIES
BAKERSFIELD
SANTA BARBARA
LOS ANGELES
SOUTHERN CALIFORNIA
SAN DIEGO

their vines over to white varieties, but began to experiment with home winemaking in anticipation of becoming professional vintners. Thus, many vintners who started their wineries on a small scale survived the resulting wine glut and today are viable and highly successful in the marketplace.

The third group of vintners consists of vintners who have had successful careers in other fields and have chosen to change their careers. Typically, these vintners have a connoisseur's interest in wine and want to produce the wine in which they are most interested.

Whatever the reason the vintners in this book entered the wine business, there is one thread which ties all of them together. THEY PRODUCE EXCELLENT WINE.

Even as diversified as their backgrounds are, and realizing that each puts out a product that is in competition with that of the other, they are a close knit, friendly, and cooperative group of people. The smaller producers, particularly in the more isolated areas of the state, are very helpful to each other. For example, in the Sierra Foothills region, if one vintner suffers a machinery breakdown, a neighboring vintner will either help repair it or loan his neighbor what he needs. Since most of the wineries in that area are small, they often share equipment, such as a bottling line.

This cooperation is in evidence on a larger scale in Sonoma County where a Vintners' Association has been formed as a promotional entity to market Sonoma County wines. Each year, there is a series of junkets to various parts of the nation — Northeast, South, Midwest, Texas, Upper Lake region, and even Alaska and Hawaii. In the key cities of each of these regions, tastings are set up by the local distributors to give the public a taste of Sonoma County wines. Through these tastings, interest is generated not only for the Sonoma County wines, but also the individual participating wineries. This in turn, aids the local distributor for these individual wineries to place the wines in the right retail market. Tastings and cooperation of this type also take place continually, although on a smaller scale, at local and regional affairs throughout California.

For the majority of the vintners in this book, grape growing and winemaking have become a seven-day-a-week occupation. It is not an easy one. There is a year-round cycle of tasks — vineyard maintenance, grape harvest and crush, winemaking, bottling, and finally, marketing. Even though they live with their wines every day, these vintners remain interesting people — they are certainly not dull or one-sided. Their outside interests range over cooking, writing, art collecting, boating, fishing, gardening, and environmental preservation — to name only a few examples. Allan Green of Greenwood Ridge

Vineyards has a career-related hobby of collecting wine cans. Dr. Martin Griffin of Hop Kiln Winery has been instrumental in bringing about environmental preservation along the northern coast of California. Both Henry Matheson of Mt. Veeder Winery and Bob Pecota of Robert Pecota Winery are avid collectors of contemporary paintings — Bob Pecota uses some of this art on the Pecota wine labels.

All of these vintners, regardless of whether they are assisted by a winemaker or perform that function themselves, love to experiment with various styles and techniques of winemaking. They frequently make a small batch of an experimental variety, not only to satisfy their own curiosity, but also to see the reaction of their staff and friends to their creation. Whether it is the use of new or old winemaking techniques, there are some very interesting new wines emerging from the small California wineries.

Charles Shaw, of Charles Shaw Winery, is an example of an innovative winemaker who is committed to producing a unique wine. He produces one of the state's only Nouveau-style wines from Napa Gamay grapes. Charles did years of research in France on that particular style of winemaking, and decided that is what he wanted to produce when he started his winery in the Napa Valley. Creston Manor Winery, with winemaker Vic Roberts, is producing a Nouveau-style wine from Pinot Noir grapes. Randall Grahm, of Bonny Doon Winery, is interested in growing the same varietals as those in the Rhone Valley of France and making wines from them, while Charles Richard grows and blends all of the Bordeaux varietals into his Cabernet Sauvignon. There are few businesses that give the individual as much freedom for creativity as there is in making wine.

This freedom may be the last bastion in America for the small businessman to create his own product — particularly where artistry still predominates over science. For most — if not all — of these vintners winemaking is not only a business but a way of life.

The most difficult aspect of the wine business is the marketing of the finished product. The supply of wine, even premium wines, still somewhat exceeds the demand, so the individual vintner is constantly fighting for a share of his distributor's time and for shelf space in the retail stores.

Both federal and state regulations present numerous obstacles to inter-state marketing of wine. Vintners cannot sell directly to stores or restaurants except in California. They must sell through individual distributors in each state where the wine is sold. All of this means a great deal of travelling not only for the vintner himself, but also for his wife and other members of the family who are involved in the winery. The distributor and his retail customers want to see who is behind the wine label. Consequently, many vintners spend one-third of their time away from the winery on promotional trips. In order to minimize this promotional work, some vintners prefer to remain small and market their products only in their immediate areas. A few small vintners depend only on their tasting rooms and an aggressive mail order program to promote their wines.

Family vintners have found that customer loyalty is strong once established. Bit by bit the consumption of fine wine is increasing. The public is beginning to appreciate the unique contribution being made by the individual small vintner. Many of the wineries highlighted in this book have had their wines served at important public occasions, including state dinners at the White House.

The families of these vintners have had to adjust to the lifestyle of the year-round, everyday business of wine growing and winemaking. Usually the wife of the vintner is involved in doing the administrative, marketing, and hospitality work for the winery. Sometimes she is also the winemaker. Grown children are frequently active in the winery, either doing marketing or learning winemaking, in preparation for eventually taking over the operation. There seems to be a whole "second generation of vintners" emerging, such as young Bob Pepi and Doug Shafer, who are now the winemakers at their families' wineries.

There are many advantages to leading the life of a vintner. Surrounded by vineyards, with wonderful cli-

mate, there is no better place for a relaxed lifestyle. The smog, the roar of cars, and the hectic life of the city were left far behind when the people in this book decided to join one of the last frontiers of individual enterprise — premium winemaking.

Many families moved into existing farmhouses on their property, which, in addition to the old winery, needed a great deal of refurbishing. Not only did this take capital investment, but a lot of hard work, much of it done by the vintner and his family. Some, like the Freys, with the help of their 12 children, built a winery from "scratch." To others, like the Tomkas, the re-opening of an old winery was a dream of their homeland come true. To another, Jay Corley, the building of a replica of Monticello was paying homage to his Virginia ancestry and his lifelong interest in the life of Thomas Jefferson.

Whatever the reason, whatever the motif, whatever the driving force of the vintners described in this book, the end result is the same — *they all produce some of the finest premium wines in America.*

It is also important to understand some of the background of the industry that has provided these people with a rich heritage and helped motivate them to become "continuing pioneers" in the production of this wonderful product of nature. The following pages provide a brief summary of the historical evolution of California's wine industry, starting when the first mission was established by Father Junipero Serra near San Diego in 1769. ❧

History of California Wine Production

Wild grapes were growing in profusion throughout California long before either the Spanish or the Americano settlers arrived. Nature blessed large portions of this part of the world with warm sunny days, cool evening ocean breezes, moderate rainfall, mild winters, and fertile soil. As civilization developed in California, these natural endowments fostered an informal lifestyle conducive to the enjoyment of wine, this most gentle of alcoholic beverages.

The wine culture of California did not begin, however, as a social custom nor as the result of commercial exploitation. Rather, it was spawned from a religious need.

When Father Junipero Serra and the other Franciscan Fathers started the string of California missions in 1769, they assumed that wine for the celebration of Mass could be readily obtained from headquarters in Mexico City. They soon found, however, that the obstacles of distance, terrain, and climate isolated them from this source. Many letters were written to church headquarters in Mexico City complaining about the situation. Receiving no help from headquarters, the Fathers turned to making wine from indigenous grapes but quickly found it undrinkable. The beverage of the local Indians, made from fermented cherries laced with wild tobacco and powdered sea shells, provided an even worse alternative.

After years of frustration, the Franciscan Fathers finally asked Mexico City to send vine cuttings so that they could start their own vineyards. These vines, of a variety called the Mission Grape, finally arrived and were planted at Mission San Juan Capistrano around 1780 — ten years after Father Serra founded the first mission at San Diego.

Grape growing and winemaking quickly became part of mission life for the Spanish priests. The Mission Grape proved well suited to the hot, arid Southern California climate. Therefore, cuttings of the grape, the planting of vineyards, and the making of wine moved north as each successive mission was established. By 1823, when the last mission was built in Sonoma, all but four of the twenty-one missions were self-sufficient in wine production. Mission Dolores in San Francisco was one of the notable exceptions due to the cool and damp climate.

Commercial Winemaking

Winemaking was never meant to be a significant function of a mission. The objective was to produce only enough for use at Mass and for drinking with the evening meal — an established custom with the Spanish-trained priests. Most of the missions were able to supply their own needs, and also sell modest quantities to local pueblos, ranchers, and Spanish-Mexican military bases. In spite of this modest objective, by 1820, the San Gabriel and San Fernando Missions in the Los Angeles basin had become the two largest wine producers in California. However, as the local population grew, the missions became unable to fulfill the needs of the local inhabitants. Consequently, a secular wine industry began to spring up in Los Angeles around 1820.

Mexico secularized the missions in 1834, a decade after the country gained freedom from Spain. Following secularization, the missions and their vineyards deteriorated rapidly. The commercial wine industry, however, began to flourish. The first commercial vineyard was planted by a Frenchman from Bordeaux named Jean Louis Vignas in what is now downtown Los Angeles. In 1818, 50 acres of vineyards existed in Los Angeles; by 1830, the acreage had grown to 100 acres. Vignas doubled that total when he planted his vineyard in 1833.

Soon after Louis Vignas' vineyards and winery started operation, immigrants from all over Europe and the eastern United States commenced planting commercial vineyards in and around Los Angeles. These early grape growers included: an American sailor who jumped ship; a Kentucky frontiersman who, accompanied by George Yount, had come west to trap furs; various Scotch, Irish, Swiss, and English vintners; and several important Mexican-born landowners.

Northern California Wine Developments

Vineyards of Mission Grapes began to proliferate in Northern California after 1840. The Los Angeles area, however, continued to predominate the state's production into the late 1800s. In 1860, the Los Angeles area still produced two-thirds of the state's wine and Mission Grapes was the major crop of the area. A decade later, this portion had dropped to a little over half, and by 1890, the Los Angeles area produced only one-tenth of California's wines.

The Northern California wine industry started to dominate in the 1860s and 1870s as the demand for fine table wines began to increase. The hot climate in the Los Angeles basin, so suitable for the Mission Grape, was not suited for growing the more refined varietals. Also, in the 1880s, Los Angeles area vineyards suffered irreparable damage from a disease called Pierce's Disease (caused by a bacteria and still a problem in certain parts of California).

Growth of the Northern California wine industry had its start in 1834, when Lt. Mariano Guadalupe Vallejo was sent to Sonoma by the Mexican government to secularize the mission and colonize the northern part of the state. He found the mission and vineyards in disrepair and quickly restored part of the mission for living quarters. Vallejo also restored the vineyards and, by 1840, was making wine. Fifteen years later, Vallejo, by then a general, was winning statewide medals for his wine.

In 1838, Vallejo awarded a land grant at the site of Santa Rosa to Señora Maria de Carillo, a widow with 12 children. This was part of the colonization program designed to buffer the Russian colony on the Mendocino Coast. Señora Carillo planted a vineyard and became well known for her wine, thus likely becoming California's first female winemaker.

Soon after Lt. Vallejo arrived, George Yount, who had originally come to Southern California to trap furs, obtained 1,200 acres in the lower Napa Valley from Vallejo. Although he primarily raised cattle and grain, Yount did plant a small vineyard from cuttings obtained from Vallejo.

At about that time, Spanish-born Antonio M. Sunol and several others planted vineyards in Santa Clara County, Soon thereafter, Rancher Robert Livermore planted grapes on his property in the valley east of the San Francisco Bay Area that now bears his name. In 1844, the Danish pioneer, Peter Lassen, planted a Mission Grape vineyard on his Mexican land grant at Vina, north of Chico in Tehama County. (The Lassen property later became famous when Leland Stanford made it into one of the largest vineyards in the world at the time.)

With the discovery of gold near Coloma in 1848, the Sierra foothills also became a focal point for wine growing as vineyards were planted and wineries built to quench the thirst of the miners.

The Haraszthy Era

The early growth of the Northern California wine industry coincided with the start of the California saga of Agoston Haraszthy de Moskesa. While outstanding contributions were made to the development of California's wine industry by a number of individuals — General Vallejo among them — none had the impact of Haraszthy's drive and enthusiasm. Born in 1812 in Yugoslavia of Hungarian ancestry, Haraszthy came to America around 1840 as a political fugitive from the Austro-Hungarian Empire. He settled in Wisconsin and almost immediately started a half dozen businesses, wrote an influential book about America for Hungarian consumption, entered politics, and introduced sheep and hops into Wisconsin.

In 1849, Haraszthy packed his family and belongings into wagons and made the long trek to San Diego. Within a year he was farming 160 acres. During the next year he started several businesses, became county sheriff, and was elected to the state legislature. In 1852, he again pulled up stakes, moved to San Francisco, and planted grapes on 200 acres he had purchased in South San Francisco. Haraszthy quickly became active in the San Francisco community, became a partner in a precious metals refining company, and was appointed assayer at the U.S. Mint.

Haraszthy found the weather on the San Francisco Peninsula too cool for commercial grapes. In 1857, he moved to Sonoma, where he bought 600 acres and planted 400 in grapes. He rebuilt an existing run-down winery and employed Chinese workers to dig wine storage caves into the hillside. He named his estate Buena Vista, a name that is still used by the winery currently operating on the original site.

With his move to Sonoma, Haraszthy began to make his unique contribution to the California wine industry. By 1860, he had put Northern California on the map, worldwide, as a growing region for premium wine grapes. He imported and planted hundreds of grape varietals and distributed thousands of cuttings to growers throughout the state. He was influential in establishing the state agricultural school at the University of California at Berkeley, wrote the first definitive books on grape growing and winemaking, and was elected president of the State Agricultural Society in 1862. Within a few years after that date, however, financial losses turned Haraszthy's investors against him. He fled to Nicaragua where he started over again, but died in an accident in 1869.

This remarkable man was not the only contributor to the development of the California wine industry. Haraszthy's close friend, General Vallejo (whose daughters married Haraszthy's sons in a double wedding) continued to experiment with grape varieties and winemaking even after he was deposed as Mexican governor of "Upper" California. Haraszthy's son, Arpid, also became influential in the California wine industry throughout his 50-year career.

Other Key Wine Pioneers

Charles Krug, who founded his vineyard in the Napa Valley in 1860, became an influential member of both the Napa and state-wide wine communities. Jacob Schram, Jacob Beringer, Carl Wente, Jacob Gundlach, Pierre Mirrasou, Charles Lefranc (Almaden), and Lefranc's son-in-law, Paul Masson, are all pioneering vintners who contributed to the development of the industry during the second half of the 1800s. Their names have been carried on by their descendants or through the label on well-known premium wines.

As the wine industry developed and the consuming public became more knowledgeable, the demand for finer premium wines increased. In the early years, wine and wine brandy were mere substitutes for hard liquor which was expensive and difficult to obtain in quantity. Consumers increasingly made comparisons with French and other European wines. It was in response to this pressure that Haraszthy and others imported a wide range of varietal grapes from Europe.

The industry experienced rapid growth starting about 1850, with grape farming spreading beyond Napa and Sonoma counties. Vineyards were planted in Sacramento, Yolo, Tehama, Alameda, and Santa Clara Counties, as well as the San Joaquin Valley and Sierra foothills.

In 1854, Kohler and Frohling — two professional musicians in San Francisco, both of German ancestry — started the first successful, large-scale wine merchandising company. They opened the first wine shop in San Francisco to serve the growing population caused by the Gold Rush. Since wine production in the mid-1850s still centered in Los Angeles, they purchased a vineyard and winery there. John Frohling moved to Los Angeles to manage winemaking operations, while Charles Kohler managed the San Francisco store.

As sales expanded, they purchased grapes from other Los Angeles growers. They also made wine for others, shipping all of these wines to the Northern California market. Expansion was so rapid they became short of storage space; at one point they leased the entire basement of the Los Angeles City Hall. Through their expansion, Kohler and Frohling were able to make improvements in grape growing and winemaking standards in the Los Angeles area. To further supply their growing need for grapes, they started the famous Anaheim Colony in the late 1850s. By the 1870s, Kohler (Frohling had died in 1862) claimed their wines were selling in every city and town of reasonable size in the United States.

In the 1870s, Charles Kohler purchased acreage in Sonoma and Fresno Counties. He planted Zinfandel in Sonoma and bottled it under that label — one of the first to do so.

Frohling and Kohler were truly among the pioneers of the California wine industry.

Phylloxera Hits

After 20 years of rapid growth, California vineyards were hit by a disease called phylloxera in the late 1870s. This very destructive root louse was first discovered in a vineyard just north of Sonoma in 1873. It was the same disease that had devastated the European wine industry during the previous decade.

The spread of phylloxera in California became of sufficient concern that in 1880 the state legislature finally passed "An Act for the Promotion of the Viticultural Industries of the State." This act established a State Board of Viticultural Commissioners and ordered the University of California to start a research program in viticulture and enology (winemaking).

The research program was undertaken by Professor Eugene Hilgard, Professor of Agriculture at U.C. Berkeley, who had recognized the seriousness of the disease several years previously and had already researched and publicized the problem. Professor Hilgard is regarded as the father of modern viticulture and enology in California. He pushed for accurate labelling, cleanliness in winemaking, regard for acid-sugar balance, low temperature fermentation, and for lighter and tastier wines.

The phylloxera epidemic was finally conquered by the end of the century through massive replanting of rootstock immune to phylloxera. There were two bright spots resulting from the epidemic. One was the advances made through research at U.C. Berkeley. The other was that the massive replanting of immune rootstock reduced the industry's dependence on the inferior Mission Grape. In 1880, over 80% of the wine in California was made from that grape. By 1890, it was below 20%. European grape varietals had finally become established in California.

During the years 1880 to 1910, a number of politicians and businessmen invested heavily in the wine industry, including Leland Stanford, George Hearst, James Fair (Fairmont Hotel), and J.P. Smith (20-Mule Team Borax). This period also saw the emergence of important Italian vintners — particularly in Sonoma and San Joaquin Counties — such as Rossi, Petri, Guasti, Sebastiani, Martini, Franzia and Gallo. The famous Italian-Swiss Colony was created at Asti in the northern end of Sonoma County during this 30-year period.

Between disease (phylloxera in the north and Pierce's Disease in the south), excessive supply, falling prices, frost, and many other factors, the business of being a vintner was not a carefree one. As a consequence, the vintners formed the California Wine Maker's Corporation (CWMA) and major San Francisco dealers formed the California Wine Association (CWA). These two organizations controlled much of the wine market for several decades. CWA later expanded into wine production by purchasing a number of wineries.

Prior to the San Francisco earthquake and fire of 1906, the practice of the industry was to ship wine in bulk to San Francisco where it would be bottled and distributed. Consequently, at the time of the fire, there were millions of gallons of wine stored in huge vats in warehouses throughout the city — almost all of which was lost in the fire. Following the loss of their huge storage tanks in the city, CWA built the largest winery in the world (at that time) on Point Richmond. It was called Winehaven.

Prohibition.

Prohibition exploded onto the scene in 1919, although there had been active attempts to outlaw liquor, wine, and beer for at least the prior decade. Production and sale of wine was restricted to medicinal and religious purposes. The affect on the industry was, of course, to drastically curtail wine production — only 100 wineries were able to stay open by serving this market. Bootlegging kept a number of other wineries open — particularly those in the remote mountain regions of Santa Cruz, Sonoma, and Mendocino Counties.

Law enforcement of Prohibition was difficult due to the gray area between legal vs. illegal production and sale of wine, grapes, or their derivatives. Vintners used many ingenious methods to try to stay alive. This included selling grape juice and concentrates; grape syrup; wine sauces, wine jellies and wine flavorings; "bricks" and "tonics"; cooking sherry and wines; prescription medicines; and many other concoctions.

Somewhat unexpectedly, Prohibition accelerated the planting and production of wine grapes. The law permitted individual citizens to make and store up to 200 gallons of wine per year. Consequently, the demand and price for grapes grew rapidly. A speculative boom in vineyard land developed. Grape-bearing acreage increased from 300,000 acres in 1919 to a peak of 650,000 in 1928. In 1929, 29,000 carloads of wine grapes were shipped east from California.

Post Prohibition

After Prohibition was repealed in December of 1933, the industry recovered slowly, since by then the Depression had set in. The number of bonded wineries in California did expand, however, from a low of 130 to 380 the day following repeal, and 804 a year later, although it dropped back to 538 by 1940.

Vintners were faced with the task of budding-over their vines back to premium wine grapes after having switched to grapes suitable for shipping to the home winemaking market 15 years previously. Further, there were relatively few vintners who knew how to grow premium grapes or make premium wines in 1934. The industry almost literally had to start from scratch.

Vintners, including the major ones such as Gallo, were unable to find experienced winemakers. They were forced to learn by trial-and-error and by reading all the printed material they could lay their hands on — much of it hidden in basements and attics for 15 years.

At this point, the University of California came to the industry's rescue. The faculty undertook research, published and distributed information on grape growing and winemaking, provided hands-on assistance in the field and at wineries, and generally played a major role in bringing the industry back to life. In 1934, the vintners formed a trade association called the Wine Institute to help in the rebuilding process. The Wine Institute continues to play a key role in the development of the industry to this day.

In the rebuilding years of the late 1930s, most of the wine produced in California was sold in bulk and then bottled and labelled by eastern and midwestern marketers. A few of the larger vintners started to make names for themselves by bottling under their own labels: Roma and Petri in the San Joaquin Valley; Cresta Blanca, Concannon, and Wente in the Livermore Valley; Beaulieu Vineyards, Louis Martini, and Christian Brothers in the Napa Valley; and Paul Masson and Almaden in the Santa Clara Valley.

Around the start of World War II, vintners began to offer varietal wines. It would take another 20 years or so before this practice would become commonplace and accepted by the wine consuming public. In fact, it was not until 1983 that the federal agency with regulatory jurisdiction over the wine industry, the Bureau of Alcohol, Fire Arms and Tobacco (BAFT), raised the content requirement for varietal-labelled wines from a minimum of 51% of the varietal grape to 75%.

During the early post-World War II period, the industry continued to evolve, but expansion was only moderate. Most of the growth that did take place occurred primarily in the Napa Valley up to 1970, after which the so-called "winery revolution" took place throughout California. In the 1970s, the industry doubled production in eight years, whereas it had taken 23 years to accomplish the previous doubling. This growth had stirred the interest of big eastern and foreign corporations interested in diversification who had begun to acquire some of the larger premium wineries in the late 1960s. Large eastern corporations entering the California wine industry included firms such as Seagrams, Coca Cola, Heublein, R.J. Reynolds, and Nestle.

A big business orientation had come to the San Joaquin Valley generic wine industry soon after World War II, 25 years before. Wine grapes for bulk generic wines had long been grown by large independent farmers who had no interest in winemaking and treated grapes as just another crop. The large bulk wine producers in the valley encouraged high vineyard yields and purchased these grapes at very competitive prices.

This trend toward corporate ownership in the premium wine segment of the industry, ironically, stimulated a counter-trend toward the family-owned winery. Coincidentally, the industry's 25-year effort to educate consumers to appreciate fine varietal wines began to pay off in the early 1970s. The public began not only to demand high-quality, unique, premium wines, but also a wider diversity of wines and wine styles. The large volume premium wine producers found it increasingly harder to meet these consumer demands — diversity in particular. Consequently, a whole new breed of vintners joined the industry and the so-called "boutique" wine market emerged.

The large premium wine vintners — located primarily in the Napa, Sonoma, Livermore, and Santa Clara Counties — are caught at the moment between the two extremes of the market. While serving the premium wine segment of the market, they must also compete from a cost standpoint with the San Joaquin Valley producers of bulk, or generic wine. On the other hand, they do not have the flexibility of the small family wineries in the boutique segment of the market. Only time will tell whether these large premium wine vintners will be able to maintain a position in the minds of increasingly more sophisticated consumers, as producers of fine quality wines. Perhaps over time they will absorb the more popular developments of the small family wineries or, better yet, provide some type of financial and technical association with these small innovative entrepreneurs.

In any event, the small family vintners are currently providing a stimulus for the development of the industry and performing a service to the consuming public. Because of it, today's wine enthusiast has by far the widest selection of quality wines that has ever been offered anywhere at any time. Tomorrow will undoubtedly bring an even wider selection of unique and high quality wines, giving even fuller enjoyment of wine with food and with social intercourse. ❧

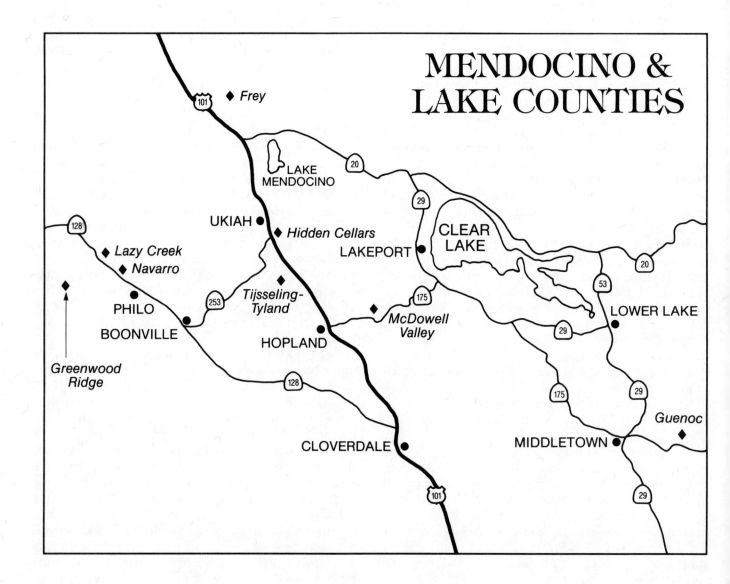

MENDOCINO &
LAKE COUNTIES

♦ Frey

LAKE
MENDOCINO

20

29

CLEAR
LAKE

128

UKIAH ●

♦ Hidden Cellars

LAKEPORT ●

20

♦ Lazy Creek
♦ Navarro

253

♦
Tijsseling-
Tyland

53

PHILO ●

175

LOWER LAKE ●

BOONVILLE ●

♦
McDowell
Valley

29

HOPLAND ●

Greenwood
Ridge

128

175

29

Guenoc
♦

CLOVERDALE ●

MIDDLETOWN ●

101

29

MENDOCINO & LAKE COUNTIES

Frey Vineyards
Greenwood Ridge Vineyards
Guenoc Winery
Hidden Cellars Winery
Lazy Creek Vineyard
McDowell Valley Vineyards
Navarro Vineyards
Tyland, Tijsseling Vineyards

Mendocino &
Lake Counties

Mendocino and Lake Counties, which until recently have been overlooked as major wine producing areas, are located in the northern part of California. Even into the second half of the 1800s, this region was considered to be at the edge of American civilization, since it lacked both water and rail transportation to major markets. At one time, the area was considered a buffer zone to the Russian settlements along the coast. With the development of truck transportation, however, and increased demand for premium wines, both Mendocino and Lake Counties have come into their own as producers of fine wines.

Today, Mendocino County's wine production exceeds that of Lake County by a factor of more than three to one, but this was not the case back in the late 1800s. Lake County had 1,000 acres in grapes while there were only 300 in Mendocino County. Since there were no railroads in Lake County, wine was hauled in barrels by horse-and-wagon over the mountains via steep and winding roads to the Napa Valley.

In 1887, the Lake County wine industry received worldwide publicity when the famous actress, Lillie Langtry, purchased a portion of Guenoc Valley east of Middletown and founded Langtry Farms. She planted a vineyard and hired a French winemaker from Bordeaux to produce Langtry Wines. She sold the property in 1912.

At about the same time, grape growing and winemaking deteriorated in both Mendocino and Lake counties due to strong competition from Napa and Sonoma wineries. By Prohibition, the 36 wineries and 5,000 acres of vineyards in both counties virtually disappeared.

The Mendocino wine industry recovered much faster than that of Lake County. Even during Prohibition, a certain amount of grapes, particularly Zinfandel, continued to be grown and shipped east to home winemakers. One of the vintners who led the resurgence of the Mendocino wine industry was Adolph Parducci. In the middle of Prohibition, he started a 100-acre vineyard and by 1938 had a winery with a capacity for 120,000 gallons (about 50,000 cases). For 30 years Parducci sold his wines primarily in bulk to wineries in Sonoma and Napa Counties.

Lake County recovered more slowly, although several thousand acres of wine grapes were being cultivated in the 1970s, the first commercial crush in modern times did not occur until 1977. Grapes were, and still are, being sold to wineries outside of the county.

Today the wine industry of both counties continues to grow. The Anderson Valley near Philo has gained national recognition for its Gewurztraminer, Chardonnay, and Pinot Noir. Lillie Langtry's ranch in the form of Guenoc Winery has again become a source of premium wines. The area around Ukiah, in the northern part of Mendocino County, has also become a major center for grape growing and winemaking. ❧

Frey Vineyards

Address: 14000 Tomki Road, Redwood Valley 95470
  □ (707) 485-5177
Tasting Room: Highway 101, Redwood Valley
  □ (707) 485-8551
Visitation: Daily, 9 AM to 5 PM
Principals: Paul and Marguerite Frey and their 12 children
Varietals produced: Sauvignon Blanc, Grey Riesling, Chardonnay, Gewurztraminer, Syrah, Pinot Noir, Zinfandel, and Cabernet Sauvignon
Production: 6,000 cases

The story of the Frey vineyards and winery is best told by the patriarch of the family — Dr. Paul Frey, who with his wife, Marguerite, also a medical doctor, manages their family of 12 children.

"We started our winery after going through several stages. First we looked for a means to pay our property taxes on our 100 acres. We felt land should at least support itself. We tried sheep: neighbors' dogs ran them to their deaths. Cattle: not enough feed in the scrub oak canyons. Pigs: too smart and too much work. So we put in vineyards [in 1967]. They provided great work — outdoor work — for our children.

"Local wineries bought the grapes and said they were good. Then, in 1978, Sunrise Winery in Santa Cruz bought our Cabernet Sauvignon and won Best Cabernet of the Year with it — only 200-plus cases. We thought 'Why not start our own winery? Grape prices are down, our microclimate seems just right for Cabernet, we could produce exceptional wine.' So we plunged into the sea of red tape and government forms. We persevered.

"The children, ages 17 to 33, run the winery. Those in college or away from home sell wine wherever they happen to be. Seven of the sons are on the ranch lending their individual talents to the work at hand. Grandchildren spill over the fields and help their fathers.

"Our older children had come under the influence of Alan Chadwick, the English organic gardener of the 'French Intensive Gardening' method. The gardens on our place always have been farmed organically. A natural course to take was to grow our grapes without the use of pesticides or herbicides. It was a serendipitous choice, as we inadvertently found ourselves the only winery making wine from organically grown grapes. Thus the large, and heretofore unknown to us, organic food market opened up. Our largest and steadiest accounts are in health food stores and restaurants in California.

"We dry farm our grapes, — no irrigation. This intensifies the flavors. We add no sulphites as preservatives to the wine. In essence, we make wine the old-fashioned way. It works for us.

"What we hate about running a winery is the paperwork. We did not foresee the magnitude and the unending boredom of paperwork. Since we do most of the work ourselves, we simply divide the paper chores among the many of us.

"What we love about our life as vintners: We feel ourselves blessed to have gotten here, to spend days in sun and breeze tending our vines, or working in the cool cellars producing the wines. The smells of the winery are varied and all are lovely. They speak of the earth...

"Some family businesses are fashioned in the father/dictator — children/worker mold. We started out as Frey and Slaves, but. . . have evolved to management by consensus by discussion. One son emerged as a superb salesman, another finds landscaping and general tidiness his forte. A daughter buys a 'selling suit' and earns college monies selling wine in her college town, chasing down accounts on her bicycle. Individual strengths and talents have firmed up into winery running assets."

Paul and Marguerite (Bebe) Frey purchased their land in Redwood Valley in 1961 after they had lived in another part of Mendocino County for several years. Previously they had both been medical doctors with the U. S. Public Health Service on the Navajo Indian Reservation in Arizona. Marguerite is Medical Director of Planned Parenthood of Mendocino County (she jokingly says all of her children were planned) during the week, and is the doctor on call at the Sonoma State Hospital on weekends.

The winery was constructed from wood and some equipment salvaged from the old Garret Winery in Ukiah when it was dismantled. Other parts of the winery building and equipment have been assembled from other pieces of usable equipment the boys could salvage. The winery may not be an architectural prize winner, but it is very functional.

Two sons, Jonathan and Matthew, worked at Fetzer Winery for a number of years, doing anything and everything. It was good training. Jonathan is the winemaker and Matthew, his assistant, is in charge of general operations and selling. Since he is very clever with his hands he has hand made quite a bit of the winery equipment. There is a homemade bottle washer and sterilizer. Matthew welded some of the stainless steel tanks from scratch, and set up the cooling system.

"As kids we planted the vineyard and sold the grapes. It was the feeling of the children that we wanted something to work with the rest of our lives. We loved this area and wanted to stay here, and growing grapes was not enough," Matthew says. They all worked at various jobs to save enough money to start the winery.

All of the organically grown grapes are hand picked at a lower sugar. In that way the grapes are high in acid and help preserve the wine. Thus, the wines do not require sulphite as a preservative. The Freys only grow about one-third of the grapes they use. The rest are purchased from certified organic vineyards.

Though this may be an informal winery, the growing of grapes and the winemaking is very serious business for the Freys. Their 1982 Cabernet Sauvignon won the prestigious gold medal in the 1985 Orange County Fair and their Zinfandel won silver medals at the same competition in 1982 and 1983. It is the only totally organic winery in the state of California. No pesticides, no herbicides, no irrigation water is used on the vineyards and no chemicals are added in the winemaking. This is a winery operation that is different in that it uses old-fashioned methods of farming and winemaking and makes premium wines. ❧

Guenoc Winery

Address: 21000 Butts Canyon Road, Middletown 95461
□ (707) 987-2385
Visitation: Thursday through Sunday, 10 AM to 4:30 PM
Principals: Orville Magoon
Varietals produced: Chenin Blanc, Sauvignon Blanc, Chardonnay, Petite Sirah, Zinfandel, and Cabernet Sauvignon
Production: 50,000 cases per year

Lillie Langtry, upon seeing her ranch in the Guenoc Valley of California, sent a telegram to a friend, saying "Am delighted. Words don't express my complete satisfaction. Join me in paradise."

Today, nearly 100 years later, paradise is still there and very much alive. The Lillie Langtry residence has been completely restored. The property has been enlarged to a working ranch of 23,000 acres including 270 acres of vineyards and a winery with all of the latest technical equipment.

Langtry Farm, as the property was called a hundred years ago, was owned by Emily Charlotte LeBreton Langtry, an English woman whose nickname was Lillie. Born on the Isle of Jersey, the daughter of a rector of the local church, she wanted to escape from the dull life on the island. At 20, Lillie married a visiting yachtsman from London and in a short time she became the toast of London. She had a scandalous affair with Albert Edward, Prince of Wales and oldest son of Queen Victoria. Since Lillie's husband was unable to provide her with satins, laces, and jewels, she decided to make a living for herself by acting.

Lillie was a woman of great charm and beauty who had capitalized not only on her acting ability, but also her business ability and had formed her own touring company of actors. She was eulogized by the literary giants of the day and painted by numerous artists. Her social charms and graces made her much in demand throughout this country and Europe. In 1888, in order to find a repose and a haven from all of the public attention, she arranged to have her San Francisco attorney purchase a 4,190 acre ranch in the Guenoc Valley. She had also wanted to establish a residency in California in order to obtain a divorce from her husband, who had become an alcoholic.

Lillie's move to Langtry Farm was not inspired solely by the desire for peace. She had also wanted to establish a residency in California in order to obtain a divorce from her husband, who had become an alcoholic.

Lillie travelled to St Helena, in the northern part of Napa Valley, in her own railroad car. From there she proceeded by carriage over the mountain ridge to take up residence on her ranch. At last, it seemed, she had found her paradise where she could retreat from social and professional engagements and do nothing but ride and breed horses. Fred Gebhard, a millionaire from Baltimore who not only had an interest in horses, but was in love with Lillie, purchased the neighboring ranch of 3,000 acres.

Life on the ranch was simple — food was either grown or hunted and a vineyard was planted so that wine could be produced. Lillie engaged Henri Deschelles from Bordeaux to be the winemaker. A modest amount of Burgundy was made — no comparison to the 50,000 cases which are now being produced on the property.

There was a little trouble in "paradise," however, and Lillie's love for Gebhard was not a lasting one. She soon lost interest in him and ran off with someone else. After her divorce was granted in 1897, she married Hugo Gerald de Bathe — a member of one of the oldest and richest families in England. When Hugo's father died, Hugo became a baron and Lillie became Lady de Bathe.

Lillie Langtry owned the Guenoc property for 18 years. She sold the ranch in 1906, and several years later retired to Monte Carlo, where, in 1929, she died at the age of 74.

The story of the Guenoc (an old Indian name) Valley picks up again in 1963, when the Magoon family, mother Genevieve and her two sons, Orville and Eaton arrived. Additional property had been acquired making the ranch much larger even than the combination of Lillie Langtry's and Gebhard's ranches.

Orville Magoon's great-grandfather was a Scottish sea captain who had sailed to the Hawaiian Islands and remained there after he married the daughter of an Hawaiian chief. The sea captain and his Hawaiian princess developed quite a number of plantations. The Magoon family's landholdings were extensive, including 34 acres in downtown Honolulu. But the government wanted the property for the University of Hawaii. Since the University then owned the Guenoc property, a gift of an alumnus, they asked the Magoons to swap land with them. In 1967, they did, and Orville and his family swapped the 34 acres for 23,000 acres in and around the Guenoc Valley. Most of the property is in Lake County, although a small portion extends into Napa County.

While continuing with his career of engineering, Orville Magoon also acts as manager of the ranch. Orville is an internationally renowned coastal engineer whose speciality is designing harbors and breakwaters. He has also been an expert witness in a number of court cases involving coastal structures throughout the world. Orville's brother, Eaton Magoon, is now a successful playwright in London. Their mother, Genevieve has since passed away. Before she died, she wrote a book about Lillie Langtry

It was not until the early 1970s that grapes were considered as a crop for the ranch. Orville, with the aid of the University of California at Davis, planted a 25-acre test plot to determine which varietals would be best suited to the soil and climate of the Guenoc Valley. In 1979, the vineyards were expanded and 270 acres were planted with Cabernet Sauvignon, Merlot, Cabernet Franc, Petite Sirah, Malbec, Chardonnay, Sauvignon Blanc, Semillon, Chenin Blanc, and Zinfandel.

In what the BATF (Board of Alcohol, Tobacco and Firearms) described as the most thoroughly researched petition it had ever received, Guenoc Valley was granted its own appellation. This is one of the few single vineyard/single proprietor appellations in the United States. As part of the investigation and research for the petition, Orville discovered some old hillside vineyards and an old stone foundation for a winery of many years ago.

Orville, with his engineering background, has used the most modern equipment in the winery and in the vineyards. Remote sensing devices were installed at key points throughout the vineyards. These sensors record temperature and send it to a central computer. The computer is voice-synthesized so that Orville can call a special telephone number from anywhere in the world and find out the temperature at given points in the vineyard. In this way Orville can have special equipment turned on for frost protection if warranted.

The 54,000-square-foot winery was completed in 1981. It is built of redwood, styled after a Langtry barn, entirely insulated, and sits on a bluff overlooking the vineyards and the ranch. The winery has a number of computers to aid in the production process. It is equipped to handle twice the present production of 50,000 cases.

The winemaker at Guenoc Winery is Bob Roman. He was formerly with Stag's Leap Winery in Napa Valley. Bob is carrying on some of the winemaking traditions and vineyard practices established by Walter and Roy Raymond, Orville's consultants when the vineyards and winery were first established. The Raymonds have since established their own winery in Napa Valley.

Bob Roman initially ages many of the red wines in large American oak uprights for about six months to pick up some vanilla characteristics from the oak. The Chardonnay, which has four hours of skin contact, is aged in lightly toasted French oak barrels. That particular French oak contributes a hint of mint to the wine. The Cabernet Sauvignon which contains some Merlot, up to 20% depending on the vintage, is aged in French oak for 24 months.

Guenoc Winery is more than just a winery. It is a winery estate in the grandest sense of the word. The ranch has three lakes, all stocked with fish, There are wild boar, bison, deer, pheasant, and quail roaming the ranch, and Orville maintains a full-time game keeper. There are gardens for produce and herbs. The Lillie Langtry House has been completely restored, with period furnishings and memorabilia of her times. (Orville has searched far and wide to obtain any objects that ever belonged to Lillie or were associated with her.) The Langtry House is not open to visitors, but is used as a guest house for invited visitors to the ranch. When there are guests staying at the Langtry House, a part-time chef is employed to prepare the meals.

Lillie Langtry would be very proud of what Orville Magoon has done, not only to preserve her memory but to expand her interest in viticulture and winemaking through the development of the excellent Guenoc wines. It is truly a modern paradise. Lillie's portrait appears on the Guenoc Winery label. It is as if her presence is felt and she is the guiding spirit for the award-winning quality wines made on "her ranch." ❧

Greenwood Ridge Vineyards

Address: 24555 Greenwood Road Philo 95466
   □ (707) 877-3262
Tasting Room: 5501 Highway 128, Philo 95466
   □ (707) 895-2002
Visitation: (Tasting Room) Daily, 10 AM to 6 PM
Principals: Allan Green
Varietals produced: White Riesling, Merlot, and
   Cabernet Sauvignon
Production: 3,000 cases per year

Grape growing is not new to the Greenwood Ridge between Philo and Elk. Many of the early settlers had small vineyards and made their own red table wine. During Prohibition, the vineyard owners and winemakers on the hill became very popular, and the hill became known as Vinegar Hill. The railroad that carried logs from the mountain ridge to the coast frequently carried loggers with empty jugs on the return trip to Greenwood Ridge and the "vinegar producer."

Over the years, many of the vineyards have disappeared through neglect and fires which have swept the area. Also, many of the grape varieties planted were not suited to long exposure to the coastal climate. A few old Zinfandel vineyards do remain and are still bearing. In recent years, however, growers have been planting grapes that do well in cool climates

Greenwood Ridge Vineyards sits on top of a coastal mountain range of the same name. The trip to the Greenwood Ridge Vineyards and winery is like going back in time. In 1840, Caleb Greenwood, who guided the first wagon trains across the Sierras, settled the nearby town of Greenwood, now called Elk. At one time, the town was densely populated by loggers who worked in the surrounding mountains. In 1890, the Elk Creek Railroad was built to handle the logging operations. At that time the railroad, with its sudden curves and fantastic grades, claimed more lives than all other railroads combined. Today, however, the mood of the area is quiet, and the ocean breezes give a sense of peacefulness to the surroundings.

Allan Green and his parents, an architect and a doctor, became intrigued with the area in 1971, and his parents purchased some land. They were living in Los Altos, south of San Francisco, and were seeking a quiet place in the country. A year later they purchased from Tony Husch, the former owner of Husch Vineyards, eight acres on top of the ridge. Husch had planted three acres of Riesling, five of Cabernet Sauvignon and some Merlot on the property.

Allan engaged a vineyard manager who pruned the vineyards and replaced dead vines. The vineyards consist of small parcels of land on the hillside protected from the strong ocean breezes. Since the vineyards are at 1,200 feet elevation, the vines are above the fog and essentially protected from frost.

In 1978 and 1979, Edmeades Winery made some experimental wine from Allan Green's grapes. The wines showed good potential, and the graphic designer found himself in the wine business — by design, so to speak, since he had designed the Edmeades wine label. The Greenwood winery was completed for the 1980 crush. The building was built into a hillside from redwood that was milled from fallen trees on the property. Allan Green's first efforts at winemaking resulted in a Gold Medal at the Orange County Fair for the White Riesling and two silvers in other competitions.

Through 1984, Allan was the winemaker. Although he has a master of art's degree from U.C.L.A., he went back to U.C. Davis for enology courses. To integrate the winery operations, Fred Scherrer, a U.C. Davis enology graduate, was engaged as winemaker and vineyard manager. Greenwood Ridge Vineyards has become known for its White Rieslings. Fred makes the Riesling in the German style, using some botrytis grapes for balance whenever possible. The result is a wine that has a good acid balance with its 1.6% residual sugar.

The Greenwood Ridge Riesling has no skin contact. The juice is settled for two days while chilling at 55 degrees in stainless steel tanks. Fermentation takes about three to four weeks at that same temperature. Fred then stops the fermentation at 1.5% residual sugar, following which the wine is racked and chilled down to 28 degrees and held for three weeks. It is then filtered, bottled, and aged for four to six months prior to release.

The good acid and sugar balance in the grapes is due to the cool growing climate and soil, similar to that of Germany and northern France. Another reason for the excellent wine, Allan believes, is that all three varieties are planted on their own root stock. The grapes are allowed to hang on the vine as long as possible to obtain the desired sugar. Since the winery is adjacent to the vineyards, little time elapses between the hand picking and the crushing of the grapes

Some years Fred Scherrer is able to make a Late Harvest Riesling from botrytis grapes. The climate of the vineyards is often conducive to the "noble rot," a mold that causes the skins of the grapes to become permeable, allowing the water or liquid inside to evaporate. The result is a raisin-like grape which is high in sugar and acid. The Late Harvest Riesling wine, usually a dessert wine, has been called "Nectar of the Gods."

As a related hobby, Allan collects wine cans and has added onto his house several times to showcase his collection. "One of the problems with canned wines has been the taste cans impart to the wine," Allan says. However, Reynolds Aluminum claims to have solved the problem. Wine in cans? Allan points out that for over 50 years wines have been marketed in cans, from small cans on airline flights to the crown-capped cans of Mother Goldstein's Kosher wine produced in New York State.

Each July, Greenwood Ridge Vineyards sponsors the California Wine Tasting Championships. Three categories of wine tasters — novice, amateur, and professional — try to identify California wines as to the varietal. They then try to identify the growing appellation, the producer and the vintage. Most wineries hold an occasional open house, but "I wanted to do something different," Allan Green says.

Bit by bit the Greens have bought additional property as the parcels have come up for sale. They are trying to put together the original ranch and reforest part of the property. They recently opened a tasting room on Highway 128 adjacent to Navarro Vineyards. The building, designed by Allan's father, Aaron Green, provides the public better access to Greenwood Ridge wines. Allan, who continues working in graphic arts, is very much involved in the winery operations and would like to see gradual growth of production. ❧

Hidden Cellars Winery

Address: 1500 Cunningham Road, Ukiah 95482
□ (707) 462-0301
Visitation: June through October: Daily, 11 AM to 4 PM
November through May: Monday through Fridays,
11 AM to 4 PM
Principals: Dennis Patton
Varietals produced: Sauvignon Blanc, Chardonnay, Gewurztraminer, Johannisberg Riesling, Late Harvest Johannisberg Riesling, Zinfandel, Petite Sirah, and Cabernet Sauvignon
Production: 10,000 cases per year

When a load of botrytised Johannisberg Riesling grapes arrived during the first crush in 1981 at Hidden Cellars Winery, the crew looked at them and then at owner Dennis Patton and said "Are you sure?" They were the worst looking grapes anyone had ever seen. But Dennis was so excited he buried his face in them. He had previously been to look at the grapes in the vineyard. They were rotten, and he considered them wonderful. In most grape growing areas, botrytised grapes are a rarity, but in Mendocino county, the grape growers encounter the problem every year and are trying to find ways to eliminate the rot.

Working with botrytised grapes during the first crush is not the normal thing to do, but Dennis Patton has never shunned a challenge and maybe he had a "hidden" feeling that the resulting wine would win a gold medal and that his Late Harvest Johannisberg Riesling in subsequent years would go on to win double golds.

Dennis, who grew up on a farm in Santa Clara County south of San Francisco, worked for a while for Consort Imports, a wine importer in San Francisco. The firm sent him to Europe, where he learned to appreciate French and German wines. He also made mental notes of how the wines tasted. Many years later his fantastic memory can still recall taste and style details.

In the early 1970s, Dennis Patton moved near Ukiah to operate a farm, which was sold out from under him several years later. This was the second time he had to face similar circumstances — his family's farm in Santa Clara County had been taken over by urban development.

About the same time Dennis became an avid home winemaker who was rapidly turning commercial, and enrolled in an extension course at U.C. Davis. "All of the people in the class had name tags with fancy winery names and everyone was a vice-president of Snooter Cellars." he recalls. The person at the registration desk asked for the name of his winery and Dennis just naturally said "Hidden Cellars!" It was hidden, as a matter of fact it was invisible — no real facilities at all.

In 1981, Dennis and a partner started making wine in an overgrown garage in Mill Creek Canyon, which was in an out-of-the-way place. They made 1,800 cases the first year. Just before that first crush, Dennis decided he should get the winery operation bonded, and hastily filled out the forms in early August. The permit arrived the day before the first grapes were crushed.

That first crush was a hectic one. Along with grapes coming from various last minute sources, working with a small crusher and a hand operated basket press, and using dairy tanks for fermentation, there was really no time to ask if things were being done right. Things must have gone right, because all of the wine's styles have become a permanent part of Hidden Cellars' line. The wines have won 28 medals in a little over four years.

Dennis attracted the attention of the Hildreth family, one of the oldest farm families in Mendocino County. They liked Dennis' aggressive attitude toward the business which he had started with pocket change and were impressed with the award-winning wines he was making. In 1983, a winery was built on the Hildreth ranch to which Dennis Patton moved his operation. The winery was literally built around the 1983 crush. As the grapes were being crushed the carpenters were nailing on the roof. "Minor obstacles" such as that have never bothered Dennis or his crew, because everyone works together.

Hidden Cellars purchases all of its grapes, because Dennis believes that no plot of ground can raise all of the varietals he wants to produce. "A cook does not limit himself to two dishes. Why should I only make two or three varietals?" he says. All of the grapes come from the surrounding countryside. The Zinfandel grapes are from a dry farmed vineyard and the Johannisberg Riesling from several miles to the north, where some of it is now naturally infected with botrytis every year.

Dennis tries to bring out the fruit of the grape in his winemaking. His Zinfandel is known for its raspberry flavor. He keeps the tannins low and the alcohol down so that the wine will age well.

Experimentation is another key to Dennis's winemaking. He is only frustrated by the fact that it can only be done once a year — he lives from one crush to the next.

Hidden Cellars has become recognized for its Late Harvest Johannisberg Riesling. The botrytis infested grapes (called the "noble rot" in France) produce a wine with a honey-like richness, which is ideal as a sweet dessert wine. Dennis plans to release a Late Harvest Sauvignon Blanc-Semillon blend next.

Custom crushing for a new brandy house is also an integral part of Hidden Cellars' operation. Hubert Germain-Robin, whose family has been making brandy in France for 200 years, and Ansley Coale, who owns a ranch in Mendocino County, have joined to form Alambic, Inc. They are producing brandy in the traditional French manner. Hidden Cellars does all of the crushing and works closely with them.

Dennis Patton feels optimistic about his winemaking future, particularly about the long-term outlook for Mendocino grapes and wines, which have been consistently winning medals. He says, "The fun is making really good wine, not just lots of it." ❧

Lazy Creek Vineyard

Address: 4610 Highway 128, Philo 95466
□ (707) 895-3623
Visitation: By appointment
Principals: Johann and Theresia Kobler
Varietals produced: Chardonnay, Gewurztraminer, and Pinot Noir
Production: 1,400 cases per year

"For me there is great satisfaction and pleasure in owning a business that allows me a consistent discourse with nature, and in that interplay one is not so much one's own boss, but is a player, both controlling and controlled by the land and the seasons of Mendocino County." These are the thoughts of Swiss-born Hans Kobler, the owner of Lazy Creek Vineyard, a small winery in Mendocino County. In the course of his life he has travelled halfway around the world to produce award-winning wines.

The road to success has not been an easy one, but one of hard work and great perseverance. Hans and his wife Theresia have always been associated with fine wines through their careers as waiter and waitress at some of the world's finest hotels. After training in various hotels in Switzerland, Hans worked in Geneva at the Beau Rivage, which sent him to London in 1948 in an exchange program with the newly opened New Claridge Hotel. After returning to Switzerland, he worked at the Simmentaler Hof in Thun, where he met Theresia, the boss's daughter.

In 1957, Hans and Theresia decided to see the world and they proceeded to move to Canada, working in Montreal, Toronto, and Vancouver. They were married in Toronto in 1959. In 1960, they went back to Switzerland for a very short time.

Wanderlust again took over, and the Koblers headed for Hollywood, California where they both found work at the Brown Derby. But the Hollywood lifestyle did not suit them. One evening, Hans and a friend left after work and drove to San Francisco. When they arrived they went to a coffee shop and asked the waitress for the names of all the fancy restaurants in town. Within hours both men had employment. They drove back to Hollywood, quit their jobs and moved with their wives to San Francisco.

Hans and Theresia worked at various San Francisco restaurants, and for the last ten years of his restaurant career, Hans was in charge of the private upper floor at Jack's, while Theresia worked at the St. Francis Hotel.

In the early 1970s, Hans and a friend were making wine on an amateur basis. In 1972, Hans, for health reasons decided to quit the restaurant business. He purchased 90 acres "way out in the country" near Philo in Mendocino County. The property had originally been owned by an Italian bootlegger during Prohibition and there was an 80-year-old make-shift winery on the property. There was also a vineyard in very bad shape, and sheep running wild.

It took a number of years and a lot of hard work to get the property back in shape — tearing out the old vines, planting new ones, refurbishing the two old winery buildings, and learning how to make wine properly. Part of the time, Hans went back to work in a restaurant to cover expenses. Theresia, with the help of a day laborer, planted most of the vines. The Koblers were determined to make a success of their new venture.

Seven years later, the winery was bonded, and they produced their first wines — two whites, a Chardonnay and a Pinot Blanc — 200 cases. Hans is the winemaker and what joy when the small production of Pinot Blanc won a gold medal in both the 1979 and 1980 Orange County Fairs!

There are 20 hillside acres planted in Chardonnay, Gewurztraminer, and Pinot Noir. They are planted in the European tradition — facing south — and although the yield per acre is not as high as on flat land, the fruit has intense flavor. Hans uses all three varietals in his production of 1,400 cases per year and sells most of the remaining grapes primarily to his neighbor, Ted Bennett, owner of Navarro Vineyards.

Hans, in his winemaking, strives for the flavor of the fruit. He ferments the Chardonnay cool and ages it only a short time in oak. The same is true for the Gewurztraminer. Hans likes to use oak to smooth out the flavor but does not like an oaky taste. Barrel aging the Gewurztraminer is unusual, but Hans feels that the wine breathes better in oak than in stainless steel. To his knowledge, there is only one other winery that uses this technique.

The farm, with its neat small farmhouse, has provided an entirely different lifestyle for Hans, Theresia, and their 18-year-old son, Norman. They raise virtually all of their food, and smoke hams and sausages, in addition to raising grapes and making wine. Norman, a recent high school graduate, was a leading Future Farmers of America member in his county. After graduating, he went to Europe on an exchange program for a year with another winery in Switzerland. Following that, he will take over some of the duties of running Lazy Creek Vineyards.

No, Hans and Theresia Kobler will not retire, just take life a little easier. Hans says that there are few occupations that give as much satisfaction as being a vintner. They want to increase production to at least 4,000 cases per year.

McDowell Valley Vineyards

Address: 3811 Highway 175, Hopland 95449
  □ (707) 744-1053
Additional Tasting Room: Highway 101 in Hopland.
Visitation: Winery and tasting room, daily, 10 AM to 5 PM both at winery and tasting room
Principals: Richard and Karen Keehn
Varietals produced: Fumé Blanc, Chardonnay, Zinfandel Blanc,Grenache, Cabernet Sauvignon, and Syrah
Production: 55,000 cases per year

Most people talk about food and wine, but few do anything about it. Karen Keehn, co-owner of McDowell Valley Vineyards, has not only created recipes to complement the wines she and her husband produce, but she has written a comprehensive booklet about the subject, and is well known and much in demand as a lecturer on food and its relationship to wines. Both of the Keehns — Richard and Karen — travel at least half of the time not only to promote their wines, but to work with chefs on recipes using wine as an ingredient and to inform the public on the herb, spice, wine and food combinations that enhance fine wines.

Richard and Karen purchased land in the McDowell Valley, 40 miles northeast of Santa Rosa, in 1970. The valley was not new to grape production. In 1852, Paxton McDowell, for whom the area is named, bought the 700-acre valley for 1,200 pieces of gold and settled there believing the land to be suitable for cultivation. By 1890, substantial vineyards and orchards had been planted . In 1906, additional vines were planted. Surrounded by mountains which temper the sun's fierceness and prevailing ocean breezes, the valley has proved to be well suited for grape growing.

It was in 1970 that Richard Keehn, a divorced father with four children, and his bride, a widowed mother also with four children, decided that all of these children should grow up in the country. Richard had retired from the Army where he was an aeronautical engineer and a test pilot.

The Keehns purchased 560 acres in the McDowell Valley. There were 360 acres of vineyards in production — among them 65-year-old Syrah vines, which today are still producing and providing the estate with Syrah. The Keehns tore out some lesser varieties and replaced them with more Syrah, Cabernet Sauvignon, Chardonnay, and Sauvignon Blanc. There are seven different soils in the vineyards — all alluvial and of gravelly loam formation, which promotes good fruit balance. No grapes are purchased, as all of the wines produced are from the estate vineyards in the McDowell Valley.

McDowell Valley Vineyards has its own appellation in this isolated valley surrounded by mountains. The property is unique in that it is an American version of a true European winery estate. It is selfsufficient. The majority of the Keehns' food is produced on the ranch — not only fruit, vegetables, and herbs, but also poultry, beef, pork, and lamb. Fish are obtained from the lake and stream on the property. Karen grinds her own flour and usually bakes eight loaves of bread a week when all of the children are home. All of the vineyard workers live in the valley as do a majority of the people who work in the winery.

For the first eight years the Keehns sold their grapes to other wineries, but then decided to complete the product and produce their own wines. In 1978, they bonded an old barn for barrel aging of 1978 Cabernet Sauvignon. The next year they crushed grapes in their striking new winery building. The winery is completely dependent on solar energy for its operations — the first of its kind in California.

The building is constructed of redwood and cement, and part of the building is concealed behind an earthen berm. The first floor contains most of the production facilities for the winery. The offices and tasting room are on the second floor with a redwood deck that stretches the full width of the building front (118 feet). From the deck, there is a spectacular view of the valley and the vineyards. There are 600 square feet of solar collectors, a complex water circulation system, and heat exchange units. Richard Keehn estimates that he has saved the consumer 50 cents per bottle of wine by utilizing solar energy in his production.

John Buechsenstein has been the winemaker at McDowell Valley Vineyards since mid-1985. A graduate of U.C. Davis, he comes from a distinguished winemaking career at various Napa and Monterey County wineries.

The Keehns' philosophy of winemaking is to capture the flavors and balance of mature fruit and to structure their wines with enough complexity so that each varietal will complement a varied range of cuisine. One of the unique wines produced at McDowell Valley is the Grenache, from 67-year-old vines planted in 1919. The Syrah, also from 67-year-old vines is complex and pairs well with a variety of foods.

Since wine should accompany food, Karen and Richard feel there is no better way to inform the public of the proper combinations than to give lectures and demonstrations throughout the country. Periodically, cooking classes are presented at the winery. These classes are led by famous guest chefs who incorporate wine as an ingredient in their dinners or luncheons. The classes are usually all-day events.

Not only do Karen and Richard work very closely together, but of their eight children, a son and daughter are also involved in the winery operation.

Karen and Richard Keehns' belief that food enhances wine, and wine enhances food, is supported by McDowell Valley Vineyards' quality wines. ❧

Navarro Vineyards

Address: 5601 Highway 128, Philo 95466
□ (707) 895-3686
Visitation: Winter: Daily, 10 AM to 5 PM
Summer: Daily, 10 AM to 6 PM
Principals: Edward Ted Bennett and Deborah Cahn
Varietals produced: Chardonnay, Gewurztraminer, White Riesling, Pinot Noir, Cabernet Sauvignon, and Late Harvest White Riesling
Production: 12,000 cases per year

Ted Bennett has always been an innovator, whether it is in the world of electronics, running a winery, using unique methods to make wine, or finding more productive growing techniques for his grapes.

In 1964, Ted Bennett was one of the three partners in the newly formed Pacific Stereo Store in Berkeley, California — the first of a chain of stores that were to change the marketing of hi-fi and stereo systems forever. Ted was in charge of marketing and conceived the idea of putting an entire system together as one consumer package, instead of selling all of the components separately. Pacific Stereo began offering customers a complete system for a single price. The rest is history. This new approach moved hi-fi systems from the hobby to the mass market.

Over the next few years, Pacific Stereo grew from one store to a nationwide chain, with advertisements not only in the nation's newspapers, but also in Life, Time, and Playboy magazines. In 1970, Pacific Stereo was about to go public with a stock offering, when CBS bought the company.

Ted remained with the corporation for a while, but became convinced that his brand of entrepreneurship was no longer needed. It was time to turn to a new vocation. He asked himself what he really enjoyed. Since he had already made a hobby of collecting wines and of home winemaking, it was a small step for Ted and his bride, Deborah Cahn, to start a winery.

Ted and Deborah decided at first to concentrate on one varietal and to find the perfect soil, climate, and location for growing that particular grape. Since they both loved Alsatian wines, the grape they choose was Gewurztraminer, a varietal predominately grown in clay in the cool grape growing region of Alsace. To concentrate on Gewurztraminer was to be a maverick, since at the time, most California winemakers were concentrating on emulating the Chardonnays of Burgundy and the Cabernets of Bordeaux.

After studying the U.C. Davis statistics on soil and climate conditions for growing Gewurztraminer, Ted and Deborah decided to purchase property in the Alexander Valley of Mendocino County. The soil is basically clay, similar to that of Alsace and the warm days and cool coastal fogs also emulate the climate of that region. They planted their first Gewurztraminer in 1974, and Navarro Vineyards and the winery became a reality.

The decision has since proved to be a right one, for the Anderson Valley has become a prime grape growing region. The warm days and the cool coastal fogs provide a long growing season, and this in turn results in grapes of more intense fruit.

Ted planted additional grapes — Pinot Noir, Chardonnay, and more Gewurztraminer. Now there are 50 acres planted in grapes on his 900-acre ranch. He plans to plant Riesling in the near future when he finds the appropriate clone for his soil and climate. Sixty percent of the grapes used in the Navarro wines are estate grown — the Riesling, some Chardonnay, and the Cabernet Sauvignon are purchased from neighboring Mendocino County vineyards.

For several years Ted experimented with various methods of spacing of the plants, and different methods of pruning and tying. He finally settled on the lyre system, which keeps the leaf canopy vertical on both sides, permitting the sun to reach more of the grapes. They ripen better and have more sugar content. The lyre system, however, requires more pruning and hand tying. He is convinced that this method is the right one,though, because on his last trip to Alsace he saw the same planting system in use there.

Navarro Vineyards has become famous for its dry style Gewurztraminer. Each lot or block of grapes is harvested separately and is kept separate through the fermenting and aging processes. The wine is cold fermented to retain the spicy varietal aromas, and then racked to German oak barrels to slowly finish fermentation. The separate lots are then tasted and blended together if desirable.

Every year, Ted and Deborah produce a Late Harvest or Botrytised Gewurztraminer, and also a Late Harvest Riesling. The weather conditions of the Anderson Valley are very conducive to the slow dehydration of the grapes causing the "noble rot." The grapes have to be hand picked, the juice is lightly pressed and allowed to ferment very slowly with a German strain of yeast. It is a long and difficult process to make Late Harvest wines, but the Bennetts feel it is well worthwhile.

Ted has spent many years experimenting with various methods of making Pinot Noir wine, and has returned to the traditional French method of *La Méthode Ancienne* (without modern machinery), which minimizes handling of the grapes. The wine is aged in oak for a minimum amount of time to preserve its fruitiness.

As the winery and the vineyards, grew Ted and Deborah have had to hire various people for the vineyard, the winery, and the tasting room. The business is still one big family, though, because Ted believes in operating his winery according to the highly participative Japanese style of management — a management practice carried over from his days at Pacific Stereo. Ted is in charge of the vineyards and the winery, while Deborah supervises the tasting room and is in charge of marketing. Seventy percent of the wines are sold either through the tasting room or through private pre-release mailings.

The Bennetts do not want their winery to grow much larger, because they want to retain the handmade quality of their wines. Ted, however, will continue to seek innovative methods of growing and harvesting grapes, and will continue to make wines, both the long-forgotten traditional ones and those produced by newly developed techniques. ❧

Tyland Vineyards

Address: 2200 McNab Ranch Road, Ukiah 95482
　☐ (707) 462-1810
Visitation: Spring, Summer and Fall:
　Monday through Friday, 11 AM to 4 PM;
　Saturday and Sunday, 11 AM to 5 PM
Principals: Dick and Judy Tijsseling
Varietals produced: Chenin Blanc, White Zinfandel, Gamay Beaujolais, Blanc de Blanc Champagne, and Muscat Canelli
Production: 10,000 cases per year

Tijsseling Vineyards

Address: 2150 McNab Ranch Road, Ukiah 95482
　☐ (707) 462-1810
Visitation: Weekends, 11 AM to 5 PM;
　Weekdays by appointment.
Principals: Herman and Alida Tijsseling, and Dick Tijsseling
Varietals produced: Sauvignon Blanc, Chardonnay, Petite Sirah, Cabernet Sauvignon, and Brut, Blanc de Blanc, and Blanc de Noir Champagnes

Most families are the proud owners of one winery and vineyard. Not so for the Tijsselings, the elder and the junior. They each own and operate a winery.

In 1965, Herman and Alida Tijsseling purchased the 8,000-acre McNab Ranch, an old sheep ranch six miles south of Ukiah in Mendocino County. The elder Tijsseling had planned to develop a recreational subdivision which was to be constructed and developed by the family real estate and construction company. The idea was abandoned because of the state of the housing market at that time.

Local farm advisors counselled the family that the micro-climate and the geography made their McNab Valley property ideal for vineyards. The land was rich in alluvial soil, drainage was good and the warm days and cool nights were a natural for grape growing.

The Tijsselings proceeded to plant grapes with Dick acting as vineyard supervisor while he still continued working with the family construction company in Contra Costa County, east of San Francisco. Dick researched the grape growing field thoroughly in order to acquaint himself with his new part-time career.

In 1972, Dick and Judy Tijsseling purchased land adjacent to the parcel owned by Dick's parents and also planted grapes. Today 95% of Tijsseling wines are from estate vineyards, and 100% of Tyland wines are estate grown. In 1975, Dick and Judy acquired another adjacent ranch, part of which was to be the site of an eventual winery.

When he began growing grapes, Dick Tijsseling also started making home wines. In 1978, Dick, who is an architectural engineer drew up the plans for an 8,000-square-foot winery to produce wines from his own grapes. At that time, he became a full-time vintner. As is his nature, everything in the winery is precisely placed and very functional — even the smallest tool has its own peg. Dick decided to name the winery Tyland because he thought it would be easier to spell than Tijsseling.

By 1981, there were 235 acres of vineyards under cultivation on the McNab Ranch, and the decision was made by the senior and junior Tijsselings to build another winery on the property. Again Dick used his architectural skills and drew up the plans. Construction started on a 24,000-square-foot winery, to which champagne making facilities were added in 1984. This time they used the family name, which by then had become well known and accepted.

Dick manages this winery for his parents, who are in their 80s and who live in the Bay Area. Herman Tijsseling comes once a week to confer with his son on operations. The younger Tijsselings live on the ranch. Dick also works very closely with Miles Karakasevic, the winemaker for both wineries. Mike is a graduate in enology from the University of Belgrade, Yugoslavia. He is an eleventh generation winemaker and is a perfectionist who sees his craft as a way of life. Miles defines winemaking "as a fine-tuning of the unique potential of the grape rather than a form of self-expression of the winemaker." He has a keen awareness for blending the various lots of each wine to achieve the maximum flavor and complexity from each varietal. In past years, Miles has produced gold medal winning wines for both wineries. He is most interested in promoting Mendocino wines.

Miles is also most enthusiastic about the champagne production of both facilities. The *Méthode Champenoise* is used for all champagne production. At the Tijsseling winery, the riddling is done by an automatic machine. The bottles to be riddled are placed in a large wooden box which is, in turn, put on a stand with a vibrator attached. This method saves manpower.

Miles makes Tyland's White Zinfandel in the very dry style. The juice has virtually no skin contact. However, after fermentation a percentage of red Zinfandel is added to the wine for further enhancement. Most of the red grapes are field crushed and the must is transported to the winery for fermentation. The stems and leaves are left behind in the field for mulch.

The two wineries have very different labels. Tyland has, as part of its logo, a sketch of the winery building. Tijsseling's logo is the Tijsseling family crest, which can be traced back 400 years in Europe. The Tijsseling family emigrated from Holland to the United States in the the mid 1950s when Dick was a youngster.

Even though the two wineries are side by side and belong to the same family, the wineries do not compete with each other. Their wines are different and serve different markets. Good things usually come in pairs, and that is certainly true for Tyland and Tijsseling wines. 🍃

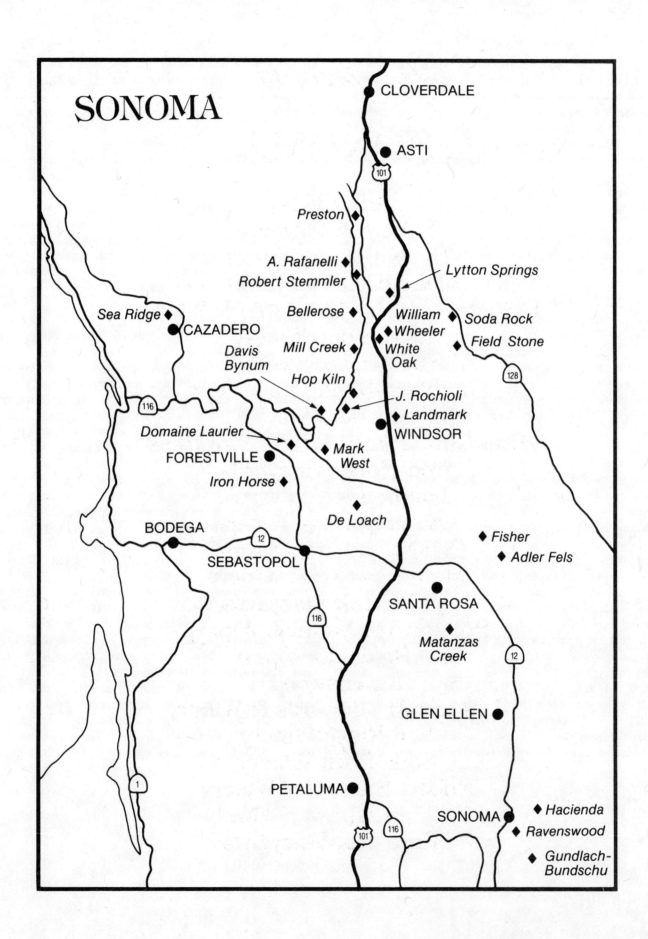

SONOMA

CLOVERDALE

ASTI

101

Preston

A. Rafanelli
Robert Stemmler

Lytton Springs

Sea Ridge
CAZADERO

Bellerose

William
Wheeler

Soda Rock
Field Stone

Davis
Bynum

Mill Creek

White
Oak

128

Hop Kiln

J. Rochioli

Domaine Laurier

Landmark
WINDSOR

116

Mark
West

FORESTVILLE

Iron Horse

De Loach

BODEGA

12

Fisher
Adler Fels

SEBASTOPOL

116

SANTA ROSA

Matanzas
Creek

12

GLEN ELLEN

1

PETALUMA

SONOMA

Hacienda

Ravenswood

101

116

Gundlach-
Bundschu

Wineries of

SONOMA

Adler Fels
Bellerose Vineyard
Davis Bynum Winery
De Loach Vineyards
Domaine Laurier Vineyards & Winery
Field Stone Winery
Fisher Vineyards
Gundlach-Bundschu Winery
Hacienda Winery
Hop Kiln Winery, Griffin Vineyards
Iron Horse Vineyards
Landmark Vineyards
Lytton Springs Winery
Mark West Vineyards
Matanzas Creek Winery
Mill Creek Vineyards
Preston Vineyards & Winery
A. Rafanelli Winery
Ravenswood
J. Rochioli Vineyards & Winery
Sea Ridge Winery
Soda Rock Winery
Robert Stemmler Winery
William Wheeler Winery
White Oak Vineyards

Sonoma County

Winemaking in the region north of San Francisco started in 1824, when grapes were planted behind the Mission St. Francis de Solano in the town of Sonoma at the south end of the Sonoma Valley. In 1834, the missions were secularized, and if it had not been for the foresight of General (then Lieutenant) Mariano Guadalupe Vallejo, the vineyards would probably have disappeared. Vallejo restored the vineyards and by 1840, was making wine. Fifteen years later he was winning state medals with his Mission Grape wine. Vallejo was well established when Agoston Haraszthy arrived in 1857, and he helped Haraszthy become settled.

Thanks to Haraszthy, Sonoma quickly became the center of knowledge on viticultural techniques. Wineries spread up the Sonoma Valley toward Santa Rosa. Jacob Gundlach started the "Rhinefarm" in 1858, bringing Riesling from Germany (the winery still operates today as Gundlach-Bundschu). In the mid-1870s, Sonoma County had more vines under cultivation than Los Angeles County and produced more than twice as much wine. There were more than 100 wineries in the Sonoma Valley, between Sonoma and Santa Rosa, in the late 1800s.

Vineyard plantings accelerated throughout the county in the late 1800s when the European demand for California wines increased due to the phylloxera epidemic there, which had created a shortage of wine. The number of wineries in the area increased from 50 to 116, and vineyard acreage tripled in the 1880s. Vineyards and wineries began to spring up in the Russian River, Bennett, Dry Creek, and Alexander Valleys.

In 1880, the famous Italian Swiss Colony experiment was founded in Asti, between Geyserville and Cloverdale at the north end of the county. This social experiment had been designed to settle penniless Italian and Swiss immigrants by paying them a wage, but deducting $5 per month to purchase stock in the colony. The experiment failed, but the winery is still operating today.

Prohibition closed down many of the wineries in Sonoma County but, as in many other parts of California, wine grape acreage continued to grow in response to the demand for grapes for the home winemaking market. By 1930, there were 30,000 acres of vineyards in the county, but the number of wineries had dwindled from 256 in 1919 to less than 25 in 1930.

For the next 40 years, vineyard acreage in Sonoma County slowly shrank so that, by the start of the "wine revolution" in 1971, there were only 15,000 acres and 20 wineries. In the ensuing 15 years, 15,000 acres of prune, pear, and apple orchards have been ripped out and pasture land ploughed under to make room for new vineyards. As a result, Sonoma County now has 120 wineries and vineyard acreage of 31,000 — slightly more acreage than Napa County. Sonoma County will likely out-distance Napa County in the future since it has considerably more land available for cultivation.

The Sonoma County vineyard that started it all — Haraszthy's Buena Vista vineyard — began to deteriorate soon after Haraszthy left for Nicaragua in 1866 under pressure from his investors. His son, Arpid, moved to San Francisco to become a wine merchant. Phylloxera finally destroyed the vineyards by 1880. It lay dormant until 1941, when a United Press newspaperman named Frank Bartholomew purchased part of the property at auction— without knowing its heritage — and after the war he revitalized Buena Vista. In 1968, Bartholomew sold the winery, but retained the vineyard. In 1973, at the age of 75, he started Hacienda Wine Cellars on the vineyard property. Hacienda is a very successful winery today under the ownership of A. Crawford Cooley, a co-owner with Bartholomew until 1976.

Another famous old Sonoma winery still operating today is the Korbel winery on the Russian River at Rio Nido. This winery was started in 1886 by the three Korbel brothers, who were from Bohemia. Originally, their business was making cigar boxes from redwood cut at their sawmill in the area. As the land was cleared, they planted vines between the stumps. In 1896, they started making a dry sparkling wine called "Grand Pacific." The Korbel family later sold the winery to the Hecks, a German family, who were champagne makers in St. Louis. The Hecks have since expanded the winery's line of champagne and brandy. They make champagne by the traditional French *Méthode Champenoise*.

One of the most well known Sonoma County wineries is Sebastiani Vineyards, which Samuele Sebastiani started in 1904, eight years after arriving in this country from Tuscany, Italy. The winery has remained in continuous operation to this day, even during Prohibition when it made sacramental and medicinal wines. Sylvia Sebastiani, the widow of Samuele's son August, is currently head of this large family winery.

There are several other old Sonoma County wineries still operating today that are worthy of mention. At Windsor, the facility operated by the Sonoma County Co-op (which ships bulk wine to Gallo in Modesto), was started in the 1870s by Kohler and Frohling, the famous San

Francisco wine merchants. Just north of Healdsburg is the Simi Winery, founded in 1876 by Giuseppi and Pietro Simi, another pair of San Francisco wine merchants. Since 1960, the Simi Winery has been owned by Moet-Hennessy, the large French wine and spirits firm. In Dry Creek Valley north of Healdsburg, is the huge Gallo vineyard and winery purchased in 1976 from the descendants of Louis and Later Frie, who founded the Frie Brothers Winery in 1880. ❧

Adler Fels

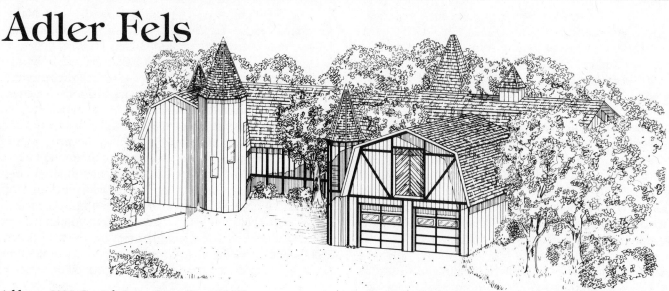

Address: 5325 Corrick Lane, Santa Rosa 95405
◻ (707) 539-3123
Visitation: By appointment only
Principals: David Coleman, Ayn Ryan, Lila Burford (Ayn's mother)
Varietals produced: Fumé Blanc, Chardonnay, Gewurztraminer, Pinot Noir, Late Harvest Riesling (if year is right), and Mélange à Deux (50% Gewurztraminer and 50% Johannisberg Riesling — *Méthode Champenoise*).
Production: 5,000 cases per year

High above the Valley of the Moon in the midst of the Mayacamas Mountains (just south of Santa Rosa) stands a large towering precipice known as Eagle Rock. This local landmark, mentioned by Jack London in his writings about the Valley of the Moon, acquired its name from its unusual shape — years of weathering have honed it to resemble the head of an eagle.

It is on a nearby mountaintop, within sight of Eagle Rock, where David Coleman and his wife, Ayn Ryan, decided to build their winery in the style of a Rhine castle complete with turrets. They combined the romantic charm of European architecture with the practicality and efficiency of a modern winery. The Colemans appropriately named the winery "Adler Fels" — the German translation of "Eagle Rock."

David Coleman, an innovative and maverick vintner, was educated in New York and studied industrial design at the Massachusetts Institute of Technology. Over the years he designed world fairs, furniture, trade show exhibits, and packaging for various products.

It was during his stint in the Army — two years of which were spent in Germany as a photographer — that David discovered fine wine. A German couple gave him a bottle of Riesling for his birthday and he decided to have a glass just to please them. "Well, I tasted it and it was wonderful," he says now.

After his discharge from the Army in the early 1970s, David moved to California and was led to the wine country through a job as a designer for a Santa Rosa printing firm. A couple of years later, while out on a business call, he drove up the driveway of a pretentious looking Tudor building under construction and asked the owner if he needed any printing. Dick Arrowood, owner of Chateau St. Jean, said "No, but I do need a label designed." Thus began David Coleman's career of designing wine labels.

Coleman designed an intricate gold-faced, embossed wine label that is still seen today on Chateau St. Jean's bottles. This led to a career of designing labels for over 40 wineries in the Napa-Sonoma area. In talking with the vintners during his years of designing wine labels, he gained knowledge of the wine business and decided that he could make just as good a product — perhaps even better. So, in 1980, he started his own winery.

At about the same time, he met Ayn Ryan, the director of marketing for a bottled mineral water concern. Today, Ayn is still involved in marketing — but now functions as marketing director for Adler Fels.

David approached Ayn's mother, Lila Burford, (who was no stranger to the wine business since she is a member of the Merzoian family who owned Chateau St. Jean) about the possibility of joining Ayn and David in their investment in his winery. Jokingly, she replied , "Yes, but only if you marry my daughter." Ayn and David did marry, and soon after Adler Fels did start a small expansion program!

Today all three — Ayn, her mother Lila, and David — are quite involved with Adler Fels. David is the winemaker and builder (the Adler Fels winery which started in 1980 was literally constructed by David); Ayn does the marketing and public relations; and both Ayn and her mother do food and wine demonstrations all over the state.

In early 1985 David added a champagne cellar down the east side of the mountain, just under the winery, to house their sparkling wine known as Mélange à Deux. Mélange á Deux is an unusual blend of 50% Johannisberg Riesling and 50% Gewurztraminer. Only fully mature grapes are used in this sparkling wine, and with carefully controlled fermentation, the result is a dry fruity sparkling wine.

Adler Fels' white wines are different, too. Coleman does not believe in putting them through a second fermentation. He says it makes the wines taste too rich. To age their Chardonnay, the Colemans use lighter flavored older oak barrels from Nevers, France instead of the usual fuller, richer flavor from Limousin. They believe this results in a wine with more subtle flavors.

The variable capacity tank now used extensively by smaller vintners was conceived and designed by David Coleman. These tanks — double jacketed with refrigeration — have a free floating top that adjusts to the amount of wine inside the tank. This keeps the wine free of air and reduces the amount of sulfur dioxide needed.

Adler Fels grows no grapes, but carefully selects the vineyards whose grapes they will use. David and Ayn believe that choosing the right vineyard is the single most important element in winemaking. They carefully analyze many factors on which to base their judgment of a small vineyard's grapes — soil, climate, location, health of the vines, and good intuition.

Getting the grapes up to the mountaintop is no small feat. Several trucks have broken down in the process, and some truckers refuse to make the trip. Grapes are now brought up on small flatbed trucks in 40-pound picking boxes rather than the more typical bulk loading gondola trucks. Use of picking boxes also reduces damage to the grapes and, therefore, the extensive use of sulphur.

The Adler Fels wine label is most unusual. Not the rectangle usually found on wine bottles, but a free form in the shape of an eagle's head. It is burgundy in color, flocked with a pattern of little eagles.

Ayn and David's goal for the winery is to continue "to select from the finest vineyards in Sonoma County and produce, consistently, the highest quality wines." Adler Fels wines have won gold medals throughout California. They "love the people connected with the wine business, but," they admit, "working and living together is not always easy." 🐌

Bellerose Vineyard

Address: 435 West Dry Creek Road, Healdsburg 95448
☐ (707) 433-1637
Visitation: By appointment only
Principals: Charles and Nancy Richard
Varietals produced: Cabernet Sauvignon, Merlot, and Sauvignon Blanc
Production: 5,000 cases per year.

A fine Bordeaux wine is the ultimate in wine enjoyment, Charles Richard concluded after many years as a connoisseur of fine wines. "Can California wines challenge the French? Is there a place for Bordeaux style wines in California?" Charles Richard asked himself, when he became a vintner. For years, Charles Richard had been a great admirer of Bordeaux wines, feeling that they have more depth and complexity. He had always wanted to emulate that style of winemaking in California.

Raised in the hotel and restaurant business, Charles took fine food and wine seriously. His Italian-born father founded a Mount Pocono, Pennsylvania resort which bore his name "Villa Charles." For a while he worked for his father in the restaurant business and was trained in Italian and French wines.

Charles Richard, however, wanted to become a musician and earned a master's degree in music and aesthetics from Lone Mountain College in San Francisco. At one time, he aspired to be a virtuoso of the classical guitar. He has performed professionally, taught music, and written a book on the history of the classical guitar repertory. In the long run, however, his interest in food and especially wine won out as a career.

Thus in 1978, he and his wife Nancy purchased a 52-acre property on a hillside overlooking the Dry Creek Valley in Sonoma County. The property is full of history. Evidence has been found that prehistoric Indians once were encamped there. The first real owner of the property fought in the Civil War and then settled on the land to farm. At first the land was planted in grains, then fruit and walnut trees, followed by grapes. Then it lay fallow — and now it is planted again in grapes.

In 1887, there was a winery on the property. It was built by then owner Captain Everett Wise, who hauled stones by wagon from the nearby Mill Creek to build a winery. Bill and Eva Passalacqua took over the property and operated a 90,000-gallon bulk winery until it was destroyed by fire in 1939. Two walls, each two feet thick, remained and are now incorporated into the building which is the Bellerose aging cellar. The building is constructed into a hillside to provide natural cooling.

The style of Bordeaux wines has not only influenced Charles Richard in his winemaking, but also in the types of grapes he has planted. There are 35 acres of Cabernet Sauvignon, four acres of Cabernet Franc, and 12 acres of Merlot. These are the basic varietals of Bordeaux. Richard has also planted smaller parcels of Malbec and Petit Verdot, both of which are traditionally used for blending a classical Bordeaux wine.

Richard points out that in Bordeaux most of the chateau vineyards consist of two to five grape varieties. The resulting wines are blended to the particular style of wine for which the vineyard is known. The principal varietal used in the wine is not designated — unlike the practice in California. For example, in California a Cabernet Sauvignon to be called such has to have 75% of that grape in the wine. In France, however, a Bordeaux can contain all or some Cabernet Sauvignon depending on the chateau and the characteristics of the varietal wines in a given vintage year.

Charles Richard has tried to emulate the Bordeaux style of wine as closely as possible. He has planted the same grapes as exist in the Medoc region of Bordeaux. The reason for having a "mixed vineyard" in California is the same as in Bordeaux. If, in a season, one grape does not do well, it can be enhanced with the blending of others into the wine to maintain a uniform style. The individual varietals ripen at different times and can, therefore, be crushed and fermented in serial fashion.

Charles Richard also uses Bordeaux methods in blending the wine. His wines emphasize a style of wine, and he tries to interpret the individual vintage, but blends to the style. In fact, his Cabernet Sauvignon has the subtitle of "Cuvée Bellerose," suggesting the eventual use of classic chateau names. The gold rose on the Bellerose Vineyard wine label is the same as the one on the Richard family coat of arms. Again, suggesting the chateau style of winemaking.

Just like Charles Richard and the grapes, Curly and Rowdy are an integral part of the Bellerose Vineyard. They are a pair of Belgian draft horses weighing a ton each and are really the "work horses" at the winery. Charles likes using Curly and Rowdy for all types of vineyard work such as clearing stones. They get to areas of the hillside vineyard where it is impossible to use tractors. On the average they eat 50 to 60 pounds of orchard grass-alfalfa hay a day, but after an especially hard day their rations are augmented with fresh oats. Charles Richard says that, "the cardinal virtues of draft horses are patience, strength, and a docile nature that allows us smaller mortals to work with giants." Charles's non-vintage table wine is called Work-horse Red.

Working with intricate and traditional French Bordeaux methods of making wine, working the land with horses, and cultivating his grapes by hand has made Charles Richard live his daily life at an even tempo. He has followed the motto of his favorite composer Verdi: "Let us return to the past and that will be progress." ❧

Davis Bynum Winery

Address: 8075 Westside Road, Healdsburg 95448
  □ (707) 433-5852
Visitation: Daily, 10 AM to 5 PM
Principals: Davis Bynum
Varietals produced: Sauvignon Blanc, Chardonnay, Gewurztraminer, White Zinfandel, Pinot Noir, Zinfandel, and Cabernet Sauvignon
Production: 17,000 cases per year

Davis Bynum's father, Lindley, had a life-long dream of owning and operating a winery. Although for many years he owned a vineyard in St. Helena, and served as a wine competition judge in the 1940s and 1950s for the Los Angeles and California State Fairs, he never achieved his dream. , His son, however, achieved it for him with one of the best known of California's small wineries.

Davis Bynum was for many years an editor with the *San Francisco Chronicle*, and in the early 1960s, he moved to Southern California to work on a newspaper there. He could not get comfortable with life in Southern California and really wanted to pursue his hobby — winemaking — instead of his career in journalism.

Winemaking began for Davis Bynum when he graduated from the University of California in Berkeley in 1951. He bought a batch of grapes from Robert Mondavi at Krug Winery and made his first homemade wine. He continued to do so year after year, making wine at home. His friends thought the product was so good that he should go commercial. This he did, in 1965, after moving back to Northern California.

Davis rented an old plumbing warehouse in Albany, near Berkeley, and installed some winery equipment — a few tanks, a crusher-stemmer and a three-and-a-half-ton wooden basket press. The press was very hard to handle and in the old horse-and-buggy days a horse would probably have been used to operate it. Nevertheless, Davis operated it by not filling it full. That first year of operation, Davis Bynum crushed one ton of grapes and made wine. He converted the office of the plumbing warehouse into a tasting room and found himself in the commercial wine business. At that time he used two labels — Davis Bynum and Barefoot Bynum for his blends.

Both wines were so well received by his customers that he decided, in 1971, to purchase a vineyard in St. Helena and build a winery there. Unfortunately, the city fathers never granted him a use permit to build a winery in his vineyard. In 1976, he sold the property.

Fans of his wine, including Howard Allen, a vineyard owner in Sonoma County whose vineyard is designated on the Bynum Chardonnay Reserve, convinced Davis to investigate the possibility of locating his winery in Sonoma County. He became aware of the fact that Sonoma County was still in its infancy, as far as wine growing and production was concerned. Also, land was much cheaper there than in Napa. Years of winemaking and critical acclaim for Davis Bynum wines have also brought out the fact that grapes grown in Sonoma County are of superior quality. He discussed the project with friends, who eventually became investors in his project, and they convinced him to establish his winery in Sonoma County.

In 1973, he purchased hillside property near the Russian River. The ranch contained a residence and a small hop kiln which Davis converted to the winery. Davis was the original winemaker for the enterprise, but eventually turned that position over to his son, Hampton. Now the winemaker is Gary Farrell, who in one year won gold medals with all three vintages of Davis Bynum Pinot Noir. Quite a feat for a small winery.

All of the grapes for the Bynum wines are purchased — 65% from growers who are shareholders in the winery and have their vineyards in the immediate vicinity of the winery. The rest of the grapes come from the Russian River area. Recently, Davis Bynum has cleared some land on the hillside above the winery and is planting Merlot.

Dorothy Bynum, Davis's wife, is an excellent artist who paints primarily in oils and is also very much involved in the winery. Her paintings and artistic talents are featured on all of the Reserve labels of the Davis Bynum wines. The paintings on the labels range from pastoral vineyard scenes to florals to still lifes of sea shells.

It is Davis Bynum's philosophy of winemaking to develop the character o grape as it is grown in the vineyard, paying strict attention to the appellation area and its growth conditions. Davis tries to bring out the fruitiness of the grapes. To this end Gary Farrell produces a very intense and aromatic Gewurztraminer. The grapes have 14 hours of skin contact and are cold fermented for 45 days, with fermentation stopping at .5% sugar. This makes a very drinkable food wine.

Davis Bynum's father may not have achieved his dream, but Davis has certainly captured a true prize in the premium winery he established. ❧

De Loach Vineyards

Address: 1791 Olivet Road, Santa Rosa 95401
  □ (707) 526 9111
Visitation: Daily, 10 AM to 4:30 PM, except major holidays
Principals: Cecil O. DeLoach, Jr.
Varietals produced: Sauvignon Blanc, Fumé Blanc, Chardonnay, Gewurztraminer, White Zinfandel, Pinot Noir, Zinfandel, Cabernet Sauvignon, and Late Harvest Gewurztraminer
Production: 45,000 cases per year

Cecil DeLoach has heard many clanging bells and seen many puffs of smoke in his sixteen years as a fire fighter for the San Francisco Fire Department. Now he is hearing different kinds of bells and seeing different kinds of puffs, plus stars as well — those are the merit awards that wine writers give when evaluating their tastings. DeLoach Vineyards has received many three- and four-bell, star and puff ratings.

Cecil DeLoach was born in Montgomery, Alabama and spent his early childhood in Macon, Georgia, where his grandfather was a Baptist minister. At the age of seven he and his family moved to San Francisco. Ultimately, he joined the fire department after a stint in the Marine Corps and some time spent as a racetrack photographer. After discharge from the Marine Corps, he attended San Francisco State University, graduating with a degree in physical anthropology. He worked in that field for a short time, while continuing his job with the San Francisco Fire Department.

"Dad wanted us boys [Mike and his brother John] to grow up in the country instead of in the city, that's one of the reasons he bought this place," said Mike DeLoach, son of owner Cecil DeLoach and director of marketing for DeLoach Vineyards.

That was in 1969, when Cecil and his wife Christine and the two boys started looking for good agricultural land. Cecil thought he would like to raise something on the property. A fellow fireman told him of some available property in Sonoma County. The land was a 24-acre ranch in the Russian River Valley, seven miles west of Santa Rosa, consisting primarily of a vineyard of Zinfandel vines planted between 1905 and 1927. Louis Barbieri, who owned the land, had not been successful in enticing his children to farm the vineyard. He and Cecil came to an agreement that Louis would continue to live in the farm-house and teach the DeLoach family how to grow grapes if Cecil purchased the property.

Cecil moved a small trailer to the ranch and lived there on his off days while learning to tend the vineyards. In 1971, the family moved to the farmhouse and the next year the DeLoaches purchased a neighboring 28 acres. Part of this property later became the site for the winery. Cecil continued his job with the San Francisco Fire Department.

The 22-acre Zinfandel vineyard, with its 60-year-old vines, is dry farmed and is still producing excellent grapes. It continues to provide the grapes for the estate bottled DeLoach Zinfandel. Since 1971, other grape varieties have been planted — Gewurztraminer, Pinot Noir, Chardonnay, and more Zinfandel. The DeLoaches also lease additional acreage for their wine production. In total they either own or operate 150 acres of vineyards.

In 1972, Cecil DeLoach, happy to have his family living in the country, started selling his grapes to the Sonoma County Cooperative Winery in nearby Windsor, California. He has been on the Board of Directors of the Cooperative since 1972, serving as its president in 1973. This exposure led to his interest in wine and winemaking. Since his job as a fireman was not a regular 9-to-5 one, he was able to take extension courses in enology and chemistry from U. C. Davis. Cecil was really leading a double life — as a fire fighter and as a viticulturist — and the possibility of becoming a vintner was not too far in the future.

In 1975, Cecil felt that he was ready to start making wine professionally, having made some successful wine on an amateur basis the previous years. He also felt that his premium grapes should be used for premium wines. That year, he kept some of his prime Zinfandel grapes, rented a nondescript metal building in a Santa Rosa industrial complex, and bought some old-fashioned, used winery equipment. The wine he made turned out well, and the DeLoaches decided they needed a winery building if they were going to be vintners.

Cecil drew up the plans for a 3,200-square-foot winery. It was designed to resemble a California mission building, and he and the boys constructed it. He figured that if the winery did not succeed, he could always put a cross on top of the building and sell it for a church. Finally, after two years of dealing with government paper work, the De-Loach winery was bonded in 1979. In 1981, Cecil retired from the San Francisco Fire Department to become a full-time vintner.

In 1984, the DeLoaches added a 6,000-square-foot addition for office space, additional winery space, and a tasting room. Again the family did most of the construction work. Cecil has always put the profits of the winery back into the business. "We've always had to go slow because everything we do is with money generated internally," Cecil says. "There is no family fortune and there is no stock portfolio to finance this winery." he continued. In seven years, the winery has grown from 9,000 cases to 45,000 cases per year. The success is not only due to the quality of the wines, but also to Cecil's determination and the family's commitment to the winery. All of the DeLoach wines are 100% varietal.

"If there is one philosophy that runs through Cecil DeLoach's winemaking it is to bring out the varietal character of the grape and to have a year-to-year consistency," says Randy Ullom, associate winemaker at DeLoach Vineyards.

DeLoach vineyards makes both a Fumé Blanc and a Sauvignon Blanc. The latter has a more grassy style, and the wine is aged three weeks in oak. The Zinfandel grapes are treated in the traditional manner of open top fermentation. After the wine is racked, it is placed in 3,000-gallon Yugoslavian uprights to finish the fermentation process and then aged in small barrels for 8 to 16 months. In addition to racking, the Zinfandel is egg-white fined for a silky finish and filtered prior to bottling.

The Pinot Noir is handled similarly to the Zinfandel. Cecil restricts the production of Pinot Noir to about two and one half tons per acre. During fermentation, about 5% of whole stems are added back into the fermenting wine. Fermentation starts at 78 degrees. At peak fermentation, the temperature is raised to 84 degrees, and then the cooling jackets on the stainless steel tanks bring the temperature back down to the low 70s. Cecil feels this spike in temperature allows for more color extraction.

DeLoach is truly a family operation Cecil is the winemaker, Mike is in charge of marketing, and Christine and daughter-in-law Rachael (Mike's wife) work together on hospitality. Hard work and perseverance have earned DeLoach Vineyards an enclave of bells and puffs of excellence reminiscent of Cecil's fire fighting days — only this time it is not an alert to tragedy, but an alert to superior quality.

Domaine Laurier Vineyards & Winery

Address: 8075 Martinelli Road, Forestville 95436
  □ (707) 887-2176
Visitation: Weekdays by appointment
Principals: Jacob and Barbara Shilo
Varietals produced: Sauvignon Blanc, Chardonnay, Pinot Noir, and Cabernet Sauvignon
Production: 15,000 cases per year.

"Domaine Laurier" means "Home of the Laurel." It was inspired by a 150-year old laurel tree that is the dominant landmark of the winery estate of the same name. Inspired by the strength and tradition which this old tree radiates, Jacob and Barbara Shilo made a commitment to produce superior quality wines using traditional French methods — but utilizing modern technology.

Traditional French winemaking philosophy has influenced the entire development of the Domaine Laurier winery. This extends from the name to the decision to produce the four varietal wines made so famous in France — Sauvignon Blanc, Chardonnay, Pinot Noir, and Cabernet Sauvignon.

Just as the ancestry of these grapes go back to Europe, so does the ancestry of Barbara and Jacob Shilo. Barbara was born in Germany and immigrated to the United States as a young girl. Her interest in fine arts, particularly painting, seemed only natural since her father was the founder and owner of a large artists' production and supply company in New York. She attended Hunter College and New York University in New York City where she lived until the early 1960s and she has continued her interest in fine art. Today she is a painter of some renown. Barbara has also had a professional writing career.

Jacob Shilo was born in Poland, grew up in Israel, and spent a part of his professional life there as an agronomist and economist. He pioneered in the settlement and development of the Upper Galilee Region of Israel. For a while he worked in a consulting firm planning agricultural projects in underdeveloped countries. On one of his trips to the United States he met Barbara. They settled in Westchester County near New York City. During this time Jacob was commuting between the United States and Israel where he managed an electronics company. Subsequently, Jacob and Barbara moved to California.

In 1977, the Shilos decided to move to a more rural area and looked for property in Sonoma County. They found a 60-acre plot near the Russian River which had some Cabernet Sauvignon and Pinot Noir grapes planted on it. The Shilos had always enjoyed wine, and Jacob had made some wine as a hobby. With Jacob's agricultural-economic background, it was relatively easy for him to become a vintner. Since becoming a vintner, Jacob has been retained by the Israeli government as a consultant on the development of its wine industry.

The cool climate of the Green Valley region of Sonoma

County — the cool mornings and warm afternoons fanned by ocean breezes — proved to be ideal for growing the four varieties in which the Shilos were interested. Pinot Noir and Cabernet Sauvignon are estate grown on 30 acres, and some Sauvignon Blanc and Chardonnay are purchased from nearby vineyards. All of the grapes are hand picked in small lots to ensure minimum handling.

There are two types of vineyards on the estate — one on the hillside and the other on bottom land. The Chardonnay is planted on a terraced hillside with drip irrigation. The bottom land is dry farmed and can be temporarily flooded by winter rains. In the heavy rains of February 1986, the bottom land vineyard was entirely covered with flood water well above the top of the bare vines. Fortunately for the Shilos and other vintners along the Russian River who were flooded, no lasting damage occurred to the vines or the vineyards.

The winemaker at Domaine Laurier is Stephen Test, who has a bachelor's degree from Stanford and a master's in enology from U.C. Davis. He follows traditional French winemaking methods. The philosophy of winemaking at Domaine Laurier is to maximize the complexity of each varietal. A large percentage of the Sauvignon Blanc and Chardonnay is barrel fermented. The complexity of the Chardonnay is further enhanced with malolactic fermentation. Both the Sauvignon Blanc and the Chardonnay are aged in French oak barrels. All lots of Chardonnay are handled separately through the aging stage and then blended together to produce the final product.

At present, the Domaine Laurier winery is in a converted barn. The Shilos have completed plans to construct a winery building in the same style as their Tudor-style home. The home, which is perched on top of a hill, was designed by a San Francisco architect and built by local craftsmen. The interior of the house, with its beautiful wood panelling, is a showcase for Barbara's paintings. The kitchen is one that anyone who likes to cook dreams of owning. Barbara is a gourmet cook and develops many recipes complimenting the Domaine Laurier wines. The Shilos enjoy entertaining in the traditional European style.

Jacob says that when he started the winery, he thought 10,000 cases a year would be economical, but with inflation those figures keep going up and his goal now is a 30,000-case winery. He says, "Bigger than that, you may lose control and sacrifice quality."

Jacob hopes that the bulk of the California wine industry will remain under individual ownership so as to encourage experimentation and ensure the production of high quality premium wines. ❧

Field Stone Winery

Address: 10075 State Highway 128, Healdsburg 95448
   ☐ (707) 433-7266
Visitation: Daily, 10 AM to 5 PM
Principals: The Wallace Johnson Family, dba Redwood Ranch and Vineyard
Varietals produced: Sauvignon Blanc, Chenin Blanc, Gewurztraminer, Johannisberg Riesling, Rose of Petite Sirah, Spring Cabernet (Rose of Cabernet Sauvignon), Petite Sirah, Cabernet Sauvignon, Late Harvest Johannisberg Riesling, and Late Harvest Gewurztraminer
Production: 12,000 cases per year

The basic interrelationship of earth, vine, and wine is represented by the unique underground building of Field Stone Winery. It is the first of its kind to be built in California in this century. The face of the winery is composed of the field stones selected from the 1976 excavation for this winery. Massive oak trees grow on top of the knoll and, except for the face of the building, there is no evidence of a structure being hidden in the hillside.

Construction of a winery, however, was not envisioned when, in the fall of 1955, Wallace Johnson and his family purchased a ranch in the Alexander Valley, north of Healdsburg. The ranch of rolling hills was perfect for raising purebred cattle, and Mr. Johnson decided to name his property Redwood Hereford Ranch. Wallace (Wally, as he was known to both friends and acquaintances), was the inventor of portable aluminum scaffolds and had manufacturing plants in the United States and abroad. He also became a very innovative rancher and grape grower.

In the early 1960s, the Alexander Valley's main crops were pears, plums, and cattle, although before Prohibition the land had been in vineyards and had produced prime grapes. Ninety years ago, Italian farmers had planted a ten-acre plot with Petite Sirah vines. This vineyard is still in existence today, and its grapes are being made into award-winning wines.

Wallace Johnson had extensive soil and temperature studies conducted on his ranch and put in test plots to determine which were the best grape varietals for the ranch. He also acquired additional property for his vineyards, bringing the ranch total to 850 acres. In 1966, 130 acres of the five best growing varietals from the test plots — Cabernet Sauvignon, Sauvignon Blanc, Johannisberg Riesling, Chenin Blanc, and Gewurztraminer — were planted. The vineyard acreage has since been increased to 145 acres. At the time of the planting, the ranch was renamed "Redwood Ranch and Vineyard."

Johnson applied his inventive genius to the invention of a mechanical grape harvester, a first in the world of viticulture. As a result, hand harvesting has been combined with the use of the mechanical harvester in the Redwood Ranch vineyards. The harvester is used at night when grape picking can be done at cooler temperatures. It takes two people to operate the harvester, instead of the usual 20 needed to hand pick the grapes.

Ten years after Wallace Johnson planted his vineyards, he decided to produce his own wines. Prior to 1976, the Johnson family sold all of their grapes to other vintners. In 1976, however, they decided to build the winery and produce wine from a select portion of the vineyards.

In the summer of 1979, Wallace Johnson died of a massive stroke. His son-in-law, John Staten, took over the management of both the ranch and the winery. He has continued Wallace Johnson's idea of a small estate winery producing a limited quantity of premium wines from the choicest grapes on the ranch.

John Staten was born in west Texas and spent part of his youth living on a sheep ranch, which makes him no stranger to the world of ranching and farming. Before taking over the management of the Redwood Ranch and Vineyard and the Field Stone Winery he had a career in academia. After graduating with a B.A. in history and philosophy from Stanford he went on to graduate school at Princeton to study ancient biblical languages and literature, and received a Ph.D. in theology. Dr. Staten has headed the religious studies departments at Reed College in Oregon and at Mills College in Oakland, California. He still teaches part-time, and is a lecturer and writer in the field of theology.

Shortly after graduating from Stanford, John Staten married Katrina Johnson, his college sweetheart. She serves as secretary-treasurer of the family corporation while also raising a family of four children.

James Thomson, who has a degree in microbiology, is the winemaker at Field Stone. He gained practical experience in winemaking working at HMR winery under André Tchelistcheff, the acknowledged dean of American winemakers. This association continues as Mr. Tchelistcheff is the consulting enologist for Field Stone and Jim Thomson.

Field Stone Winery is known for its red wines, particularly its Petite Sirah from century-old vines. The vines are a one-of-a-kind clone, tracing their history back to the Rhone Valley. Wine derived from these vines emphasizes the fruitiness and the varietal character of the grapes. Blending techniques of the Rhone Valley are utilized in producing the Petite Sirah. A small percentage of a neutral white grape — Chenin Blanc — is blended into the crusher with the Petite Sirah. After fermentation the wine is aged for about 14 months in French and American barrels. The Petite Sirah has been a consistent medal winner.

Sauvignon Blanc is a relative newcomer to the list of wines made by Field Stone. The grapes are harvested at the peak of their ripeness. The wine is given fifteen hours of skin contact and cold fermented to capture the fruitiness of the grape. It is then aged in new French oak standing barrels,

Although viticulture and winemaking were not John Staten's first vocation, he has fallen in love with them. He is carrying on in the best tradition of his late father-in-law, who had a 30-year-long "love affair" with the land — the earth, the vine, and the wine. 🍇

Fisher Vineyards

Address: 6200 St. Helena Road, Santa Rosa, 95404
□ (707) 539-7511
Visitation: By appointment only
Principals: Fred and Juelle Fisher
Varietals produced: Chardonnay and Cabernet
Sauvignon
Production: 7,000 cases per year

At the turn of the century, it was "Bodies by Fisher" for the carriage trade. Today it is elegant wines from Fisher Vineyards. The same heritage of craftsmanship which is a family tradition is used today in crafting fine wines.

Fred J. Fisher, II is a native of Detroit, Michigan, the son of a chairman of a major bank and the grandson of a founder of the Fisher Body Corporation. Early in life he learned respect for fine craftsmanship and for hard work. After graduating with honors in engineering from Princeton University, he went on to Harvard for an M.B.A.

In 1956, Fred joined the army to "see the world." While on various tours of duty in Europe and the Far East, he learned about the wines of the countries where he was stationed and became a lover of wines. Back in the United States he worked for many years in private industry, but always had the ambition of owning and running his own business.

This ambition became a reality when, in 1973, he purchased a small and picturesque valley in the Sonoma Mayacamas Mountains. The property had been homesteaded in 1888, and grapes were grown there for many years. At first he thought he would plant a small vineyard as a hobby, but he became so intrigued with raising grapes, and possibly making wine that he planted 18 1/2 acres of Chardonnay and Cabernet Sauvignon — the two wines he

enjoyed most. To add to his knowledge, he took classes in viticulture and winemaking at U.C. Davis. In 1975, the vineyard was the scene of his marriage to Juelle Welch Lamb, a native of Utah.

Fred Fisher made his first Cabernet Sauvignon in the fall of 1977. Two years later, Fred realized his ambition to own his own business by building a winery to make uniquely crafted wines. A close friend, architect Bill Turnbull, himself a winery owner, designed the building for Fred. The exterior was constructed from two large redwood trees which were felled on the property, and the interior is panelled with Douglas fir, also from trees that had to be felled to make room for the winery. The winery building has won numerous design and construction awards including citations from the California chapter of the AIA and the American Wood Council as one of the outstanding California buildings of the decade.

To complete his quest for excellence, he engaged Henryk Gasiewicz as winemaker. Henryk has a perfect palate and often serves as a judge in wine competitions. Henryk makes wines by the taste of his palate, not by chemistry or book formulas. While working at Fisher as cellarmaster, Henryk met a member of the French winemaking family of *Domaine de Comte Lafon.* The following year, he went to France for six months to study their winemaking techniques.

To increase his grape growing capacity and add blending complexity Fred Fisher purchased an additional vineyard of 70 acres on the Napa Valley floor near Calistoga in 1975. Chardonnay is mainly grown on this property which has entirely different characteristics than those grown on the side of the mountain at Fisher Vineyards. The mountain vineyards are at elevations of 900 to 1,400 feet, with well drained soils. The steep mountainside vineyards produce grapes of exceptional quality grown in stressed circumstances.

Henryk strives for elegance and balance in his winemaking. The Chardonnay has minimum skin contact before fermentation. He partially barrel ferments the juice in small oak barrels for a light oaky character. All of the lots of wines are fermented and aged separately and blended after aging. The Chardonnay is barrel aged for eight months. Henryk and Fred Fisher feel that the real art of winemaking is in the blending.

The Fisher Cabernet Sauvignon is from the hillside vineyards near the winery. It is aged in small French Nevers oak barrels for two years, bottled and aged another year prior to release.

Just as his grandfather strived for excellence in his product — Fisher car bodies — Fred Fisher strives for excellence in the Chardonnay and Cabernet Sauvignon wines from his vineyards. ❧

Gundlach-Bundschu Winery

Address: 2000 Denmark Street, Vineburg 95487
☐ (707) 938-5277
Visitation: Daily, 11 AM to 4:30 PM
Principals: Jim Bundschu
Varietals produced: Chardonnay, Gewurztraminer, Sonoma Riesling, Kleinberger, Pinot Noir, Merlot, Zinfandel, and Cabernet Sauvignon
Production: 40,000 cases

Over 125 years of grape growing expertise and excellence stand behind the label of one of the oldest commercial wineries in California. Although the winery was idle for over 50 years, grape growing on the Gundlach-Bundschu Rhinefarm never ceased, nor deteriorated, but always improved.

Jacob Gundlach left Germany in 1850 to come to California for the Gold Rush as so many other Europeans were doing. His ship was wrecked off the coast of Africa, and he ended up in Rio de Janeiro for a short stay, arriving in California a year after departing Germany and too late for the Gold Rush. Gundlach worked for a short time as a brewer in San Francisco, while he searched for property with soil and climate conducive to growing wine grapes.

Near the town of Sonoma he found a climate and soil that was reminiscent of the south slopes of the Rhine west of Frankfurt. He proceeded to plant 400 acres of vineyards and built a stone winery into the limestone hillside. The coolness of the earth on three sides of the winery were to keep the barrels of wine cool and humid through the hot Sonoma summers. Gundlach called the wine estate the Rhinefarm, and the small community that grew up around it was named Vineburg. The community still exists today with its own Post Office. Gundlach-Bundschu Winery has P.O. Box 1.

The business and the reputation of the German winemaker flourished, and in 1862 Gundlach took on a partner — Charles Bundschu — a fellow Bavarian. The two worked very well together, making fine wine which won awards all over the country and in Paris. They established a large cellar and offices in San Francisco to better merchandise their wines. In 1872, Charles Bundschu married Gundlach's daughter, Francesca. The marriage had been prearranged when Bundschu first joined the partnership and when Francesca was still a child.

The 1906 San Francisco earthquake and its resulting fires leveled the Gundlach-Bundschu cellar and offices in San Francisco. All of the wine inventory was destroyed, but five months later a new building was being constructed, and it too flourished until Prohibition delivered that fatal blow, as it did to many other California wineries.

Although the Gundlach-Bundschu winery was forced to close, a few wineries remained open, and Carl and Walter Bundschu (whose wife Sadie was a strict Prohibitionist) worked as winemakers at a nearby wineries making wine for medicinal purposes. The Rhinefarm vineyards continued to raise grapes and sold them to wineries making wine for medicinal and sacramental purposes and also to grape juice manufacturers. With the repeal of Prohibition, many Sonoma and Napa wineries reopened, and many were eager to purchase the high quality grapes from Bundschu's Rhinefarm.

For the next 38 years, the Bundschu's continued to improve their vineyards, plant new acreage, and sell grapes — upholding a long established standard of quality and excellence. It was not until the late 1960s that Jim Bundschu, great-great-grandson of Jacob Gundlach, decided to resume the tradition of making wines. The old winery was reopened and completely refurbished, with new modern equipment and modern technology. The original building with Bonded Winery Number 64 is the second oldest licensed winery in California. The two-foot-thick walls still provide natural insulation and cooling for the winery. Since the reopening, an addition to the winery has been built.

Jim Bundschu, who has a degree in Economics from the University of California at Berkeley, grew up in the vineyards and is thoroughly familiar with grape growing. Knowing that vines have been growing successfully on the property for over 125 years, he tends to practice the old tried and true methods of farming. Jim believes that "good wine is born in the vineyards and raised in the winery." Eighty-five percent of all Gundlach-Bundschu wines are estate grown.

Gundlach-Bundschu winery is known for its red wines and its German style whites. Lance Cutler is the winemaker, and he prefers to produce his reds with an intense character. He is proudest of the Special Reserve Cabernet Sauvignon. The fruit is grown in limestone soil at the top of a hill on the property. The fruit ripens early and is very intense in flavor and color, with a considerable amount of tannin. Lance Culter blends very little Merlot into any of the Cabernets produced at Gundlach-Bundschu because he wants to preserve the unique characteristics of the Cabernet Sauvignon. Sixty percent of Gundlach-Bundschu production is in red wines, primarily Merlot and Cabernet Sauvignon.

The Gundlach-Bundschu Rieslings are also well

known. The winery is the only one in the United States to produce a Kleinberger wine — a German clone of Johannisberg Riesling. The wine is made in a Riesling style and is very fruity. Their Sonoma Riesling is a blend of Rieslings — Johannisberg, Sylvaner, and Kleinberger.

The Rhinefarm vineyards have always been a family operation and continue to carry on this early California wine tradition. ❧

Hacienda Winery

Address: 1000 Vineyard Lane, Sonoma 95476
☐ (707) 938-3220
Visitation: Daily, 10 AM to 5 PM
Principals: A. Crawford Cooley, Robert A. Cooley, Steven W. MacRostie
Varietals produced: Chenin Blanc, Sauvignon Blanc, Chardonnay, Gewurztraminer, Pinot Noir, Zinfandel, Cabernet Sauvignon, and Vintage Port
Production: 25,000 cases per year

On the entrance to the property known today as Hacienda Winery is a marker which proclaims "Here is Where It All Began." The vineyard land surrounding Hacienda Winery is one of the oldest commercial grape producing properties in California. The surrounding land was originally planted in 1857 by a Hungarian nobleman (some have disputed his nobility), Count Agoston Haraszthy, who had collected over 100,000 grape cuttings from France, Italy, Germany, and Spain. One of Hacienda's vineyards was planted originally in 1862. Today it is planted in Chardonnay and Pinot Noir.

The property was originally a part of the Buena Vista Winery and Vineyards founded by Count Haraszthy in the early 1860s and passed through various hands in subsequent years. At one time a huge mansion also graced the property. When the last owner of the residence — a Mrs Johnson — died in 1920, she willed the house and its surroundings to the state of California, provided that the state would take care of her collection of cats and let them live in the house. The state did until the cats died out.

The mansion then became a home for wayward women. In 1926, the state built an infirmary for the institution. One night in the late 1930s the mansion burned down and it was never rebuilt. The infirmary was turned into the Sonoma Valley Hospital. The Spanish-style building of white stucco with a red tile roof, remained the only hospital in Sonoma until the late 1950s. For a while, the building was a nursing home.

In the late 1870s the original Buena Vista Winery and surrounding vineyards had started to decline. This was accelerated by the infestation of phylloxera, the collapse of the wine cellar in the 1906 earthquake, and Prohibition in the 1920s. In 1941, Frank Bartholomew, executive vice-president of United Press International, purchased the Buena Vista property. War interrupted his efforts to restore the winery — he was UPI chief of the Pacific theater of operations. After the war, however, he succeeded in restoring Buena Vista as a well-respected winery. Frank Bartholomew sold Buena Vista in 1968, but retained the portion which is now Hacienda Winery and its vineyards.

After selling Buena Vista, Frank still wanted to operate a winery, so he converted the former hospital building into a winery in 1973. The 14-inch-thick walls provided excellent insulation and the red quarry tile floor was suited to easy maintenance for a winery. He added some colonial charm to the building and installed modern crushing and fermentation equipment. As the winery operations became too much for him he recalled a friend's interest in the wine business. As a consequence he prevailed upon his friend, Crawford Cooley, to became general manager of Hacienda winery in 1976. The following year Crawford purchased the majority interest.

Crawford Cooley's roots are deeply entwined in the settlement and development of California. His mother's family, the Elliots, came from the South to California in the second overland party to the state in 1845. His father's family came from Ohio and settled in Sacramento, lured by the Gold Rush of 1849. By 1853, the Cooleys had moved to a farm in Cloverdale and planted prunes, citrus, some other produce and vineyards.

Crawford's father attended Stanford University, and after graduation set up a law practice in San Francisco. Crawford also went to Stanford; he was an economics major and after graduating, entered the world of business. He was vice-president of Chromatic, a research and development firm founded by three Nobel prize winners, working on the development of color television. From there, Crawford moved to Litton Industries and then on to Draper, Gaither and Anderson in Palo Alto, California, a venture capital firm specializing in the electronics industry. In the early 1970s Crawford and his wife Jess moved their family to Marin County to be closer to the family properties in Sonoma County.

Crawford Cooley continues to manage the old family ranch in Cloverdale. The ranch has 12 acres of Sauvignon Blanc and Cabernet Sauvignon which are used by the winery. This ranch vineyard is one of the oldest grape producing vineyards in the state.

The 45 acres of estate vineyards around the winery itself produce Chardonnay, Cabernet Sauvignon, and Pinot Noir. The Pinot Noir grapes are over 20 years old and only produce one and a half tons per acre. Additional grapes are purchased from contract growers in Sonoma County.

Steven MacRostie is the winemaker at Hacienda, and has been since 1974. He has developed the operation from a 1,000-case winery to its present 25,000 cases. Steven grew up in Sacramento and graduated from Washington's Whitman College with a degree in biology and a minor in chemistry. He was going to be a doctor. Two years in Italy with the U.S. Army altered his course. In Italy he learned the language, traveled and developed a passion for wine. Upon his return to California, he entered U. C. Davis, where he earned a masters in enology in 1972.

Since Steven believes very strongly that grapes are the key to successful winemaking, he has an ongoing search for grapes which meet his criteria. He is interested in the clone of the vineyard, the yield per acre, and the soil and climatic conditions. He is constantly looking for hillside or bench-land grown grapes with a yield of two to five tons per acre.

Steven's favorite wine variety is Gewurztraminer. He has the grapes harvested when they are just getting a russet glow and are between 21.5 and 22 degrees Brix. "That is when their spicy flavors are at their best," he says. The crushed grapes have three hours of skin contact and are fermented at 50 degrees in stainless steel tanks. There is no oak aging and the wine has .75% to .90% residual sugar.

The award-winning Hacienda Chenin Blanc grapes come from the Clarksburg area, southwest of Sacramento. Mechanical harvesting at night allows the grapes to arrive at the winery in the morning still cool. After crushing, Steve lets the juice rest with three hours of skin contact to increase varietal intensity. The wine is fermented in stainless steel tanks to .8% residual sugar. There is no oak aging. The slight amount of sugar gives the wine good balance. All Hacienda wines complement food, but still have complexity.

Robert Cooley, Crawford's son, joined the Hacienda organization in 1979 and became its national sales manager in 1982. A champion cow horse rider, he now crosses the United States on the wine circuit instead of the rodeo circuit.

Although Hacienda is a creation of the 1970s, its vineyards date back to the 1860s when commercial winegrowing began in Northern California. Count Haraszthy's aim was to provide California with excellent wine grapes, Hacienda today is making excellent wines and continuing this heritage. 🍂

Hop Kiln Winery, Griffin Vineyards

Address: 6050 Westside Road, Healdsburg 95448
□ (707) 433-6491
Visitation: Daily, 10 AM to 5 PM
Principals: Dr. L. Martin Griffin, Jr.
Varietals produced: Sauvignon Blanc, Johannisberg Riesling, Gewurztraminer, Chardonnay, Napa Gamay, Cabernet Sauvignon, Petite Sirah, Zinfandel, and Sparkling Johannisberg Riesling
Production: 10,000 cases per year

Hop Kiln is the most famous landmark in Sonoma County. The structure is on the registry of National Historic Trust Buildings and it has been used as a backdrop for four movies. Today the building is a winery, but at the turn of the century it was a hop kiln.

Dr. Martin Griffin purchased the 240-acre sheep ranch in 1960 with a building that was practically falling apart — the hop kiln. Dr. Griffin, who grew up on a dairy farm in

Utah, purchased the property with an eye toward eventual retirement. That however, was not to be.

A graduate of Stanford Medical School, Dr. Griffin was a cofounder of the Ross Valley Clinic in Marin County where he practiced internal medicine for 19 years. After retiring from medical practice he went into wildlife conservation work. He was cofounder of the Audubon Canyon Ranch and the Kent Island Wildlife Preserves near Stinson Beach north of San Francisco. Dr. Griffin also helped establish Hawaii's first state park for nature conservation on the island of Maui. Later he worked on a wildlife preservation project in Nepal.

During visits to India, Dr. Griffin became interested in public health, and, in 1971, earned a master's degree in the subject from the University of California. At the present time, he is public health officer at Sonoma State Hospital and is in charge of the clinic for the 2,000 employees. All of this, of course is in addition to supervising the running of the Hop Kiln Winery.

Shortly after he purchased the Sonoma Hop Kiln ranch, he started to restore the building with the help of two friends, Fred Ross and George McGeary. It was in bad need of repair since the ridgepole connecting the two sections of the barn had collapsed and later one of the three towers blew down in a windstorm. In order to finance this project he had to find a way to make the building pay for itself. Even though he came from a teetotalling background, he decided to turn it into a winery.

There were already grapes on the property which were about 100 years old. When the building was used as a hop kiln, from about 1905 to the early 1940s, the Petite Sirah and Zinfandel which grew on the property were made into wine for the workers. Shortly after Dr. Griffin purchased the ranch he added more vineyards because the ranch has several micro-climates suitable for grape growing. One section has a cool climate similar to the Rhine valley of Germany and is ideal for growing Johannisberg Riesling. The other part of the ranch has the same climate as the sunny hillsides of France and Italy and is well suited to Petite Sirah and Zinfandel. There are now 65 acres planted in vineyards.

Dr. Griffin is a great believer in preserving the past as he has not only done with the restoration of the hop kiln, but also with the preservation of his residence on the property. He purchased an old Victorian built in 1873, had it cut into four pieces, and moved it to its present site on the ranch. The house, which needed repair, has been restored to its original splendor.

Dr. Griffin first became interested in wine when he lived in Italy for a short while. He studied the winemaking techniques in Tuscany and Sicily and became intrigued with the whole process. Later, in 1977, he went to Germany to learn the wine and champagne making process there.

By 1974, Hop Kiln had been completely restored and turned into a winery. Dr. Griffin became its first winemaker with the crush of that fall. "A friend and I made the first wine," he recalls. "There were grapes everywhere, even in the bathtub." With the release of Petite Sirah and Johannisberg Riesling in 1975, the Hop Kiln Winery was to become an integral part of the Sonoma wine scene.

Dr. Griffin sees nothing strange in combining a career in public health with that of a vintner. After all, it was Louis Pasteur who was the chief winemaker of France during his time. Most of the winemaking techniques Dr. Griffin learned in Europe have been utilized at the winery. There is open top fermentation of the reds, similar to the process used in Italy and the whites are made in the German style. Dr. Griffin's theory is that wine must taste good at every stage of its development — when the grapes are picked, when they are crushed, when fermentation begins, and as the wine is aging.

In 1979, Hop Kiln started making sparkling wine in the *Méthode Champenoise* from Johannisberg Riesling grapes, the favorite grape in Germany for making champagne. Hop Kiln is still one of the few wineries bottling the cuvée and riddling and disgorging it entirely by hand. The wine is left on the yeast for two to three years and is made in a very dry style (Sehr Trochen). The aging cellars for the champagne are old hop kilns in the winery, consisting of massive rock and limestone walls 16 inches thick. Each kiln is 30 x 30 x 30 feet. Before use, however, 40 years of hops-drying grime had to be scrubbed, the rock walls "pointed up," and a concrete floor installed. Each year, Hop Kiln has increased its champagne production, although it is still sold only at the winery.

Several years ago, Dr. Griffin turned over the winemaking duties to Steve Strobl, who had taken courses in enology at U.C. Davis and worked at several other wineries in the area. Steve's wife Jo Anne is the manager of the winery. Several of Dr. Griffin's children are involved in the marketing of Hop Kiln wines.

To Dr. Griffin the greatest satisfaction is not the wines themselves or the awards they have won. It is the fact that he has helped save and preserve two old buildings — the hop kiln and the Victorian residence. "They are part of our heritage and have a lot of good values that have almost been forgotten," he says. The hop kiln certainly has not been forgotten. Instead of being a slowly deteriorating, obsolete building, it is now, 78 years later, serving a useful purpose as a winery involved in the making of premium wines. ❧

Iron Horse Vineyards

Address: 9786 Ross Station Road, Sebastopol 95472
□ (707) 887-1507

Visitation: Tuesday through Saturday, by appointment only

Principals: Barry and Audrey Sterling, and Forrest Tancer

Varietals produced: Fumé Blanc, Chardonnay, Pinot Noir, Cabernet Sauvignon, and Brut, Blanc de Blanc, and Blanc de Noirs (Sparkling Wines)

Production: 25,000 cases per year

Iron Horse — in years past it was the name of a railroad stop in Sonoma County. Today it is the name of the brand of sparkling wine that President Reagan once served to Mikhail Gorbachev at a summit meeting in Geneva. Iron Horse Sparkling Wines, in fact, are served at many important world functions, as well gracing the dinner tables of many Americans. Iron Horse Vineyards also produces an array of excellent still wines, made from the 135 acres of estate grown grapes.

Iron Horse Vineyards and Winery is located on gentle sloping hillsides in Green Valley, 65 miles north of San Francisco. The site had originally been selected for vineyards by Rodney Strong, Sonoma winemaker and founder of Sonoma Vineyards. He felt that the area, with its warm days and cool Pacific coast breezes, would be good for early ripening grape varieties, such as Chardonnay and Pinot Noir. In 1971, Forrest Tancer was hired by Strong to plan and develop the vineyards on the Iron Horse ranch.

Forrest Tancer, who grew up in the Alexander Valley area of Sonoma County, has a degree in political science from the University of California at Berkeley. While going to school he worked during the summers in the vineyards and after graduation from college he took a semester in viticulture at Fresno State. He decided to broaden his education, and he and his wife spent time in the Peace Corps in Brazil.

After returning to California, he worked for Rodney Strong for five years, in the summers in the vineyards, and in the fall and winter as cellarmaster of Sonoma Vineyards. When Audrey and Barry Sterling purchased Iron Horse they asked Forrest to remain as vineyard manager. That same year Forrest, his wife Kate and their young daughter moved back to Alexander Valley and took over the family ranch, where Forrest began improving the vineyards and planting new grapes.

By 1978, with the Iron Horse vineyard plantings complete and the vines bearing fruit, Forrest and the Sterlings formed a partnership to develop a small winery using only estate grown grapes. There are 110 acres of grapes on the 300-acre Iron Horse ranch and 30 acres on Tancer's Alexander Valley ranch. The trio would combine the tonnage of the Sterlings vineyards and Tancer's Alexander Valley grapes. Forrest planned the construction of the winery and became the winemaker.

The Sterlings are both Californians and graduates of Stanford University. Barry, who had accelerated his studies in the lower grades, entered Stanford at the age of 16 and graduated at 22 with a law degree, having passed the bar before graduation. In the summer of 1952 after graduation, Barry and Audrey were married and they moved to Washington, D.C. where Barry joined the Judge Advocate General's Corps and served as an attorney on the legal staff of the Pentagon.

Upon completion of his military service, Barry Sterling returned to Los Angeles to practice corporate law, founding his own firm in 1960. On his first trip to Europe at the age of 30 (the trip was a birthday present from Audrey), he fell in love with France and vowed one day to live there. In 1966, he joined a prestigious Los Angeles law firm and was sent to Paris to represent American and European clients.

It was during the time that the Sterlings lived in Paris that their knowledge of and love for fine wines expanded. The apartment where they were living had a wine cellar with room for 10,000 bottles. Barry collected more than 4,000 bottles of the finest European wines.

In 1967, the Sterlings made an offer on a wine chateau in Bordeaux, but due to appellation problems had to withdraw the offer. In 1974, Barry, Audrey, and their two children, returned to California where they resumed a search for vineyard property.

Two years later, in a driving rainstorm, they saw Iron Horse for the first time. Although the property and the Victorian house needed extensive renovations, the Sterlings sensed that this property had great potential. Forrest Tancer was asked to stay on to run the operation. Together he and Audrey managed the vineyards and the winery while Barry continued his law practice in Los Angeles, coming home on weekends. In 1984, Barry retired from his law practice to take on the full-time job of general operations manager and director of marketing. Recently, daughter Joy, after a career in journalism and as a TV news director, has taken over the job of marketing.

After acquiring Iron Horse, Audrey Sterling, who had always been a great hostess, became even more involved in entertaining. First, however, there was the charming Victorian to be remodeled — in nine months' time — as

Audrey informed the carpenters. "After all, a house should take no longer than a baby," she recalls telling them. The house was pulled apart, restored and put back in place. Today it is one of the showcases of Sonoma County. Audrey had patios built, flower beds planted and two greenhouses constructed so that she might always have fresh flowers for the table and for her guests. Audrey adores flowers and has whatever flower is in season blooming in abundance. On the patios she can easily seat and serve 100 guests.

When the Sterlings purchased Iron Horse, Audrey had not cooked in over 25 years. However, she found she had to do so since there was no help available in the immediate vicinity. Now she has a full-time live-in cook who prepares the dishes from menus specified by Audrey. Regardless of whether she is entertaining 2 or 300, Audrey's food preparations are works of art designed to pair with Iron Horse wines.

Not only have Iron Horse wines been served at important occasions, but they have also won many awards. The sparkling wines are all made in the *Méthode Champe-noise*. The grapes for these wines are hand picked into small containers, and pressed rather than crushed to extract low yields of juice without harsh overtones. A *liqueur de Tirage* is added to create a second fermentation in the bottle. The wines receive daily attention from Claude Thibaut, who grew up on his family's Champagne property, and has been a member of the Iron Horse staff since 1983.

The Sterlings and Forrest Tancer like the style of Iron Horse Wines to be crisp and steely — an austere style similar to the French. "We make wines to suit our own palate and to complement food," says Audrey. "They are not big wines," she continues. In years of entertaining, whether in her charming Victorian home in Sonoma County or her country estate in the South of France, doing simple French country cooking, Audrey Sterling has become an expert in wine and food.

Today, Iron Horse Vineyards is a well-respected name in premium wines. The property has certainly come a long way from being a whistle-stop on a railroad. 🐾

Landmark Vineyards

Address: 9150 Los Amigos Road, Windsor 95492
□ (707) 838-9466
Visitation: By appointment only
Principals: William R. Mabry III
Varietals produced: Chardonnay
Production: 23,000 cases per year

William R. Mabry III is the president and winemaker of Landmark Vineyards, a position he has held since 1974. He is one of the youngest vintners in California. He actually started making wine before he was legally allowed to drink it!

Bill Mabry became interested in viticulture and winemaking while planting his family's Sonoma Valley vineyard in 1971. Colonel Mabry, Bill's father, had retired from a career in the Air Force, and he and his wife, Maxine, had settled in Sonoma, near Buena Vista Winery. Since the soil and the climate was suited to viticulture, they decided to plant grapes. Bill helped plant the first vineyard, and became interested not only in grape growing, but in winemaking, too. He became a home winemaker and, as a result, quickly changed his college major from criminal justice to viticulture. He went on to U.C. Davis to study that and enology.

In 1974, while still in school, Bill planted his second vineyard in the Alexander Valley on the east side of Sonoma County. Two years later Bill and his family purchased the home vineyard property in the Russian River Valley and built a small winery there. This third property was once a part of a Spanish land grant and still has a number of historical markers on the property. Part of the property consists of one of the oldest houses in the county, along with a row of century old cypress trees that line the driveway to the Spanish-style house. The house and the driveway are the logo of the Landmark Vineyards wine label.

Bill, in the past ten years or so, has made all types of varietals — reds as well as whites. His first love, though, is Chardonnay and all of the estate vineyards have been budded over to Chardonnay. There are a total of 154 acres — 77 in the Russian River Valley, 60 in Alexander Valley and 17 in Sonoma Valley — all producing Chardonnay.

Because he can utilize grapes from three different growing conditions, Bill is able to blend one of California's most complex Chardonnays. It is a challenge to balance the different characteristics to make one premium wine. Since all of the vineyards have now reached their ten year mark, the resulting wines are full-bodied and age well. Although he blends all three vineyards together for the Sonoma County Chardonnay, he also produces an Alexander Valley Chardonnay solely from that vineyard.

Bill barrel ferments a portion of his Chardonnays, anywhere from 20% to 50% depending on the vintage. Landmark's 1983 Sonoma County Chardonnay won three gold medals and a platinum in the International Wine Review.

When asked what he likes about his life as a vintner, Bill replies, "I love the lifestyle, the variety of wearing many hats, such as being a vineyardist, a winemaker, a president of a business. The lifestyle allows me to have contact with many different people, as well as giving me the solitude of working in the cellar and the outdoors. There is always something new to do and something new to learn." With each vintage of Chardonnay, Bill Mabry is ready to face a new challenge. ❧

Lytton Springs Winery

Address: 650 Lytton Springs Road, Healdsburg 95448
  □ (707) 433-7721
Visitation: Daily, 10 AM to 4 PM
Principals: Richard Sherwin
Varietals produced: Zinfandel, and for 1987, Sauvignon Blanc and White Zinfandel
Production: 9,000 cases per year

"Lytton Springs Winery's primary goal is to elevate Zinfandel to its rightful status as a 'primary' California red wine," says Richard Sherwin. He feels that the unique character of Zinfandel is overlooked. It is the most widely planted red grape in California because it has adapted well to climate, soil and growing conditions. Dick Sherwin has tried to maintain a consistency of style in his Zinfandel for easy recognition of the product. His Zinfandel is a big, full-bodied wine that has won many gold medals

Dick Sherwin, a Southern Californian, is a multi-talented professional having worked in advertising, real estate, graphic arts and publishing. He is co-publisher of *Wine World* magazine, founded in 1970. With the creation of the magazine, Dick became interested in all phases of wine and winemaking.

That same year, Dick toured Northern California with his former wife and met her aunt and her uncle, Walt Walters. Walt and Dick discussed the possibility of acquiring a vineyard. They scanned the local real estate ads and found one for sale. Neither one really knew what they were looking at when they toured the vineyard. "We called the vines bushes and we had never heard of Zinfandel," he laughingly recalls. Dick purchased the 50-acre plot of Zinfandel vines with an adjacent 12 acres. Little did he know the potential of those Zinfandel vines.

Walt, who had just retired from the navy, agreed to oversee the property and to act as vineyard manager. It was to be strictly a farming operation. The Zinfandel vines were 80 to 90 years old, planted on a hillside and dry farmed. The first year, the grapes were sold to Mondavi for red wine. The second year, Paul Draper of Ridge Winery purchased Dick Sherwin's grapes and designated the wine as Lytton Springs on the Ridge label. He had been scouting Sonoma County for Zinfandel grapes grown on hillsides in stressed situations. The Lytton Springs Zinfandel quickly became one of Ridge Winery's best wines.

Although the business relationship with Ridge Winery was ideal, it became evident to Dick and Walt that, if they were to make the vineyard a viable entity they would have to convert the grapes to wine themselves. In the mid-1970s Dick started formulating plans for a winery. He severed his ties with Wine World so that there would not be a conflict of interest.

The winery became a reality in 1977. Dick Sherwin was extremely fortunate in buying used winery equipment from a Denver winery that was going out of business. For $25,000 he purchased all equipment necessary for a 5,000-case winery. He built a steel-type Butler building on his property to house the winery. Since then, Dick has added additional French and American cooperage.

When Dick established his vineyards, he also became interested in the process of winemaking and took some courses in the subject. In the meantime, Walt took viticulture courses at U.C. Davis.

Each year, from 1977 to the early 1980s, the demand for Lytton Springs Zinfandel increased, and so did the production. Since 1980, Dick has had to go to outside sources to purchase additional grapes for his wine. However, he purchases only from growers who have the same type of grapes as are in his own vineyard. Although industry sales of Zinfandel started declining in the early 1980s, Lytton Springs' sales only leveled off. In 1981, Dick made a lighter style wine to conform to consumer trends, but he found his customers much preferred the heavier, big Zinfandel style.

Dick will conform, however, to the current trend to white wines by making a Sauvignon Blanc and a White Zinfandel. He is cutting back somewhat on the production of Zinfandel and using more estate grown grapes. Additional equipment will be added for the white wines.

Since the death of Walt Wlaters in early 1986, Dick has taken on the position of winemaker, along with Darrell Holbrook. "It is a joint effort with each contributing to the final product," says Dick.

The winemaking process for the Zinfandels at Lytton Springs is an uncomplicated one. The big, fruity wine comes from the fully ripened (25 to 28 degrees Brix), almost Late Harvest grapes from non-irrigated hillside vineyards. After the wine is fermented, it is aged in oak for one year. Dick and Darrell do no fining or filtering, but do do plenty of racking. The aging starts in large uprights and then finishes in small American and French barrels.

Lytton Springs' wine label was one of the first to use four colors. Dick Sherwin wanted the label to have a distinctly California look, and not try to emulate the "French look." "California makes the best wines in the world, why shouldn't we have the best looking labels?" Dick says.

Although in recent years red Zinfandel has seen a decline, Dick has always enjoyed a steady clientele for his Zinfandel, even though the bottom line dictates that he also produce a White Zinfandel. If the white style is similar in feeling to the reds, he should have another winner on his hands. &

Mark West Vineyards

Address: 7000 Trenton-Healdsburg Road, Forestville 95436 □ (707) 544-4813

Visitation: Daily, 10 AM to 5 PM

Principals: Robert C. and Joan C. Ellis

Varietals produced: Gewurztraminer, Johannisberg Riesling, Chardonnay, Pinot Noir Blanc, Pinot Noir, Zinfandel, and Blanc de Noirs Champagne

Production: 18,000 cases per year

The saying "Go West, young man," still applies, even to the seekers of new lands in the 20th century. The urge to move west (or northwest) for Joan and Bob Ellis began in 1972, when a trip to downtown Alamo, California, where they were living, brought them to the reality that they no longer lived in an uncluttered small town. Alamo, located about 50 miles east of San Francisco, had bowed to urban development and installed its first traffic light. The Ellises decided it was time to move.

In looking about for a less hurried, "countrified" environment, they investigated all sorts of places, including a cattle ranch in New Mexico. However, they realized that that was going to be very difficult for Bob, since he is a pilot with Pan American Airlines.

Bob's parents, who lived in Sonoma, asked the Ellises if they had ever considered raising grapes. Over the years, Bob and Joan had become wine connoisseurs, and Joan was a gourmet cook. After numerous wine appreciation courses, Joan's interest in wine had become more than casual. The idea of growing grapes and living in the country was an intriguing one for the Ellises.

The next step was to look for land, and they did this very systematically. They visited the offices of various county agents, got brochures, and started looking at land. Whenever they found acreage to their liking, they would check it out with the University of California at Davis to assess the land's possibilities for growing grapes. The land they finally settled on was 116 acres near the Russian River, a few miles south of Healdsburg in Sonoma County. Not only was the land ideal for raising grapes, but it also had quite a history connected with it.

In 1840, Mark West and his family settled in Sonoma County on a 6,000-acre land grant he had received from the Mexican government. The land grant was located between the Russian River and a stream the Indians called Potiquiyomi, later renamed Mark West Creek. West was an English-born carpenter who had come to California to seek his fortune. He had landed in Mexico first, stayed long enough to learn Spanish, and then worked his way up to Monterey, California. There he met and married Guadalupe Vasquez, a native daughter of California. In 1840, he moved to the Sonoma land grant, built an adobe house, and became a craftsman in the area. West died in 1849. The adobe built by West has long since gone, and all that remains of one of the first settlers in the area is the ever-flowing stream — Mark West Creek.

It is part of this rich agricultural area that Bob and Joan Ellis bought for their vineyard and winery, and they named it Mark West after the original settler and the creek that runs on the edge of their property. Sixty acres of grapes were planted — Chardonnay, Johannisberg Riesling, Gewurztraminer, and Pinot Noir. All of these grapes are well suited to the cool climate of the area. There are plans to expand the vineyard.

Bob Ellis continues to fly for Pan Am, but he is also the vineyard manager. Joan, after taking several short courses in enology at U.C. Davis, became the winemaker for Mark West. She also takes care of most of the administrative duties of the winery. Her previous business experience in accounting and real estate has proved a valuable asset in this task.

Joan believes that a good wine is made in the vineyard. "If the the quality of the grapes is good, you have the potential for a good wine." The quality and style are often determined when the grapes are picked. Once the wine is made and bottled, the natural acids determine the longevity of the wines. Joan Ellis prefers to age a superior wine rather than release and market it immediately when bottled.

Mark West produces five types of wine from Pinot Noir grapes. One is a hearty red, similar to the French Burgundies, another is a blend that is marketed as a table wine, the third is Pinot Noir Blanc, a blush table wine, the fourth is Blanc de Noirs, a *Méthode Champenoise* sparkling wine; and the fifth is Angelique, a dessert wine.

Angelique is a fortified wine with berry juice added. As a child, Joan helped her mother make wine in their home in Connecticut and she remembers the wonderful berry aroma from this wild grape and wild berry combination. Joan uses the extra Pinot Noir juice from the sparkling wine, fortifies it with brandy and adds a touch of raspberry.

Bob and Joan's goal for the winery is to produce 30,000 cases a year, while maintaining their quality. 🍇

Matanzas Creek Winery

Address: 6097 Bennett Valley Road, Santa Rosa 95404
□ (707) 528-6464
Visitation: By appointment only
Principals: Sandra and William MacIver
Varietals produced: Chardonnay, Sauvignon Blanc, and Merlot
Production: 11,000 cases per year

Since barrel fermentation plays an important role in the making of Matanzas Creek's white wine, the new winery building was designed with this in mind. All of Matanzas Creek's Chardonnay is barrel fermented, as is a substantial portion of the Sauvignon Blanc. David Ramey, who has a long and distinguished winemaking career, joined Matanzas Creek just as the foundation for the new building was being poured and he had the opportunity to lay out the cellar and laboratory facilities.

The 22,000-square-foot building was designed by architect Paul Hamilton under the direction of Sandra and William MacIver. The striking new building is nestled snugly into the hillside of Bennett Mountain in the Bennett Valley of Sonoma County. The earth colored structure, surrounded by large oak trees, has a large reception area, gourmet kitchen, dining room, offices, a completely outfitted laboratory, fermentation area and two barrel aging rooms. The first floor is built into the hillside for natural cooling.

Matanzas Creek Winery was founded by Sandra MacIver in 1977. A former resident of New Orleans, Louisiana, she came to California in the late 1960s to study art at Mills College in Oakland. After living in Oakland for a while, she decided to move to the country to pursue a career in the bustling California wine industry. With great determination and her father's support she purchased property in the Bennett Valley and planted a Cabernet Sauvignon vineyard. That was at the time when prices for

that grape were at a premium. When the vines came of bearing age, however, prices had dropped substantially and as Sandra says, she "could not sell them for love or money." Like so many other growers, Sandra started a winery to use her own grapes.

In 1977, Sandra converted an existing dairy barn on the ranch to a small winery. Sandra had dreamt of owning a winery and had become acquainted with fine wines through her father's magnificent wine collection. (Sandra's father is Edgar B. Stern, president of Royal Street Corporation, which owns the prestigious Stanford Court Hotel in San Francisco.) After Sandra and Bill were married in 1979, Bill became general manager of the vineyard and winery operation.

As production increased, a larger building was needed that would allow room for further expansion. David Ramey designed a new barrel storage system for Matanzas Creek utilizing a palette system that eliminates the need for stacking and allows for easy movement of the barrels to the work area. With David's system, many more barrels can be stacked in a small area.

David Ramey has had the most influence on the production of Matanzas Creek's award-winning Chardonnay, the premier varietal produced. Using estate grown grapes and also some grapes grown in climatic conditions that match the Sonoma Valley, David ferments all of the Chardonnays in barrels. No sulphur dioxide is added to the juice prior to fermentation. The wine is left on the lees for the entire period of barrel aging. The yeast lees are stirred periodically, and some of the lots of Chardonnay go through malolactic fermentation. Chardonnay from different vineyards are blended for complexity.

In making the Matanzas Creek Merlot, David blends some Cabernet Sauvignon and some Cabernet Franc into it for smoothness. Since David spent some time in France working for various chateaux, he uses the Bordeaux style of winemaking for the Merlot. This includes 12 to 30 days of skin contact, and gentle pumping over during fermentation.

The Matanzas Creek wine label was designed by Sandra, who is an accomplished calligrapher. The logo is a 16th-century woodcut of a grapevine.

Both of the MacIvers are actively involved in wine industry activities. In 1985, Sandra was president of the Sonoma County Winegrowers Association. Sandra and Bill not only promote Matanzas Creek's award-winning wines, but try to further the California wine industry as a whole. "Being vintners gives us the opportunity to promote agriculture and to be on the cutting edge of the revival of this nation's wine growing heritage..." says Sandra MacIver. ❧

Mill Creek Vineyards

Address: 1401 Westside Road, Healdsburg 95448
  □ Tasting Room (707) 431-2121; □ Office (707) 433-5098
Visitation: Daily, 10 AM to 4:30 PM
Principals: Charles W. Kreck, Vera H. Kreck,
  James (Bob) R. Kreck, William (Bill) C. Kreck
Varietals produced: Sauvignon Blanc, Chardonnay,
  Gewurztraminer, Cabernet Blush, Cabernet
  Sauvignon, Merlot, Gamay Beaujolais, and Pinot Noir
Production: 12,000 cases per year

Mill Creek's tasting room was constructed in 1982 as a replica of an old mill, complete with a small pond and a water wheel. The two-story building is constructed mostly of redwood. The trusses, beams, and bar top are all from one tree felled on the Kreck ranch on Mill Creek Road, and were sawn by Bob and Bill Kreck using a portable Alaskan saw. This tasting room was the final stage of construction for Mill Creek Vineyards and the end of a long road in the establishment of one of the most respected wineries of Sonoma County.

Charles and Vera Kreck and their three children — Bob, Bill and Christine — arrived in Sonoma County in 1949. They had purchased a cattle ranch at the lower end of Alexander Valley east of Healdsburg. Soon, however, the family moved west of Healdsburg to the Mill Creek area. Bob and Bill spent their school years there, and in the summertime helped around the farm — building lakes,

clearing brush, and giving a hand wherever needed.

In 1965, the Kreck family purchased another small farm. That year Charles and the boys planted their first vineyard — Cabernet Sauvignon. By 1969, the Kreck family was ready to expand the vineyard operation and purchased a prune ranch with the right climate, soil, and water for grape growing. This ranch now includes the present winery and tasting room. In the years that followed, Charles, Bob and Bill tore out the prune trees, prepared the soil, and planted 65 acres of Cabernet Sauvignon, Chardonnay, Pinot Noir, and Merlot grapes. All of the Mill Creek Vineyards grapes are estate grown except the Gewurztraminer.

By 1974, the final phase of the project began — to build a winery to utilize all the grapes the Krecks were growing. They converted an old 6,000-square-foot barn into a small, efficient winery. New concrete floors had to be poured, insulation and air conditioning installed, and winery equipment had to be purchased and put in place. Included in the winery equipment were temperature-controlled stainless steel tanks and French, American, and Yugoslavian oak barrels and casks for aging. The last phase of the winery was the construction of the tasting room in 1982.

Mill Creek Vineyards is still very much a family operation. Charles Kreck is involved in the overall decision-making although Bob and Bill run the day-to-day operations. Bob Kreck is the winemaker, in charge of everything from "vine to the bottle" and Bill Kreck handles the business and marketing aspects of the winery, or everything from "bottle to the bank," as Bill puts it.

Bob Kreck produces some very distinctive wines. His Gamay Beaujolais has a crisp light finish. The grapes are picked with sugar at 22 degrees Brix and fermented in stainless steel for five days. At pressing, the sugar has dropped to 6% at which point there is not a great deal of tannin. There is a secondary fermentation which softens the wine and brings the sugar to zero. After fermentation, the wine is filtered to remove the heavy solids, and it is then aged in American oak for two months.

Mill Creek Vineyards' Gewurztraminer is off-dry with a hint of residual sugar but pleasantly fruity. Bob adds some Muscat to the Gewurztraminer for added complexity. He also blends about 5% Merlot into the Cabernet Sauvignon.

Mill Creek Vineyards was one of the first to make a Blanc de Noir wine and uses the word "blush" on their label. The Krecks have the official trademark on the word and it may not be used by other wineries except by license. The Krecks' original purpose for this action was to control the quality of the product. Samples of wine have to be submitted to the Krecks for approval before the trademark and the word "blush" can be used on the label.

Developing nature's product to its fullest potential is the purpose in Bob Kreck's winemaking. Bob and his father became home winemakers when they started planting vineyards. In the early days of the winery Charles was also involved in the winemaking, and consultants were engaged to help make the final product.

The family has strict control over all phases of the winery operation, from the planting of the grapes to the placement of its wines in the marketplace. There is a feeling of continuity for the product. The Kreck family has set a production limit of 15,000 cases per year to ensure control over their premium wines. ❧

Preston Vineyards & Winery

Address: 9282 West Dry Creek Road, Healdsburg 95448
□ (707) 433-3372
Visitation: Monday through Friday, by appointment only
Principals: Louis D. Preston
Varietals produced: Chenin Blanc, Sauvignon Blanc, Cuvée de Fumé, Gamay Beaujolais, Zinfandel, Syrah-Sirah, and Cabernet Sauvignon
Production: 20,000 cases per year

The Prestons live with their grapes every day. They have a complete understanding of how well-made wine is a blend of the best of nature and the skill of the winemaker. The first class winemaker at Preston Winery is Tom Farella, the vineyard manager is John Clendenen,
and Louis Preston, with his managerial background, has the ability to manage a winery estate.

In 1973, Lou and Susan Preston founded Preston Vineyards and Winery after converting a family prune ranch of 120 acres into vineyards. The ranch is located at the north end of the Dry Creek Valley in Sonoma County. The soil and climate of the region are well suited to Zinfandel, which has been grown on the property even prior to Prohibition. A few acres of that varietal were in existence on the property when the Prestons started their vineyards.

The prune orchards were gradually torn out, and the 120 acres of Preston vineyards today consist of 13 different varieties of grapes including Sauvignon Blanc, Zinfandel, and Cabernet Sauvignon. A great emphasis is placed on the grape growing itself, and Lou has carefully chosen the varietals that do best for his particular soil and climate. He feels that quality wines begin in the vineyard. Lou also wanted to grow and produce something a little different. After talking with his neighbors, he found that the ranch at one time contained a small vineyard of Petite Sirah. Lou again planted Petite Sirah in well drained gravel-like soil.

Prior to 1973, Lou Preston had completed the M.B.A. program at Stanford University and joined a large accounting firm in San Francisco. One of his accounts was Beaulieu Vineyard in Napa Valley. He became fascinated with the entire operation and wanted to be on the "other side of the desk." This inspired Lou and Susan to consider seriously the possibilities of becoming vintners.

Lou took winemaking courses at U.C. Davis and in 1975 crushed 20 tons of Zinfandel on an experimental basis. He used the old prune dehydrator as an aging cellar and continued making wine with the facilities available until the spring of 1983, when a new winery building was completed. The building has separate fermentation areas and aging cellars — all temperature controlled. Open tank fermentation for the Zinfandel takes place outside of the winery.

Lou Preston has an exceptionally well-developed pal-ate, and he is constantly fascinated with the myriad of flavors and textures which are characteristic of the grapes in the Dry Creek Valley. Lou, and his winemaker Tom Farella, have become masters at creative wine blending. One example is the Cuvée de Fumé which is 75% Sauvignon Blanc blended with Chenin Blanc and Semillon. The flavor is unique with some grassiness, good fruit, and complexity. There is also extensive clonal blending in the production of the Preston Zinfandel.

Susan Preston, who grew up in Calaveras County, is very much involved in food and wine. To beautify and landscape the new winery and office building she has created an edible landscape. In this way, she hopes to show winery visitors not only the connection between food and wine, but also how easy it is to grow some of the produce we eat every day. Her culinary talents are enhanced with all of the fresh herbs and produce from her extensive garden.

Lou and Susan Preston replanted grapes in a pioneering grape growing area and are very conscious of the fact that well-made wine is a blend of nature's product, enhanced by the patient skill of the vintner. This patient skill and blending ability has created award-winning premium wines for Preston Vineyards and Winery. 🐿

A. Rafanelli Winery

Address: 4685 West Dry Creek Road, Healdsburg 95448
☐ (707) 433-1385
Visitation: Daily, 9 AM to 5 PM, by appointment only
Principals: A. Rafanelli
Varietals produced: Zinfandel, Cabernet Sauvignon, and Gamay Beaujolais
Production: 4,000 cases per year

If there ever was or is a one-man operation it is the A. Rafanelli Winery. Not only is Americo "Am" Rafanelli the proprietor, but he is also the vineyard master, winemaker, marketing director, and, when there are visitors, its tour guide.

Americo — so named because his Italian parents were so glad to be in America — comes from a winemaking family. His father owned a winery in downtown Healdsburg and even continued making wine right through the Prohibition. Am says that "when the neighbors turned us in, the revenue agents would come out and fine us." But it seems that they never really broke up the operation. One time the agents noticed that the wine was spilling out of one of the tanks. It seems that they had come just as Am's father was transferring wine from one tank to another. The agent simply lifted the hose and put it back in the tank. "It was one thing to make a pinch, another to waste good wine."

Prohibition did not shut down the Rafanelli winery, but eminent domain did in the late 1940s. Healdsburg High School took over the vineyards and winery operated for decades by the elder Rafanelli and his son. The elder Rafanelli then went to work as a carpenter.

It was not until 1955 that Am acquired a parcel of land on the west slopes of Dry Creek Valley in Sonoma County. He kept adding to that parcel of land, five to ten acres at a time. Most of today's 100 acres were planted in prunes. Little by little, Am pulled out the orchards and began planting vines — mostly Gamay Beaujolais, Zinfandel, and French Colombard. Today there are over 30 acres in grapes.

For years, Rafanelli sold all of his grapes to larger wineries. He continues to sell a good portion. All of the French Colombard, for example, is sold since Am makes no white wine.

In 1972, Am made his first wine in the bonded basement of his home while, at the same time, he was remodeling an old horse barn on the property with the intention of turning it into a winery. The redwood sided barn is completely insulated. It has a fermenting room, and an aging room on the first floor. The loft was turned into the bottling, labelling, and packaging room.

Rafanelli knows winemaking like the back of his hand and still does it in the same old style his father used, with minor modifications. "I ferment in open redwood tanks," he says. "It was done that way in the old days." There is no modern mechanical machinery. Am uses a basket press and a small stemmer crusher, all done by hand.

The wine is kept from seven to nine days in open fermenters. "During that time I punch the grapes down every four hours (day and night) with a paddle 12 by 18 inches wide." He keeps the skins on the grapes during this time because the skin contact gives the right amount of color he wants for the wine.

Another traditional method Rafanelli uses is not filtering the wines. "That's my style," Am says. He does rack his wines every three months. The wines are aged in French and American oak.

Being a small one-man operation does have its advan-

tages. Since he produces three different varietal wines, he can crush at different times. The Gamays first, then the Zinfandels, and finally the Cabernet Sauvignon. Am has 30 acres in Gamay and Zinfandel.

He does hire help when it comes to bottling and labelling. These are hand operations, but with help, Rafanelli can bottle 300 cases of wine in a day.

Rafanelli is known for his Zinfandels. Since he uses his own grapes, he can closely control the way the grapes are grown. While the grapes are reaching maturity, Am thins out the second growth to encourage the full development of the clusters. This also helps the sugar content of the grapes and assures a better quality. He does help pick the grapes. "I want to see what I am going to crush," he says. "I go out and test the grapes while they are still on the vine for sugar and acidity."

Rafanelli enjoys every aspect of the business of winemaking. The one-man operation works well for him. The wines are literally handmade. "I control everything," he adds with a twinkle in his eye. 🍂

Ravenswood

Address: 21415 Broadway, Sonoma 95476
　☐ (707) 938-1960
Visitation: By appointment only
Principals: Joel Peterson, W. Reed Foster
Varietals produced: Chardonnay, Merlot, Zinfandel, and Cabernet Sauvignon
Production: 10,000 cases per year

"And the Raven, never flitting, still is sitting, still is sitting…shall be lifted — nevermore." Unlike the raven in Edgar Allen Poe's poem, ravens are not a symbol of bad luck for Joel Peterson. At Joel's first crush (he was working at Joe Swan's winery), there were two uninvited guests — two ravens who continuously harassed him during the entire crush. He outlasted the ravens: they did not harm him or the grapes he was crushing, and Joel decided that they were a good luck symbol of perseverance and survival. So when he started his winery, he named it Ravenswood, and on the winery's label, there are three ravens in a circle

Joel learned to appreciate wine as a young teenager since his father, the head of the San Francisco Wine Club, would occasionally permit him to participate in his semi-weekly tastings. There was a strict agreement that if Joel did participate, he was not to swallow any of the wine. The taste of the fine European wines, however, lingered in

Joel's memory and were to be very useful in the creation of his own wines many years later.

Joel not only followed his father's footsteps in wine appreciation, but also in a scientific career. After graduating from Oregon State University, he embarked on a career in immunology, doing tissue cultures and cancer research. However, his job became more one of desk work rather than research, which he loved, so he turned to his second love — wine.

He started making home wine, worked part-time in a wine store, and started writing articles about wine. In the early 1970s, Joel decided to move to Sonoma County to do a stint as an apprentice to Joe Swan, who had a one-man winery operation. It was not a giant step for Joel to go from biochemistry to winemaking. In subsequent years he worked at several other wineries.

In 1976, Joel decided to start his own winery. The first crush was eight tons, but the winery has grown every year since those meager beginnings. In 1981, he moved his operation to its present location just south of the city of Sonoma. Joel still works part-time as a medical technologist at the Sonoma Hospital. This extra income will enable him to expand his winery operation and move his winery to another location in the future. Joel has started looking for vineyard land with a winery building.

Currently, all of Ravenswood's grapes are purchased. Much of the Zinfandel comes from the Dickenson and Old Hill Ranches where it is grown on 80-year-old vines. Joel buys Zinfandel grapes from five different vineyards and blends where he feels it necessary. The North Coast Zinfandel that he uses is not a product of a hot climate, but has a longer ripening season, resulting in a more complex wine.

Joel believes that winemaking is an art form with special techniques, not something that can be done by a scientific formula. "I am not in the food processing business. If I were, I might as well be making mayonnaise," he says. The old Burgundy and Bordeaux styles and the wines he remembers from his childhood have influenced his winemaking.

All of Joel's red wines are fermented on their own yeast in large, open redwood fermenters. Sometimes this takes 25 to 30 days until the cap sinks. No sulphur is added during this process. During the fermentation process, 15% of the stems are added back to the Zinfandel. After fermentation, the reds are aged in French oak barrels for at least two years. The second year they are racked with nitrogen which stimulates gravity flow. The wines are fined with egg white, but generally not filtered. Joel adds about 10% Merlot to his Cabernet Sauvignon for smoothness.

The Chardonnay soaks on the skins for 12 hours. It is then fermented in French Limousin barrels and allowed to undergo malolactic fermentation. The wine usually remains on the primary yeast (or lees) for three to four months before racking. It is then aged in French Limousin oak barrels for approximately ten months. The Chardonnay is fined with skim milk.

David Lance Goines, a well known Berkeley graphic artist and painter, designed Ravenswood's label in the style of a traditional Japanese family crest. The three ravens joined by a ring symbolize the work, strength, and commitment it took for Joel to start a winery on the proverbial shoestring — a winery whose wines are becoming more recognized by the public and critics alike. In the spring of 1986, Ravenswood's Cabernet Sauvignon was featured on the cover of *Wine Spectator*. 🍂

J. Rochioli Vineyards & Winery

Address: 6192 Westside Road, Healdsburg 95448
　□ (707) 433-2305
Visitation: Daily, 10 AM to 5 PM
Principals: Thomas M. Rochioli and Joe Rochioli
Varietals produced: Sauvignon Blanc, Chardonnay, Pinot Noir, Zinfandel, and Cabernet Sauvignon
Production: 3,000 cases per year

This story of third generation Italian-Americans in the wine business is not the typical one, although it starts out like most of the others. Grandpa (Joe Rochioli) came over from Tuscany in the early 1930s, did manual labor and saved enough money to buy a ranch. Actually, he bought the ranch of his employer. There the usual story deviates.

Originally, Joe, Sr. planted hops and prunes in the rich river bottom soils and grapes on the rolling hillsides on the ranch. In the 1950s, he and his son Joe, Jr. removed the prunes and planted the entire ranch with low-yield varietal grapes. They were pioneers in their time, since planting low-yield grapes was then unheard of.

"Young" Joe had no ambition to be a winemaker. He merely wanted to grow premium grapes and sell them to a variety of vintners. He had prepared himself to be a rancher by obtaining a degree in agricultural science from California Polytechnic University at San Luis Obispo.

It took a third-generation Rochioli, Tom, and his Irish wife Theresa to convince Joe, Jr. to create a winery. Tom did not initially follow in his father's or grandfather's careers of agriculture. Tom graduated in finance and accounting from California State University at Sacramento, and went to work for the Bank of America. Working with many accounts in the wine business made him homesick for the vineyards and he felt that he really wanted to be "on the other side of the desk."

The growth of the grape and wine industry in Sonoma County impressed young Tom, and he had visions of a wine being produced from the family-raised grapes. After all, the wineries using Rochioli grapes were consistently winning medals. Being a good businessman, he put together a ten-year plan for a winery. After a year of study, Tom and his father decided that starting a winery was an opportunity they could not let pass by.

The conservative Italian father agreed to try making wine on a limited basis, although for years he had made wines in the "back of the barn in his private cellar in the true Italian fashion." The first crush was in leased space at a neighboring winery in 1982. The winery's first releases won medals in every competition they entered.

The next year, an old family orchard and vineyard were cleared to make room for a winery building and tasting room. The new rustic looking redwood building blends into the landscape of old trees and vineyards.

Rochioli's consulting winemaker is Gary Farrell who

used to work with these same grapes at another winery. As Tom says, "Gary knows these vineyards," and has been involved in producing winning wines from them. Theresa Rochioli runs the tasting room and also does some of the marketing of the wines.

They started out small — 2,500 to 3,000 cases per year — but will expand. They will never become so big, though, that they lose control over the production of premium wines. Although the Rochiolis still sell grapes to other wineries, they retain a portion of the "cream of the crop" grapes from their 80 acres for their own winery. Tom's winemaking philosophy is that fine wines are "grown" in the vineyards, and then special care must be taken to transfer that quality into the bottle.

All of the wines are aged in French oak. The Pinot Noir is of Burgundian style. The Cabernet Sauvignon is made in a Bordeaux style. The Sauvignon Blanc is styled to be intense and fruity. The Chardonnay is barrel fermented and made complex to give it aging potential. In the future the Rochiolis plan to plant some Gewurztraminer to round out their wine selection.

Joe, Jr. says that he thinks his father would have been happy with the fact that the Rochioli family now has a winery. "It is in the Italian blood to make wine." ❧

Sea Ridge Winery

Address: P.O. Box 287, Cazadero 95421
□ (707) 847-3469
Tasting and Sales Room: 935 Highway 1, Bodega Bay 94923 □ (707) 875-3329
Visitation: Tasting room: Daily, 10 AM to 6 PM;
Winery: By appointment only
Principals: Tim Schmidt and Dan Wickham
Varietals produced: Sauvignon Blanc, Chardonnay, Pinot Noir, and Zinfandel
Production: 5,000 cases per year

The Cazadero hills, 1,100 feet above the Pacific Ocean in western Sonoma County, have traditionally been home to sheep, cattle, and redwoods. In recent years, however, some of the agricultural emphasis in the cool climate area, fanned by sea breezes, has changed. Now grapes are being grown. At the present time, there are about 100 acres in grapes, spread among a dozen small vineyards, and there is room for many more.

Mickey Bohan, a rancher in the Cazadero hills, started growing grapes more than ten years ago. His vineyards were successful even though viticulture experts from the University of California advised him against the venture. The coastal region of Sonoma County, which still does not have an official appellation designation, did not come into prominence, until Dan Wickham and Tim Schmidt planted their eight-acre vineyard of Pinot Noir and built their Sea Ridge Winery in the late 1970s.

Dan Wickham, winemaker at Sea Ridge, hails from Michigan where, at the age of ten, he crushed and fermented some wild American grapes. His teetotalling Christian Scientist parents were not his most enthusiastic fans, although his younger sister thought his wine was wonderful. Dan became a marine biologist and came to California to grow lobsters. He earned a Ph.D. from U.C. Berkeley for his discovery of a parasite that is wreaking havoc with the Dungeness and Alaskan King Crab fisheries.

Tim Schmidt, a Sonoma County native, also studied marine science — first at Duke University and then at U.C. Berkeley. He received a master's degree from the University of Canterbury in New Zealand. Tim stayed in New Zealand for a while, working and teaching at the University of Canterbury in Christchurch, New Zealand.

The two marine scientists met in 1974 while they were both working at the Bodega Marine Laboratory. They both had an interest in wine and started making home wine together. Four years later they purchased 40 acres in the Cazadero hills where they constructed the winery and planted vineyards.

The cool climate, they decided, was similar to the climate of Burgundy where the grapes often have to struggle to ripen. Also the soil, which contains a lot of limestone, is similar to that of Burgundy. The soil is one of the reasons for the excellence of Burgundian wines.

It took a lot of hard work on Dan's and Tim's part to construct the winery. First, roads had to be built, and redwood stumps cleared in order for them to construct the 3,000-square-foot winery. It is not a fancy building, but it is functional. As Tim says, "You do not have to have a million dollars to build a winery. Nor does it have to look like a French chateau to produce fine wine."

With the construction of the winery, Tim resigned his position at the Marine Laboratory to work full-time at the winery and manage the vineyards. Tim and his wife Susan, who works part-time as a registered nurse, live in an apartment attached to the winery while they are building a house on the property. Dan, who is the winemaker, still works part-time as a marine biologist and lives near Bodega Bay.

Burgundy's climatic conditions not only influenced

Dan and Tim's choice of land, but Burgundy also greatly influences their style of winemaking. Their production methods are ancient and classic — sometimes out of necessity. The first few years there was no electricity on the property, so Dan and Tim literally made the wines by hand — with no power equipment.

The Pinot Noir, for which they have become well known, is fermented with the skins for about three weeks in open redwood fermenters. The cap formed by the skins is punched down three times a day to extract color and flavor. The wine is then aged in 60-gallon French oak barrels. The Chardonnay is fermented and aged in small French oak barrels. The acids are reduced and smoothed by secondary (malolactic) fermentation.

The Pacific Ocean is and continues to be an integral part of the life at Sea Ridge Winery. The marine life theme is reflected in the design of the Sea Ridge Winery label. It features the *Tibia fusus* seashell native to the Phillipines, and was chosen by Dan and Tim for its graceful lines. Dan and Tim have recently opened a combination marine museum, art gallery, and tasting and sales room at Bodega Bay. Each month there is a new exhibit on the Pacific Coast fishing industry, and the art exhibit rotates periodically. There are also two aquariums of local marine life.

Dan and Tim plan to expand their Pinot Noir vineyards, while continuing to purchase Zinfandel, Chardonnay, and Sauvignon Blanc grapes from their neighbors in the Cazadero and Fort Ross hills. They use only grapes from the cool coastal region. All of Sea Ridge's wines are 100% varietal. ❧

Soda Rock Winery

Address: 8015 Highway 128, Healdsburg 95448
□ (707) 433-1830
Visitation: Daily, 10 AM to 5 PM
Principals: Charles Tomka, Jr. and Charles K. Tomka, Sr.
Varietals produced: Sauvignon Blanc, Chardonnay, Gewurztraminer, White Zinfandel, Zinfandel, Cabernet Sauvignon, and Late Harvest Riesling (Sweet Frances)
Production: 10,000 cases per year

"Just like home — just like in the old days," says Charlie Tomka pointing to the barrels of wine at Soda Rock Winery. The old days and the original home are many miles and another world away.

The Tomka family — consisting of Charlie, Sr., his wife Etza, and their young son Charles — arrived in the United States in 1957. They were refugees from the totalitarian government of Hungary and were forced to flee during the Hungarian revolution. The All Saints Church in Carmel sponsored them and saw to it that Charlie gained employment. That was not hard for Charlie, since he had had a varied career in his homeland.

As the first son of a Rumanian landowner, he had been given unique educational opportunities, and graduated from horticulture school with additional skills in agronomy, viticulture, winemaking and floriculture. Upon graduation from school, he was appointed gardener to the court of King Carol and worked for Queen Marie in the palace gardens. Those were marvelous days between the two big wars, when Charlie was given the chance to show his artistic landscaping talents to beautify the grounds of the royal palace. It was difficult for him to leave his position, but he was needed at home, and family has always been most important to Charlie.

The years that followed were really training for Charlie's later life. He worked in vineyards and wineries in Hungary, where he served as wine inspector for the government and was in charge of buying wine to be sold for export.

When the family arrived at Carmel in 1957, Charlie secured a job doing landscaping at the prestigious Highlands Inn. Although he did not know a word of English, he quickly learned with the help of one of the staff members who spoke Hungarian. The only word for food he knew was hot dog and he ate a lot of hot dogs in his early days in America.

Not long after that, Charlie and Etza started their own nursery and landscaping business, the Broadway Nursery. Charlie landscaped many of the homes in Pebble Beach. People would wait two or three years just to avail themselves of Charlie's services. If a newcomer asked a resident who did their landscaping the reply was always "Charlie with the green truck." And that green truck had beautiful lettering and floral paintings on it, all done by Etza.

After 14 years in Carmel, the family moved to Menlo Park, where Charlie not only did landscaping for private homes, but designed many of the gardens of public and commercial buildings.

Charlie and Etza traveled whenever the opportunity presented itself. They wanted to see and learn more about their new homeland. When it came time for Charlie to retire in 1980 he wanted to go back to the Ozarks. They purchased 180 acres and moved to Missouri to semi-retire.

In the meantime, young Charles had become self-sufficient and quite adept at remodeling old Victorian houses. He would buy one in a rundown condition, restore it, then sell it at a profit. He had moved to Sonoma County, and, in 1981, was looking for a large building where he could do his woodworking. He had passed the old Soda Rock building many times, until one day it struck him that since it was for sale it might be converted into just the woodworking shop he was seeking. He also considered renovating the old building for housing.

The winery was in a rundown condition and had not been operated during the last ten years. Previous to that it had been an operating winery since the early 1900s. A large vineyard had been started in the 1880s, and a winery building was added later. Soda Rock Winery can be considered a historical landmark since it was built with rocks from a dismantled school and is the only remains of a community named Soda Rock that existed there in the early 1900s. There was even a U.S. Post Office named Soda Rock.

After arranging to purchase the property, Charles called his father in Missouri and asked him to come and look at his new acquisition. When Charlie and Etza took one look at the winery, Charlie said, "Just like home." It seems that he had always wanted to make wine again and own a winery. He was hooked. He immediately sold his property in Missouri, moved back to California and the Tomkas were in the wine business.

The entire family pitched in to clean up and refurbish the old equipment. There was an old basket press, open top redwood fermenters, and tall redwood tanks for aging. "Just like home," says Charlie. The Tomkas have added some new equipment — stainless steel fermenters for the whites and some small French oak barrels for aging. The outside, of course, has been re-landscaped by Charlie. Etza has designed signs and embellished the old Soda Rock wine label with her drawing of grape vines. The scene of Mt. Helena in the background of the logo is the same as the previous owners used.

Soda Rock Winery purchases most of its grapes, although there are four acres of vineyards planted with Gamay and Chardonnay. Charlie Tomka is still the winemaker, using the same methods he learned as a young man in Transylvania and practiced in Hungary. Open top fermentation for the reds and lots of skin contact is the by-word for Charlie Tomka's winemaking. The reds are aged for at least two years, first in large casks and then in small barrels. Although Charlie, going with current trends, does make a variety of white wines, his reds — particularly his Zinfandel — are as smooth as chocolate. "Just like home," he says with great satisfaction. ❧

Robert Stemmler Winery

Address: 3805 Lambert Bridge Road, Healdsburg 95448
□ (707) 433-6334

Visitation: Daily, 10:30 AM to 4:30 PM

Principals: Robert Stemmler and Trumbull Webb Kelly

Varietals produced: Sauvignon Blanc, Chardonnay, Pinot Noir, Cabernet Sauvignon, and Late Harvest Sauvignon Blanc

Production: 12,000 cases per year

When he opened his winery in 1977, Robert Stemmler vowed never to make Pinot Noir again. He had not been pleased with the Pinot Noir he had made while winemaker at Charles Krug in the 1960s. Robert felt that the wine had a nice nose, but not enough flavor to back it up. Fate intervened and changed his mind. Today, his Pinot Noir is one of the most sought-after wines throughout the country.

Robert Stemmler was born and raised in Germany in a winemaking family. He graduated from Bad Kreuznach Wine College and worked in the German wine industry before coming to California. In the 1960s and 1970s he worked as winemaker at Charles Krug, Inglenook and Simi before going out on his own to do consulting work and problem-solving for some of the leading Napa and Sonoma County wineries.

In 1977, Bob Stemmler and his partner Trumbull Kelly, founded and built their own winery. Trumbull Kelly, a native of Minnesota, had spent 25 years working with the California Youth Authority as its educational program director. He had plenty of experience traveling and appearing before groups of people, making his transition to marketing for the new winery an easy one.

Early on, Bob and Trumbull decided to limit the winery's production, so that they might be able to do most of the work themselves and control the entire operation — at first, they limited production to Sauvignon Blanc, Chardonnay, and Cabernet Sauvignon. Pinot Noir was added later. When conditions are right Bob also makes a Late Harvest Sauvignon Blanc, a dessert wine with nice acid balance.

Bob Stemmler firmly believes that the wine is only as good as the vineyard which produces it. All of the Pinot Noir he had worked with at other wineries had come from growing areas that, in Bob's opinion, did not have the proper soil and growing conditions. One day in 1982, one of his growers had some Pinot Noir grapes available. The grapes had been dry farmed with a low yield per acre. They were also high in acid despite their maturity. Bob, not one to give up, decided to make one more attempt at Pinot Noir. The result is history. The wine won gold medals at tastings all the way from San Diego to New York. It was an immediate hit and helped put the Stemmler Winery on the map. He now has a long-term contract with that particular grower for Pinot Noir grapes.

All except 5% of Robert Stemmler Winery's grapes are purchased. (There is just a four-acre plot of Chardonnay planted around the winery.) Bob, through his contracts with the growers, has strict control as to the yield per acre (the lower the yield, the higher the acid and the better the resulting wine). He does not allow any spraying within eight weeks of harvest since he feels there is too much residue left on the grapes. Also he feels that too much water on the grapes (irrigation) leaves the fruit watery.

Bob uses all American oak for the aging of his wines. However, he insists that the wood be air dried, which takes two to three years. He does not like kiln dried barrels since they "are bitter and unbalanced." He uses American barrels instead of French ones, because he is making wine in America and wants to use American products.

No sulphur is used in the fermentation of the Stemmler wines. Bob uses natural yeast in the fermentation process and does no fining of his wines. Overworking the wine, Stemmler insists, can rob it of flavor, character, and depth. He only filters before bottling. In the Pinot Noir fermentation, Bob includes some uncrushed berries for richness of flavor. All of the wines are made in a traditional European style, designed to accompany food. Bob likes to give the wines only a light touch of oak. "Too much oak hides the natural taste of the wine," he says.

After graduating from wine college in Germany, Bob Stemmler paid a visit to the Cluny Museum in Paris and saw a woodcut of a medieval scene depicting grape crushing. The work, entitled "Le Vendage," was done by an unknown 15th century artist of the Flemish school. Today, a reproduction of that woodcut is a part of the Robert Stemmler Winery label.

A wine, which he vowed not to make again, has made Robert Stemmler's reputation as one of the "Princes of Pinot Noir." Not only is he producing it, but he is again this year expanding its production. 🍇

William Wheeler Winery

Address: 130 Plaza Street, Healdsburg 95448
  □ (707) 433-8786
Visitation: By appointment only
Principals: William and Ingrid Wheeler
Varietals produced: Sauvignon Blanc, Chardonnay, White Zinfandel, Zinfandel, and Cabernet Sauvignon
Production: 16,000 cases per year

Like chefs, winemakers are always experimenting with new ingredients. This is particularly true in producing a varietal that is blended from different vineyards. The William Wheeler Winery Sauvignon Blanc, for instance, is a blend of grapes from three different regions in Sonoma County. Julia Iantosca, who is their winemaker (and, incidentally, one of the few women winemakers in the industry), enjoys the challenge of blending because she feels it is the real art of winemaking.

The Wheeler Sauvignon Blanc grapes come from Dry Creek, Russian River, and the Alexander Valley. The grapes of the first two areas are characteristically grassy and intense. To modify this assertiveness the winery purchases grapes from the Alexander Valley, where the fruit tends to have a more floral quality. Depending on the assertiveness of the wine, Julia may also blend some Semillon in for roundness and a soft fig-like aroma. This was done with the 1984 Sauvignon Blanc.

For Julia, the ideal sugar level for picking Sauvignon Blanc grapes is 22 degrees Brix. After harvest the grapes are crushed with little or no skin contact. Pasteur Chardonnay yeast is added to the juice for a quick, moderately cool (55 to-60 degree) fermentation in stainless steel tanks. Eighty-five percent of the wine goes into French oak barrels for four to five months of aging while the rest remains in stainless steel to preserve the fresh fruitiness. The finish of the wine is crisp with a light oak richness.

This is only one of the five wines of which Julia Iantosca is the "chef and caretaker." She strives to produce wines which are companions with food — wines that do not overpower whatever is chosen to be served with them.

The William Wheeler Winery has two locations — vineyards and fermentation facility are in the mountains above the Dry Creek Valley, and red wine barrel storage, offices and tasting room are in a building owned by the William Wheelers in downtown Healdsburg.

William Wheeler was born in St. Louis, Missouri, where in the 1870s his grandfather started an outfitting company to supply the flood of pioneers passing through on the way West. By the time Bill's grandfather sold the business in 1920, he had acquired an extensive collection of Western American literature. He stamped each book with his personal library seal, the three intertwined W's that stood for William Webb Wheeler. These three W's are, now the logo of the William Wheeler Winery wine label.

Bill Wheeler grew up in Southern California, graduated from Yale with a history major, took graduate work at the London School of Economics and the Sorbonne, and received an M.B.A. in finance and international business from Columbia University in New York. In 1965, Bill Wheeler entered the State Department and spent the next four years in Argentina, Brazil, and Columbia as a Capital Development Officer in charge of lending money to public and private sectors of these developing countries. While posted in Rio de Janeiro, Brazil he met his wife Ingrid. They were married in London and proceeded to move to Columbia.

Ingrid Wheeler was born in Hong Kong to a Scottish mother and Norwegian father who was in the shipping business. During World War II, their home in Hong Kong was destroyed by bombs, and rather than face life in a Japanese concentration camp, Ingrid's father organized an escape through China for a group of Norwegians. They walked for 103 days from Hong Kong to Chunking, being guided by a network of Chinese friends. From Chunking they flew over the Himalayas into India.

After the war, in 1946, the family returned to Hong Kong. Ingrid attended school in Hong Kong and then went to boarding school in London. She also studied at La Combe in Rolle, Switzerland and finished her education in Cannes. It was while visiting her older brother in Rio that she met William Wheeler.

After Bill's tour of duty with the State Department, the Wheelers moved to San Francisco where Bill worked with the international venture capital group of the Bank of America. On a visit to Healdsburg and the Dry Creek Valley, the Wheelers fell in love with the area. After a thorough study of growing conditions and the financial aspects of raising grapes, the Wheelers purchased 175 acres with the purpose of establishing a vineyard.

In preparation for this venture Bill and Ingrid spent a harvest in France as working guests at Chateau Malecasse, learning all they could not only about the French method of grape growing, but also winemaking. Upon their return, in 1973 and 1974 they planted 20 acres of Cabernet Sauvignon (doing almost all of it themselves on weekends) on terraced hillsides at 1,500 feet elevation. In 1981, ten acres of Zinfandel were planted at 800 feet elevation, also on terraced vineyards.

In 1975, the Wheelers started selling some of their first harvest to local Sonoma County wineries and continued to do so until 1979. At that time, Bill wanted to do the whole thing from the growing of grapes to the finished product. That year and the next he did some custom crushing at another facility and in 1981 built a 4,500-square-foot fermentation cellar on the property. At the same time, he purchased the downtown Healdsburg building for a red wine aging cellar. The Wheelers with their two children also moved full-time to the ranch.

Bill and Ingrid Wheeler both spend a considerable amount of time marketing their wines since they are sold in 30 states, Jamaica, and England. Bill is a member of the Board of Directors of the Sonoma County Winegrowers' Association, one of whose functions is to act as one promotional voice for its member vintners. The Wheelers' weekends are frequently occupied with wine events and wine related social activities, which both of them enjoy.

Since 1982, Julia Iantosca has been with the William Wheeler Winery. She was raised in Southern California, majored in microbiology at San Jose State and decided to transfer to U.C. Davis in 1977 for their winemaking courses. Julia loves every aspect of winemaking, including hauling heavy hoses and cleaning tanks. Wine is very much a part of her life, since she is also married to a winemaker. Her husband Bob is the assistant winemaker at Freixenet, the new Spanish sparkling wine facility in Sonoma County.

Food and wine have always been a part of the life of Ingrid and Bill Wheeler. That is one of the reasons why they designed their style of wines with food in mind. The Wheelers, along with Julia Iantosca as their winemaker, will continue to provide premium wines designed specifically for the dining table. ❧

White Oak Vineyards

Address: 208 Haydon Street, Healdsburg 95448
□ (707) 433-8429
Visitation: Daily, 10 AM to 4 PM
Principals: Bill Myers
Varietals produced: Sauvignon Blanc, Chenin Blanc, Johannisberg Riesling, Chardonnay, Zinfandel, and Cabernet Sauvignon
Production: 9,000 cases per year

Many people have migrated to Alaska to seek gold, drill for oil, or become lumberjacks or salmon fishermen. For Bill Myers it was the other way around. He is a native Californian, but had gone to Alaska at the age of seventeen. In Alaska he was a building contractor and a commercial fisherman, and it was there that he developed an interest in wine. It was this interest and his enterprising spirit that prompted him, in the late 1970s to move his family to Healdsburg in northern Sonoma County. He felt that winemaking presented an opportunity to be creative and that that area in particular grew premium grapes due to the diversity of growing regions within the area.

Before starting into winemaking, Bill Myers built a small laboratory to research and test various grapes from selected vineyards in northern Sonoma County. This research, which not only consisted of test tube experimenting, but also of making single barrels of wine from selected grapes, helped him determine which vineyards consistently produced good fruit. Bill was looking for the combination of a conscientious grower and unique plots of land planted with the correct varietal for the soil and climatic conditions. "We took samples from over a hundred different vineyards and made a single barrel of wine from about a third of these," Bill recalls.

Not only did all of this experimentation result in a variety of wines, but it also was the determining factor in the careful selection of vineyards which were to supply grapes for the winery that Bill Myers was to build. These vineyards are under long term contract and supply grapes each season. Bill strongly believes that good wine begins in the vineyard.

In addition to buying grapes on a long contract basis, in 1983 Bill Myers purchased six acres in the Alexander Valley in northern Sonoma County. The vineyard, originally planted in 1968 with the same clones as the famous Robert Young Vineyard, is equally divided between plantings of Chardonnay and Cabernet Sauvignon. Bill had been making small lots of wine from the vineyard since 1979 and was impressed with this example of the right varietals planted in the right area.

After two years of experimental winemaking, in 1981 Bill Myers designed and built his winery specifically for the production of small quantities of superior wines. Since the winery is in a residential section, Bill designed it to look like just another residence. The facility is designed so that small lots of grapes can be fermented and handled on an individual basis. This results in virtually handmade wines.

In 1983, Paul Brasset, who had 15 years of experience at various wineries, joined White Oaks as the winemaker. He, too, shares Bill's philosophy of hand-making small batches of varietals. Selected lots of each varietal grape are fermented separately and may or may not be blended, depending on the balance desired by Paul and Bill. Balance is the key word in the winemaking techniques of White Oak Vineyards. Abundant fruit is balanced with subtle oak flavors.

White Oak Vineyards Sauvignon Blanc is cold fermented in stainless steel and then aged in French oak barrels for three to four months. Several lots of wine are usually blended together for balance and complexity and to avoid an overly grassy taste.

Bill Myers, who loves being a vintner because that means he is usually dealing with happy people, does not want his winery to grow to more than 10,000 cases per year, so that most of the wines can still be "hand produced." Bill still owns a fleet of salmon fishing boats in Alaska, so every year he hosts a salmon feast featuring hours-old fish flown in from Alaska — and his latest wines. ❧

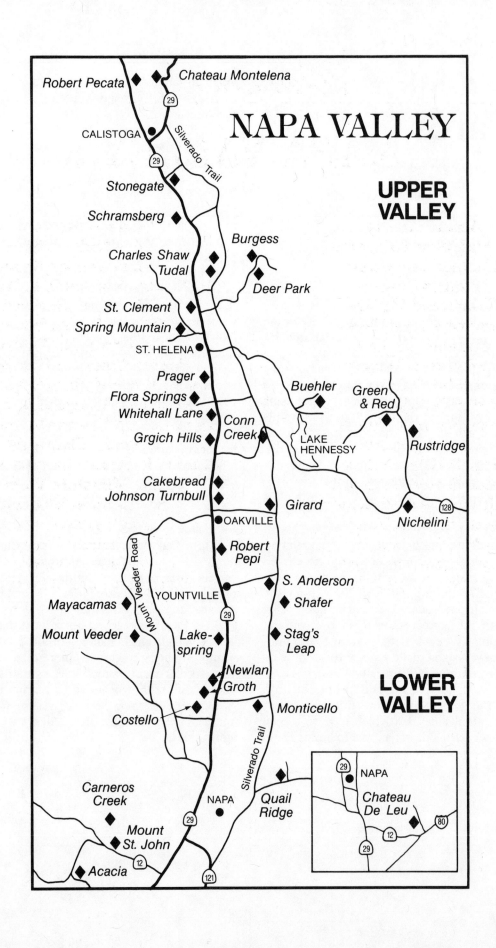

Wineries of

NAPA VALLEY

Acacia Winery
S. Anderson Vineyards
Buehler Vineyards
Burgess Cellars
Cakebread Cellars
Carneros Creek Winery
Chateau De Leu
Conn Creek Winery
Costello Vineyards
Deer Park Winery
Flora Springs Winery
Girard Winery
Grgich Hills Cellars
Green & Red Vineyard
Groth Vineyards & Winery
Johnson Turnbull Vineyards
Lakespring Winery
Mayacamas Vineyards
Mont St. John Cellars

Chateau Montelena
Monticello Cellars
Mount Veeder Winery
Newlan Vineyards & Winery
Nichelini Vineyard
Robert Pecota Winery
Robert Pepi Winery
Prager Winery & Port Works
Quail Ridge Cellars & Vineyards
Rustridge Vineyard & Winery
Schramsberg Vineyards And Cellars
Shafer Vineyards
Charles F. Shaw Vineyard & Winery
Spring Mountain Vineyards
St. Clement Vineyards
Stag's Leap Cellars
Stonegate Winery
Tudal Winery
Whitehall Lane Winery, Ltd.

Napa Valley

Much has been written about the physical characteristics of the Napa Valley and its ideal climate and soil for the growing of premium wine grapes. The Valley might better be understood, however, as a "way of life." The climate is perfect for the "good life," and the physical setting of the Valley is idyllic — sufficiently so, that one could not blame the residents if they were to usher out the visitors each evening and close the gates. Every Napa Valley label on a bottle of wine seems to give it the aura of a "superwine."

How did this "bigger than life" image of the Napa Valley come about? It had a rather inauspicious start which did not portend its ultimate status as the center of California's premium wine industry. The first vine cuttings (of the lowly Mission grape) were brought to the Valley in 1836 by a frontiersman-cattleman named George Yount, who never made more than 200 gallons of wine per year. He had obtained the cuttings from General Vallejo in Sonoma and then brought them by mule to the neighboring Napa Valley. The Valley was still frontier land and would remain so for several more decades, with Indian skirmishes and at least one Indian massacre by the white settlers.

Napa Valley's wine history really started with Charles Krug when he moved to the Valley in 1860 and planted grapes — 24 years after Yount had settled there — on land north of what is now St. Helena. Krug, a native of Germany, had come to San Francisco by way of Philadelphia to become the editor of the first German newspaper in San Francisco. He gave that up and planted a vineyard next door to Agoston Haraszthy in South San Francisco. Realizing that this endeavor would not work, due to poor climate conditions, he went to work for Haraszthy at the San Francisco Mint. Haraszthy, too, gave up his vineyard and moved to Sonoma in 1857. Charles Krug moved with him and worked for Haraszthy in the latter's Buena Vista winery until he moved to his property in the Napa Valley. Krug went on to become influential in the development of the Napa Valley and the California wine industry. He was an active member of the first State Viticulture Commission.

Other pioneering vintners began to settle in the Valley, including Jacob Schram in 1862. Schram was a barber by trade in his native Germany. He worked in that trade in San Francisco before buying land near Calistoga, where he planted imported German Rhine grapes. The winery continued in operation until Prohibition. It was reactivated in 1965, when Jack and Jamie Davies purchased the property and began producing champagne in the *Méthode Champenoise* under the Schramsberg label.

Jacob Beringer, another familiar name in the Napa Valley wine industry, came to work for Charles Krug in 1869. He was one of the few early settlers of the Valley who had received training in winemaking, both in his native Germany and in France. In 1875, he purchased property and two years later started his own winery. His brother joined him in 1884.

Jacob Beringer built a home for his family, calling it the "Rhinehaus." It was modelled after his family's home in Mainz, Germany and is still a Napa Valley landmark. The Beringer winery has continued to operate to this day, although the family sold it to the Nestle Company in 1971.

The Christian Brothers Winery, another Napa Valley landmark, actually started in Martinez in 1882. It moved its Novitiato to the slopes of the Mayacamas Mountains near Napa in 1930. Today this French teaching order, (founded in 1680) is the largest church-owned wine producer in the world and is the largest vintner in the Napa Valley. Christian Brothers currently operates five wineries, three in the Napa Valley and two in the San Joaquin Valley.

In spite of the expanding wine industry, the agricultural interests of the Napa Valley continued to be field crops and cattle until about 1870. It was during the next decade, however, that grape and wine production took over the economy of the Valley, with vine production expanding ten-fold. This drastic increase caused an over-supply of grapes and wine, and prices dropped significantly. Before the demand could catch up with the supply, the phylloxera epidemic hit Northern California, and many vintners failed or converted their land to orchards and field crops.

Just as the wine industry was getting back on its feet, it was hit by Prohibition. Napa Valley grape growers, like those in Sonoma and elsewhere, switched to lower quality grapes which could be readily shipped to home winemaker markets in the east. Following Repeal, the Napa Valley grape growers and winemakers were slow to recover due to the Depression. They started by replanting the Cabernet Sauvignon vines which had been torn out, and by 1940, the Valley led the state in the production of that varietal. By then, the Valley's reputation for Cabernet Sauvignon had returned.

Growth in grape and wine production did not return to the Napa Valley until the late 1960s. The 1970s saw a dramatic increase in both vineyard acreage and the establishment of new wineries. Close to 150 new wineries have started in Napa County since 1965, and grape acreage has almost tripled from 11,000 acres to 30,000.

The Napa Valley, while small (only two to five miles wide by 25 miles long) has a wide range of climates. Thus, it is able to produce very fine Burgundian style wines — Chardonnay and Pinot Noir — at the south end and Bordeaux-type grapes such as Cabernet Sauvignon at the upper end. The surrounding mountain slopes also support these and other varietals.

Napa Valley has assumed the role as the leader in the California wine industry in overall quality grape growing and winemaking. It does indeed represent a way of life, which also exemplifies the spirit of the entire California wine industry in its striving to further enhance one of life's true pleasures — fine wine with fine food in the company of fine people. 🍐

Acacia Winery

Address: 2750 Las Amigas Road, Napa 94559
□ (707) 226-9991
Visitation: Weekdays by appointment only
Principals: Paul Perret
Varietals produced: Chardonnay and Pinot Noir
Production: 32,000 cases per year

It takes 100 days from grape set to maturity for Pinot Noir in the Carneros region at the south end of the Napa Valley. Michael Richmond, the Director of Winery Operations at Acacia Winery, places as much emphasis on the proper growing of the grape as he does on the winemaking techniques.

The Carneros region has in recent years become famous for its Chardonnay and Pinot Noir. The climate and soil of the area at the north end of San Francisco Bay have greatly influenced the flavors of the grapes grown there. The cool winds and fog from the Bay raise the acid level of the grapes and make them more intense and well balanced. The resulting wines are more complex.

Even though the cool climate of the Bay influences the grape growing, the Carneros grapes ripen earlier than those grown in the warmer portions of the Napa Valley. The marine influence moderates the winter to summer variations and provides warmer winters and springs than is experienced further up the Valley.

Michael Richmond, Paul Perret, and several other investors founded the winery in the Carneros region in 1979 to take advantage of the soil and climate which are producing exceptional Pinot Noir and Chardonnay in the area. The Acacia Winery building was built in 1982. There are 44 acres in vineyards adjacent to or near the winery.

Equipped with teaching credentials, Mike Richmond, originally from Port Arthur, Texas, came to California in 1970 looking for work. Not finding any work in the education field, he took a job conducting guided tours at Freemark Abbey Winery in the Napa Valley and over a period of years worked for several other Napa wineries in various capacities.

Paul Perret is currently president and general manager of Acacia. Before deciding to seek out a satisfying lifestyle in the wine industry, Paul was a partner in a major San Francisco law firm. Paul Perret is also the owner of Perret Vineyards, located in the Carneros region.

Michael Richmond maintains close supervision of the

vineyards from which Acacia acquires its grapes. Michael believes that constant monitoring of the growing progress of the grapes is of ultimate importance to Acacia. Since sugar is made in the grape leaves, Acacia vineyards' leaf canopies are periodically moved and retied for optimum sun exposure for the leaves. At the same time, the leaf canopy protects the fruit from over-exposure to the sun. "The fruit needs light, but not direct sunlight," says Mike Richmond. In cooler climates, such as the Carneros region, a more elaborate trellis system is required.

Since there is a variety of soil and a variety of microclimates in the various Acacia vineyards, all wines are labeled as to their vineyard designation. There is a distinct difference in the wines produced from each vineyard even though they are within a one-mile radius of each other. There are variations even within the same vineyard. Consequently, Larry Brooks, the winemaker at Acacia, ferments the grapes from within a designated vineyard in small lots and then blends the lots back together. Wines from individual vineyards, however, are never mixed.

Larry Brooks and his assistant winemaker, Wade Mills, strive for a consistency and individual vineyard identity in their winemaking. They have established winemaking criteria which includes a constant checking of the ripening

grapes to determine the proper time for harvesting. The fermentation process also follows criteria set up over the years of making award-winning wines. Larry typically adds 7% of uncrushed berries to the Pinot Noir fermentation for complexity. The wine is fermented at a warm temperature to enhance the texture and complexity of the wine. The fermented Pinot Noir is aged in French oak barrels until spring, then racked and put back into small barrels and bottled in August. Larry does not strive for extreme fruitiness in either the Pinot Noir or Chardonnay.

Acacia produces wines which pair well with food. The distinct vineyards designation provides different flavors within a varietal. "After all, you would not flavor everything in your cooking with cumin," says Mike Richmond. Just as a choice of spices in cooking is used to bring out the flavors of food, Mike feels that the various pigments in the wines give them a distinctive character and flavor. That is why Acacia has taken so much care to produce four Pinot Noirs and four Chardonnays, each with distinctive characteristics of its own.

Today Acacia Winery is still following its original commitment to produce only the two prime Burgundian wines — Chardonnay and Pinot Noir. 🍂

S. Anderson Vineyards

Address: 1473 Yountville Road, Napa 94558
  □ (707) 944-8642
Visitation: By appointment only
Principals: Stanley B. and Carol G. Anderson
Varietals produced: Chardonnay and Blanc de Noirs Champagne
Production: 4,000 cases per year

Fill and drill! Even though Dr. Stanley Anderson, a well known Southern California dentist, and his wife Carol, a dental hygienist have changed careers they are still very much involved with filling and drilling — filling their bottles of champagne and drilling out their tunnel for their magnificent champagne cellar.

Stan attended dental school at the University of Pacific in San Francisco and became enamoured with the Napa Valley on many weekend trips he took to the valley. At the time he says he was not a connoisseur of fine wines, but did enjoy the free tastings. Stan, who is a highly motivated and active person, spent years racing yachts, a hobby which he enjoyed while practicing dentistry. After receiving 22 awards in international yacht races, Stan was ready

for a new challenge. Also, he was seeking something to interest him and keep him busy when he eventually retired.

In 1971, the Andersons found "just what the doctor ordered" — a 30-acre former vineyard and prune orchard in Napa Valley. They were going to become involved in grape growing. And involved they became! The ranch had been planted in vineyards in the 1860s, but by the turn of the century it was a prune farm. It remained such until 1971, when it was purchased by the Andersons.

Stan and Carol had the prune trees and their roots cleared from the property. Over the next several years they started planting 20 acres of vineyards, primarily in Chardonnay. The soil was particularly wellsuited to Chardonnay. Starting in 1975 with the first harvest, the Andersons sold their grapes to the premium wineries in the Napa Valley. However, each year they would hold back a small portion of the grapes for their own experimentation. In 1978, an additional 20-acre dairy property was added, and Pinot Noir and more Chardonnay were planted.

Stan had been a home winemaker for six years. Carol Anderson went back to school to U.C. Davis to study enology. She was there at the same time as the Anderson's two daughters were undergraduates. In 1978, when Carol finished her studies, it was time for the Andersons to establish a winery. Then life became very hectic.

Stan practiced dentistry in his Pasadena office Monday

through Thursday, and the Andersons were at the winery Friday through Sunday. Each Thursday afternoon they would drive 400 miles to Napa, arriving in the middle of the night, and working at the winery Friday through Sunday. Late Sunday afternoon it was time to drive the 400 miles back to Southern California so that Stan could be in the office at 9 AM on Monday. They led double lives, maintained two homes and had two sets of friends. For over five years the Andersons drove 50,000 miles a year up and down Interstate Highway 5.

Unfortunately, life got a little too hectic, and Stan suffered a heart attack in 1985. He retired from dental practice and now lives full-time in the remodeled farm house on the property. Both Stan and Carol work full-time in the winery and the vineyards, although they do employ a vineyard manager and an assistant winemaker. But Stan and Carol share the major part of the winemaking.

All of the Chardonnay is from the estate vineyard. Stan and Carol have planted their vineyard with closer spacing than typical California vineyards. This results in less tonnage per acre, but the system produces a more intensely flavored grape. No irrigation or fertilizer is used. The Pinot Noir grapes for the Blanc de Noir, however, are purchased from selected growers.

Each year the Andersons completely sell out their production of Chardonnay. The style of the wine is Burgundian, with emphasis on the fruit, avoiding excessive oak. Half of the grapes are fermented in stainless steel and the other half in oak. The components are then blended together and aged in oak.

Carol and Stan Anderson have always loved champagne and had done quite a bit of experimental work on producing champagne. They knew the techniques required, but they needed a cellar for aging.

On the Anderson's 50-acre ranch, there are two hills of solid rock. Stan decided to tunnel into the rock to build his champagne cellar. He contracted with the person who had the most experience at building tunnels — Alf Burtleson. Not only had Alf dug tunnels for other wineries and San Francisco city projects, but he helped build the underground rapid transit system, BART, in San Francisco. For the tunneling job at S. Anderson vineyards, Alf Burtleson used a Welsh coal-mining machine to get through the solid rock and build the tunnels and caves Stan wanted. The temperature in the resulting champagne cellar never varies.

The champagne cellars are a showpiece in themselves, with three separate rooms for aging. The middle cellar with its cathedral ceiling, candelabras attached to the walls, and a natural raised ledge resembling a stage has provided a setting for concerts. Formal dinners are also served in the cellar on very special occasions.

The Blanc de Noir champagne is made in the *Méthode Champenoise* with the wine resting on the yeast for at least two years in individual bottles. The bottles are all riddled (turned) every day by hand. The first release of S. Anderson Blanc de Noir got a three star rating shared only by Domaine Chandon and Schramsberg. The Anderson Blanc de Noir is consistently rated as one of the top champagnes made in this country. It takes about three years from the making of the wine for champagne to its actual release to the consumer.

In the future, Stan and Carol plan to expand their production to Blanc de Blanc, Brut, and Rosé champagnes. There is room in the cellar for expansion. They also plan to build a new winery building in front of the hill which houses the cellar.

Stan Anderson shuns the highly mechanized methods of production of some of the larger wineries. He and Carol like to handcraft their wines and give them the same individual attention as they did their dental patients. "After all, Michelangelo didn't paint the ceiling of the Sistine Chapel with a roller," says Stan. "I'm not in a hurry either." ❧

Buehler Vineyards

Address: 820 Greenfield Road, St. Helena 94574
□ (707) 963-2155
Visitation: By appointment only
Principals: John P. Buehler, Sr. and Helen Buehler; John P. Buehler, Jr. and Lisa Buehler
Varietals produced: Pinot Blanc, Chardonnay, White Zinfandel, Zinfandel, and Cabernet Sauvignon
Production: 30,000 cases per year

Situated in the mountains on the eastern side of the Napa Valley, high above St. Helena, is a chateau-style winery in the true sense of the French word. Buehler Vinyards is comprised not only of extensive vineyards, but also has an entire living and working complex of buildings. The courtyard with its plantings of flowers and shrubbery is the focal point for the four French chateau buildings — the winery, the office, the aging cellar, and the residence.

In 1972, when John Buehler, Sr., a then recently retired vice-president of the Bechtel Corporation, purchased the original 145-acre hilltop site, it had never been cultivated. John Sr., a West Point graduate, had retired as a full colonel from the Army Corps of Engineers before joining Bechtel to work with hydroelectric dam projects and the development of rapid transit systems.

The development of the vineyard, however, John Buehler, Sr. left to his son. The land is in a frost-free micro-climate high above Lake Hennessey. John Buehler, Jr. found that the soil and climate were ideally suited to a variety of grapes. However, he did not want to plant the same grapes as everyone else. "I wanted to try something a little different with the Pinot Blanc," he said. He is the only producer of an estate bottled Pinot Blanc in the Napa Valley.

In addition to the eight acres of Pinot Blanc, John planted 27 acres of Zinfandel and 26 of Cabernet Sauvignon. A drip irrigation system was installed, but it is only used to help establish new plantings. Now the vines are all dry farmed. At first John sold his grapes to the leading Napa and Sonoma wineries, then decided to produce his own wines. He felt that having control of the grapes would be a great asset in producing premium wines. At this time, all the grapes for his wines except Chardonnay are estate grown.

Construction of the Buehler winery began in 1978 and was ready for that year's crush. A barrel storage building and an office building were added later. Also, since John's young family was growing, a second storey was added to the residence in the early 1980s.

John Buehler is committed to red wines and strongly believes that there is a "trend back to the reds." The Buehler wines are food wines and are designed to be drinkable at time of purchase, although the reds and the Chardonnay also age well.

Heidi Peterson, one of the youngest winemakers in California (she is in her late 20s), is in charge of producing the Buehler wines. Although quite young, she has had more than ten years of winemaking experience. Her father, Richard Peterson is the president of Monterey Vineyard, and it was his influence that fostered her interest in wine. At 16, Heidi began working in a vine nursery in St. Helena and during high school and college summers worked at various wineries.

In 1980, Heidi graduated with a degree in enology from U. C. Davis and worked the crush in Germany. After her return to the states she worked briefly at Franciscan Vineyards, and then went to Australia to work the crush. Not only has she experienced firsthand the making of wine in Europe and in Australia, but she also served as winemaker at several Napa Valley wineries before joining Buehler Vineyards.

Heidi Peterson structures the Buehler Zinfandel in a claret style. The wine is usually aged one year in French oak before bottling. The Cabernet Sauvignon, which has a deep color and rich taste, is aged for 18 to 20 months in French oak. The Pinot Blanc is partially fermented in the barrel and partially in stainless steel. The two lots of Pinot Blanc are then blended together and aged in French oak for a totally dry wine.

John Buehler, Sr. is involved in the overall planning and operation of the winery estate, while John, Jr. is in charge of day-to-day operations and marketing throughout the United States.

Lisa Buehler's artistic ability has been a great asset to the winery. A Stanford graduate, she studied art in Switzerland and has used her talents to design the winery labels as well as other graphics for the winery. Lisa also creates and prepares many recipes which pair the Buehler wines with complementing foods.

The Buehler Vineyard is truly a chateau winery estate perched high in the mountains of Napa Valley where the soil and the climate is ideal for producing estate wines.

Burgess Cellars

Address: 1108 Deer Park Road, St. Helena 94574
□ (707) 963-4766
Visitation: Daily 10 AM to 4 PM, tours by appointment
Principals: Tom and Linda Burgess
Varietals produced: Chardonnay, Zinfandel, and
  Cabernet Sauvignon
Production: 30,000 cases per year

Burgess Cellars is perched on a Howell Mountain ridge overlooking the upper Napa Valley. The view from the winery and nearby home is spectacular. "Almost like being in a plane coming in for a landing," commented Linda Burgess.

The atmosphere is not too far removed from that of the Burgesses' former occupations in aviation, although the work and lifestyle is completely different. Tom, who was born in Akron, Ohio, graduated from Miami University with a degree in aeronautics. After graduation he became a U.S. Air Force pilot and traveled to various parts of the world. He was always drawn to the vineyards and to the wine of the country, regardless of where he was in the world — Europe, Australia or California.

In 1967, Tom became a corporate pilot based in New York. On one of his numerous trips across country to San Francisco, he met Linda, a native Californian, who at the time was a stewardess with United Airlines. Two years later they were married. Although they traveled to many different parts of the world, they always found themselves saving part of their free time to visit the Napa Valley, going to wineries and tasting the wines.

In the early 1970s, Linda and Tom decided that they wanted to do something on their own instead of working for others. Tom wanted to create a product which would make a statement of quality and style. But the question was: "What and where?" On their travels the Burgesses had begun collecting wines, and this interest in wine eventually led them to the decision to become vintners. "Actually," says Tom, "both flying and winemaking have a lot in common. They are technically oriented and have a diverse daily activity."

In 1972, Linda and Tom purchased the old Rossini winery and vineyard property on the western side of Howell Mountain. The property was originally homesteaded by the Rossini family around 1880 who established a vineyard on the steep mountainside and built a winery. The wines that were produced at the time were taken by horse-drawn tank wagons down to the Napa Valley to be either sold in bulk or bottled.

Following Prohibition it was not until 1943 that the owner at the time started making wine again from the old vineyards. In 1965, barrel rooms and a retail sales area were added to the winery. However, the facility was not large enough for the owners of the early 1970s — Souverain. Consequently, they sold it to Linda and Tom Burgess who considered the property perfect for their purposes.

Since purchasing the property, the Burgesses have replanted all of the old vineyards and added some new acreage. Twenty-one acres of Cabernet Sauvignon and Cabernet Franc were planted on the steep mountainside at 1,000 feet elevation. Due to the steep slope of the vineyard there is a constant battle against erosion to maintain the terraces. The soil is primarily volcanic, well suited to the two varieties of Cabernet.

In 1979, Tom and Linda purchased an additional 50-acre parcel on the valley floor in Yountville, midway in Napa Valley. The soil and climate there is wellsuited for the cultivation of Chardonnay.

Although the winery buildings were in existence and in operating condition when the Burgesses purchased the property in 1972, Tom has added a great deal of modern equipment to the operation. He was the first Napa winery to use the Westphalia centrifuge, and later was an early user of the Bucher tank press, now a standard at most wineries. Tom, like many other vintners, has selected a specific French barrel cooper, Jacques Damy of Mersault,

rather than use barrels from several coopers in a specific region of France.

Bill Sorenson, a native Missourian who like the Burgesses fell in love with California, is the winemaker at Burgess Cellars. Sorenson worked with a construction firm in Fresno and became fascinated with wine on his numerous trips to the Napa Valley. He decided to enroll at California State University in Fresno and graduated with a degree in enology in 1972. After graduation he came to Burgess Cellars to create, in conjunction with Tom and Linda, wines that form a "total impression."

Tom Burgess strongly believes that it is vital not only to grow grapes that are best suited to particular soils, but also to produce wines which bring out the varietal characteristics of those grapes. To this end, he and Bill Sorenson work with the vines, harvest the grapes at peak of maturity, and make wines which have good body and a long, complex finish.

The Cabernet Sauvignon is obtained from "stressed" mountain grown vines which produce small berries and low yields per acre. The juice is fermented on the skins in stainless steel until the sugar is reduced to 2 to 3 degrees Brix. The skins are then removed to prevent excess tannins and the wine is fermented until dry. After fermentation and light filtration, a small amount of Cabernet Franc or Merlot is blended into the wine. It is then aged for two to three years in French oak. The Zinfandel, all from purchased mountainside grapes, is fermented in much the same process.

The handpicked Chardonnay grapes are crushed into temperature controlled stainless steel tanks with skin contact for the first six hours. It is then barrel fermented in small oak barrels. Only about 25% of the Chardonnay is put through malolactic fermentation, for balance. Tom and Bill Sorenson believe that a small amount of malolactic enhances the rich and complex character of the Chardonnay.

The entire Burgess family is involved in the winery's operation. Linda is in charge of the winery office and does local marketing. The two teenage sons, Steven and Jim, help out in the summer. Tom not only oversees the operation, but also coordinates the marketing of Burgess Cellars wines throughout the country.

Tom does not want the winery to grow, since it is almost at capacity. In the future he would like to get involved in redoing the varietal regulations, which he feels need upgrading. ❧

Cakebread Cellars

Address: 8300 St. Helena Highway, Rutherford 94573
□ (707) 963-5221
Visitation: Daily 10 AM to 4 PM
Principals: Jack and Dolores Cakebread
Varietals produced: Sauvignon Blanc, Chardonnay, and Cabernet Sauvignon
Production: 30,000 cases per year

"We're just having so much fun," says smiling Dolores Cakebread as she shows guests through the new Winery Home at Cakebread Cellars. All of the hard work of establishing vineyards, building a winery, completely gutting and remodelling a 100-year-old farmhouse, creating new gourmet dishes to pair with the Cakebread wines, and maintaining three homes would be enough to drive most of us into a nervous breakdown. Not Dolores Cakebread. She is enjoying every minute of it.

As a matter of fact, husband Jack Cakebread, who operates several businesses and is perpetually on the go, and son Bruce, who is the winemaker, are both constantly on merry-go-rounds. They all love it — the more activity the better. As Bruce says, "We're a team, we all work together."

Jack Cakebread is a doer and has been successful at the things he is doing. He grew up in Oakland where his family had peach, apricot, and almond orchards in Contra Costa County. Eventually he purchased his father's automotive garage in Oakland. He left the garage for a short time for a career in the Air Force with the Strategic Air Command in North Africa. In 1950, he married his high school sweetheart, Dolores.

Running a garage was not exciting enough for Jack, although he is an excellent auto mechanic and the garage is a very prestigious one. He began studying photography with the late Ansel Adams and this led to the eventual creation of Cakebread Photography in 1959. Twelve years later Jack got a photographic commission which was to bring yet another enterprise into the Cakebreads' life. In 1971, he was engaged to shoot the pictures for Nathan Chroman's book *The Treasury of American Wines.*

While traveling the then undeveloped Napa Valley in early 1972, shooting pictures for the book, Jack and Dolores visited some old family friends, the Sturdevants. The elderly couple was getting ready to sell their farm and retire. The farm of 35 acres was mostly pasture with a few acres in vineyards. The Cakebreads made an agreement with the Sturdevants which said that if they could buy the farm and turn it into a vineyard, the Sturdevants could live in the farmhouse for the rest of their lives. And they did, until both passed away.

It was time for an additional career for Jack Cakebread. He took viticulture and enology courses at U.C. Davis. For the next several years, Jack and Dolores spent many weekends planting their 33 acres of vineyards in Cabernet Sauvignon and Sauvignon Blanc. They both continued to work 12 hours a day in the garage and photography business. Jack made the first commercial wine in 1976 with some pre-Prohibition equipment. That same year, the vineyard planting was also completed and an irrigation system with a reservoir was built. Realizing that the water table was close to the surface, Jack Cakebread designed a system using subterranean perforated tile pipes leading into a pump. Computer-driven pumps kick into action when the water level warrants, carrying the overflow to the reservoir. An old barn was converted into a winery building and a small laboratory was constructed.

Vegetables and gardening have always been a family tradition of the Cakebreads. Dolores, who was born in Wisconsin, came to California with her family as a young girl and became enchanted with farming and cooking. After she and Jack were married she became a regular participant in Bay Area cooking classes. The more she raised vegetables and herbs the more involved she became in culinary efforts.

After the three Cakebread sons were out of college, Dolores took a year off from the family businesses to complete the professional cooking curriculum at Le Cordon Rouge in San Rafael, California. Although there was a strong emphasis on butter and cream at the school, Dolores' cooking has moved away from fats and cholesterol. She is applying the professional principles she learned to salt-free, low calorie food preparation as a complement to the Cakebread wines.

In 1978, Bruce Cakebread, the youngest of the three sons, joined the winery as winemaker. Bruce started college at California Polytechnic at San Luis Obispo where he was majoring in pomology (the science of growing fruits and nuts). About the same time his parents purchased the vineyard property in Napa Valley. Bruce decided to specialize in grape growing instead, and transferred to U.C. Davis where he started in viticulture. However, while working for his father in 1976, assisting in the winemaking, he started thinking of himself as a potential winemaker. After graduation from U.C. Davis with a degree in enology in 1978 he took over the winemaking duties at Cakebread Cellars.

As the vineyards came into full maturity and production expanded, the winery also needed to be expanded. In 1980, William Turnbull designed a redwood building which looked as if it had been there for many years. Although rather simple on the outside, it is equipped with the latest in winemaking technology. The Cakebread winery building has won The Wood Council and the California Architect awards.

William Turnbull also designed the new Winery Home. The rehabilitated century-old Sturdevant house is a soaring Japanesque structure. Not only is the house a hospitality center with a completely equipped professional kitchen, but it also serves as the Cakebread residence when they are at the winery.

In 1985, the Cakebreads purchased 11 acres of Rutherford benchland and have planted it with Cabernet Sauvignon and Cabernet Franc. After extensive studies, Jack and Bruce decided on the percentage of Cabernet Franc to plant so that the blend would be done in the vineyard in the growing, instead of in the winery after the wines are made. All of the Chardonnay is still purchased from Napa Valley growers.

Much of the harvesting is done at night with mechanical harvesters, and the grapes are field crushed in a German Mortl crusher with the juice coming to the winery in stainless steel tanks.

In his winemaking, Bruce has tried to steer away from making the Sauvignon Blanc over-assertive. Since most of the harvests have been running early, he is able to use grapes which show perfect ripeness and good acid balance. The Sauvignon Blanc after cold stainless steel fermentation, is aged in oak for five to seven months. The Chardonnay, which is mostly fermented in stainless steel with a little barrel fermentation, on the other hand is aged for seven to nine months in oak. The Cabernet Sauvignon which is also cold fermented, is aged in French oak barrels anywhere from 18 months to two years. However, the reserve Cabernet receives four years of aging.

Cakebread Cellars is still very much a family operation. Jack does all of the administration, marketing, and vineyard management; Bruce does the winemaking; and Dolores is in charge of the hospitality and does a lot of the promotional work. It is one big happy, enthusiastic family that can well be proud of its many accomplishments — most important of which is making some of the finest wines in California. ❧

Carneros Creek Winery

Address: 1285 Dealy Lane, Napa 94558
□ (707) 253-9463
Visitation: By appointment only
Principals: Francis Mahoney and Balfour Gibson
Varietals produced: Chardonnay, Pinot Noir, Merlot and Cabernet Sauvignon
Production: 20,000 cases per year

"Technology has arrived in the field of winemaking, but the answer to excellent wine is still in the vineyards," says Francis Mahoney as he stands on the balcony of Carneros Creek Winery overlooking his vineyards. He has long been dedicated to making fine wines in the Burgundian and Bordeaux tradition.

Francis Mahoney was born and raised in San Francisco and received a B.A. from the University of San Francisco. He taught public school in that city prior to entering the wine industry. While working for Connoisseur Wine Imports in San Francisco, he developed a palate for Burgundian wines. Francis went on to U.C. Davis to study enology. Then he made some wines commercially for Connoisseur Imports, and he subsequently became vineyard manager for Mayacamas Winery.

Early in 1970, Francis Mahoney set out in search of a dream. His love for Burgundian wines created a desire to produce a world class Pinot Noir. He was convinced that the low rating of California Pinot Noirs was due to improper growing conditions and a lack of understanding of the grape. He reasoned that the missing links must be the lack of similar soil conditions, climate, and the same clone as in Burgundy.

The Carneros region of lower Napa Valley seemed to be the answer to his dream. Carneros was originally a Mexican land grant given to Nicholas Higuerra in 1838. He called his property *Rancho El Rincon de los Carneros*, after the Spanish word for sheep — carnero. In 1860, vines were planted in the area and flourished until phylloxera and Prohibition forced many growers to plant fruit trees and raise cattle. After Prohibition Louis Martini purchased 200 acres in Carneros for grape growing and in 1960, Rene di Rosa established the famous Winery Lake Vineyard in the area.

In 1973, Francis Mahoney and his partner Balfour Gibson purchased acreage in Carneros, planted nine acres of Pinot Noir grapes, and built a small chateau-like winery. Long-term contracts were arranged with grape growers to provide the remainder of grapes needed for Carneros Creek wine production.

Shortly after starting production, Carneros Creek embarked on a major research project in conjunction with the Univeristy of California at Davis to determine which clonal selection would produce a Pinot Noir of Burgundian calibre. Twenty clones of the grape were selected for an experimental plot in Carneros Creek's vineyards. Careful records are kept as to amount of production per vine, size of fruit, and the resulting wine. These records are helpful in long-range planning.

The results of this test plot and the studies convinced Francis Mahoney that superior Pinot Noir from the Carneros is one that is blended from wines (from different clones) all possessing complementary characteristics. Acting on this belief, Francis has planted five clones from which to make his Pinot Noir wine. Eleven new acres were planted in these Pinot Noir clones.

Since the yields from these clones is rather small, Francis Mahoney uses the traditional French method of spacing the vines closer together for added tonnage per acre, yet not decreasing the quality.

In keeping with the Burgundian practice of first promoting a wine-producing region and then the particular chateau which produces the wine, Francis Mahoney was instrumental in forming the Carneros Quality Alliance.

The Carneros Alliance encompasses the area just north of San Pablo Bay (a part of the greater San Francisco Bay) including a part of the lower Napa Valley and a part of the lower Sonoma Valley. Included are numerous vineyards and wineries. The Alliance is co-ordinating marketing efforts of the area and consumer information. Francis Mahoney was elected the Alliance's first president.

Francis Mahoney, who is the winemaker for Carneros Creek, strives for consistency in the production of all of his wines. He is still on the course of producing the finest Burgundian style Pinot Noir in California, and he firmly believes that the wine originates in the vineyard. That is why over a period of the last 15 years he has been so concerned with improvements in the Pinot Noir grape.

Chateau De Leu

Address: 1635 W. Mason Road, Suisun 94585
☐ (707) 864-1517
Visitation: Daily, 10 AM to 4:30 PM
Principals: Keith and Marian Lamb, Scott and Carole Lamb
Varietals produced: Chardonnay, Sauvignon Blanc, Chenin Blanc, French Colombard, and White Pinot Noir
Production: 12,000 cases per year

Wineries, just like any other businesses, are occasionally sold. Such was the case in 1985 with the Tudor-style winery known as Chateau De Leu in Green Valley, near Suisun City, east of the Napa Valley. The property, including 80 acres of vineyards had been owned by Benjamin Volkhart III, whose father had replanted a 70-year-old vineyard in 1954 and had raised grapes for a number of years. The Volkharts sold their grapes primarily to Napa Valley wineries. In 1981, Benjamin Volkhart III decided to construct a chateau-style winery in order to produce his own wine from these grapes.

Green Valley, although a small area one mile long and four miles wide, is well suited to grape growing. It has a micro-climate of its own, although similar to the southern end of the Napa Valley known as the Carneros District. The valley is bordered on the east and the west by mountains, but is open at the southern end to the Suisun Bay from which it receives its cooling breezes and sea fogs. Grape growing in the valley dates back to the early 1880s with over 2,000 acres in grapes at the turn of the century.

The new owners of Chateau De Leu — Keith and Marian Lamb — along with their son Scott and daughter-in-law Carole, purchased the winery and 40 of the original 80 acres of the property in the fall of 1985. They had been looking for vineyard property and a winery for the about eight years. The Lambs had studied vineyard management, winemaking, and winery operation and had searched the length of California and into Mexico for just the right spot. When they finally found the winery and vineyard they were looking for, the property was practically in their backyard.

Keith and Marian Lamb had been living in Sacramento, about 60 miles from Chateau De Leu. Keith is a retired attorney who specialized in business law with emphasis on agricultural problems and represented large farming corporations in the Sacramento Delta. Through his association with these agricultural concerns he became interested in grape growing and the winemaking process. His 20 years as the general counsel for the Sacramento Restaurant Association made him aware of the opportunities as well as the problems of sales and distribution of wines within the restaurant industry.

Scott Lamb was an economics major at U.C. Davis and also took some enology and viticulture courses, thus furthering the family's interest in owning a winery. After college, Scott worked in advertising and sales promotion. Marian Lamb and Scott's wife, Carole, have each contributed their own expertise to this new venture — graphic design, advertising and promotion, plus bookkeeping and office management. Steve Devitt, winemaker for Chateau

De Leu, acquired his skills at U. C. Davis and at his family's winery.

Although the Lambs purchased the winery, the vineyards were split, with 40 acres going to the Lambs and the Volkharts retaining the other 40 acres. All of the grapes used in the Chateau de Leu wines are estate grown from this property (considered one large estate).

White wines are a speciality of Chateau De Leu. The grapes are picked at cool morning temperatures and field crushed to maintain freshness. They are then racked into stainless steel tanks where they retain skin contact for 24 to 48 hours. The juice is then fermented in stainless steel tanks, with a portion fermented in French oak barrels. They are also aged in French oak for about eight months.

Although the Lamb family is new to the operation of a winery, they do not lack enthusiasm for their product or shun the hard work involved. They have come to realize that running a winery is a full-time, seven-day-a-week job. The Lambs hope to increase their production to the 25,000 cases capacity of the winery in the near future. Like the name Chateau De Leu — Chateau of Gold — the Lambs have found their gold at the end of the rainbow — a family working together. ❧

Conn Creek Winery

Address: 8711 Silverado Trail, St. Helena 94574
 □ (707) 963-5133
Visitation: By appointment only
Principals: Bill and Kathy Collins
Varietals produced: Chardonnay, Zinfandel, and
 Cabernet Sauvignon
Production: 20,000 cases per year

Kathy and Bill Collins became part of the Napa Valley scene with a big bang, figuratively speaking. They had to use a half a stick of dynamite on each old vine in their newly acquired vineyards to uproot the non-producing ones so that new vines could be planted. It took permits from sheriffs of two counties before they could start their "big bang" operation and join the world of grape growers.

Bill Collins is a native of Colorado. He graduated from the Naval Academy and spent eight years in the submarine service. While in the Navy he was sent to California, where he was eventually discharged. In 1957, Bill joined Lockheed and worked on the Polaris project. In the 1960s Bill became a manufacturer's representative in the electronics field. He worked with a series of manufacturers in the Silicon Valley and still represents some European companies.

In 1967, Bill and Kathy purchased 54 acres on the Napa Valley floor, which they replanted with Cabernet and Zinfandel. However, some of the 60-year-old Zinfandel vines on the property were still producing well and were left intact. The grapes are still being used in the Conn Creek Zinfandel. In 1970, the Collinses purchased another 58 acres in Yountville and planted Chardonnay and Pinot Noir.

As a grower, Bill has been a leader in developing improved relations between growers and vintners.

In 1975, Bill and Kathy decided to enter the field of winemaking. They leased a 90-year-old winery to begin making wine after their attempt to purchase another winery had failed. The old pink building was decrepit and cramped, but they made wine with their first winemaker, John Henderson, who had come along with the inventory the Collinses purchased from the failing Lyncrest Vineyards. Conn Creek continued in this mode of operation, but using their own grapes, until 1979, when having outgrown the old winery building, Bill and Kathy decided to construct their own winery.

A modern 14,000-square-foot French-style winery was constructed on Silverado Trail where one of Conn Creek's vineyards is located. The building utilized a revolutionary design, employing thick styrofoam/Gunite walls in order to achieve energy savings without sacrificing beauty.

The majority of the Cabernet Sauvignon and Chardonnay used in the winery are estate grown. All of the Zinfandel comes from Conn Creek's vineyards. Also planted are

Cabernet Franc and Merlot used in blending with the Cabernet Sauvignon. The balance of the grapes come from premium grape growers in the Napa Valley.

Shortly after Conn Creek Winery moved to its new facilities, it acquired a new winemaker. Daryl Eklund, who grew up in a small town where his dad was in logging, follows the principle that if you want something you have to work for it. He is very much involved with wine, not only working hard at the winery, but he usually spends his weekends at wine tastings or wine related events.

As the grapes arrive at the winery for crushing, each lot is tagged separately and handled individually from fermentation through aging. Eventually the separate lots are assessed and Daryl Eklund decides on the final blends. He tries to achieve consistency in his winemaking.

Conn Creek's Chardonnay is 40% barrel fermented, and the remainder is fermented in stainless steel. The wine is aged in small French oak barrels and blended before bottling for a buttery complexity.

Daryl and Bill are both of the belief that the wine should be drinkable when released. To achieve this they bottle age all of their wines — the Chardonnay for one year and the reds for two years. The style of wine Conn Creek produces improves with age in the bottle.

Kathy Collins is very actively involved in the winery. She has an excellent palate and participates in all of the tastings and final blending decisions. She is also in charge of hospitality for the winery, and does a great deal of entertaining for visiting wine and wine related dignitaries.

Conn Creek Winery and Vineyards started off with a bang and has been going strong ever since. The winery is particularly well regarded for their Zinfandel and Cabernet Sauvignon. ❧

Costello Vineyards

Address: 1200 Orchard Avenue, Napa 94558
☐ (707) 252-8483
Visitation: By appointment only
Principals: John and Mieke Costello
Varietals produced: Sauvignon Blanc and Chardonnay
Production: 10,000 cases per year

"We buy no grapes and we sell no grapes," So speaks John Costello, owner of Costello Vineyards. He wants to control his wines from the vine to the bottle. All of the grapes used in Costello wines are estate grown.

John, who grew up in the midwest on a dairy farm, has a background in agriculture and economics, having graduated with an economics degree from the University of Kansas. John Costello rekindled his interest in farming when he moved to the San Francisco Bay Area of California in 1961. He purchased three citrus and avocado groves in Southern California and had eventually planned to build a home on one of the ranches.

In 1968, John met and married Mieke, who is a native of Holland. She had lived in Paris and Lausanne, both as a student and later as a professional interpreter. Mieke is proficient in five languages and had just taken a job with Pan Am in San Francisco. Her first day in the city she looked for an apartment and found one in the building owned by John Costello.

It was Mieke's love for wine and John's desire to move to the country which first attracted them to the Napa Valley. Mieke, who had always lived in metropolitan areas, had no desire to move to a ranch in southern California, but was willing to move to the country as long as it was close to the city. Napa Valley, with both an international population and reputation, seemed to be the ideal spot for the Costellos.

In 1978, John Costello purchased an abandoned orchard which, at one time, had grown prunes, pears, and apples. All of the old trees were pulled up, grapes were planted, and a house for the family was built that same year. Before he purchased this plot, John had done a thorough investigation of the climatic and soil conditions of the property and found it to be ideally suited for Chardonnay and Sauvignon Blanc grapes, both of which like the cool climate of the lower Napa Valley. The area does not get much coastal fog which can cause rotting of the grapes instead of ripening. John takes pride in avoiding the use of pesticides in the vineyard.

There are 40 acres of Chardonnay and seven acres of Sauvignon Blanc in an adjoining vineyard. John had also originally planted Gewurztraminer, but found this too hard to sell and is T-budding it over to Chardonnay.

The Costellos soon found that a winery was needed to round out their profit picture. Besides, John wanted to produce the complete product instead of just selling grapes. He felt that "if you grow good grapes you should get good wine." He proceeded in 1982 to build a winery and to take courses in winemaking.

Since he makes both the Sauvignon Blanc and the Chardonnay in the French style it was only natural to use the consulting services of cellar masters from Burgundy. Each year a winemaker from one of two chateaux in Burgundy visits the Costello vineyard and advises John on the crushing and fermentation process. John gets the benefit of French knowhow, and the winemakers enjoy the experience of working with modern state-of-the-art equipment.

Costello Sauvignon Blanc is light and fruity, not a grassy variety. This style is partly due to the fact that the grapes are picked with slightly less sugar and some light oak aging — one-third in large oak French casks, one-third in once-used small French barrels, and the other third in stainless tanks. The Chardonnay, also on the fruity side, is aged in a similar manner. Sauvignon Blanc is fermented in stainless steel, and Chardonnay in a combination of French oak and stainless steel.

Mieke, who loves international gourmet cooking, is in charge of the bookkeeping for the winery and the vineyard. John's son Greg joined the family business and took over the marketing function in 1984, after graduating from the Naval Academy and fulfilling his tour of duty requirements. The two younger boys, Phil and Paul, are high school students and are a great help at crush and bottling times.

John feels that there are few industries in which the entire family can be involved from the growing of a product to the finished manufacturing.

In the future John hopes to also make Cabernet Sauvignon from purchased grapes, and for this he plans to enlarge the winery, which already has some of the latest equipment available on the market. 🍇

Deer Park Winery

Address: 1000 Deer Park Road, Deer Park 94576
 ☐ (707) 963-5411
Visitation: By appointment
Principals: David and Kinta Clark, Robert and Lila Knapp
Varietals produced: Sauvignon Blanc, Chardonnay, Zinfandel, and Petite Sirah
Production: 5,000 cases per year

One day in 1972 David Clark decided he had had enough of corporate life, sitting behind a desk in San Diego and trying to climb the ever-present corporate ladder. He had been raised on a cattle ranch and decided to return to the life in the country. As David says, "I would rather have dirt under my fingernails than ink. I enjoy my tractor."

David and his wife Kinta came north to the Napa Valley where David served an apprenticeship at both Cuvaison and Clos du Val wineries. He continued to work at Clos du Val until 1979 when he and his wife formed a partnership with his sister and her husband, Lila and Bob Knapp, and bought the old Deer Park Winery located in the hills northeast of St. Helena in Napa County.

The old winery was built in 1891. Emil Leuenberger, married to the daughter of John Sutter, purchased the 160-acre parcel at a sheriff's auction for $987 in gold. The winery, which the family built, became the original Sutter Home Winery and remained so until 1909, when the Sutter family decided to move to the floor of the Napa Valley south of St. Helena.

Three Italian families purchased the winery for only $25 in gold in 1909 and owned it until purchased by John

Ballentine in 1922. Since this was in the midst of Prohibition, the Ballentines were unable to make use of the facility until 1934. From then until 1960 the family produced mostly bulk wines. For the next 19 years, until the Clarks purchased the property, the winery was unused, though much of its equipment and cooperage was still intact and usable.

The winery, like many built in the late 19th century, was built into a hillside to take advantage of the cooling effect of below ground storage and also to utilize gravity flow from the crush on the second floor to the fermentation and aging barrels on the first floor. Even when Dave bought the winery, there was no electricity or drainage for the floor. He put in both electricity and a modern drain.

When David bought the winery, he also found large quantities of old but usable equipment packed into the two storeys of the building and also lying around outside. He has restored an old press so that it does all of the pressing at the winery, disassembled and cleaned old wooden storage tanks so that they could be used. As time goes on, he is reclaiming more and more of the old equipment. "The winery contains enough material for a museum," David says.

Along with the winery purchase was the land surrounding it — 48 acres. So far about three and one-half acres have been planted in the varietal which interests Dave the most — Sauvignon Blanc. He plans to plant two acres of Chardonnay and a half acre of Petite Sirah. The other 42 acres contain trees and rocks of all sizes, making it impossible to plant more vines.

David Clark has decided to make his "wine statement to the world" in his Sauvignon Blanc. He describes his style of the wine as "light, crisp, and steely." It is a dry wine with just the right amount of sugar to balance the acidity. This makes for a fruitier wine, but not a lot of "grassiness." He cool ferments the wine at about 60 degrees and does some barrel aging. In David's judgement, his Sauvignon Blanc has sufficient balance between acidity and fruitiness that it does not reach its peak until after two or three years.

Since Dave does not grow Zinfandel, he buys it from several growers in the Napa Valley. Each vineyard is treated separately and then blended together to achieve a consistent style year-after-year.

David knows the style of wine he wants to achieve for each varietal. Having no formal education in winemaking, he likes to experiment with his own techniques to achieve it. Whatever style he wants in the wine determines his winemaking procedures. David says he "relies on his taste rather than on book learning."

Deer Park is not a one-person winery. David's wife Kinta does the paperwork for the winery and helps at crush time. She is also an avid gardener. While gardening may be her avocation, Kinta's vocation and true love is designing and making authentic period costumes for antique dolls, which she sells throughout the western states.

The life of vintners is enjoyed by Kinta and David Clark. They plan to increase production to 8,000 cases, although staying with the four varietals they now produce. As David says, "Winemaking gives me the satisfaction of converting products of the soil into one of life's true enjoyments." &

Flora Springs Winery

Address: 1978 West Zinfandel Lane, St. Helena 94574
 □ (707) 963-5711

Visitation: By appointment only

Principals: Jerry and Flora Komes, Mike and Rose Komes, John and Carrie Komes, Pat and Julie Garvey

Varietals produced: Sauvignon Blanc, Chardonnay, and Cabernet Sauvignon

Production: 17,000 cases per year

Flora Springs is the story of the rebirth of a winery estate in the true European sense of the word — an estate where grapes are grown, where the wine is made, and where a family works together to produce the wine.

The winery building and the vineyards were started in the 1880s by two Scottish brothers, William and James Rennie. They had planted 60 acres of grapes and unfortunately had only two crushes before the phylloxera disease ruined their vines. For almost 50 years the property lay idle, and the lovely old stone building set into the hillside became a ghost winery.

In 1934, Louis Martini, Sr. purchased the old Rennie winery to age his Cabernet Sauvignon and also to make sherry at the facility. He liked the property and moved his family into the small house next to the winery. They soon outgrew this home and he built a much larger one a short distance from the winery. After Martini's death, the estate fell into disuse and the winery fell into further disrepair.

For the Komes family, it all started in 1977 when Jerry and Flora Komes decided to buy some vineyard property near St. Helena on the west side of the Napa Valley. Jerry Komes, who had just retired as president of the Bechtel Corporation, had selected the raising of grapes as his retirement avocation and a source of retirement income. Flora Komes, a native of the island of Oahu in Hawaii, liked the property they selected because it gave her a chance to further her hobby of gardening, as is evidenced today by the many colorful annuals and perennials planted on the estate.

Jerry Komes hired a property manager to revive and expand the 60 acres of estate vineyards. It took two years of pruning, draining and replanting to get the vineyards back into reasonable production. The grapes were sold to wineries in the Napa Valley, and he had no intention of making wine. In the meantime, Jerry's daughter Julie and her husband Pat Garvey also bought some vineyard property nearby, as did son John and his wife Carrie. With grape production going well in all the vineyards, it was obvious that a vineyard manger was needed to run the operation. This became the job of Pat Garvey, who had been an administrator at a community college. He has always loved the outdoors and was glad to trade paperwork for viticulture.

The time was right for the entire family to become involved in the operation, and with this in mind, John and Julie approached their father one day in 1978 with the idea of building a family wine business. John had become involved with home winemaking, and the prospect of converting the abandoned, century-old ghost winery into a successful commercial operation was an intriguing one. He owned a contracting business in the East Bay and enjoyed restoring old buildings, which he still does on a limited basis.

Both John and Pat moved their families to the "wine estate." John remodeled another smaller winery on the estate and converted it into a home for his family. Pat and Julie moved with their family into the cottage built by Louis Martini, and the elder Komeses live in the larger house on the property.

Flora Springs Winery is truly a family affair — named in honor of Flora Komes and the natural springs on the property. It is a great example of how six members of one family, each from different professional backgrounds, can work together and adjust to new vocations. John was the original winemaker, but now has the duties of general manager of the entire operation. Pat is the vineyard manager and Julie, who also had a career in the educational field, is the marketing director.

The first task was to restore the old winery so that it was operational. This required a new roof and more supports for the building which had suffered extensive damage in the 1906 earthquake. The building did not need a cooling system since it is built into the hillside with 24-inch-thick field stone walls. In 1982, the original building was enlarged further into the hillside for more fermentation space.

Flora Springs had its first harvest in 1978. The family picked the grapes, crushed and made 250 cases of wine. This bottling was for family and friends to test the marketability of the wine. The answer came the next year when the Chardonnay won a Gold Medal at the Los Angeles County Fair. John said there was an advantage to starting out cold. "We felt free to exercise some of our ideas of winemaking without all of the fear of failure."

Pat Garvey, desiring to keep the grapes fresher and cooler and the workers more comfortable, decided to harvest at night instead of the heat of the day (sometimes 95 degrees). Night harvesting is not a new innovation for people with mechanical harvesters, but had not been done with hand pickers before. An intricate lighting system was devised by Pat to light up several rows at the same time. Since about 80% of the Flora Springs vineyards' grapes are sold to other wineries, it means that the cool fresh grapes arrive at the wineries at 9 AM. Flora Springs grapes are crushed at the winery as soon as the gondolas are filled, regardless of the time of night.

There has also been a large project to improve the old hillside vineyards, including the installation of 4,000 feet of drain tile. Erosion can be a problem since there are four springs on the property. In total there are 300 acres of vineyards, 100 on the estate itself and the rest within a short distance. Only 15% to 20% of the prime grapes are used to produce the Flora Springs wines — Sauvignon Blanc, Chardonnay, and Cabernet Sauvignon. The remainder is still being sold to other vintners.

In 1980, Ken Deis, who was educated in enology at California State University, Fresno, joined Flora Springs as winemaker. The basis of his winemaking has been the ability to experiment using different yeast strains, fermenting some lots in stainless, others in barrels. Another asset to his success at Flora Springs is being able to work closely with Pat. They both believe strongly that the wine is only as good as the grape itself.

The Sauvignon Blanc is fermented for about 15 days in stainless steel tanks. Then half of it is aged in a combination of small French and American oak barrels while the other half ages in large French oak casks. Ken says that the small amount of American oak adds a distinctive character which blends well with the softer French oak aging. This aging takes four months, and then the wine is bottled.

Flora Springs produces an "estate" Chardonnay, which begins its fermentation in stainless steel to preserve its fruitiness and completes its fermentation in oak to add complexity. They also produce a unique barrel fermented Chardonnay in small quantities. In the latter, the grape juice is put into stainless steel tanks just long enough for innoculation with yeast. It is then immediately transferred to French oak barrels. After ten days of fermentation the wine is then aged for six months in small French oak barrels.

The Komes family's goal for the winery is about 20,000 cases. At that size it can still retain the individuality of a true "estate winery" with total family involvement. 🐾

Girard Winery

Address: 7717 Silverado Trail, Oakville 94562
  □ (707) 944-8577
Visitation: Monday through Friday, 12 noon to 5 PM
  Saturday and Sunday, 12 noon to 5 PM
Principals: The Stephen A. Girard Family
Varietals produced: Chenin Blanc, Sauvignon Blanc,
  Chardonnay, and Cabernet Sauvignon
Production: 14,000 cases per year

The oak-leaf cluster on the label of Girard Winery wines was inspired by the oak grove surrounding the winery — a lovely setting for the stone building. The oak grove sits in the middle of the Girard vineyards. The brick red background color was inspired by the red soil of the property.

The Girard winery and vineyards are owned by the Stephen A. Girard family — Stephen Girard, Sr., Stephen Girard, Jr., who is the general manger of the operation, and Stephen, Jr.'s three sisters.

The Girard family has always had an interest in wine. The senior Girard had established a very fine cellar of wines from around the world. The family moved to California in the early 1960s, where the the senior Girard was a vice president of Kaiser. In the early 1970s, Mr. Girard and the family started looking for his retirement venture. Since they had an interest in wines and enjoyed the Napa Valley, a grape growing venture seemed natural. They also wanted a family place in the country where they could all come together and share a common interest.

They searched for quite a while to find the right vineyard since they had set up specific qualifications for the land they wanted to purchase. They wanted an established vineyard on the side of the Napa Valley where there was better drainage and lighter soils. Those conditions would produce smaller amounts of fruit per acre which meant greater complexity and flavor for the grapes.

In 1972, the Girards found such acreage in Oakville on the Silverado Trail. There were 44 acres of gently sloping vineyards surrounding an oak grove where the future winery would be located. The soil is very rocky, thus providing excellent drainage. For some strange reason rocks "kept growing" in the vineyard and were removed each year to form the wall which now surrounds the entire ranch. The existing vines of Chardonnay and Cabernet Sauvignon had been planted by the previous owners in 1968. However, the vines had not received good care. Sound vineyard management breathed new life into the vineyard, and in 1977, a planting of Chenin Blanc vines was added.

For many years the Girard grapes were sold to the Robert Mondavi Winery, where they went into the private reserve bottlings. The Girard family decided that since these grapes were of such good quality, why not complete the process and build their own winery? Thus, in 1980, they built a 5,000-square-foot winery building with field stone facing. The operation was complete, but they needed a manager, preferably someone in the family. The senior Girard was still working full-time with Kaiser. So the task fell to Stephen Girard, Jr., who at first decided to take on the project on a part-time basis since he was involved in his own career.

Stephen Girard, Jr. is a graduate of the University of Washington with a degree in finance. He spent four years in the intelligence arm of the Navy during the Viet Nam war. Prior to coming to the winery, Steve was a negotiator for a defense supplier in Southern California for nine years.

Fred Payne, who had worked under Mike Grgich at Chateau Montelena, and also under Warren Winiarski at Stag's Leap Wine Cellars, became the winemaker at Girard Winery. Fred has a degree in chemistry from Occidental College and did postgraduate work at U.C. Davis.

The Girard wines are made to accentuate balance. Fred wants all components in the wine to come together to form one taste, instead of having the various components fight each other. Part of this is achieved by controlling the acid and sugar balance in the grapes. In other words, knowing the right time to harvest. All wines are cool fermented for good fruit extraction. "All of our Chardonnay is barrel fermented," says Steve Girard. "This gives the wine a creaminess," he adds. All of the wines are aged in small French oak barrels.

Girard Winery makes a very dry Chenin Blanc using the estate grown grapes in addition to purchased grapes for this wine. Steve also manages the two vineyards from which the Chenin Blanc grapes are bought. Since Chenin Blanc vines are prolific producers, Steve adheres to vigorous pruning to reduce the tonnage per acre, while increasing the intensity of the fruit. After cool fermentation the Chenin Blanc wine is aged in small French oak barrels for about five weeks.

In 1982, the Girard family purchased 440 acres of hillside property on the western side of the Napa Valley. When this property was purchased, it was heavily forested. A road has been cut and 30 acres planted in Cabernet Sauvignon, Chardonnay, and Cabernet Franc. A stream was dammed to form a lake for vineyard irrigation.

Steve Girard believes that Pinot Noir grapes should be grown in a cool climate and thinks the Napa Valley is too hot for the growing of this grape. With this in mind, the Girards have purchased a five-acre plot in Oregon south of

Eugene and are planting Pinot Noir. Until these vineyards come into production, Steve is purchasing Pinot Noir grapes in Oregon and having them transported in refrigerated trucks to the winery.

What started out for Stephen Girard, Sr. as a retirement venture has grown into a full-scale vineyard and winery operation. Girard wines have consistently won medals in the major competitions. They have been served at State dinners at the White house, and President Reagan took some of the wines to China with him. One of the reasons the Girard Winery has been highly regarded for its wines is the consistent quality of the product. The Girards believe this comes from the fact that the same people who make the winemaking decisions also make the vineyard decisions. ❧

Grgich Hills Cellars

Address: 1829 St. Helena Highway, Rutherford 94573
    ☐ (707) 963-2784
Visitation: Daily, 9:30 AM to 4:30 PM
Principals: Mike Grgich and Austin Hills
Varietals produced: Chardonnay, Fumé Blanc, Johannisberg Riesling, Zinfandel, and Cabernet Sauvignon, Late Harvest Johannisberg Riesling
Production: 30,000 cases per year

"American wines are moving up in quality," So says an expert in the field and one of the "Deans of American Winemakers." Miljenko (Mike) Grgich won world acclaim when the 1973 Chardonnay he made for Chateau Montelena won in a blind tasting over the most prestigious French White Burgundies (Pinot Chardonnay). The tasting, staged by wine expert Steven Spurrier, took place in Paris on May 24, 1976. A befitting victory in the year of America's Bicentennial. The victory also endearingly won Mike Grgich the title "Mr. California Chardonnay." The defeat of the French by a California Chardonnay was the top story in newspapers and magazines all over the country. Mike Grgich certainly did not stop there. He has gone on to other accolades.

In 1980, Mike Grgich's Chardonnay won the best wine over 220 other Chardonnays world wide. This was at a blind tasting in Chicago where wines from all over the world were entered — the "Great Chicago Chardonnay Showdown." This time the Chardonnay was made in Mike's own winery.

Mike Grgich, one of eleven children, was born in the Croatian area of Yugoslavia, where his father owned vineyards. Mike says that his first experience with winemaking was when he was three years old — he was stomping grapes. When he grew up, he studied enology and viticulture at the University of Zagreb.

After the war, he left his native land due to political pressures, immigrating to California in 1958 via Germany and Canada. He knew when he left Yugoslavia that his ultimate goal was to make wine in California. Even at that time, California had become known for premium wines. When he arrived in California, he worked for a short time for Souverain and Christian Brothers before joining André Tchelistcheff at Beaulieu as a wine chemist. "André had brought the French influence in winemaking to the Napa Valley," Mike recalls. After nine years at Beaulieu, Mike moved down the road to Oakville in 1968 to join a young new winery founded by energetic young Robert Mondavi.

Mike contrasted working at Beaulieu and working at Mondavi as the former had art, but the latter had action. And lots of action, as Mike recalls. Mondavi was the first to import different oak barrels for use in the winery. He emphasized the importance of different oaks in the flavors and the maturity of wine. Robert Mondavi also taught Mike the art of wine promotion and how to present wine to the public in a definite and realistic way.

One day, after tasting a superb Zinfandel made by an old Italian winemaker, Mike became convinced that there is a lot of instinct to winemaking — knowing what and when to do certain things. The Zinfandel wine he had tasted was made in that fashion — "without a lab, no centrifuge, no nothing," Mike recalls. "And it was wonderful." He came to realize that the less change a wine goes through the better the ultimate product will be.

After working for Mondavi for four years, Mike Grgich moved again, this time to Chateau Montelena where he remained for another five years. In 1973, he made his famous California Chardonnay. There his fame began.

Austin Hill, a member of the Hills Brothers coffee family, was greatly impressed with Mike's achievement. Austin Hill owned a vineyard in the Napa Valley and recognized an opportunity to combine his business background with a life-long interest in wine. He wanted to build a winery to make first class wines. What better way to do this than to form a partnership with one of the premier winemakers in the world. Mike Grgich and Austin Hill formed a partnership and broke ground for the new winery on July 4, 1977. In the spirit of patriotism and high hopes for the new winery, Independence Day was chosen for this celebration. Mike blessed the winery site with a bottle of his famous 1973 Montelena Chardonnay. Each year since then a unique Fourth of July celebration is held to celebrate the Grgich and Hill partnership.

The majority of the grapes used in the Grgich Hills winery are either from the Hill vineyards or from the Grgich Hills Cellars vineyards — one adjacent to the winery and the other in Yountville. The Yountville property also contains a 100-year-old Victorian house which the Grgiches have remodeled. Mike has tried to retain the old charm of the house, but has added some modern conveniences, such as a central heating system and a jacuzzi.

Over the years, Mike Grgich has developed his own style of winemaking. "Temperature is one of the most important things in winemaking…fermenting, aging or drinking," he says. He considers himself as a caretaker of the wines, not a manipulator. Like a baby-sitter, he is a "wine-sitter." If a wine is made correctly it will age well, he adds.

Each varietal wine which Mike Grgich makes is structurally different and has its own distinct characteristics. Mike says that if all of the whites were made alike, they would most likely taste alike. That was the way it was when he first came to California.

Today not only is Mike Grgich's Chardonnay known all over the world, so are the rest of his wines. Because of their popularity, Mike has had to put his wines on an allocation basis in order to service his accounts throughout the United States.

"Wine is not to make money, but a labor of love," says Mike Grgich, and that love shows in the quality of his wines. ❧

Green & Red Vineyard

Address: 3203 Chiles Pope Valley Road, St. Helena 94574 □ (707) 965-2346

Visitation: By appointment only

Principals: Jay Heminway and Pam Wilder

Varietals produced: White Zinfandel, Chardonnay, and Zinfandel

Production: 2,000 cases per year

"Wine broke out, babbling, bubbling over their speedy black ship, it was sweet, it was fragrant, its odor was divine." This is part of a 6th century BC poem by Homer entitled "Hymn to Dionysus" in honor of the god of wine. The story of the abduction of Dionysus by pirates is illustrated on the Green and Red wine label. The original painting was part of a 6th century BC wine cup.

The story, according to Homer, was that the pirates, against the better advice of the helmsman who had recognized Dionysus as the god of wine, tried to tie him up. Dionysus immediately changed into a raging lion, and the ship's hull filled with wine. A grapevine with clusters of grapes was entwined with the ship's mast. The terrified sailors jumped overboard and were instantly transformed into dolphins.

Not only is this scene on the Zinfandel label, but there are porpoises on the Green and Red labels for White Zinfandel. As one wine shop, Trumpet Vine of Berkeley, California commented on first seeing the label, "Oh, a wine with a porpoise [purpose]."

Jay Heminway has had a lifelong interest in the classics and art, having graduated from U. C. Berkeley with a B.A. and an M.A. in fine arts, majoring in sculpture. He spent a year in Italy studying on a Fulbright scholarship. Prior to this, Jay spent some time working in vineyards in France, and it was there that he further learned to appreciate fine wines.

When Jay came back to the U.S., he taught at U.C. Berkeley and started making wine at home in his spare time. He became so interested that not only did he want to make wine, but he also wanted to grow his own grapes. In 1970, he bought 160 acres in Chiles Valley in the hills above the east side of the Napa Valley. The valley was named for Colonel Joseph Chiles, who in the 1850s was a farmer in the area and a whiskey maker of some renown.

The property purchased by Jay was in a run down condition with a house that needed refurbishing and a barn that had burned in 1965. At one time, vineyards had been planted on part of the property. Replanting of 16 acres started in 1972 on ground that had originally been a vineyard at the turn of the century.

Pam Wilder, who has a degree from the Corcoran School of Art in Washington, D.C., is a painter who works mostly in oils. Although primarily a painter, she finds herself more and more involved in the winery, doing the bookkeeping and taking care of hospitality duties. Her culinary efforts to pair their wine with food is greatly enhanced by the large vegetable garden Pam and Jay plant and cultivate every year.

The vineyards range in elevation from 900 to 1,500 feet. The contours of the land make it possible to have two different vineyards at different elevations and with different sun exposures. The vineyards are also in two different micro-climates, providing the opportunity to grow two varietals — Chardonnay and Zinfandel. The soil contains red iron oxide veined with green serpentine. Thus the name Green and Red Vineyard.

In 1977, Jay rebuilt the barn, extended it into the hillside, and made other additions so that the structure could become the winery. The resulting building is composed of a number of rooms, each used for a different process of winemaking — stainless steel fermentation, oak fermentation, barrel aging, and bottle aging.

Pam and Jay do all the vineyard and winery work themselves. The grapes are hand-picked into lug boxes and hand-sorted before putting the berries into the crusher. "That way we can eliminate any moldy or bad grapes," Pam says.

The Zinfandel is fermented in open-top stainless steel tanks with the cap being punched down two to five times daily. After fermentation over 10 to 15 days, the pressed wine is moved to settling tanks and remains on the lees until malolactic fermentation is finished, usually around Thanksgiving. The wine is aged in small American and French oak barrels for 12 to 16 months and then bottle aged for another year before release.

The Chardonnay grapes are also hand picked and hand culled. After a light press, 80% of the juice is fermented in stainless steel, while the remainder is fermented in French oak barrels. The wine is aged and settled on the lees through the winter with no malolactic fermentation. After six months of barrel aging, the wine is bottled and then aged another six months before release.

The White Zinfandel of Green and Red Vineyards is done in a completely dry style, making it compatible with many foods. The grapes are harvested at 20 degrees Brix, not overripe, and left on the skins for one to four hours. The wine is cold fermented in stainless steel until completely dry. A small portion of the wine, however, is fermented in oak barrels, adding a hint of oak to the flavor of the wine.

Hard work has been the story behind the success of Green and Red Vineyards' award-winning wines. Pam still recalls with a chuckle her first task at the winery. It was to get down into a large oak upright through a small door and scrub it clean. Claustrophobia almost got to her. To avoid having to do this task again, Pam says she put on ten pounds.

Pam and Jay enjoy working in the vineyards and seeing each harvest, with their help, produce quality wines. They are convinced that the grapes make the wine and try for a balanced wine that emphasizes the qualities of the fruit. The results are wines that complement food and yet still have a character of their own. ❧

Groth Vineyards & Winery

Address: P.O. Box 412, Hillview Lane, Oakville 94562
☐ (707) 255-7466
Visitation: Monday through Friday, 9 AM to 5 PM
Principals: Dennis and Judy Groth
Varietals produced: Sauvignon Blanc, Chardonnay, and Cabernet Sauvignon
Production: 24,000 cases per year

Dennis and Judy Groth believe that anything worth doing is worth doing right. That was the motivating factor in their search for the right vineyards, the proper winemaker for the new winery, and a consistent style of quality wines.

Both Dennis and Judy grew up in the Bay Area, and it was only natural that they developed an extensive interest in California wines. Dennis Groth worked for one of the large accounting firms — Arthur Young in San Jose. Later he became president of the international division of Atari. However, when Atari had a change in management, Dennis Groth's job was eliminated. After spending eight years in the fast pace of corporate life, he decided to devote himself full-time to his own wine business, and, in 1984, moved to Napa to be a vintner. Being a vintner would give him the opportunity to concentrate all of his efforts on creating his own product — wine.

In preparation for the creation of the winery, Judy and Dennis searched for quality vineyards which would provide the fruit for the style of wine they liked and wanted to make. They not only tracked down the vineyards already producing that type of grape, but also which wineries were using these grapes. They tasted the wines from these vineyards and those of neighboring vineyards as well. They also checked the soil and climatic conditions which produced the type of grapes they wanted. All of these tests helped them decide to buy two pieces of property — the Oakcross Vineyard for Cabernet Sauvignon grapes and the Hillview Vineyard for Sauvignon Blanc grapes — a total of 165 acres.

In addition to Sauvignon Blanc, the Hillview Vineyard also has some Merlot grapes. Chardonnay was planted at Oakcross Vineyard and will be used in the 1987 production. Currently they are purchasing Chardonnay grapes. Groth intends, however, to produce wines only from estate grown grapes.

There was another ingredient necessary for a successful winery — a winemaker of some renown. The Groths were lucky in being able to hire Nils Venge, previously the winemaker at Villa Mt. Eden. Nils Venge, a graduate of U.C. Davis in viticulture and enology, has been in the industry for 20 years. He had worked for a decade with the grapes of the neighboring Oakcross Vineyard and had produced some award-winning Cabernet Sauvignons.

At Groth, Nils is continuing the same traditional methods of producing Cabernet Sauvignon with one exception — adding 10% Merlot for a softer wine. Venge's style of winemaking is oriented toward wines that complement food. This style goes back to his adolescent days when he tasted wine daily at his home in Los Angeles. His father, Pers Venge, was a wine importer and educated his son in the finer food wines.

The Groth Winery is still under construction and will be at the Oakcross Vineyard. Crushing and fermentation in jacketed steel tanks set in the open in the middle of the vineyard is already taking place at the facility. Aging in the Groth's own oak barrels takes place in rented space as does bottling and shipping.

Since going into the wine business, Judy Groth, an accomplished cook, has had a better opportunity to use her culinary skills, experimenting in the use of wine in cooking and pairing wine with food. Another member of the family, daughter Elizabeth, a recent graduate of U.C. Berkeley, is the public relations director for the winery.

The Groths' aim is to maintain a constant quality of their wines, so that year after year they will be known for consistently the same style of estate wines. 🌢

Johnson Turnbull Vineyards

Address: 8210 St. Helena Highway, Oakville 94562
□ (707) 963-5839
Visitation: By appointment only
Principals: Marta and Reverdy Johnson, William Turnbull, Jr. and Mary Turnbull
Varietals produced: Cabernet Sauvignon
Production: 2,500 cases per year

"Let me in live in my house by the side of the road...and be a friend of man." The 100-year-old farmhouse on the edge of the Johnson Turnbull Vineyards could well be the type of house Sam Walter Foss was thinking of when he wrote his famous poem. The house in this case has been the gathering place for two families who enjoy working together. It is the perfect weekend retreat, since both the Johnsons and the Bill Turnbulls live in San Francisco. However, one or the other is there every weekend tending to the winery.

Reverdy Johnson and Bill Turnbull, the former a lawyer and the latter an architect, became friends when they both worked on the Sea Ranch development project on the Pacific Coast north of San Francisco. Both men came from farming backgrounds in the East and had always enjoyed life on a farm. Their ambition was to own a piece of land and raise a crop.

In 1977, Marta, Reverdy, and Bill decided to purchase a 21-acre Cabernet Sauvignon vineyard which needed refurbishing in Napa Valley. "The buildings were totally rundown" says Marta, but Reverdy and Bill saw the potential of the land and there was a house they could remodel.

Little by little the trio ripped out some of the old Cabernet vines, and, since the soil and climate were excellent for that particular grape, they replanted the vineyard with Cabernet Sauvignon.

The first couple of years after planting the vineyard, Marta, Reverdy, and Bill used some of the grapes and made wine for their own home use. They also sold some of the grapes to local wineries.

In 1979, there was an overabundance of grapes on the market and since the wine the Johnsons and Bill Turnbull had made was successful, they decided to establish a winery. Bill Turnbull redesigned the old barn on the property into a small efficient winery. There is a laboratory, fermentation room, and an aging cellar with a library ladder. For several years, Marta Johnson, who is five feet tall, had the task of topping the barrels once a week. Since an aluminum ladder is not the safest thing in the world, Bill designed the cellar with stacks of barrels on each side like a library.

Johnson Turnbull Vineyards buys no grapes and uses only what is grown on the estate vineyard. In that way there is total control not only of the vineyard, but also the winemaking. Reverdy and Bill continue to be joint winemakers, with the aid of Lawrence Wara, a consulting enologist. Kirstin Anderson, a recent U. C. Davis graduate, has been engaged to take over Marta's duties and has become assistant winemaker.

The Cabernet Sauvignon is fermented in stainless steel and then aged first in large American oak uprights for eight to nine months. It is then transferred to small French oak barrels where the wine ages another 12 to 15 months.

Bill and Reverdy gutted and remodeled the old farmhouse, with the two families doing all of the work themselves — even the children were involved. The bunkhouse was used for living quarters while the remodelling was going on. The house has a spacious living room and country kitchen which are wonderful places for both families to gather. The glassed in dining porch has a splendid view of the vineyards.

The logo on the Johnson Turnbull winery label is the

family crest of Bill Turnbull — a bull with his head turned looking over his shoulder

Even though the production of Johnson Turnbull is limited, their Cabernet Sauvignon has gained an excellent reputation. It is even part of the futures program of MacArthur Liquors in Washington, D.C. Just like buying futures on the stock market, wine enthusiasts buy futures of certain vintages from select wineries. It guarantees the consumer the wine he wants, and it also provides additional working capital to the vintner.

Reverdy and Bill plan to expand the production of the winery to an eventual goal of 5,000 cases per year. For the present, they are enjoying their farmhouse and winery retreat. "It's a wonderful place for friends and family to come together," says Marta. 🐚

Lakespring Winery

Address: 2055 Hoffman Lane, Napa 94558
  □ (707) 944-2475
Visitation: Daily, 10 AM to 3:30 PM
Principals: Frank, Harry, and Ralph Battat
Varietals produced: Chenin Blanc, Sauvignon Blanc, Chardonnay, Merlot, and Cabernet Sauvignon
Production: 18,000 cases per year

If you are planning to build a winery, it is a nice idea to let the winemaker design the building. After all, he has to work there. This is exactly what the Battat brothers — Frank, Harry, and Ralph — did when they built their winery in 1980.

The Battats are no newcomers to the field of food and agriculture as they own the Liberty Gold Fruit Company which is primariluy involved in producing processed and canned foods for the overseas market. In the late 1970s, they decided to diversify and create a business which serves the U.S. market. Frank Battat had been interested in wines for a long time as a wine collector and convinced his brothers they should become vintners.

Randy Mason, the winemaker at Lakespring Winery, designed a very functional building of 13,000 square feet of cellar, warehouse, and office space. There is also a conference room which can double as an entertainment and tasting center.

The cellar has a very open feeling. On the south side are temperature controlled stainless steel fermenting and holding tanks. On the opposite side are rows of French Nevers and Limousin oak barrels. The east side of the cellar is lined with French oak puncheons and behind them 2,000-gallon German oak ovals used for finishing the Sauvignon Blanc.

All phases of the winemaking have been planned with great care. The grape receiving area is stainless steel for easy clean up. The crusher is Italian, and the press is German. The pumps and filter have all been chosen for efficiency and quality. The bottling line is the latest state-of-the-art equipment from Italy. Lakespring bottled wines are bottle aged on the property in a separate temperature controlled warehouse.

There are seven acres of Chardonnay planted next to the winery. Although not the main source of grapes, the estate Chardonnay is blended into the wine. Randy and the Battats feel that they can make better wines by purchasing grapes. In this way, they can procure grapes from different soils and micro-climates. Blending these various lots, they feel, gives their wines a more fruity flavor and adds to the complexity of the wines.

Since Lakespring makes five different varietals, the Battats feel they would have to own five different vineyards, and still that does not guarantee quality. To them, that is not efficient farming. They are thoroughly familiar with farming techniques since they have been connected with farming 550 acres in the San Joaquin Valley for over 25 years.

Frank Battat is directly involved with the winery, doing administration work and all of the out-of-state marketing. Lakespring wines are marketed in 30 states. Lee, Frank's wife, is in charge of sales in California.

Randy Mason, who has been with Lakespring Winery since its inception, is a graduate in enology from U. C. Davis. He started his college education as pre-veterinarian, but stayed a fifth year and completed the enology program. His pre-med background has been an asset to his winemaking.

Randy tries to bring out the fruit in all of the varietals he makes. The Sauvignon Blanc, with grapes from San Luis Obispo and Napa Valley, is 100% varietal. The Chenin Blanc is finished off-dry with 0.5% residual sugar. The wine is aged one month in oak for roundness. Randy does not do a malolactic fermentation for the Chardonnay. After crushing and 18 hours of skin contact the juice is pressed off for fermentation. Forty percent of the juice is fermented in small oak barrels. After fermentation, the two lots are blended and then aged in wood for six months. The wine, which is a blend of various vineyards, has good acid balance.

Lakespring wines are primarily created to be food

wines. Thus the wines are dry, because a dry, crisp wine livens food flavors. They are also subtly oaked so that they will not overpower food. "And, the wines are also fruity because wine is basically a food, and the best flavors which accompany foods are other foods," adds Randy Mason.

From the inception of the winery, the Battats have limited the quantity of the winery because they feel that the best wines are made by one person, and one person can only do so much. They would rather have quality than quantity. ‌

Mayacamas Vineyards

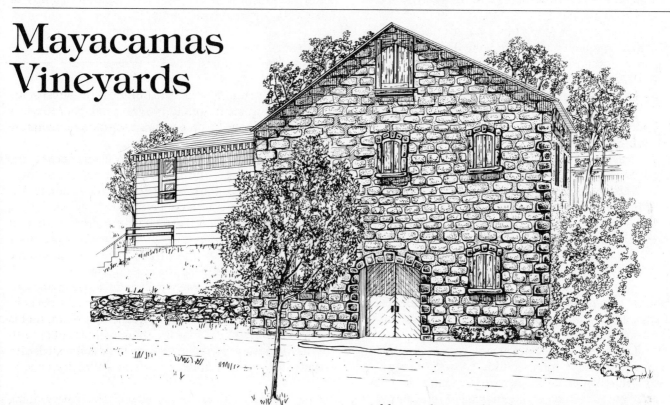

Address: 1155 Lokoya Road, Napa 94558
☐ (707) 224-4030
Visitation: By appointment only
Principals: Robert and Elinor Travers
Varietals produced: Sauvignon Blanc, Chardonnay, Pinot Noir, Zinfandel, Cabernet Sauvignon and Noble Semillon
Production: 5,000 cases per year

Mayacamas is the name of the mountain range which separates the Napa and Sonoma Valleys, and it is also the name of a winery which is located in this mountain range. The word "Mayacamas" is the Spanish adaptation of the local Lokoya Indian word meaning "howl of the mountain lion." Cougars and bobcats still roam the mountains. Two rampant lions in a stately English design within the letter "M", a design inspired by the former owner, are part of the Mayacamas wine label.

The Mayacamas Winery, although known by another name, then, was built in 1889 by John Henry Fisher, a German immigrant. Fisher, who was a sword engraver in his native country, came to San Francisco and became a

pickle merchant. He bought the Mayacamas property and not only built a winery, but also a small distillery. Vineyards of Zinfandel and a grape called "Sweetwater" were planted. Fisher sold the property after the turn of the century, and like so many other wineries of the region, it fell into disuse.

In 1941, an Englishman, Jack Taylor, and his California wife purchased the property and refurbished the winery and part of the vineyards. He converted the old distillery into a home for his family and made additions to the winery. Since stainless steel tanks were unheard of at that time, he built concrete tanks with epoxy lining for his fermentation tanks. These square tanks on two levels of the winery are still in use today. Taylor pulled out all of the old vines and replanted the vineyards with Chardonnay and Cabernet Sauvignon. He also gave the winery the name Mayacamas (it had been known as the Fisher Winery) and used the "English" lions as a logo on the label.

In 1968, the Fishers sold the property to Robert and Elinor Travers. Bob and Elinor, both Stanford graduates, had been involved in the world of investment and banking but wanted to live in the country and become involved with agriculture. For over a year, before purchasing Mayacamas Vineyards, Bob had apprenticed himself to Joe Heitz, a leading winemaker in the Napa Valley. He did all sorts of winery chores and learned the business from the "ground up." The more involved he became, the more he was convinced that owning a vineyard and a winery was to be his life's work.

The 2,000-feet elevation of the Mayacamas vineyards proved to be excellent for grape growing. The soil is high in acid and volcanic rock — the area having once been the crater of an extinct volcano. This type of soil allows the vine roots to go down into the ground as much as ten feet. The soil, combined with a micro-climate of warm days and cool nights, produces an intensely fruity grape. Bob and Nonie, like their predecessor, tore out a portion of the vines and replanted to basically two grapes — Chardonnay and Cabernet. Although there are some other varietals grown on the 50 acres of vineyards, these two grapes form the majority of the acreage. Another fine acres are being planted.

The Traverses work as a team. Bob handles the winery and vineyards. Nonie is responsible for all bookkeeping and accounting, handles much of the hospitality and correspondence work, and plays a key role in wine tasting appraisals and decisions. She has frequently been seen picking grapes, bottling wine, and doing myriad other tasks around the winery.

The Traverses have decided to concentrate efforts mainly on producing and becoming known for only two wines — Chardonnay and Cabernet Sauvignon. Bob Travers describes his method of winemaking as "old-fashioned in a classical style." He uses no centrifuge or fining in his red winemaking. The Chardonnay, fermented in the concrete tanks, is made in the Burgundian style with French oak aging.

Mayacamas Cabernet is of the Bordeaux style. Depending on the vintage, Merlot or Cabernet Franc may be added for more complexity or to soften the wine. The juice is fermented on the skins for up to ten days, then aged in oak for 28 to 32 months and bottle aged for at least one year. The average time from vintage date to the time of release is four years. Mayacamas Cabernet Sauvignon has great aging potential, and this sought-after wine is usually sold out shortly after release. Some retailers throughout the country limit their customers to one or two bottles per purchase.

The Sauvignon Blanc is made in a Graves style to accentuate the fruitiness of the grape. A small percentage of Semillon is added to the Sauvignon Blanc for smoothness. It is aged in large oak casks for about ten months. This allows the wine to breathe without becoming over-oaked. "All fruit in wines is diminished by barrel aging," Bob Travers says. For this reason, he carefully monitors the aging progress of his wines.

Some years, the Travers produce a Noble Semillon, a dessert wine made from Botrytised grapes. If the "noble" rot is not present on the grapes, Bob induces it artificially. The picked grapes are placed on trays and sprayed with the Botrytis mold. The grapes are left on trays inside the winery where temperature and humidity can be controlled. After ten days they are crushed, fermented, and made into wine.

Although the production of Mayacamas Vineyards and Winery is small, the Traverses feel that they can control the operation most efficiently at this level. As plantings are increased, the purchase of outside grapes will be reduced. Bob and Nonie expect this will further improve the quality of two of the most sought after wines produced in California — Mayacamas Chardonnay and Cabernet Sauvignon. ❧

Mont St. John Cellars

Address: 5400 Old Sonoma Road, Napa 94559
  □ (707) 255-8864
Visitation: Daily, 10 AM to 5 PM
Principals: Louis Bartolucci
Varietals produced: Sauvignon Blanc, Chardonnay, Gewurztraminer, Johannisberg Riesling, Pinot Noir, Petite Sirah, Zinfandel, Cabernet Sauvignon, and Muscat di Canelli
Production: 10,000 cases per year

"When I started in the business," Louis Bartolucci reminisces, "most wine was sold in bulk." It seems that in the early 1930s, a retailer would buy barrels of wine — a red, a white, and a port or sherry. His customers would bring their own bottles and fill them from the spigot on the barrel. They were charged according to the size of the bottle. Wine was shipped east in tank cars and was put into barrels or bottles at the destination. Some of the eastern dealers, however, were watering down the wine until the Internal Revenue Service intervened. Most of the reputable dealers refused to buy California wine which was not in bottles and labeled "Bottled in California." Consequently, wine in bottles and designated by place of origin became popular.

Louis Bartolucci is a real pioneer in California wine producing and is part of a three generation wine family in the Napa Valley. Louis' father Andrea, Sr. and the latter's brother-in-law left the Tuscany region of Italy in 1913 to come to San Francisco to work on the construction of the French Pavilion in the Pan Pacific Pavilion. After the completion of the job, Andrea moved to Napa Valley to work in a magnesium mine. In 1919, he sent to Italy for his wife and small son, Louis. They landed in New York and came across country by train.

The reunited family settled in St. Helena, where Andrea became a grape shipper during harvest and a woodsman during the rest of the year. He had certainly come a long way from making wine in the small vineyard in Italy which had been part of his wife's dowry. After moving several times, the family settled in Oakville in the heart of the Napa Valley. In 1922, there was an auction of 24 acres with a winery next door, where the Bartolucci family was living. Andrea put in a bid and it was accepted. Since this was during Prohibition, Andrea produced sacramental and cooking wines which he marketed in San Francisco. He

was also shipping grapes to families in the Bay Area for home winemaking.

After the repeal of Prohibition, Andrea, Sr. purchased additional properties in Napa Valley as well as in Lodi in the San Joaquin Valley. In the 1930s, Louis joined his father in the family wine business, and together they built a new stone winery and named it the Madonna Winery — Mont St. John Cellars located in the shadow of Mont St. John. At that time wine sold for nine cents a gallon. At one time, the Bartoluccis were the 12th largest wine producers in California.

Following a tour of duty at Mare Island in World War II, Louis Bartolucci returned to the family business and operated it with his brothers until they sold the vineyards and winery in 1971 to Oakville Vineyards. When the operators of Oakville Vineyards did not succeed in the business, the Bartoluccis took the property back and ultimately in 1976 sold it to United Vintners.

Following the 1971 sale, Louis' son Andrea (known as Buck) took the money from his share of the stock and purchased 160 acres in Los Carneros on the south end of the Napa Valley. Buck felt that the soil and climate would prove the area to be a prime grape growing region. He was not wrong, since today it is recognized as one of the prime viticulture regions in California. For the next several years, Buck proceeded to plant Pinot Noir, Zinfandel, Chardonnay, Johannisberg Riesling, Gewurztraminer, Muscat di Canelli, and Sauvignon Blanc. He has recently added Cabernet Sauvignon. By 1979, his grapes were ready for wine production.

Louis Bartolucci had planned to retire, but found that a pretty boring idea. He drew up plans to build a winery with his son Buck. The two men literally built the winery by themselves, even doing all of the wiring. With an interruption of a couple of years, Mont St. John Cellars is back in the family business which was originally started in 1922.

All of the latest equipment was installed in the winery and all space has been utilized for efficiency. The winery was designed to handle large amounts of grapes without a waiting period. Twenty-ton lots can be crushed at one time and then immediately pumped into one stainless steel tank.

Buck, who is a graduate in viticulture and enology from Fresno State and has taken additional courses at U.C. Davis, is the winemaker. After picking the Pinot Noir grapes at 22 degrees Brix, Buck ferments the juice at a fairly cool fermentation — 75 degrees. To extend the fermentation time he adds some new wine. The alcohol in the new wine extracts the color and flavor from the fermenting juice. It also extends the fermentation time.

Buck has tried to minimize the number of moves a wine makes during its fermenting and aging periods. "Too many moves oxidize the wine," he says. Buck filters the wine before bottling.

Mont St. John Cellars is one of the oldest wineries in the Napa Valley and uses some of the old time-tested traditions in winemaking with new 1980s approaches. The region of grape growing is the "new" and the time-honored tradition of the Bartolucci family is the "old." 🍂

Chateau Montelena

Address: 1429 Tubbs Lane, Calistoga 94515
▢ (707) 942-5105
Visitation: Daily, 10 AM to 4 PM
Principals: James L. Barrett, Laura G. Barrett, Lee Paschich, Ernest Hahn
Varietals produced: Cabernet Sauvignon, Zinfandel, Chardonnay, and Johannisberg Riesling
Production: 30,000 cases per year

In 1976, the year of America's Bicentennial, California wines won hands down over their French counterparts at a tasting on May 24th. The tasting was staged in Paris by Steve Spurrier, a transplanted Englishman who owns a wine shop and runs a wine school for the French Restaurant Association. He arranged to have a blind tasting of California Chardonnay against the French White Burgundies made from the Pinot Chardonnay grape and California Cabernet Sauvignon against the most prestigious French red Bordeaux, including one by Mouton Rothschild. The nine French judges drawn from the Who's Who in the French wine scene agreed the best Chardonnay and the best Cabernet Sauvignon were made in California. The Chardonnay was Chateau Montelena, vintage 1973, and the Cabernet was Stag's Leap, vintage 1973.

Jim Barrett, Chateau Montelena's general manager and part owner, happened to be in France on a wine tour of the chateaux with 30 other California vintners when he heard the news. "Not bad for kids from the sticks," he said. Excitement ran high for the rest of the tour and although there was a very free exchange of winemaking information, the French became a little more reserved than usual.

The best world class Chardonnay had been made by winemaker Mike Grgich, a native of Yugoslavia who had been trained at the University of Zagreb. Mike Grgich's 1973 Chardonnay had already won in several blind tastings in the United States over its French competitors. The French victory, plus the other awards the wine had received, earned Mike Grgich the title of "Mr. Chardonnay." The wine was made in a most unconventional French style — a blending of two vineyards, Napa and Alexander Valleys.

The stunning victory of Chateau Montelena's Chardonnay skyrocketed the little known winery to national and international fame, although the winery had a long history in the annals of California winemaking.

Chateau Montelena had its beginnings in 1882 when Alfred L. Tubbs founded the winery. Tubbs, a state senator, owner of a whaling fleet, and builder of the first "rope walk" on the West Coast for China Clippers, wanted a winery estate fashioned after the great chateaux of Bordeau. The winery building was modeled in the chateau style by a French architect. The front was constructed of imported stone, and the rear and side walls were made of native stone walls which are three to 12 feet thick, extending into the hillside. This produced natural cooling for the wine cellar.

A perfectionist in all of his endeavors, Mr. Tubbs sailed to France and returned home with selected varietal vine cuttings and a winemaker, Jerome Bardot. One hundred acres of vineyards were planted. The vines flourished, and Mr. Bardot made some outstanding wines which gained considerable renown in Northern California.

During Prohibition, the vineyards fell into disuse and neglect, and the winery became dormant. It stayed that way for a considerable number of years. In the late 1950s Yort Franks and his wife owned the property and lived in the upstairs of the winery building (which today is the front and houses the tasting room).

The Chinese couple longed for their native gardens and lakes of northern China, their ancestral home. They decided to recreate some of these surroundings in their Napa Valley home by creating an artificial lake at the foot of the winery chateau. Jade Lake is surrounded by weeping willows. Arched bridges connect the islands where red lacquered pavilions are in contrast to the green foliage. Ducks and geese paddle lazily around the Chinese junk which floats peacefully on the lake.

In 1972, the current owners, led by Jim Barrett, resurrected the winery to full operation. Mike Grgich was the first winemaker and teacher of the present one, Bo Barrett, son of the principal. Bo is also the general manager of the operation.

Bo had worked in the vineyards, all of which were replanted, and was drawn more and more to winemaking, which he believes is not a one-man operation. "Although one person makes the final decisions, it is a consensus of all of the people involved in the process," says Bo Barrett.

Just as the vineyards of Chateau Montelena were unique a hundred years ago, so they are today. Lying at the foot of Mount St. Helena, the vineyards contain three basically different types of soils — alluvial, volcanic, and sedimentary. The vineyards are planted in Cabernet and Zinfandel, and each varietal may have as many as seven different lots in the vineyard — different as to ripening time, and sugar and acid levels. Consequently each lot is fermented and aged separately and then evaluated for final blending. "By making each of the lots separately we maximize their individual quality and create a master blend that gives us a finished wine with more power and dimension than any of the components," says Bo. All of this attention to the final blend of Cabernet Sauvignon has made Chateau Montelena famous for that varietal.

Bo Barrett believes in emphasizing the fruit first and foremost in his winemaking. He believes that the oak in the wine should be evident, but not overwhelming.

Even though Chateau Montelena gained world recognition with its 1973 Chardonnay, it has not sat back and rested on its laurels. Each year it is a different ballgame, and Bo Barrett is always looking for "the next hit" in his production of chateau-type wines. 🍃

Monticello Cellars

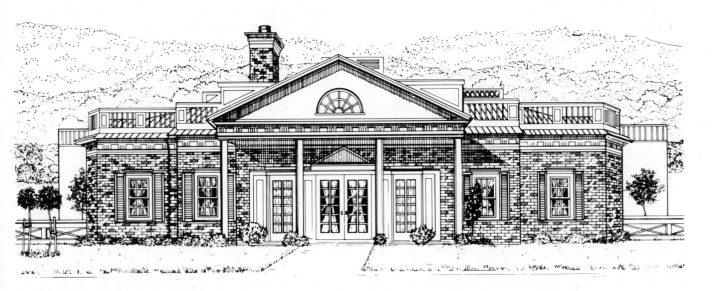

Address: 4242 Big Ranch Road, Napa 94558
 ☐ (707) 253-2802
Principals: Jay Corley
Visitation: Daily, 10 AM to 4:30 PM, by appointment
Varietals produced: Sauvignon Blanc, Chardonnay, Gewurz Traminer, Cabernet Sauvignon, and Late Harvest Gewurz Traminer
Production: 20,000 cases per year

"Good wine is a necessity of life," said Thomas Jefferson who had a great interest in wine. He had a vineyard at Monticello and made wine. Jefferson was a stickler for quality and excellence, which he felt could only be obtained through total involvement with whatever task was being performed. As in all of his other endeavors, Jefferson was personally involved in the vineyards and farming operations at Monticello.

Jay Corley, president of Monticello Cellars, traces his heritage back to Bedford County in Virginia. He, however, was born in Illinois, where his grandfather was a physician and owned a farm. It was this farm which first kindled Jay Corley's interest in agriculture, along with his Virginia ancestors' involvement with farming.

A Stanford alumnus, Corley began his business career in 1957 by becoming involved in insurance, mutual funds, and financial planning. In association with Howard Edgerton, a Los Angeles savings and loan executive, he formed The Corley Company which insured many real estate developments in Southern California. Corley also had real estate interests which included Century Park in Century City.

Eventually Corley became a private investor in several successful companies. In 1960, he was instrumental in founding National Systems Corporation of Newport Beach. At first a tiny mail order business, NSC evolved into the National Education Corporation, a hundred-million-dollar business. Jay Corley became its president.

Wanting to fulfill an almost life-long dream of being involved in agriculture, Jay Corley purchased a 200-acre plot in the southeastern section of Napa Valley early in the 1970s. Prior to buying this property Jay had a series of soil analyses and weather studies done. He found that there were different soils on the property which would add to the complexity and fruitiness of the grapes he intended to grow there.

Jay Corley became known in viticulture circles for his innovations in grape growing in the early 1970s. He installed underground sprinkler systems in the vineyard. There is also an underground drainage system. Corley was one of the first to use metal stakes in the vineyards and planted the vines closer together at that time, using eight-foot by ten-foot spacings.

Corley has divided the vineyards into 15-acre blocks of responsibility. Each block is assigned to an individual who prunes and harvests it. In this way, Jay feels he gets a better product because people take pride in their individual plot.

Until 1980, Monticello sold all of its grape production to the leading Napa Valley wineries. However, Jay Corley decided he wanted to produce the finished product and built a winery building with all the latest modern equipment. The building was finished for the 1982 crush. Today, the winery uses a third of the vineyard's production, while two-thirds of the grapes are still sold to other wineries.

Alan Phillips, an honor graduate of the University of California at Davis, is the winemaker at Monticello Cellars. He participated in the design and supervised the construction of Monticello's sophisticated holding tank system. The system consists of a cluster of four small tanks positioned over the press to hold the grapes. This allows the free run juice to drain quickly while holding the bulk of the grapes for the desired skin contact. The system makes it easier to handle small batches of grapes.

Jay Corley and Alan Phillips have structured Monticello's wines to be food wines patterned after the Burgundian and Alsatian styles. There is an emphasis on lower alcohols and a balance between the fruit and oak. As Alan Phillips explains, "The oak in our wines is used like a spice in food; it brings out the flavors of the fruit, but does not overpower it."

Monicello makes two Chardonnays, each with its own style. One is barrel fermented using slighty riper fruit and aging the wine in oak for ten months. The other, the Monticello Jefferson Ranch Chardonnay, is especially made for lighter cuisine. It is fermented in stainless steel with slightly less ripe grapes and is aged in oak for five months. The Gewurz Traminer is an off-dry style with 0.7% residual sugar and a good acid balance. The wine is aged four months in large German oak ovals. There are also two Monticello Cabernet Sauvignons — one has more Merlot blended in than the other, making the former more drinkable with lighter foods.

Shortly after the completion of the winery, a replica of Monticello was built for use as executive offices and the hospitality and culinary center. The dining room, with its crystal and silver chandeliers, is decorated in colonial blue and white, and is used for wine and food tastings. The decor of the entire building is patterned after Monticello with the same woodwork, color schemes, and colonial furnishings.

Since Monticello's emphasis is on food wines, it may be the only winery with a full-time professional culinary director. Even before Jay Corley built the Jefferson House, as the hospitality center is called, he commissioned Richard Alexei to develop recipes and menus to complement the wines of Monticello Cellars. Alexei is a well-known food and wine writer and cooking instructor. He is a regular contributor to *Wine Country* magazine and has appeared on food and wine programs throughout the nation. Not only does Richard Alexei enjoy preparing new recipes to complement Monticello wines, but he has done considerable research into recipes of colonial times to pair with the wines. Food and wine seminars are held periodically in the Jefferson House.

Each year in April, on a Sunday afternoon, Jay Corley invites his friends to a great celebration at Monticello Cellars. It is a birthday party to commemorate Jefferson's birthday. Food in the spirit of colonial times is developed by Richard Alexei and is served with the Monticello wines — such as Onion Gruyère Tart and Virginia Smithfield Ham with Biscuits served with Gewurz Traminer.

Thomas Jefferson was one of America's first viticulturalists and a fervent wine enthusiast. It is this enthusiasm, coupled with the Jeffersonian quest for excellence, which Jay Corley and Monticello Cellars are upholding with their quality food-oriented wines. ❧

Mount Veeder Winery

Address: 1999 Mount Veeder Road, Napa 94558
☐ (707) 224-4039
Visitation: Monday through Friday, by appointment only
Principals: Lisille and Henry Matheson
Varietals produced: Chardonnay and Cabernet Sauvignon
Production: 5,000 cases per year

"Consistency in wines comes from the vineyard, but there are vintage differences," explains Henry Matheson, owner of Mount Veeder Winery. He also believes that wine is basically made by the time it hits the crusher. In Henry's opinion, the vintner and winemaker only process the wine — they do not create it.

Mount Veeder Winery was founded in 1965, when 60 vines were planted in a former cow pasture. All but two of the vines survived, providing a good omen for future plantings. Since the mid-1960s, 20 acres of vines have been planted with Cabernet Sauvignon, Cabernet Franc, Merlot, Malbec, and Petit Verdot. Mount Veeder was one of the first vineyards planted with all of the varietals used for blending in the traditional Bordeaux manner.

By 1971, there were enough grapes to encourage the owners to build a small winery, and in 1973, the winery became a reality. It was built into the hillside to take advantage of natural cooling. The two-story building provides for barrel storage on the first floor and offices and winemaking laboratory on the second floor.

Henry and Lisille Matheson moved to California from Miami, Florida in 1982, when they purchased Mount Veeder Winery. Henry wanted to become involved in an agricultural product. He was familiar with agriculture since he grew up on his family's coconut farm in the southern part of Florida. Henry had been involved in various forms of employment from boating and scuba diving to real estate. The buying and selling of land was not what Henry wanted to do for the rest of his life.

Finally, in 1980, Henry knew that grape growing was the answer to his quest for a career. He and Lisille, who were married in 1979, spent the next year and a half looking for vineyard property on the East Coast. Fate, however, interfered when they got bumped from a flight in Pittsburg and were given free tickets to California as a form of compensation.

The Mathesons drove up and down the Napa Valley and were unimpressed. An advertisement in the Wall Street Journal, however, caught Henry's eye. It was an advertisement for the sale of Mount Veeder Winery. While he had no intention of buying it, he called the owner to discuss how a property of that size should be managed. The Mathesons ended up purchasing the property in 1982.

Mount Veeder Winery was exactly what Henry and Lisille had been looking for — a winery small enough for almost a one-man operation and a residence on the property surrounded by vineyards. With those physical characteristics they could run the vineyard with a hands-on approach.

Mount Veeder Winery and vineyards are located on the slopes of an extinct volcano in the Mayacamas Mountain range that lies between the Napa and Sonoma Valleys. The shale and volcanic soil provide excellent drainage. Since the vines are all planted on hillside property and receive no irrigation, their root systems are very deep. The roots absorb minerals from the soil which contribute to the complex flavors of the grapes. Also, since there is no excess moisture to go into the fruit, the berries are small with a large ratio of skin to pulp, resulting in deeper color and more varietal character for the wine.

Since the Mathesons came to Mount Veeder they have added four acres of vineyards to the existing 18 acres. They also grafted over two acres of Zinfandel to Chardonnay and in 1983 produced the first Chardonnay.

The nonirrigated vines grow at an elevation of 1,000 to 1,600 feet. At this altitude, they are above the frost line in the winter and the fog line in the summer. This provides the vines with morning sun. The surrounding mountains help shield the vines from intense late afternoon heat. Although the temperatures of Mount Veeder vineyards are cooler than the Napa Valley floor, the grapes usually ripen a week earlier.

Henry Matheson and winemaker Peter Franus decided that the quality of the wines would be enhanced by harvesting the grapes at a lower sugar content. This has resulted in better structured wines with rich flavors, but without high alcohol or overripe flavors.

Mount Veeder Winery, which is well known for its Cabernet Sauvignon, uses all estate grapes and blends all five traditional Bordeaux grapes into the final wine — 85% Cabernet and the remainder Merlot, Cabernet Franc, Malbec, and Petit Verdot. Peter, who is an enology graduate from Fresno State, likes to give the Cabernet Sauvignon about 12 days of skin contact during fermentation. The wine is fermented in stainless steel tanks and then moved to small French oak barrels where it ages for about two years. After bottling, the wine receives two more years of aging.

Peter and Henry make their Chardonnay in the traditional *sur lie* method. The grapes are harvested at sugar levels of slightly less than 23 degrees Brix, and are crushed and left with skin contact for about 24 hours. The must is then pumped into 60-gallon French Nevers and Vosges oak barrels for 100% barrel fermentation. The wine remains on the lees for six months. After bottling, the Chardonnay receives another eight months of aging.

Lisille Matheson has a journalism and advertising background and is very much involved in the winery, since she is in charge of the winery's sales program. She also does all of the public relations work and writes the winery's newsletter. This, and the two small Matheson children — Harper and Hank — keep Lisille very busy.

When Henry Matheson is not totally occupied with the winery, he attends to his art collection which he started shortly after graduation from Washington University in St. Louis, Missouri. Over the years, his collection has changed emphasis from Cubism to the contemporary California art movement. The paintings grace the walls of the office in the winery as well as the walls of the Mathesons' home.

Mount Veeder has been consistently recognized for its high quality Cabernet Sauvignon. This is due to the use of estate grown grapes. The Mathesons and Peter Franus follow many of the same vineyard and winemaking procedures of the small French winery estates, year after year. This makes for consistency in the quality of wine. ❧

Newlan Vineyards & Winery

Address: 5225 St. Helena Highway, Napa 94558
  □ (707) 944-2914
Visitation: By appointment only
Principals: Bruce and Jonette Newlan and family
Varietals produced: Sauvignon Blanc, Chardonnay, Pinot Noir, Cabernet Sauvignon, and Late Harvest Johannisberg Riesling
Production: 3,500 cases per year

Although Bruce Newlan grew up in the city of Long Beach, California, farming and grape growing was a part of his and his wife's Jonette's heritage. Both of their grandfathers were farmers. Bruce's grandfather owned grape orchards in the San Jaoquin Valley. In his teens, Bruce spent many summers helping his grandfather prune and harvest grapes.

After graduating from Fresno State with a degree in physics and electronics, Bruce joined the Navy and served for four years as an electronics officer, part of the time on the cruiser Essex. After the Navy, Bruce and Jonette moved to Northern California where Bruce was employed as a missile engineer at Lockheed.

In the 1960s, Bruce became involved with wine, first as a home winemaker, and then as a grower of grapes. In 1967, he and Jonette purchased land at the southern end of Napa Valley. He proceeded to plant 11 acres of his favorite wine grape — Cabernet Sauvignon. He kiddingly says he planted that varietal so that he could enjoy his own wine.

In 1972, Bruce purchased another piece of property,

north of the original vineyard and planted Pinot Noir. Over the years he has experimented with various clones of Pinot Noir on that property and in the late 1970s, has grafted over to an excellent wine grape. In 1975, the Newlans purchased aother vineyard. This third vineyard is two miles south of Yountville and is planted in Chardonnay and Sauvignon Blanc.

For many years, Bruce Newlan sold his premium grapes to various wineries in the Napa Valley. Since these wineries were winning awards with his grapes, Bruce decided to retain some of the choicest grapes and make his own wine. In 1977, he started a winery. Bruce was familiar with winemaking since he had done so for many years. However, he took some short courses at U.C. Davis to add to his technology.

Bruce is known primarily for his excellent Cabernet Sauvignon and his Pinot Noir, but also for his Late Harvest Johannisberg Riesling. This intensely flavored botrytised wine is picked when the grapes are at 35 degrees Brix. Although it is a very time-consuming wine to make, Bruce enjoys doing so.

Jonette Newlan spends a great deal of time with winery work, taking care of all correspondence and bookwork. As a former high school teacher, she is quite familiar with paperwork. She is constantly amazed with the amount of government forms a winery is required to fill out each month. Also, if wine is sold out-of-state, each individual state has an additional set of monthly forms to be completed. "It's a never ending circle," says Jonette.

Dan and Jim, the two youngest Newlan boys (there are two older ones) are involved in the winery with their dad. Dan works in the winery and Jim is the chief winery and vineyard mechanic.

Bruce has seen the Napa Valley grow over the last 20 years but still enjoys his vineyards and prefers to keep his winery small where he can control the quality of his wines.

Nichelini Vineyard

Address: 2349 Lower Chiles Valley Road, St. Helena 94574 □ (707) 963-3357
Visitation: Saturday and Sunday, 10 AM to 6 PM
Principals: Jo-Ann Nichelini Meyer
Varietals produced: Chenin Blanc, Sauvignon Vert, Napa Gamay, Zinfandel, Petite Sirah, and Cabernet Sauvignon
Production: 4,000 cases per year

There is a rule on the federal government's books that a convicted felon cannot make wine. That, however, did not stop Anton Nichelini, whose crime in this day and age would not have warranted a conviction.

Sixty years ago, during Prohibition, Anton Nichelini's wife Caterina made the mistake of selling a 35-cent jug of wine to a federal agent. Because the wine was from her husband's winery, he was sentenced to jail. He did not go to jail, but lived in the Plaza Hotel in Napa, across the street from the jail. He was a "trusty" and did gardening. Caterina would often visit him, and they would have a picnic on the lawn of the hotel.

After Prohibition, Anton could not get a license to operate a winery because he was a "convicted felon" in the eyes of the law. That did not stop him.

Anton Nichelini and his wife Caterina were both from Switzerland and first lived in Sonoma after coming to this country. In 1890, he homesteaded the land where the present Nichelini winery is located in the Chiles Valley east of St. Helena and over a ridge of hills. Vineyards were established and a winery was built with native stone into the side of the hill with a residence on top. (Passing on the road, State Highway 128, only the residence is visible.) The Nichelinis raised 12 children on this land and established a reputation for making wines in the old Italian-Swiss style. Anton had served a winemaking apprenticeship in France before coming to the United States.

In the early 1900s, more than 100 Italian workers had been imported into the area to work the manganese mines. "They worked for a dollar and a quarter a day and their room and board. The board included bread and wine," Jo-Ann Meyer recounts. Caterina Nichelini worked night and day baking enough bread to satisfy their needs, and Anton made the wine. Most of the workers drank a gallon a day. Prohibition struck one blow, and the closing of the mines after World War I struck the other.

One scheme Anton used to fool the government agents during Prohibition was to siphon off the 200 gallons allotted for family use. At night he would remove wine, seal it, and then top the tank from a secret hidden tank. All that worked until that fateful day when Caterina sold wine to the federal agent.

When Grandpa Nichelini was denied a license to operate a winery, the oldest son, William Anton, obtained the license for him and Anton continued to make wine. William Anton took over the winery when his father died in 1937. Up until that time, William had lived in Oakland where he worked as a surveyor. William's son James Nichelini, who began working at the winery in 1947, took over the operation and continued until his death in April 1985.

Now there is a fourth-generation Nichelini operating the winery. Jo-Ann makes wine just as a her great grandfather did a hundred years ago. Some modern equipment has been added, but basically the style of winemaking is the same as has been passed on from generation to generation. The Roman press used until 1957 is kept on display. The press is about five feet square with a 40-foot long pressure lever. It is believed to be the only one of its kind in this hemisphere. The old press pictured in front of the winery is the logo for the wine label of Nichelini Vineyard.

Jo-Ann Nichelini Meyer, who learned winemaking from her father, is married to an electrician and has two sons. The family is refurbishing the old homestead and plans to move in the near future. That way Jo-Ann can be close to the winery.

To continue making wine in the old Italian style is Jo-Ann's commitment of style. The wines are full-bodied, dry, and flavorful. Nichelini vineyard is one of the few producers of a Sauvignon Vert. In most wineries the grape is used for blending, but Jo-Ann makes it into a very dry, light wine.

Jo-Ann wanted to make wine since she was six years old. She is proud of her family history and wants to teach her children to be vintners. She loves working hard and being involved in what she considers an art. Jo-Ann appreciates the fact that her family is very supportive of her efforts. Jo-Ann wants to keep the winery small in order to best serve the loyal customers of Nichelini wines. ❧

Robert Pecota Winery

Address: 3299 Bennett Lane, Calistoga 94515
□ (707) 942-6625

Visitation: Monday through Friday, 9 AM to 5 PM, by appointment

Principals: Robert Pecota

Varietals produced: Sauvignon Blanc, Cabernet Sauvignon, and Muscat Blanc (sweet)

Production: 20,000 cases per year

"Winemaking is a poetic endeavor…a sense of balance and rhythm is the key…we follow the season from birth of budding grapevine to harvest and revel in the exhaustion of a task fulfilled. We are integrally tied to the cycles of the seasons. A combination of sensitivity to the elements and hard work yield the joy and exhilaration we feel in our efforts…" These are the thoughts on winemaking by Robert Pecota, owner of a winery at the northern end of the Napa Valley and a writer of poetry.

Bob has always had a love for, and an appreciation of, good food and wine, especially aromatic foods. This stems not only from his family background, but also from his career. The son of immigrant Russians, he has always been conscious of food since his father loved to cook and exposed him to many food experiences. Both of Bob's parents immigrated to the United States shortly before the Russian Revolution of 1917. Although they had lived only 20 miles apart in Russia, they met in New York. Bob's father engaged in various occupations from owning his own drayage company, to working in the garment industry, to owning dry cleaning stores, to owning a dairy farm in New Jersey.

The lure of new business adventures brought the small family of three to San Francisco. After engaging in more businesses and becoming the father of 11 children, Bob's father decided to become an evangelist, concentrating his ministry in the Midwest, which required him to be away from home for extended periods. Bob says that his father was actually more of a philosopher than a minister.

Robert Pecota earned a master's degree in economics from the University of San Francisco and worked for the M.J.B. Coffee Company for several years as a coffee buyer. When the coffee business became flat, he decided to take a position with Beringer, where he was in charge of grape purchasing. He also got some cellar experience there to add to his knowledge of winemaking, since for years he had been a home winemaker. While looking at land and grapes for Beringer, he kept eyeing a parcel of land at the north end of Napa Valley. In spite of Bob's efforts, the retired couple who owned the vineyard property sold their grapes on contract to wineries other than Beringer. When they finally decided to give up grape growing and move to a smaller retirement community, they asked Bob if he was interested in buying the home and vineyards. He was and he did. He completed construction of the winery in 1978.

At that time, the 35 acres of vineyards were in Petite Sirah, and Bob grafted them over to Sauvignon Blanc and Cabernet Sauvignon. Today, all of the Pecota Sauvignon Blanc and some of the Cabernet Sauvignon is estate grown. The soil and climate produce Cabernet Sauvignon grapes vines which are lush in fruit with lower tannins. Additional Cabernet grapes as well as the grapes for the Muscat wine are purchased.

Bob Pecota tries to emphasize the clearness of the fruit in all of his wines. He uses the traditional techniques of Bordeaux in his style of winemaking. All of the wines made are 100% varietal. The Sauvignon Blanc fermentation is started in stainless steel, then racked to oak barrels from Nevers, France. The wine is fermented and then aged in barrels for six months. Bob considers the Nevers oak barrels to have the tightest grain and the most subtle oak flavor. The sediments are allowed to settle, and then the wine is racked. Similar procedure is used for the Cabernet Sauvignon; however, it is aged for at least 18 months. Kathy Joseph, who holds a master's degree in enology from University of California, Davis, is the winemaker at Robert Pecota.

The winery also produces an unusual dessert wine, Muscato di Andrea, named after Bob's daughter. It is made in the "Auslese style," and is light and fruity to blend with any fruit-based dessert.

Robert Pecota is not only a wine connoisseur. He also likes to write poetry, enjoys jazz, and collects Napa Valley art. The art has become part of his wine labels. Each year a different work of art is featured on the label — the original being an oil painting, watercolor, or graphic art. The idea of art on the label was originally started by Baron Rothschild, and Bob has found that people identify the art with his wine. Art and wine go together. The Muscato di Andrea wine will have its own series of art labels starting in 1986. Each year, a different artist will be commissioned to paint a new portrait of Andrea. The wine and Andrea will grow up together.

"It is the human hand superimposed on the gift of lush fruit that is our challenge and love," says Robert Pecota. "We will never make the ultimate wine, but we try with each and every vintage." ❧

Robert Pepi Winery

Address: 7585 St. Helena Highway, Oakville 94562
□ (707) 944-2807
Visitation: Saturday and Sunday, 11 AM to 4:30 PM;
  Weekdays, by appointment only
Principals: Robert A. Pepi and Robert L. Pepi
Varietals produced: Semillon, Sauvignon Blanc,
  Chardonnay, and Cabernet Sauvignon
Production: 20,000 cases per year

When, in 1966, Robert A. Pepi and his wife Aurora bought the 70-acre vineyard near Oakville in the Napa Valley, they intended it as their semi-retirement property. They had planned to raise grapes and sell them to local vintners. The property already had 15 acres planted in Cabernet Sauvignon. "At that time, Cabernet was the king of all grapes" says Robert Pepi, and so he decided to plant more.

The purchase of the vineyard was the realization of a dream for the Pepis, whose family roots were in farming in the Tuscany region of Italy. The family had been grape growers and winemakers in Italy, but abandoned that occupation when they emmigrated to America in the early 1900s.

Robert Pepi's father came to San Francisco in 1922 and established a successful fur dressing business serving major taxidermists throughout the United States. Robert learned the business and joined his father, where he continued to work until 1981.

Over time, Pepi found that his vineyard soil was much better suited to the cultivation of Sauvignon Blanc grapes. It was a difficult decision, but recognizing the consumer trend toward white wine in the late 1970s, he completely T-budded the Cabernet vines over to Sauvignon Blanc. There are also ten acres of Chardonnay and a small acreage

of Semillon. Semillon is tradionally used as a blend with Sauvignon Blanc, but the Pepis also produce a 100% Semillon wine.

In 1979, the Pepis, joined by their son Robert L. and his wife Jennifer, decided to build a small winery and make it a family business. The younger Pepis took enology and viticulture courses at the University of California, Davis.

The winery building, which was finished in 1981, is constructed of locally quarried stone and situated on a 75-five foot knoll above the vineyards. Taking advantage of the hillside, the first floor of the winery is partially underground. The interior of the winery is primarily redwood panelled. Glass partitions in the second floor offices and tasting room permit a clear view of winery operations at all times.

Papa Pepi is as proud of the winery as he would be of a new son. After all, his son, Robert L.,and the Pepis' wine consultant, Tony Soter, designed the building. The younger Pepi and Soter have been friends since college days.

Robert L., the younger Pepi, is the winemaker. He concentrates over 50% of the winery's production on Sauvignon Blanc. Robert uses some techniques of Bordeaux winemaking with an emphasis on a softer, more complex style. The wine is aged in large 1,600-gallon French oak tanks rather than the conventional small 60-gallon variety. This method of aging allows the wine to develop more slowly and to mature without the rapid extraction of oak flavors. Robert makes Semillon by the same process.

He, however, utilizes several winemaking techniques in making Chardonnay. A portion is fermented in stainless steel to capture the fruity quality. A portion is fermented in barrels for oak flavor, and a portion undergoes malolactic fermentation for softness and complexity. These are then blended and aged in French oak barrels. The

Pepis also produce a small quantity of Cabernet Sauvignon from purchased grapes. As the senior Pepi says, "A true Italian has to make some red wine."

Jennifer Pepi is the vineyard manager. Under her supervision, a part of the Sauvignon Blanc acreage has been changed to a new and unconventional trellis system. She says the use of Y-shaped trellises enables the sunlight to be filtered onto the grapes, which results in a more even ripening and a better balanced fruit.

Within a few years, all of the white grapes used by the Robert Pepi Winery will be estate grown, while Cabernet Sauvignon grapes will be purchased from the Vine Hill Ranch which borders the famous Martha's Vineyard — known for its Cabernet Sauvignon grapes.

The entire family works together — the two men in the winery, Jennifer overseeing the vineyards, and Aurora using her culinary skills to create recipes which will blend with their wines.

Robert L. Pepi says that "there is a real sense of accomplishment in taking what nature has provided and transforming it into a product like wine — something that can reflect the winemaker's taste and what he feels the consumer will enjoy." 🍇

Prager Winery & Port Works

Address: 1281 Lewelling Lane, St. Helena 94574
  □ (707) 963-3720
Visitation: By appointment only
Principals: Jim and Imogene Prager
Varietals produced: Three different varietal Ports, Chardonnay and Cabernet Sauvignon
Production: 6,000 cases per year

There is a certain elegance and romance to the thought of serving a glass of port, the wine which was named after the city of Oporto, as was the country in which it originated. In days past, gentlemen after dinner used to retire to the drawing room to have a glass of port and smoke a cigar. Those times have changed. Today port is enjoyed at the dinner table as a dessert wine, or after dessert with some nuts and cheese.

Although not produced on the scale of Chardonnay, Zinfandel, or Cabernet Sauvignon, there are several innovative people producing Port in California. One of them is Jim Prager in Napa Valley.

Jim fell in love with the Napa Valley after he and his wife, Imogene, had taken a trip to the Valley in the spring of 1974. Jim and Imogene, both graduates of the University of Southern California, had lived in southern California most of their lives. Not long after their visit to the Napa Valley, however, Jim called a family meeting with his wife and seven children. After much discussion, it was decided that Jim should take a gamble and change lifestyles — from a successful insurance broker to that of a vintner. The entire "family crew" pledged to help and help they did.

The next year, the Pragers purchased a piece of land with an old carriage house on it which had been constructed in 1865. One of the first things that Jim did was to shore up the foundation of the building and put in a new concrete floor. The next project was restoration of a lean-to about 30 feet in front of the carriage house. With some more remodeling, these two buildings became the winery in 1979 — the carriage house is the press and fermenting room.

The transition from wine drinker and collector to winemaker has not been an easy one for Jim Prager. He has, however, blazed his own trail in port making. Lacking formal training as a winemaker, he read everything he could find on ports. While visiting U.C. Davis for some advice, he also had the opportunity to taste some port made from the Cabernet Sauvignon grape. The port was smooth and semi-dry. This convinced Jim to make port.

Most winemakers think about dinner wines when they fashion a wine from red grapes, but not Jim Prager. He is thinking after-dinner and port wines. Jim makes three kinds of port, each from a different red grape — Cabernet Sauvignon, Petite Sirah, and Pinot Noir.

In general, ports are high in alcohol and residual sugar when compared to table wines. Prager says that his ports average 18% alcohol and about 4% sugar. That is lower in both categories than most California ports and certainly lower than the Portuguese.

Only about 2% of the grapes Jim uses are estate-grown on a half-acre plot next to the winery. These are the Cabernet Sauvignon used for the estate port. He pays his growers a bonus for high sugar content in the grapes, which are usually picked at the end of the harvest season.

The grapes are brought to the winery, crushed, stemmed, and fermented on the native yeast. Then Prager adds grape brandy to the fermenting wine. This slows the fermentation process because it kills the yeast cells. Eventually fermentation stops before all of the sugar in the juice is converted by the yeast into alcohol. Jim ages his port for two or more years in oak before bottling. He does a minimum of racking and no filtering, as he feels that the lees (sediments in the wine) add flavor to the wine. Jim says his port does have to be decanted, but will last in the bottle for a month after it is first opened.

Although the making of port is Prager's main concentration, he does produce two table wines — Chardonnay and Cabernet Sauvignon. The former is made in a Burgundian style and the latter in a Bordeaux style, both with as little handling as possible.

Jim Prager was instrumental in founding and forming the 14-member California Port Producers Association and acted as its chairman. He feels that in the next few years there will be a renewed interest in dessert wines by Americans.

"I'm a frustrated artist," says Jim Prager. "My wife, a music graduate, and all of the kids play musical instruments. I can't play a note, but wine is an art form, so maybe I am expressing my art in the wines." ❧

Quail Ridge Cellars & Vineyards

Address: 1055 Atlas Peak Road, Napa 94558
☐ (707) 226-2728
Visitation: April through October: Weekends, 11 AM to 4 PM; Weekdays by appointment only
November through March: by appointment only
Principals: Elaine Wellesley and Leon Santoro
Varietals produced: Chardonnay, French Colombard, Merlot, and Cabernet Sauvignon
Production: 8,000 cases per year

Just as "too many cooks spoil the broth," there are few, if any, winemaking "teams" in the United States or even Europe. Not so for Quail Ridge — both partners, Elaine Wellesley and Leon Santoro, are the winemakers. Not only are they a team, but they are an international team. Elaine is English. Leon is Italian. They make French style wine from California grapes.

Elaine Wellesley, who is related to Richard Colley Wellesley (1760-1842), the first Duke of Wellington, was born in Durban, South Africa. She was educated at Cambridge University and worked as a journalist for Reuter Press Service covering Kenya, Zaire, and Rhodesia. In 1969, she moved to Los Angeles and worked as a book and script editor.

Elaine's interest in wine grew out of her interest in food and culinary techniques. Although she had taken many courses in wine appreciation, she felt that the best way really to understand a wine was to have the experience of making it. Thus, she could observe the development from juice to wine. Between 1970 and 1975, she and her husband became heavily involved in home winemaking — learning not only the modern, but also the traditional techniques.

In 1976, she and her late husband — film production manager Jesse Corallo — moved to the Napa Valley. After extensive study of micro-climates, they purchased land on the slopes of Mt. Veeder and planted grapes. In preparation for a career in commercial winemaking, Elaine obtained a degree in enology and viticulture from U.C. Davis. The first wine was made in 1978 — a rich full bodied Chardonnay from the grapes planted on the slopes of Mt. Veeder.

Following the tragic death of her husband in a vineyard brushfire in March 1981, Elaine regrouped her winery operation and relocated in the old Hedgeside Winery near the Silverado Country Club northeast of Napa. In 1981, Leon Santoro joined the winery as a partner and co-winemaker. The winery was composed of a 100-year-old sandstone building and a 340-foot-long "L"-shaped cave, hand hewn by Chinese workmen in 1885. The sandstone building was designed by Hamden W. McIntrye, California's preeminent winery architect. He had designed and built the Inglenook and Christian Brothers wineries, as well as other prominent ones in the Napa Valley.

Leon Santoro, who was born near Rome, gained his first winery experience at an early age helping his family produce their own wines in Italy. In 1967, his family moved to the United States and Leon, after earning a B. S. in chemistry at a New York university, became a food chemist in a large New York corporation. Leon wanted to do research, but the company wanted him to be a supervisor. This did not suit him. So he turned down the position and headed to California, where he worked first for Louis Martini and then Stag's Leap.

The two winemakers met at a seminar on winemaking in the late 1970s. While working at Stag's Leap, Leon had admired Quail Ridge's style of Chardonnay. Elaine and Leon's winemaking philosophies were virtually identical, and so it was natural that the two would form a partnership.

The old Estee Winery, which became Quail Ridge in 1981, is perfectly suited for the style of wine Elaine and Leon are making. "The temperature in the cave is usually 52 degrees and the humidity is consistently high," says Elaine Wellesley, "perfect for the type of wine we are making. It makes our barrel fermentations more stable and requires little topping since there there is little evaporation."

Elaine and Leon try to produce more complex and refined wines. To achieve this they blend from different vineyards of the same area — similar to the style of French winemaking. "In the end, the art of winemaking lies in the blending. Otherwise, winemaking could be reduced to a recipe and that would be no fun," Elaine says.

Chardonnay has always been the focal point of Quail Ridge. Except for a half acre of experimental Pinot Noir, all 17 acres at Quail Ridge are in Chardonnay grapes. The Quail Ridge Chardonnay is all fermented in French oak barrels resulting in a big, complex wine. Elaine and Leon also produce a Sonoma Chardonnay which is fermented in stainless steel tanks "to preserve the delicate, natural apple fruitiness of the grape," and then aged in oak. Elaine says that there is even a third "Chardonnay" of sorts. It is actually a French Colombard fermented in the same barrels as used for the Chardonnay.

Similar principles of blending are also applied to the making of Cabernet Sauvignon. Fruit from the Napa Valley floor and from the hillsides of Mt. Veeder are blended to create the balance desired by Elaine Wellesley and Leon Santoro. The valley fruit provides the finesse while the mountain fruit provides the structure of the wine.

Elaine and Leon are making a journey back in time — blending wine in traditional methods, fermenting in caves dug out with pick and shovel, and using time-consuming barrel fermentation. They both like to supervise the making of wine from the crushing of the grapes to the bottling of the wine. Elaine says that seeing each bottle corked and labelled is like a mother saying to her children "Now go off and make mother proud." Elaine Wellesley's and Leon Santoro's objective is to achieve a unique niche in hand-crafted, premium wines. ❧

Rustridge Vineyard & Winery

Address: 2910 Lower Chiles Road, St. Helena 94574
□ (707) 965-2871
Visitation: Daily, 10 AM to 5 PM
Principals: Grant and Stanton J. Meyer
Varietals produced: Chardonnay, Johannisberg Riesling, and Zinfandel
Production: 6,000 cases per year

What is the connection between Kentucky and Napa Valley? Rustridge is the tying link. It is the unique combination of a thoroughbred horse ranch and vineyard and winery. Kentucky cooperage barrels hold the wine for aging and a thoroughbred stallion named "Napa Valley" from Kentucky stock was recently added to the ranch's residents of eight mares. Eight foals were born on the ranch this last spring — all potential race horses.

Lucille Meyer is in charge of the thoroughbred operation while her sons Grant and Stan preside over the vineyard and winery. Mrs. Meyer, a native of San Francisco, had been in the real estate business for several years, when one day in 1972 she found herself showing a client a 450-acre ranch in Chiles Valley east of St. Helena. She immediately fell in love with the property and vowed to buy it herself if her client did not. They did not and she did.

The Meyers made several starts at creating a vineyard with bad luck. The first planting failed because the planting was too late in the season, the summer was unusually hot, and the root stock was second grade. Attempt number two also failed due to the drought of the mid-1970s, although a dam had been constructed as a water scource for the ranch. The third attempt fared much better with a drip irrigation system. By 1979, Rustridge grapes were being harvested and sold to the Napa Valley wineries. As were the thoroughbreds, the vineyard operation was "off and running." By that time, 60 acres of the property were in vineyards producing Johannisberg Riesling, Chardonnay, Zinfandel, and some Sauvignon Blanc and Cabernet Sauvignon.

Stan and Grant Meyer were in their teens when the first grapes were planted and since they both had been intrigued with grape growing, the prospects of operating a winery was only a natural progression for these interests. Stan majored in viticulture and agricultural economics at U.C. Davis while Grant majored in engineering at Napa College.

In 1984, Stan and Grant decided to convert the old hay barn into a winery. The boys had learned some carpentry skills from their father, and the whole family helped with the project. Stan became the winemaker with help from his wife Diane and Jeff Booth, a consulting winemaker. Grant became involved in marketing and promotion.

The first Riesling that Rustridge made won a silver medal at the Orange County Fair and subsequent medals in other competitions. The Rustridge wines emphasize the fruitiness of the grape. Stan's Zinfandel is made in a lighter style. The grapes are picked early to exhibit more fruity qualities. After fermentation, the wine is aged in Kentucky oak for one year.

There is still a definite connection between horses and wines. Mrs. Meyer, who still works as a consultant in the real estate field, has raced a horse at Bay Meadows, the local San Francisco racetrack, since August of 1985. She and the winery have been involved at the annual Ascot Day at the racetrack. Ascot Day pairs Napa Valley wineries and San Francisco restaurants to provide not only a day of racing but of food and wine. Rustridge wines are served in the Turf Club at the racetrack.

The entire family was involved in the design of the Rustridge wine label. Its design is simple and clear-cut.

The Rustridge label depicts a thoroughbred horse as a tribute to the ranch's history. The rust line that runs through the horse represents the rust ridge, the chaparral-covered knoll for which the ranch was named. The black line represents the solid fencing that surrounds the vineyard and the winery. The gold line symbolizes the fine soil that is responsible for the growth of the grapes.

Although Rustridge is a fairly new winery, tucked in a valley beyond the beaten path of Napa, its wines are beginning to win awards. Stan and Grant Meyer plan to expand their production to 9,000 cases in the next few years. ❧

Schramsberg Vineyards & Cellars

Address: Schramsberg Road, Calistoga 94515
□ (707) 942-4558
Visitation: Tours by appointment only, no tastings
Principals: Jamie and Jack Davies, Managing Partners
Varietals produced: Champagne by *Méthode Champenoise*: Blanc de Blancs, Blanc de Noirs, Cuvée de Pinot, Crémant Demi-sec, Reserve
Production: 50,000 cases per year

"Madame, your duty is clear. Take off your shoes and stockings and stomp the grapes!" said André Tchelistcheff to Jamie Davies. She did—and that was the beginning of the first vintage of Schramsberg. Jamie Davies became intimately involved with the winery from that first day of the crush.

Schramsberg champagne has become the most famous American champagne which has graced the tables of five U.S. summit conferences, and the last four American presidents have toasted numerous heads of state with Schramsberg champagne, including Queen Elizabeth, the Emperor of Japan, and the presidents of France and Mexico.

Since that beginning, when the crusher broke down in front of the assembled press and various dignitaries from the wine industry — including André Tchelistcheff, the "Dean of American winemakers"—Jamie Davies and her husband Jack have pioneered the American champagne industry. They were the first to produce only champagne in the traditional French *Méthode Champenoise*, instead of treating champagne as a sideline of wine production. "When we started there was hardly a single American

champagne producer, who grew his own grapes, made his own wines and produced sparkling wines from them — and produced nothing else," says Jack Davies.

Jack Davies is a native Californian, a Stanford graduate, and a graduate of the Harvard Business School. In 1965, he purchased the old defunct Schramsberg property which included a winery, aging caves, and a hundred-year-old house. It was a challenge to both Jack and Jamie Davies not only to make this "ghost" winery and house a working entity, but also to establish and pioneer a new aspect of the California wine business. It was their goal to produce champagne in the *Méthode Champenoise* as close to the French product as possible, not only in the method of production, but also in the grapes used.

At age 42, Jack Davies had rapidly climbed the executive ladder through: Kaiser Aluminum, Mckinsey & Co., Fibreboard Corp., and Ducommun, Inc. where he was a vice-president. He walked away from success to accept a challenge in an industry where he felt he could make a real contribution. Jack Davies believed the wine business offered him an opportunity not only in producing a single unique product, but also to put into practice his own theories on business management. However, it has not been a one person show. Jamie Davies, Jack's wife, has been every bit as much involved. Prior to moving to the Napa Valley, Jamie ran her own art gallery.

Over the years, Jack and Jamie Davies had developed an interest in wines after having joined the San Francisco Wine and Food Society. They had also developed a quality wine cellar. In the early 1960s, the Davies joined a group of investors in a winery near Saratoga in the Santa Cruz Mountain area. At the same time, they purchased an adjacent plot and started planting grapes. They had now progressed from casual wine lovers to serious participants in the industry. However, after several years, their interest diminished, and Jack and Jamie liquidated their investment in the wine industry. The episode did pave a way to their future desire to be vintners, however.

When Jack and Jamie finally decided to act on their

desire, they looked at several wineries which were for sale in Napa Valley at the time. One day, Jerome Draper, Sr., a prominent Napa Valley grape grower, took them to see the old Schramsberg property. The Davies immediately wanted the property and began negotiations to buy it. In August of 1965, the final papers were completed, and the Davies owned Schramsberg.

Schramsberg winery was originally started in 1862 by German immigrants, Jacob Schram and his wife Annie. Jacob Schram originally made his living as a barber. With the help of Chinese laborers, he planted one of the first vineyards in the Napa Valley and a few years later established a winery. Chinese laborers also dug tunnels 175 feet deep into the side of the mountain to provide aging cellars which are still in use today. Schram's wines became renowned all over the United States. After Schram's death, his son operated the winery which closed with the advent of Prohibition.

Champagne making by the *Méthode Champenoise* is not new in California. It dates back as far as 1855, when Benjamin Davis Wilson established a champagne cellar near the San Gabriel Mission in Southern California. There were difficulties in deciding which grape varieties to use and where to obtain bottles which could hold the pressure. One of the most successful at true champagne making in Northern California was Arpid Haraszthy, the son of the famous pioneer vintner in Sonoma. Others followed, but Prohibition put an end to champagne production.

The first years of operation were not easy for the Davieses. They had taken over a defunct winery whose equipment was old and run-down, the grounds and existing vineyards needed lots of work, and it was a tremendous job to make the house livable. "We had to acquire knowledge fast. Jack took short courses in winemaking," says Jamie. She made the house livable and took over the rennovation of the grounds.

Jack, who remained the winemaker for the first seven years, learned very quickly. He knew the type of product he wanted to create — a champagne which would go with food — from an apéritif to dessert. "From the beginning, we vintaged our wines and focused on their 'wineness,' or their individuality," he says. Jack also supervised the planting of 40 acres of vineyards — Chardonnay and Pinot Noir — on the property. Several years later, the first vintage of 250 cases of Blanc de Blancs was released.

Gradually, more acreage has been planted, the winery has had additions, the cellars have been enlarged by two-thirds, and all new equipment was purchased. Twenty-one years after the initial founding of Schramsberg, production is at 50,000 cases per year, and sales are 30,000. There is a waiting list of retailers and restauranteurs who want to sell Schramsberg champagnes. Due to the aging time, production continues to exceed sales. It will be several years before sales volume will reach the 1985 production level.

Jack Davis, in addition to the estate vineyards, purchases grapes from about ten different growers with whom he has long-term contracts. Until fairly recently, Schramsberg's production was limited by the availability of Chardonnay. However, as more of that varietal was being grown and became available, the Davies have been able to increase production.

Greg Fowler is now the winemaker at Schramsberg and works closely with both Jack and Jamie Davies. The *Méthode Champenoise* is strictly followed. Jack believes that the preparation of the blend of still wine (cuvée) is most important in creating the individual style of the champagne. "We don't simply take any white wine and put bubbles in it," he says. He is, first of all, making the finest table wines, before they ever become champagne.

After fermentation, the wines remain in stainless steel tanks for one to six months. They are then filtered and blended to make the cuvée. Tastings for the blend take place from October through December with a panel consisting of Jack, Jamie, Greg Fowler, and Dan Holm — the production manager. A precise amount of sugar and yeast is added to the dry wines, depending on which champagne is being made. For instance, the Blanc de Blancs, a blend of Chardonnay and Pinot Noir, is very dry and requires very little sugar addition. The wine is next poured into bottles which are capped with stainless steel caps. The bottles are laid down for aging from two to four years in the tunneled cellars.

Jack Davies is a problem solver as well as a champagne maker. Finding that tin caps corrode in his cellars, he switched to stainless steel ones, which he imports from France. He also uses mechanical riddling machines. A great deal of the riddling, however, is still done by hand. Jack feels that there are some vintages which do better with hand riddling. "There is no substitute for the human touch," he says.

Jack also designed a new vacuum system to deliver the grapes from the trucks to the presses, minimizing damage to the grape skins. The wines also flow by gravity from the winery to the bottling line in the cellars.

Schramsberg produces five kinds of champagne: Blanc de Blancs, a blend of Chardonnay and Pinot Noir; Blanc de Noirs, a blend primarily of Pinot Noir with some Chardonnay; Cuvée de Pinot, a blend of Pinot Noir and Napa Gamay; Crémant Demi-sec, a dessert champagne; and Reserve, a limited bottling of each year's choicest harvest.

The Cuvée de Pinot is unusal in that it is a salmon colored champagne, completely dry. Most rosé still wines and champagnes are off-dry or slightly sweet. The Cuvée de Pinot combines the fruitiness of the Pinot Noir and the Napa Gamay grapes.

The Crémant Demi-sec is a unique dessert champagne made from the Flora grape — a hybrid grape developed at the University of California, Davis. It is cross between Gewurztraminer and Semillon, with a delightful floral bouquet. "The Crémant is made to especially comple- ment sweet desserts," says Jamie Davies. Only half of the effervescence of usual champagne making is added to the Crémant. The result is a more "creamy" champagne. It, as well as the Flora grape, is an American first.

Another innovation of Jack and Jamie Davies is to age their champagne longer. The Reserve, for instance, is aged anywhere from four to six years. Many of the Schramsberg champagnes are aged for four years.

Both Jack and Jamie are very much involved in all aspects of the winery. Jamie, too, does a great deal of traveling to promote Schramsberg champagnes and give lectures on food and champagne. Jack does all of the marketing and travels widely not only in this country, but also abroad. Schramsberg champagnes are sold in Europe as well as the Far East.

Jack and Jamie Davies have certainly brought in- dividuality and excellent technical and managerial prac- tices to the wine industry. Over the years, the Davies have not lost sight of their purpose and goals to make American *méthod champenoise* champagne equal in quality with the finest French champagnes. Most critics say they have surpassed that goal, for Schramsberg is recognized as mak- er of one of the finest champagnes, worldwide. ❧

Shafer Vineyards

Address: 6154 Silverado Trail, Napa 94558
  □ (707) 944-2877
Visitation: By appointment only
Principals: John Shafer, Elizabeth Shafer, and four
  children
Varietals produced: Chardonnay, Merlot, and Cabernet
  Sauvignon
Production: 15,000 cases per year

In 1972, John Shafer, a 47-year-old senior vice-president in charge of long-range planning with a Chicago publishing firm, decided to do some planning of his own and start a second career. He and his wife Elizabeth (Bett) had grown tired of the same routines of daily life and yearned for a change while they were still young enough.

Being a thorough researcher, John looked into all sorts of possibilites and became intrigued with the then- booming California wine industry. A trip to California and the Napa Valley convinced them that this was where they wanted to live. John and Bett started looking for vineyard property and purchased 209 acres, 35 of which were planted with 50-year-old vines. The vineyard was in a run-down condition and needed quite a bit of work, but the property was considered prime. It is located in the Stag's Leap area, a minature valley-within-a-valley at the foot of the Stag's Leap Palisades on the eastern side of the Napa Valley.

The soil of their vineyard was ideal, similar to that of Bordeaux, for the growing of Cabernet Sauvignon grapes. The western exposure and the hilly terrain were important factors in growing excellent grapes.

After moving from Chicago with their four grown chil- dren, Bett and John spent the first few years replanting the vines in their run-down vineyard. They planted mostly Cabernet Sauvignon with some Zinfandel (which has since been T-budded over to Cabernet) and Merlot.

Most of the vineyard land is steep hillside terrain, which called for terracing. There is good sun exposure, natural frost control, and efficient drainage to produce excellent grapes. These hillside vineyards, however, de- mand a lot of extra attention. Planting, cultivation, and harvesting must all be done by hand or specially man- ufactured equipment.

The Shafers were content to learn everything they could about grape growing and had no initial intention of getting into winemaking. They sold their grapes mostly through a cooperative. John soon saw that wineries would pay a good price for good grapes, but not a premium price for great grapes. In the meantime, Stag's Leap Wine Cel- lar's Cabernet Sauvignon took top honors in a 1976 Paris tasting. The judges declared the wine superior to even its French counterpart. The wine was made from grapes from the vineyard neighboring the Shafers' property.

As time went on, encouraged by the superior quality of their grapes and also having added an additional vineyard of Chardonnay, they decided not only to grow grapes but also to make wine.

From 1978 to 1980, until the construction of their win- ery was complete, the Shafers produced wine from their grapes at a neighboring facility.

The winery is equipped with sufficient fermentation and storage capacity to allow simultaneous crushing and fermenting of all varietals. This has proved invaluable, since in their particular micro-climatic growing conditions, they often have various grape varieties ripen at the same time. With enough fermentation space, the fruit can be harvested and processed at the optimum time. In addition to stainless steel fermentation tanks, there are large oak uprights and several hundred French and American oak barrels for aging.

Doug Shafer had not really planned to be winemaker at his parents' winery when he went to U.C. Davis to take a degree in enology. For the first two years out of college he taught at a junior high school in Tucson, Arizona, but then returned to the Napa Valley to work as an apprentice winemaker at Lakespring Winery. Doug came to the Shafer winery, in 1983 and really likes the size of the winery because it gives him a chance to stay on top of the product from beginning to end. He says that good winemaking depends on attention to details and follow-through.

Shafer Vineyard's wines emphasize fruit and balance. Doug tries to make a Cabernet Sauvignon which has rich flavors and a velvety texture, balanced by firm acidity. The soft tannins give the wine a smooth finish. The Merlot is usually blended with a small percentage of Cabernet Sauvignon for a milder and softer style. Chardonnay, which is about 20% of their production, has a balance of fruitiness and oak.

The whole family is involved in the Shafer vineyard and winery operation. Bett is in charge of all the bookwork and oversees the hauling of grapes to the crusher during the harvest period. John manages the winery and the vineyard and is in charge of the marketing. Son Doug is the winemaker, while daughter Libby Shafer Cafaro works part time at marketing in addition to raising two young sons.

John wants his family winery to remain the size it is today, so that personal attention can be given to the estate grown grapes. Managing a vineyard and a winery is a full-time occupation, but one in which John Shafer has found a rewarding second career. 🍇

Charles F. Shaw Vineyard & Winery

Address: 1010 Big Tree Road, St. Helena 94574
□ (707) 963-3232 or □ (707) 963-5459
Visitation: Daily, 10 AM to 4 PM
Principals: Charles F. and Lucy Shaw
Varietals produced: Fumé Blanc, Chardonnay, Napa Gamay, Gamay Nouveau, and Gamay Blanc
Production: 25,000 cases per year

When establishing a new winery, to make a commitment to produce only one wine takes some guts, but when that wine is one that is not generally produced in its traditional French method, it takes a "heck" of a lot more guts. The wine: Gamay Nouveau and Napa Gamay. The vintner: Charles F. Shaw.

Charles Shaw is the only vintner in California who is producing a Gamay Nouveau and Napa Gamay in the traditional *maceration carbonique* technique perfected in the 19th century in France in the province of Beaujolais.

Some other California wineries are using the technique with other varietals, but not with a Napa Gamay, which is the closest grape to the Fleuries and Brouillys of Beaujolais. The Gamay Beaujolais, as known in this country, is a clone of the Pinot Noir grape.

A native of Michigan, Chuck Shaw is a 1965 graduate of West Point. He spent some time in the Army, leaving the service with the rank of captain to attend Stanford University's Graduate School of Business. While at the Business School, he had a special project to study some of the wineries of Northern California. It was during this project that he first became acquainted with wine. After graduation, Chuck joined a Houston banking firm, and he and his wife, Lucy — a native of Texas — were assigned to the Paris office of the bank.

While living in Paris, Chuck and Lucy toured the French countryside and became more and more interested in wines — particularly those of Beaujolais. Also while living in Paris, Lucy attended the *l'École Cordon Bleu*. The more the Shaws learned to know and love the fresh taste of the wines of Beaujolais, the greater the desire for Chuck to own his own winery.

In 1974, on a trip back to the United States, Chuck came to California and purchased some property above Lake Hennessey in the mountains east of the Napa Valley with the idea of establishing a winery when the Shaws returned from France. When they did return, they sold that parcel of land and purchased another one on the Napa Valley floor. Lucy thought the original property was too isolated, and the new acquisition had another great advantage.

The enticing factor of the property the Shaws purchased in 1978 from Charles Crocker of San Francisco, was the fact that Napa Gamay grapes were growing on its vineyards. The vines had been planted in 1974 on land that had been a thoroughbred horse breeding and training farm. Napa Gamay was the grape Chuck wanted to grow and to use in the old winemaking techniques of the Beaujolais region of France.

Chuck Shaw was well prepared for his new venture as a vineyard supervisor and winemaker. While in France he had made charts of the climate and growing conditions of grapes similar to the Napa Gamay. He had observed the winemaking techniques and had probably read everything there was on the subject. When he came back to California, he brought with him an entire library on how to grow and make Gamay Nouveau and Napa Gamay using the *maceration carbonique* technique.

An existing barn on the property was remodelled and additions made, and a residence was built for the Shaw family, which now includes five children. Since the Shaws had spent some time on Nantucket Island off the coast of Massachusetts and liked the Cape Cod architecture, all of the buildings on the winery estate are designed in that style. The gazebo featured on the label of the Shaw wines was built in 1981 by MGM, when part of the movie, *Yes, Giorgio* starring Luciano Pavarotti, was filmed on the estate.

Both the Gamay Nouveau and the Napa Gamay are made by the *maceration carbonique* technique originally developed centuries ago in France. The grapes are carefully harvested by hand into small picking boxes to avoid crushing the skins. When the small boxes arrive at the winery,

the grapes — whole clusters with the stems — are placed in specially designed square stainless steel fermenting tanks. (In France concrete tanks are still used.) Any free running juice is removed and fermented separately. The tank is sealed. Under a blanket of carbon dioxide, fermentation takes place inside of the whole berries.

Chuck varies the fermentation time for each wine. The Gamay Nouveau takes three to four days to complete the fermentation process, resulting in a lighter colored wine. The Napa Gamay, on the other hand, takes up to ten days and results in a darker wine with more tannins. After the period of maceration the grapes are lightly pressed and the fermentation continues for a short period of time. The wine is placed in large French oak uprights for storage and aging. The Napa Gamay has the longer aging period. Chuck prefers the large oak uprights because they do not emit as much oak flavor. Oak flavor detracts from the fresh fruitiness of the Gamay.

The Gamay grapes are harvested in September or early October and the Nouveau Gamay is released in mid-November — the same as in France.

Since Chuck Shaw was essentially producing wine from only one grape with a little-known technique, in 1982, he decided he had to broaden his line of wines. First of all he joined the "blush" wine market by making Gamay Blanc, and after having acquired an additional piece of land, he planted Sauvignon Blanc and several clones of Chardonnay.

That same year, Ric Forman — a well-known winemaker with 11 years experience in the Napa Valley (primarily at Sterling Vineyards) — joined the Shaw winery. Ric had made a name producing white wines, and he created the award winning Fumé Blanc and Chardonnays for the Shaw Winery. Chuck prefers the Fumé style for the Sauvignon Blanc grape because it is lighter and contains less alcohol. It is fermented in stainless steel and aged in large French uprights.

Chuck Shaw has always wanted to use the Fleurie clone of Gamay. After a long try, he was able to procure some vines and has planted them with the approval of the USDA. What started out as an experimental planting one day may well be a new varietal in California.

Lucy Shaw is also very much involved in the winery, working with tastings, supervising the gift department of the tasting room, and, of course, using her culinary expertise to create dishes that complement the Shaw wines.

Charles Shaw has done a lot to make the wine-consuming public aware that there is a California Gamay Nouveau equal to the French Nouveau Beaujolais. Both the Gamay Nouveau and the Napa Gamay have won critical acclaim and numerous awards. Not only has he made a name for himself with the Gamay wines, but also with his award-winning Chardonnay and Fumé Blanc.

Spring Mountain Vineyards

Address: 2805 Spring Mountain Road, St. Helena 94574
□ (707) 963-5233
Principals: Michael Robbins
Visitation: Daily, 10:30 a.m to 4:30 PM
Varietals produced: Sauvignon Blanc, Chardonnay, and Cabernet Sauvignon
Production: 25,000 cases per year

Many visitors to Spring Mountain Vineyards would probably look around for Angie, Emma, Julie, Lance, Melissa, and all of the rest of the characters of the popular TV series *Falcon Crest*. The house, gardens, pool area, and the winery are used in the filming of this TV series starring Jane Wyman. It is not just a set. It is a very serious working winery with its owners, Michael and Susan Robbins, living in the old Victorian home on the property.

Originally, wine was a hobby with Michael Robbins, who grew up in Des Moines, Iowa and is a graduate of the Naval Academy in Annapolis, Maryland. After spending time in the Navy, he attended law school and then became a real estate marketer and consultant in Northern and Southern California. While working with ALOCHA, he was involved in the development of Twin Towers in Century City and the Golden Gate Center in San Francisco.

On numerous trips to France, he became enamoured with the lifestyle of chateau owners and hoped he could duplicate that for himself and his wife in the Napa Valley. Mike had become just as enchanted with the Napa Valley and its potential as a world class wine producing area as he had been with the chateau areas of France.

In 1962, Mike Robbins purchased the present St. Clement property which included an old Victorian house with a wine cellar in the basement. Mike and his wife had purchased the property as a second home and were commuting from San Francisco every weekend. The house was completely remodeled, and in 1968, the old wine cellar was reactivated and wine was being produced under the Spring Mountain label. Mike's dream of the French type of wine chateau had come true.

Spring Mountain wine production outgrew the basement wine cellar, and Mike wanted larger facilities and a larger house. In 1976, he sold the property and purchased the 258-acre 19th century hillside estate of Tiburcio Parrot. The estate has a lovely Victorian house and an old wine cellar which had been tunneled into the mountain side in the late 1880s, probably by Chinese laborers. There was a winery with vineyards on the estate from 1885 to 1894.

Mike Robbins built a new winery in the Federal Victorian style in front of the old cellars, incorporating them into the winery. The old tunnels are now used for wine aging in small barrels. The latest crushing, pressing, and fermentation equipment were installed in the winery. This turned into a multi-million dollar project.

The house, as seen on television, was also completely restored with a new kitchen, new plumbing, heating, and air-conditioning. All of the original woodwork and moldings were either refinished or replaced in their original form. There are still 40 original stained glass windows in the house, including the magnificent front door panels. Mike has taken up the hobby of making stained glass and is gradually putting stained glass windows and ceiling in the offices of Spring Mountain above the winery.

Greg Vita is the winemaker at Spring Mountain Vineyards. He uses all estate grown grapes either from the vineyards on Spring Mountain or from Robbin's other vineyards located on the Napa Valley floor. Greg tries to blend the Cabernet Sauvignon toward the traditional Bordeaux style, using a combination of Cabernet Sauvignon,

Merlot, and a little Cabernet Franc. The Merlot adds smoothness, and the Cabernet Franc increases the complexity.

Spring Mountain also produces wine under a second label — Falcon Crest.

Although the winery estate is highly visible to the American public, Susan and Mike Robbins do enjoy life as vintners. Even with all of its publicity, Spring Mountain is a serious producer of excellent and highly rated wines.

St. Clement Vineyards

Address: 2867 St. Helena Highway, St. Helena 94574
☐ (707) 963-7221
Visitation: Monday through Saturday, 10 AM to 3 PM, by appointment only.
Principals: Dr. William J. Casey and Mrs. Alexandra Casey
Varietals produced: Sauvignon Blanc, Chardonnay, and Cabernet Sauvignon
Production: 10,000 cases per year

If there was ever a dream of a winery estate, St. Clement fits the bill. It looks as if it jumped right out the pictures of a book and has all of the elements of glorious fantasies — vineyards surrounding a dream of a Victorian house, and behind the house a newly constructed stone faced winery with all of the latest technical equipment available. Many people have looked at the house, one of Napa Valley's most famous landmarks and remarked, "I wonder if it's for sale. If so, I would like to own it."

From the road, this unmarked winery looks like a symbol of gracious country living, not like a winery. As a matter of fact, the winery is not visible from the road. All that is visible is the charming 1878 landmark home which appears on the label of St. Clement. Until recently, the winery was in the basement of the house.

The house was built in 1878 by Fritz Rosenbaum, a German immigrant who had come to San Francisco and established a stained glass making business. He moved to the Napa Valley and continued making stained glass, providing decorative windows for many of the large homes in the Valley. As was the custom with many European families, he also made wine in his basement for personal use. To facilitate this production he built a stone cellar under his house and planted a vineyard on the hillside around the house.

Until the turn of the century, mostly white wine was made in the stone cellar of the house and sold to two hospitals. The home passed through the hands of various owners in the next 60 years until, in 1968, Michael and Shirley Robbins of southern California purchased the property as a second home. They began meticulously to restore the house and the hundred-year-old vineyards and found themselves in the wine business before they knew it. The old stone cellar with its huge oak vats was reactivated for winemaking by Mike Robbins. However, the Robbins longed for a larger wine estate and eventually purchased the 19th-century Tiburcio Parrott estate which became known as Spring Mountain Winery (Falcon Crest).

In 1975, Dr. William Casey, a San Francisco eye surgeon, and his wife, Alexandra, purchased the charming house and property from Mike Robbins. Included with the sale of the house were two thousand gallons of wine which had been made by Mike Robbins. This provided a start for St. Clement wines. Dr Casey hired a consulting enologist, and together they made a few hundred cases of wine in the stone cellars under the house. Bill Casey's scientific and medical background were helpful in Bill's initial winemaking experiences.

Bill Casey was born in Maryland and graduated from Johns Hopkins Medical School. Alexandra is from California. The name St. Clement comes from Clement, the patron saint of mariners. It was the name given to a small island in the Chesapeake Bay near the eastern shore of Maryland where English settlers landed after their harrowing Atlantic crossing. The Casey family ancestral property was nearby.

Alexandra Casey, an excellent gourmet cook, often pairs the St. Clement wines with traditional eastern shore food when it is available on the West Coast. She especially enjoys their Sauvignon Blanc with Maryland seafood.

During the first several years of the St. Clement winery's operation, Bill Casey engaged the services of Charles Ortman to assist in the winemaking duties. He also helped train the present winemaker, Dennis Johns, who had previously been employed at Sterling Vineyards. In 1980, Dennis took over the winemaking duties at St. Clement, gaining great acclaim for his Sauvignon Blanc.

In the meantime, it was obvious to the Caseys that the stone cellar under the house would never be large enough or operationally efficient for a full-scale winery. Plans were drawn up for a winery to be built behind the house. The building was completed in early 1982. It is constructed into the hillside, partially underground for natural cooling. It is faced with native stone set by a family of Italian stonemasons — father and five sons. The winery is solar water heated and earth cooled — completely energy efficient. The aging cellar is underground in the hillside for natural cooling.

St. Clement has been recognized for consistently fine quality wines. Since St. Clement purchases most of its grapes, it is a real challenge for Dennis Johns to blend from the various lots of grapes and still maintain a consistency of style. However, Dennis welcomes the challenge and feels that he can obtain a greater complexity in the St. Clement wines by blending wines whose grapes came from different soils and different micro-climates. He ferments and ages each lot separately. In this way he has a larger variety to choose from for his ultimate blending. Dennis Johns believes that one of the few skills left in winemaking in this technical age is the art of blending.

Dennis Johns believes that being a good winemaker means paying attention to the fruit and being able to develop the fruit to its fullest potential. "Oak aging is only a complement to the fruit, and we should never lose sight of the fruit. After all, it's not oak juice. Excellence starts with nature's hand," he says as he reflects on his style of winemaking at St. Clement Vineyards. Dennis and Bill Casey want the wines to tell their own story — unfold their complexity as they are consumed.

Bill Casey also stresses the aging potential of St. Clement's wines and the qualities which enhance the enjoyment of food. For this reason the white wines — Sauvignon Blanc and Chardonnay — have strong acid backbones which give them the character which stands up to food. The Cabernet is also structured toward acidity and low tannins.

St. Clement winery, although only ten years old, has already established a tradition of excellence which befits its image of stability and quality as exemplified by its stately Victorian mansion. ❧

Stag's Leap Wine Cellars

Address: 5766 Silverado Trail, Napa 94558
□ (707) 944-2020
Visitation: Daily, 10 AM to 4 PM
Principals: Warren and Barbara Winiarski
Varietals produced: Cabernet Sauvignon, Sauvignon Blanc, Chardonnay, White Riesling, Merlot, and Petite Sirah
Production: 40,000 cases per year

It is very difficult for the French to admit that their wine is not the best. That is exactly what happened when a California Cabernet Sauvignon was declared the winner of a prestigious blind tasting organized by Steven Spurrier, a noted English wine authority. The tasting was held in Paris on May 24, 1976. At a rematch with the French, held a year and a half later, in San Francisco, the same Cabernet Sauvignon came out on top again. The winning winery was Napa Valley's Stag's Leap Wine Cellars, and the winemaker was owner Warren Winiarski.

More than any other grape, Cabernet Sauvignon has become synonymous with Napa Valley. However, there is still considerable controversy over where to grow the "great Bordeaux" grapes and exactly how to make the wine. Every vintner has a different idea — some of which are award-winning ones. One vintner who is recognized as an expert in making Cabernet Sauvignon is Warren Winiarski.

Warren Winiarski, whose last name means son of a vintner, is of Polish ancestry. He acquired a taste for wine through his father, a home winemaker. Warren also became a home winemaker in the Chicago area, where he lived and taught political science at the University of Chicago. His interest in wines and winemaking were constantly growing. Through his contacts with others in academia, particularly Dr. Maynard Amerine of U.C. Davis,

Warren lined up a job at Souverain Winery in Napa Valley. He left his teaching career in 1964, moved his wife Barbara and family to California, and began to learn winemaking from the bottom up. He dragged hoses, cleaned out tanks, and did whatever else was necessary. After two years at Souverain, Warren Winiarski became one of the first employees of the newly constructed Robert Mondavi Winery in Napa Valley. At Mondavi, Warren learned more about winemaking and had the opportunity to taste fine wines from many different areas of Napa Valley.

It was not Winiarski's intention to work at someone else's winery forever. In 1970, he and Barbara purchased 45 acres at the southern end of the Napa Valley east of the Silverado Trail. A taste of a neighbor's homemade wine from his own Cabernet Sauvignon grapes convinced Warren that that part of the Napa Valley was perfect for growing the style of Cabernet which he wanted to produce. The neighbor was Nathan Fay. In early 1986, the Winiarskis purchased the Fay vineyard, bringing their total vineyard acreage to 115 acres.

The land which Warren purchased was gradual hillside terrain with good drainage and wellsuited to Cabernet Sauvignon, which he proceeded to plant. By 1972, Warren had established his winery and named it Stag's Leap Wine Cellars, after a local geographic landmark — a nearby rock formation which is called Stag's Leap.

The first vintage of his Cabernet Sauvignon was a lean one from new-bearing vines. The next year's vintage, however, made international news at the Paris tasting in 1976.

The rest is ongoing history.

Although at first Warren was attracted to a "big style" wine, when he made the 1973 vintage, he had introduced the criterion of moderation in his winemaking. Through years of making Cabernet Sauvignon, he has developed his own criteria for the wine.

Warren says he takes "an iron fist and velvet glove approach to the Cabernet Sauvignon. I like to take the richness and strength of the varietal and modify it with elements of balance and harmony." Merlot is usually the balance Warren uses for a smooth and subtle Cabernet wine. "The Merlot is a grace note, not a theme in itself," he adds.

Stag's Leap Wine Cellars' master of winemaking also blends Semillon with his Sauvignon Blanc. "It is an element of composition which adds aroma and taste. The Semillon also modifies the aggressiveness of the Sauvignon Blanc," Warren comments. Stag's Leap's Chardonnay is fermented partially in stainless steel and partially in oak barrels. He believes that the wine can become too flabby under California conditions, if totally barrel fermented.

The addition of the Fay Vineyard, which originally led Warren Winiarski to that part of Napa Valley, will give additional support to the firm structure of Cabernet Sauvignon he has already established. For a man who started his professional winemaking career with a top winner, he has certainly kept up the reputation. ❧

Stonegate Winery

Address: 1183 Dunaweal Lane, Calistoga 94515
□ (707) 942-6500
Visitation: Daily, 10:30 AM to 4 PM
Principals: James C. and Barbara G. Spaulding
Varietals produced: Sauvignon Blanc, Chardonnay, Merlot, and Cabernet Sauvignon
Production: 15,000 cases per year

Pressing a single grape is easy since the juice flows freely from the crushed berry with gentle pressure. Put several tons of grapes together, however and the grapes become like people squeezed into a subway train. Those in the middle of the car, like the juice in the middle of the press, have a hard time getting out. In winemaking, the remedy used to be to apply more pressure to get the juice out. This method, however, tends also to squeeze out the harsh flavor components of the skin and stems and results in a harsh wine.

David Spaulding, general manager and winemaker of Stonegate Winery, like other California wineries, is using a soft press technique to avoid harshness in his wines. A sophisticated membrane press with soft pressings is used to gently coax out the delicately flavored juice. The grapes are also gently tumbled in the press, to allow air to circulate between the grapes. "This is almost as good as squeezing each grape by hand," David Spaulding says.

The Spaulding family has been involved with commercial grape growing and winemaking since 1969. Prior to that time, Jim Spaulding, David's father, was a journalist in Milwaukee where the family was living. He specialized in writing about medical science and wrote a regular column entitled, "Report on your Health."

Jim Spaulding first encountered grapes while working in his father's Concord grape vineyard in southwestern Michigan in the mid-1930s. Thirty years later, he planted a small experimental vineyard around his home north of Milwaukee and made home wine. He had obtained vines from the University of California at Davis and also from the New York State Experiment Station at Geneva, New

York. The French hybrids survived the bitter Wisconsin winter, but the European Rieslings and Pinot Noirs and Cabernets needed special winter protection. Because of the cold winters and humid summers the grapes did not ripen properly, and the birds and raccoons had a field day with the grapes.

When the University of California at Berkeley offered Jim Spaulding a chance to teach journalism, Jim took it. Not only did he want to teach, but he was going to be close to the Napa Valley where he could really grow grapes and make wine.

In 1969, the Spauldings purchased hillside property above Calistoga at the northern end of Napa Valley. They cleared the prune and walnut trees and proceeded to plant 20 acres in grapes. Jim continued to teach in Berkeley, commuting up to Napa on weekends. Barbara learned to prune the vines and generally took care of the vineyards.

In 1973, the Spauldings purchased a piece of land at Dunaweal Lane and Highway 29, the main road in the Napa Valley. The property consisted of several buildings, including an old house. The small outer buildings were initially used for the winery operations. In 1979, however, a new building was erected to house the winery operations. At the present time David Spaulding and his wife, Kathleen Iudice-Spaulding, who were married in 1983, are living in the house and remodeling it.

The name Stonegate for the winery was originated by Barbara Spaulding. It was a choice of the moment. The printers called her for a name to put on their first wine labels and Barbara quickly thought of the name Stonegate. She has always been intrigued with the long association of stone with wineries and vineyards. Eleven years later, the Spauldings hired masons to build a stone gate at the entrance to the winery. Volcanic quarry stones were cut, crafted and set to match exactly the drawing on the label.

About half the grapes used to make Stonegate wines come from estate vineyards which total 35 acres. There is also a small vineyard surrounding the winery on the Napa Valley floor. The hillside vineyard has 12 acres of several plots of Cabernet Sauvignon that are dry farmed on steep slopes. These stressed grapes produce a complex wine which is not high in alcohol. In the same vineyard four acres of the stoniest soil are planted with Merlot, and the four remaining acres contain Chardonnay.

The vineyard around the winery contains Sauvignon Blanc. For the remainder of their grapes, Cabernet Sauvignon, the Spauldings have contracts with grape growers who have the same soil and climatic conditions as their own. Two of these vineyards are located next door to the hillside property owned by the Spauldings. The Spauldings also buy some Chardonnay from the Carneros district.

David Spaulding, who took winemaking courses and worked under the supervision of consulting enologists over a number of years, has initiated a program of aging Stonegate's Cabernet Sauvignons for five years. After fermentation, the wines are aged for at least 18 months in a combination of French and American oak. Depending on the vintage, 10% to 15% Merlot is usually added for smoothness. Since the wine is very complex, the extra bottle aging time makes it more drinkable at time of purchase, although the wine will continue to age well.

Since there was a trend to lighter wines, in 1982 David made a leaner and crisper Chardonnay, but found that customers preferred a bigger more complex wine, so he went back to making it in the old style. The Chardonnay ages nine months in oak.

Stonegate is truly a family operation. Barbara still occasionally helps in the vineyard, but most of her time is taken up managing the office and traveling to wine tastings. David is the full-time winemaker, and his wife Kathleen is the marketing director.

By limiting the number of varietals grown and produced by Stonegate Winery, the Spaulding family can better supervise and control the quantity and quality of their wines.

Tudal Winery

Address: 1015 Big Tree Road, St. Helena 94574
□ (707) 963-3947
Visitation: By appointment only
Principals: Arnold and Alma Tudal
Varietals produced: Cabernet Sauvignon
Production: 3,000 cases per year

Arnold Tudal, who was a vegetable farmer from 1946 until 1973, used to harvest one acre of radishes every four days. He still harvests — now bunches of grapes and only one crop a year.

Arnold and his brother-in-law farmed an area of Alameda County known as Bay Farm Island. They produced all types of vegetables and salad greens for the entire San Francisco Bay Area. However, in the early 1970s, urban development and urban taxation forced the Tudals to change their lifestyle. The Bay Farm Island farm became a part of Harbor Bay Isle, an exclusive commute community for San Francisco.

World War II brought Arnold Tudal, a native of Lynn, Massachusetts and the son of a French father and a French-Canadian mother, to the west coast. At 18, he was an aerial gunner stationed at the Alameda Naval Air Station, where he was assigned to a squadron aboard an aircraft carrier.

It was while working at a defense job at the Naval Air Station that Alma Cerruti met the young flyer from Massachusetts. When the war ended they were married and Arnold joined the family truck farming business. He knew nothing about the business, but worked hard to learn everything he could. It turned out that he had not one, but several green thumbs.

In the early 1970s, they were encouraged by their children to look at property in the Napa Valley, and after numerous trips to the valley, they found just what they wanted on the floor of the Napa Valley near Calistoga. It was a ten-acre site with a declining walnut orchard. "The first year I picked walnuts. When I saw the return, I said this is insane," recalls Arnold.

After talking with several vintners in the Napa Valley, and on the advice of Louis Martini, Arnold decided to tear out the walnut orchard and plant grapes. John, the Tudal's son, took a semester off from college and helped his dad clear the land and plant the vines.

They planted Cabernet Sauvignon, which was best suited for their soil and the type of climate they have. The climatic conditions of the ten acres planted in grapes is most unusual. There are actually three different micro-soils within the ten acres. It is as if the grapes had been planted in three different vineyards. The grapes from the three different soils are crushed, fermented, and then blended together to make the wine that ultimately goes into the bottle.

The first harvest in 1975 yielded 800 pounds of grapes, and Arnold made home wine with the aid of textbooks, wooden tubs, and a canoe paddle. The next several years the yield increased considerably, and he sold grapes to the Louis Martini Winery. He kept reading books on how to make wine and took several short courses at U.C. Davis.

Arnold, who had been used to growing multiple crops during a month, had a lot of time on his hands. He had built a beautiful workshop, but that still did not keep him busy. So he decided to make wine on a commercial basis. It was quite a traumatic undertaking to dismantle his workshop and turn it into a winery. In the fall of 1979, the winery was bonded, and Tudal's Cabernet Sauvignon has been winning gold medals ever since.

The Tudals love to entertain and have their children and grandchildren come for visits. With this in mind they put their efforts into building their dream home. Both new technologies and old traditions are incorporated in the 4,000-square-foot house. The water tank from the old vegetable farm was dismantled, hauled to the Napa Valley, and reconstructed as an outdoor deck. Part of his father-in-law's barn has been recycled as indoor panelling. "It really is part of the family heritage," Alma comments.

The kitchen is equipped to take care of any cook's fancy, and Alma is at ease serving anywhere from two to two hundred guests. The oak-floored kitchen has both electric and gas stoves. The adjoining pantry is as big as most kitchens, with floor-to-ceiling shelves, a chopping surface, its own sink, and refrigerator. She makes her own pasta in an adjoining room.

Alma raises all of her own herbs and vegetables and cooks from "scratch." Her mother, who is 85 and lives with the Tudals, enjoys helping Alma cook as they did in the "old days." Alma regards cooking as a way of showing love, and that is part of her Italian heritage.

Alma helped in the planting of the vineyard and still does her share in the winery — keeping all the books and records and using her culinary talents to pair food with wine.

The logo on the Tudal wine label is a Cabernet Sauvignon leaf, which has five segments with a letter in each joined representing Arnold, Alma, and their three children, who are all partners in the winery.

Arnold plans to try a new method of planting grapes this

spring — closer spacing like the traditional French system. He also wants to convert an old barn into an aging room in preparation for producing some Chardonnay.

Arnold has become as committed to making fine wines as he once was to growing premium produce. Tudal produces fine Cabernet for honest pleasure. As Arnold says, "Don't make a flowery story out of a glass of wine. Just drink it and enjoy it." 🐝

Whitehall Lane Winery, Ltd.

Address: 1563 St. Helena Highway, St. Helena 94574
☐ (707) 963-9454
Visitation: Daily, 11 AM to 5 PM
Principals: Alan and Charlene Steen, Arthur and Bunnie Finkelstein
Varietals produced: Chenin Blanc, Sauvignon Blanc, Chardonnay, Blanc de Pinot Noir Merlot, Pinot Noir, Cabernet Sauvignon, and Late Harvest Johannisberg Riesling
Production: 22,000 cases per year

Building — construction and reconstruction — have all been and still are a part of the lives of two brothers — Art Finkelstein and Alan Steen. Art was an architect and builder who designed and built the winery, and is now the winemaker of Whitehall Lane Winery. Alan did mostly reconstruction as one of the leading plastic surgeons in the Los Angeles area. He is now in charge of marketing and the vineyards at Whitehall Lane. The two brothers are still in the building and reconstruction business — continuing to build a reputation for quality wines and continuing to reconstruct an old vineyard with new vines.

Alan Steen and Art Finkelstein came into the wine business with definite philosophies. They wanted to make fine quality wines which would be drinkable early and produce these wines at affordable prices.

The two brothers are a unique pair, with varied professional backgrounds and a myriad of interests. Their dry sense of humor has helped them in a business which occupies their time seven days a week.

The original family name of Art and Alan was Maraslavsky — when the family emigrated from Russia many years ago. The family, however, wanted a more American sounding name, so they decided on Finkelstein. Alan took the name one step further and kept the Steen. Art and Alan grew up in Rock Island, Illinois and came to Southern California in their twenties to go to college.

Each of the brothers had their own careers in Southern California before becoming vintners. Art, who is the winemaker, was a well-known architect and had his own con-

tracting business. He, at one time or another, was a professional blue-grass mandolin musician, a potter, a caterer, and even worked as a pool cleaner. Years ago, Art became interested in home winemaking and was very active in the Cellarmasters Guild in the Los Angeles area. He kept winning many of the top amateur awards and was in great demand to give lectures to other home winemakers.

Alan, a plastic surgeon in Palos Verdes and the older of the two brothers, has just as many varied interests as his brother. He holds a master's degree in biochemistry. To help put himself through medical school, Alan played the piano professionally. He is also an extremely fine gourmet cook. Having been interested in wines for over 30 years, Alan had seriously considered buying a winery at some point in his life. After all, there was already a winemaker in the family. In the mid-1970s, he and his wife Charlene came to the Napa Valley frequently to vacation and found themselves looking for vineyard property. An earnest search began in 1977 and culminated two years later in the purchase of the property for Whitehall Lane.

In 1979, the two brothers purchased a prime vineyard site in the Napa Valley on Highway 29, a few miles south of St. Helena. The property had just come on the market, and the brothers snatched it up. That was the beginning of the Los Angeles to San Francisco commute for Art and Alan. Art come north three days a week to design and oversee the construction of the winery, returning to his own business for the rest of the week. Alan practiced medicine three days a week and spent the other four days supervising the planting of the vineyards. Both families moved onto the property into houses next to each other — one into an old farmhouse (Alan and Charlene) and the other into a reconverted barn (Art and Bunnie).

Although the 26 acres of vineyards they purchased had vines, they were disease-ridden. The vines had originally been planted in 1935. After tearing out all existing vegetation, the soil was turned over to a depth of four feet and fumigated. The 26 acres were planted with Chardonnay, Chenin Blanc, Sauvignon Blanc, and one acre of Merlot.

In 1980, the winery building was finished and Art permanently moved to the Napa Valley. He is the full-time winemaker for Whitehall Lane. Alan continued his practice until 1983, when he retired and moved north to take charge of all of the marketing and the vineyards. After all, Alan says, "pruning is just a natural extension of my former profession." All of Whitehall Lanes white wines are from estate grown grapes.

The winery building which Art designed is completely energy efficient in heating and cooling. There are solar panels to heat the water. The sunny side of the building is up against an earthen berm to prevent excessive heat. There is a night air exchange and massive insulation. Labor-saving devices were also installed to enable Art to crush 350 tons of grapes a year with the help of only one or two workers.

Art Finkelstein tries to emphasize fruitiness and varietal character in his winemaking. Some of the whites are off-dry which makes them good sipping wines.

The wine Art enjoys making the most is Pinot Noir. The grapes are picked in one-half ton lots, which is small by most standards. Because of this picking technique, very little juice accumulates in the gondola to oxidize on the way to the crushing machine. After the grapes are stemmed and crushed, they are placed in small shallow plastic bins and left uncovered for fermentation. This open fermentation allows the must to heat up slower than usual for Pinot Noir, thereby creating a fruitier wine. Every six hours the grapes are turned by hand. The wine is aged for six months in American oak. This process makes a lighter style of Pinot Noir — more like a Beaujolais, not too complex and not too much tannin.

Since the Whitehall Lane red grapes are all purchased, the Cabernet Sauvignon is often a blend of many vineyards. Although each lot is handled separately, a small amount of estate Merlot is added for smoothness.

The two families are very close and work well together. Bunnie, Art's wife, is in charge of the winery office. Charlene, who is a practicing attorney, lends a hand with government forms and any legal matters that arise, as well as providing the winery's financial planning. She is also a ventriloquist, making her a star at winery parties.

Owning and operating a winery is hard work and has been a building experience for both families. In the six years of operation, they have build a reputation for quality wines. ✺

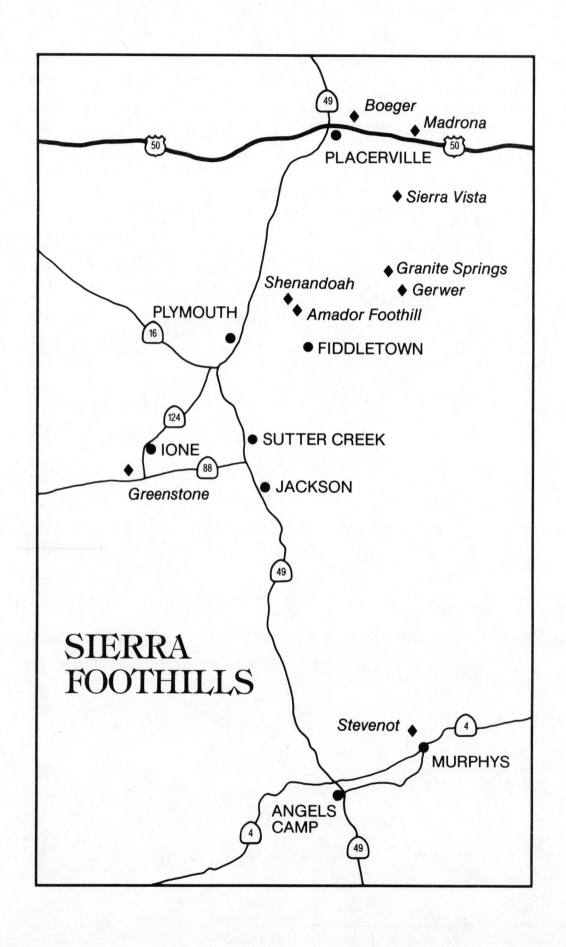

49
Boeger
50
Madrona
50
PLACERVILLE

Sierra Vista

Granite Springs
Shenandoah
Gerwer
Amador Foothill

PLYMOUTH
16
FIDDLETOWN

124
SUTTER CREEK

IONE
88
Greenstone
JACKSON

49

**SIERRA
FOOTHILLS**

Stevenot
4
MURPHYS

ANGELS
CAMP
4
49

Wineries of the
SIERRA FOOTHILLS

Amador Foothill Winery
Boeger Winery
Gerwer Winery
Granite Springs Winery
Greenstone Winery
Madroña Vineyards
Shenandoah Vineyards
Sierra Vista Winery
Stevenot Winery

Sierra Foothills

Whenever one thinks of premium wines in California there are two names which are synonymous — Zinfandel and Amador County. Situated in the Sierra foothills, Amador County is but one of six counties that has been on the California wine scene for almost 150 years. Even today, winemakers in Southern California have Zinfandel grapes from Amador County shipped to them by refrigerated trucks so that they can make premium Zinfandel.

Grape growing is not new to the Sierra Foothill region — Amador, Calaveras, El Dorado, Nevada, Placer and Tuolumne Counties — since the vines and grape growing arrived shortly after the start of the Gold Rush in 1849. With the discovery of gold near the now famous Sutter's mill in El Dorado County the population of the region exploded, as did the thirst of the miners. For a time, wine was being shipped to the Gold Country from Southern California (since that was the largest producing area of wine at the time) via San Francisco, where it was bottled.

Grape growing started soon after the discovery of gold in order to meet the demand for wine and brandy. Many people who were unsuccessful in gold mining started planting and farming vineyards. In 1849, there were no wineries in the Sierra Foothills, but by 1880, thirty-one years later, there were 100 in El Dorado County alone. At that time, there were more wineries in the Sierra Foothills than in Napa Valley.

By 1920, grape production in the area had reached its peak with 5,000 acres under cultivation. Unfortunately, all were destroyed, first by phylloxera, then by Prohibition. The land was replanted with pear and apple orchards. The latter crop made the area famous until the late 1960s. The area is still known for its apples, and several of the wineries of the Sierra Foothills actually make an "Apple Chardonnay."

In the late 1960s, the University of California at Davis began to conduct experiments to determine which grape varietals would grow best in the Sierra Foothills. One of these experimental plots was established on land belonging to what is now Gerwer Winery. In 1972, Greg Boeger planted a vineyard and reactivated a century-old winery. Others soon followed.

While the area is known for its Zinfandel, the microclimates and soil conditions make it suitable for a great variety of grapes from Rieslings, which do best in cool climates, to Cabernet Sauvignon, which like more warmth. Even within one vineyard — such as Boeger Winery's — variations in climate and soil are sufficient to make it suitable for cultivation of more than one varietal. Since the elevation of the vineyards in the area vary from 500 to 3,000 feet, a great variety of grapes can be grown. However, it is some of the 100-year old Zinfandel vines, primarily dry farmed on hillside terrain, that have made the present Sierra Foothill region of California famous for its fine wines. ❧

Amador Foothill Winery

Address: 12500 Steiner Road, Plymouth 95669
  □ (209) 245-6307
Visitation: Saturday and Sunday, 12 noon to 5 PM, or
  by appointment
Principals: Ben Zeitman
Varietals produced: Sauvignon Blanc, White Zinfandel,
  Zinfandel, and Cabernet Sauvignon
Production: 8,000 cases per year

"Working with Zinfandel grapes that come from a vineyard that is over 100 years old can be like trying to tame an old beast," says Ben Zeitman. But once you know how to "tame it" you can produce a refined delightful wine.

Ever since Ben Zeitman started as a home winemaker in the early 1970s he has been fascinated with Zinfandel, especially those grapes from older vines. They have exceptional complexity and fruity aromas. His first attempts at winemaking were with Zinfandel grapes from Amador County.

For the first 20 years of his professional life, Ben worked as a chemist with the National Aeronautics and Space Administration. A graduate of San Jose State University, he worked on such diverse projects as the release of hormones under stress and the development of life support systems. It was this training in chemistry that also provided a valuable background for his winemaking.

In 1980, he felt that he needed a change of vocations and decided to trade one set of test tubes for another — from NASA chemist to full-time winemaker. He had purchased 20 acres of vineyard property from his to-be neighbor, Leon Sobon of Shenandoah Vineyards, the year before.

Twenty percent of Amador Foothill's wines are estate grown. Much of Zeitman's red Zinfandel grapes are purchased from very old vineyards — 70 to over 100 years old. The vineyards are located in Amador County — one being in Fiddletown, an old gold mining center, the others being in the Shenandoah Valley. He buys from these same vineyards year after year and feels that these grapes, which have been dry farmed, make a fruity complex wine. Often these dry farmed grapes are shrivelled and look a little like raisins, as a result of their struggle for life in a harsh environment. All of this results in a complex Zinfandel wine.

Ben Zeitman tries to manipulate the fermentation as little as possible, pulling off the skin at just the right time. He feels that wines can be over treated and he does not use a lot of "cellar material."

Many vintners produce a White Zinfandel, mostly because the public wants it, and because it sells well. Ben, however, has another good reason for doing so. He feels it is a good way to utilize the grapes of his young Zinfandel vines, and it is a good way to use "black skin grapes in a white wine boom." Amador Foothill Winery's White Zinfandel has just enough sugar content to balance the acid. Ben also makes a Sauvignon Blanc, labeled as Amador Fumé, which is a dry style of Sauvignon Blanc that is cold barrel fermented.

The split-level winery was built into a north-facing hillside to take advantage of energy-efficient features. All the walls, roof, and doors are insulated. The roof has a sprinkler system which is used on hot days to reduce heat transmission into the winery. Fast growing locust trees have been planted on the south side to provide shade. A friend of Zeitman's helped design a natural air convection cooling system for the winery, which keeps the cellar cool the year around without the use of expensive mechanical cooling systems.

Ben regards his wines basically as food wines. This led him to commission artist Linda Laing-Seiferheld to create colorful labels that pair each varietal with food. Each label illustrates a cooking herb — such as rosemary, dill, chives — which complement that particular wine.

Ben Zeitman, along with his bride of a couple of months, Katie Quinn, who was the former assistant winemaker at Gundlach-Bundschu, hopes to expand the winery to produce 10,000 to 12,000 cases per year. They both, however, will continue to take a big interest in producing an elegant Zinfandel. ❧

Boeger Winery

Address: 1709 Carson Road, Placerville 95667
□ (916) 622-8094

Visitation: Wednesday through Saturday, 10 AM to 5 PM

Principals: Greg and Susan Boeger

Varietals produced: Chenin Blanc, Sauvignon Blanc, Semillon, Chardonnay, White Zinfandel, White Cabernet, Merlot, Zinfandel, and Cabernet Sauvignon

Production: 10,000 cases per year

There was, and there still is "gold in them thar hills." El Dorado County in the Sierra Foothills was once the site of the Gold Rush of 1849. Today, nearly 150 years later, the region is again getting attention by producing some of the state's gold medal-winning wines.

El Dorado County has a long history of winemaking. When gold was discovered in Coloma in 1848, grape vines were planted soon afterwards to quench the thirst of the '49ers. As the gold supply diminished, the miners turned to farming, and vineyards multiplied. By 1880, over 100 wineries were in operation. One of these was the Fossati Winery and Distillery, founded in 1857. A fire destroyed the original winery, but in 1872, the Fossatis rebuilt the

winery using stones cleared from their vineyards. This building is today on the "National Register of Historic Buildings," and is the tasting room at the Boeger Winery.

Boeger Winery is the oldest of the new breed of wineries in El Dorado County. Phylloxera and Prohibition had extinguished the wine industry in the region until the late 1960s, when the University of California planted several vineyard test plots in the Sierra Foothill counties. By the early 1970s, the grape rush started and Greg Boeger was the first to establish a new vineyard and a winery.

Greg was not new to the wine business. He is the grandson of Anton Nichelini, a Swiss-Italian who founded a winery and vineyards in the Napa Valley in 1883. That winery is still in operation today. As a youngster Greg worked at the family winery, helping his cousin Jim Nichelini with winemaking. The Nichelini winery is currently owned and operated by Jim Nichelini's daughter, Joanne Meyer.

After graduation from U.C. Davis with a Masters in Agricultural Economics and a minor in Viticulture, Greg and his wife Susan decided to start a winery. They spent two years looking for property, during which time Greg worked as an agricultural statistician for the U.S.D.A. In

1972, in partnership with Susan's parents, Dr. and Mrs. George Babbin, they bought a 70-acre orchard near Placerville. The property included the old Fossati winery building.

The Boegers tore out some of the old orchards of apple and pear trees and cleared out brush and timber. They originally planted 20 acres and then planted another 15 — all with the varietals used in making their wine. Greg also manages several other vineyards in the area and purchases grapes from these vineyards. He has recently planted a vineyard on 20 acres of leased land at 3,000 feet elevation adjacent to Madroña Vineyards.

The area of El Dorado County, at an elevation of 2,000 to 3,000 feet, is well suited for grape growing. The days are warm, and the cool evening breezes from the high Sierras moderate the vines' temperature, preventing overripe fruit and excess sugar content. The soil is fractured rock, and the vines have to struggle for life. This combination makes for very intense fruit and a very smooth wine.

In 1973, Susan and Greg built a modern winery designed to blend with the architecture of the original gold country buildings. The building is equipped with all of the latest modern equipment needed for temperature-controlled fermentation and aging.

Greg Boeger, who is the winemaker, believes in making a red wine which is drinkable when released, but will also age well. To achieve this, he tries not to extract every last drop of juice from the grapes. The juice is fermented at reasonably cool temperatures for a softer wine. Greg says that "control of fermentation temperature and not too much skin contact" achieves a now drinkable style of wine. He uses the same techniques for the whites.

"Grapes grown in this climate do not need extended skin contact." he emphasizes. The climatic conditions and the elevation keep the acid level up and produce a fruity wine.

Although Greg follows traditional methods of winemaking, he also likes to experiment. Part of this experimentation consists of blending various varietals, which annually become his famous red and white table wines — Hangtown Red, Hangtown Gold, and Sierra Blanc. Hangtown was the name given to Placerville in the gold mining days. Hangtown Red is usually a blend of the red grapes which come from some old vines planted in the area in the 1930s. The wine is made in the same style as the wine orginally produced at the old Fossati winery — otherwise known as a good spaghetti wine. Boeger Winery is particularly known for its Merlot, which was recently served at a White House dinner for the President of Algeria.

Boeger Winery is a family operation. Susan is in charge of marketing. She has designed and coordinated a wine marketing seminar, which she annually gives at U.C. Davis. The Boeger children, aged 11 and 13, help in the vineyards at crush and bottling time.

Greg does not want the winery to grow to any great extent. He would rather devote his extra time to perfecting the growth of different varietals which would also be suited to the El Dorado climate. At present, he has a test plot of Flora, Muscat Canelli, and Symphony. He is also growing some Johannisberg Riesling, which he hopes to make into wine shortly. Cabernet Franc and Petite Verdot are also planted and will eventually be blended into his Cabernet Sauvignon to enhance its fruitiness and to soften the wine. 🍂

Gerwer Winery

Address: 8221 Stoney Creek Road, Somerset 95684
    □ (209) 245-3467
Visitation: Weekends, 11 AM to 5 PM, or by appointment
Principals: Vernon and Marcia Gerwer
Varietals produced: Chardonnay, Chenin Blanc, Sauvignon Blanc, White Zinfandel, Ruby Cabernet, Petite Sirah, and Cabernet Sauvignon
Production: 4,000 cases per year

El Dorado County is still a place where neighbor helps neighbor — just as they did in the pioneer days when the frontiers were first settled. This is especially true among the vintners in the county. Since most of them are small they depend on each other for equipment, advice, and just plain friendship.

Marcia and Vernon Gerwer were both salespeople for a craft and hobby manufacturer until 1978, when they decided to become vintners. They were both "farm kids" — Vernon grew up on the dairy farm of his Swiss-born father, and Marcia grew up on a farm near Sacramento. Today, Marcia's father owns and farms the land adjoining their present winery. Marcia and Vernon met in 1953 at a Nevada state 4-H convention at Lake Tahoe. Most of their adult years, however, have been spent in the city.

The Gerwers had some previous experience with grape vines. In 1967, the U.C. Davis School of Viticulture decided to conduct an experiment to determine which grapes were most suitable for growing in the granite soil of the Sierra foothills. Marcia's dad agreed to provide the land

and urged Marcia and Vernon to farm the test plot under the supervision of U.C. Davis. Twelve varieties were planted, and all did well and made exceptional wine. This test plot, which contained quite a bit of granite, was a quarter of a mile from the acreage the Gerwers were later to purchase. During this time of experimenting, they found that they enjoyed viticulture and winemaking.

In the intervening years from 1967 to 1978, Marcia and Vernon travelled across the United States, selling craft products in Florida, Ohio, and Colorado. But they kept returning to El Dorado County and eyeing that parcel of 40 acres near Marcia's dad's property which ultimately became their home and the winery. The land had a good southern exposure, rather steep slopes, suitable soil for a vineyard, and a good home site.

Presently, there are four and a half acres in Ruby Cabernet, three and a half in Sauvignon Blanc, a little in Petite Sirah and a little in Semillon. The Gerwers hope eventually to have 20 acres under cultivation.

The area where the Gerwer winery is located is still an old-fashioned farm community with neighbor helping neighbor. Vernon's pre-planting costs were low, since he had a lot of help from neighbors and family.

There are several vineyards and wineries in the area, all of them small. Since they are small, they share bottling equipment and supplies Thus, they get a better price on their supplies and enjoy a neighborly camaraderie. For example, when the aging barrels need cleaning, Vernon goes to the vineyard that last had the steam cleaner and picks it up for his own use. Then, he stores it until the next person needs it.

Bottling day is a big day around a small winery. Everybody helps out, including family members, friends, and neighbors. With 10 helpers, the Gerwers can fill 4,000 bottles in a day. Filling and corking is done automatically, but it still takes people-power to load and unload the bottling machine. In the late afternoon, Marcia always has a big chili supper ready for the crowd.

Twice a month the grape growers and winemakers of the Sierra foothills get together for their wine tasting. Wines are sampled from unlabeled bottles and identified only after they have been scored. These "blind tastings" enable them to judge each other's wine. "It's one way we work together so that everyone benefits," Vernon says.

Ruby Cabernet, one of the grapes developed by U.C. Davis, takes on a unique character when grown in the granite soil of the Sierra foothills at an elevation of 2,600 feet. The resulting wine has a deep, intense ruby color and has very strong cabernet characteristics.

Eventually, the Gerwers plan to grow 75% of the grapes for their projected wine production of 8,000 cases per year. However, they plan to continue making small lots of the exceptional red wines which do well in their granite soils.

The Gerwer Winery label features the family crest. The original wooden crest occupies a place of honor in the family home in Switzerland. The burgundy-colored background of the label was chosen as a symbol of the deep, intense wines that are produced in El Dorado County.

"The undertaking of this venture has turned out to be rewarding and everything we expected," says Vernon Gerwer. The farm is almost self-sufficient. The house is heated with solar energy, and most of the food — meat, vegetables, and fruit — are grown on the farm. The Gerwers hope to prove that it is still feasible to "live from the land" in the 1980s. "With our small acreage, we are a real Mom-and-Pop operation, helped by our four children, six grandchildren, and our neighbors and friends," says Vernon, with a satisfied smile. ❧

Granite Springs Winery

Address: 6060 Granite Springs Road, Somerset 95684
  ☐ (209) 245-6395
Visitation: Saturday and Sunday, 11 AM to 5 PM; by
  appointment during week
Principals: Les and Lynne Russell
Varietals produced: Sauvignon Blanc, Chenin Blanc,
  White Zinfandel, Zinfandel, Petite Sirah, and
  Cabernet Sauvignon
Production: 7,500 cases per year

The saying "hard as a rock" is certainly one which Les Russell, owner and winemaker of Granite Springs Winery, knows well. After all, he dug down ten feet into solid granite to construct his winery in El Dorado county in the Sierra foothills. Actually, there was quite a bit of jack-hammering and blasting to get the foundation of the winery deep enough to utilize the natural cooling of the granite mountainside. It is no wonder that Lynne and Les Russell named their winery Granite Springs.

Les Russell did not get into the wine business until 1979, although he grew up on a ranch in El Dorado County. After graduation from college at Sacramento State in the mid-1960s, he worked as a park ranger in Santa Cruz County. During his free time, he helped out at the David Bruce Winery in the Santa Cruz mountains, working in every phase of the winery's operation. This was good basic training for what was to become his livelihood 15 years later. He always carried the dream of one day owning and operating his own winery.

Most of Les's working life, previous to Granite Springs Winery, had been in the parks and recreation field. He did some consulting in the public recreation field and taught at the University of Nevada. For the six years prior to coming to the Sierra foothills, he was Director of Recreation and Parks for the City of Novato. He was involved in planning and administration and had written a 20-year master plan for the the city's park and recreation development. The passage of Proposition 13 brought an end to all his plans, however. There was no funding, and that meant no growth. Work was no longer challenging for Les Russell. It was time to move on.

And, move on he did. Les bought a 40-acre plot in the Sierra foothills with the intent of establishing a winery. He and his wife Lynne, who was in civil engineering, and their three daughters moved to El Dorado County in 1979.

When the Russells arrived at the home and winery site,
there was nothing but bare ground and the trailer which they were to live in. The land had been cleared of trees in the early 1920s, so planting was not too much of a problem. The next year saw the transformation of the bare land, with the planting of 23 acres of grapes — Cabernet Sauvignon, Zinfandel, Sauvignon Blanc. The Russells purchase Chenin Blanc, Muscat, and Petite Sirah from other local vineyards.

In order to sustain their livelihood for the first couple of years, Lynne worked in an engineering office and as a graphic artist. It took a lot of hard work, however, to clear the land, plant the vines and build the winery. Les and Lynne did most of the hard manual labor involved, which cut the $6,000-per-acre cost usually budgeted for preparation of the soil and irrigation facilities in half. Excavation for the winery began in the spring of 1981, and it was ready in the fall for the crush.

Les has a major commitment to red wines in his vineyard plantings, not only because the granite soil of El Dorado County is well suited to the red, but also because he, like some of his fellow vintners, believes that there is a trend back to the reds.

Les is the winemaker, having taken courses at U.C. Davis and being helped by his experience at David Bruce Winery. Lynne takes care of the administrative duties and the marketing. The wine business is a full time, seven-day-a-week job for both. It used to be baseball in the spring for Les's recreation department — now it is cultivation of the vines. Summer used to be devoted to recreation for the kids — now it is devoted to irrigation. Fall meant football — now it means harvesting and crushing. Les is still involved in a seasonal business, but the emphasis is now different.

Both traditional and new methods are used in the Russells' wine making techniques. Red wines start in open redwood fermenters and are often punched down by hand to keep the skins in contact with the fermenting juices. This practice also gives the wine deep rich colors and results in a full bodied wine. Whites are fermented in temperature controlled (cool) stainless steel tanks to preserve the delicate bouquet of the white grapes. Both techniques emphasize the unique characteristics of the El Dorado region grapes.

Granite Springs' colorful label features the California Quail and the state flower: the golden poppy. The design was inspired by Lynne Russell's label design for an entry in a home winemaking contest. Lynne also has had some experience as a graphic artist.

Les and Lynne Russell want to expand their production to 9,000 cases per year, and Les would eventually like to make some dessert wines, particularly using the Muscat grape and also producing a Petite Sirah Port wine. 🙂

Greenstone Winery

Address: Highway 88 at Jackson Valley Road, Ione 95640 □ (209) 274-2238

Visitation: Saturday and Sunday, 10 AM to 4 PM; July and August: Wednesday through Sunday, 10 AM to 4 PM

Principals: Durward and Jane Fowler, Stan and Karen Van Spanje

Varietals produced: Chenin Blanc, French Colombard, Sauvignon Blanc, Fumé Blanc, White Zinfandel, Rose Zinfandel, Barbera, Zinfandel, Zinfandel Port, and Creme Sherry

Production: 8,000 cases per year

A nationwide search for the perfect vineyard and winery site was conducted for several years in the mid and late 1970s by Durward and Jane Fowler and Stan and Karen Van Spanje. The two couples have been friends for years and are now business partners.

Durward and Stan met during their college days at California State University, Long Beach when they were both studying for a career in public education. Most of their fellow collegians drank beer and rum colas, but Stan and Durward liked and drank wine, which was not the "in thing." After graduating from college, they met and married their respective wives and all four taught in the Orange County School System.

"The boys'" interest in wine continued, and their appreciation of wine grew. One year, "the girls" gave them a home winemaking kit, and they caught the winemaking bug. The Fowler's garage became the winemaking workshop. They soon became discontented with their amateur

status, however. The two couples began serious consideration of the possibility of not only owning a winery, but also of growing their own grapes.

The Fowlers and the Van Spanjes did not know where they wanted to locate. They had decided, however, that they desired to move away from Southern California to a rural environment where their young children could grow up in the country.

In 1979, Stan and Karen took a leave of absence from their jobs to look for vineyard property. They traveled to the East, South, and Midwest to seek the perfect soil and climate for grape growing. However, every summer for several years, the Fowlers and the Van Spanjes found themselves returning to Northern California on the same mission. Stan and Karen were about to end their cross-country sojourn and return home when they happened upon the Jackson Valley in Northern California at the foot of the Sierra Nevada Mountains. The valley and the surrounding area was like Shangri-la to them. There were several vineyards already established in the area (some of the neighboring Zinfandel vines were over 100 years old), and luckily they found suitable property for sale.

The two husbands resigned their jobs, and the families moved to Ione, near Jackson Valley, a small town that had been famous during the gold rush days. Jane and Karen continued their professions as school teachers while the husbands started planting the vineyards.

Near the property are several dry lakes of clay which affect not only the soil, but also the temperature. In the summer they provide natural air conditioning and absorb heat in the winter. The grape growing conditions of Greenstone's vineyard are similar to those located at 1,000 foot elevation even though they are located at only 500 feet. Warm days and cool breezes from the Delta ensure a climate which is conducive to high acid content in the grapes.

In 1980, Durward and Stan planted French Colombard, followed by Chenin Blanc, Zinfandel, and Palomino. There are now 23 acres of grapes, and plans call for the planting of 10 more acres, mostly in Sauvignon, Blanc, Cabernet Sauvignon and Muscat D'Canelli.

The construction of the winery began in 1981, and it was ready for that fall's crush. The winery is constructed of wood and field-stone to resemble an elegant French barn. Stan is the winemaker. He took short courses in enology at U.C. Davis and also worked with some of the local vintners. Durward is in charge of the vineyards.

Greenstone's French Colombard is the only Colombard produced in the Sierra Foothills. The vines are grown in shallow loamy soil, which produces stressed grapes — grapes from vines that have to work harder to survive and produce fruit. The French Colombard is fermented and aged in stainless steel with no oak contact. It has won a medal in every competion in which it was entered —

including seven gold medals, two of which were in successive years at the Orange County Fair.

Not only does Greenstone produce a White Zinfandel, but also a Rose Zinfandel. The Rose has two- to four-hour skin contact during fermentation, and then some of the red Zinfandel wine is added back in for flavor and additional color.

Both Stan and Durward have always enjoyed sherry, and they decided to build the winery to include a place to age sherry. Instead of aging in a cool temperature, sherry has to be aged in a warm environment. Stan purchases Palamino, Mission, and Tokay grapes for the sherry. He ferments these and then fortifies the wine with grape spirits. It is then aged in oak barrels under the peaked roof of the winery. Sherry needs almost to cook in order to give the sherry the caramalized taste.

The two families are committed to the winery. Although the wives teach during the week, they are both involved in the tasting room and create recipes to complement Greenstone's wines.

Stan's and Durward's immediate goals are to plant more vineyards and expand the production of the winery to about 20,000 cases per year. 🍇

Madroña Vineyards

Address: Gatlin Road, Camino 95709
☐ (916) 644-5948
Visitation: Saturday, 10 AM to 5 PM, Sundays, 1 PM to 5 PM, or by appointment
Principals: Dick and Leslie Bush
Varietals produced: Chardonnay, Johannisberg Riesling, Gewurztraminer, White Zinfandel, Merlot, Zinfandel, and Cabernet Sauvignon
Production: 8,000 cases per year

At an elevation of 3,000 feet, Madroña vineyards are the highest in California. The winery's name is taken from the large Madrone tree on the property — a tree that grows profusely in the Sierra foothills at this elevation.

The experts had predicted that only certain varietals could be grown on his land, but Dick Bush was out to prove them wrong. He had studied the climate and vegetation of the area for the past 20 years and was convinced that the sunny days and cool nights would prove ideal for growing a wide range of varieties of grapes. Therefore, Dick planted many of the same varieties that do well in the upper regions of both Napa and Sonoma Valleys.

Doing scientific studies was not new to Dick, who has a Ph.D. in Materials Science from Stanford University, has worked as a research engineer for Ford, and has been a computer programmer and a math and science teacher. At a certain point in his life, however, he decided he simply wanted to grow grapes. In 1972, he purchased 52 acres five miles east of Placerville. Most of the property is on gently sloping hillsides at 3,000 feet elevation.

For the next two years, he and his wife Leslie, an elementary school teacher, prepared the land and planted the six varietals which were later to become the basis of their estate wine. While the vines were maturing, the Bush family — Dick, Leslie, and their four children — moved to the Congo in Africa for several years, where Dick and Leslie taught at the American School of Kinshasa.

In 1976, Dick and the family returned to the Placerville area. By then, their vines had matured, and they started selling their grapes to many wineries throughout the state. Over the next four years, however, Dick experienced several difficulties in selling grapes. This experience, plus his desire to prove that premium wines could be made from grapes grown at a high elevation, led him to the decision to build a winery. The Bushes, with the help of their two sons and two daughters, built the winery themselves, except for the concrete slab, the steel beams, and some stone work, (they have also done most of the major construction on their home).

The winery is partially built into a hillside to provide

natural cooling. Dick has installed a greater number of stainless steel tanks than is typical for a winery of Madroña's size. This permits him to ferment a number of varietals at the same time. Dick, who had taken short courses at U.C. Davis and also worked with Boeger at his winery, was the winemaker from 1980 to 1985, when Mark Foster joined Madroña Vineyards as the full-time winemaker.

Mark has a degree in enology from U.C. Davis and had previously worked as assistant winemaker at Chalone Vineyards. This is the third career for Mark Foster, who has masters degrees in biology and computer science. He has worked as a limnologist in Arizona, analysing the state's lakes and rivers, and he also spent three years as a computer programmer. Winemaking gives Mark a chance to combine his scientific and logical background with his love of the outdoors. He seems to provide a perfect match to Dick's approach to winemaking, since Dick and Mark both have scientific backgrounds.

Dick credits the climatic conditions at Madroña to the successful production of grapes which possess a strong varietal character and an excellent balance between sugar and acid. Although the vineyards have snow every year, the Bushes have not had a killing frost since they have been raising grapes. The uniqueness of the Madroña vineyards is highlighted by the presence of both Gewurztraminer and Zinfandel vines, a rare combination.

Mark adheres to the French traditions of winemaking. His Chardonnay is produced in the Burgundian style, while the Cabernet Sauvignon emulates the Bordeaux style. Some Merlot and Cabernet Franc are blended with the Cabernet Sauvignon to create a more complex and elegant wine.

Mark has developed a unique style in making Zinfandel. By making full use of the grape, he has created a concentrated varietal raspberry character in his wine.

Every three or four years, the Johannisberg Riesling becomes infected with Botrytis, which enables Dick and Mark to produce a Late Harvest Riesling. Dick hopes to induce this "noble rot" — a condition where the grapes turn almost to raisins and have a high sugar content — on an annual basis with the use of overhead sprinklers.

Dick Bush's main interest is still his vineyards. He likes to experiment with different varietals and wants to prove that the Sierra Foothills are an excellent place to grow a wide variety of premium wine grapes. 🍇

Shenandoah Vineyards

Address: 12300 Steiner Road, Plymouth 95669
  ☐ (209) 245-3698
Visitation: Daily, 11 AM to 5 PM
Principals: Leon and Shirley Sobon
Varietals produced: Sauvignon Blanc, White Zinfandel, Zinfandel, Cabernet Sauvignon, Orange Muscat, Black Muscat, and Port
Production: 25,000 cases per year

There is something about becoming interested in home winemaking that changes one's life forever. That was certainly true for Leon Sobon, a Lockheed engineer, who at the age of 43 gave up a good paying job to start a different career and lifestyle.

Leon had grown up in New York state, earned a ceramic engineering degree from Alfred University in New York, and had worked at Lockheed and Hewlett-Packard for 19 years. In the late 1960s, Leon and some friends started making wine at home, sharing equipment and making wine by consensus. Whoever was home on the week-ends was autmoticaly elected to crush the grapes. This became quite a project for the Sobons — it took over their garage, and a cellar was dug next to the building to store the wine.

Winemaking fascinated Leon, and it did not take long for him to decide that this is what he wanted to do for the rest of his life. He spent his vacations at several nearby wineries volunteering for any task available. Making wine was considerably more interesting than his 9-to-5 job, even though he headed a research team that had discovered a brighter phosphor for use in color television and a luminescent material which significantly reduces X-ray dosage.

It took three years for him to convince his wife Shirley, a registered nurse, and their six children to change their lifestyles and move to the country. He knew he had won when Shirley told him one day that she was taking some business courses, because, "she might need to know something about keeping books."

The Sobons started looking for inexpensive land on which to grow grapes. They found it in rural Amador County — rich in history from the gold rush days. Agricultural land was selling at $400 per acre in 40-acre parcels. That was in 1974. But by the time the Sobons were ready to buy — three years later — the price had risen to $2,000 per acre.

In 1977, Leon and Shirley bought 74 acres complete with a stone house overlooking the Shenandoah Valley They moved in early August, just before the crush. "That was the year of the drought, grapes were in short supply, and I didn't have a winery," Leon recalled. His neighboring vintners and grape growers all got together and made sure he obtained grapes. He was able to make some wine, and Shenandoah Vineyards was born.

In spite of the helpful neighbors and the beautiful surroundings, it was not as easy as all that. There was a great deal of hard work ahead for the Sobons. After being a housewife for 20 years, Shirley went back to work as a nurse (working the night shift) until the winery was self supporting. Leon planted the vineyards and readied an old building to become the winery. Recently, he has added a storage and fermentation room to the original winery, doubling the capacity of the winery. Since 1978, production has grown between 50% to 100% per year.

Although the Sierra foothills are known for Zinfandel, Leon Sobon has chosen not to raise any Zinfandel grapes. He buys them from the neighboring vineyard because the vines are very old and produce better fruit than the new ones he could have planted. Shenandoah Vineyards does have 17 acres planted in Sauvignon Blanc and Cabernet Sauvignon.

In addition to making the traditional tablewines, Leon loves to experiment — that attribute is left over from his engineering research days. This experimentation has led him to produce award-winning dessert wines. There is an Orange Muscat, a Black Muscat, and two styles of Zinfandel Port. One is in the style of a rich Ruby Port and the other in the style of a true vintage Port.

Leon finds that there has been an increasing interest in dessert wines in recent years, especially among the more sophisticated and adventurous wine drinkers. Leon says that his sales of dessert wines have doubled every year since he started production, and he intends to make additional varieties.

Shenandoah Vineyards is an operation in which the entire family is involved. Leon is the vineyard manager and winemaker. Shirley takes care of the financial aspect. The second son Paul works full-time assisting in the winemaking. David, the oldest son, is in charge of sales and marketing in California. The other four children help out on week-ends when they are home from school. Leon says, "Everybody does his share — especially at crush and bottling time."

Leon's plans for the future include planting 15 more acres of grapes (although he has not decided on which variety), and to continue making not only tablewines, but unique dessert wines as well.

To enhance the attractiveness of the winery to visitors, the Sobons created an art gallery in the tasting and aging rooms of the winery. Interesting works of local artists are displayed on the walls and are available for sale. This helps Shirley and Leon fulfill their desire to help foster art and encourage talented artists.

Home winemaking did change the course of the Sobons' life. There is much hard work involved in owning a winery. It is not a 9-to-5 job, but it is a job he enjoys. "I'll never be rich as a winemaker, but I'll be happy, " he says, smiling. 🙢

Sierra Vista Winery

Address: 4560 Cabernet Way, Placerville 95667
□ (916) 622-7221
Visitation: Saturday and Sunday, 11 AM to 5 PM or by appointment
Principals: John and Barbara McCready
Varietals produced: Fumé Blanc, Chardonnay, White Zinfandel, Zinfandel, Cabernet Sauvignon
Production: 4,000 cases per year

Sierra Vista — just as its name implies — is located in the foothills of the Sierras, with a breathtaking view of the mountains to the east and (on a clear day) the coastline to the west.

John McCready, like so many of his fellow vintners in the Sierra foothills, is not only an engineer by profession, but also has the common heritage of being a home winemaker. John has a Ph.D. in Electrical Engineering from the University of Missouri. He worked for NCR in southern Ohio and currently is a member of the engineering faculty at California State University, Sacramento.

In 1967, his career in home winemaking started when he skimmed through a book on the subject which his wife, Barbara, was giving to her brother as a Christmas gift. He was so fascinated with the art of winemaking that he started to experiment with potato wine, then turnips, gradually branching out to cherries and other fruits before trying his hand at grapes. While living in Ohio, he made some wine with French hybrid grapes, but deep down he knew he would not be happy until he could press his own grapes in California.

Coincidentally, John's sister, Enid Reeves, owned a ranch in El Dorado County, next door to what was to become the ranch the McCreadys purchased. Enid was aware of the fact that previous to Prohibition there had been a number of vineyards in the area, and the remains of one was just a ridge away from her property. The vineyard had been mostly destroyed by fire in 1930.

John researched the area extensively, even though the U.C. Davis experts did not think the area was very well-suited for grape growing, especially not for Cabernet Sauvignon, one of the grapes John wanted to plant. They felt that the climate was too cool for the grapes to ripen properly. However, John kept coming back to the property adjoining his sister's, and in 1972, purchased 70 acres for his vineyards, winery, and homesite.

In 1973, John and his family — Barbara and their two daughters — moved to California. John started clearing the land and planted five acres of Cabernet Sauvignon grapes. This was followed by the planting of Zinfandel, Semillon, and Sauvignon Blanc, and additional Cabernet Sauvignon. Now there is also a small plot of French Syrah which is made into a French Rhone-style wine. A vineyard of Chardonnay has also been recently planted.

John found that the rocky, granite-type soil at 2,800 and 2,900 feet elevation produces lush fruity grapes with excellent balance. The shallow, well-drained hillsides and the wise use of pruning shears ensure low yields per acre, but top quality grapes. Warm days and cool nights give the grapes the right sugar-acid balance.

The ranch has three micro-climates which John has utilized in his plantings. Cabernet Sauvignon and the French Syrah are planted in the warmest region. On a cooler slope are the Zinfandel, Sauvignon Blanc, and the Semillon. Chardonnay is planted in the coolest vineyard.

Since Sierra Vista is a hilltop winery, the water table is low, and drip irrigation is used where necessary. The grapes are picked by hand and laid into small boxes, a process which allows for as little handling as possible and facilitates sorting.

The McCready's started producing wine in 1977 in a garage-like building at the foot of the property. The building, which is heavily insulated, became too small for the winery's production. In 1983, the McCreadys added a barrel storage building, which was constructed from wood milled on the ranch.

John McCready follows three rules in his winemaking: (1) Wine grows in the vineyard; (2) fine grapes make fine wine; (3) each unnecessary step in wine processing reduces the quality of the wine.

John uses open tank fermentation for most of his reds, punching down the cap by hand (the skins floating on top) to bring out the flavors. The whites are cold fermented in stainless steel tanks.

To make the White Zinfandel, the grapes are picked early in the morning and rushed to the winery in small batches. If the grapes were allowed to wait in the vineyards, the skins would begin to break down, and more color would emerge when pressed. The grapes are pressed immediately and then fermented in stainless steel tanks. The resulting wine is off-dry.

Barbara McCready does the marketing and bookkeeping for the winery. John is still involved in his engineering profession by teaching at California State University, Sacramento.

In the future the McCreadys plan to plant more vineyards so that all of their wines will be from estate grown grapes. They also plan to expand their winery production.

Stevenot Winery

Address: 2690 San Domingo Road, Murphys 95247
    □ (209) 728-3436
Visitation: Daily, 10 AM to 5 PM
Principal: Barden E. Stevenot
Varietals produced: Chenin Blanc, Fumé Blanc, Chardonnay, White Zinfandel, Zinfandel, Cabernet Sauvignon, and Muscat Canelli
Production: 45,000 cases per year

The old saying, "Thars gold in them thar hills," holds very true for Barden Stevenot of Stevenot Winery in Calaveras County — a county in which there were numerous gold mines during the gold rush. The legendary Morgan Mine, a gold mine on Carson Hill — a few miles south of Angels Camp — is owned by Barden Stevenot and his family and was recently reopened for mining.

However, gold mining is not the only success in Barden Stevenot's life. His winery grew from 2,200 cases in 1978 to its present 45,000 cases, which bespeaks of Barden's commitment to perseverance and hard work. He was one of the first producers of White Zinfandel and today half of the Stevenot Winery production is in White Zinfandel. It could be considered another gold mine of sorts.

Wine growing and winemaking is not new to Calaveras County. In 1869, it was the fourth largest grape growing region in the state. Grapes were grown and wine was made to satisfy the thirst of the miners. Grape growing in the area declined in the early 1900s and was completely destroyed by Prohibition. It started up again in the 1970s with the planting of vineyards and the establishment of small wineries. Currently, Stevenot is the largest winery in the Sierra Foothills.

Barden Stevenot is a fifth generation Californian of French and Italian descent. His family can be closely tied to the history of Calaveras County since the days of the '49ers and the discovery of gold in the region. Several Carson Hill mines have been in and out of the hands of the Stevenots more than once.

Barden's great-great-grandfather, Gabriel Stevenot, came to California from Nancy, France in search of gold. Gold had initially been discovered in the area in 1848 by James Carson. In 1851, Carson Hill was the site of the largest mine in California. The largest nugget ever discovered in North America was taken from Carson Hill in 1854 — it weighed 195 pounds. People believed that the legendary "mountain of gold" had been found at last.

Many battles, with guns and otherwise, were fought over the ownership of mines on Carson Hill. Gabriel Stevenot claimed he owned one-half of the Morgan Mine. He bought the Reserve Mine on Carson Hill and worked it until 1865. At the same time, Gabriel's son, Emil, who was born in France and educated in mining engineering in Strasbourg, came over and joined his father in the mine operation. Emil continued to operate mines in the area until 1889.

Nothing was heard of the mining operations or its connection to the Stevenot family until Emil's brother Archie took the job as mine superintendent of the newly organized Carson Hill Gold Mines prior to World War I. In 1919, the mine became famous when a shoot of ore discovered, which eventually netted $5 million. The mine closed in 1942, but was purchased by the Stevenot family in 1952. Barden, after many geological studies, has recently reopened the mine in partnership with a Canadian mining firm. There is reported to be enough gold still in the mine for operations to continue for the next ten years.

Both sides of Barden's family had done a little home winemaking, but at the time Barden did not show great interest in the venture. He acquired an active interest when a friend of his, Louis Preston of Preston Vineyards, planted a vineyard and established a winery in Sonoma County in the early 1970s. At the time Barden was involved in real estate development and had spent time as Vice President and General Manager of Kirkwood Meadows in the Sierra Foothills — where he was responsible for the development of the ski area.

In 1969, Barden purchased the Shaw Ranch. It seems that when he was a youngster growing up in the area, he visited the Shaw ranch periodically and was charmed by its setting and its swimming pool. Twenty-five years later he purchased the ranch.

There are also many turn-of-the century buildings on the ranch — the house, some of the barns, and a small cabin known as the Alaska House. The owner of the ranch built this cabin, which had a dirt floor, as a replica of the cabin he saw and visited in Alaska. It became Mr. Shaw's private retreat from the world, where he could sit and meditate. Today the Alaska House is the tasting room for the Stevenot Winery. A sod roof has been added to keep the building cool. Barden has remodelled the old ranch house and lives there.

The property was a rundown cattle ranch, which had been established in 1860, and Barden let it lay fallow until 1974, when Lou Preston encouraged him to plant grapes. Sixteen acres of Chardonnay and Cabernet Sauvignon were planted. There were some vines in a hillside vineyard which had been planted at the turn of the century. An additional nine acres have been planted with Zinfandel. The estate grapes are used in the Stevenot wines, though most of the grapes are purchased from neighboring vineyards.

Barden Stevenot did some home winemaking after planting the vineyards. In 1977, he turned the old hay barn into a winery where the first wines were made in 1978. Since then a large redwood-sided storage and office building has been added to the winery complex.

During the first year, Barden was the winemaker and remained so for several years. He made only the wines he enjoyed. In 1979, however, he followed the trend of a small group of vintners who were making white wine from Zinfandel. This was utilizing an over-abundance of Zinfandel. The wine was a hit with consumers and has been in great demand ever since. From that success the winery grew. In 1982, Steve Millier, a graduate of Fresno State, joined Stevenot as winemaker.

The basic philosophy of Stevenot winemaking is to encourage blending, but blending the same varietal from several small vineyards located in the immediate region. "We blend wines on the premise that we can make a better whole out of separate parts. All varietally labeled wine is 100% varietal," says Barden Stevenot. Blending is Steve Millier's forte, and "he is a master with a watchful eye who can read the wines perfectly," adds Barden.

The Stevenot winery still makes many wines which are particular favorites of Barden Stevenot, including Muscat Canelli. This wine, which is high in acid and has a full fruity taste, looks like gold in a glass — a good way of describing Barden's Stevenot wines from the Gold Country. ❧

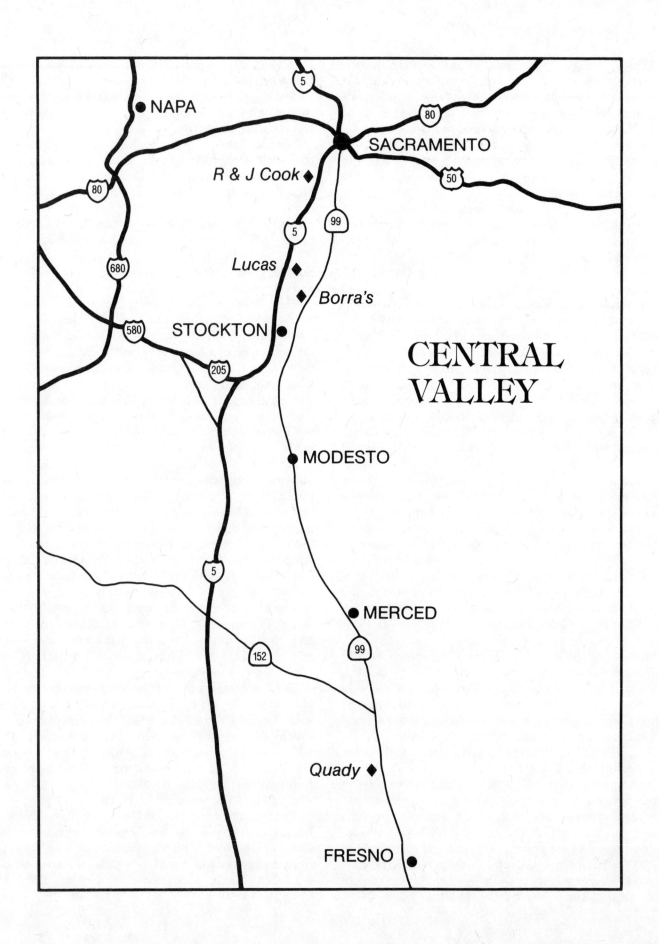

NAPA

SACRAMENTO

R & J Cook ◆

Lucas ◆

Borra's ◆

STOCKTON

CENTRAL
VALLEY

MODESTO

MERCED

Quady ◆

FRESNO

Wineries of the
CENTRAL VALLEY

Borra's Cellar
R. & J. Cook
The Lucas Winery
Quady Winery

Central Valley

From the standpoint of sheer volume, the San Joaquin and Sacramento Valleys of central California are the heartland of California grape growing and winemaking. Well over 60% of the state's wine is produced in this region — primarily in the San Joaquin Valley, which extends from Kern County in the south to San Joaquin County in the north.

Wine growing started in 1850 in the Central Valley near Stockton, when Charles Weber, who founded the city, planted the first vineyard with Mission grape cuttings from Southern California. However, it was another pioneer, George West, who established and developed the wine industry in the San Joaquin Valley.

West orginally came to California in 1850 to mine gold, which he did successfully for several years. In 1852, he started a vineyard with Mission grapes, but a year later planted some 40 different varietals. In 1858, he built a winery and crushed his first vintage.

West's operation grew steadily with vineyard and winery expansion. By 1890, he owned wholesale houses in San Francisco and New York. His wines — brandy, port, sherry and Madeira — were considered the best produced in California. West was an exponent of quality control in manufacturing and was one of the first in the industry to age his wines.

Vineyard acreage in the San Joaquin County expanded in the late 1800s — from 225 acres in 1875 to over 4,000 by 1890. The other major grape growing counties of the San Joaquin Valley — Fresno, Madera, and Kern — developed much later than San Joaquin County due to lack of readily available water and transportation. The first vineyard in this southern part of the Valley was planted by Francis Eisen near Fresno in 1875. Local residents ridiculed his efforts and predicted they would be able to eat his entire harvest in one sitting. Through use of irrigation, however, he prevailed.

These four counties, plus several others, have over 200,000 acres of wine grapes under cultivation. This comprises 60% of California's total wine grape acreage. The growth of the wine industry in the Central Valley has indeed been remarkable.

The varietals produced in the Central Valley are those that thrive in very warm climates and are not dependent on cool evening breezes. French Colombard, Chenin Blanc, Carignan, and Grenauche fit these growing qualifications. They are four of the top seven wine-producing grapes in California. These grapes are used primarily in the so-called generic wines, although they can be, and frequently are made into premium wines. The region below Sacramento has become recognized for its production of premium Chenin Blanc grapes. The San Joaquin Valley also has the largest acreage of Zinfandel (another of the top seven varietals) in California, producing 40% of the wine made from this grape in the large bulk-type wineries.

The Alicante Bouchet grape saw an explosive growth in the San Joaquin Valley during Prohibition. Since the grape was very thick-skinned, it was ideal for shipment to home winemakers in the East. It was particularly popular with the Italian home winemakers because it resembled the heavy red wines of southern Italy. In 1938 there were more than 38,000 acres of this grape in the Valley. Today only 3,200 acres remain in all of California.

The Sacramento Valley which today is known for its growing of premium Chenin Blanc, was the scene of large vineyards in the late 1800s. Leland Stanford, an entrepeneur and founder of Stanford University, had the largest vineyard in the world in the area. The property called Vina, situated on the Sacramento River in Tehama County, consisted of 3,500 acres of vineyards, two acres of cellars under roof, and 800 employees. The climate, however, was not conducive to premium grape growing, and the entire operation ceased in the early 1900s.

Today, only the counties benefitting from the cool breezes of the San Francisco and Suisun Bay grow what are considered premium grapes. They are located west of the Sacramento-Lodi region. These vineyards are primarily planted with Chenin Blanc, Cabernet Sauvignon, and Sauvignon Blanc. &

Borra's Cellar

Address: 1301 East Armstrong Road, Lodi 95240
□ (209) 368-5082
Visitation: By appointment
Principals: Stephen and Beverly Borra
Varietals produced: Barbera and White Barbera
Production: 1,000 cases per year

Grapes have been growing continuously for the past 65 years on the property at 1301 East Armstrong Road in Lodi, which was settled by Joe Manassero when he immigrated from the Piemonte region of Italy in the early 1900s. Today, his grandson Stephen Borra is still living on the property raising grapes and making wine as his grandfather did. The Lodi area, recently granted its own appellation designation, has rich soil and an abundant water supply.

Joe Manassero planted Carignane, Zinfandel, Mission, Palomino, and Tokay grapes. He made wine as a hobby, as was the custom with most Italian families, using old Italian methods and aging the wine in the cool basement of his farmhouse. While Steve was growing up, he did not really pay much attention to the winemaking process. Years later, when he married and settled into the farmhouse which had been passed down through the family, he developed an interest in learning the old ways.

Steve Borra worked for 18 years for Pacific Telephone Company. In 1983, he decided to take early retirement to devote full time to his 30-acre farm and an irrigation company which he had started. Since he had been a home winemaker for nine years, he also wanted to turn his hobby into a commercial venture.

The original farm is still planted in grapes. When he completed the winery in 1975, Steve used the old Carignane grapes in his first crush in honor of his grandfather. That was the first and last time those family grapes, which had been planted by his grandfather in 1925, were used. The vines were old, and they had not been producing well, so Steve decided to pull them out and replant with Barbera grapes.

Today the ranch consists of 12 acres of Barbera and 15 of Tokay, which are sold as table grapes. There is also one acre of Zinfandel, which was harvested for the first in fall 1986 and made into wine.

Steve took winemaking a step at a time, growing a little each year. He read books on winemaking and took some short courses at U.C. Davis. The first year Borra's Cellar produced 200 cases and has grown a little ever since. Steve's first release won medals at the Los Angeles County and Orange County Fairs and helped encourage the Borras' winemaking efforts. Steve bought used equipment from other wineries, and his family — wife Bev, son Steve, Jr., and daughter Gina — helped with crush, bottling, and labeling.

Since it is high in acid, the Barbera grape is well suited to the hot climate of the San Joaquin Valley. Over the years, Steve has learned that drastic pruning and thinning of the grape crop produces better wine. "It allows the harvest to begin approximately four to six weeks early, reducing fruit spoilage and retaining the natural fruit acids," says Steve.

The old farmhouse, no longer the Borra's residence since they built a new home next door, is still an integral part of the winery. It not only houses the tasting room, but also the offices for the winery and Steve's other agricultural businesses. Bev, who does the bookkeeping for the various family businesses, also has a bookkeeping service which is located in the farmhouse. In the fall, the old house doubles as the "bottling plant."

Crush takes place on a concrete pad at the back of a building a few yards from the farmhouse. Being a small operation, Steve says, gives him a chance to inspect every grape going into the crusher. "That's quality control," he adds.

The Red Barbera ferments on its own yeast in large open redwood tanks. After fermentation, it is aged in American oak barrels for two to three years. The aging takes place in the basement of the old farmhouse where Steve's grandfather made his wine many years ago.

The grapes for the White Barbera are crushed, then run over screens, and lightly pressed. Yeast is added and the White Barbera is cold fermented then bottled.

An integral part of the winery property is the three-storey tank house with a 60-year-old grapevine arbor which was constructed and planted by Joe Manassero, Steve's grandfather. The tank house and the huge grapevine are pictured on the Borra's Cellar label.

Steve and Bev Borra plan to expand their winery to 10,000 cases per year and to make white wines — Sauvignon Blanc and Chenin Blanc — beginning in 1987. They will also produce some Cabernet Sauvignon, Zinfandel, and White Zinfandel.

Grape growing and winemaking have been a part of the Borra family for three generations, and Steve says that the most rewarding part of the business is "seeing my wines enjoyed, either alone or with food." ❧

R. & J. Cook

Address: Netherlands Road, Clarksburg 95612
□ (916) 775-1234 or (916) 775-1811

Visitation: Weekdays, 10:30 AM to 4 PM; Saturday and Sunday, 11 AM to 4 PM

Principals: Roger and Joanne Cook

Varietals produced: Chenin Blanc, Sauvignon Blanc, Merlot Blanc, Merlot, Petite Sirah, and Cabernet Sauvignon

Production: 50,000 cases per year

The Delta Queen steamboat pictured on the wine label of R. & J. Cook's wines depicts a real steamboat which used to travel up and down the delta waterway from San Francisco to Sacramento, the state capital. The boat carried mail, cargo, and passengers. Clarksburg, a town 12 miles south of Sacramento, was a regular port of call. The Delta Queen does not run on the delta waterway anymore. She was transferred to duty on the Mississippi.

In recent years, the delta, particularly the Clarksburg area, has become known for the excellent Chenin Blanc grown there. Chenin Blanc wine has also made R. & J. Cook well known.

Although the delta is famous for its hot weather, the area around Clarksburg has the same weather and temperature as the north end of the Napa Valley. Clarksburg has the same cool marine breezes as Napa with west winds blowing from San Francisco across Suisun Bay into Clarksburg. The rich bottom land on the river banks provide good soil for grape growing.

R. & J. Cook stands for Roger and Joanne Cook, who have grown up in the Clarksburg area, where their families are involved in farming operations. Roger is a fourth generation farmer. His father grows grapes on his farm across the slough from Roger and Joanne's property.

In 1968, after doing climatic and soil studies of their property, Roger and Joanne started planting 115 acres of grapes on their ranch. Previous to the planting of the vineyards, they had been raising produce of all types and selling them to the wholesale market.

All of Cook's grapes were sold to prominent Napa and Sonoma wineries, who won awards, particularly with the Chenin Blanc.

As the price of grapes went down in 1978, due to an overabundance of grapes on the market, Roger and Joanne suddenly found that the market for their grapes had almost disappeared. They realized that the situation was not going to get better for a while. The Cooks felt that they could better merchandise the finished product — wine — than their grapes. Roger proceeded to build a winery, doing most of the construction himself. In 1979, Roger and Joanne were in the wine business.

Over the years, production has grown from 7,000 cases in 1979 to the present 50,000 cases, and they are utilizing the majority of their own grapes, still selling some to Napa and Sonoma wineries.

In 1983, Roger applied for and received the appellation for Clarksburg as a new viticulture area. Now it can be used not only to designate Cook wines, but also on wines of other grapes grown in the area.

The entire family is involved in the winery. Roger oversees the operation, Joanne does the administration and marketing, and the two sons, in their late twenties, work in the winery or wherever they are needed. Steve Birtwhistle, a U.C. Davis graduate, is the winemaker. He has traveled extensively in Europe and Australia studying winemaking methods.

In order to preserve the fruitiness of the grapes, they are picked at night, when the temperature is coolest. Roger uses a mechanical harvester, which with three men, does the same work as 50 individual pickers. The harvested grapes are immediately brought to the winery for crushing and fermentation.

The varietal that has made the Clarksburg area and the R. & J. Cook winery famous is Chenin Blanc. The Cooks produce three Chenin Blanc wines — a very dry, a semi-dry, and an extra dry or private reserve. The extra dry is fermented in stainless steel tanks. When the fermentation is half complete, the wine is transferred to French oak barrels and allowed to ferment dry. Properly stored, this wine will age as well as a Chardonnay.

The Merlot Blanc is Roger and Joanne's answer to White Zinfandel, since they do not grow any Zinfandel. The Merlot grape has a distinct flavor, and the color of the wine is a lovely peach. The flavor is further enhanced by the addition of a little Chenin Blanc and a little Muscat, which adds fruitiness to the wine.

Roger and Joanne Cook are excited about being part of a new viticulture area and are trying to make people aware of this region of grape growing. In a business where there is lots of competition, especially foreign competition, they are helping to make the American public aware of California wines — wines from other regions of California. This is the way they have grown and survived in the industry.

The Lucas Winery

Address: 18196 North Davis Road, Lodi 95240
□ (209) 368-2006
Visitation: By appointment
Principals: David and Tamara Lucas
Varietals produced: White Zinfandel and Zinfandel
Production: 1,000 cases per year

There are 30 acres of grapes growing on the Lucas property — 18 acres of Zinfandel and the rest of Tokay. Since Dave and Tamara Lucas feel that "good wine begins in the vineyard," they do not consider themselves grape growers but wine growers. Not only are they wine growers, but they are Zinfandel wine growers, since that is the only wine they produce. The Lucases have spent years researching, experimenting, and perfecting the art of making Zinfandel — both white and red.

Working with the land was not new to Dave and Tamara Lucas when they purchased their 30-acre vineyard near Lodi in 1976. Dave, who has a B.S. in Agriculture from California State University, Chico and a Master's Degree in International Agriculture, spent part of his career in India with the Peace Corps advising remote tribes about rice and potato production. After the Lucases were married, they were stationed in Iran — Dave with the Peace Corps and Tamara teaching school.

When they returned from Iran, Dave worked for a Lodi agricultural co-op, and they settled in the Lodi area, on the property they had purchased. The ranch needed a lot of refurbishing. Not only were the farm buildings in bad disrepair, but the Zinfandel grapes planted in the 1920s were in sad neglect. Tamara took courses in construction, and Dave, who wanted to see the finished product of his grapes, took winemaking classes through U.C. Davis extension.

At the present time, the Lucases sell all of the Tokay grapes and about half of the Zinfandel. Home winemakers and winemaking shops from as far away as Boston purchase the Lucas Zinfandel grapes. At harvest time, the grapes are picked by a special crew and carefully packed into shipping boxes, then shipped by refrigerated trucks across the country.

This is not a new venture for some of the grape growers in California, but dates back to the turn of the century when grapes were shipped to home winemakers throughout the country — first by rail and now in refrigerated trucks. Zinfandel grapes lend themselves especially well to being shipped long distances if kept under refrigeration. The climate in Lodi allows Zinfandel grapes to ripen and color uniformly, which reduces the chance of spoilage.

In 1978, after Tamara remodeled the barn and Dave had made a barrel of Zinfandel which was an instant success in the neighborhood, the Lucases decided to make wine as a small commercial venture. A few years later, Dave changed jobs, becoming the grape buyer for the Mondavi tablewine facility near Lodi. This gave him an opportunity to observe winemaking techniques on a large scale throughout California. The Lucases have increased production to approximately 1,000 cases per year — a level they expect to maintain.

Making only one varietal has given Dave and Tamara the opportunity to familiarize themselves with the various techniques of making an award-winning Zinfandel.

The red Zinfandel is produced in a unique manner beginning with not one, but three different harvest dates. The first pick occurs when the grapes are at 19 to 20 Brix sugar, resulting in high acid and a fresh raspberry bouquet. The second harvest is when the sugar has reached 21 to 23 Brix which results in a typical claret style of red wine. The last harvest is at 25 to 26 Brix, when the grapes are higher in sugar but lower in acid. At this point the grapes are also more intense in flavor — a richer blueberry jam taste. The blending of the three harvests results in a more complex wine.

The grapes are field crushed and then fermented in open stainless steel tanks for about five to six days. Twenty percent of the wine, however, is left on the skins for about 28 days to give the wine softer tannins and greater richness. The red wine is barrel aged in four different French oaks for 14 months, blended again, and then bottled. The wine is also bottle-aged for six to eight months prior to release.

The Lucases also make a very unique dry White Zinfandel on a very limited production. The wine is fermented in new French oak barrels until very dry. For added complexity the dry wine is left in contact with the lees for approximately 30 days. This is the "sur lie" method of winemaking used in France to produce the finest white table wines.

The Lucases enjoy raising grapes and operating a winery, and it is most rewarding at harvest time. As Tamara Lucas says, "That is the time when the grower and the winemaker extend and complete the whole process of winegrowing."

Quady Winery

Address: 13180 Road 24, Madera 93637
☐ (209) 673-8086
Visitation: By appointment
Principals: Andrew Quady
Varietals produced: Essensia (Orange Muscat), Elysium (Black Muscat), and California Port (Zinfandel)
Production: 12,000 cases per year

Fine dining is nearly impossible without an appropriate accompanying wine. The right choice of wine complements the foods being served. In the case of desserts, however, the most popular accompaniment has been coffee or tea, both of which provide a contrast in flavor to the dessert. The bitterness of coffee seems to remove the sweet aftertaste left by the dessert, placing coffee in direct competition with most desserts. In the last five years there has been considerable interest in pairing desserts with dessert (sweet) wines. After all, the British learned this several hundred years ago with their use of port.

Andrew Quady was born in St. Louis, Missouri and came to California at the age of six. After attending college in Southern California, and earning a chemical engineering degree, he worked for an explosives manufacturer in Southern California. Andy credits his bomb-making experience with starting him in the wine industry.

As a chemical engineer, he worked all day in the explosive industry and became terribly depressed. He would come home at night and relax with a glass of wine. He appreciated the moment of relaxation offered by the sip of wine. One day he decided that since he appreciated wine so much, why not make his own? That was the answer he was seeking as an alternative lifestyle. He quit his job and enrolled in the graduate enology program at U.C. Davis.

Following his enology training, he worked for a Lodi vintner, where in 1975 he made his first port from Amador County Zinfandel. This effort was the start of a career which was to ultimately earn him the title of "The Muscat King of California."

Andy Quady observed a trend toward dessert wines. He decided to focus his efforts on this niche in the market place. In 1975, he built a winery to produce dessert wines exclusively.

After years of research, Andy believes he has found the right wine to produce for dessert wines. He found that desserts are sweeter and more intensely flavored than the preceding courses and require a sweet wine to complement the desserts. The wine must also be flavor intensive and have a favorable balance of acid and alcohol. Consequently, he believes his Essensia and Elysium — both Muscats, the former orange and the latter black — satisfy these requirements.

Andy first started producing port from Amador County grapes. He has also planted some typical Portuguese port varietals found only along the Douro River in Portugal to produce wine for his vintage port. These grapes are planted in Amador County and are under contract to Quady.

Five years after making his first port, Andy started developing dessert wines using the orange and the black Muscat grapes. Prior to that, vintners had shied away from the Muscat grape, because it was used chiefly in bulk wine. The Essensia, made from the Orange Muscat, has an aroma and taste of orange blossoms. The Black Muscat has a reminder of chocolate, and is named Elysium.

Both Essensia and Elysium are fermented in stainless

steel. The fermentation is stopped at about 12 to 13 brix sugar. After fermenting, fortified wine spirits are added and the wine is then allowed to age in oak barrels before bottling. The wine then ages six more months in the bottle before release.

Dessert is more than simply eating. By creating a dessert wine, Andy Quady has created an additional reason to stay at the table, enjoy wine and good conversation. The dessert wines Essensia and Elysium are often substituted for dessert or may be used as an after dinner drink.

Andy Quady has expanded his dessert wine production from zero to 12,000 cases per year, creating a market when there was virtually none. Today he is recognized as the foremost producer in America of dessert wines. ❧

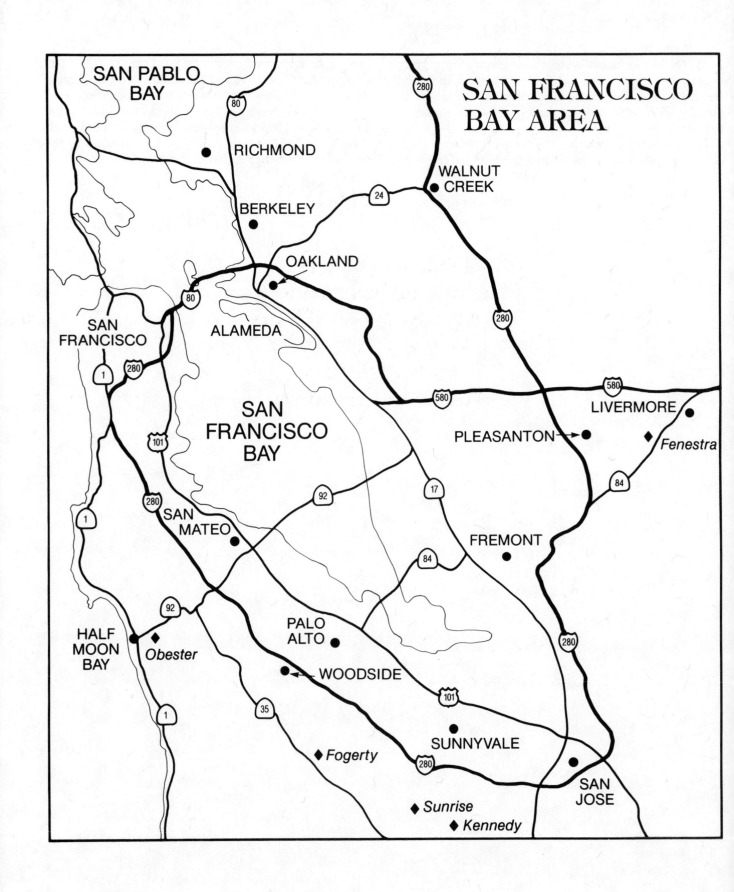

SAN FRANCISCO BAY AREA

SAN PABLO BAY

RICHMOND

BERKELEY

OAKLAND

WALNUT CREEK

ALAMEDA

SAN FRANCISCO

SAN FRANCISCO BAY

PLEASANTON

LIVERMORE

Fenestra

SAN MATEO

FREMONT

HALF MOON BAY

Obester

PALO ALTO

WOODSIDE

Fogerty

SUNNYVALE

SAN JOSE

Sunrise

Kennedy

Wineries of the

SAN FRANCISCO BAY AREA

Fenestra Winery
Thomas Fogarty Winery
Kathryn Kennedy Winery
Obester Winery
Sunrise Winery
Woodside Vineyards

San Francisco Bay Area

During the 1870s and 1880s — the peak period of evolution for the California wine industry — the San Francisco Bay Area was equal in importance to the Sonoma-Napa areas. The principal centers for grape growing and winemaking were in and around San Jose and the Livermore Valley. Vineyards and small wineries stretched up into San Mateo County to the Woodside-Portola Valley area. Leland Stanford had vineyards and a winery (now the Stanford Barn, a shopping complex) in Palo Alto long before he established the university which bears his name.

The first vineyards and winemaking activities in the area were at the Santa Clara Mission and Mission San Jose in the late 1700s. By the early 1800s, these two missions were producing about 2,500 gallons (1,000 cases) of wine and brandy per year. This small production, by today's standards, was sufficient for the Mission's use as well as for supplying Mission Dolores in San Francisco and several other missions in Northern California. Mission Dolores could grow no grapes due to the cool climate of San Francisco.

By the middle of the 19th century, various vineyards had been established in the San Francisco Area. Robert Livermore planted vineyards in the valley and near the town which bears his name. In 1849, Elias Beard acquired 30,000 acres of what had been the property of Mission San Jose (the missions had been secularized in 1834), including its deteriorating vineyards of Mission grapes. He quickly established a winery with a capacity of 20,000 gallons (8,000 cases). In 1852, Joseph Palmer planted 200 acres that contained European varietals. At the same time a Frenchman, Antonio Delmas, also imported and planted European varietals in his San Jose vineyard. Palmer and Delmas became the first growers of non-Mission grapes in the San Francisco Bay Area.

A milestone in the development of the Bay Area wine industry was the arrival from France of Charles Le Franc, who started the New Almaden Winery southwest of San Jose and planted the largest acreage of vineyards in Santa Clara County, south of San Francisco. Upon his death, Le Franc's son-in-law, Paul Masson, took over the operation of the enterprise.

Expansion of the wine industry continued throughout the 19th century in all areas of the San Francisco Bay Area. Leland Stanford expanded his vineyards and added a winery in another county in the Bay Area. The Livermore Valley expanded when Dr. George Bernard created a vineyard and winery near the town of Livermore in 1879. Five years later, Carl Wente, Sr. purchased an interest in the Bernard winery. Wente rapidly expanded his holdings. James Concannon settled in the Livermore Valley in 1883 and created the winery which today bears his name. James Wetmore started his Cresta Blanca Winery there in 1887.

Expansion in all areas of the region continued until urban development overtook the area. The few wineries in the area today, with the exception of the Kathryn Kennedy and Thomas Fogarty wineries, depend chiefly on purchased grapes. Grapes from small vineyards of one to four acres in the Portola-Woodside area are used by Woodside Winery.

Unfortunately, the glorious viticultural past will likely never return to the San Francisco Bay Area. ❧

Fenestra Winery

Address: 83 E. Vallecitos Road, Livermore 94550
  □ (415) 447-5246
Mailing Address: 14124 Buckner Drive, San Jose 95127
  □ (408) 258-1092
Visitation: Saturday and Sunday, Noon-5 PM; Open
  house invitation 4 times a year
Principals: Lanny Replogle and Fran Replogle
Varietals produced: Chardonnay, Sauvignon Blanc,
  White Zinfandel, White Riesling, Cabernet
  Sauvignon, Zinfandel, and Merlot
Production: 2,500 cases per year

Dr. Lanny Replogle is a man whose dream has come true. For 13 years, he and his wife Fran made wine at home every fall. The first batch they made was awful. "It was full of hydrogen sulfide," according to Dr. Replogle, a Ph.D. in organic chemistry from the University of Washington and a chemistry professor at San Jose State University.

That first bad batch of wine did not discourage the Replogles. Each fall they bought Zinfandel grapes, picked, stemmed, and crushed them with the help of friends, and bottled their own wine. The wine-making bug had bitten them, and year-by-year their wine improved. Lanny started trying different grape varieties and experimented with new techniques.

In 1976, after 15 years of experience as an amateur winemaker who had become an expert, he decided to become a commercial vintner. There was just one problem. He did not own a winery. So he struck a deal with Stony Ridge Winery in the Livermore Valley. He would be their consultant in winemaking if they would let him use part of their extensive facilities to make his own wine. In the early 1970s, during summer vacations, Lanny had worked as a consultant to Paul Masson Winery in Saratoga, developing techniques to improve the efficiency of grape crushing.

But making wine and having your own label was only part of Lanny's dream. He wanted to operate his own winery. In August of 1980, Lenny's dream came true. The Replogles moved their operation to an old winery building near Livermore. At one time the Livermore Valley southeast of San Francisco was one of the most prestigious wine producing areas of California. A hundred years ago there were some 30 wineries in the valley. The building they moved into was in disrepair, to put it mildly. The 1890 building had holes in the roof and a floor littered with cow manure and sawdust. But this did not discourage Lanny and Fran. The building did have a concrete floor and drains and would make a good home for their winery.

The two-storey brick, wood, and concrete winery was built into the hillside, a common practice in the 1890s. This provided natural cooling since part of the building is underground. Also, the design would make wine-moving easier since gravity would allow the flow of wine after the crushing and fermenting on the top floor to be drained into barrels on the first floor. This technique was common in the old days before the electrical pump became the efficient way to move liquid.

The Replogles grow no grapes. Thus, each fall, long before the harvest, Lanny visits potential sources for grapes in the Napa Valley, nearby Livermore Valley, and Monterey County. Trucks from the vineyards bring the grapes to the winery where they are crushed and the liquid is transferred to stainless steel tanks for fermentation. After fermentation the wine is removed from the tanks, allowed to settle, and then is put into oak barrels for aging. White wine receives less contact with oak, but reds are allowed to age in the barrels from one to two years, depending on the variety.

Lanny Replogle's goal for his wine is finesse. By this he means an elegant intensity with a balance of flavors. He also wants to produce wines that are drinkable early — not requiring years of aging. He wants to be known for fine varietal wines. His wines have already won gold and silver medals in state competitions.

Fran Replogle is in charge of marketing and public relations for the winery. She publishes a quarterly newsletter that features information on their new releases, wine tips, and how to serve Fenestra wines with food. Fran is also quite a cook and enjoys sharing her wine and food tips. She is a firm believer in the theory that food goes better with wine — but the right wine. Since she leads a busy life — marketing, public relations, bookkeeping for the winery, and mother of two boys — she has learned that a recipe that calls for "chill overnight" means to her, "one hour in the freezer and get on with it."

The Fenestra wine label is in four colors, showing the winery at a distance as seen through an open arched window framed by brick. After all, Fenestra is the Latin word for window.

Lanny Replogle's dream has come true. The joys of winemaking are only occasionally overshadowed by some of the regulatory aspects of the business, he says. Both Fran and Lanny continue to love the physical activity and creative aspects connected with being vintners. ❧

Thomas Fogarty Winery

Address: 19501 Skyline Boulevard, Woodside 94062
  □ (415) 851-1946
Mailing address: Alpine Road, 5937 Alpine Road,
  Portola Valley 94025
Visitation: First Saturday of each month, 1 PM to 4 PM,
  by appointment
Principals: Thomas J. Fogarty, M. D.
Varietals produced: Chardonnay, Gewurztraminer,
  Pinot Noir, and Cabernet Sauvignon
Production: 7,500 cases per year

"Wine making is a little science and a lot of art," says Dr. Thomas Fogarty, well-known cardiovascular surgeon and inventor of surgical instruments. Although there is a lot of art to making and blending wines, Dr. Fogarty also believes in the scientific side of winemaking as evidenced by the fact that his winery has a fully equipped laboratory.

Dr. Fogarty, who grew up in Ohio and trained in Oregon, came to Stanford University in the late 1960s to work with Dr. Norman Shumway, a pioneer in heart transplants. About the same time, Fogarty purchased 320 acres on the inland side of the Santa Cruz Mountains. He had become interested in wines and knew the Santa Cruz Mountains had a long history of vineyards and winemaking. The property has an elevation ranging from 1,000 to 2,200 feet and is well-suited to growing the cooler orientated varietals, such as Pinot Noir and Chardonnay. The area has warm days and receives cool afternoon ocean breezes flowing over the mountain. This small area, in the midst of urban development below it, is an agricultural haven.

Tom Fogarty had had a long and ongoing interest in agriculture and thought a vineyard would be a good outlet for this interest. He also took up home winemaking as a hobby to gain experience as a vintner.

By 1975, Tom was ready to plant vineyards and in 1981 to build his winery. He wanted to concentrate primarily on the varietals of Burgundy, which he knew would do well on his property — Chardonnay and Pinot Noir. Fourteen acres of these two grapes were planted in 1978, and ten more are currently being added. Tom plans eventually to have 50 acres in vineyards in various parcels on his property. In this way he can blend, if he desires, the various lots from varying soils and microclimates. At the present time, the Fogarty winery buys 80% of its grapes from the cool growing regions of Napa and Monterey Counties.

The winery, a handsome redwood structure, looks, from the front, like a residence. It is a two-storey building, designed by Tom Fogarty, built into the hillside, with a crushing platform on the lower level. The winery, at 2,000 feet elevation, has a spectacular view of the San Francisco Bay Area.

A Fresno State graduate in enology, Michael Martella, is the winemaker at the Fogarty Winery. He follows the traditions of Burgundian winemaking. Jim Varner, a U.C. Davis graduate with experience at the Krug and Bob Varner wineries manages the vineyards. The other important member of the staff is George Burtness, a Stanford M.B.A., who is the general manager of the entire operation. George is very familiar with winery operations, since he himself was at one time a part-time vintner.

Michael Martella's winemaking has proven to be very successful. Fogarty wines have won many medals in the past few years, including medals at the California, San Francisco, and Orange County Fairs. Thomas Fogarty Winery has been particularly recognized for its Chardonnays and Pinot Noirs.

Tom Fogarty, although a full-time practicing cardiovascular surgeon, spends as much time as possible at the winery. He not only takes part in the weekly strategy meetings, but living on the property gives him a chance to observe the proceedings on a day-to-day basis. In the spring, he helps prune the vines.

Not only is Tom Fogarty making a positive statement in the wine world, but he hopes that his commitment to the Santa Cruz Mountains as a winegrowing region will help the world become a little more aware of that area. ❧

Kathryn Kennedy Winery

Address: 13180 Pierce Road, Saratoga 95070
☐ (408) 867-4170
Visitation: By appointment only
Principals: Kathryn Kennedy
Varietals produced: Cabernet Sauvignon
Production: 800 cases per year

In the early 1970s, there was persistent pressure from the Saratoga City Council for Kathryn Kennedy to sell her land so that a connecting road could be constructed to the neighboring housing development. After all, the city fathers stated, the seven acres did not include her residence and were laying fallow and unused. Since she was living alone on the property, and her children had left home, there was no reason for Kathryn to keep this land, the council claimed.

Kathyrn Kennedy was not going to be defeated so easily. First, she investigated the legitimacy of the necessity for an access road to the neighboring development. She found that there was an existing access road available. She won the argument with the city council, and then evaluated possible ways to put the seven acres to good use. Kathryn considered a small Christmas tree farm or possibly a kiwi ranch, since that fruit was becoming popular. But she kept eyeing the property across the street and observing the elderly gentleman tending Cabernet Sauvignon grapevines.

"Why not plant a vineyard?" she asked herself. The man across the street seemed to be doing financially well selling his grapes to several wineries. The vines had been there for over 20 years and were still flourishing. Kathryn decided it must be a good place to raise wine grapes.

Not being a person to plunge into something blindly, she decided to learn about viticulture. In 1972, she went to U.C. Davis and took courses in viticulture. The next spring she planted 3,300 vines on their own root stock.

Since the vineyard is on the inland side of the Santa Cruz Mountains, the area has a warm, dry growing season. Kathryn prunes her vines heavily to reduce the amount of fruit per acre. This method stresses the vines and produces heartier fruit. Another stress factor is dry farming, which means depending only on rainfall for water. Although Kathryn's son, Marty Mathis, has now joined her in the vineyard and winery work, she still hand prunes a portion of the vineyard.

After six years of growing and pruning, Kathryn was ready for her first harvest. By that time, the crop that had seemed to be a good investment six years earlier was considerably down in price. Also, there was a trend away from red wines. Her only choice, then, seemed to be to make her own wine from her grapes. She converted her ex-husband's workshop, which was the size of a two car garage, into a winery by insulating the walls and buying winery equipment. The first year she hired a consultant as a winemaker. After that, her son Marty became proficient and took over the job as winemaker.

Kathryn Kennedy's wines are practically hand made. The grapes are hand picked into small lug boxes and immediately taken to the winery for crushing. Marty ferments the grapes in open top fermentors in small lots — one ton at a time. The grapes have a minimum of 12 days of skin contact, with the cap being punched down three times a day. A small basket press is then used for a soft press to extract the juice. The wine is then aged in small oak barrels for a minimum of 18 months. Kathryn and Marty use 80% French oak and 20% American. Extra gentle racking and egg white fining results in a clear, fruity Cabernet, but one that ages well.

Although the property adjacent to Kathryn Kennedy's home had been a problem 15 years ago, she met the challenge and is very pleased with the results. Even though she makes only one varietal, Cabernet Sauvignon, it is rated as premium quality. She believes that the best wines are made in the vineyard. "In the winery they are only refined, without diminishing their delicate qualities," she added.

Obester Winery

Address: 12341 San Mateo Road (Highway 92), Half Moon Bay 94019 □ (415) 726-9463

Visitation: Friday through Sunday, 10 AM to 5 PM

Principals: Paul and Sandra Obester

Varietals produced: Sauvignon Blanc, Chardonnay, and Johannisberg Reisling (under the Obester label) White Zinfandel, Zinfandel, and Cabernet Sauvignon (under the Gemello label)

Production: 10,000 cases per year (8,000 at Obester and 2,000 at Gemello)

The Obester Winery is really a Tale of Two Wineries and three generations of the Gemello family. It all started in 1912, when an Italian emmigrant John Gemello and his wife Teresa arrived on the San Francisco Peninsula by train from the East Coast. They were penniless and unable to speak English.

John Gemello knew winemaking, having made wine for his family in Italy and also having worked at a winery in Asti. He and his wife then moved to France where he was a grower of grapes. A freak hailstorm wiped out their wine crop and the young couple decided to pack their belongings and head for the land of opportunity — America.

John's first job in America was at Almaden Winery, and he later settled at Monte Bello Ridge on the Peninsula where he grew grapes and made wine. That was until 1920, when federal legislation wiped out his livelihood — just as the hailstorm had done in France.

For the next five years, Gemello worked on a ranch and saved enough money to buy a 55-acre ranch in Mountain View and later established his winery there. Twenty-two of the acres were planted in plum and cherry trees, the fruits of which were a great temptation for winemaking. But the law was the law, and so Prohibition was in effect. Within a month after the repeal of Prohibition, however, Gemello rolled out oaken barrels of aged wine for sale. He always said he had a "good haystack."

In the 1950s, Gemello passed the family winery on to his only son and retired from winemaking — although not entirely.

One fall night in 1975, Gemello's winemaking bug was to reappear. The "grandfather" of winemaking, now in his mid-90s, was living with his granddaughter, Sandy Obester and her husband Paul. His wife had passed away, and the Obesters tried to keep this energetic man busy at various activities. One night, while they were sitting around the dinner table, Sandy said, "Let's have Grandpa show us how to make wine." Her thought was to make a small batch in the garage of their home in Palo Alto.

John Gemello agreed enthusiastically and said, "Fine. We'll need a ton of Zinfandel." That was the only proportions he knew how to work with. Sandy and Paul talked him down to half a ton — still a great amount of wine for a garage project. "We really were just going to start a barrel as a hobby," Paul recalled.

The next year they did crush a ton, and by 1977, Paul and Sandy decided to become serious vintners. They started looking for property for a winery and settled on the present winery site just east of Half Moon Bay. A haybarn was converted into the winery. The property also contained a house for their living quarters and the carport was converted into the tasting room. They started on a shoestring, having sold their home in Palo Alto, and taking a larger mortgage in order to obtain cash to buy winery equipment.

By the crush of 1979, Paul Obester had a decision to make — whether to continue his successful career with an electronics company in Silicon Valley or become a full-time vintner. He had always wanted to operate his own business, and he had a masters degree in business management from Stanford. The winery won. As Paul says, "I am never going to get rich running a winery, but there is a certain pride in producing your own product."

Grandfather Gemello continued to help out and teach both Paul and Sandy winemaking in the European traditional way. Although he needed a crutch to get around, his mind remained sharp and active until he died at the age of 99 in 1981.

In 1982, the Obesters acquired the old Gemello Winery from Sandy's Uncle Mario. Sandy is the winemaker there, producing reds under the Gemello label, while Paul continues as winemaker at the Obester Winery. The Mountain View facility is also used to store some of the Obester wines, since the "old haybarn" is not large enough for storage.

Since the establishment of the winery, both Paul and Sandy have taken courses at U.C. Davis and one of their sons is taking his degree in enology and plans to join the family winery. There will be a fourth generation winemaker in the family.

The Obesters do not grow any grapes. They tried it on their land in Half Moon Bay, but the vines were flooded out in 1982. They do work closely with their growers, however, and stress the quality of the grape as the most important part of wine making. As Grandpa Gemello said, "You can make bad wine from bad grapes, good wine from good grapes, but you can't make good wine from bad grapes." By keeping in close contact with their growers in both Monterey and Mendocino Counties they know just when to harvest. Another important factor for good grower-vintner relationship is the practical one that Paul has established. He pays top dollar for top grapes and he pays on time.

Even though the Obesters learned wine making in a traditional European style, they have branched out into an innovative style of their own. Particularly, their white wines are consistent gold medal winners. Obester's Sauvignon Blanc is 100% varietal with partial barrel fermentation. With their Rieslings, the Obesters pioneered a new California-style using a cold fermentation to give the wine a fruity style. This style is a good balance for shellfish — just the right balance of sugar and acid.

The Obesters have recently bought 70 acres in the Anderson Valley of Mendocino County and hope in the future to grow their own grapes. Paul and Sandy believe that this is the right region for the quality of grape that is the hallmark of their wines. ❧

Sunrise Winery

Address: 13100 Montebello Road, Cupertino 95014
□ (408) 741-1310
Visitation: Friday through Sunday, 11 AM to 3 PM
Principals: Ronald and Rolayne Stortz
Varietals produced: Chardonnay, Pinot Noir, Zinfandel, and Cabernet Sauvignon
Production: 2,500 cases per year

A visit to Sunrise Winery is liking taking a trip back into history. There is not only a winery and a ranch house but a large recreation area with hiking and riding trails and picnic facilities as well. The entire property, known as the Picchetti Ranch Area, is a 307-acre parcel which is managed by the Midpeninsula Regional Open Space District.

The site is named for Italian immigrant brothers Vincenzo and Secondo Picchetti who settled the area in the 1880s. Vincenzo Picchetti had been working for the Jesuits at Villa Maria, and the church helped him obtain some property he could farm. The ranch house was built in 1886 and the brick winery was added in 1896. They farmed and established a winery as did several other immigrants who had settled on the Monte Bello Ridge. Wine merchants from San Francisco used to drive wagons loaded with redwood tanks to the wineries in the Santa Cruz Mountains and purchase wine in bulk from various wineries to blend into their own product.

The winery was operated under the Picchetti Brothers label until 1963. But it had gone through hard times before it closed — the phylloxera epidemic, Prohibition, and the mechanization of agriculture. Orchards gradually replaced the vineyards, and today only three acres of old Zinfandel vines remain.

In 1976, Sunrise Winery was established in the Santa Cruz Mountains by two home winemakers. Ronald and Rolayne Stortz joined Sunrise Winery in 1977. The Stortzes had always enjoyed wine and were enthusiastic home winemakers. Ronald Stortz has an accounting practice in

San Jose, and his wife Rolayne worked as a medical technologist until the early 1980s when the winery became her full time occupation.

In 1978, a fire completely destroyed their winery near Santa Cruz. Although one of the partners left, the winery was rebuilt. In 1983, however, the other partner, Keith Hohlfeldt became winemaker for David Bruce winery.

Ron and Rolayne stuck with it. They had come to realize that the Santa Cruz winery was inadequate. Consequently, in the fall of 1983 they moved the operation to the old Picchetti winery. Ron and Rolayne had been talking with the Midpeninsula Open Space District about the old winery since 1981 and finally negotiated a 25-year lease on the buildings and on the three acres of 80-year-old Zinfandel vines.

A lovely old hand-carved wine barrel, dating back to the turn of the century, sits at the winery. It was part of the California exhibit at the 1904 World's Fair in St. Louis. Mr. Picchetti purchased the barrel from a neighboring winery in 1908, and it has been on the property ever since.

Rolayne Stortz makes the wines with the help of consulting winemaker Lanny Replogle of Fenestra Winery. Each wine is made using traditional methods of winemaking to bring out the varietal character of each grape. "There is a certain joy in following the whole process of winemaking." she says. "Also, there is an element of suspense because you're never sure how it will turn out."

All of the grapes, except for the Zinfandel grown on the property, are purchased, mostly from the Santa Cruz mountains, Sonoma County and San Luis Obispo. Rolayne works closely with the growers and uses only hand-picked grapes.

The Pinot Noirs and Zinfandels ferment on wild yeast. Somtimes yeast is added as necessary. This is often the case when grapes come from small vineyards which did not use pesticides.

Rolayne and Ronald hope to plant about 40 acres in grapes on the property in the future and would like to increase their production to 10,000 cases per year. ❧

Woodside Vineyards

Address: 340 Kings Mountain Road, Woodside 94062
   □ (415) 851-7475
Visitation: By appointment, and invitational tastings
Principals: Robert L. and Polly Mullen
Varietals produced: Chardonnay, Pinot Noir, Zinfandel, and Cabernet Sauvignon
Production: 1,000 cases per year

Each weekend from September to late October, friends of Bob and Polly Mullen are invited to help with the picking, crushing, and stemming of grapes from about 12 vineyards in the Woodside area to make the Woodside Vineyards wine. It is purely a labor of love and fun, and everyone enjoys it. During the weekdays of harvest time, help is also hired to pick grapes.

Grape growing and winemaking are not new to this area of the San Francisco Bay Peninsula, which is within commuting distance of San Francisco. From the early 1870s onward, there were numerous small vineyards and wineries in what is today the Woodside community. In 1889, there were 800 acres planted in grapes. There was a ready local market for this wine with the many lumber mill crews in the area.

Phylloxera, the dreaded virus root disease, killed many of the vineyards in the early 1900s, and Prohibition struck a final blow to many of the wineries in the area. Most of the small winery buildings have long since deteriorated, but a few have been converted to elegant homes.

Polly and Bob Mullen, owners of Woodside Vineyards, grew up in the midwest and were high school sweethearts. They married and moved to California in 1954. Prior to coming to California, they had not experienced the enjoyment of wine. The first day on his new job, Bob was taken to lunch, and wine was served with the meal with the explanation "You're a Californian now." From then on, wine became very much a part of the Mullens' life. They went to many wine tastings, and at one such tasting in 1959, they met Bev and Bob Groetzinger, who had been producing wine from grapes grown on their home property. Soon after, the two couples went into partnership and, in 1960, started making wine together.

At the same time, Polly and Bob looked for property on which not only to build a house, but also a small winery. What they found was a piece of land in Woodside that already had a vineyard on it. Bob negotiated with the real estate agent and the owner of the property to let him harvest the grapes before he actually purchased the land. One could call it a trial marriage with grapes. The trial marriage proved a success, and, in 1963, after the Mullens' home and winery was completed, the Woodside winery was bonded. ❧

The property is in a rural residential community, so the winery is designed to fit unobtrusively into the living area complex. It is dug into a small hillside next to the house with the carport on top. At crush time, the carport is used for crushing, and the juice descends by gravity flow through a trapdoor in the carport deck into the fermentation tanks below.

Two varieties of grapes are grown on the two acres of Mullen vineyards — Pinot Noir and Chardonnay. They also have a working arrangement with nine small local vineyards. In exchange for tending the vines during the year — pruning, plowing, training, and harvesting — the Mullens secure the grapes. Two of these small vineyards are the remaining portion of the 100-year-old La Questa Vineyards, which was part of the Groetzinger property. These vineyards were planted in Cabernet Sauvignon over 100 years ago. They are still producing and are the primary source of this varietal for Woodside Vineyards.

In 1970, the Groetzingers moved to London, leaving the Mullens as sole owners of the winery. In honor of the old vines and their former partners, all of the Mullens' Cabernet Sauvignon bears the label La Questa.

Each year the Woodside Village Church gives a blessing of the grapes. The Mullens reciprocate by donating part of their red wines to the church for use as sacramental wines.

As the winery and its output grew, Bob Mullen had to make a decision. His hobby was turning into a second business. Since he had a demanding and full-time career as western regional manager of the Armstrong Company, he could not devote the time necessary to the development and operation of the winery. He needed a winemaker, which he found in the person of Frank Churchill. This arrangement has worked out beautifully for both Frank and Bob.

Frank lives in San Francisco and commutes to Woodside three times a week. On the other days, he heads north to attend classes in enology at U.C. Davis. Previously, he worked at Paul Masson, but he enjoys his position at Woodside Vineyards because he can "take charge of each barrel as if it were my own."

Bob and Polly Mullen do not want their winery to grow. They relish the contact with the 100 or so friends who participate in the grape picking each season. Polly always serves a buffet at the end of each working session, and the harvest becomes a social gathering as well as hard work. Bob has the satisfaction of enjoying two professional careers — one in the world of big business, and the other in the creation of truly fine wines which can be enjoyed by his family, his friends, and his customers. ❧

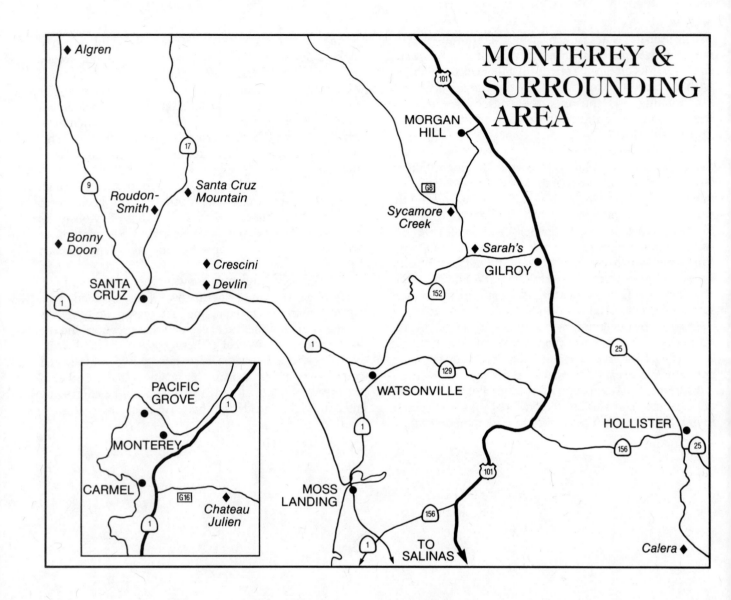

MONTEREY &
SURROUNDING
AREA

◆ Algren

101

17

9

MORGAN
HILL

Roudon-
Smith ◆

◆ Santa Cruz
Mountain

G8

Sycamore ◆
Creek

◆ Bonny
Doon

◆ Crescini

◆ Sarah's

GILROY

SANTA
CRUZ

◆ Devlin

152

25

1

1

129

WATSONVILLE

HOLLISTER

PACIFIC
GROVE

1

1

156

25

MONTEREY

MOSS
LANDING

101

CARMEL

G16

◆
Chateau
Julien

1

156

1

TO
SALINAS

Calera ◆

Wineries of

MONTEREY & SURROUNDING AREA

Ahlgren Vineyard
Bonny Doon Vineyard
Calera Wine Company
Chateau Julien
Crescini Wines
Devlin Wine Cellars
Roudon-Smith Vineyards
Santa Cruz Mountain Vineyard
Sarah's Vineyard
Sycamore Creek Vineyards

Monterey & Surrounding Area

Monterey became the first capital of California almost 200 years ago under Spanish rule. It remained the capital under Mexican rule until early statehood, and was the focal point for social, economic, and political development in California long before either Los Angeles or San Francisco became influential.

Today the counties surrounding Monterey — Monterey, Santa Cruz, San Benito, and Santa Clara — continue to be focal points for the continuing development of premium grape growing and winemaking in California. This region has 33,000 acres of grapes under cultivation, more than either the Napa or Sonoma regions. Over 90% of these vineyards are in the fertile Salinas Valley, which extends for more than 100 miles from Monterey Bay in the north to Paso Robles in the south. The valley is bordered on the west by the Santa Lucia Mountains and on the east by the Gabilan Range.

The history of this region is like a microcapsule of the history and development of the California wine industry. The Carmel Mission planted the first vineyard in the region soon after the mission was founded in 1770. Not long thereafter, the Soledad and San Juan Bautista Missions also planted vineyards. The Spanish and Mexican governors of California awarded huge land grants to their subjects throughout the Salinas and Santa Clara Valleys. In the 1850s, American immigrants took over much of this land, legally and otherwise, and began to develop its agricultural potential.

The Salinas Valley. in particular, experienced drastic ownership changes in the 1850s because entire 20,000 acre ranches were sold just to pay off back taxes. Land previously used for livestock quickly became seas of grain. With the development of the railroad in the area, other crops which had to be quickly marketed were developed. Today the Salinas Valley produces a wide variety of vegetables, including lettuce, artichokes, and tomatoes for which this fertile valley is particularly well known.

At the south end of the Salinas Valley, starting around Greenfield and extending beyond Kings City to the Monterey County border, are thousands of acres of wine vineyards planted to take advantage of the cool evenings created by the slightly higher elevations and ocean breezes. These vineyards were developed primarily by Almaden, Mirassou, and Paul Masson as their production grew and urbanization took over their Bay Area vineyard properties.

There are three other grape growing areas of significance in the extended Monterey region. The areas include the Santa Cruz Mountains and its famed Chaine d'Or, the San Benito area south of Hollister, and the San Martin-Gilroy area south of San Jose. Two of these, Santa Cruz and San Benito, produce some of the finest Pinot Noir and Chardonnay made in North America.

The Santa Cruz Mountain wine growing area is located high on the ridges between the San Francisco Bay and the Pacific Ocean. While the area has never been known to have more than 1,000 acres in grape cultivation at any one time, the quality of the wine produced from grapes grown in this area has been recognized worldwide for almost 100 years. The area specializes in Chardonnay, Cabernet Sauvignon, Zinfandel, and Pinot Noir. The term "Chaine d'Or" was coined by Paul Masson and others before the turn of the century, because they saw the area as a source of exceptional wine grapes and world-class wines.

The San Benito River Valley south of Hollister also became known as a source of fine wine grapes. The upper slopes of the Gabilan Range, with its deposits of chalky soil and cool clean evening breezes, has become a source of Pinot Noir grapes superior to none.

At the southern end of the Santa Clara Valley in the hills west of Gilroy lies the fourth winegrowing area in the Monterey region. While small, this Hecker Pass and Uvas Valley area's wine making history dates back to the late 1800s when local ranchers and Italian immigrants started raising grapes. Many of these wineries are active today, frequently making use of the original vines planted in the late 1880s. ❧

Ahlgren Vineyard

Address: 20320 Highway 9, Boulder Creek 95006
  □ (408) 338-6071
Visitation: Periodic tastings, by appointment only
Principals: Dexter and Valerie E. Ahlgren
Varietals produced: Semillon, Chardonnay, and
  Cabernet Sauvignon
Production: 1,500 cases per year

There are many different family-owned winery buildings in California — old wineries which have been refurbished, newly designed state-of-the-art ones, and ones which, through the ingenuity of its owners combined old equipment with modern techniques. The winery of Dexter and Valerie Ahlgren is one of the latter, having been built as part of the Ahlgrens' home in the Santa Cruz Mountains.

In 1969, Valerie became interested in home winemaking. She started making mead, elderberry wine, and beer as a hobby. The hobby progressed further and by 1972 she had interested her daughter, Dennelle, and her husband Dexter, in her winemaking projects. That year they crushed two tons of Zinfandel in their driveway and made wine in the garage.

The project was a success and the Ahlgrens decided to become serious about winemaking. Consequently, they bought some property in the Santa Cruz mountains, and establish a vineyard. The acreage they purchased had been a vineyard 100 years ago; grapes, on a commercial basis, had been grown in that region for many years. Before Prohibition, there were 2,000 acres in vineyards in the area, while today there are only a little over 200.

Not only did the Ahlgrens want to build a winery, they also wanted to build a home. Dexter, who was the city engineer for the city of Los Altos on the San Francisco Peninsula, had established his own consulting firm and was ready to leave urban sprawl for a place in the mountains. At the time, Valerie taught English and speech at nearby De Anza College.

An architect friend helped them design an energy efficient home and winery. Solar panels and a wood-burning stove heat the home. The winery, built into the side of their hillside property, is located in the cellar where it is naturally cool, while the residence is upstairs. Dexter and Valerie are "do-it-yourselfers," and on weekends over a period of three years, they hand-built their home and winery. They spent six months milling all the lumber from redwood trees which they had purchased from their neighbors. Recycled doors and windows were used in the house. Openings were designed to fit these surplus fixtures. The maple floor of their home came from a school gymnasium which was being dismantled.

In the course of all of this building, Valerie set out 300 vines of Chardonnay in an area which she and Dexter had cleared for a vineyard. The property is located at an elevation of 1,500 feet elevation and receives coastal fogs and warm days, well suited to grape growing. Unfortunately there was one problem to this idealistic setting in the mountains: the ground water contains salt which is not tolerated by grape vines. They were forced to construct rain water collectors and a 125,000-gallon water tank for both vineyard and household use. The Ahlgrens lost much of the first plantings to drought and are replanting their vineyard with Chardonnay grapes which will start producing estate wines in the next few years. For the first couple of years, Valerie is using drip irrigation with rainwater from the water tank reservoir, but the vineyard will ultimately be dry farmed.

Presently, the grapes must be purchased. Most come from the Santa Cruz Mountains; some from the Napa Valley. The Chardonnay is from the famous Ventana vineyard in Monterey County.

Valerie, Dexter, and Dennelle (who is the assistant winemaker) believe in using old-fashioned methods to produce their wines. There is only one stainless steel tank, which is used strictly as a holding tank prior to bottling. There is also a classic roller crusher and an antique double ratchet basket press. Small wooden fermenters with open tops are used for fermenting the red wine.

The roller crusher is used for the whites — Semillon and Chardonnay. After pressing, the juice goes into the tank for settling and then it is transferred into barrels for fermentation. The Chardonnay goes through malolactic fermentation for complexity and stability. The Cabernet Sauvignon is fermented in small open-top fermenters with the cap being punched down frequently. After fermentation, the wine is aged in small American oak barrels.

Although the Ahlgrens use a great deal of old-fashioned equipment and traditional techniques in their wine making, they do utilize modern technology when they feel it contributes to the end product. Modern stainless steel bottling equipment, although not automatic, assures that no excess oxygen gets into the bottle. The wine labels include hand lettering and are signed by Valerie and Dexter, the winemakers.

Winemaking is a joint effort for the three Ahlgrens.

Dennelle, who took some courses at the University of California at Davis and worked at various wineries in the Santa Cruz mountain area, takes care of most of the cellar work. They try to extract the best from each vintage and use a handmade approach to winemaking. Although the Ahlgrens' production is small, they take great pride in the premium wines they make. ❧

Bonny Doon Vineyard

Address: 10 Pine Flat Road, Bonny Doon 95060
☐ (408) 425-3625

Visitation: Summer: Tuesday through Sunday 12 noon to 6 PM
Rest of year: Saturday and Sunday, 12 noon to 5:30 PM

Principals: Alan Grahm, Randall Grahm

Varietals produced: Marsanne, Chardonnay, Vin Gris Viognier, Pinot Noir, Syrah, Cabernet Sauvignon, and Muscat Canelli

Production: 9,000 cases per year

Marsanne, Viognier, Syrah — these are not the usual varietals grown for winemaking in California. Randall Grahm of Bonny Doon Vineyard is not the usual winemaker, either. Why these varieties? "Because it is exciting. It's never been done, except for some Syrah. I love Rhone wines. I'm bored with what people in California are doing[making]....Cabernet...and Chardonnay to pay the bills... but I don't think they really represent what California is capable of doing," said Randall Grahm, 33, who is one of the most innovative winemakers in California and is a true wine adventurer.

Randall Grahm's interest in wine evolved over a period of years in three different stages. While a student in philosophy at U.C. Santa Cruz he attended weekly wine tastings. Then, while on a visit to Denmark, he saw a woman making wine in her bathtub and was impressed. The third influence was working for a Beverly Hills wine shop where he was exposed to fine old French wines. Drinking these fine French wines was not enough. He wanted to make what was in the bottle — he wanted to do something creative. His palate had been excited by the great wines of Europe, particularly of the Rhone Valley.

Like so many other vintners, Randall Grahm believes in the cliché that great wine begins in the vineyard. This conviction caused him to go to the University of California at Davis to earn a degree in plant science in 1979. "Being a city kid and not knowing anything about plants or grape growing," Randall says "I felt that viticulture would be a good background for winemaking." After all,

he knew the style of wine he wanted to make.

After searching for vineyard land in California, Oregon and Washington, Randall returned to the Santa Cruz area for his search and found what he wanted near the small town of Bonny Doon. Although there is an average of 50 inches rainfall per year in the area, the climate is very similar to the Rhone Valley in France. With the aid of his father, Alan Grahm, who is an importer in Los Angeles, he purchased 48 acres of land. After clearing the property of trees, Randall planted 22 acres of grapes.

In addition to Chardonnay and Pinot Noir, Randall planted the Bordeaux varieties — Cabernet Sauvignon, Cabernet Franc, Merlot, Malbec, and Petit Verdot — as well as Syrah, Cinsault, Marsanne, Roussanne, and Viognier, all varietals of the Rhone Valley. He believes that the white, Marsanne and Viognier, will gain as much acceptance in California as they have in the Rhone. The first bottlings of Marsanne will be released this year.

In order to get enough stock of the Viognier, Randall purchased cuttings from the New York State Experimental Station in Geneva, New York and propagated new vines. He did the same with the Marsanne and Roussanne.

Randall Grahm planted his vineyard in the European style — much closer together than Americans were doing. Instead of the usual 450 vines per acre he has 1,700 per acre on either a 3-feet x 8-feet or 6-feet x 4-feet spacing. The European theory is that the quality of the grape improves when it is denser because the vine has to fight harder to get its nutrients — stressed grapes. He also uses a different trellis method which calls for hedge trimming, thereby exposing more of the fruit to direct sunlight. Sunburn has not been a problem in the woodsy location of the vineyards close to the Pacific Ocean.

In order to gain winemaking experience, Randall worked for a time at other wineries in the Santa Cruz Mountains while still tending his vineyards. In 1981 and 1982, Grahm produced the Bonny Doon wines from purchased grapes at other facilities until his winery could be completed. In 1983, a former equipment rental shed was renovated and transformed into the winery. In 1985, a fire caused by faulty wiring destroyed a portion of the winery, which then had to be rebuilt. The winery was fronted by a rustic bar and restaurant which Randall converted to a tasting room. As he says, it is in downtown Bonny Doon: "As a matter of fact, we are downtown Boony Doon."

Not only are the viticulture practices of Randall Grahm

unorthodox, but his winemaking techniques are as well — when compared to the usual practices in California. He believes that a Chardonnay should be light, lively, and delicate. All of the Chardonnay is barrel fermented. To minimize the risk of the wine picking up too much oak flavor he leaves the wine on the lees. The wine is racked only if there is a problem, otherwise it is left until bottling. This "sur lie" technique is used for all Bonny Doon white wines. In this way, the wine is not subjected to as much oxidation. The method also works well in promoting malolactic fermentation.

Vin Gris is the French term for white wine made from red grapes. In 1984, Randall made a Vin Gris of 81% Pinot Noir and 19% Chardonnay. This year it is a Vin Gris of Grenache. The usual California method of making these wines is to cold ferment the juice with little or no skin contact. Randall Grahm, on the other hand, treats this wine like his other whites with the "sur lie" method of fermentation.

Pinot Noir is a notoriously difficult wine to make, and here, too, Randall Grahm does things his own way. He picks 75% of the grapes at 21.5 degrees Brix. The grapes are completely destemmed, partially crushed, and then the fermentation process is started. Randall punches down the cap several times a day during fermentation. When the wine approaches dryness, he picks the other 25% of the grapes and dumps the whole berries into the fermentor. In this way the fermentation time can be extended to about 20 days. The wine is put into the barrel with heavy lees and racked only when necessary.

Each year Bonny Doon also produces a proprietary red wine which is a blend of all of the Bordeaux grapes.

Randall Grahm, who has proved that a small winery doing things differently from the norm can be successful, does not march in the band of most vintners — he brings his own music and, most of the time, his own drummer.

Calera Wine Company

Address: 11300 Cienega Road, Hollister 95023
□ (408) 637-9170
Visitation: 9 AM to 5 PM, by appointment only
Principals: Josh and Jeanne Jensen
Varietals produced: Chardonnay, Pinot Noir, and Zinfandel
Production: 10,000 cases per year

Calera means "lime kiln" in Spanish. Josh Jensen of Calera believes that in order to produce a true and fine Burgundian style Pinot Noir, the grapes must be grown in limestone soil. For years, California winemakers have been trying to emulate the French Burgundies. According to the critics, only a few have succeeded — one of the stars is Calera's Pinot Noir as created by Josh Jensen and Steve Doerner, owner and winemaker respectively. In the fall of 1984, Jensen's Calera 1982 Selleck Pinot Noir won the Platinum award as the best Pinot Noir in America at the American Wine Competition in New York.

Josh Jensen is a native of California. He graduated from Yale in 1966 with a degree in history, and the following year was doing graduate work at Oxford, where he was first introduced to the fine Burgundies of France. While at Oxford he was a member of the rowing team. He is still active in sports, competing in a French 80 mile-a-day, three-day bicycle trek each summer. He competes very favorably every year and hopes not only to beat the French at bicycle racing soon, but also at producing the best Pinot Noir.

After leaving Oxford in 1969, Josh Jensen spent two years in France, studying the techniques of making Burgundies (Pinot Noir). He worked two consecutive crushes and was an apprentice to several winemakers in Burgundy. After reading all he could about the Pinot Noir grape and observing the French techniques, he became convinced that the limestone soil in which the grapes were grown was a major contributing factor to the excellence of the French Burgundies.

Upon his return to California in 1972, Josh, equipped with geological maps, went up and down the state seeking property for sale having limestone soil on which to establish his vineyards. It took two years for Josh to find that type of property. It is located at 2,200 feet in the Gabilan Mountains, south of Hollister, in San Benito County (90 miles south of San Francisco), and it had a limestone kiln on the property. The kiln had been built at the turn of the century, and the remains are still visible. There is the right amount of limestone in the soil for the growing of Jensen's Pinot Noir grapes. Also, since the property is located on a plateau 30 miles from the Pacific Ocean, it gets cooling breezes which are necessary for grape growing in warm climates.

Josh spent a year clearing out oak and pine trees and underbrush to ready the land for planting. In 1975, he finished planting 24 acres of Pinot Noir grapes in three distinct vineyards, each parcel with its own natural boundaries. He named the three vineyards Selleck, Reed, and Jensen. In 1984, an additional 12 acres of Pinot Noir and the first six acres of Chardonnay were planted alongside the other vineyards. These new vineyards began bearing in 1986. Calera's Zinfandel grapes are purchased from a neighboring vineyard.

In 1977, Josh Jensen purchased a nearby never-completed rock crushing plant which proved to be perfect for his winery operation. Since the plant was built in a terraced fashion it allowed for natural gravity flow of the wine, from crushing on one level to fermentation on the next, to aging on the third and bottling on the fourth. This proved to be advantageous to the Pinot Noir grapes, since they are quite fragile and easily oxidized. They do not like too much handling.

Since the winery, or old rock plant, is located on the San Andreas earthquake fault, Josh had to reinforce the foundations, including the sinking of 30-foot concrete pillars, before he could commence operations. Steel beams had to be added to strengthen the retaining walls. Seven hundred cubic feet of concrete were poured to make the structure earthquake safe.

On the same property there was also a residence which enabled Josh, Jeanne, and their four children to live near the winery. They still retain a part-time residence in San Francisco.

In 1978, Calera produced its first estate wines with Josh Jensen the winemaker. As the production of the vineyards and the winery grew, Steve Doerner, a graduate of U.C. Davis with a degree in biochemistry, was engaged as winemaker. He and Josh work very closely together.

When the Pinot Noir grapes arrive at the top level of the winery they are put into the crusher which is movable on wheels, much like a railroad car. The crusher is positioned over the stainless steel tank which will receive the crushed grapes. The Pinot Noir grapes, however, are not crushed. The crusher only acts as a means of transport.

Steve Doerner says that since Pinot Noir is notorious for fast fermentation, the fermentation process is different. Whole grapes, including the stems, are put into the open top stainless tank. This slows the fermentation process and spreads it out over a period of about ten days to two weeks. Through this extended skin contact, the wine gets additional color. "In this way," Steve says, "the sugars are released over a period of several days." Natural yeast is used for the fermentation, and the cap is punched down twice a day. When the cap falls, the juice is lightly pressed and transferred through gravity flow to a holding tank on the next level down. Then the wine goes into the barrels with the lees for aging. It is racked one month before bottling. Egg white fining is used just prior to bottling.

The Calera Chardonnay is 100% barrel fermented, after being crushed and lightly pressed. Each varietal is treated differently and can receive maximum attention since Calera only produces three varietals. Steve relies on the natural yeasts for the fermentation of all of the wines. Steve and Josh follow the rule that lab work is done in the lab and not in the winery. They do not want to experiment with their wines, especially their precious Pinot Noir.

Josh Jensen's persistence in proving that the soil is the key to excellent Pinot Noir has proven that a first class Burgundian style Pinot Noir can be made in California. After all, it did win the best American Pinot Noir award in 1984. ❧

Chateau Julien

Address: 8940 Carmel Valley Road, Carmel 93923
□ (408) 624-2600
Visitation: Monday through Friday, 8:30 AM to 5 PM
Saturday and Sunday, 1 PM to 4 PM
Principals: Robert and Patricia Brower
Varietals produced: Sauvignon Blanc, Chardonnay,
Johannisberg Riesling, Merlot, and Cabernet
Sauvignon
Production: 20,000 cases per year

Chateau Julien is a handsome white building of French and Spanish architecture complete with turrets, stained glass windows, wrought iron fixtures, oak panelling, and antique furnishings. It sits on the bend in the highway in Carmel Valley. The homeowners are proud to have this building in their neighborhood. It is beautifully landscaped and seven acres of vineyards will be planted at the back of the winery in the near future.

Pat and Bob Brower, both in their thirties, are originally from New Jersey and New York respectively. Their backgrounds were in the transportation and oil industries, but they had always dreamed of owning a winery. After several trips to the West Coast, driving up and down the wine growing areas and not finding an appropriate winery for sale, they decided to purchase property and build their own. Both Pat and Bob liked the wines they had tasted which had been made from Monterey County grapes. They decided that this was the fruit they wanted to use in

their own winery, and that they would locate their winery near where the fruit is grown.

When Pat and Bob moved West to become vintners, several members of their combined family — aunt, uncle, and several cousins — came with them to work in the new facility. The people who work at Chateau Julien are "like an extended family," says Pat.

The winery building is not only the facility for making wine, but it also contains: offices; a test kitchen where cooking classes are frequently conducted; a hospitality center for dinners, wine tastings, and wine seminars; and a complete sales room with gift shop. Anything and everything concerned with wine is under one roof. There also have been several weddings held at the winery and in its gardens.

Since its beginning in 1984, Chateau Julien has conducted extensive cooking and wine appreciation classes. The object of this "wine and food adventure" is to teach consumers how to cook with wine and how to pair wine with food. The classes emphasize the different flavors which can be achieved when cooking the same basic dish with different varietals. "There is a great difference cooking a chicken with Sauvignon Blanc versus using Chardonnay," says Tim Siemsen, Marketing Director of Chateau Julien. Frequently, guest chefs from the Monterey-Carmel area restaurants are featured at the all day cooking seminars.

Bill Anderson, a Stanford and U.C. Davis enology graduate, is the winemaker at Chateau Julien. In his short tenure since the official 1984 opening of the winery, he has produced some unique and award-winning wines. The Chateau Julien Chardonnays are from four different vineyards with three being vineyard-designated, the other going into the proprietary blend. Bill strives to make soft, round, subtle wines that are very drinkable fresh, but will also age well. To this end, he barrel ferments the Chardonnay, either totally or partially, depending on the vintage.

Chateau Julien's Sauvignon Blanc is fermented in stainless steel with no oak aging. Bill likes to retain the acid in the wine for a crisp finish.

In its first years of existence, Chateau Julien has won numerous medals and has had its wine served at the White House. The 1982 Merlot, which was served at a White House State dinner, was chosen the "Most Desirable Merlot in the Nation" at the American 1984 Wine Championships. 🍃

Crescini Wines

Address: 2621 Old San Jose Road, Soquel 95037
☐ (408) 462-1466
Visitation: Weekends only, by appointment
Principals: Richard and Paulé Crescini
Varietals produced: Chenin Blanc, Merlot, and
    Cabernet Sauvignon
Production: 900 cases per year

Each year as Richard and Paulé Crescini made more and more wine, the romance, intrigue, and mystique of winemaking grew and became stronger for them. Also each year, crush time created the urge to do further experimentation and to make more and different styles of wines. Finally, in 1980, the Crescinis decided to make wine on a commercial basis and became a bonded winery.

The Crescinis had been making wines for family and friends in their garage since 1975. Richard, as a small boy, became intrigued with winemaking while watching his Italian grandfather, who had settled in the Santa Cruz area, make wine in the traditional Italian style for family use. In later years he took courses at U.C. Davis to enhance his winemaking techniques.

Not only do the Crescinis have a common interest in winemaking, but they have common career interests as well. Both Richard and Paulé have full-time occupations in the field of radiology. Richard, who has a degree in health science, is the manager of the radiology department of a local hospital, while Paulé, who has a degree in radiological technology, is chief radiology technologist at another local hospital.

In 1980, Richard and Paulé converted an old horse barn on his property into the winery. They purchase grapes from two regions of Napa Valley and from Monterey County — the Merlot and Cabernet Sauvignon from the former, and Chenin Blanc from the latter. Even though Richard is planning to expand the capacity of the winery

he will still continue to purchase grapes. The Crescinis have planted a small vineyard of Gewurztraminer to enable them to produce this varietal wine — a favorite of theirs — for their own use.

Having a small winery operation Richard Crescini and his wife Paulé can take the time to hand process each wine. They select individual small lots of grapes from various areas of vineyards in California, and they experiment with each wine they produce to get the optimum of fruitiness and complexity.

The Crescini Chenin Blanc is in a dry style. It is fermented in 60-gallon French oak barrels on the lees and stirred up every two weeks. This French "sur lies" method helps give the Chenin Blanc some complexity and a soft oakiness. After fermentation, it is also aged in French oak barrels.

Working with small lots of wine, no more than 700 gallons at a time, gives Richard the opportunity to employ several strains of yeast in the fermentation. Sometimes as many as three different yeast strains may be used — 75% of one, 15% of another, and 10% of a third. This diverse use of various yeasts results in more fruity wine with lots of berry taste. Also, the amount of tannins tend to be less. The reds are fermented in stainless steel and aged in 60-gallon French oak barrels. Usually, the Cabernet Sauvignon has 3% to 5% of Merlot added for softness, and the Merlot has 3% to 5% of Cabernet Sauvignon for complexity.

Richard and Paulé Crescini plan to expand their winery in the near future and build a new tasting room. Although operating a small winery in their spare time is hard work, it is a rewarding effort for them. Richard enjoys tracking the development process from the juice to the finished wine, and they both enjoy having the family involved in the various activities of the winery. Currently, most of their wine is sold in the Santa Cruz-Soquel area, thereby giving them more time to devote to the making of fine wines. 🍃

Devlin Wine Cellars

Address: P.O. Box 728, Soquel 95073 □ (408) 476-7288
Tasting Room: 2815 Porter Street, Soquel 95073
Visitation: Tasting room, daily, 12 noon to 5 pm
Principals: Charles Devlin
Varietals produced: White Riesling, Chardonnay, White Zinfandel, Merlot, Cabernet Sauvignon, and Muscat Canelli
Production: 5,000 cases per year.

Most boys at age ten want to become firemen, doctors, or astronauts when they grow up. But not Charles Devlin. From the time he can remember he wanted to be a winemaker and maybe someday own a winery.

Chuck grew up near Soquel where his father is an orthopedic surgeon. As a high school student he worked during the summers at the nearby Bargetto Winery in the Santa Cruz mountains. After graduation from high school, Devlin went on to U.C. Davis to graduate in 1975 with a degree in fermentation science. In the next few years he worked for several wineries, including Louis Martini in Napa Valley and Lords & Elwood in Santa Clara. He also spent time at the Wiederkehr Winery in Arkansas.

In 1978, Chuck started his own winery in a wooden barn on his parents' 30-acre ranch in the hills near Soquel overlooking the Monterey Bay. The winery building is not pretentious, and as Chuck says, "I've put money where it counts — into the wine, not into buildings. We buy only the best grapes, barrels, etc., — all of those things that influence the taste of the wine."

Devlin's winery is not high tech as are those of the "big boys." His presses and fermentation tanks are adequate, definitely not high capacity. His first crush in 1978 totalled only 16 tons. Quite a feat, however, for a one-man operation, but not unusual for a man of his stamina. Chuck, who competed for 15 years in judo and freestyle wrestling, was a member of several national and international judo teams and is the holder of a black belt.

As with most small operations, the bottles are filled and corked by hand. Is there quality control? "Yes. I pull out anything that looks funny," Chuck said. Labels have been the "stickiest part of winemaking so far," he added. It seems that the manufacturers of labels do not tell you about the kind of glue necessary for the label to adhere to the bottle, and the glue suppliers do not apprise you of the special kind of paper needed for their glue.

Even with all the problems of running a small winery, Devlin's wines — whites as well as reds — have been consistent gold medal and sweepstake winners at the major competitions. His wines were chosen as a gift of premium quality wine by the University of California and presented to Chairman Deng Xiaoping of the People's Republic of China.

Devlin raises no grapes, but buys from older dry farmed hillside vineyards. He does not try to emulate French theories of making wine or produce a French style of wine. Chuck uses California grapes and tries to produce a superior American product.

Devlin Wine Cellars' Cabernet Sauvignon and Merlot tend to be on the fruity side since they are fermented at cooler-than-normal temperatures. Another contributing factor to this pleasant fruity taste is a minimum amount of handling of the grapes. Since the winery has extra equipment available, it can handle crush and fermentation when the grapes are ready to be picked.

His philosophy of marketing is unique also. He uses no distributors or brokers, but sells his wines directly within a 100-mile radius of the winery. Chuck's wife Cheryl, who has a degree in agro-economics from U.C. Berkeley, handles most of the marketing chores — servicing each of their accounts, delivering the product, and stocking the shelves. Devlin's attractive tasting room in downtown Soquel is an important outlet for his wines.

Devlin Wine Cellars' labels feature local artists, which vary from time to time. Two artistic works of his young son Thomas (painted at age 18 months and three years) are featured on the Chardonnay and the Cabernet Sauvignon. Even at that young age the modernistic paintings reproduced are quite professional looking. Other more seasoned local artists used on the labels included Phil Haysmer and Chris Carothers.

When asked what is his greatest enjoyment from being a winemaker, Charles Devlin replies, "The pleasure of drinking great wine and being able to offer it to the public at reasonable prices." ❧

Roudon-Smith Vineyards

Address: 2364 Bean Creek Road, Santa Cruz 95066
□ (408) 438-1244
Tasting Room: 2571 Main Street, Soquel 95073
Visitation: Saturday, 10 am to 4 pm, by appointment
only. Tasting Room: Wednesday through Sunday, 12
noon to 5 pm
Principals: Robert and Annamaria Roudon, James and
June Smith
Varietals produced: Pinot Blanc, Chardonnay, White
Zinfandel, Pinot Noir, Zinfandel, Petite Sirah, and
Cabernet Sauvignon
Production: 10,000 cases per year

Compatible as "peas in a pod" is a good description of
the relationship of the two couples who are the working partners of Roudon-Smith Vineyards.

The winery idea was actually conceived in the late
1960s by Bob and Annamaria Roudon as an alternative
lifestyle to hectic corporate life in Los Angeles. Although
Bob was from an anti-alcohol Texas background, he became interested in French and German wines when he
was serving in Germany with the U.S. army in the early
1950s. It was during that time that he met and married
Annamaria who was born and raised in Pfalz, West Germany — a large wine producing region not far from the
French region of Alsace.

After returning to the U.S. and attending university in
New Mexico, Bob Roudon entered the aerospace industry
in Los Angeles. During the next few years the Roudons
made several trips to France and Germany to learn more
about winemaking. Bob also learned to appreciate California wines and began making wine in his garage. He
attended U.C. Davis for courses in viticulture and
winemaking. By 1967, he became determined to make a
living as a vintner. In 1971, the Roudons moved to Santa
Clara Valley, where Bob was hired by Jim Smith to work at
Amdahl Corporation.

Jim Smith was born and raised on a dairy farm in Wisconsin and still loves the land with the passion of an
agriculturist. While on a summer work furlough from the
University of Wisconsin, Jim met June at a church social.
It was love at first sight. June and Jim were married and
moved to the San Fernando Valley where Jim worked in
engineering. June at the same time worked as a cosmetics
consultant, which gave her sales experience.

In 1971, the Smiths came to Northern California where
Jim began working for a pioneer in the electronics field —

the Amdahl Corporation. They hired him to develop the
manufacturing system, and he was authorized to hire one
other person. That person was Bob Roudon.

From the beginning of their association, they talked
wine. At the time, Jim was looking for a farm in the Santa
Cruz area, because land was cheap and Bob also was looking for land in the country to cultivate grapes.

A small parcel of land, 12 acres, was purchased in the
Santa Cruz mountains in 1972. This was to become the
first Roudon-Smith winery.

The Roudon-Smith quartet was to learn by doing. The
first year they planted Chardonnay grapes on the sunny
slopes of their property above the Branciforte Creek. These
grapes were never made into wine, however, because they
had provided excellent food for the Santa Cruz Mountain
deer. They quickly found out that fences were needed.
Research also told them that the rows of estate grapes were
too widely spaced, and that some of the rows were even
planted in the wrong direction.

The two Silicon Valley engineers began leading hectic
lives — commuting over the hill at dawn and in the
evening, working on the building of the Roudon house on
weekends (the basement of which was the first winery),
crushing grapes, and making serious wines.

The wives soon became involved in the effort. June
Smith put her marketing experiences to good use placing
the wines with distributors and into the restaurant trade.
Annamaria Roudon, who had worked in Los Angeles in
advertising and graphic arts, put her talents to use as the
label and brochure designer.

After several years, the wines really took on a distinctive character. The facilities became too small, and in
1978, a new building to house the winery was constructed
on Scotts Valley's Bean Road. The winery was a success,
and Bob and Jim quit their jobs to become full-time vintners.

The present facility is not pretentious, but is filled with
appropriate equipment for producing handmade wines.
The Roudon-Smiths do not want to grow much bigger
than their 10,000 case goal. They pride themselves in
seeking out individual vineyards capable of providing the
basis of fine wines. In making their wines they attempt to
capture the unique character of each vineyard within its
growing region. Only 3% of the Roudon-Smith wine is
estate grown, the rest coming from vineyards in Napa,
Sonoma, and Monterey counties.

Bob and Jim try to produce wines in the classical manner. As in Europe, most of the wines are fermented with
their own yeast. The Chardonnay is barrel fermented and
the red wines — especially the Zinfandels — are bottled
with no cellar treatment other than racking. Bob's admira-
tion for Zinfandel is long-standing, and he feels that only

American oak fermentation can preserve the unique berry-fruit and spice character of this grape.

Even today, after 14 years, the personal chemistry of the close associations of the owners still works. It is a team effort. Bob Roudon is the winemaker. Jim Smith is vineyard and production manager. June Smith is in charge of sales and public relations, and Annamarie Roudon is the graphic designer and controller.

It took guts and sacrifices to give up comforts over the past decade of launching the winery, but the Smiths and the Roudons did it. They have a freedom from "big pressures" and a four-way compatibility which Annamarie describes as "rare and wonderful."

The Roudon-Smith wine label has as a symbol an ancient Roman amphora which symbolizes the elegance and artistry that complements their wines. 🍃

Santa Cruz Mountain Vineyard

Address: 2300 Jarvis Road, Santa Cruz 95065
□ (408) 426-6209
Visitation: By appointment only
Principals: Ken D. Burnap
Varietals produced: Chardonnay, Pinot Noir, Merlot, and Cabernet Sauvignon
Production: 3,500 cases per year

Each of us has a time in our life when we would like to be doing something entirely different. Often it calls for a complete change in living and working habits — a complete change in lifestyle. Ken Burnap made such a change because a certain varietal wine had dominated and consumed his interests. He was obsessed with the idea of ultimately making award-winning Burgundian style Pinot Noirs.

Ken Burnap grew up in Texas and for many years worked with his father in construction. They were considered "Boomers," moving around the country wherever there was construction work to be done. Eventually, Ken settled in Orange County and opened his own construction business. In addition, he founded and operated the popular Hobbit Restaurant in Orange, California, just outside of Los Angeles.

One day Ken decided that he was tired of the restaurant business and all of the problems that go with running a food operation. He wanted to take some time off to pursue his hobby of winemaking. He also wanted to research anything and everything about the Pinot Noir grape.

First, he brushed up on his French, so that he could read about the Burgundian grape — how it is grown and how the wine is produced. For three years, starting in 1969, he made semi-annual trips to France to observe the growing season and the crush and winemaking procedures.

At the same time, he started looking for property on which to establish vineyards and eventually build a winery. His research took him all over the state, and he finally found what he had been looking for in the Santa Cruz Mountains. Not only was the soil and climate to the specifications he wanted, but there was an established vineyard on the property — of Pinot Noir. There had been a continuous vineyard on the property since 1863, when Zinfandel was planted. David Bruce, another vintner in the Santa Cruz Mountains, had purchased that particular property in the early 1960s and had eventually torn out all of the Zinfandel vines. Bruce proceeded to plant Pinot Noir on its own root stock instead of using grafts onto disease resistant stock. The advantage of using the varietals own root stock is that the fruit produced is more intense.

Ken Burnap purchased the property in 1972 and started building a winery. The building is constructed partially into the hillside, with three levels to utilize gravity flow from crushing, to fermentation, to barrel aging. In this fashion, the rather delicate Pinot Noir grapes receives as little handling as possible.

First released was the 1975 Pinot Noir, which, though the production was small, received critical acclaim by many wine writers. Ken Burnap smiled and said his dream was becoming a reality. His smile also hinted at the memory of that first vintage and all the mishaps that were connected with it. The grapes were gathered by volunteers who used garden shears, and some of those volunteers got into the poison oak. The grapes were fermented on their own yeast, which was not the approved method by U.C. Davis at the time. The wine was fermented at too high a temperature, and at the time the winery building was not completed for barrel aging of the wine.

All of these mishaps proved to contribute to a superior product — Santa Cruz Mountain Vineyards Pinot Noir. The wine, especially the 1981 and '83 vintages, has won many gold and silver medals in wine competitions, including a gold at the Orange County Fair. The Cabernet Sauvignon as well has received many medals and is made in a strict Bordeaux style.

All of the red wines are fermented in open top fermenters with the cap being punched down periodically. The

Pinot Noir is still fermented on its own yeast. The Cabernet and Merlot are both 100% varietal.

Ken Burnap grows about 30% of his grapes, purchasing the Cabernet Sauvignon and Chardonnay from the Santa Cruz Mountains and the Merlot from San Luis Obispo County. Recently Ken has planted more vineyards near his original property.

The research of Pinot Noir is far from over for Ken Burnap. Each vintage provides him with a new challenge —new pruning methods, new techniques to try. The job is never finished, but each year Ken produces a superior Pinot Noir. ❧

Sarah's Vineyard

Address: 4005 Hecker Pass Highway, Gilroy 95020
　☐ (408) 842-4278
Visitation: By appointment only
Principals: John and Marilyn Otteman, Steve and Donna Hicks, and Craig and Debbie McManigal
Varietals produced: Chardonnay and Johannisberg Riesling
Production: 2,000 cases per year

"Wine is a woman. She grows, matures, and refines with age." These are the terms in which Marilyn Otteman, vintner and winemaker of Sarah's Vineyard, thinks of her wines. Marilyn regards wine as a living, breathing thing and is convinced that wines are affected by the environment. She says, "First, nature infuses the grapes and their environment with its own special magic.

Then the winemaker enters the picture. "Marilyn believes that winemaking is as much an art as it is a science. "Through the entire process of harvesting, fermenting, aging, and bottling, the winemaker balances instinct and judgement with technical expertise."

Marilyn, and her husband John — with the help of their partners — started the winery in 1978, although they had bought the 10-acre vineyard property and its existing house the previous year. They planted seven acres of Chardonnay, which Marilyn features as her premier estate wine. When the time came to plant a vineyard and establish a winery, Marilyn chose the Hecker Pass area at the base of the Santa Cruz Mountains in Santa Clara County.

Sarah, Marilyn's "other spirit", (her winemaking spirit) is housed in an immaculate small winery which has touches of elegance that bespeak gracious living, such as fresh flowers, classical music, and sometimes even candlelight. All of these are merely amenities, however, since Marilyn is truly devoted to making fine Chardonnay.

Marilyn regards her Chardonnay as a growing woman. The way she describes the aging of her two distinctly different Chardonnays — from two separate vineyards — is like two ladies growing up. One grows up as a dignified young woman, becomes very sophisticated, has numerous affairs, and reaches maturity in her early thirties. The other, also in her early thirties, is stately, quite reserved, and only gives you a hint of her potential. Each Chardonnay has a different essence and complexity, and takes a different path to maturity and drinkability. One Chardonnay is upfront and exciting. The other must be contemplated to be appreciated.

Marilyn ages her Chardonnay in oak barrels, half of which are bought new each year. Most vintners retire their barrels after five years, but Marilyn prefers to replace them more often. She is very selective in the oak barrels she uses — all French. Marilyn says that "some types of oak enhance the structure of the wine, like a picture frame, while other types perk up the wine, like adding certain spices to food."

Marilyn named her winery Sarah. She describes Sarah as a woman of vitality, energy, and complexity. "Every woman has these attributes, thus enabling them to play all of the roles of life," Marilyn explained.

The seven acres of Chardonnay were planted with the help of friends, some of whose names are on signposts among the vines. "Almost everything at the winery is done by hand," explains John. Although John is very much involved in his own business, he good-naturedly keeps the equipment running and supervises sales and the business aspect of the winery — while Marilyn "takes care of Sarah." The partners in the winery are a part of Marilyn's (Sarah's) family and are always willing to lend a helping hand when called upon to do so.

The Chardonnay, fermented in oak, is made in a classical style. It is a complex wine which goes well with food. Marilyn also produces a Johannisberg Riesling from purchased grapes.

Sarah's label is a very distinctive one. It features fine engraved detail scroll work drawn by an engraver from Smith and Wesson, the arms manufacturer. John happens to be a collector of antique small arms. Marilyn says over the years she "has modified the original drawing to emulate a Fleur de Lis — the symbol of life, as old as 4,000 BC."

Marilyn wants her winery to stay small. She is deliberately limiting her production and would rather "produce quality than quantity." Even though at times Marilyn Otteman's description of her wines as women may be unusual, she is recognized for producing fine Chardonnays.

Sycamore Creek Vineyards

Address: 12775 Uvas Road, Morgan Hill 95037
□ (408) 779-4738

Visitation: Saturday and Sunday 12 noon to 5pm
   Weekdays by appointment

Principals: Terry Parks and Mary Kaye Parks

Varietals produced: Johannisberg Riesling,
   Gewurztraminer, Chardonnay, Gamay Blanc, Napa
   Gamay, Carignane, Zinfandel, and Cabernet
   Sauvignon

Production: 5,000 cases per year

On the east side of the Santa Cruz mountains and west of Morgan Hill lies a peaceful valley in which grapes have been growing for centuries — wild ones as well as cultivated. It was the wild grapes that the Spaniards found growing there when they first reached the valley; therefore they named the valley "Uvas," the Spanish word for grape.

Many of the existing vineyards in the Uvas Valley were planted in the early 1900s and belonged to a winery known as Marchetti Cellar. Prohibition forced it to close, although some of the old vineyards remained — unattended and overgrown with weeds.

In 1975, Terry Parks and his wife Mary Kaye purchased the property, rebonded it, and named it Sycamore Creek Vineyards. Sycamore Creek bisects the property. On one side of the creek are seven acres of Zinfandel and Carignane planted in the early 1900s. On the other side are new vineyards of Chardonnay and Cabernet planted by the Parkses after tearing out walnut trees.

The original Marchetti wine cellar, which was carved into the sloping creek bank, was still in existence when Terry and Mary Kaye purchased the property. The Parkses were both teaching school at the time they decided to purchase the winery and change their lifestyle. "When we bought this place we didn't really know what we were going to do with it," Terry said. After looking at the possibilities and opportunities the wine business had to offer, Mary Kaye and Terry came to the conclusion that this was an opportunity to get into a business where they could control their destinies, instead of working for somebody else. It also meant that they could raise their two small sons in the country and in a "family business."

At the time they purchased the Marchetti property the Parkses owned another ranch. They decided to sell it, however, in order to provide the funds needed to rebuild the old winery. Terry had been a home winemaker who knew what style and type of wine he liked. To him, winemaking "is made up of scientific elements, some components of good housekeeping, and providing the right environment for the product."

A mixture of old and new produce the wines of Sycamore Creek Vineyards. The old vineyards are dry farmed. The new plantings require a minimum of irrigation. Only 25% of the grapes used by Sycamore Creek are estate grown, however.

Although the Uvas Valley had long been known as a stronghold of Italian winemaking families whose forte was dry red wines, Terry Parks chose to make a variety of whites along with the reds grown on the property. Deviating from the traditional path of buying grapes from local growers, he started buying white grapes from Monterey County, and today about 65% of Sycamore Creek's production is white wine.

Since Terry believes that good winemaking is, in part, a function of good housekeeping and fastidious quality control, he prefers stainless steel fermentation to barrel fermentation for his Chardonnay. "Barrel fermentation is just too messy," he says. "If you start with good grapes you can ferment in stainless and get better temperature control," he added.

Sycamore Creek is also one of the few wineries in California to produce white wines without the addition of sulfur dioxide. These are done in the German style using cold fermentation.

Terry and Mary Kaye Parks have recently released their first blush wine — Gamay Blanc. The grapes are picked at 21 Brix sugar. The wine, made in a German tradition, is pressed with very little skin contact, cool fermented, and sterile filtered. The cool fermentation brings out the strawberry-like flavor of the wine.

The Sycamore Creek wine label is a deep cream color bordered in gold with a black engraving of the old Marchetti winery buildings.

The Parkses plan to keep their winery on the small scale so that they can control production and emphasize quality. Their wines have won many gold and silver medals at competitions throughout the state.

Terry and Mary Kaye like the lifestyle of being vintners. "I never wanted to have a factory in my back yard," Terry says. "It took me two years to get out of the seven-day-a-week routine, and realize I was my own boss. Now, however, I am running my life, not my life running me." ❧

Caparone ◆

York
Mountain → ◆

Martin Brothers ◆◆
◆ Eberle

Pesenti ◆

PASO
ROBLES

101

46

SAN LUIS OBISPO ●

◆ Creston Manor

◆ Chamisal

58

SANTA MARIA ●

SAN LUIS OBISPO
&
SANTA BARBARA
COUNTIES

1

LOMPOC ●

101

246

Sanford ◆
Vega ◆

Ballard
J. Carey

LOS OLIVOS

Gainey

SOLVANG

Santa Ynez
Valley

101

154

SANTA BARBARA ●

Wineries of

SAN LUIS OBISPO
&
SANTA BARBARA
COUNTIES

Ballard Canyon Winery
Caparone Winery
J. Carey Cellars
Chamisal Vineyard
Creston Manor Vineyards & Winery
Eberle Winery
The Gainey Vineyard
Martin Brothers Winery
Pesenti Winery
Sanford Winery
Santa Ynez Valley Winery
Vega Vineyards Winery
York Mountain Winery

San Luis Obispo & Santa Barbara Counties

Grape growing and winemaking in the region from Paso Robles in the north to Santa Barbara in the south started at the Santa Barbara Mission in 1782. Although the Santa Barbara area has long since ceased to be a significant factor in grape growing and wine production, the northern parts of Santa Barbara County and San Luis Obispo County have become prime areas of premium wine production.

This region is comprised of four distinct areas, each with its own unique micro-climate and soil conditions. The areas from north to south are: Paso Robles, Edna Valley, Santa Maria Valley, and the Santa Ynez Valley.

Of the four, the Santa Ynez Valley has the most dramatic history from a winemaking standpoint. Spanish Franciscan Fathers came to the Valley and built the Santa Ynez Mission in 1804 near what is now Solvang. Vineyards were planted and wine was made for the mission's use. Although a fire destroyed the mission in 1812, it was rebuilt. The life of the Santa Ynez Mission as the center of the community was short-lived, however, since the Mexican government secularized the missions in 1834. As a result, the vineyards deteriorated soon thereafter.

One hundred and fifty years passed from the initial vineyards at Santa Ynez Mission, however, before the region again saw a significant attempt at grape growing. Beginning in 1970, as the demand for premium wine increased, ranchers and dairy farmers started planting grapes. Most of the grapes were sold to wineries throughout the state. In the late 1970s, with an over-abundance of grapes, coupled with the grower's desire to produce the finished product, wineries became established throughout both San Luis Obispo and Santa Barbara counties.

Santa Ynez Valley Winery, founded in 1976, was one of the first wineries in the Santa Ynez Valley. The Santa Maria and Edna Valleys just north of Santa Ynez continued primarily to grow grapes. It is only recently that growers in these two areas have begun to make their own wines.

Limited grape growing and winery construction also developed in the northern part of the region, particularly in and around Paso Robles. That area's York Mountain Winery, established in 1882, became famous when it made some wine for Ignacio Jan Paderewski, the famed pianist who was to become president of Poland. He had a vineyard, primarily of Zinfandel, at a ranch he owned near Paso Robles and had the grapes processed into wine at York Mountain under the Paderewski label. One of the early wineries established in the area in the modern era of grape growing was Pesenti Winery in 1934.

Each of the distinct areas of the region has its own unique climatic conditions, the most unusual being the Santa Ynez Valley. The valley, which is the only one on the West Coast that runs east to west, is also bounded by the Pacific Ocean on two sides. As a result, the valley receives late afternoon ocean breezes from two directions. Warm days with cool afternoon breezes are a desirable condition for grape growing.

On the other hand, the Paso Robles area is at a higher elevation and further from the ocean. Within the area are two distinct growing regions — the gentle rolling hills east of Highway 101, and steep hillsides and bottomlands west of the highway. The latter are particularly well suited for what is termed "stressed grapes," which are dry farmed, thereby producing wines with intense fruitiness and great complexity.

Although grape growing and winemaking is expanding rapidly in what is commonly known as the South Central Coast region, it still only represents a small portion of California's total premium wine production. Currently, there are 30 wineries in the area with 13,000 acres planted in wine grapes. The wineries produce about 250,000 cases of wine each year. ❧

Ballard Canyon Winery

Address: 1825 Ballard Canyon Road, Solvang 93463
▫ (805) 688-7585
Visitation: Daily, 11 AM to 4 PM
Principals: Dr. Gene Hallock and Rosalie Hallock
Varietals produced: Fumé Blanc, Chardonnay, Johannisberg Riesling, White Cabernet Sauvignon, Zinfandel, Cabernet Sauvignon, and Muscat Canelli
Production: 20,000 cases per year

"It's a wonderful place to visit. The people are so friendly," states a typical letter addressed to the Ballard Canyon Winery. "We are constantly getting fan mail from the people who visit our winery," says Dr. Hallock. He welcomes receiving fan mail, particularly after being a dentist for many years.

Ballard Canyon has long been known for its hospitality since the 1880s. In Gold Rush days, Ballard Canyon was a stop on the stagecoach route on the famous Mission Trail from Southern California to Sonoma. This early history of California is depicted on the Ballard Canyon wine label. The label was designed by Santa Barbara artist Janice Blair, and it shows a stagecoach with horses racing through the countryside.

Dr. Gene and Rosalie Hallock both grew up in farming states, Wyoming and Nebraska respectively. They had no real interest in a winery as such when they purchased property in Ballard Canyon near the charming town of Solvang. Their objective had been to have a place to retire to the country, eventually.

The climate and soil of the Ballard Canyon area of the Santa Ynez Valley proved to be well suited to grape growing. Since the Hallocks had enjoyed premium wines, they were naturally attracted to raising grapes. Thus, in 1974, when they purchased their acreage, they persuaded family members and friends to help them plant grapes. Within three years, 50 acres of Johannisberg Riesling, Sauvignon Blanc, Chardonnay, Cabernet Sauvignon, and Muscat Canelli had been planted. All are now used in producing estate wines. The Zinfandel is made from purchased grapes.

At first, the Hallocks only intended to sell their grapes, but like so many others who started growing grapes, they wanted to be involved in the finished product. In 1978, they constructed a winery, which included a hospitality room. One portion of the winery is surrounded by a large redwood deck, where visitors may relax and sample the Ballard Canyon wines while looking out over the vineyards.

Fred Holloway, an enology graduate from California State University, Fresno is the winemaker at Ballard Canyon. Fred's Fumé Blanc is 100% Sauvignon Blanc. Following pressing, the juice is divided into thirds. Two-thirds are fermented and aged in French oak barrels, while the other third is fermented in stainless steel. The blending of these Sauvignon Blanc components produces a fruit-rich wine with unusual floral quality.

All of the lots are then aged in French oak. Ballard Canyon wines have received 85 major medals in competitions over the last seven years.

Several years ago, Dr. Hallock gave up his dental practice to devote his full time to the winery. He has taken over the marketing duties and works with the various brokers and distributors who sell the wine. Dr. Hallock is a member of the board of directors of the Santa Barbara Vintners Association, which was formed by the 23 wineries in the area.

Daughter Mary Hallock is the winery internal operations manager who also manages the Vintage House, a satellite tasting room in Solvang (ten miles away).

"The most rewarding thing about being a vintner is the wonderful and friendly people you meet," says Rosalie Hallock. This feeling of friendliness and hospitality prompted the Hallocks to establish an annual harvest festival the first three Saturdays in October. The festival is by reservation only and includes a country barbecue, wine tasting, chef demonstrations, live music, dancing, and grape stomping.

It is Gene and Rosalie Hallock's belief that wine and friendship go together. ❧

Caparone Winery

Address: 2280 San Marcos Road, Paso Robles 93446
▢ (805) 467-3827
Visitation: Daily, 11 am to 5 pm
Principals: Dave and Mary Caparone
Varietals produced: Merlot and Cabernet Sauvignon
Production: 3,000 cases per year

Dave Caparone makes wine using old-fashioned methods interspersed with modern technology. His philosophy is to start with good grapes and do as little as possible to them. The result is big, rich, and intense red wines. Dave makes only red wines.

Dave holds a master's degree in fine arts with a music major, and has worked in residential construction and real estate. After living in the country for 20 years and working outdoors as part of his job doing environmental studies for Caltrans, the agency that handles California's state highway system, Dave decided to follow his dream of self-employment. He had been a home winemaker for several years and decided to go commercial when he purchased 58 acres of land northeast of Paso Robles.

This acreage, which Dave is gradually planting in red varietals, lies in a small valley with a unique microclimate. Very warm days and cool night sea breezes make the area suitable for growing Zinfandel. At the present, there are four acres planted in that varietal, and some small plantings in Nebbiolo and Brunello. The latter two varietals are from the Piemonte and Tuscany regions of Northern Italy and are considered two of Italy's finest wines. The current release of Merlot and Cabernet Sauvignon are from purchased grapes grown in the Santa Maria Valley in northern Santa Barbara County. The harvest and crush of 1985, however, did yield enough Zinfandel for Dave to make his first commercial wine of that variety.

Dave is just as particular about the grapes he uses as he is about his winemaking techniques. When it gets close to harvest time, he can be seen walking through the rows of vines of his contract growers, testing for proper grape maturity. He tries to extract as much flavor from the grapes as possible, and a timely harvest is most important.

Since Dave practically hand-makes his wines, the quality of the fruit is most important. In his winemaking, Dave leaves the grapes on the skins for an unusually long time and ferments the wine at a higher-than-normal temperature. He feels that this technique results in a smooth wine, not one that is harsh or overly tannic. The red wines are then aged in small barrels. Dave does not filter his wines. He only racks and then bottles them.

When the grapes are available, Dave makes a late harvest Botrytis red wine. The latest is a Late Harvest Gamay made from grapes that were picked at the unheard-of time of January 18 — harvest season had been over for three months, but these grapes had been left on the vines!

Many small wineries like Caparone Winery use a bottling truck, a large tractor trailer that contains all equipment necessary for bottling, foiling, and labelling. It saves the considerable investment needed for a bottling line which, in a small winery, is used only a few days a year. Also, the bottling truck, being highly automated, can complete the bottling job in about half the time it would take the vintner to do it even with help of friends and relatives. There are several of these concerns in California.

An interest in conservation and the environment prompted Dave to design and build his own residence — a home completely energy-sufficient with the use of solar energy. The winery, too, has energy-saving devices.

Dave enjoys every aspect of his job as a vintner, even the marketing. He feels personal contact with the people selling his wines is most important. And, Dave has not lost his interest in music. He can frequently be found on the weekends playing in a jazz band at local social affairs or at jazz festivals.

Dave likes working for himself and being involved in a new viticulture area. Eventually, his vineyards will produce two little-known varietals, Nebbiolo and Brunello, to add to the list of California wines. ❧

J. Carey Cellars

Address: 1711 Alamo Pintado Road, Solvang 93463
□ (805) 688-8554
Visitation: Daily, 10 AM to 4 PM
Principals: Dr. James C. Carey, Jr. and Dr. Joseph S. Carey
Varietals produced: Sauvignon Blanc, Chardonnay, Cabernet Blanc, and Cabernet Sauvignon
Production: 6,000 cases per year

"Ii is our hope that the judicious use and appreciation of [wine] will contribute to the evolution of mankind as the problem solving beings of the universe and help them in their quest." These are the thoughts of Dr. James C. Carey, Jr. as he talks about wine and the family winery.

Dr. James Carey feels that a premium wine is part of the food industry, not the alcohol industry. He would rather see people drink less alcohol, but drink a better quality wine. He points out that one 4-ounce glass of wine, blended with a meal, is actually treated by the body as food and metabolized without any significant increase in blood alcohol levels. "Many physicians still prescribe a glass of wine as a mild appetite stimulant, source of vitamins and iron, and a mild nighttime sedative," he says.

The winery was originally owned by three "Dr. J. Careys" until the death of the elder Dr. J. Campbell Carey in 1984. The Carey family has had a long tradition of farming in Illinois. Dr. J. Campbell Carey retired from a long career as an obstetrician and moved to California in 1977. He purchased a 25-acre piece of property near Solvang and planned to retire there. The property included a house, an unused dairy barn, and two vineyards that had been planted in 1973.

As many people do, Dr. Carey found himself working harder after retirement than before. He was fascinated by the vineyards and by the property's potential. In the next few years, he planted — by hand — an additional vineyard. The property is now comprised of three vineyards, each unique in that each has a different micro-climate and different soil composition. All three are dry farmed, which causes roots to reach quite deep, resulting in grapes with intense fruit flavor.

In 1978, the Careys converted the old red barn on the property into a winery to utilize their grapes rather than sell them to other wineries. Although a winemaker had been engaged, Dr. Carey, Sr., with his scientific background, took great interest in the winery. He also supervised the entire vineyard operation.

At one time or another, the whole Carey family has become involved in the winery operation. Dr. Jim's daughter was the first office and sales manager. She, however, has gone East to pursue an acting career. Jim Carey III, Dr. Jim's son, is the California marketing director. At the present, Mary Louise Carey, the senior Dr. Carey's widow, at age 79, still keeps the books and is the controller of the winery. Dr. Joseph is president of the winery, and Dr. Jim is the general manager. Both of the doctors continue to practice medicine. Dr. Joseph is a heart surgeon in Torrance, and Dr. Jim is a plastic surgeon in Santa Barbara. Since the winery is only an hour's drive from Santa Barbara, Dr. Jim is at the winery twice a week to oversee daily operations.

Scott Meyer is the winemaker at J. Carey Cellars. He has worked for several wineries in California and Europe. Scott says he welcomes the challenge presented by three vineyards every harvest. Conditions are never the same, but he does strive to maintain a consistent style for the wines. Since Sauvignon Blanc is planted in all three vineyards, Scott has the opportunity to blend lots for greater complexity. J. Carey Cellars has also become known for its complex Chardonnay, which is mostly barrel fermented with one to two years of French oak aging.

"As a family, especially as a family of three generations of physicians, we feel it fitting that wine be used in religious ceremonies, to mark special occasions, and at mealtimes. We hope that when people do this, they will appreciate and continue to increase their knowledge of the winemaking process." These are the thoughts of Dr. James Carey as he talks about wine. ❧

Chamisal Vineyard

Address: 7525 Orcutt Road, San Luis Obispo 93401
□ (805) 544-3576
Visitation: Wednesday through Sunday, 11 AM to 5 PM
Principals: Norman and Carolyn Goss
Varietals produced: Chardonnay
Production: 5,000 cases per year

Chardonnay, the wine; Chamisal, the winery; and cello, the instrument. Like the three B's — Bach, Beethoven, and Brahms — these three C's are music to the ears of Norman Goss, a former cello player with the Los Angeles Philharmonic. His love for the cello came early in life, because he grew up in a musical family. His love for wine came not too long thereafter, and the winery is now the pride and joy of his life.

In the early 1930s, Norman Goss and his family traveled from California to Europe. While in Switzerland, they were invited to a luncheon given by the famous Polish pianist, Ignacio Paderewski. A special wine was served for these special visitors from California — the first bottling from Paderewski's vineyard near San Luis Obispo.

In 1933, Norman returned to Europe for six years to study at the Paris Conservatory of Music. While in France, he further learned to appreciate food and wine — both of which were to play a vital role in his life.

Norman Goss joined the Los Angeles Philharmonic in 1940. He also played with the Pasadena Symphony for several years. In 1941, Norman decided to further his interests in gourmet food by opening the first of a series of Stuft Shirt restaurants. The restaurants became known throughout Southern California not only for their innovative cooking, but also for their extensive California wine list. That was long before the time when people recognized California as a major wine producing area of the world.

Over the years, Norman Goss observed the wine buying trends of his restaurant customers — the shift from red to white. Chardonnay seemed to be fast becoming the favorite wine. Thus, when the Gosses as a family thought about a change of lifestyle, it was a natural progression to turn from the restaurant business to wine — to the idea of planting a vineyard.

The search for suitable grape growing land began, and Norman remembered that wine from long ago — from the Paderewski vineyards near San Luis Obispo. The rich soil, cool climate, and abundant water supply of the Edna Valley south of San Luis Obispo made it an ideal location for a Chardonnay vineyard. In 1972, the Goss family purchased acreage there and proceeded to plant grapes — 47 acres of Chardonnay and 10 of Cabernet Sauvignon (which have since been grafted over to Chardonnay.)

Since the vineyard and, later, the winery, were to become parts of a total family operation, the two Goss children proceeded to seek an education in viticulture and its related fields. Tom Goss, who was always a farmer and businessman at heart, enrolled at Cal Poly San Luis Obispo in Agricultural Business Management, while simultaneously working at Chamisal. Allyn Goss enrolled at U.C. Davis in Wine Marketing and Sales, classes which were an asset to her when she began marketing Chamisal wines.

The Edna Valley proved to be all that Norman Goss had dreamed it would be as the location of a Chardonnay vineyard. It is "phylloxera-free" of the common root louse so often found to be a problem in other areas of California and Europe. This permitted the Gosses to plant the vineyard on their own varietal roots. Recent research has shown that vines planted this way provide more varietal flavor. The stock that was chosen by the Gosses was from cuttings originally imported from the Côte d'Or area of France.

These vines, although sparse-bearing, are known for their high quality fruit. Because of low production, Tom Goss, the vineyard manager, developed a unique pruning method to increase production. The result was a large number of small bunches of grapes with a high skin-to-juice ratio. Since most of the Chardonnay flavor lies directly beneath the skin, more skin means more flavor.

In 1980, Norman Goss decided to build a small winery to produce wine from his own grapes, which had been winning awards for several years. The name Chamisal was chosen for the winery because it was the Spanish name given to a native shrub growing on the property. Scott Boyd, who had been a winemaker at Roudon-Smith in the Santa Cruz Mountains, was hired as winemaker for Chamisal. Scott brought with him winemaking experience and an enology background gained at Cal Poly and at U.C. Davis.

Chamisal Chardonnay grapes are immediately delivered to the winery for crushing upon harvest. There is some skin contact for optimum flavor, and fermentation is both in stainless steel tanks and oak barrels, with the two being aged separately. Some of the wine goes through malolactic fermentation. All of the Chardonnay is aged in French oak and sterile filtered. The various lots of Chardonnay are blended together for the final product.

Currently, Chamisal uses only a portion of the grapes it grows. However, Norman Goss hopes to increase production to 10,000 cases per year, so that he can utilize most of his vineyard's grapes. Like the great chateaux of France, he will still produce only one wine — Chardonnay. Norman Goss has made beautiful music with his cello, has produced gourmet food in his restaurants, and now makes outstanding Chardonnay. ❧

Creston Manor Vineyards & Winery

Address: Highway 58 at 17-Mile Marker, Creston 93432 ◻ (805) 238-7398

Tasting Room: Highway 101 and Vineyard Drive, Templeton 93465

Visitation: Tasting Room: Daily, 10 AM to 6 PM
Winery: By appointment only

Principals: Lawrence and Stephanie Rosenbloom

Varietals produced: Sauvignon Blanc, Chardonnay, Pinot Noir, and Cabernet Sauvignon

Production: 13,000 cases per year

Is there such a thing as a special wine for the stars of Hollywood? Certainly not, but a great number of them — Ruta Lee, Alex Trebek, Ed McMahon, and Lucille Ball, to name a few — are staunch supporters and active promoters of Creston Manor wines. Ruta Lee is even one of the stockholders. Wayne Rogers, a co-star of the long-running TV series M*A*S*H*, supplies some of the grapes used in Creston Manor wines. He specializes in growing premium grapes in the Edna Valley about 50 miles away from the mountain location of the winery.

Creston Manor is one of the newest wineries in California. It is located high in the La Panza Mountains of San Luis Obispo County at an elevation of 1,700 feet and is frost-protected by coastal fogs. The vineyard and ranch is only 18 miles from the ocean, as the crow flies. By road it is much farther, going through winding canyons with beautiful vistas. The climate and the limestone soil are well-suited to grape growing.

The winery and vineyard were originally founded and owned by two couples from the Los Angeles area — Larry and Stephanie Rosenbloom and Christina Crawford (of *Mommy Dearest* fame) Koontz and her husband, David. The latter had been looking for vineyard property, and Larry wanted a ranch. In 1980, the two men found exactly what they were looking for in the old Indian Creek cattle ranch of 479 acres. The Koontzes are no longer involved in the enterprise, however.

Two years later, 95 acres of the property had been planted with Chardonnay, Sauvignon Blanc, Pinot Noir, and Cabernet Sauvignon. The Rosenblooms plan to expand the vineyards to 150 acres in the near future. For irrigation, three lakes and a reservoir on the property are used. Irrigation is used even though the area gets an average of 17 to 20 inches of rainfall a year. There are six distinct soil types in the vineyards from clay to limestone to volcanic shale. All contribute a special character to the grapes which ultimately add complexity to the wines. For the first few years, until the new vines reached maturity, all grapes were purchased from nearby vintners in the Edna Valley and the Paso Robles area. Starting this year, some estate grapes will be used.

An old ranch building was remodeled and became the winery. It has a specially built platform to enable the Pinot Noir grapes to go directly into an open top fermenter to be made into a nouveau-style wine with the use of a process developed in Burgundy, France called "*maceration carbonique.*"

Victor Hugo Roberts is the talented winemaker at Creston Manor. He is a 1979 graduate of U.C. Davis with a degree in enology. He also keeps a close check on the vineyards, since he and his wife Leslie, a registered nurse, live on the property. The wines which Vic has produced have already won over 30 medals and have caught the attention of the critics as well as the general public. The Cabernet Sauvignon and the Chardonnay have been completely sold out early in the year.

The Petit d' Noir (Nouveau style) is only one example of Vic Roberts' style of winemaking. He tries to meld French traditional techniques with California innovations. Vic explained the process in the following manner:

"After the grapes are hand-picked in the fields into half ton bins they are transported to the winery, where they are inspected for fruit cleanliness, sugar, acid, and pH. The grapes with the stems are then placed into 2,300-gallon open-top oak tanks. When the tank is one-third full two pounds of freeze-dried yeast is added for fermentation of the free running juice.

"When the tank is full of grapes, it is sealed to allow internal berry fermentation. In other words, the berries primarily ferment on their own yeast from the inside out. After fermentation — the juice has fermented inside the whole berries — the free juice is drained. Grape clusters, with the stems, are removed to be crushed lightly. The must is then placed into a stainless steel temperature-controlled tank to finish the fermentation process which takes about nine to 13 days. A bladder press with soft pressings then extracts the juice from the must. The juice goes back into the tank for settling for one week, after which it is lightly filtered and bottled. The entire process takes about 45 days from harvest to bottling. The wine has an excellent red color and a fresh taste."

Each November there is a race at Creston Manor to release the Petit d'Noir earlier than the French Nouveau Beaujolais. There is great pageantry to take the wine by stagecoach to the Los Angeles market; after all, this Nouveau Pinot Noir is one of the few made like it, and probably the only Californian of its kind. Last year, the Creston Manor wine beat the French by 48 hours. The entire undertaking is a symbol of the pioneering spirit of the American West and the innovativeness of California wines.

Vic Roberts likes to blend some Semillon with the Sauvignon Blanc. Both the Sauvignon Blanc and the Creston Manor Chardonnay are fermented in stainless steel and then barrel aged for about three to four months. The regular Pinot Noir and Chardonnay are barrel aged in French and American oak for 24 to 30 months. All wines except the Petit d'Noir are bottled aged before release.

In addition to the planned additional vineyard plantings, Larry and Stephanie plan to bore into the hillside next to the winery and build a 40-by-70-foot tunnel. This is to be used for barrel aging of the red wines, similar to the chateaux in France. When completed, the tunnel — aging cellar — will have enough room for 5,100 cases of wine.

Creston Manor has grown by leaps and bounds from its first release in 1982 of 1,200 cases to 20,000 cases in 1986. It has taken a great deal of hard work and perseverance on the part of Larry and Stephanie Rosenbloom — from the hand planting of vines, to helping with the harvest and crush, manning the bottling line, and now being heavily involved in the marketing. Stephanie is in charge of all marketing activities. Larry, who spends three days a week at the winery, is still involved in his insurance business in Los Angeles.

Creston Manor wines are enjoyed by the Hollywood stars, and the wines, too, are stars — on the California wine scene. ❧

Eberle Winery

Address: 3.8 miles east of Highway 101 on Highway
46, P.O. Box 2459, Paso Robles 93447
□ (805) 238-9607
Visitation: Winter: Daily, 10 AM to 5 PM
Summer: Daily, 10 am to 6 pm
Principals: W. Gary Eberle
Varietals produced: Chardonnay, Cabernet Sauvignon
Blanc, Cabernet Sauvignon, and Muscat Canelli
Production: 8,000 cases per year

"It is much easier to reason with Cabernet than to reason with your teenage daughter," says Gary Eberle, as he talks about his vocation as winemaker and vintner — although Gary, who is a former defensive tackle for Pennsylvania State, could easily and forcefully reason with anybody.

Gary grew up in western Pennsylvania and received a B.S. in Biology from Penn State. He went on to Louisiana State University for a master's in zoology and to U.C. Davis for a Ph.D. He majored in fermentation science at Davis, not only because he had a great interest in wine, but also because his brother was about to start a winery and needed a winemaker.

Interest in food and wine has been part of Gary Eberle's heritage. Wine was always served at meals at the home of his Jacobin-Polish mother and German father, as was a great variety of cuisine. Gary further became interested in gourmet food while living in New Orleans. He still enjoys cooking and has inaugurated a series of gourmet candlelight dinners at the winery to showcase food and wine.

Gary's half brother, Cliff Giacobine, had been a successful businessman, and in the early 1970s wanted to establish a business that would be of interest to the entire family and would involve them with producing a product. They found and purchased land east of Paso Robles, planted 700 acres of grapes, and built a winery, the Estrella River Winery. Gary Eberle became the winemaker, and his wife Jeanie became involved in sales.

During the next few years, Cliff's Winery grew by leaps and bounds. Instead of being directly involved in the winemaking process, Gary found himself writing work orders and winemaking formulas. He realized that this was not the type of winemaking he wanted to be doing. He wanted to do hands-on winemaking — to be involved in the crush, the fermentation, and the racking.

In 1982, Gary Eberle purchased property about four miles east of Paso Robles, planted a vineyard, and constructed a modern redwood winery on a knoll overlooking the vineyards and the countryside.

Since his vineyards have only recently become of bearing size, Gary has had to purchase grapes from nearby vineyards. The climate and soil is particularly wellsuited to the two varietals which Gary planted — Chardonnay and Cabernet Sauvignon. The Cabernet from the Paso Robles area is high in fruit and soft in tannins, resulting in a wine that can be drunk early. Since the Cabernet has enough complexity, Merlot does not have to be added to the wine. Gary Eberle considers Cabernet Sauvignon to be the king of grapes, and it is his favorite grape to work with.

The Eberle Chardonnay has 12 to 16 hours of skin contact. It then is given a light press and fermented in stainless steel at 50 degrees. The wine is settled and barrel aged for at least four months.

Each year, Gary makes a Muscat Canelli from purchased grapes. It is not an extremely sweet wine, with only 5% sugar and 10% alcohol. Gary, who has been greatly influenced in his career by Robert Mondavi, wants to make the perfect Muscat Canelli. According to critics, he has succeeded.

Jeanie Eberle is still involved in wine marketing. She has expanded her marketing capabilities to include not only the Eberle wines, but has established her own marketing firm for about 20 other wineries. Darien Eberle, who is a college student, helps her father at the winery whenever she can. She shares not only her father's sense of humor, but also his interest in food and wine.

In the last couple of years Gary Eberle has discovered the importance of personal appearances at tastings and distributor meetings. Since Eberle wine is widely distributed in all parts of the United Sates, Gary found himself away from the winery a great deal. He decided too much of his valuable time was being spent in the car, driving to or from the airport or to the ultimate destination. Consequently, he bought a plane, took flying lessons, and now flies to his meetings throughout the country.

The Eberle wine label reflects Gary's love of Cabernet Sauvignon in its ruby red color. The boar on the label was inspired by the name "Eberle," which means boar in the Schwebish German dialect.

Gary Eberle wants his winery to grow at a reasonable rate, but never to be so large that he cannot manage it himself and be actively involved in the winemaking. ❧

The Gainey Vineyard

Address: 3950 East Highway 246, Santa Ynez 93460
□ (805) 688-93460
Visitation: Daily, 10 AM to 5 PM
Principals: Daniel J. Gainey
Varietals produced: Sauvignon Blanc, Johannisberg
Riesling, Chardonnay, Merlot, and Cabernet
Sauvignon
Production: 10,000 cases per year

From the vine to the wine. "An integral part of enjoying wine is the understanding of the process." This was, and is, the belief of Daniel J. Gainey when he built his winery in 1984. He designed his winery to facilitate showing visitors how wine is produced. Regularly scheduled tours demonstrate the process step-by-step, from the various varietals growing in the field to the final bottling, labelling, and packaging.

Each person visiting the winery may join a short 20-minute well-organized tour which begins in a model vineyard. The vineyard shows six varietals with six different styles of trellising for the vines. Also shown are different irrigation techniques. From there, the tour moves to the huge, fully automated crusher, then on to the stainless steel tanks where the fermentation takes place. Next, there is a view of the barrel room with racks of French and German oak barrels. Finally, the visitor sees the bottling line and a huge aging cellar which holds 40,000 bottles. The entire tour is narrated by well-trained Gainey personnel.

The Gainey family, which owned Jostens (a manufacturing concern specializing in scholastic jewelery), had owned farms in Minnesota and Arizona before coming to California in 1962. Daniel Gainey and his father purchased an 1,800-acre ranch in the Santa Ynez valley to raise diversified crops — sugar beets, wheat, flower seeds, and cattle. This also gave the Gaineys an opportunity to capitalize on their interest in, and love for, Arabian horses. Daniel Gainey's father was one of the founders of the Arabian Horse Registry. The Gainey Fountainhead Arabians have become recognized worldwide as one of the top breeds of Arabians.

Several years ago, Daniel Gainey and his ranch foreman Barry Johnson decided to further diversify the ranch's crops. Since the Santa Ynez Valley was becoming known for its vineyards and wineries, they decided to put in some test plots of wine grapes. At first they sold the cuttings through their nursery to other growers. After several years of declining sugar beet prices, Daniel and Barry did some statistical analysis and decided that they needed to diversify even further. This led them to build a winery and sell wine directly to the public.

In 1983, Daniel Gainey planted 54 acres of grapes — Sauvignon Blanc, Semillon, Chardonnay, Johannisberg Riesling, Merlot, and Cabernet Sauvignon — with the intention not only to raise grapes, but also to construct a winery and tasting room.

Robert Lamb Hart of San Francisco was commissioned to design the winery building, which features Spanish architecture and Mexican tiles, and is furnished with French country antiques. The winery, itself, is equipped with the latest and most efficient equipment available. There is an unusual bottling line which fills the bottles from the bottom up, thus minimizing the amount of air entering the bottle. This also minimizes spoilage of the wine.

Robin Gainey, Daniel's wife, who is a gourmet cook and has studied cuisine in France, wanted to showcase wine and food. To do this, the Gainey's added a culinary wing to the winery. This includes a kitchen with all of the latest equipment. Not only is the kitchen used for winery dinners, but periodically chefs from well-known restaurants in Los Angeles teach cooking classes at the winery. There are also wine appreciation courses taught by Ric Longoria, Gainey Vineyards winemaker, and by visiting wine experts.

Ric Longoria joined Gainey Vineyards as winemaker in 1985. He is no stranger to the Santa Ynez Valley, since he grew up in Lompoc some 30 miles away. After graduating from U.C. Berkeley with a degree in sociology, he worked at various Northern California wineries before coming back to the Santa Ynez Valley and working as winemaker at Santa Ynez Valley Winery and J. Carey Cellars. "He knows the soil, the climate and the type of grapes the valley produces," says Daniel Gainey.

The style of Gainey wines are basically wines to be enjoyed with food. The Johannisberg Riesling, with 2% residual sugar, on the other hand is a good sipping wine and an accompaniment to desserts. One of the first wines Ric made after coming to Gainey Vineyards was Erin Vin Gris, a blush wine of 90% Pinot Noir and 10% Chardonnay. It was named in honor of the new Gainey baby who was christened in the winery.

Daniel Gainey has a commitment not only to his wines but also to the valley in which he has lived for over twenty years. He wants to produce something of value from the land and to share with his visitors the knowledge of how it is produced. ❧

Martin Brothers Winery

Address: Buena Vista Drive, Paso Robles 93446
  □ (805) 238-2520
Visitation: Daily, 11 a.m to 5 PM
Principals: The Martin Family
Varietals produced: Chenin Blanc, Sauvignon Blanc,
  Chardonnay, Zinfandel, and Nebbiolo
Production: 7,000 cases per year

For the better part of a century, a beverage has been produced on the property now known as Martin Brothers Winery. Until the early 1970s, it was a successful dairy farm. When the sales and distribution system of milk changed, the owners were forced to give up the milk business, sell the cows, and eventually sell the farm which had fallen into disrepair.

In 1981, the Martin family purchased the 83-acre property just east of Paso Robles off Highway 46 with the purpose of establishing a winery. Wine and its merchandising were not new to the Martin family. Wine was always a food beverage in the Martin household in Ojai, California, since the senior Martin, Edward, was the advertising manager of Padre Vineyards in the late 1930s.

It was not until many years later that the family, particularly the two brothers Tom and Nick (Edward), became interested in establishing a winery. Tom, an ex-marketing executive of the Mattel Corporation, had succeeded his father, Edward, Sr., as president of the outdoor advertising company headquartered in Paso Robles which was founded by his father and owned by the Martin family. The younger brother Nick had by then become an established winemaker.

Nick graduated with a B.A. in english literature from the University of California at Santa Cruz in 1973. His first job was as cellarman at Mirassou Winery in San Jose. He became so fascinated with the entire process of producing wine that he went back to college at U.C. Davis for a degree in fermentation science. After graduation in 1978, he was employed as winemaker for the Lambert Bridge Winery in Sonoma County where he produced award-winning wines.

The two Martin brothers felt that the Paso Robles area was a good spot to locate a winery. The area was growing high quality grapes, producing award-winning wines, and had an emerging and enthusiastic wine community.

It was no easy task to transform the old dairy farm into an estate winery. In 1982, they prepared 15 acres of sloping hillside and planted them with Chardonnay and Sauvignon Blanc. A year later, 45 more acres were planted with Chenin Blanc, Sauvignon Blanc, Chardonnay, Semillon, Zinfandel, and an Italian varietal called Nebbiolo.

The dairy buildings on the property were remodeled into a winery. The feed barn was completely gutted on the inside, and a new structure was built within the old one. This resulted in 14- to 18-inch-thick walls which provide a natural insulation for the winery. Although it is very compact in structure, all of the latest equipment have been provided. The milk barn was converted to the storage area and offices for the winery. What is now the parking lot for winery visitors was once the old wash-down area.

The farmhouse on the property was remodeled as a residence for Nick and his wife Patrice Boyle, the daughter of a Los Angeles newspaperman. Patrice, who graduated from Santa Clara College, worked in newspaper graphics prior to marrying Nick in 1976. She is now Director of Marketing, Sales, and Public Relations for the winery.

Until their vines are in full production, Nick purchases the majority of the grapes used for Martin Brothers wines. The 1985 Sauvignon Blanc, however, was made from estate wines.

Nick purchases his Zinfandel from an old Italian dry-farmed Paso Robles vineyard which produces stressed grapes that result in a fruity wine. "We consider these little grapes our jewels," Tom Martin comments. Paso Robles has a history of growing Zinfandel which dates back to the turn of the century. Nick makes his Zinfandel in a light, fresh, style, which is drinkable early.

Martin Brothers Winery is the only California winery producing Nebbiolo as a varietal wine. The Nebbiolo grape (considered the Cabernet of Italy) is the basis of many of the finer wines of the Piemonte region of Italy. It has been grown in California for over 50 years and used as a blending grape in the larger wineries in California. Currently, Nebbiolo grapes are being purchased from Stanislaus County. The grape takes its name from the Italian word *nebbia*, meaning "fog." It grows best in a region where there is a good deal of morning fog in September such as Paso Robles.

Not only is the Nebbiolo a unique wine, but so is the label on the bottle. Each year the label features a drawing or painting by either Leonardo da Vinci or Michelangelo. The 1982 Nebbiolo label was a sepia colored line drawing by da Vinci, and the 1983 label depicts a famous Michelangelo painting. Tom Martin, who went to school in Florence, thinks this is a nice touch for the time-honored Italian grape.

The Nebbiolo wine, as made by Nick Martin, is light and fruity with just an edge of tannin for character. The grapes are fermented on the skins in stainless steel tanks for about 12 days. After pressing, the wine is aged in small French barrels for 6 months and then transferred to 1,000-gallon oak uprights for an additional four months of aging. Nick believes this brings out the complexity of the wine without the addition of excessive oakiness.

Each year, the Martin Brothers produce an interesting generic wine called Mozart in honor of the Paso Robles annual Mozart Festival, held during the month of August. The wine is released at a "Springtime in the Vineyards" charity party the first Sunday in May. All proceeds from the party, plus a portion of the sale of the wine, benefits the Mozart Festival. The party features music — a Mozart string quartet plays in the winery — arts and crafts, food and Martin Brothers wine.

The Mozart wine is an off-dry blend of Chenin Blanc, Sauvignon Blanc, Chardonnay, and a little Muscat Canelli. Each year the percentage of the blends varies, but it is consistently a much sought-after wine.

In the next few years, the Martin brothers plan to expand their production to 12,000 cases per year and produce 85% of their wines from estate grown grapes. They plan to keep it a family operation with Nick as winemaker and vineyard manager. The senior Edward Martin, Chairman of the Board of American Commercial Bank of Ventura, will continue to heap praise on the family's efforts.

Ten years ago, few people outside of Paso Robles had heard of wine made in the area. Today, with wineries like Martin Brothers, Paso Robles wines are receiving considerable attention and respect. ❧

Pesenti Winery

Address: 2900 Vineyard Drive, Templeton 93465
□ (805) 434-1030
Visitation: Daily, 9 AM to 5 PM
Principals: Victor Pesenti and Aldo Nerelli
Varietals produced: Gewurztraminer, Johannisberg Riesling, Grey Riesling, White Zinfandel, Zinfandel, Cabernet Sauvignon Blanc, Cabernet Sauvignon Rose, and Cabernet Sauvignon
Production: 25,000 cases per year

"In our family, there is a tradition of fine winemaking as well as a spirit of discovery, leading us to improve on the quality of our father's wines while seeking new wines for today's tastes." These are the thoughts of Aldo Nerelli as he reflects on his family's history of winemaking in the Templeton-Paso Robles area.

Frank Pesenti first planted grapes in 1923 on the rolling hillsides outside of Templeton. The climate, rainfall, and soil of the area seemed to be right for the Zinfandel and Cabernet which Frank Pesenti planted. From time to time, the Pesentis and the Nerellis have added to the original plantings. Some of the original plantings are still producing excellent grapes. All of the 75 acres of Pesenti vineyards are dry farmed, producing a robust wine.

In 1934, after the end of Prohibition, Frank Pesenti built a winery. Additions were made to the building in 1941 and 1947. Three generations of winemakers — grandfather Frank, son Victor Pesenti, son-in-law Aldo Nerelli, and now grandson Frank Nerelli — have all made wine in the same building.

Not only is Frank Nerelli making wine in the same building, but he is using much of his grandfather's original equipment. He ferments his red wines in concrete tanks built in the late 1940s before the extensive use of stainless steel. During fermentation, Frank punches down the cap twice a day in the old Italian style of winemaking. The red wines are then aged and stored in huge 12,500 gallon redwood tanks.

Frank Nerelli says he has learned winemaking from tried-and-true family experience, and he tries to follow the Old World methods interspersed with some modern technology. The Pesenti Zinfandels and Cabernet Sauvignons have won medals in many of the major wine competitions, including the prestigious Los Angeles County Fair.

One of the new innovations in the Pesenti vineyards is a German field crusher called a Mortl — probably the only one being used in San Luis Obispo County. With crews of pickers and this crusher, 20 tons of grapes can be worked in one day. The grapes are crushed in the field. Leaving the stems in the field, the juice and the must is then transported in the field crusher to the winery for fermentation.

Although most of the wines produced by Pesenti are in the bolder Italian style, Frank Nerelli has joined current customer trends towards lighter blush wines by producing a White Zinfandel and both a Blanc and a Rose Cabernet Sauvignon.

Both of the families, the Pesentis and the Nerellis, love the wine business. After all, it is a family tradition. ❧

Sanford Winery

Address: 7250 Santa Rosa Road, Buellton 93427
□ (805) 688-3300
Visitation: Monday through Saturday, 11 AM to 4 PM
Principals: Richard and Thekla Sanford
Varietals produced: Sauvignon Blanc, Chardonnay, Pinot Noir-Vin Gris, and Pinot Noir
Production: 20,000 cases per year

Do you ever judge a wine by its label? With literally hundreds of wines, all with different labels and all competing for shelf space at the wine shop, it is a difficult to decide which wine to buy. Labels are one of the main concerns in the marketing of wine. There is no sniff, scratch-and-sip test before purchase; consequently, something must attract the customer to a wine with which he or she is not familiar. Representative of the loveliest ways this problem has been solved are the beautiful Sanford Winery wine labels created by Sebastian Titus.

When Richard Sanford first thought about marketing his new wines, he, too, was faced with the problem of identity for his product. Since he and his wife, Thekla, have always been interested in art and the environment, it was only natural that they would commission the well-known artist and wine label designer Sebastian Titus to design a series of flowers for their wine labels.

The flowers, each different for the four varietals Richard produces, are all wildflowers grown in and around the Sanfords' 738-acre Rancho Jabali in the Santa Ynez Valley. The same flower on the varietal does not continue from year to year; instead, new flowers are painted each year, signed and dated by the artist. Thus, in four years there have been twelve of these superb wildflower paintings which are available in poster form from the winery. The superb quality of the art work is only a hint of the fine premium wine contained in the bottle.

Richard Sanford, a native of Southern California, has always had an interest in the land and a fondness for growing things. In 1965, he graduated from the University of California at Berkeley with majors in geography and geology. After completing Naval Officer Candidate School, he served as a navigator aboard a navy destroyer during the Viet Nam war. Upon his return to Santa Barbara, Richard worked briefly in the video communications field, but the attraction of working with the land was irresistible. With an interest in wine, it was only natural that he should turn to grapes and grape growing for his permanent career.

Although he had no formal training in viticulture or enology, he did use his scientific background to study the climatic conditions of the Santa Ynez Valley, where he wanted to locate permanently. He compared these to the climates of Burgundy and found the two very similar.

The Santa Ynez Valley is very unique in topography as well as climate. Most of the mountain ranges in the Western Hemisphere run north to south. In the Santa Ynez Valley the coastal range runs east to west, permitting the prevailing westerly ocean breezes to cool the warm central coast valleys of California. The Santa Ynez Valley is one of the coolest grape growing regions in California, and Richard decided it was perfect for the growing of the two famous Burgundian grapes — Chardonnay and Pinot Noir.

Together with a partner, Michael Benedict, Richard Sanford planted a vineyard on the west end of the Santa Ynez Valley in 1971. This was one of the first new grape growing projects in the valley since Prohibition. In the mid — 1970s the two men converted an old dairy barn into a winery. In 1980, the partnership was dissolved, and Richard decided to establish his own vineyards and winery.

Richard and his bride, Thekla Brumder, whom he had married the year before, searched throughout California for an appropriate vineyard and winery site but kept coming back to the Santa Ynez Valley. The climate caused by the transverse mountains was perfect for the types of grapes they wanted to grow. In 1983, they purchased the magnificent 738-acre Rancho Jabali with its rolling hills and beautiful vistas.

Thekla Sanford shares her husband's enthusiasm for the outdoors and native art. Born in Wisconsin, she graduated from the University of Arizona with a degree in fine arts. While living in Arizona, she fell in love with the native Southwest and Mexican art. This interest is still reflected in the Sanfords' art collection. It also inspired them in the design of their future winery building.

In 1982 and 1983, Richard leased space at the Edna Valley Winery to produce his wines. Since then he has leased space in an industrial complex in nearby Buellton, where he and winemaker Bruno D'Alfonso are making wines in the traditional Burgundian style with modern technology.

All of Sanford Winery's grapes are purchased from the Central Coast region and the Santa Ynez Valley. In these regions the acid level is very high in the grapes, resulting in a fruity and complex wine. To smooth out the wine, they all go through malolactic, or secondary fermentation.

Bruno D'Alfonso, the winemaker at Sanford Winery, has a degree in soil science from California Polytechnic in San Luis Obispo. While in college, he developed a taste for wines and decided he wanted to be a winemaker. He furthered his education by earning an enology degree from U.C. Davis. It was while working at Edna Valley Winery in 1982 and 1983 that he got to know Richard Sanford and joined his enterprise in 1983.

Both Richard Sanford and Bruno D'Alfonso put strong emphasis on barrel fermentation. All of the white wines are barrel fermented in 60-gallon French oak barrels. A portion of the Sauvignon Blanc, however, ferments in American oak barrels. The Pinot Noir is fermented in open top stainless steel tanks and then is aged in oak for 18 months.

One of the most innovative of the Sanford Winery's wines is the Pinot Noir-Vin Gris. The Pinot Noir grapes are crushed and pressed immediately into French oak barrels for fermentation. After the wine is completely dry, it is aged in French oak barrels for four months. To complement the reddish-copper hue and fruitiness of the Vin Gris, Richard and Thekla selected a painting of wild strawberries as the first Vin Gris label.

The Sauvignon Blanc's pungent quality is enhanced by fermentation in a combination of French and American oak. It, too, goes through secondary or malolactic fermentation. "By using both French and American oak, the natural grassy quality is subdued, and the herbal roundness and earthiness are accentuated," says Richard Sanford. The California wild rose, the lupine, the Pacific Coast iris, and the monkey flower have all adorned the Sauvignon Blanc label.

The California poppy, growing wild on the Sanfords' ranch has been used on the Sanford Winery's Chardonnay.

Since all of the Sanford wines have a high acid balance, they are good food wines. Richard and Thekla are both avid cooks and enjoy pairing food with their wines.

Land has been cleared and stakes put in for the first planting of 15 acres of vineyards. Eventually Richard Sanford plans to have 70 acres in vines, which will supply about half of the grapes for his winemaking. Many of the vineyard and winery workers reside on the property and are busy preparing for the building of the winery, which Richard hopes will be complete for the crush of 1988. It is going to be a lengthy process because he plans to have all of the adobe bricks made right on the ranch. He chose adobe brick for the winery not only because of the visual effect, but because they provide natural insulation. The proposed winery of two buildings is to be Southwestern in style with a fountain and large patio linking the buildings. Shortly, a carpentry shop will be established on the ranch to not only restore some of the existing old ranch buildings, but also to help build the winery.

Regardless of where Richard Sanford makes his wines, the beautiful labels on the bottles are only an enticement to the premium, first class wines inside. 🍃

Santa Ynez Valley Winery

Address: 343 North Refugio Road, Santa Ynez 93460
☐ (805) 688-8381
Visitation: Daily, 10 AM to 4 PM
Principals: The Boyd B. Bettencourt family, The Gifford Davidge family, The Erik Brander family
Varietals produced: Sauvignon Blanc, Semillon, Chardonnay, Gewurztraminer, Johannisberg Riesling, Merlot, Cabernet Sauvignon, and Orange Muscat
Production: 12,000 cases per year

The sites of the first college in California and the first commercial vineyard in the Santa Ynez Valley are both a part of the history of the Bettencourt and Davidge properties which are located next to each other in the Santa Ynez Valley a short distance from Solvang.

The 200-acre combined property was originally part of a 36,000-acre land grant during California's Mexican era. In the early 1800s, the first college of the state was built there and operated on the site for over 80 years. The *El Colegio de Nuestra Señora del Refugio* seminary provided education for many priests. The buildings of the seminary were of wood and adobe. A fire destroyed some of the wooden parts; however, some of the remaining parts were incorporated into the Bettencourts' residence. The living room still contains the altar of the chapel, and the present kitchen pantry was the confessional.

For many years, both the Davidge and Bettencourt properties were farmed separately. The Bettencourt portion had been a dairy for over 50 years. In 1969, the two families decided to plant vineyards on part of the combined acreage as an experiment to see if grapes would successfully grow in that particular micro-climate.

The vineyards of the Santa Ynez Valley Winery are located in a low spot of the valley with the river nearby. The area is warm during the day and quite cool at night, with considerable morning fog in the spring and summer months. The experimental planting proved that both climate and soil were suitable for grape growing, and the Davidges and Bettencourts proceeded to expand their vineyards. Today there are 110 acres in grapes. All of the wines are estate grown.

From the growing of grapes it was a logical step to build a winery. The old dairy barn on the Bettencourt property became the winery and much of the dairy equipment, such as stainless steel tanks, is utilized in the operation of the winery.

Santa Ynez Valley Winery was immediately recognized for its excellent Sauvignon Blanc, which over the years has won numerous awards and medals. Another innovative wine which was first introduced in 1976 is the Blanc de Cabernet, one of the first blush wines on the market. A third wine which has helped Santa Ynez Valley Winery gain its excellent reputation is the Johannisberg Riesling. It is made in three styles — off-dry, sweet, and Late Harvest. The cool climate and summer fogs in the valley produce a high acid and good sugar level for the Riesling grape.

Mike Brown is the winemaker at Santa Ynez Valley Winery. He is a native Australian who graduated from the University of Adelaide and also received a master's degree in enology from U.C. Davis. He has worked in both Australian and California wineries.

Mike gives special attention to the Sauvignon Blanc. He partially ferments it in French oak barrels and then ages the entire lot of wine in French oak for four to nine months. A small amount of Semillon is blended into the Sauvignon Blanc to help the aging and give the wine richness. Mike also makes a 100% Semillon varietal.

The Blanc de Cabernet is produced by fermenting the free run juice of the Cabernet Sauvignon. It is a beautiful salmon color, and the resulting wine has a fresh fruity taste reminiscent of strawberries.

Santa Ynez Valley Winery is experimenting with making a port wine made from Cabernet Sauvignon grapes. The juice is fermented with the skins, then pressed off and fortified with brandy aged in oak.

As pioneers in grape growing, the Davidges and the Bettencourts have helped make a lot of wine history in the Santa Ynez valley in the last 17 years. They hope to continue to be one of the leaders in the future by developing new products and new wines, such as Santa Ynez Valley Winery's new port wine. ❧

Vega Vineyards Winery

Address: 9496 Santa Rosa Road, Buellton 93427
   ☐ (805) 688-2415
Visitation: Daily, 10 AM to 4 PM
Principals: William and Jeri Mosby
Varietals produced: Johannisberg Riesling, Gewurztraminer, Chardonnay, and Pinot Noir
Production: 7,000 cases per year

If walls could talk, what a story they would tell! They would relate part of the history of the Santa Ynez Valley and how an old carriage house was turned into a winery.

Located among the rolling hills of the only valley in California that runs from east to west is Vega Vineyards.

The vineyards trace their winemaking history back to the early days of California. The Rancho de la Vega, or "Ranch of the Meadow," was constructed in 1853. The ranch and its 8,000 surrounding acres were a part of the dowry of Micaela Cota in her marriage to Dr. Ramon de la Cuesta.

The historic 13-room adobe house has three-foot thick walls built with redwood timber hauled through the rugged Gaviota Pass ten miles south of the ranch. The first cultivation priority of the de la Cuestas for their land was to plant a vineyard. Some of the original vines are still bearing fruit today.

In the subsequent years, the ranch and parcels of its lands were sold several times. For a number of years after the war, and until the Mosbys purchased the property in 1976, the ranch was a horse farm.

Bill and Jeri Mosby, natives of Oregon, had been living in Lompoc (about 30 miles distant) where Bill is still practicing dentistry. Bill was a home winemaker for many years, and in 1971 he took the first step to becoming a vintner. He and Jeri purchased some property across the river from the present Vega ranch. There he planted a small vineyard of White Riesling. The property known as River Ranch, has had additional vineyards planted in Riesling, Gewurztraminer, Pinot Noir, and some Chardonnay.

In 1976, the Mosbys purchased the old Rancho de la Vega adobe and some of its surrounding lands. Like the original owners — the de la Cuestas — the Mosbys' first priority was to plant vineyards. Their first planting was Johannisberg Riesling. A decade later, 75% of Vega's wines were estate grown from the combined 34 acres of the two ranches.

Since the Santa Ynez Valley is situated east to west, it receives the cooling breezes of the Pacific Ocean. Those cooling breezes mixed with warm days, are the essential climatic elements for premium grape growing. In addition, the soil — alluvial sandy loam on the River Ranch and decomposed shale on the other — provide soil that is suitable for root penetration and excellent drainage.

The first restoration project Jeri and Bill attempted after acquiring the Vega property was to restore the old carriage house. Bill had in the back of his mind that it might be transformed into a winery building. In that way he could realize his own dream of making wines from the grapes he grows. However, a 100-mile-an-hour windstorm swept through the Santa Ynez Valley in the spring of 1977 and leveled the historic old building. Not to be deterred, the Mosbys, with the help of modern technology and modern materials, completely restored the carriage house to its 1860 Victorian facade. The little red building, which has had a small addition on the side, is quite adequate for the winery, lab, and tasting room. There is even capacity for

expanded production. In 1979, Bill's dream became a reality, and Vega became a bonded winery.

Most of the family is involved in the Vega Vineyards Winery. Bill, who still practices dentistry in Lompoc three days a week, is the winemaker, and son Michael, a graduate of Cal Poly-San Luis Obispo, is the vineyard manager. Another son, Gary, also inherited his father's love of wine. He graduated with a degree in enology from U.C. Davis and is now the winemaker at Edna Valley winery. Jeri is in charge of hospitality and does most of the bookkeeping.

Bill Mosby's philosophy of winemaking is to handle the grapes as little as possible. Both the Johannisberg Riesling and the Gewurztraminer are crushed, pressed, and then fermented in cool, 50-degree, jacketed stainless steel tanks. The wines are sterile filtered before bottling and aged in the bottle two to four months prior to release. The Gewurztraminer is made in the Alsatian style — very dry.

The Pinot Noir is hand-picked from estate vineyards. The grapes are then placed in small open top stainless steel fermenters and inoculated with Montrachet yeast. The wine is fermented at fairly warm temperatures to extract the maximum fruity character. Bill uses gravity flow to transfer the wine to barrels for aging. He believes that pumping it into barrels would injure the wine. Pinot Noir is aged for 12 to 18 months, fined with egg white, and then bottled.

Vega's Chardonnay is partially barrel fermented and aged in French Limousin barrels, where malolactic fermentation occurs concurrently with the aging.

Jeri and Bill have a ten-year plan. They want to expand their vineyards so that all of the Vega expanded production of 10,000 cases will be from estate vineyards. This year they will plant an additional ten acres of Chardonnay.

The Mosbys are also restoring the old adobe ranch house. This is turning into quite a project since it literally needs refurbishing from the floor supports upward. The old carriage house no longer houses carriages, but in its Victorian splendor, it houses wines for the carriage trade.

York Mountain Winery

Address: York Mountain Road, Templeton 93465
   ☐ (805) 238-3925
Visitation: Daily, 10 AM to 5 PM
Principals: Max Goldman
Varietals produced: Chardonnay, Merlot, Pinot Noir, Zinfandel, and Cabernet Sauvignon
Production: 5,000 cases per year

The first winery in the South Central Coast area was established in 1882 on land originally deeded by President Ulysses S. Grant to Andrew York. For more than 100 years, York Mountain Winery remained in continuous operation by three generations of the same family. During Prohibition, the Yorks made and sold grape juice. The winery building was constructed of hand-formed bricks which were kiln baked on the York property. The timbers for the structure were brought overland by wagon from Cayucos, ten miles away on the coast. They were taken from a dismantled pier at Cayncos, where northwestern lumber schooners used to deliver their cargo.

In the 1920s the winery became famous for the Zinfandel it had produced for Ignacio Jan Paderewski, the world famous pianist and later president of Poland. Paderewski owned a ranch and vineyard, the San Ignacio Ranch, outside of Paso Robles and had his grapes transported to the York Mountain winery for crushing and processing.

In 1970, Max Goldman, a well known New York State champagne maker, purchased the historic property from Wilford York. Max Goldman, who has a degree in chemistry from Whittier College, started his winemaking career just after the Depression as a chemist doing lab work for Roma Winery in the San Joaquin Valley. In the late 1950s, he moved his family to New York State where he was the winemaker for Great Western. He later became a vice president of production for that organization. Max also has served as a consultant to the champagne industry all over the country. He is also a past president of the American Society of Enologists and on the board of directors of the Wine Institute.

After purchasing the York property in 1970, he was successful in inducing his son Steve to join him in the winemaking and operation of the winery. Steve, who has a B.A. in liberal arts from Colorado State University, agreed to the life of a vintner because it would enable him to continue his interests in the outdoors. Steve now is the full-time winemaker.

York Mountain has its own appellation. The area of about 3,000 acres has 35 acres in vineyards — probably one of the smallest appellations in the United States. York Mountain's vineyards are planted primarily in Zinfandel, Chardonnay, Cabernet Sauvignon, and Pinot Noir. Steve has recently planted more grapes on the property, which will increase the estate wine production in a few years.

At the beginning of its history, the winery was known as the Ascencion winery, named after the Ascencion school in the area. The name was later changed to York and Sons and then to York Mountain Winery. In honor of that first name, Steve Goldman has decided to reintroduce the Ascencion label for some of the wines. The logo of the old winery building is used for both the Ascencion and York Mountain labels.

Steve Goldman is a firm believer that the harvest dictates the style of winemaking. He "lets the grapes do the talking." Max agrees with him and adds that over the last 50 years there has been a great improvement not only in grape varieties, but also in the grapes themselves. He also believes that the winemaker and the viticulturist have to work very closely together.

Steve tries to make complex wines. In order to do this he uses some of the old techniques inherent in York Mountain winemaking, such as open top fermentation for the reds. The York Mountain product line will soon be expanded to include a Pinot Noir Blanc champagne and three port wines — two made from Merlot and one from Zinfandel.

The entire Goldman family is involved in the winery. Max still acts as a consultant to son Steve, who is not only the winemaker but also the vineyard manager. Daughter Suzanne Semones is in charge of the tasting room. Steve's wife Cindy lends a hand wherever she is needed and also uses her culinary talents to produce jellies, mustards, and wine vinegars for sale in the tasting room.

The Goldmans have tried to preserve the heritage of the historic winery by assembling a variety of original winery equipment for display in the tasting room, which resembles an old-fashioned country store. The historic past and the new wines of York Mountain Winery form a happy combination. ❧

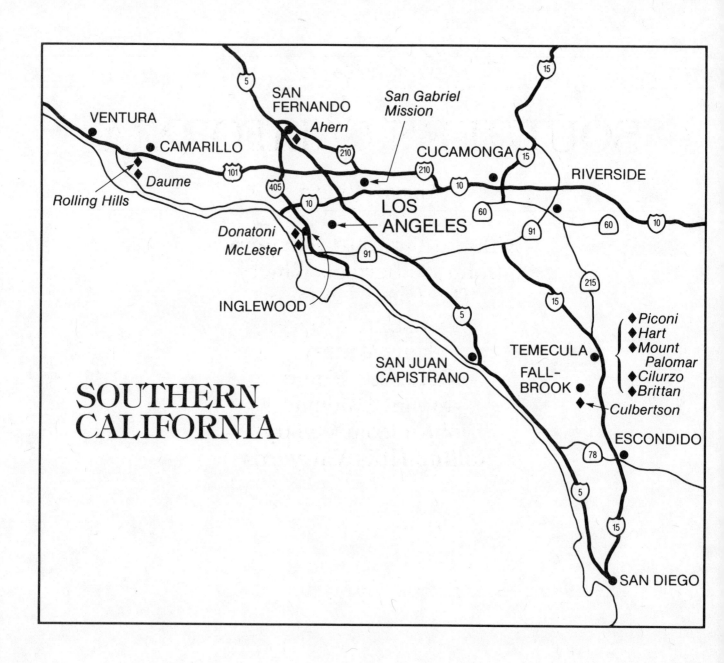

Wineries of

SOUTHERN CALIFORNIA

Ahern Winery
Britton Cellars
Cilurzo Vineyard & Winery
John Culbertson Winery
The Daumé Winery
Donatoni Winery
Hart Winery
McLester Winery
Mount Palomar
John Piconi Winery
Rolling Hills Vineyards

Southern California

It is hard to imagine that about 175 years ago Los Angeles and its surrounding areas were not only the starting point of the California wine industry but also was the largest producing wine area in the state until the 1870s. It all started with the San Gabriel and San Fernando Missions in the early 1800s. In 1830, the San Gabriel Mission was the largest wine producer in California, producing the equivalent of about 6,000 cases of wine per year — the same as a small winery does today. The Mission also had 175 acres of vineyards, which is about the same as many of the family wineries of today. The San Fernando Mission, the second largest wine producer, had a capacity of about one-third of that of San Gabriel.

At about this same time, a secular agricultural industry grew up in what is now downtown Los Angeles. Corn and grapes were the principal crops. At one time there was a vineyard on the property of the present Los Angeles railroad station. Politicians strongly urged a diversification of crops, expressing concern about the over-dependence of the local economy on wine grapes. However, they did admit that the alternative of procuring wine and brandy from Mexico or Europe was undesirable.

The most popular local drink, in addition to wine, was *aguardiente*, a grape brandy. Another local favorite — the only California invented wine beverage — was Angelica, which was a blend of unfermented grape juice and grape brandy.

The first American to plant grapes in California was Joseph Chapman, who in 1824, planted 4,000 vines in what is today downtown Los Angeles. The first professional vintner in California, however, was a Frenchman named Louis Vignes. He had cuttings shipped from Europe via Boston and planted sufficient vineyards to almost double the grape production in California at the time. Vignes was also the first vintner to age his wines. By 1840, he was shipping his wine by ship along the coast of California where it was selling for as much as $2 per gallon at Santa Barbara, Monterey, and San Francisco.

Although the Gold Rush was a great economic boom for Northern California, it was also an economic boom for the Los Angeles vintners as well. They shipped both wine and grapes by ship to San Francisco to quench the thirst of the gold miners in the Sierra Foothills.

By 1863, Los Angeles had a population of 4,000, and 1,000,000 grape vines. Most of these vines were Mission grapes, since none of the European varietals seemed to survive the desert heat. Today, Mission grapes are still grown in Southern California. They are used in the blending of bulk wines.

In 1855, a cooperative vineyard and winery was established around Anaheim, populated with German immigrants. Although they had a rough time getting started, by the mid-1880s the colony was producing about 400,000 cases of wine per year. Success was short lived, since by the end of the 1880s all of the vines had been destroyed by a disease which became known as the "Anaheim Disease."

Urban development and smog has made any major existing grape growing around Los Angeles insignificant. The six premium wineries in the immediate Los Angeles area all purchase their grapes from elsewhere. Cucamonga, a grape growing center since 1830, is also suffering from smog and urban development. The Temecula Valley area, however, which has similar climate and soil to the upper Napa Valley, has become the center of premium wine production in Southern California. ❧

Ahern Winery

Address: 715 Arroyo Avenue, San Fernando 91340
□ (818) 365-3106
Visitation: Daily, by appointment
Principals: Jim and Joyce Ahern
Varietals produced: Sauvignon Blanc, Chardonnay, Zinfandel, and Cabernet Sauvignon
Production: 5,000 cases per year

Two centuries ago, wine was made in the San Fernando Valley northeast of Los Angeles at the San Fernando Mission. When the missions were secularized in 1834 and wine started to become a commercial enterprise in California, the importance of "mission wine" declined. Today, however, wine is again being made in the San Fernando Valley at the Ahern Winery, the only winery in the Valley.

Jim Ahern's winery is not located in an ivy-covered brick building surrounded by rolling hills with vineyards, but in an industrial complex where his neighbors are a transmission repair shop, a shoe factory, a discount clothing store, and an automotive and aircraft balancing shop. It does not take a particular building or ambience to produce premium wines, only the know-how and the proper equipment.

Even though Jim Ahern's winery does not have the romantic atmosphere usually associated with winemaking, he does employ traditional techniques in making wine. He even uses some of the same techniques as the Indians did centuries ago when making wine at the San Fernando Mission. The grapes are pressed on a modern version of the basket press, much the same as was used at the Mission. They are processed by a modern electric crusher which separates the stems. "The Indians never had that kind of equipment," Ahern says. Modern technology has also added many steps in the winemaking process, especially lab testing at various stages. Ahern Winery has a fully equipped lab to check pH and sugar levels, yeast cultures, and fermentation.

Jim Ahern's interest in wine began when he was stationed in Europe with the navy. He adopted the European custom of drinking wine with his meals. In later years, working all over the world as a mechanical engineer for various construction companies, he always became acquainted with the local wines. At that time, however, he did not have a desire to make wine.

One weekend in May 1970 when he and his wife, Joyce, were in San Francisco she spotted a home winemaking shop. For $7.95 Joyce purchased a kit for Jim to try his hand at winemaking. Within weeks, he bought a second kit and some French oak barrels, which he stored in the spare bedroom. It was probably the only "small winery" with wall-to-wall carpeting.

In subsequent years, Jim Ahern became more and more fascinated with winemaking. He took courses in enology at U.C.L.A. and at U. C. Davis and began winning gold medals in home winemaking tastings and contests. He and John Daumé were the driving forces in the founding of a Cellarmaster Club for home winemakers in the Los Angeles area, and Jim was the first president of the club.

The Ahern Winery, founded in 1978, was designed by Jim to be basically a one-man operation. At that time, he retired from his engineering job, which was constructing radar stations in Alaska, and became a full-time vintner. Jim designed special fork lifts and other equipment to enable him to handle the winery by himself, although Joyce does lend a helping hand many times. In addition to that extra pair of needed hands, Joyce also handles the office work for the winery.

Jim Ahern purchases his grapes from Santa Barbara and San Luis Obispo Counties. The grapes are hand picked early in the morning when they are cold and then immediately trucked to the Ahern Winery. They are still cool when they arrive at about two o'clock in the afternoon.

Jim Ahern's style of winemaking is to produce big, robust whites and reds — wines that age well. Jim tries to extract a lot of fruit and complexity from the grapes. He does this by fermenting the reds on the skins for as long as 21 days. The whites are crushed and left with skin contact for approximately 18 hours before pressing and yeast inoculation. Sauvignon Blanc and Chardonnay are barrel fermented and aged in 60-gallon French oak barrels and large French oak upright casks for eight to nine months.

The maximum capacity of the winery is 6,000 cases, which Jim and Joyce Ahern will reach in the near future. Jim still wants to remain a small premium winery so that he and Joyce can handle the entire production process. It is pride in the ultimate product which makes all of the hard work and long hours put in by Jim and Joyce Ahern worth every minute. Winemaking has become a way of life for the Aherns. ❧

Britton Cellars

Address: 40620 Calle Contento, Temecula 92390
□ (714) 676-2938
Visitation: Saturday and Sunday, 11 AM to 5 PM,
Weekdays, by appointment
Principals: Tom and Echo Freestone,
Bob and Debbie Britton
Varietals produced: Chenin Blanc, Sauvignon Blanc,
Chardonnay, White Riesling, Zinfandel Pearl,
Cabernet Pearl, and Merlot
Production: 9,500 cases per year

The Britton winery, with its stained glass windows and its redwood siding, looks as if it is a building out of yesteryear and has been in the Temecula Valley for a long time. From the exterior it gives the impression of being a lovely stop on a stagecoach route.

That is not true. It is the newest winery in the Temecula area, having been completed for the crush of 1984.

In the early 1980s the Freestones and Brittons purchased an existing vineyard just off the main highway in the Temecula Valley. The 20 acres were planted in White Riesling, Chardonnay, Sauvignon Blanc, and Cabernet Sauvignon. The two families had a new interest in winemaking.

With the vineyard producing premium grapes, it was only a natural progression that the two couples should build a winery. Tom Freestone took some time off to work at nearby Hart winery to learn winemaking. Tom also took

classes at U.C. Davis. He is now the winemaker at Britton Cellars.

Tom Freestone, who was engaged in his own spa business at the time the two couples purchased the vineyard, took a leave of absence from his business to help construct the winery. He has since sold his spa business. Tom is an excellent craftsman and handcarved the wood decorations in the winery. In the future, he plans to carve several large casks in the traditional wine symbols of Europe.

Bob Britton is a retired fireman, and in addition to the winery, is also involved in real estate.

The beautiful stained glass windows are also Tom's creation. He says that a desire for stained glass windows inspired him to make the ones in the winery. He had obtained a commercial price for them, which was above the winery's budget — so he decided to make them himself. Tom is general manager of the winery and takes care of day-to-day operations.

Echo Freestone was instrumental in furthering her husband's interest in wine, since she worked for a time in a wine shop. The Freestones have always enjoyed wine with dinner and regard it as a food beverage. Tom is not a conformist and drinks whichever wine suits his mood with a meal, not what the experts say goes together.

Tom and Bob enjoy the life of vintners, especially the people they encounter. They eventually plan to expand the production of their winery to 15,000 cases and will release Zinfandel and Cabernet Sauvignon as soon as the aging process is finished. ❧

Cilurzo Vineyard & Winery

Address: 41220 Calle Contento, Temecula 92390
☐ (714) 676-5250
Visitation: Daily, 9 AM to 5 PM
Principals: Vincenzo and Audrey Cilurzo
Varietals produced: Chenin Blanc, Sauvignon Blanc, Chardonnay, Pinot Noir, Petite Sirah, Cabernet Sauvignon, Late Harvest Johannisberg Riesling
Production: 8,000 cases per year

"Lights, action, roll the cameras," is a familiar phrase to Vince Cilurzo, who has been a lighting director with ABC Television for over 20 years. He is the lighting director for the MERV GRIFFIN SHOW, DANCE FEVER, and ENTERTAINMENT TONIGHT, and has worked specials for Dean Martin and Frank Sinatra. He was also involved with the lighting for President Reagan's first inauguration.

In the 1960s the Cilurzos began traveling south of Los Angeles to spend weekends in the Temecula area. A friend told them to buy land there and plant grapes, because he felt one of these days it would be another Napa Valley. Audrey and Vince followed the friend's advice and purchased 52 acres east of Temecula near Rancho California.

Break, an organization which had done typography studies for Rancho California, was hired by Vince to study weather and soil conditions of his newly acquired 52 acres. By 1968, the first vines — Petite Sirah — were planted. It was the first commercial planting of premium grapes in Southern California in modern history. Although, the vineyard experts had discouraged the growing of reds in the Temecula area, they flourished on the Cilurzo property and Vince has been producing reds since he started the winery.

The Temecula appellation encompasses an area ten miles square. Its climate is similar to the Napa Valley, with warm sunny days and cool dry nights.

In 1978, the Cilurzos built a Spanish-style adobe home, totally solar-powered, at the summit of their property. That same year, Vince built a small cellar into the side of the hill as the start of a winery. The winery has since been enlarged to a modern structure of 13,000 square feet, and, being partially underground, it keeps an even cool temperature without expensive air-conditioning.

Vince, until recently, has been the winemaker. In 1985, he hired Dave Hopkins, en enology graduate from California State University, Fresno as winemaker, and put him in charge of production. (Vince spends four days a week in Los Angeles continuing his career as a lighting director.) Vince Cilurzo has the winemaking philosophy of doing as little as possible to the wines. He strives for subtle, well-balanced wines.

The Cilurzo Chardonnay is fermented in stainless steel tanks equipped with an inner stave system. Lightly toasted French Limousin oak staves are arranged inside the tank so that the ratio of wine to wood is the same as in the barrel. Having complete temperature control during the entire fermentation "on the wood" produces a deep, mellow, and complex wine. The wine is then aged in small French oak barrels.

When conditions are right, Vince Cilurzo produces a Late Harvest Johannisberg Riesling. So far, he has been able to procure the Botrytis grapes almost very year. Fermentation of this wine is very slow, anywhere from eight to ten months in temperature-controlled stainless steel tanks at 30 to 35 degrees.

Vince also makes a proprietary red and white wine called Vincheno. The name is a blending of the Cilurzo children's names — Vinnie and Chenin. Vince and Audrey's daughter Chenin was named after the Chenin Blanc wine first made by the Cilurzo Winery in the year of her birth.

Audrey Cilurzo is very involved in the winery. Almost every week there is a special dinner at the Cilurzo home for either a wine related or industrial group. Audrey, an excellent cook, usually prepares a seven-course meal, served with complementing Cilurzo wines. The food is served by the two teenage Cilurzos in the Spanish-style dining room of the home.

Although Vince Cilurzo may wear two hats, he is as enthusiastic about his lighting endeavors as he is about being a vintner — a pioneer in a little-tapped wine growing region of California. ❧

John Culbertson Winery

Address: 2608 Via Rancheros, Fallbrook 92028
□ (619) 728-0156
Visitation: Weekends, by appointment only
Principals: John and Martha Culbertson
Varietals produced: Natural, Brut, Brut-Rosé, Blanc de Noir, and Cuvée de Frontignan (all sparkling wines in *Méthode Champenoise*
Production: 9,500 cases per year

Special occasions call for a toast of "bubbly" and the occasion is even more special if the sparkling wine is made in the *Méthode Champenoise*. However, champagne does not have to be restricted to special occasions; it is an enjoyable drink at any time from brunch to lunch to aperitif to dinner through dessert. There is a style of champagne not only for every occasion, but to accompany any type of food — anything from Beef Wellington to Chinese Stir Fry.

There has always been a certain aloofness and mystique associated with champagne, but for no valid reason. The champagnes themselves range from very dry to slightly sweet — from those made from Chardonnay to Pinot Noir to Muscat Canelli. The wines are basically the same as used for still wines, only the method of production is different. The difference between sparkling wine and champagne is merely that the latter is made in the Champagne region of France — although the term is used all over the world to describe sparkling wine made by the *Méthode Champenoise*.

John Culbertson Winery is one of the foremost producers of champagne in this country. Twenty-five medals were awarded to the Culbertson champagnes at major competitions in 1985 alone, including seven to the Brut Rosé and six to the Blanc de Noir.

The winery is located in Southern California, 50 miles north of San Diego in Fallbrook, a center for avocado and citrus growing. Not only is this a rather unlikely location for a champagne cellar, but the winery is located in the middle of an 80-acre avocado and citrus grove. The ranch, named "Ragalo del Mar," which means gift from the sea, is owned by John and Martha Culbertson. Both are natives of the San Diego area.

John Culbertson is president and owner of Martech International, a firm that provides deep sea diving services to the oil exploration industry. Since the headquarters of the firm is based in Houston, Texas, John commutes to Houston frequently. John was an underwater demolition specialist in the navy and extended that speciality into his present career.

It was while John's firm was working off the coast of Australia that John and Martha Culbertson first became interested in wines. This interest grew when business reasons caused them to move to Singapore in 1971. The move permitted them to experiment not only with Australian wines, but also the wines of Bordeaux, Burgundy, and Champagne. Both John and Martha were delighted with the way the sparkling wines of Champagne paired with Martha's gourmet cooking. This experience caused John and Martha to start dreaming of owning their own winery, and maybe even producing champagne.

The idea at the time may have seemed a little beyond fulfillment since Houston, Texas is not exactly the place to start a winery. John, who is a very persistent person, did not give up that easily. He did some research work on Texas grape growing in conjunction with Texas A & M University, and he had even selected a name for his future winery.

In the meantime, in 1975, John and Martha had purchased an 80-acre avocado ranch in the Fallbrook area, thinking they might eventually make that their permanent home. The next year they decided to make the move from Houston and built a home on the property. They dug a cellar under the residence to be used for John's winemaking. He had taken some extension courses from U.C. Davis, and some of his first home winemaking was champagne. The first cuvées were made in that cellar. From there, the winery operation progressed to a series of construction trailers to the present facility.

By 1981, they decided to make only champagne in the traditional *Méthode Champenoise* and built a winery in the avocado grove below the residence. The cellar was constructed into the hillside with underground bays, each ten feet high and holding 12,000 to 14,000 bottles.

Martha Culbertson has gained fame in the last few years as one of the most creative new restaurateurs in Southern California. She is a pupil of Julia Child, Simone Beck, and Jacques Pepin. Martha is a founder of the American Institute of Wine and Food, and several years ago she established the acclaimed Fallbrook Grocery. The restaurant started as a carry-out deli, with a few tables on the patio for sit-down eating, and in a few years it has grown into one of the most "in" eating establishments between San Diego and Los Angeles. The Fallbrook Grocery has recently been remodelled for additional dining space.

In 1982, Ron McClendon, a graduate of U. C. Davis,

joined the Culbertson winery as winemaker and general manager. Since both John and Ron are innovative winemakers, a blend of grapes is used to make the still wine — cuvée — which ultimately becomes the champagne. For instance, the Blanc de Blanc might contain: 14% Chenin Blanc, 6% Sauvignon Blanc, 30 % Chardonnay, and 50% Pinot Blanc. The percentages and the number of varietals vary from year to year. One of the most interesting Culbertson champagnes is the Cuvée de Frontignon — a blend of Muscat Canelli, Chenin Blanc, and Pinot Blanc. It is a wonderful accompaniment to desserts since it contains 3% sugar but also has good acid balance.

The Culbertsons currently purchase most of their grapes. Twenty acres of Chardonnay vineyards have been planted on the ranch, and the first harvest of these vines will be in 1986. The whites — Pinot Blanc, Sauvignon Blanc, Chenin Blanc, and Chardonnay — are from the Temecula area, 25 miles away. The Pinot Noirs comes from San Luis Obispo.

Making champagne in the *Méthode Champenoise* is like producing two wines. The grapes are hand-picked at 18% to 19% sugar. This is lower than normal winemaking, and the practice evolved in the Champagne region of France because the climate frequently did not permit the grapes to ripen to a higher sugar content. The grapes for Culbertson champagnes are picked early, usually in August, at the lower sugar level.

At that time, the various varietals, Chenin Blanc, Sauvignon Blanc, Chardonnay, Pinot Blanc, Pinot Noir, and Muscat Canelli are made into still wines. In November, John Culbertson, Ron McClendon, and Jon McPherson, the assistant winemaker, sample the various wines and determine the blend to be used for each of the five champagnes to be produced. Each year the blend varies with the vintage.

In January, the wines decided upon in November are blended in huge vats. Sugar and yeast is added for the secondary fermentation. This second fermentation creates the bubbles in the champagne. The champagne bottles are carefully filled. A "pop bottle" cap is placed on the bottle to withstand the terrific pressures caused during secondary fermentation which usually takes about 90 days.- (Occasionally a bottle will burst from the pressure.) The bottles are then stacked in the underground bays to undergo secondary fermentation and to age the respective cuvées — the wine blend of the champagne. This aging — *en tirage* — takes anywhere from 18 months to four years, again depending on the cuvée.

The process to remove the yeast is the same in all *Méthode Champenoise* wineries. The bottles are put into a rack, called a riddling rack, neck down, so that the spent yeast, which has settled along one side of the bottle, may be forced to the neck. Periodically the bottles are turned — *riddled* — to enable the yeast sediments to flow downward. When all of the yeast has been collected in the neck of the bottle, the bottles are taken to a special cold room for *disgorging* — the removal of the yeast. The neck of each bottle is dipped into a solution which freezes the neck of the bottle and the plug with the sediment of yeast is removed. A predetermined *dosage* — mixture of sugar and brandy — is added not only to replace the frozen liquid which was extracted, but also the amount of sugar used determines the ultimate dryness of the champagne. Culbertson's Natural Champagne has no sugar added to it.

Making champagne is not only time consuming, but it is also very costly. In order to reduce some of the costs, John Culbertson uses a computerized riddling machine to help the yeast settle in the neck of the bottles. Bottles are put into a large crate, and a machine turns the crate according to a predetermined program. This technique was developed in France to cut costs and is now used in the larger champagne cellars throughout the world.

Each harvest and each cuvée bring new challenges and new innovations for the Culbertsons. Martha is constantly experimenting with new food combinations to complement the Culbertson champagnes, and John is always refining the product. He plans in the future to make a sparkling burgundy wine also in the *Méthode Champenoise*. The past few years of excellence, critical acclaim, and awards indicate that Culbertson champagnes are "the bubbly" to drink at any time — and will help make any occasion special. ❧

The Daumé Winery

Address: 279 Aviador Street, Camarillo 93010
□ (805) 484-0597 or (818) 884-8586
Visitation: By appointment only
Principals: John E. Daumé
Varietals produced: Sauvignon Blanc, Chardonnay, Vin Gris (dry blush wine from Pinot Noir), and Pinot Noir
Production: 2,000 cases per year

"A fine dinner wine is like a lady you take out to dinner. She demands and appreciates your attention," says John Daumé. Consequently, he makes strictly dinner wines. They are dry and are made in the French tradition.

John Daumé, in addition to producing wines, is considered the wine guru for many amateur winemakers in Southern California. He is the inspiration behind a number of wineries founded in the last ten years.

John grew up in Detroit, where he attended medical school, but ultimately opted for a career in retailing. He was a buyer of furniture for Gimbels in New York, and later, when he moved to Southern California, he became a buyer for Bullocks.

In 1970, John began to experiment with home winemaking. He was able to put his medical education to good use in this new hobby, which later became his vocation.

Wanting to expand his hobby, John became more and more involved with the "winemaking scene." This led to his opening of the Home Wine Shop in Woodland Hills in 1972 — a shop selling all necessary supplies to the home wine and beer maker. He also formed a Cellarmasters Club for the home winemakers to permit them to exchange ideas and encouragements. Out of the 150 members of John Daumé's Cellarmasters Club, 15 have opened their own award-winning wineries.

In 1982, John Daumé decided to commercialize his winemaking by opening a winery in Camarillo in Ventura County north of Los Angeles. The winery is located in a steel-framed building in an industrial park surrounded by other types of manufacturing businesses, including the Rolling Hills Winery. John still operates the Home Wine Shop and buys as much as 20 tons of grapes a year for use by the Club's home winemakers.

John Daumé makes dinner wines in the strictly French tradition. The Chardonnay is 100% barrel fermented, and then barrel aged with heavy lees contact. The Sauvignon Blanc is treated like the Chardonnay — barrel fermented and aged — to downplay the fruitiness, but emphasize the complexity of the wine.

Stainless steel tanks have essentially one purpose in John Daumé's winery. They are used for transferring the wine from one function to another. The Vin Gris, however, is fermented in stainless steel to retain the fresh fruitiness with French oak barrel shavings added for complexity and flavor.

The Pinot Noir, in a classic Burgundian style, is intensely fruity. John Daumé makes two wines from the Pinot Noir grapes. The first, Vin Gris, a blush-type of wine, is made with little skin contact. The juice is pressed off and fermented completely dry. The skins of the Vin Gris are then added back to the Pinot Noir for fermentation. John likes to ferment his Pinot Noir in small batches so that he can more easily punch down the cap in the traditional manner. After fermentation, the wine is then pressed off and racked into barrels for aging.

John Daumé does not grow any grapes, but purchases them from the Santa Maria and Paso Robles areas. He feels that the climate in these two growing regions of California is the most similar to that of Burgundy.

It is hard to believe that these exquisite French-style dinner wines are produced in an industrial complex and not in a French chateau. However, that is part of California winemaking ingenuity. John Daumé does not want his winery to grow. At the present size, he can do most of the work himself. However, friends and members of the Cellarmasters Club lend a helping hand at crush and bottling times. He still wants to retain time to help and encourage home winemakers "to do their thing." 🐛

Donatoni Winery

Address: 10604 La Cienega Boulevard, Inglewood 90304
  ☐ (213) 645-5445
Visitation: First Saturday of each month, 10 AM to 5
  PM, or by appointment
Principals: Hank and Judy Donatoni
Varietals produced: Chardonnay and Cabernet
  Sauvignon
Production: 1,200 cases per year

The roar of the planes overhead does not bother Hank Donatoni as he is tending to chores in his winery located across the street from Los Angeles International Airport. He is used to the roar of the plane engines, since he is a pilot for United Airlines, flying mainly 727s. Besides, when he comes off a flight, it is an easy "hop" to his winery. The winery is located in an industrial complex at the end of the runway. There is an ordinance in Los Angeles prohibiting the operation of a winery within the city limits. However, there are two blocks of La Cienega Boulevard next to Los Angeles International Airport that are in Los Angeles County, where light manufacturing is permitted.

Hank Donatoni, who is of Italian heritage, grew up in Southern California and watched his family make wine when he was a boy. As he grew up he enjoyed wine, but the thought of making wine had not entered his mind until he and his wife Judy purchased a house in Topanga Canyon, north of Los Angeles, in 1968.

Along with the house there was a one-half acre vineyard of Zinfandel. Hank bought a book on how to make wine. That fall, he crushed 12 gallons of wine and made his first estate bottled Zinfandel. The next year, like any good vineyard manager, he pruned his vines and increased production considerably. Eventually, as do most home winemakers in the Los Angeles area, he joined the Cellarmasters Club, an organization for home winemakers in Southern California.

Hank, who has a degree in business administration from Northrup College, received his flight training in the navy. When he left the navy in the late 1950s, the field of business administration was not too promising. He applied to United Airlines for a flying job and was put on their waiting list. In 1959, he was hired as a junior officer and has been with United ever since, making the rank of captain several years ago. Judy Donatoni, as a stewardess for United Airlines, is also a flying member of the family. Since she is the mother of five children, she is not on a regular schedule, but takes relief jobs, a situation which provides time to care for her family and further her excellent culinary interests.

All of Donatoni's grapes are purchased. The Cabernet Sauvignon comes from a contract grower in San Miguel near Paso Robles. The grapes are picked in the early evening and trucked to the winery, arriving in the middle of the night so that they are still cool and ready for fermentation.

The Chardonnay, on the other hand, comes from Monterey County, where Hank has a contract with a grower to pick the grapes at a high sugar level. He lso has an agreement with a large winery there to do the crushing and pressing. It gives Hank a chance to obtain a blend of juices from several vineyards, thereby adding complexity to his wine. Only the juice is trucked to Los Angeles in refrigerated trucks. That method is advantageous to Hank in several respects. In this way, not only does Hank obtain very fresh juice, but he does not have the problem of disposing of the residual skins and stems in an urban area.

In Hank's mind there are three wines: White and Red; and then there is Chardonnay. He ferments various lots of Chardonnay separately, and lets each one go through secondary malolactic fermentation in French oak barrels. He then blends the lots together to achieve the complexity he desires.

Hank and Judy want their winery to expand at a modest pace. However, sometime in the future they would like to retire, move to the Paso Robles area, and build their own winery. 🐌

Hart Winery

Address: 32580 Rancho California Road, Temecula 92390 □ (714) 676-6300

Visitation: Saturday and Sunday, 11 AM to 4 PM, or by appointment

Principals: Travis and Nancy Hart

Varietals produced: Chenin Blanc, Sauvignon Blanc, Chardonnay, Cabernet Blanc, Merlot, and Cabernet Sauvignon

Production: 6,000 cases per year

Travis Hart has been involved in several pioneering enterprises — from mapping the ocean currents to growing grapes in a newly discovered region of California.

A third generation Californian, Travis Hart was born in Holtville in the Imperial Valley of California. He graduated from San Diego State with a degree in political science and a teaching credential, which he later used. A stint in the army in Germany first acquainted Travis with wine, a beverage he was not familiar with since he grew up in a teetotalling family. From Germany, he toured Italy and became very fond of their red wines, particularly when paired with food. To this day, he enjoys drinking Zinfandel with his meals, as he feels it best represents the Italian type of wine.

Upon return to California, he, as well as his wife Nancy, taught in the Carlsbad (on the Pacific Coast, 30 miles from Temecula) school system. Nancy still teaches there. Travis, however, was extremely interested in the sea and in oceanography and obtained a position as a marine technician at Scripps Research Center at La Jolla. For five years he collected and studied oceanographic data.

After that, Travis returned to teaching and furthur developed his interest in wine. He became a home winemaker and also started looking at property in the much talked about Temecula Valley, an area for potential grape growing. The predictions made in the early 1970s — that this region of Southern California would become a center for the growing of premium wine grapes — turned out to be right.

In 1973, Travis and Nancy Hart, with a partner, purchased 12 acres east of Temecula for the purpose of raising wine grapes. After all, Callaway Vineyards had just been established next to their property and had a huge winery under construction. The Harts proceeded to plant grapes on 11 of the acres they had purchased. Today their vineyard provides about 25% of the grapes they use in their winery. The remainder is purchased from nearby vineyards in the Temecula Valley. The unique climate of the Temecula Valley, combined with its granite soil, gives Hart wines a smoothness which makes them good food wines. One exception to the use of Temecula Valley grown grapes is the Cabernet Sauvignon which comes from a little further away at elevation 2,400 feet and about 15 miles from the ocean.

At first, Travis and Nancy sold grapes to home winemakers in the area. However, as Travis became more and more interested in the winemaking process himself, he wanted his own winery. In 1979, he took a year's leave of absence from teaching to build a winery on his property. By the next summer the winery was finished, the crush started, and Travis never returned to teaching.

In his winemaking, Travis tries to extract the best varietal characteristics from the grapes. The Hart Winery's Sauvignon Blanc has a very subtle hint of oak and is made in a very dry style. Depending on the vintage, a portion of the Sauvignon Blanc may be barrel fermented. The same is true for the Chardonnay. Both have oak aging.

Tropical storms, combined with Santa Ana winds, sometimes occur in the Temecula Valley. When this occurs, the grapes may rot, causing botrytis. If that is the case, Travis will make a Late Harvest Zinfandel.

There is a considerable early history of California associated with the Temecula Valley — it was on a stagecoach route, the Anza expedition came through the area, and one of the first railroads was built there. It has taken modern pioneers like Travis Hart, his wife Nancy, and his family to help establish a new industry for the area — premium winemaking. ❧

McLester Winery

Address: 1067-D South La Cienega Boulevard,
Inglewood 90304 □ (213) 641-9686
Visitation: Saturday Noon to 5 PM, Monday through
Friday, by appointment
Open house once every quarter by invitation
Principals: Cecil McLester and Marcella Mattson
McLester
Varietals produced: Fumé Blanc, Sauvignon Blanc,
Zinfandel Rose, Merlot, Zinfandel, Cabernet
Sauvignon and Muscat Canelli (Suite 13)
Production: 3,000 cases per year

"Ready for landing on runway 13. Ready for takeoff on runway 4." These may not be the exact instructions from the control tower to the pilot but similar ones are being issued across the street from McLester Winery. The winery is located in an industrial complex at the east end of the runways of Los Angeles International Airport. Outside of the winery, the plane noise is so severe that it is hard to hold a conversation. However, once inside the boutique winery with its pleasant tasting area, the outside surroundings are completely forgotten.

Cecil and Marcy McLester have honored their location and their many clientele in the aerospace industry by naming their two proprietary wines Runway Red and Runway White. The wines feature a label with a 747 bearing down on a runway flanked by vineyards. Actually, there are no vineyards in the landing pattern, although most flights do traverse over vineyards elsewhere in California.

McLester Winery is surrounded by a wood shop, an air freight company, and a welding operation. However, there are two other wineries — Donatoni and Palos Verdes — in the same block. As is the pattern with most vintners, these three are very supportive of each other and frequently hold joint open houses.

Cecil McLester first became acquainted with wine while he was in college at North Texas State University. Most of his fraternity brothers were beer drinkers, but Cecil was not fond of beer. He and a couple of his fraternity brothers started drinking Gallo Rosé. When they ran low on funds they stretched the wine by combining it with Strawberry Kool-Aid. It was not a sophisticated beginning to wine appreciation, but in later years Cecil did develop a more sensitive palate.

Years later, in the early 1970s, Cecil decided to try his hand at home winemaking. His first batches turned out very well and he supplied the wine for his group's annual Christmas party. With that kind of encouragement he could do no less than go commercial. His commercial efforts, too, have been very rewarding. One of his first wines, a 1981 Zinfandel, won a medal in the first show McLester entered. The wines have been winning medals ever since, and McLester has become well known for his reds.

McLester Winery is a two person operation. Cecil still has a full-time job as a military sales account manager for Motorola Semiconductor. Most of his work is in the Los Angeles area. This enables him to also be close to the winery. Marcy, who had quite a wine collection when she met Cecil, had been interested in premium wines for a long time and was delighted to be involved in the winery. Marcy does all of the administrative work for the winery, working with accounts and with an extensive customer mailing list. Periodically she writes a newsletter directed to their supporters.

Grapes from the Paso Robles and Amador County areas are trucked to the winery in refrigerated trucks. The Zinfandel comes from Amador County. The grapes are crushed at the winery, and the pomace is removed by a local waste disposal contractor. The winery, with its white walls, is the epitome of cleanliness.

Cecil McLester's speciality is red wines. He makes Zinfandel and Cabernet Sauvignon in the classical French way. Using open top fermentors he ferments the grapes at a warm temperature. Instead of punching the cap down, Cecil pumps the wine over three times a day for one week. In order to get a soft press, he uses a small basket press. The wine is then held in large tanks with the lees for four weeks. Then it is pumped into French and American oak barrels for 18 to 24 months of aging. The Zinfandel ages in American oak. Cecil likes to use various woods for complexity. "The finish is different. The French oak smoothes the wine and the American brings out the tannin," he says. Before bottling, Cecil lightly fines the wines and blends the various barrel contents together. The results are big fruity wines.

Suite 13, a medal winner in several tasting competitions including the Orange County Fair, is made from the Muscat Canelli grape. The wine has a good acid balance giving it a fresh crisp finish. The Suite 13 label shows a fuschia to denote freshness.

Having a winery in the city has its advantages Marcy points out. The McLesters are avid theatergoers and also enjoy recreational cycling around the Los Angeles area — activities in which they could not participate if they were located out in the winegrowing areas.

Being located next to the L. A. airport is an ideal location for the McLester Winery. Their clientele can either fly in or drive in. The McLesters particularly value support from customers in nearby office and industrial complexes.

Mount Palomar

Address: 33820 Rancho California Road, Temecula 92390 □ (714) 676-5047

Visitation: Daily, 9 AM to 5 PM

Principals: John H. and Olivia Poole, Peter Poole

Varietals produced: Chenin Blanc, Sauvignon Blanc, Chardonnay, Johannisberg Riesling, Gamay Beaujolais,Cabernet Blanc, Cabernet Sauvignon, and Cream Sherry

Production: 15,000 cases per year

Prior to the 1960s, the majority of the agricultural land of the Temecula Valley was owned by Vail Ranch. It constituted 80,000 acres. The land then was divided and sold to large corporations such as Kaiser Aluminum, Richfield Oil, New York Central Railroad, and others. In the mid-1960s, these corporations subdivided their plots of land into parcels of more than 200 acres, which in turn were sold to individuals. One of these parcels was purchased by John Poole, a pioneer vintner in the Temecula Valley.

Kaiser commissioned the University of California at Davis to do a climate and soil study of the Temecula Valley and test-plant some of the acreage in various grape varietals. It was determined that the Valley was suitable for grape growing. Twenty years later, with an abundance of vineyards, the Temecula Valley was approved as a grape growing appellation.

John Poole was the founder and owner of radio station KBIG, the Catalina Island station. He also had interests in 12 other radio and TV stations in Southern California and Minnesota. John, who came to California at the age of one, wanted to get out-of-doors to a more relaxed lifestyle, and he particularly wanted to work with a product connected with agriculture. John had already decided he wanted to grow grapes. Many years of European travel and the European heritage of his wife, Olivia, made wine a part of daily meals and family life. Grape growing furthered his original interest in wine.

Mount Palomar vineyards, at an elevation of 1,400 feet above sea level, are situated halfway between the Pacific Ocean and Palm Dessert. The warm dry days, coupled with late afternoon cool ocean breezes, provide favorable grape growing conditions. The area is even well suited to

Johannisberg Riesling, a grape that prefers cooler climates. In Temecula Valley, as in all of the other grape growing regions of California, there are many micro-climates which provide the vintner with the opportunity to grow a variety of grapes.

Subsequently, John Poole planted 160 acres of vineyards with various varietals. Since that time, some varieties have been grafted over and some acreage has been replanted. John discovered that some grapes did not do as well as he had hoped, and the demand for some of the varieties he had planted decreased with the consumer's varying tastes. Also, some of the lesser producing acreage has been sold. After "fine tuning" the property, John now has 103 acres of premium vineyards, and 90% of the wines are produced from estate grown grapes.

In 1975, the first Mount Palomar wines were produced by John Poole in the tractor shed on the premises. Shortly thereafter, Joseph Cherpin joined the winery as winemaker.

Joe Cherpin made his first wine at the age of 12 under the guidance of his French-born father Louis Cherpin, founder of the Cherpin Winery in Fontana, California. Eventually, Joe took over the winemaking and management of the family business. He later was cellar master at the Cucamonga Vineyard, a well known champagne producer. Last year, Joe went back to France to visit relatives in the winemaking region and to learn more about French winemaking techniques.

As a partial result of this visit, Joe produced a Gamay Beaujolais in the Nouveau style using the traditional French *"maceration carbonique"* technique. The wine is released on the same day as the Nouveau wine in France. It is a fragrant and fruity wine meant to be enjoyed while still young.

Mount Palomar Winery also produces a cream sherry. The sherry is aged for one year in an outdoor solera. The sun oxidizes the wine and caramelizes the sugar. This method of making sherry has been used over the centuries.

The winery, with Joe Cherpin as winemaker, has received many medals over the years and helped put the Temecula Valley on the California wine map. One of Mount Palomar's consistent winners is their Chenin Blanc. It has 1% residual sugar to balance the acid, giving it a crisp finish.

Mount Palomar winery is built into a hillside for natural cooling. The building was constructed in 1975 and has had additions in 1978 and 1981. There is a separate barrel storage building on a grade below the winery. The fermented juice flows by gravity through a pipe to the barrel room, and after aging is pumped back for bottling.

Peter Poole, John's eldest son, joined the winery in 1978 after graduating from the University of Washington with a degree in botany. He has worked at various tasks throughout the winery and has designed the winery's label. Peter is now president and operations manager of the winery.

John Poole has built his winery with a visitors' center and outdoor picnic areas. There are secluded spaces with tables for 100 picnickers. The visitors' center has a large tasting room, deli foods, and gift shop. John wants the winery visitors to enjoy the facilities, and he can often be found conducting tours of his winery.

Not only has John Poole enjoyed being involved in agriculture and overseeing the production of one of nature's products, but he has been a real pioneer of the development of the Temecula region. ❧

John Piconi Winery

Address: 33410 Rancho California Road, Temecula 92390 □ (714) 676-5400

Visitation: Saturday and Sunday, 10 AM to 5 PM

Principals: John and Gloria Piconi

Varietals produced: Chenin Blanc, Fumé Blanc, Chardonnay, Johannisberg Riesling, Rose of Cabernet, Merlot, Petite Sirah, and Cabernet Sauvignon

Production: 7,000 cases per year

"Wine is really something beyond the comprehension of man. No matter how sophisticated we get, man can never create wine chemically. Nature has to do the work." So speaks a man who knows science and winemaking. Although the two work interdependently with each other, Dr. John Piconi strongly believes that premium grapes make premium wine.

Wine has always been very much a part of the Piconi family. John is from an Italian family and grew up in Pittsburg, Pennsylvania. His father and mother made wine every year from Muscat and Alicante grapes shipped by refrigerated rail cars from California. Winemaking was always an occasion, and John loved the aroma of wine around the house.

After a year's duty in Viet Nam, John brought his wife Gloria and their children to the West Coast where John did a residency in urology in San Diego. While John was in Viet Nam, Gloria stayed in Pittsburg with her mother-in-law, learning many of the old-fashioned Italian cooking techniques. These have remained with Gloria over the years and gave her the experience to teach cooking classes.

While living in San Diego, John started making wine at home. He drove up to the Paso Robles area each year to get his grapes. John's medical training, combined with his observations of his parents' techniques in winemaking, made the process very easy for him.

John always wanted to own a winery at some point in his life. After moving to Fallbrook, north of San Diego, in 1978, to establish a medical practice, he continued with his home winemaking. The demand by friends for his product became so great that he was about to exceed his amateur legal limit of 200 gallons per year.

An opportunity presented itself for him to form a partnership with a friend in Temecula (about 30 miles away) to establish a winery. The friend had been growing grapes for a number of years. However, the partnership did not work out and was dissolved after a couple of years, although this venture got John even more interested in winemaking.

John and Gloria purchased a piece of land east of Temecula in 1981, and planted six-and-a-half acres of vineyards along the contours of the sloping hills of his property. This type of planting, following the contours of the land, avoided the concentrated heat which builds up on the Temecula Valley floor. The Temecula Valley is located about 20 miles from the Pacific Ocean and receives the sea breezes in the late afternoon after warm sunny days.

In 1982, the Piconis built their own winery from plans that John had designed. He spent quite a bit of time inspecting other wineries in California to determine the most efficient winery design. Part of the winery is built into the hillside, utilizing the natural cooling available underground. The partial underground area is used for winemaking, cellaring, and storage. John Piconi custom-designed stacking devices for his small French oak barrels. The wall of barrels is designed with catwalks. Each barrel sits on casters which allow for easy turning and cleaning in place. Individual barrels can be removed with a forklift independently without disturbing the others.

Since most of John Piconi's vines are still young, he purchases a great deal of his grapes from neighboring vineyards. The close proximity of the grapes to the winery reduces shipping time, and crushing takes place within a short time after picking.

There has always been a myth that Southern California does not produce premium red wine. John Piconi, along with the other vintners in the Temecula Valley, has put that myth to rest. John Piconi's red Petite Sirah has won a gold medal at the Orange County Fair, and each of his Cabernet Sauvignon vintages have won a medal every year.

John Piconi is the winemaker with the assistance of his oldest son, Tom, who has taken over most of the day-to-day duties. Since John's mother and father still love winemaking, they come out each year from Pittsburg to help work the crush. John Piconi still has a very active medical practice.

Wine is very much a part of the day-to-day life of the Piconis, especially at dinnertime. "Our dinnertime frequently lasts two hours," says John. They do not drink a lot of wine, but it is a time for family togetherness at the end of the day. "Wine has been married to food and that's the way it should be enjoyed, as an accompaniment to food," he adds.

Why did John Piconi build a winery? He wanted to leave a heritage and tradition to his five children — a family business which they could take over one day. After all, he asks, what would they do with a medical practice? ❧

Rolling Hills Vineyards

Address: 167-L Aviador Street, Camarillo 93010
□ (805) 484-8100
Visitation: By appointment only; open house by invitation twice a year
Principals: Edward A. Pagor, Jr.
Varietals produced: Chardonnay, Pinot Noir, Merlot, Zinfandel, and Cabernet Sauvignon
Production: 1,000 cases per year

Rolling Hills may be a small winery, but that does not keep Ed Pagor from winning gold medals with his Chardonnay and Zinfandel at the prestigious Los Angeles County and Orange County Fairs. The other Rolling Hills wines have also been consistent medal winners at other wine judging competitions.

Rolling Hills describes the rolling hillside vineyards which Ed and Eve Pagor own in Temecula, south of Los Angeles. They purchased the property in 1979 and have planted 5 acres of Johannisberg Riesling there. The Pagors made their first wines from these grapes for the 1986 crush. At the present time all of the grapes used at Rolling Hills are purchased — the Pinot Noir and Chardonnay from Santa Maria, Zinfandel from Amador County, and the Cabernet Sauvignon from Temecula.

The Rolling Hills winery, started in 1980, is located in Camarillo north of Los Angeles in an industrial park. "You do not need a large operation to make good wine," says Ed Pagor as he squeezes between barrels and other equipment in his 1,200-square-foot winery.

Ed Pagor, who is a sales representative for a Swiss aluminum manufacturer, wants to keep the winery small. Having grown up in New Jersey of Italian heritage, Ed was accustomed to having wine with his meals. His interests in wines and winemaking were furthered when he spent a year studying languages at a university in northern Italy. While there he also traveled to France and Germany to become acquainted with more varietals. After moving to Southern California, he became a home winemaker and joined a home winemaking club, the Cellarmasters.

Most of Rolling Hills wines are produced in small lots — 249 cases. With this small amount of grapes for each varietal, Ed can do the majority of the work himself. Eve, his wife, usually accompanies him to the winery on weekends to help with the chores and do the bookwork. Friends, the two Pagor daughters, and their friends are usually enlisted to help at crush and bottling times.

"The red wines are full-bodied and geared to people who are familiar with the complexities of red wines," Ed comments. He feels that the type of oak used for aging is one of the important contributing factors to the distinctive tastes of his wines. The oak barrels for the Chardonnay are imported from the Limousin province of France. "That type of oak is excellent for aging Chardonnay," Ed says. For the reds he uses a combinations of American and French oak barrels.

Ed uses traditional methods in his winemaking. He uses a basket press so as not to overwork the grapes. The reds are fermented at warm temperatures in open top fermentors and the juice is pumped over the cap.

Although winemaking is quite time consuming, both Ed and Eve Pagor enjoy what they are doing. There are two other small wineries located near them, thereby providing a community of interest and support. ❧

Current Trends

During the course of the interviews with vintners, a number of interesting observations were developed regarding current trends in the wine industry. These focus primarily on the role of the small vintner and on the growing awareness of the differences in style and quality among varietal wines.

Search for "Niche" Markets

The small vintners are clearly trying to appeal to the tastes of the more sophisticated wine-lover. They are emphasizing the nuances of winemaking styles and the basic flavors of the grape within a given varietal wine. Most varietals can now be made in styles that make them enjoyable as a drink by themselves, as an apéritif, as a companion to food, or as an accompaniment to dessert.

The smaller vintners are attempting to develop "niche" markets for themselves within a few varietal wines, focusing on wine sophisticates who have strong preferences for wines with a certain level of sugar, oak, tannin, acid, alcohol, color, complexity, fruitiness, smoothness, bigness, intensity, and so forth. The style selected is frequently dictated by the vintner's personal preference. Fortunately, technology has provided vintners with the appropriate chemical, mechanical, and biological tools to produce these characteristics at will.

Today's Varietals

While the larger producers of premium wine continue to offer a broad line of varietals, the smaller ones no longer feel compelled to do so. The small wineries typically limit themselves to one to four of the major varietals — Chardonnay, Sauvignon Blanc, Chenin Blanc, Gewurztraminer, or Johannisberg Riesling among the whites, and Cabernet Sauvignon, Zinfandel, Merlot, or Pinot Noir among the reds. A number of these smaller wineries offer several styles of the same varietal in order to cater to individual tastes. Acacia Winery, for example, makes four styles of Chardonnay and four of Pinot Noir.

Several vintners are gaining uniqueness through specializing in less popular wines. Charles Shaw, for example, makes a Nouveau-style Gamay. Jim Bundschu at Gundlach-Bundschu is the only American producer of the German varietal Kleinberger. The Martin Brothers Winery is one of the few California producers of wine from the Nebbiolo grape, a well respected varietal from the Piemonte region of Italy.

Other small vintners specialize in varietal wines from grapes normally used in blending. These include Merlot, Cabernet Franc, Semillon, Carignane, and Barbera. The latter three, plus French Colombard and Chenin Blanc, are the major blending grapes grown and used by the bulk wine producers in the San Joaquin Valley. However, they are also grown in the cooler coastal regions where they are made into delicate premium wines. The cooler growing climate brings out their varietal flavor.

The much-publicized trend toward white wines has also brought to the market a wide range of so-called blush wines made from various varieties of red grapes. Until recently, Rosé wines were a blend of red and white wines, frequently of whatever was left over in the storage tanks. This ceased to be acceptable as a premium wine (if it ever was) with the advent of White Zinfandel in the mid-1970s. Vintners now offer a wide range of blush wines made from Cabernet Sauvignon and Pinot Noir and such lesser-known grapes as Charbono, Gamay, Merlot, Barbera, and Petite Sirah.

Sources of Grapes

The quality and characteristics of the grapes from which the wine is made is a major factor in determining the characteristics of the final product. When purchasing grapes, therefore, the small vintner searches out growers that employ vineyard practices and vineyard locations that are most likely to produce premium quality grapes. The small vintner is willing to pay up to ten times as much per ton as the bulk wine producer, if he or she can obtain grapes with the right fruit, acid, and sugar balance.

Lighter, More Complex Wines

The association of wine with good food was also evident among the vintners. They are producing lighter, but more complex wines. Complex Chardonnays, for instance, are being produced through a combination of blending wines from different vineyards and partially fermenting the wine in both oak barrels and stainless steel tanks. Since today's now-type lifestyle calls for wines that are drinkable when purchased, vintners are producing red wines with less harsh tannins and better acid-sugar balance. They are also aging their wines in the bottle for longer periods before releasing them for sale.

Labelling

Until varietal wines became important in the mass market, wine labels were borrowed from European labels — typically those of a geographic wine region. It didn't matter whether the bottle contained a varietal or a blend of varietals. Names such as "Chablis," "Sauterne," "Burgundy," "Moselle," or "Rhine" were used routinely with only a modicum of effort being made to relate a style of wine with the label. Today, this is no longer acceptable for premium wines, although it is still practiced for generic wines.

The term "Champagne" on a label still presents a rather confused picture. Historically, its use was restricted to sparkling wine produced in the Champagne region of France by the *Méthode Champenoise*. However, both terms — "Champagne" and "sparkling wine" — have been used by California producers since the making of sparkling wine was first attempted by Benjamin Wilson in 1855 at San Gabriel, by Pierre Sainsevain in 1857 at San Jose, and by Arpid Haraszthy at Buena Vista in 1863. Sainsevain avoided the issue by calling his product "Sparkling California," while Haraszthy called his attempt "Eclipse." Korbel used the label "Grand Pacific" when it introduced its sparkling wine in 1896.

Today, several of the leading sparkling wine producers are using the term "Champagne" to describe sparkling wine made by the old French *Méthode Champenoise*. They feel this distinguishes their premium product from the more common sparkling wines made by the lower cost, bulk processing methods. Use of the term "champagnes" also avoids association with the recent trend by makers of wine coolers to use the term "sparklers."

Another label whose use has become confused is the term "claret." It was originally used by the English to describe a light red French wine — usually a blend of red and white wines. While this is still the accepted definition, vintners frequently use it on all shades and hues of blended red wines — although other vintners prefer the more straightforward descriptor, "California Red Table Wine" for such wines. In recent years, there has been a mini-trend back to producing proprietary blends in the French chateau style. How to name such proprietary blends presents somewhat of a problem since the public has become educated toward varietal titles as a measure of quality.

Premium wine labels show not only the name of the varietal, but also the geographic source of the grapes. In general, the more specific the designation of the source of the grapes, the more valuable the wine. Consequently, growers are applying for official grape-growing appellations that delineate as small an area as possible. Vintners in the Carneros district — which overlaps the south end of Napa and Sonoma Counties — for example, have formed the Carneros Alliance to promote the quality of grapes of that region. Similarly, individual vintners have applied for, and received, a viticultural designation for their single vineyards (for example, McDowell Valley Vineyards in Mendocino County and Guenoc Winery in Lake County).

California Varietal Grapes

With the emphasis in California on varietal wines — unlike France with its emphasis on chateaux and regional wines — a wide range of publications have become available dealing with the varietal grapes grown in California. One informative publication of this type is the California Grape Acreage Report, issued yearly by the U.S. Department of Agriculture and State of California Department of Food and Agriculture. The following tables were derived from that report and a companion report entitled Grape Crush Report.

The tables provide, in capsule form, a picture of the principal varietals being grown in California, the extent to which they are grown, and where they are grown. The last table shows the price per ton paid in 1985 and the yield per acre for each varietal. Collectively, the tables show the unique characteristics of the premium wine grape growing industry of the coastal and foothill counties relative to those of the generic or bulk wine industry of the San Joaquin Valley.

Clearly, the growth and change that has taken place over the past ten years in the California wine industry has been close to phenomenal. While vineyard expansion essentially ceased by 1984, there is no evidence that suggests that the industry has matured. The experimentation that is currently taking place, both by the small vintners as well as the large ones, will undoubtedly reap benefits to wine consumers for several decades to come. Progress toward higher quality and more complex wines will materially enhance the mutual enjoyment of food and wine.

Table 1

CALIFORNIA WHITE WINE GRAPES
Acreage Growth—1976 to 1985 by Varietal

Varietal	1976			1985			Percent Growth 1976–85
	Total Acreage	Percent of White Varietals	Percent of Total Varietals	Total Acreage	Percent of White Varietals	Percent of Total Varietals	
French Colombard	23,485	29.7	11.2	73,241	37.5	21.4	211.9
Chenin Blanc	17,338	22.0	8.3	41,462	21.2	12.1	139.1
Chardonnay	10,869	13.8	5.2	27,424	14.0	8.0	152.3
Sauvignon Blanc	3,526	4.5	1.7	15,383	7.9	4.5	336.3
Johannisberg Riesling	6,210	7.9	3.0	10,046	5.1	2.9	63.4
Gewürztraminer	2,025	2.6	1.0	3,983	2.0	1.2	96.7
Semillon	2,002	2.5	1.0	3,039	1.6	0.9	51.8
Emerald Riesling	2,025	2.6	1.0	2,928	1.5	0.9	44.6
Palomino	2,425	3.2	1.2	2,702	1.4	0.8	11.4
Gray Riesling	1,516	1.9	0.7	2,436	1.2	0.7	60.7
Burger	1,130	1.4	0.5	2,307	1.2	0.7	104.2
Pinot Blanc	1,339	1.7	0.6	2,265	1.2	0.7	69.2
Malvasia Bianca	655	0.8	0.3	1,842	0.9	0.5	181.2
Muscat Canelli	899	1.1	0.4	1,657	0.8	0.5	84.3
Sylvaner	958	1.2	0.5	1,233	0.6	0.4	28.7
Other	2,372	3.0	1.1	3,316	1.7	1.0	39.8
Total White Varietals	78,775	100.0	37.6	195,264	100.0	56.9	147.9
Total Red Varietals	130,681	-	62.4	147,792	-	43.1	13.1
Total All Varietals	209,456	-	100.0	343,056	-	100.0	63.8

The acreage of white wine grapes has grown by almost 150% during the past nine years. The greatest absolute growth in acreage has occurred with the two white bulk wines, French Colombard and Chenin Blanc, followed by the two white premium wine grapes, Chardonnay and Sauvignon Blanc. Since 1976, acreage of white grapes has grown seven times more than that of red grapes.

Table 2

CALIFORNIA RED GRAPES

Acreage Growth—1976 to 1985 by Varietal

Varietal	1976 Total Acreage	1976 Percent of Red Varietals	1976 Percent of Total Varietals	1985 Total Acreage	1985 Percent of Red Varietals	1985 Percent of Total Varietals	Percent Growth 1976–85
Zinfandel	21,672	16.6	10.3	25,367	17.1	7.4	17.1
Cabernet Sauvignon	17,395	13.3	8.3	22,617	15.2	6.6	30.0
Carignane	16,132	12.3	7.7	16,341	11.1	4.8	1.3
Grenache	12,350	9.5	5.9	15,701	10.6	4.6	27.1
Barbera	14,615	11.2	7.0	14,825	10.0	4.3	1.4
Ruby Cabernet	10,555	8.1	5.0	10,577	7.2	3.1	0.2
Rubired	7,271	3.5	3.6	8,076	5.4	2.4	11.1
Pinot Noir	7,067	5.4	3.4	7,816	5.3	2.3	10.6
Petite Sirah	4,733	3.6	2.3	5,105	3.5	1.4	7.9
Alicante Bouschet	2,841	2.2	1.4	3,210	2.2	0.9	13.0
Gamay Beaujolais	2,426	1.9	1.2	2,526	1.7	0.7	4.1
Merlot	1,742	1.3	0.8	2,497	1.7	0.7	43.3
Napa Gamay	2,342	1.8	1.1	2,452	1.7	0.7	4.7
Mission	2,277	1.7	1.1	2,314	1.6	0.7	1.6
Carnelian	1,519	1.2	0.7	1,592	1.1	0.5	4.8
Other	5,744	4.4	2.7	6,776	4.6	2.0	18.0
Total Red Varietals	130,681	100.0	62.4	147,792	100.0	43.1	13.1
Total White Varietals	78,775	-	37.6	195,264	-	56.9	147.9
Total All Varietals	209,456	-	100.0	343,056	-	100.0	63.8

Except for Merlot, Cabernet Sauvignon, and (to a lesser extent) Zinfandel, red grape acreage grew very little during the nine-year period. Red wine grapes, as a percent of the total of all wine grapes, has dropped from 62.4% to only 43.1%, since 1976.

Table 3

CALIFORNIA WINE GRAPE ACREAGE—1985
San Joaquin Valley vs. Coastal/Foothill Regions by Varietal

| Varietal | SAN JOAQUIN VALLEY | | | COASTAL/FOOTHILL | | | Total Varietal Acreage |
	Total Acreage	Percent of Varietal	Percent of Region	Total Acreage	Percent of Varietal	Percent of Region	
French Colombard	67,770	92.5	33.8	5,471	7.5	3.9	73,241
Chenin Blanc	28,669	69.1	14.2	12,793	30.8	9.0	41,462
Chardonnay	650	2.4	0.3	26,774	97.6	18.9	27,424
Zinfandel	16,354	64.5	8.2	9,013	35.5	6.4	25,367
Cabernet Sauvignon	2,448	10.8	1.2	20,169	89.2	14.2	22,617
Carignane	13,511	82.7	6.7	2,830	17.3	2.0	16,341
Grenache	14,106	89.8	7.0	1,595	10.2	1.1	15,701
Sauvignon Blanc	2,657	17.3	1.3	17,726	82.7	9.0	15,383
Barbera	14,441	97.4	7.2	384	2.6	0.3	14,825
Ruby Cabernet	10,250	96.9	5.1	317	3.1	0.2	10,577
Johannisberg Riesling	65	0.6	0.0	9,981	99.4	7.0	10,046
Rubired	8,040	99.6	4.0	36	0.4	0.0	8,076
Pinot Noir	15	0.2	0.0	7,801	99.8	5.5	7,816
Petite Sirah	1,973	38.6	1.0	3,132	61.4	2.2	5,105
Gewürztraminer	6	0.1	0.0	3,977	99.9	2.8	3,983
Alicante Bouschet	2,877	89.6	1.4	333	10.4	0.2	3,210
Semillon	1,239	40.8	0.6	1,800	59.2	1.3	3,039
Emerald Riesling	2,337	79.8	1.2	591	20.2	0.4	2,928
Palomino	2,309	85.5	1.1	393	14.5	0.3	2,702
Gamay Beaujolais	0	0.0	0.0	2,526	100.0	1.8	2,526
Merlot	70	2.8	0.0	2,427	97.2	1.7	2,497
Napa Gamay	350	14.3	0.2	2,102	85.7	1.5	2,452
Gray Riesling	227	9.3	0.1	2,209	90.7	1.6	2,436
Mission	2,035	87.9	1.0	279	12.1	0.2	2,314
Burger	2,082	90.2	1.0	225	9.8	0.2	2,307
Pinot Blanc	36	1.6	0.0	2,229	98.4	1.6	2,265
Malvasia Bianca	1,364	74.0	0.7	478	26.0	0.3	1,842
Muscat Canelli	1,021	61.6	0.5	636	38.4	0.4	1,657
Other	4,303	33.3	2.2	8,614	66.7	6.0	12,917
Total All Varietals	201,205	58.7	100.0	141,851	41.3	100.0	343,056

The San Joaquin Valley contains almost 60% of the total acreage of wine grapes grown in California. The San Joaquin Valley grows over 85% of six of the 12 top wine grapes. The Coastal/Foothill regions produce over 90% of 11 of the 13 major premium wine varietals (except for Zinfandel and Petite Sirah).

Table 4

CALIFORNIA RED AND WHITE WINE GRAPE ACREAGE
by County—1976 and 1985

County	Region	1976 Red Grape Acrge	1976 White Grape Acrge	1976 % Total Calif. Acrge	1985 Red Grape Acrge	1985 White Grape Acrge	1985 % Total Calif. Acrge	% Growth Red Grapes	% Growth White Grapes	% Growth Total
Madera	SJ	12.4	4.9	8.2	13.6	26.4	11.6	9.6	440.7	131.2
Fresno	SJ	15.9	9.4	12.1	17.0	21.2	11.1	6.5	125.1	50.5
Kern	SJ	12.9	10.0	11.0	14.5	21.3	10.5	12.1	112.5	56.0
San Joaquin	SJ	21.2	3.7	11.9	22.4	13.3	10.4	5.2	256.8	42.6
Sonoma	C/F	11.9	6.4	8.7	15.5	15.6	9.1	31.0	144.0	70.5
Napa	C/F	10.7	7.3	8.6	14.2	16.1	8.9	32.7	119.9	68.1
Monterey	C/F	7.4	12.6	9.5	8.0	22.3	8.8	8.4	78.1	52.3
Stanislaus	SJ	7.3	4.6	5.7	7.7	9.4	5.0	5.7	103.9	43.9
Merced	SJ	4.9	4.4	4.4	5.0	10.1	4.4	2.5	128.7	62.5
Tulare	SJ	4.5	4.4	4.3	4.9	9.7	4.3	8.9	119.9	63.7
Mendocino	C/F	4.9	2.4	5.5	5.5	5.6	3.2	12.5	132.0	51.8
Santa Barbara	C/F	1.7	2.0	1.8	1.9	7.3	2.7	13.1	265.2	50.4
San Luis Obispo	C/F	2.0	0.8	1.3	2.4	3.2	1.6	20.5	280.5	98.0
Sacramento	C/F	1.5	0.8	1.1	1.7	1.9	1.0	8.6	127.5	50.6
San Bernardino	SJ	2.7	0.8	1.7	2.7	0.8	1.0	0.6	0.5	0.5
Lake	C/F	1.6	0.3	0.9	1.9	1.3	0.9	16.4	400.4	71.1
Riverside	C/F	0.7	0.9	0.8	0.8	2.3	0.9	5.3	139.5	80.6
San Benito	C/F	1.2	1.0	1.1	1.2	1.2	0.7	1.5	18.9	9.4
Alameda	C/F	0.3	0.8	0.5	0.4	1.6	0.6	58.6	106.3	93.7
Amador	C/F	0.7	-	0.4	1.2	0.4	0.5	60.6	Inf.	113.8
Glenn	C/F	0.8	-	0.4	1.1	0.4	0.4	28.0	Inf.	74.3
Yolo	C/F	0.2	0.3	0.2	0.3	1.1	0.4	82.0	277.2	210.5
Santa Clara	C/F	0.7	0.4	0.5	0.7	0.7	0.4	12.6	83.4	37.4
Kings	SJ	0.7	-	0.3	0.8	0.5	0.4	7.9	Inf.	75.0
Solano	C/F	0.4	0.2	0.3	0.5	0.6	0.3	23.9	181.1	77.7
Other	Other	1.4	0.3	0.8	1.9	1.0	0.9	40.0	253.8	77.1
Total Acreage		130.7	78.8	100.0	147.8	195.3	100.0	13.1	147.9	63.8

Note: SJ = San Joaquin Valley & San Bernardino County

C/F = Coastal/Foothill Counties and Sacramento Valley

The San Joaquin Valley counties make up seven of the ten top wine grape producing counties in California, and provide 57% of both the red and white wine grapes grown in California. Sonoma, Napa, and Monterey, the other three largest wine producing counties of the top ten, contribute an additional 25% of the total. Since 1976, Madera County has experienced the greatest growth in absolute terms, while Yolo County achieved the largest growth in percentage terms.

Table 5

PERCENT WINERY GROWN GRAPES
of Total Grapes Crushed by Wineries (1985)

Varietal	Grapes Crushed (Thousands of Tons)			Percent of Total	
	Total	Grown	Purchased	Grown	Purchased
Pinot Blanc	8.0	3.7	4.3	46.2	53.8
Napa Gamay	13.1	5.3	7.8	40.5	59.5
Chardonnay	82.2	32.1	50.1	39.1	60.9
Petite Sirah	21.4	8.3	13.1	38.8	61.2
Merlot	8.3	2.9	5.4	34.9	65.1
Cabernet Sauvignon	72.0	24.8	47.2	34.4	65.6
Sauvignon Blanc	56.3	18.7	37.6	33.2	66.8
Muscat-Alexandria	47.8	15.8	32.0	33.1	66.9
Gewürztraminer	15.3	4.8	10.5	31.4	68.6
Johannisberg Riesling	31.4	8.1	23.3	25.8	74.2
Carignane	119.2	30.1	89.1	25.3	74.7
Pinot Noir	31.7	7.9	23.8	24.9	75.1
Thompson Seedless	505.9	111.0	394.9	21.9	78.1
Zinfandel	123.4	18.6	104.8	15.1	84.9
Semillon	17.1	2.3	14.8	13.5	86.5
Emerald Riesling	21.7	2.9	18.8	13.4	86.6
Rubired	64.7	8.4	56.3	13.0	87.0
Ruby Cabernet	75.7	9.5	66.2	12.5	87.5
Barbera	125.5	12.9	112.5	10.3	89.7
Chenin Blanc	298.6	28.9	269.7	9.7	90.3
Grenache	126.7	11.4	115.3	9.0	91.0
French Colombard	585.4	46.1	539.3	7.9	92.1
Tokay	150.3	7.2	143.1	4.8	95.2
Muscat Blanc	9.2	0.2	9.0	3.6	96.4
All Reds	859.8	160.8	699.0	18.7	81.3
All Whites	1207.7	161.0	1046.7	13.3	86.7
All Varietals	2067.5	321.8	1745.8	15.6	84.4

Less than 20% of the red wine grapes crushed by wineries are estate grown, and less than 15% of the white grapes are grown by the winery. Wineries making premium wine tend to grow a higher percentage of their grapes than those who make bulk wine, with the premium varietals Pinot Blanc, Napa Gamay, and Chardonnay having the highest percentage grown by the winery (all less than 50%).

Table 6
1985 WINE GRAPE PRODUCTION
Price per Ton & Price per Acre (Ordered by Price per Acre)

Varietal	Acres (Bearing)	Production Tons	Tons Per Acre	Price Per Acre $	Price Per Ton ($)		
					All Wineries	San Joaquin Wineries	Coastal County Wineries
Chardonnay	22,847	82,204	3.6	3,251	900	200–400	650–1200
Merlot	1,955	8,299	4.2	2,566	610	25–125	350–950
Pinot Noir	7,429	31,681	4.3	2,280	530	—	380–800
Cabernet Sauvignon	20,430	72,002	3.5	1,866	535	100–250	400–850
Sauvignon Blanc	13,299	56,299	4.2	1,852	440	60–300	400–700
Pinot Blanc	2,136	8,034	3.8	1,539	405	95–100	350–950
Gewürztraminer	3,974	15,342	3.9	1,470	375	275	300–550
Zinfandel	24,775	123,370	5.0	1,345	270	150–225	300–400
Muscat Canelli	1,532	9,200	6.0	1,291	215	95–165	400–760
Semillon	2,827	17,146	6.1	1,280	210	70–360	450–800
Chenin Blanc	38,980	298,619	7.7	1,155	150	95–165	270–400
Napa Gamay	2,447	13,096	5.4	1,112	205	60–70	275–325
French Colombard	68,313	585,393	8.6	1,058	125	90–140	250–350
Johannisberg Riesling	9,732	31,374	3.2	1,040	325	50–125	350–550
Grenache	14,047	126,682	9.0	828	90	65–110	240–440
Barbera	14,804	125,386	8.5	816	95	65–100	300–500
Petite Sirah	5,093	21,359	4.2	748	180	75–125	350–450
Carignane	16,300	119,169	7.3	715	100	60–140	200–250
Mission	2,310	11,638	5.0	495	100	90–110	—
All White Varietals	179,056	1,207,669	6.7	1,286	190	95–165	430–820
All Red Varietals	141,792	859,832	6.1	1,068	175	80–180	350–750
All Varietals	320,848	2,067,501	6.4	1,184	185	90–170	235–785

There are very significant price differentials paid by wineries for grapes among the various varietals and between the San Joaquin Valley and Coastal/Foothill regions. The tons of wine grapes obtained from an acre of vineyard also varied significantly, from 7.7 tons per acre for Chenin Blanc to 3.2 tons per acre for Johannisberg Riesling. On a price per acre basis, Chardonnay sold for almost three times the average of all grapes. Coastal/Foothill wineries paid three to five times more than did San Joaquin wineries for the same varietal grapes.

Introduction to Recipes

Over 200 years ago, the Franciscan Fathers, who had come to California, would sit down after a hard day's work and enjoy their evening meal with a glass of wine. Today, California wines are being similarly enjoyed — not only by Californians, but by wine lovers throughout America, and all over the world. Wine is thought of today, as it was by the Mission Fathers, as a gentle alcoholic beverage that enhances the enjoyment of good food and good company, and ultimately, the enjoyment of life itself.

It was only natural to seek out the people who produce premium wines in assembling this collection of wine-complementing recipes. Fine wines are created and blended by taste. Vintners who are able to blend fine wines are also able to create delicious meals and to match the two up perfectly. Robet Pepi (Pepi Winery) emphasizes that wine with food accomplishes two things: it increases the flavor of food and cleanses the palate between bites of food.

The close family ties and the lifestyles of the small California family wineries make them excellent sources of a unique combination of family recipes with family-created wines. Joel Petersen of Ravenswood, for example, feels that his winemaking is in large part a result of his enjoyment of interesting food. "Think of a beverage to go with the food you have prepared. Most of the time, milk and orange juice won't cut it," Joel says. "Realizing this early in my life, thanks to my father's love of wine and food, has led me to a fuller appreciation of how wine and food enhance each other."

For the most part, the recipes provided by vintner families and presented herein are easy to prepare. They reflect the busy life of the vintner. The recipes, and the stories behind them, give good insight into the lifestyles of the people who comprise the California premium wine industry. Most of the recipes are family favorites. Many have been handed down through several generations, giving the collection a rich sampling of "old country" heritage.

Gloria Piconi (Piconi Winery), for example, recalls with warm feeling the time when her mother-in law taught her how to make bread in the old Italian style. As she de-scribed the recipe to me, I realized she was sharing a treasured part of her life. But then, that's what recipes are — treasures.

Many of the vintners have Italian backgrounds as is evidenced in many of the recipes included in this collection. For the hearty and brave souls, there is the traditional garlic Bagna Cauda. Also there is the Italian fish stew, Cioppino, which is often served with pasta. Much of the seasonings used in the recipes are typical Italian ones and the resulting dishes are usually served with a hearty red wine such as Zinfandel.

There are geographical variations on traditional ethnic recipes as evidenced in Tatjana Grgich's (Grgich Cellars) Sarma — a recipe for cabbage rolls. This version from her native Yugoslavia calls for sauerkraut in addition to the white cabbage usually found in Eastern European recipes for cabbage rolls.

Hans and Theresia Kobler (Lazy Creek Vineyards), who were born in Switzerland and trained in some of the finest European hotels, have created some simple-to-prepare versions of restaurant entrées that reflect the culinary style of their homeland.

Most of the American-born vintners are California transplants, and they have brought other types of American cuisine along with them. John Staten (Field Stone Winery) is a native Texan and his wife, Katrina, often prepares "Tex-Mex" dishes from recipes gleaned from her mother-in-law's file. Sandra McIver (Matanzas Creek Winery), a native of New Orleans, likes to serve New Orleans Gumbo for an informal supper party. There is no lack of individuality and variety in this recipe collection.

Winemaking is, in fact, a way of life. It involves the entire family in the cultivation of the grapes, the operation of the winery and the marketing of the end product. It is also a year-round occupation. Food styles and preparation times are consequently very much geared to the demands of the winemaking seasons.

Winter is the time when the wines are aging in the winery cellars which leaves more time for entertaining and dining at a leisurely pace. Starting with the Thanksgiving-Christmas holiday season, there are many dinner parties, small and large. Lucy Shaw (Charles Shaw Vineyards and Winery), who attended Cordon Bleu in Paris, likes to entertain with dinner parties for eight. She likes the ease of preparing much of her menu ahead of the guests' arrival and is particularly fond of her easy-to-prepare entrée, Peppered Beef Tenderloin.

Winter is also the time for working in the cool wine cellar, topping the wine barrels and doing blending. To take the chill off after working in the cellar all day, heartier foods such as pastas and soups are prepared for everyday meals. Many families make soup the mainstay of their meals, regardless of the time of year. Consequently, there are soups for all seasons in the collection — from an old-fashioned German Farina Soup to a very modern California Fresh Asparagus Soup.

In the spring, the vines need pruning and training, but promotional trips must also be taken to market the previous year's vintages. Food preparation is more on a do-it-yourself basis. Most of the premium wine regions of California are in close proximity to the coast so that fresh seafood is readily available. In the spring, much of the local seafood, particularly salmon, becomes available and lighter meals are the norm. Many times seafood is also combined with pasta and some vegetables for a quick yet very satisfying meal.

New wines are released in the spring and numerous tastings and open houses are held by the wineries. The vintners and their wives do a lot of experimentation with food to create just the right hors d'oeuvre to accompany the new releases. One such combination is Fran Replogle's (Fenestra Winery) Smoked Salmon Mousse created to accompany Fenestra's Sauvignon Blanc. The masked flavor of the otherwise strong smoked salmon is ideal with this wine.

In the summer, the vineyards are green, the climate is mild with warm breezes, and food and wine is center stage at many outdoor gatherings. The mild-to-warm weather, almost nine months of the year, has greatly influenced the vintners' style of entertaining. There is something very relaxing about living in close proximity to a vineyard. "Bill and I much prefer to entertain with a barbecue on the patio, rather than a formal dinner inside. We feel this lends itself to a more relaxed, comfortable atmosphere for our guests," says Yvonne Kreck, wife of the co-owner of Mill Creek Vineyards. Most of the vintners take great pride in preparing the meats to be barbecued. Dr. Fogarty (Thomas Fogarty Winery) makes chicken marinated in an oriental sauce his speciality.

The fall is crush time and the busiest season of all, which means simple-to-prepare meals that can be kept on a standby basis. That is when soups, such as Barbara MacCready's (Sierra Vista Winery) Potato Soup. or long-cooking stews satisfy hungry appetites. "Good food is a must; hearty food a necessity," comments Valerie Ahlgren (Ahlgren Vineyard) when asked about the type of food she prepares at crush time. Main dishes that can simmer all day on the back burner and be served when work is finished are the order of the day. Some of the

vintner families prefer a hearty pasta dish. Usually a slice of crusty sourdough French bread and some type of green salad will complete a "stick-to-the ribs" type of meal.

A number of family wineries involve both the husband and wife. They are a team with each having specific duties to perform. In some households this is also true for the preparation of meals, as at the home of Roger and Joanne Cook (R. & J. Cook). Roger cooks all the meat, fish and poultry, while Joanne prepares the rest of the meal. He, too, enjoys grilling meat on the barbecue, and the Cooks often entertain with a picnic or evening meal on the levee above their winery and home. Joanne's specialty is desserts. "I love to eat them as well as make them," she says. "I was raised by a mother who made everything from scratch," she continues. "It becomes a way of life, although it is a rather old-fashioned way of baking. I use no mixes of any kind."

Many of the vintners have gardens and raise their own vegetables and fruit. An herb and spice gardn is a *must* for many of the vintners. For example, everything is home-grown — meat, vegetables, fruits, herbs and fish — on the Keehn's ranch (McDowell Valley Vineyards). Dolores Cakebread (Cakebread Cellars) grows all her own produce and has three herb beds. Raising vegetables is an overture to cooking for Dolores. Susan Preston (Preston Winery) decided to landscape their winery with edible plants, not only for their own use, but to show visitors which produce is grown in California.

I have found that vintner families frequently grow their own herbs and spices and have an exceptional sense of how to use them to enhance the wines they produce. For example, Joel Peterson (Ravenswood Winery) favors his Mother's Lamb Stew recipe which uses a variety of flavors and spices —orange and lemon rind, cinnamon, cloves and coriander — and finds this recipe an excellent companion to a substantial Merlot. The citrus characteristics of the lamb stew accent the spiciness of the Merlot. On the other hand, his own recipe for Prawns and Vermouth includes very subdued flavors of sun-dried tomatoes and cream — well matched with a full-bodied Chardonnay.

Pasta, because it is simple to prepare, is standard fare with most vintner families. Additionally, there is a wide variety of pasta dishes that can include seafood, vegetables, cream sauces, cheese sauces and Italian meat sauces. The majority of the pasta is homemade. Pasta and wine just seem to go together naturally.

Chicken is another favorite dish, not only as a family meal, but also for dinner parties. This reflects the trend to lighter food and the ease of its preparation. The chicken recipes contained in this book show some of the innovative creations of the vintners, for example Marcia Gerwer's (Gerwer Winery) Orange Minted Chicken served with White Zinfandel. The fruitiness of the wine complements the orange and mint flavors of the chicken dish. There is also a traditional European chicken dish from Etza Tomka (Soda Rock Winery) — Hungarian Chicken Paprikash.

With the emphasis on wine to go with food, more and more vintners are extremely conscious of how well their wines pair with different dishes. They experiment continually to evaluate which meats or seafood, spices, cheese, sauces, and even vegetable combinations best complement their wines. Karen Keehn (McDowell Valley Winery) has made a complete study of the appropriate spices to use with the wines they produce. She recommends that "the stronger the food flavors, the stronger the wine flavors should be." For foods with sweetness or tartness, Karen suggests a wine with some residual sugar, such as a Riesling or Gewürztraminer, to balance the food. Her research has shown her that, for instance, green peppercorns are better than black with Cabernet Sauvignon. Some of the best flavor complements for wine she has found are wild rice, nuts, and orange zest. Karen Keehn uses wine to supply acid when making sauces and dressings.

Deborah Cahn Bennett (Navarro Vineyards) has researched foods to go with Gewürztraminer. She likes to serve Chinese dishes with that wine, since the various flavor components of that cuisine, spices such as ginger, anise and sesame, and the wine complement each other. Jeri Mosby (Vega Vineyards Winery) likes Gewürztraminer with sausages and sauerkraut. She says that the sage and marjoram in the sausages and the tartness of the sauerkraut combine well it. Richard Alexei, Culinary Director of Monticello Cellars, serves their Gewürz Traminer with foods that are slightly sweet, such as Smithfield ham and Onion Gruyère Tart.

"Wine is a personal thing . . . it should suit yourself and your mood," are the thoughts of Aurora Pepi (Pepi Winery). "I drink red with everything," says Richard Sherwin of Lytton Springs Winery. He does, however, drink white wines occasionally with fish. He thinks that food and wine are purely subjective decisions. "Some people like a light, sweet wine with everything," he says. Dick observes, however, that over time the more seasoned wine connoisseur tends to narrow his or her preference toward the drier, bigger style red or white wines.

Most vintners and their wives love to cook and enjoy entertaining, not only family and friends, but also clients, wine critics, distributors and other business associates. There are many wine tastings, food preparation demonstrations and industry events in which they participate. Whether it be a formal dinner or a barbecue for the family, the food and wine showcase each other. The food has to be good because it complements some of the best wines America has to offer.

For the most part, the recipes in this book are presented as written by the vintner. I have edited them only for clarity and ease of preparation by the reader. The accompanying wine labels show which of the vintners' wines are served with the particular recipe. Since the publication of this book, new vintages of the same wine may have been released and the particular vintage on the printed label may no longer be available. The same varietal wine, however, will be available in all but a few cases.

To further aid the reader, menus have been provided by several of the vintners. Each has been designed to complement the particular wines suggested. ❧

♈ VINTNERS' MENUS ♈

(denotes that the recipe is in Vintner's Choice)*

Light Summer Supper

by Lisa Buehler; Buehler Vineyards, St. Helena

Avocado Soup*
Pinot Blanc
London Broil Salad*
Tomato Couscous*
Zinfandel

Barbecue on the Levee

by Joanne Cook; R. and J. Cook, Clarksburg

Barbecued Ribs and Chicken Breasts*
Homemade Potato Salad*
Platter of Raw Vegetables
Garlic Bread
Cabernet Sauvignon
Orange Chiffon Cake*

Summer Luncheon or Supper

by Elinor Travers; Mayacamas Vineyards, Napa

Mayacamas Walnuts*
Chardonnay
California Cold Seafood Platter*
Steamed Broccoli
French Bread
Sauvignon Blanc
Kumquat-Ginger Mousse*
Noble Semillon (botrytised Semillon Wine)

Spring Dinner

by Robin Gainey; The Gainey Vineyard, Santa Ynez

Spring Salad with Blueberry Vinaigrette*
Johannisberg Riesling
Veal Medallions in Fresh Tomato Cream*
Blanched Snow Peas, Buttered Baby Carrots
Chardonnay
Champagne Sorbet*

Saturday Night Company Dinner

by Lucy Shaw; Charles F. Shaw Winery, St. Helena

Layered Seafood Aspic*
Chardonnay
Peppered Beef Tenderloin with Béarnaise Sauce*
Southwestern Wild Rice*
Stir-Fried Vegetables
Domaine Elucia — Proprietor's Reserve
Green Salad*
Napa Valley Gamay
Ice Cream Pecan Balls with Fudge Sauce*
Coffee

Dinner for Guests at Lillie Langtry House

by Margaret Clark, Chef; Guenoc Winery, Middletown

Sautéed Artichokes*
Chardonnay
Filet Mignon with Confit and Red Wine Sauce*
Fried Potato Slices
Green Beans
Cabernet Sauvignon
Chocolate Chestnut Cake*
Petite Sirah

Lunch in the Country

by Students of San Francisco Culinary Academy;
created for Landmark Vineyards, Windsor

Sautéed Eggplant Rolls
Endive with Caper Cream
Smoked Salmon Canapés
Brut Champagne
Two Bell Pepper Soup*
Chardonnay
Paella Sonoma*
Alexander Valley Chardonnay
Salad of Garden Lettuce, Radicchio, Oranges
and Niçoise Olives
Sonoma County Chardonnay
Russian Cheesecake*

Ranch Dinner

by A. Crawford Cooley; Hacienda Winery, Sonoma

Grilled Wild Boar*
Honey Glazed Chestnuts*
Pineapple Slaw*
Cabernet Sauvignon
Blueberries and Raspberries in Whipped Cream

Family Favorite

by Karen Keehn; McDowell Valley Vineyards, Hopland

McDowell Pâtè Maison with Crackers*
Marinated Mushrooms and Cherry Tomatoes
Zinfandel
Fresh Garden Greens with Walnuts
and Tomato/Basil Dressing
Chicken with Rosemary Wine Sauce*
Sourdough Bread
Zinfandel
Plum-Sirah Sorbet
Bittersweet Chocolate Cookies

Jefferson Birthday Buffet

by Richard Alexei, Culinary Director; Monticello Cellars, Napa

Smithfield Ham and Biscuits
Onion Gruyère Tart*
Gewurz Traminer
Tomato Salad with Balsamic Vinaigrette
and Fresh Basil
Grilled Ratatouille
Domas
Rosemary Garlic Toast
Sauvignon Blanc
Virginia Veal in Tarragon Chardonnay Sauce
with Fresh Morels and Fettucine
Cornmeal Graham Bread
Chardonnay
Cheese: Morbier, St. Andre, Chevrebleu
Cabernet Sauvignon
California Strawberries
Polish Walnut Cookies
Kolacski
Orange Tea Cookies*
Coffee

Special Occasion Dinner

by Jamie Davies; Schramsberg Vineyard and Cellars, Calistoga

Champagne Oysters on Tagliarini*
Blanc de Noirs — Champagne
Grilled Marinated Rabbit*
Vegetables of the Season
Cuvée de Pinot — Champagne
Filbert Roll with Ginger Cream
Crement — Champagne

Dinner at the Winery House

by Dolores Cakebread; Cakebread Cellars, Rutherford

Spinach Balls with Mustard Sauce*
Sauvignon Blanc
Wild Mushrooms and Chicken on Assorted Lettuces
Chardonnay
Grilled Rack of Lamb with Persillade*
Classic French Beans*
Carrots with Fresh Fennel
Cabernet Sauvignon
Chocolate Truffle with Raspberry Purée

A California Entrée and Dessert

by Dr. Alan Steen; Whitehall Lane Winery, St. Helena

Chicken Coins in Tarragon Cream Sauce*
Steamed Swiss Chard
Popovers*
Chardonnay
Rich Nectarine Tart*
Late Harvest Johannisberg Riesling

⚱ HORS D'OEUVRES ⚱

Laced Cheese Wafers

Makes 20 to 25 pieces

Serve with Merlot

Recipe contributed by Bett Shafer, Shafer Vineyards, Napa

Bett Shafer suggests you watch the baking of these wafers so that they do not burn. This is a simple appetizer to prepare.

½ lb. Monterey Jack cheese

seasoning salt or other ground herbs, optional

Cut Monterey Jack cheese into ¼ inch cubes. Place on ungreased Teflon baking sheet. Bake in preheated 350° oven for 8 to 10 minutes. Remove wafers with spatula. Optional: Sprinkle with seasoning salt.

Author's note: As the cheese is baking it melts into a lace wafer.

Wine Cheese Spread

Makes 2 cups

Serve with Chenin Blanc

Recipe contributed by Marcia Gerwer, Gerwer Winery, Somerset

One day a group who had come to the winery to taste wines brought this original cheese spread with them and shared it, as well as the recipe, with the Gerwers. Marcia has used this spread at their wine tastings ever since.

½ lb. Monterey Jack cheese

2 8-oz. pkgs. cream cheese, softened

2½ oz. shredded Parmesan cheese

½ teaspoon dried marjoram

½ teaspoon dried dill

½ teaspoon seasoned salt

3 tablespoons butter, softened

½ cup Chenin Blanc

Finely grate the Monterey Jack cheese. Add the softened cream cheese and Parmesan cheese and mix well. Combine cheese mixture with the herbs, seasoned salt and softened butter. Beat in the wine until mixture is smooth. Pack in lightly oiled mold. Cover and chill in refrigerator for several hours or overnight. Turn out on a serving platter, surrounded by crackers and tiny bunches of grapes.

Serve with Chenin Blanc

Ham-Stuffed Mushrooms

Serves 4 to 6

Recipe contributed by Jo-Ann Nichelini Meyer; Nichelini Vineyard, St. Helena

Jo-Ann Meyer suggests topping each mushroom cap with a small piece of thinly sliced cheese — Cheddar, Mozzarella or Monterey Jack — just before baking, for a variation to the original recipe.

½ lb. whole mushrooms

2 tablespoons butter

1 cup cooked and finely chopped ham

1 tablespoon minced chives or green onions

¼ cup sour cream

2 teaspoons lemon juice, optional

sliced olives and fresh chopped parsley for garnish

Remove stems from mushrooms and finely chop enough to make ½ cup. In a large skillet lightly sauté the caps in butter and arrange in a buttered baking dish. Mix together ham, chives, sour cream, lemon juice, if used, and chopped stems. Pile some of the mixture inside each mushroom cap. Bake in preheated 350° oven for 10 minutes. Garnish and serve.

Author's note: If using cheese, add it about 3 minutes before total baking time has elapsed, just long enough to melt the cheese.

Serve with Chardonnay

Mini-Salmon Crêpes

Makes 60

Recipe contributed by Brigit Poole; Mount Palomar Winery, Temecula

This recipe makes 60 mini-crêpes or 30 regular size. The crêpe batter may also be used with other seafood or meat fillings. Chopped green onion in the batter gives additional flavor.

FILLING

1 7¾- oz. can salmon

8 oz. cream cheese, room temperature

1 tablespoon capers

dash of hot pepper sauce

1 teaspoon freshly ground black pepper

fresh dill for garnish, or dried dill weed

CRÊPE BATTER

4 eggs

¼ teaspoon salt

2 cups flour

2 cups milk

½ cup melted butter

½ cup finely chopped green onion

butter

To make filling: Drain and flake salmon in a small bowl. Cream the cream cheese with an electric mixer. Add capers, hot pepper sauce and ground pepper. Blend until smooth. Fold in flaked salmon and refrigerate until ready to use.

To make crepe batter: Combine all crepe ingredients in a blender and blend for about 1 minute. Scrape down sides and blend for another minute. Let batter rest for about ½ to 1 hour before cooking.

To cook crêpes, heat a large flat-bottom pan over medium-high heat. Brush with butter. Pour in about 1 tablespoon batter, using the back of a tablespoon gently spread in a circular motion to form a mini-crepe about 3 inches in diameter (3 to 4 crêpes can be made at the same time in the pan). Cook crepe until bottom is browned, carefully turn with a spatula and brown on other side for a few seconds. Remove from pan and place on a sheet of plastic wrap. Continue to make crêpes with remaining batter, adding more butter to pan as necessary.

To assemble place a spoonful of salmon filling on one side of each crepe, garnish with a small sprig of fresh dill or a sprinkling of dry dill. Fold in half and arrange on platter. Crêpes may be made ahead and refrigerated covered for several hours before serving.

Mayacamas Walnuts

Serves 8

Serve with Chardonnay

Recipe contributed by Elinor Travers; Mayacamas Vineyards, Napa

Elinor Travers likes to serve these nuts as an hors d'oeuvre with a glass of wine. There are many versions of this recipe, but Elinor likes her combination of spices.

2 cups walnut halves

4 tablespoons butter

½ teaspoon minced fresh thyme

½ teaspoon chili powder

½ teaspoon minced fresh marjoram

chives to taste

In a large frying pan warm all ingredients. Stir and cook over low heat until walnuts are coated and warm. Do not brown the nuts. Serve.

Author's note: If fresh herbs are unavailable use dried ones. Do not use salt. The spices give the nuts enough flavor and there is sufficient salt in the chili powder.

Artichoke Frittata

Makes 16 pieces

Serve with Chardonnay

Recipe contributed by Bett Shafer; Shafer Vineyards, Napa

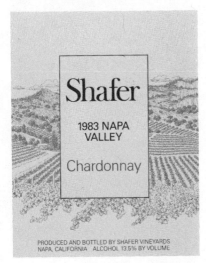

The sharp Cheddar cheese in Bett Shafer's frittata makes a tangy complement to Chardonnay.

3 6-oz. jars marinated artichoke hearts, drained and finely chopped

½ lb. sharp Cheddar cheese, grated

4 eggs, lightly beaten

6 single soda crackers, finely crushed

1 medium onion, finely chopped

dash of Tabasco sauce

salt and pepper to taste

Mix all ingredients well and pour into a buttered 8-inch square baking pan. Bake in preheated 325° oven for 1 hour. Cut into 1-inch squares and serve hot. May also be served at room temperature.

Author's note: Salt may be omitted, since the cheese and the artichoke hearts contain salt.

Warm Crab-Spinach Spread

Makes 1 cup

Recipe contributed by Rolayne Stortz; Sunrise Winery, Cupertino

Rolayne Stortz says that this is a traditional Thanksgiving appetizer at her house.

1 tablespoon olive oil	2 tablespoons Chardonnay
¼ cups shallots, minced	⅓ cup Parmesan cheese, grated
1 clove garlic, minced	salt and pepper to taste
½ lb. fresh cooked crabmeat	¼ teaspoon oregano, crumbled
1 bunch fresh spinach, cooked, squeezed dry and chopped	½ cup sour cream

Heat oil in 8-inch skillet; add shallots, garlic, crabmeat and spinach and cook gently for a few minutes. Stir in Chardonnay, Parmesan cheese, salt, pepper and oregano. Cook gently for a few minutes. Stir in sour cream and heat gently. Do not boil. Serve warm as a spread for crackers or bread.

Author's note: If fresh cooked crab is not available, substitute 1 7½-oz can of crabmeat.

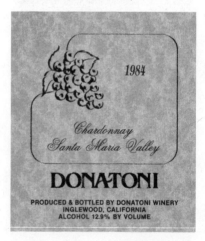

Spinach Dip with Vegetables

Serves 6 to 8

Recipe contributed by Judy Donatoni; Donatoni Winery, Inglewood

Judy Donatoni and her friend Sonya Wing created this dip to serve with vegetables. It is most attractive served in a hollowed-out red cabbage. The dip is best when prepared 24 hours in advance.

1 10-oz. pkg. frozen spinach (or 2 cups fresh chopped spinach)	½ cup minced scallions, white part only
1 cup sour cream	½ teaspoon Beau Monde seasonings
½ cup mayonnaise	
½ cup minced parsley	½ teaspoon dried dill weed
	salt and pepper to taste

Cook frozen spinach according to package directions and drain thoroughly. If using fresh spinach, cook for 3 minutes and drain thoroughly.

In a medium-sized bowl mix together remaining ingredients. Add the spinach and stir thoroughly. Cover and refrigerate overnight or longer. Place dip in a hollowed-out red cabbage. Serve with raw vegetables such as zucchini sticks, carrot sticks, celery sticks, cucumber slices, cauliflower flowerets, broccoli flowerets, snow peas, radishes.

Author's note: If Beau Monde seasoning is unavailable, ¼ teaspoon celery powder and ¼ teaspoon onion powder may be substituted.

Cloved Lobster Canapés

Makes 20 pieces *Serve with Chardonnay*

Recipe contributed by Shirley Sarvis for Sanford Winery, Buellton

This canapé was especially created for a recent wine tasting to complement the newly released Chardonnay.

- ½ cup unsalted butter
- 4 oz. lightly poached fresh Maine lobster, finely diced
- salt and freshly ground black pepper, to taste
- ⅛ teaspoon ground cloves, or less, to taste
- 1½-inch rounds thinly sliced sweet French bread, crusts removed and lightly buttered

In a medium-sized bowl stir together butter, lobster, salt, pepper and cloves. Taste carefully as you season the lobster butter. Add only enough cloves to give the slightest taste. Do not mask the flavor of the lobster. Pile deeply and loosely on bread rounds. Center each with a grinding of black pepper, if desired.

Crab and Cheese Dip

Makes 1½ cups *Serve with Blanc de Noirs*

Recipe contributed by Carole Anderson, S. Anderson Wine Cellars, Napa

Do not let the simplicity of this recipe fool you. It is delicious and foolproof! Any leftovers may be reheated the next day.

- ⅔ of a ½ lb. brick of Velveeta cheese
- ¾ cup mayonnaise
- 8 oz. fresh cooked crabmeat or 1 7½-oz. can crabmeat
- 4 tablespoons finely chopped green onions

In a medium-sized saucepan over low heat melt the cheese with the mayonnaise, stirring as the cheese melts. When thoroughly blended remove from heat. Add the crabmeat and onions and stir to blend. Serve warm with toasted rounds of French bread for dipping.

Smoked Salmon Mousse

Makes 1 cup *Serve with Sauvignon Blanc*

Recipe contributed by Fran Replogle, Fenestra Winery, Livermore

Fran Replogle creates recipes that take no time at all to put together. This one "takes 4 minutes to make — a lot faster than shopping for the ingredients."

- 4 oz. smoked salmon, cut in pieces
- ½ cup whipping cream
- dash of white pepper
- 1 teaspoon lemon juice
- ¼ cup melted butter, preferably unsalted

In a blender or food processor process salmon, whipping cream and pepper until smooth. Fold in lemon juice and melted butter. Put in crock or small bowl and store in refrigerator until ready to serve. Serve with crackers.

Author's note: This makes a mild spread with a wonderful smoked taste.

Serve with Sauvignon Blanc

Sautéed Mushrooms á la Charles

Serves 6 to 8

Recipe contributed by Charles Richard; Bellerose Vineyard, Healdsburg

Charles Richard says this recipe works best with large, broad-capped white mushrooms found in any supermarket.

1 lb. white mushrooms, large, broad-capped

2 tablespoons olive oil

2 tablespoons butter

1 green onion, chopped

salt and pepper

⅓ cup grated Parmesan cheese

¼ lb. Monterey Jack cheese

chopped parsley

Cut off stems of mushrooms, not merely flush with the cap, but to a slight depth within the cap. In a heavy skillet, heat the olive oil and the butter, add the chopped green onion and the mushrooms stem side down first. Sauté for about 5 minutes over medium heat. Turn mushrooms over and sprinkle with a little salt and pepper. Into the shallow cavity of each cap place a little grated Parmesan cheese. Next, place a square of Monterey Jack cheese in each cap. Cover pan and continue to heat until the cheese melts, about 3 to 4 minutes. Watch so that cheese does not run. Sprinkle with a little parsley. Place mushrooms on serving plate and serve with toothpicks.

Serve with Chardonnay

Chicken Mushroom Spread

Makes 50 pieces

Recipe contributed by Aurora Pepi; Robert Pepi Winery, Oakville

Aurora Pepi says this is an easy recipe to prepare and an excellent way to use leftover chicken.

1 cup cooked chicken breast meat (about 1½ chicken breasts)

¼ cup blanched almonds

½ cup quartered, cooked mushrooms

2 tablespoons mayonnaise

salt and pepper to taste

¼ teaspoon nutmeg

Cut chicken into 1-inch pieces. With metal blade in place on food processor, add chicken, almonds, mushrooms, mayonnaise, salt, pepper and nutmeg. Process with two or three pulses until evenly chopped. Add more mayonnaise to bind if necessary. Spread on small pieces of toast or sliced bread. May also be used to fill miniature cream puffs.

Author's note: For a variation, substitute curry powder for the nutmeg.

Shrimp Mold

Recipe contributed by Judith Tijsseling, Tyland Vineyards, Ukiah

Serves 8

Serve with White Zinfandel

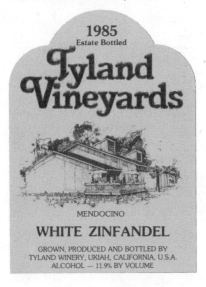

Prepare this in the morning, pour into a decorative mold and chill. To serve, unmold on lettuce leaves and surround with crackers. This, with a glass of White Zinfandel is a favorite afternoon snack for guests at the Tijsseling house. It is often served on the porch overlooking the Tyland vineyards and winery.

1 10½-oz. can cream of mushroom soup

1 cup mayonnaise

1 envelope plain gelatin

1 tablespoon hot water

1 green onion finely chopped

½ cup chopped celery

8 oz. bay shrimp, rinsed and drained (or canned shrimp, drained, rinsed and drained again)

Combine soup and mayonnaise. Dissolve gelatin in hot water and add to soup mixture. Add onion, celery and shrimp. Pour into mold and chill until firm, 4 to 5 hours.

Crabmeat may be substituted for the shrimp, or half crabmeat and half shrimp may be used.

Author's note: It is suggested that the shrimp and/or crabmeat be rinsed and drained well to remove salt since the soup and mayonnaise both contain sufficient salt for the recipe.

Serve with Chardonnay

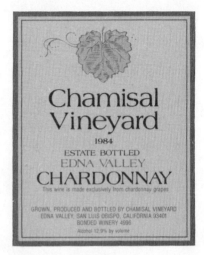

Avocados in Chardonnay

Serves 6

Recipe contributed by Carolyn Goss; Chamisal Vineyard, San Luis Obispo

This unusual and colorful first course is very light eating, especially on a hot summer evening.

3 avocados	**1 pimiento pepper, cut in ¼-inch slices**
salt and white pepper to taste	**Chardonnay**

Peel and cut each avocado lengthwise into ½-inch wide slices. Lightly sprinkle the slices with salt and white pepper. Line 6 small bowls with the slices so that they stick up in the air forming a crown. Put 4 slices of pimiento pepper in each bowl and fill with Chardonnay. Serve with crackers on the side.

Author's note: If fresh pimiento peppers are not available, canned pimiento strips may be used.

Serve with Chardonnay

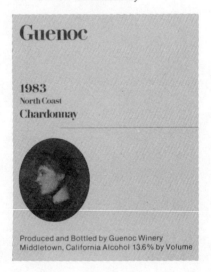

Sautéed Artichokes

Serves 4

Recipe contributed by Margaret Clark; Guenoc Winery, Middletown

The mildness of the artichokes and the chicken subtly combined with pesto are an excellent flavor combination. For a pesto recipe, see Pesce con Pesto (page 308) or use your own favorite recipe. In this dish artichoke bottoms and stems are sautéed, a preparation that may be new to many. Getting down to the edible portions of a large fresh artichoke may seem intimidating but is really fairly simple. Directions are given below.

4 large artichokes	**3 cloves garlic, minced**
vinegar or lemon juice	**½ teaspoon grated lemon rind**
2 to 3 tablespoons olive oil	**salt and freshly ground pepper to taste**
1 cup chopped cooked chicken	**¼ to ½ cup grated Parmesan cheese**
½ cup pesto sauce	
½ cup pine nuts	

Cut off tops of artichokes with a sharp knife, then pull off leaves or, with a small paring knife, turn and trim until lightest yellow-green portions of the artichoke bottoms appear. Remove artichoke stems, discarding the slice at end where it was cut from the plant. Cut each artichoke bottom in half and with a teaspoon, scoop out fuzzy thistle centers. Slice stems and artichoke bottoms into ¼ inch slices and immerse in cool acidulated water (1 tablespoon vinegar or lemon juice per quart of water) while preparing other ingredients.

To cook, heat olive oil until very hot (not smoking) in a large sauté pan. Drain and dry artichoke slices, and cook until light brown all over, on moderately high heat. Flip to brown other side and add chicken to heat. Add remaining ingredients, except cheese, and stir to blend and heat through. Sprinkle with cheese and serve.

Author's note: For extra color, add ⅛ cup finely chopped red peppers or pimiento to the sautéing and sprinkle chopped parsley on top along with the Parmesan cheese just before serving.

Spinach Balls with Mustard Sauce

Serves 8 to 10

Serve with Sauvignon Blanc

Recipe contributed by Dolores Cakebread; Cakebread Cellars, Rutherford

Over the years Dolores Cakebread has studied with many professionals in the culinary arts field, and as a result has developed many recipes that complement Cakebread wines. This is one of them. The sauce is simple to prepare, but must be started an hour before serving time. The spinach balls can be made as far in advance as is convenient and baked at the last minute.

2 bunches fresh spinach, washed and blanched

1 cup herb stuffing mix, crushed

2 green onions, chopped

⅛ cup grated Parmesan cheese

2 small eggs

4 tablespoons butter, melted

1 finely chopped shallot

dash of nutmeg

MUSTARD SAUCE

2 tablespoons dry mustard

2 tablespoons white vinegar

⅓ cup Sauvignon Blanc

1 to 2 tablespoons sugar, to taste

1 egg

3 tablespoons Dijon mustard

salt and white pepper to taste

Make spinach balls: Combine all ingredients and mix well. Shape into 1-inch balls; cover and refrigerate or freeze until ready to bake. Bake on an ungreased cookie sheet in a preheated 350° oven for 10 to 15 minutes. Serve with Mustard Sauce. Allow 3 to 4 per person.

Mix dry mustard and vinegar in a small bowl and let sit for 1 hour. In a saucepan mix wine, sugar, egg and Dijon mustard. Add dry mustard mixture. Cook over low heat, mixing constantly until light, fluffy and thick. Add salt and white pepper to taste. Add a little more Sauvignon Blanc if too hot or too thick.

Serve with Sauvignon Blanc

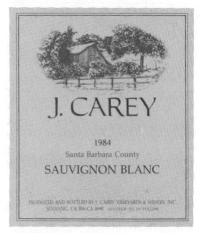

Scallops Flambé

Serves 4

Recipe contributed by Dr. James C. Carey, Jr.; J. Carey Vineyards & Winery, Solvang

Since Dr. Carey lives near the ocean, he often prepares and serves the fruits of the sea. If using bay scallops be careful not to overcook them. This is also an excellent luncheon dish. Serve with warm sourdough bread.

1 lb. whole bay scallops or sliced sea scallops	1 tomato, peeled, seeded and chopped
5 tablespoons butter	1½ cloves garlic, minced
1 onion, sliced	salt and freshly ground pepper to taste
1 shallot, minced	
3 tablespoons cognac	½ cup Sauvignon Blanc

Rinse scallops under cold water and pat dry. Heat butter in a medium-sized skillet over moderate heat. Add onion and shallot and cook until translucent. Add scallops, raise heat and brown lightly. Pour on cognac and flambé. When flame dies down, add tomato and garlic and season with salt and pepper. Pour in the Sauvignon Blanc and simmer for 5 to 6 minutes, stirring gently. Transfer the cooked scallops to four warmed scallop shells and keep warm. Raise heat and reduce sauce. Strain through a sieve and pour over scallops.

Serve with Chardonnay

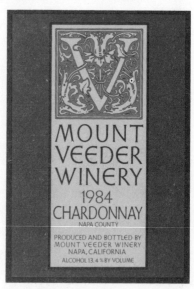

Baked Salmon with Piquant Sauce

Serves 8

Recipe contributed by Elaine Bell for Mount Veeder Winery, Napa

This first course dish was created for the 1985 Auction Wine Cellars Dinner in Napa.

8 6-oz. salmon fillets	**SAUCE**
½ cup soft butter	
salt and pepper to taste	1 large English cucumber, cut lengthwise, seeds removed, and sliced
	¼ cup fresh lemon juice
	½ cup chopped parsley
	¼ cup sliced green onions
	¼ cup olive oil
	salt and pepper to taste

Butter a large flat baking dish with half the soft butter. Place the salmon fillets in the dish and spread each piece with some of the remaining butter. Sprinkle with salt and pepper. Bake in a preheated 350° oven for 10 minutes, or until fish is done. Cool and then chill the fish.

To prepare the sauce, place cucumber slices, lemon juice, parsley, green onions and olive oil in a blender or food processor. Purée until smooth. Season with salt and pepper. Serve sauce on the side with the salmon.

Prosciutto-Stuffed Clams

Serves 6 to 8

Serve with Sauvignon Blanc

Recipe contributed by Stephanie and Larry Rosenbloom; Creston Manor Vineyards and Winery, Creston

The Rosenblooms try to use fresh local ingredients in their cooking. In this recipe they use the local Pismo clam but any fresh clam may be used. The Sauvignon Blanc is the perfect companion for the prosciutto and spices used in this clam appetizer.

18 to 24 fresh clams in the shells

½ cup butter at room temperature

3 shallots, finely chopped

1 teaspoon finely minced garlic

½ cup finely chopped parsley

1 tablespoon finely chopped fresh basil

1 cup soft bread crumbs

½ cup grated Parmesan cheese

2 tablespoons dry white wine

¼ cup finely chopped prosciutto

¼ teaspoon hot red pepper flakes

salt and pepper to taste

2 tablespoons olive oil

Chill clams quickly in freezer for easy opening, but do not freeze. Open clams and remove from shells, saving about 24 half-shells for stuffing. Chop clams, rather coarsely in food processor.

In a medium-sized saucepan combine chopped clams with butter, shallots, garlic, parsley, basil, bread crumbs, 6 tablespoons of the Parmesan cheese, wine, prosciutto, pepper flakes, salt and pepper to taste. Cook over medium heat, stirring gently, just long enough to blend the ingredients.

Stuff the clam shells with the mixture and sprinkle with a touch of Parmesan cheese. Place clam shells in a shallow baking dish. Sprinkle with olive oil. Bake in preheated 425° oven for 15 minutes. Place under preheated broiler for a few seconds for a final glaze.

Cured Meats and Fish with Melon

Serves 4

Serve with Sauvignon Blanc

Recipe contributed by Bruce LeFavour for Stonegate Winery, Calistoga

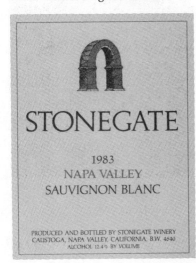

This combination of meats, salmon and melons is excellent with a Sauvignon Blanc or a Chardonnay. Gravlax is salmon cured with a special mixture of salt and sugar. If it is not available, smoked salmon will do as well. For best results, chill the melons beforehand.

4 ¾-inch slices each cantaloupe and honeydew melon

6 ripe figs, halved

4 thin slices gravlax or smoked salmon

1 shallot, minced

8 paper-thin slices prosciutto

8 thin slices "duckham" or other non-smokey pork ham

4 large sprigs of dill

Arrange the melons and fig halves on 4 chilled salad plates. Place the gravlax or smoked ham on the honeydew melon and sprinkle with a bit of chopped shallot. Place the prosciutto on the cantaloupe and the "duckham" or other ham on the figs. Garnish each plate with a sprig of dill and serve.

Salmon Mousse

Serves 6 to 8

Recipe contributed by Barbara Shilo; Domaine Laurier, Forestville

Barbara Shilo serves this appetizer often since it is very simple to prepare and makes an elegant presentation. Allow at least 12 hours for the mousse to set.

1 tablespoon water	1 cup dairy sour cream
1 tablespoon cognac	2 cups boned, skinned, poached salmon
2 tablespoons lemon juice	
1 envelope unflavored gelatin	½ teaspoon white pepper
1 small onion studded with 1 clove	1 teaspoon dried dill weed
	salt to taste

In a small saucepan combine water, cognac and lemon juice. Add gelatin and let stand until softened. Heat and stir over low heat until gelatin is dissolved. Meanwhile, boil onion in water for 8 minutes. Drain, reserving ¼ cup of the water and the onion. Discard clove and cut up onion.

In blender or food processor, combine salmon and sour cream. Blend until smooth. Add onion, reserved water, pepper and dill. Blend until smooth. Add gelatin and blend. Season to taste with salt if necessary. Pour into oiled 3-cup mold. Chill 12 hours to overnight.

Author's note: Substitute ¼ teaspoon fresh dill for the dried dill, or use both if more dill flavor is desired. Serving suggestion: Unmold the mousse on leaf lettuce and decorate with cold steamed asparagus spears and pimiento strips.

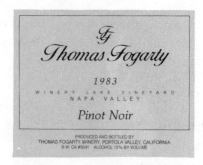

Calf Liver Pâté

Serves 10 to 12

Recipe contributed by Rosalee Fogarty; Thomas Fogarty Winery, Portola Valley

This recipe originated with Rosalee Fogarty as a way to use an abundance of venison liver, which she had stored in her freezer (one of Dr. Fogarty's hobbies is deer hunting). Any kind of liver may be used for this pâté with good results.

2 lbs. calf liver (or venison liver)	8 hard-boiled eggs
1 cup chicken broth	5 tablespoons butter
10 slices bacon, chopped	1 tablespoon salt
2½ cups finely chopped onions	1 teaspoon freshly ground pepper
	4 tablespoons sherry

In a saucepan simmer liver in chicken broth for 20 minutes. Then drain liver and cut into 2-inch pieces. Cook liver and bacon in a skillet until bacon is crisp. Remove both from skillet, leaving the drippings. Cook onion in the bacon drippings until lightly browned.

In a food processor, combine liver, bacon, onions, eggs, butter, salt, pepper and sherry. Mix to desired texture. Serve on lettuce as a first course or with crackers as an hors d'oeuvre.

Author's note: This is especially good made with chicken livers, or half chicken livers and half calf liver.

Layered Seafood Aspic

Serves 8   *Serve with Chardonnay*

Recipe contributed by Lucy Shaw; Charles F. Shaw Vineyard and Winery

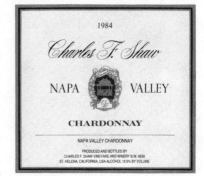

Lucy Shaw, an accomplished gourmet cook, serves this seafood aspic as a first course at a dinner party. This salad may be molded in 8 individual ring molds or in one large mold and then sliced for service. Allow time for each layer to chill thoroughly.

LAYER 1

1 10-oz. can tomato soup

1 10-oz. can water

1 10-oz. can Bloody Mary
   Cocktail mix

1 teaspoon tarragon

2 envelopes gelatin

2 tablespoons lemon juice

¼ cup water

½ cup tiny bay shrimp

GARNISH

8 large cooked shrimp with shell
   and head

lemon slices

LAYER 2

2 envelopes gelatin

2 tablespoons lemon juice

¼ cup water

1 4-oz. pkg. cream cheese

½ cup mayonnaise

½ cup sour cream

4 diced green onions

2 cups well washed spinach leaves

½ cup parsley

½ teaspoon anchovy paste

½ teaspoon capers

Layer 1: Heat soup, water, Bloody Mary mix and tarragon in medium-sized sauce-pan. Dissolve gelatin in lemon juice and ¼ cup water. Add to soup mixture, stir to combine and remove from heat. Place bay shrimp in mold. Fill mold ½ full with soup mixture. Chill until well set. Make the next layer.

Layer 2: Dissolve gelatin in lemon juice and water, and in a small saucepan heat until clear. Place the rest of the ingredients of layer 2 in food processor and process until completely blended and all vegetables are in minute pieces. Sauce will be green. Add gelatin to green mixture and pour into mold. Chill until very firm.

To serve: Unmold and garnish with whole shrimp and twisted lemon slices.

McDowell Pâté Maison

Recipe contributed by Karen Keehn; McDowell Valley Vineyards, Hopland

Karen Keehn not only serves this pâté at family gatherings but also at winery functions. The pâté may be refrigerated for several days.

1 lb. beef hamburger

1 lb. pork sausage

1 10-oz. pkg. frozen chopped spinach

1 small onion, chopped

4 tablespoons butter

3 slices white bread, crusts removed

⅔ cup Syrah (or Zinfandel)

1 cup cooked peas, puréed

½ cup grated Parmesan cheese

1 egg

2 tablespoons combined fresh chopped sage and rosemary

1 teaspoon fresh cracked pepper

⅔ cup pistachios

2 lbs. bacon, thick sliced

6 hard-boiled eggs

Meats should be ground quite fine using a meat grinder or food processor. Defrost spinach and squeeze out all of the water.

In a medium-sized skillet over medium-high heat sauté onion in butter until translucent. Tear bread in pieces, place in a bowl and soak in the wine. In a large bowl combine finely ground meats, sautéed onions, butter, puréed peas, spinach, Parmesan cheese, uncooked egg, herbs and pepper. Fold in the bread, wine and pistachios and work mixture with fingers or a large fork until ingredients are well blended.

Line the bottom and sides of 2 large loaf pans with sliced bacon, saving some to cover the top. Place ¼ of the mixture in the bottom of each pan; place 3 hard-cooked eggs, end to end, in each pan and press into pâtè mixture. Add remaining pâtè and press down firmly to compress mixture. Cover tops with bacon strips. Cover with foil.

Place both pâtè pans in a larger pan. Pour water in large pan to come halfway up the smaller pans. Bake 1½ to 2 hours in preheated 350° oven. Cool, leaving foil in place. Place weights on top to compress the pâtè. Remove from pans when cool, wrap in plastic wrap and store in refrigerator. Peel off bacon before slicing and serving.

Pâté de Poisson avec Sauce au Citron
(Fish Pâté with Lemon Sauce)

Recipe contributed by Kinta Clark; Deer Park Winery, Deer Park

Serves 6   Serve with Sauvignon Blanc

Kinta Clark's fish appetizer is an eye-appealing delight. The pâté itself must be prepared a day in advance. The sauce should be made at the last minute.

1⅓ lbs. red snapper fillets	**SAUCE**
2 egg whites	2 egg yolks
½ teaspoon salt	1 tablespoon water
¼ teaspoon pepper	1 tablespoon butter
1 tablespoon fresh lemon juice	1 tablespoon flour
1 cup heavy cream	⅔ cup chicken broth
⅓ cup chopped parsley	2 tablespoons lemon juice
⅓ cup chopped watercress	½ cup cream, whipped

Day before: Rinse and dry fillets. Cut into 1-inch chunks. In food processor, combine fillets, egg whites, salt, pepper and lemon juice. Process until finely chopped. Put in refrigerator and chill 30 minutes.

Generously butter 6 custard cups. Return fish mixture to food processor. With motor running, quickly add cream in a thin stream. Remove half of the mixture to a bowl. Add parsley and watercress to mixture remaining in processor and process until mixture turns green.

Preheat oven to 350°. Spoon half of the green mixture into the cups, then spoon the white mixture on top. Cover each cup with a small piece of foil. Place cups in a large baking pan. Pour enough hot tap water into the pan to come halfway up the cups. Bake 30 to 40 minutes, or until a knife inserted in the center comes out clean. Let the fish cups cool on a wire rack and refrigerate overnight.

Next day, to make sauce: Mix egg yolks with water and set aside. In small saucepan over medium heat, melt butter, stir in flour and cook, stirring, until well blended. Stir in chicken broth and lemon juice, and continue cooking and stirring until thickened. Remove from heat. Stir a small amount of sauce into egg yolks, stirring rapidly. Slowly pour mixture back into saucepan and cook for about 1 minute, stirring constantly. Remove from heat and fold in whipped cream. Serve sauce luke warm.

To serve, loosen pâtès from sides of cups. Pour off any excess liquid. Invert pâtès onto serving plates. Spoon sauce around base of pâtès. Garnish with watercress.

Serve with Chardonnay

Fresh Asparagus Soup

Serves 6 to 8

Recipe contributed by Julie Garvey; Flora Springs Winery, St. Helena

This soup may be served at a luncheon accompanied by hard rolls and a salad or it may be served as a first course for dinner.

1 tablespoon butter	dash of pepper
8 oz. fresh mushrooms, sliced	2 cups chicken broth
3 large leeks, white part only, sliced	2 cups milk or light cream
1 lb. asparagus, cut into 1½-inch pieces	1 12-oz. can whole kernel white corn or fresh corn cut from 2 ears of white corn
3 tablespoons flour	1 tablespoon pimiento, chopped
½ teaspoon salt	dash of saffron

In a large saucepan, melt butter and sauté mushrooms, leeks and asparagus until tender, about 10 minutes. Add flour, salt and pepper. Stirring constantly, add the chicken broth and the milk or cream. Heat until thickened. Do not boil. Add white corn, pimiento, and saffron and continue to heat. May be poured into a casserole and kept warm in the oven until ready to serve.

Serve with Fumé Blanc

El Dorado
1984 FUMÉ BLANC
Dry Sauvignon Blanc
SIERRA VISTA

Potato Soup

Serves 4

Recipe contributed by Barbara MacCready; Sierra Vista Winery, Placerville

This recipe was handed down by John MacCready's maternal grandmother whose family farmed hogs in Missouri, so of course, the recipe uses bacon and bacon fat. At the winery, Potato Soup is a favorite harvest dinner since it is easy to prepare and satisfies the hearty appetites that the harvest produces. The soup is served with French bread and a green salad.

¼ lb. bacon, minced	salt and pepper to taste
½ cup celery, sliced thin	1 tablespoon flour
1 medium onion, sliced thin	2 eggs, beaten
2 cups water	1 cup milk
1½ cups cubed raw potatoes	

Fry the bacon until crisp, reserving at least 2 tablespoons of bacon drippings. In a large saucepan, cook the celery and onion in the 2 cups of water until tender, about 15 minutes. Add the potatoes, salt and pepper, crisp bacon, and the 2 tablespoons of reserved bacon drippings. Cook until potatoes are done.

To thicken soup, mix 1 tablespoon of flour with a little water and add to the soup mixture. Let soup boil to mix well. Soup will be very thick at this point. Dribble in the eggs and 1 cup of milk. Heat thoroughly, but do not boil. Serve.

Curried Asparagus Soup with Coconut

Serves 6

Serve with Sauvignon Blanc

Recipe contributed by Susan Preston; Preston Vineyards and Winery, Healdsburg

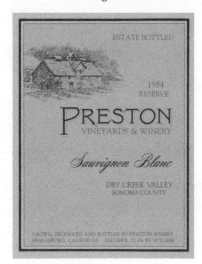

Susan Preston is a gourmet cook who likes to experiment with different combinations of foods, especially fresh vegetables. She has an extensive vegetable garden and has also planted edible landscaping around the winery to emphasize to visitors the relationship between wine and food.

1 lb. asparagus	1 quart homemade chicken broth
3 tablespoons unsalted butter	¼ cup shredded sorrel, optional
1 tablespoon peanut oil	1 cup cream
1 onion, chopped	¼ cup milk
1 tablespoon grated fresh ginger	1 fresh coconut
1½ teaspoons curry powder	salt to taste
sprinkling of cumin seeds	freshly ground pepper to taste

In a medium-sized saucepan cook asparagus in a small amount of water until barely tender. Drain and set aside. In another medium-sized saucepan heat butter and peanut oil. Sauté onion, ginger, curry and spices until onion is limp. Add chicken broth, asparagus and sorrel and bring to a boil. Simmer 20 minutes. Purée the mixture in a food processor. (May be cooked up to this point a day ahead.)

Extract milk from coconut (with a skewer or ice pick pierce the three black dots at the top and drain). Open the coconut, using a knife or hammer. Save the coconut milk. Grate the meat in a blender and measure out 1 cup.

Reheat puréed mixture and stir in cream, coconut milk, salt and pepper. Heat but do not boil. Spread grated coconut on baking sheet and brown under broiler for 1 or 2 minutes. Serve soup hot, garnished with a little toasted coconut.

Avocado Soup

Serves 6 to 8

Serve with Pinot Blanc

Recipe contributed by Lisa Buehler; Buehler Vineyards, St. Helena

This soup is good either hot or cold and freezes well, too. It can be stretched with a little more chicken broth or cream.

2 Hass avocados, peeled and pits removed	½ cup cream
	1 cup fresh orange juice
2 cups chicken broth	½ cup chopped tender celery
1 teaspoon minced orange zest	

Put the avocados, 1 cup of chicken broth and the orange zest into the bowl of a food processor and process until a perfectly smooth paste is formed. Pour mixture into a large bowl. Then place the other cup of chicken broth, cream, orange juice and celery into the food processor bowl and process until celery is very fine. Transfer this mixture to the bowl with the avocado mixture and whisk both together. Serve either heated or cold.

Serve with Merlot

Serve with Chardonnay

Hearty Lentil Soup

Serves 4 to 6

Recipe contributed by Eve Pagor; Rolling Hills Vineyards, Camarillo

This is an old Italian family recipe from Ed Pagor's family. It contains no meat, but is still a hearty and satisfying meal.

1 large onion, chopped	2 tablespoons chopped parsley
2 tablespoons olive oil	salt and pepper to taste
8 cups water	½ cup cooked elbow macaroni, optional
2 cups (12 oz.) lentils, washed	freshly grated Parmesan cheese
4 carrots, sliced	
5 stalks celery, sliced	

In a Dutch oven heat olive oil and sauté the diced onion until browned. Add water and bring to a boil. Add lentils, cover and simmer for 10 minutes. Add carrots, celery, parsley, salt and pepper to soup. Cover and simmer for an additional 40 minutes or until lentils are soft. Add macaroni and heat through. Ladle into soup bowls and sprinkle soup with grated Parmesan cheese. Serve with French bread.

Author's note: For an even heartier soup substitute chicken broth for part of the water.

Brazilian Cream of Pumpkin Soup

Serves 6 to 8

Recipe contributed by Ingrid Wheeler; Wheeler Vineyards, Healdsburg

Ingrid Wheeler learned to prepare this soup when she and her husband were living in Rio de Janeiro. She prefers making her own pumpkin purée, even though it does take a little more time. The pumpkin purée can be made and frozen for later use.

1 medium large pumpkin, about 3 lbs.	1½ teaspoon salt
3 tablespoons butter	¾ teaspoon ground ginger
1½ tablespoons finely chopped onion	¼ teaspoon nutmeg
2¼ tablespoons flour	¼ teaspoon white pepper
4½ cups scalded chicken broth	3 egg yolks
	1½ cups heavy cream
	chopped parsley

Cut the pumpkin in half crosswise and remove any seeds and stringy membranes. Place pumpkin halves in a large glass baking dish and bake pumpkin halves skin-side up in a preheated 325° oven for 1¼ hours or until tender. Remove pulp with a spoon and strain through fine disk of a food mill. A 3-lb. pumpkin will yield about 2¼ cups of purée. At this point the purée may be frozen.

In a large saucepan over medium-high heat melt the butter and sauté the onion until tender. Stir in the flour and mix thoroughly. Cook the roux over low heat, stirring until foamy. Remove the pan from the heat and add the pumpkin purée, the scalded chicken broth, salt, ginger, nutmeg and white pepper. Return the pan to the heat and cook the mixture, stirring with a wire whisk, until it is thick and smooth. Lightly beat the egg yolks and combine with the cream. Add to the pumpkin mixture in the pan. (For a less rich soup the cream can be added separately to the desired consistency.) Heat soup to just below the boiling point. Do not boil. Adjust seasonings if necessary and serve topped with chopped parsley.

Garden-Fresh Gazpacho

Serves 8 to 10

Serve with White Zinfandel

Recipe contributed by Lynne Russell; Granite Springs Winery and Vineyard, Somerset

Ladle this refreshing soup into chilled bowls for a flavorful first course to be enjoyed, perhaps, while steaks are grilling.

6 large ripe tomatoes	½ cup red wine vinegar
2 sweet red or green peppers (or 1 of each)	½ cup olive oil
2 medium yellow onions	2 cups canned tomato juice
2 large cloves garlic	salt and freshly ground pepper to taste
2 large cucumbers	

Wash and prepare the vegetables. Peel and coarsely chop tomatoes, saving the juice. Core, seed and coarsely chop peppers. Peel and coarsely chop onions and garlic. Peel and coarsely chop cucumbers.

In a bowl, whisk together vinegar, olive oil, reserved tomato juice and canned tomato juice. In a blender or food processor purée the vegetables in small batches, adding tomato juice mixture as necessary. Do not purée completely. The gazpacho should retain some of its crunch. Stir in the remaining tomato juice mixture. Add salt and freshly ground pepper to taste. Cover and chill for at least 4 hours.

German-Style Farina Soup

Serves 4

Serve with Pinot Blanc

Recipe contributed by Annamaria Roudon; Roudon-Smith Vineyards, Santa Cruz

Annamaria Roudon came to the United States as a bride in the 1950s and brought with her many of her family's German recipes. This one, Farina Soup, is a little more hearty than bouillon, but not so filling that it will detract from the remainder of the meal.

½ onion, chopped fine	1 can water
2 tablespoons butter	2 tablespoons finely chopped parsley
4 tablespoons farina (old fashioned Cream of Wheat)	1 egg, lightly beaten
2 10-oz. cans chicken broth	freshly grated nutmeg

In a medium-sized saucepan over medium heat, sauté onion in butter until golden brown. Lower heat and add Cream of Wheat slowly, stirring constantly. Then add chicken broth slowly, stirring constantly so that the Cream of Wheat will not lump. Stir in water, and simmer for 20 minutes. Just before serving, add parsley and stir in beaten egg. Heat to warm, but do not boil. Ladle into serving bowls and top with a dash of nutmeg.

Serve with Chardonnay

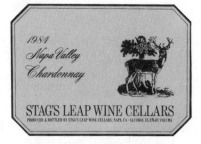

Wild Mushroom Soup

Serves 6

Recipe contributed by Barbara Winiarski; Stag's Leap Wine Cellars, Napa

Barbara Winiarski serves this traditional dish for Christmas Eve dinner or Polish Vigilia, which is a meatless meal of seven to eleven courses. This version of mushroom soup was handed down from Warren Winiarski's grandparents.

¼ lb. wild mushrooms, preferably *boletus edulis*

8 cups beef broth

1 cup finely chopped onions or shallots

4 tablespoons butter

salt to taste

sour cream for garnish

Soak the mushrooms overnight in cold water to cover. Drain the mushrooms but reserve the soaking liquid. Put the liquid through a fine cloth or a coffee filter.

Rinse the mushrooms well in cold water to remove any remaining trace of sand. Slice the mushrooms and put them in a 3-quart saucepan. Add the beef broth and the mushroom-soaking liquid. Bring to a boil and simmer for 4 hours.

Heat the butter in a heavy skillet and cook the onion in it, stirring frequently until golden brown. Add the flour and stir for a minute or 2. Add this to the soup and stir well. Continue to simmer until thickened slightly. Season with salt, if necessary, and serve in individual cups. Top each serving with a tablespoon of sour cream.

Author's note: You can substitute cultivated mushrooms for the wild, but the soup will taste quite different. The *boletus edulis* called for is highly prized in Europe. There are varieties that grow in the United States, but it would take a knowledgeable hunter to find them.

Serve with Sauvignon Blanc

Zucchini Soup

Serves 8 as first course

Recipe contributed by Judy Groth; Groth Vineyards and Winery, Oakville

Judy Groth, who likes to cook with wine, serves this hot version of zucchini soup as a first course or as an entrée with French bread and a salad.

4 lbs. zucchini, cut into chunks

1 lb. bacon, cut into pieces

2½ cups chicken broth

½ cup Sauvignon Blanc

1 onion, chopped

2 cloves garlic, crushed

1 bay leaf

4 dashes Tabasco sauce

salt and pepper to taste

Put ingredients into a large pot and bring to a boil. Simmer for 30 minutes. Let cool, remove bay leaf, and then process in a blender or a food processor. Reheat to serve.

Author's note: This is a fairly thick soup. If thinner soup is desired, add more chicken broth before reheating and serving.

Greek Lemon Soup

Serves 12

Recipe contributed by Juelle Fisher; Fisher Vineyards, Santa Rosa

Serve with Chardonnay

Juelle Fisher serves this soup in small bowls as a starter for a dinner party. The rice may be placed in individual bowls just before serving or stirred into the soup. The tangy flavor of the soup is an excellent complement to the Chardonnay served with it. The soup may be served hot, warm or cold.

10 cups chicken broth	**1 cup heavy cream**
8 tablespoons fresh lemon juice	**salt and white pepper to taste**
10 egg yolks	**1 cup cooked rice (warm)**
4 egg whites	**chopped parsley**

In a large saucepan bring chicken broth and lemon juice to a boil. Remove from heat. In a bowl beat the egg yolks. Add the cream to the yolks and then slowly add ½ cup of the hot stock. Gradually add egg yolk mixture to the remaining broth. Reduce heat to a simmer and return soup to heat, stirring slowly for 5 minutes or until the soup coats the back of a spoon. Add salt and pepper to taste. Beat egg whites until soft peaks form. Slowly whisk the beaten egg whites into soup. The soup should be frothy. Gently fold in the warm cooked rice. Serve in individual soup bowls, garnish with chopped parsley.

Another way of serving is to place 1 to 2 tablespoons of hot rice in each individual bowl and then spoon hot soup over the rice. Garnish with parsley and serve.

Author's note: This recipe can easily be cut in half to serve 6.

Cream of Spinach Soup

Serves 4

Recipe contributed by Susan Robbins; Spring Mountain Vineyards, St. Helena

Serve with Sauvignon Blanc

This easy to prepare soup makes a tasty start to a spring meal.

9 bunches of young spinach	**salt and pepper**
3 cups chicken broth	**strips of lemon zest for garnish**
3 tablespoons whipping cream	

In a large kettle bring salted water to a boil. Drop in washed spinach. Bring water back to a boil and cook for 3 minutes until spinach leaves are tender and beginning to wilt. Remove from heat and drain spinach in a colander. Run cold water over spinach to preserve color.

Purée spinach in food processor. Return to pan and add 3 cups chicken broth, cream, salt and pepper. Heat through, but do not boil. Serve in individual soup bowls. Decorate with lemon zest.

French Onion Soup á la Parks

Serves 8

Recipe contributed by Mary Kaye Parks; Sycamore Creek Vineyards, Morgan Hill

In the fall, Mary Kaye Parks likes to serve this soup for lunch with a salad. The use of Chardonnay helps to smooth out the soup.

5 cups thinly sliced onions

3 tablespoons butter

1 tablespoon vegetable oil

1 teaspoon salt

¼ teaspoon sugar

3 tablespoons flour

3 10-oz. cans hot condensed beef bouillon

3 10-oz. cans hot water

½ cup Chardonnay

salt and pepper to taste

2 oz. Swiss cheese, cut in thin slivers

1 tablespoon grated onion

16 slices French bread, toasted

½ cup Parmesan cheese, grated

1 tablespoon butter, melted

Cook the sliced onions in 3 tablespoons butter and 1 tablespoon oil for 15 minutes in a covered saucepan. Add the salt and sugar and continue cooking uncovered over very low heat for 35 more minutes. Sprinkle with flour and cook, stirring, for 3 minutes.

Remove from heat and add hot bouillon and water. Mix well. Add wine and season with salt and pepper to taste. Simmer partly covered for 35 minutes. Bring soup to a boil and pour into an ovenproof tureen. Stir in cheese and grated onion.

Float toast slices on top and sprinkle grated cheese on top of bread. Drizzle melted butter on top of bread slices and place under broiler until the top is brown.

Seafood Bisque

Serves 10

Recipe contributed by Cheryl Devlin; Devlin Wine Cellars, Soquel

Cheryl finds Seafood Bisque a lovely way to start any meal. Serve it with Chardonnay and warm French bread

1¼ cup butter

¾ cup flour

1 20-oz. can whole clams

1 cup Chardonnay

1 quart milk

1 pint heavy cream

1 bunch green onions, chopped

3 shallots, chopped

2 cloves garlic, minced

1 lb. medium-sized prawns, shelled and deveined

2 lbs. fresh, cooked crabmeat

⅓ cup dry sherry

chopped parsley for garnish

seasonings to taste: thyme, rosemary, white pepper, cayenne pepper, paprika, nutmeg

Melt the ¾ cup butter in a large Dutch oven or heavy-bottomed saucepan. Add flour and cook until flaky and paste-like — 2 to 3 minutes. Drain liquid from clams and add ½ cup Chardonnay to it. Add the wine mixture slowly to the butter-flour mixture. Blend until smooth. Slowly stir in milk and cream and cook over medium-low heat until soup is thickened, about 5 to 7 minutes.

In another large pan, melt remaining butter. Add green onions, shallots, and garlic and sauté until wilted. Add the shrimp, crab and clams. Cook until shrimp is slightly pink and crab and clams are heated through. Add seafood mixture to the soup, stir in remaining ½ cup of Chardonnay and the sherry. Heat through, but do not boil. Add seasonings to taste and garnish with chopped parsley.

Author's note: Fresh, cooked crabmeat is often available in seafood markets. However, if fresh crabmeat is unavailable, canned may be substituted.

Harvest Corn and Pumpkin Soup

Serves 12   *Serve with Gewurztraminer*

Recipe contributed by Richard Alexei, Culinary Director, Monticello Cellars, Napa

This soup is reminiscent of colonial days in Virginia. Richard Alexei has provided a traditional Early American soup with a 1980s update.

1 medium onion, coarsely chopped

2 tablespoons butter

3 lb. piece of pumpkin (hubbard, banana or other orange-fleshed squash may be substituted) seeds removed, peeled and cut into chunks

2 to 3 fresh jalapeño peppers, stems removed, cut lengthwise, seeds and veins removed

1½ quarts well-flavored chicken stock

1 cup Gewurztraminer

6 ears fresh corn (6 cups frozen kernels may be substituted), kernels removed

salt

1 cup whipping cream

1 tablespoon fresh chopped cilantro

sour cream and cilantro leaves for garnish

In a 4-quart casserole or heavy saucepan over medium-chigh heat sauté onion in butter until translucent and lightly browned. Add pumpkin, peppers, chicken stock and Gewurztraminer. Bring to a boil. Cover and simmer ½ hour or until pumpkin is tender. Add corn kernels and simmer 5 minutes more. Cool mixture so that it is easy to handle.

Purée the mixture in a blender or food processor until soup is emulsified but retains some texture. (This may be done in two batches.) Taste soup and add salt if necessary. To this point the recipe may be prepared a day in advance.

Before serving, heat soup to boiling point and simmer a few minutes. Stir in cream and chopped cilantro just before serving. Heat to warm, but do not boil. Garnish each serving with a dollop of sour cream and a fresh cilantro leaf.

Serve with Chardonnay

Mexican Corn Soup

Serves 4 to 6

Recipe contributed by Jeanne Jensen; Calera Wine Company, Hollister

This Mexican Corn Soup is Jeanne Jensen's version of a traditional "South of the Border" dish.

4 to 5 cups fresh corn, cut and scraped from the cob (about 8 to 10 ears)

1 cup water

¼ cup butter

3 cups milk

salt

1 cup cubed *Quesillo de Oaxaca* (Mexican braided cheese found in Mexican markets) or any soft-type cheese that melts, such as Mozzarella or Fontina

1 chile poblano, peeled, seeded and chopped (optional)

tortilla chips for garnish

Process corn kernels and pulp in processor with water for 10 seconds to break down the hulls. Then purée through a food mill to extract the pulp and "milk" only. Discard hulls.

Put mixture into medium-sized saucepan with butter and cook over medium heat stirring constantly for 5 minutes. Add milk and salt to taste. Let soup simmer 15 minutes, stirring well occasionally to avoid sticking to bottom of pan. Add chopped chile. Turn off heat. When ready to serve, reheat over very low heat. Add cheese. Allow a few minutes to let cheese melt. Serve in soup bowls with tortilla chips.

Serve with Chardonnay

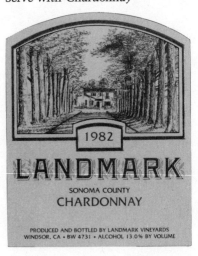

Two Bell Pepper Soup

Serves 8

Recipe created by Students of San Francisco Culinary Academy for Landmark Vineyards, Windsor

Landmark Vineyards commissioned the creation of six luncheons by students of the San Francisco Culinary Academy, requesting they use fresh ingredients available in Sonoma County and that the dishes be paired with Landmark wines. The four student chefs for the October 1985 luncheon were Nancy Thorne, Paul Weakland, Larry Bhe and Jan-Marc Baker. The visual success of this dish depends on preparing two soups and keeping them separate until the moment they are served.

6 medium red bell peppers

6 medium green bell peppers

3 shallots, chopped

½ onion, chopped

2 tablespoons butter

1 cup white wine

6 cups chicken stock

2 cups heavy cream

salt, white pepper and sugar to taste

Roast red and green peppers separately in preheated 400° oven, turning occasionally, for about 1 hour until evenly brown or black. Remove from oven and put each group in a separate paper bag. Close bag and allow peppers to steam for about 10 minutes. Remove peppers from bag, remove their skins and seeds. Work over bowl to catch the juices.

Using two soup pots, sauté half the shallots and onion in each pot in a tablespoon of butter over low heat until transparent. Add peppers and pepper juices, one color in each pot. Stew until hot. Add ½ cup wine to each pot and reduce by half. Add 3 cups chicken stock to each pot, bring to a boil and simmer for 1 hour.

Purée the soups separately in a blender until smooth. Strain into clean pots and add 1 cup of cream to each soup. Simmer and season to taste. Chill soups in refrigerator.

To serve, use wide shallow soup bowls. With one 4-oz. ladle in each hand, simultaneously pour the two soups into each bowl so that the red soup and green soup rest side by side. Serve.

Jo-Ann's Clam Chowder

Serves 8

Recipe contributed by Jo-Ann Nichelini Meyer, Nichelini Vineyard, St. Helena

Serve with Sauvignon Vert

This clam chowder is substantial enough to serve as the entrée for a light supper or lunch, in which case add a tossed green salad and sour dough bread to round out the meal. As a starter for a full meal, serve it up in moderate portions or appetites will lag.

6 to 7 slices bacon	3 teaspoons lemon juice
1 cup sliced celery	4 tablespoons butter
½ cup diced bell pepper	1 teaspoon garlic salt
¾ cup chopped green onions	¼ teaspoon pepper
1½ cups fresh clams, chopped	1½ cups water
4 potatoes, peeled and diced (3 cups)	3½ cups milk
	3 to 4 teaspoons cornstarch
½ cup finely chopped fresh parsley	dash of Worcestershire sauce

In a large frying pan, cook the bacon until medium crisp. Remove bacon and dice it; leave bacon drippings in pan. Sauté celery, bell pepper and green onion in drippings until limp. Drain celery mixture and place in a large pot or Dutch oven. Add clams, potatoes, parsley, lemon juice, butter, garlic salt, pepper and water to the pot. Bring to a boil, cover and simmer for 15 minutes. Add 3 cups of milk to the pot. Mix remaining ½ cup milk with the cornstarch and add to pot. Bring to a boil, stirring constantly. Simmer for 5 minutes, add Worcestershire sauce and serve.

Author's note: If desired, 1 to 1½ cups half-and-half may be substituted for part of the milk for an even richer soup.

▾ SALAD ▾

Serve with Napa Valley Gamay

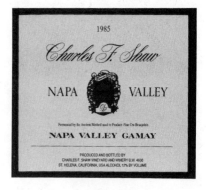

Green Salad

Serves 8

Recipe contributed by Lucy Shaw; Charles F. Shaw Vineyard and Winery, St. Helena

This pleasant, refreshing salad is served as a palate cleanser after the main course. The Gamay wine is a nice fruity accompaniment to the salad. A cheese tray would make a nice addition.

1 head butter lettuce	½ cup chopped walnuts
1 head red leaf lettuce	½ cup sliced strawberries
1 bunch fresh spinach	⅓ cup vinaigrette dressing

Wash and dry the greens. Tear into pieces and put in a large bowl. Add the walnuts and strawberries. Pour dressing over the mixture. Toss and serve.

Serve with Cabernet Sauvignon (the dinner wine)

Wilted Lettuce Salad

Serves 4

Recipe contributed by Katrina Staten; Field Stone Winery, Healdsburg

Katrina Staten serves this salad as an accompaniment to a standing rib roast of beef along with baked potatoes.

5 slices bacon, cut into strips	2 hard-boiled eggs, chopped into small pieces
¼ cup vinegar	6 young green onions, chopped in small rounds
¼ cup water	salt and ground pepper to taste
2 rounded teaspoons sugar	
1 large head red leaf lettuce, rinsed well, dried and torn in large pieces	

Sauté bacon in small frying pan until crisp. Remove bacon and drain; retain bacon drippings. Mix together vinegar and water and add with the sugar to the drippings, stir well to combine the mixture. Place lettuce, eggs, and onions in a large wooden salad bowl. Add salt and ground pepper to taste.

Bring dressing mixture to a quick, hot boil, stirring constantly. Add bacon crisps to salad. Pour bubbling dressing over salad greens, tossing gently and quickly to wilt the lettuce. Serve immediately.

Spinach Salad

Recipe contributed by Fred Holloway; Ballard Canyon, Solvang

Serves 2

Serve with Cabernet Sauvignon

The warm dressing poured over the spinach wilts the spinach leaves and melds the flavors.

4 cups fresh spinach leaves	¼ cup vinegar
4 slices bacon	dash of salt
¼ red onion, chopped	½ teaspoon freshly ground pepper
4 oz. mushrooms, sliced	1 hard-boiled egg, chopped
2 tablespoons Dijon mustard	
3 tablespoons sugar	

Wash and dry spinach. If leaves are large tear in half. In a medium-sized skillet fry bacon. Remove bacon after it is cooked, leaving drippings in the skillet. Fry onion in drippings over medium heat for 3 minutes. Add mushrooms and sauté. In a separate bowl combine the mustard, sugar, vinegar, salt and pepper. Increase heat to medium high. Crumble bacon with onion and mushrooms in skillet. Add vinegar sauce and bring to a boil. Remove from heat. Pour over the spinach and toss. Top with chopped hard-boiled egg and serve immediately.

Red and Black Salad

Recipe contributed by Lila Burford; Adler Fels, Santa Rosa

Serves 6

Serve with Fumé Blanc

This is a pretty summer salad to serve as a first course. Lila Burford uses lemon in the marinade-dressing to complement the Fumé Blanc.

	MARINADE
1 cup pitted black olives	
6 tomatoes, cut in wedges	1 teaspoon salt
2 onions, halved and sliced	2 teaspoons sugar
½ cup chopped parsley	⅛ teaspoon turmeric
1 bunch, green leaf lettuce	¾ teaspoon cumin
	¼ teaspoon black pepper
	6 tablespoons olive oil
	4 tablespoons lemon juice

In a medium-sized bowl combine olives, tomato wedges, onion slices and chopped parsley. In a mixing cup combine marinade ingredients and pour over tomato mixture. Cover and refrigerate for several hours, gently stirring occasionally to combine flavors. To serve wash, rinse and pat dry green lettuce leaves, place on six salad plates. Spoon tomato mixture on top, dividing evenly among the six plates.

Author's note: Use lemon juice rather than vinegar in a salad dressing when you are serving wine. Vinegar tends to conflict with and overpower wine.

Serve with Pinot Noir (with lamb) or the dinner wine

Endive and Beet Salad

Serves 2

Recipe contributed by Ken Burnap; Santa Cruz Mountain Vineyard, Santa Cruz

Ken Burnap, as a vintner, has made numerous trips to France. He is always amazed at the simplicity of French food. This salad is served throughout France at large and small restaurants alike.

VINAIGRETTE DRESSING

⅓ cup olive or salad oil

3 tablespoons wine vinegar

¼ teaspoon dry mustard

1 tablespoon chopped fresh basil

1 medium red onion, sliced thin

8 thin slices English cucumber

1 4-oz. can red beets, drained and julienned

freshly ground black pepper

In a small bowl combine vinaigrette ingredients. Add onion and cucumber slices. Marinate in the refrigerator for several hours.

To serve, arrange endive leaves on two salad plates, top with onion and cucumber slices, and spoon on some of the vinaigrette. Top with julienned beets and some freshly ground black pepper.

Serve with Sauvignon Blanc, or the dinner wine

Grandma's Cranberry Salad

Serves 6

Recipe contributed by Mieke Costello; Costello Vineyards, Napa

This recipe has been in John Costello's family for several generations. It is always served at holiday time, and may also be used simply as a relish to accompany poultry or meats.

12 oz. (1 bag) fresh cranberries, coarsely chopped

2 ribs celery, finely chopped

½ cup walnuts, finely chopped

1 cup sugar

juice and grated rind of 1 orange

juice of ½ lemon

1 3-oz. package lemon gelatin

½ cup boiling water

Combine chopped cranberries, celery, nuts, sugar and grated orange rind in a bowl. Stir and let stand about 30 minutes. Some natural juice will come from the cranberries.

Dissolve gelatin in ½ cup boiling water, cool slightly and add orange and lemon juices. Combine juicy cranberry mixture with gelatin mixture. Pour into a mold or a bowl and chill for several hours in the refrigerator, or until set. Serve on lettuce as a salad, accompanied by mayonnaise, or serve as a relish with poultry or meats. This will keep several days in the refrigerator if stored covered.

Spring Salad with Blueberry Vinaigrette

Serves 6

Serve with Johannisberg Riesling

Recipe contributed by Robin Gainey; The Gainey Vineyard, Santa Ynez

The blueberries add a pleasant sweetness to this varied-lettuce salad. Mâche, a soft French lettuce also known as lamb's lettuce, grows wild in the Santa Ynez Valley.

12 leaves red lettuce

12 leaves butter lettuce

12 leaves radicchio

2 cups mâche (any other soft lettuce may be substituted)

1 cup sunflower sprouts

½ lb. firm white mushrooms, sliced

1 pint fresh blueberries

BLUEBERRY VINAIGRETTE

6 tablespoons safflower oil

3 to 4 tablespoons blueberry vinegar, depending on tartness

¼ teaspoon freshly ground pepper

½ teaspoon salt

2 tablespoons minced parsley

2 tablespoons minced shallots

Wash and dry lettuce leaves; break into pieces and combine with sunflower sprouts and mushrooms. Combine vinaigrette ingredients. Add just enough vinaigrette to coat the salad lightly. Serve on individual plates garnished with blueberries.

Author's note: Availability may dictate what you put in this salad, but it is best to use soft types of lettuce to blend with the delicate flavors of the dressing. If fresh blueberries are unavailable, use frozen ones that have been thawed and well drained.

Prosciutto and Peas

Serves 4

Serve with White Zinfandel

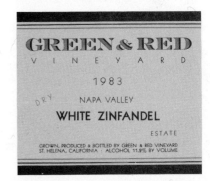

Recipe contributed by Pam Wilder; Green and Red Vineyard, St. Helena

Pam Wilder invented this recipe at the suggestion of a friend who loves raw peas. It is a good solution to the problem of too few peas in the garden for full-sized servings of vegetables for a meal. In this recipe, the saltiness of the prosciutto and the sweetness of the peas combine well with the tart wine.

12 thin slices prosciutto

1 cup fresh shelled peas

extra virgin olive oil

chopped parsley

freshly ground black pepper

lettuce leaves

Divide prosciutto into four portions and arrange on lettuce leaves on individual plates. Sprinkle with peas. Drizzle with olive oil. Garnish with chopped parsley and black pepper. Serve as a first course with French bread.

Serve with White Zinfandel, or the dinner wine

1985 WHITE-ZINFANDEL
El Dorado
SIERRA VISTA

Fruit Salad with Lime Dressing

Serves 4

Recipe contributed by Barbara MacCready; Sierra Vista Winery, Placerville

Barbara MacCready usually serves salads after the main course, so that the vinegar taste will not interfere with the enjoyment of the dinner wine. There are times, however when she likes to serve a salad to complement the main course. Fruit Salad with Lime Dressing is particularly well suited to a meat or poultry dish which has a rich sauce.

Bibb lettuce leaves	**12 strawberries, cut in half**
1 papaya, sliced	**¼ cup lime juice**
1 kiwi, sliced	**2 tablespoons honey**
1 banana, sliced	**¾ cup sour cream**

Arrange lettuce leaves on four salad plates. Place fruits on top of lettuce, distributing them evenly. Mix lime juice thoroughly with the honey. Add sour cream, slowly beating until the right consistency for dressing is reached. Taste and adjust dressing by adding more lime juice or more honey.

Author's note: Other fruits in season, such as peaches, pineapple, or berries, may also be used.

Serve with Sauvignon Blanc, or the dinner wine

HACIENDA
1984
SONOMA COUNTY
Sauvignon Blanc

Pineapple Slaw

Serves 6

Recipe contributed by A. Crawford Cooley; Hacienda Winery, Sonoma

Pineapple Slaw is prepared with red cabbage and is an ideal accompaniment to grilled or barbecued meats. It is often served at barbecues at the Hacienda Winery.

1 medium red cabbage, coarsely shredded (about 12 cups)	**1 cup mayonnaise**
½ grated carrot	**¼ cup sour cream**
½ cup finely chopped onion	**1½ teaspoons tarragon vinegar or regular red wine vinegar with a pinch of tarragon**
½ cup finely chopped red bell pepper	**¼ teaspoon crushed red pepper flakes**
1 8-oz. can pineapple chunks, drain juice, reserving ¼ cup	**1 slice dried pineapple, slivered**
	sweet red pepper rings

In a large bowl combine cabbage, carrot, onion and red pepper. Chop pineapple chunks and add to cabbage mixture. Mix mayonnaise, sour cream, vinegar, and red pepper flakes in a small bowl. Whisk in reserved pineapple juice. Pour over cabbage and mix thoroughly. If dressing is not thick enough add more sour cream. Garnish with dried pineapple and red pepper rings.

Miner's Salad

Serves 4

Recipe contributed by Barden E. Stevenot; Stevenot Winery, Murphys

Serve with White Zinfandel

Barden Stevenot enjoys preparing foods reminiscent of the days of the '49ers, since both his winery and his gold mine are located in Gold Rush Country. Miner's lettuce, which grows wild in that area, resembles the four-leaf clover in appearance, and has a tangy flavor similar to watercress.

1 cup dried lentils	1 teaspoon grated lemon peel
2 cups Zinfandel	5 teaspoons red wine vinegar
1 clove garlic, minced	6 teaspoons sesame oil
½ teaspoon cumin	**GARNISH**
¼ teaspoon black pepper	tomato wedges
	watercress or miner's lettuce
	sesame seeds, lightly toasted

In a bowl, cover lentils with cold water and soak for ½ hour. Discard any lentils that float. Drain and transfer lentils to a pot of rapidly boiling, lightly salted water. Reduce heat and cook for 10 minutes or until lentils are tender. They should retain their shape and not be mushy. Drain lentils and transfer to a bowl. Add Zinfandel and marinate for 2 hours. Drain off wine and add remaining salad ingredients. Toss lightly. Garnish with tomato wedges, watercress or miner's lettuce and sesame seeds.

Author's note: It is believed that this salad recipe was brought to California by the French miners who came during the Gold Rush. Sesame oil and seeds, however, were probably an influence of the Chinese laborers who came to the area later.

Potato Salad

Serves 6

Recipe contributed by Joanne Cook; R. & J. Cook, Clarksburg

Serve with Fumé Blanc or the dinner wine

Joanne Cook serves this potato salad at many of their barbecues. It is an old family recipe.

2 lbs. potatoes (about 6 medium)	2 tablespoons chopped parsley
6 hard-boiled eggs	fresh ground pepper, to taste
3 dill pickle halves	dash of garlic powder
1 2.2-oz. can sliced black olives	½ cup mayonnaise
¼ cup chopped red onion, optional	¼ cup mustard
	chopped parsley
	paprika

Boil potatoes in their jackets. Cool and slice the potatoes. Chop 5 of the eggs and the pickles. In a large bowl combine the sliced potatoes, chopped eggs, pickles, olives, optional onion, and chopped parsley. Season with pepper and a dash of garlic powder. Make a dressing by combining the mayonnaise and mustard. Add to the potato mixture, combining with light strokes so as not to break up the potato slices. Slice the remaining egg and lay it on top of the salad. Sprinkle with paprika and some additional parsley.

Serve with White Zinfandel, or the dinner wine

Green Pea Salad

Serves 6 to 8

Recipe contributed by Polly Mullen; Woodside Vineyards, Woodside

Polly Mullen often serves this salad with seafood, particularly salmon. The fresh mint and sour cream mixture provide an interesting flavor combination that is an excellent complement to any fish.

2 lbs. fresh peas, shelled

1 medium jicama, peeled and chopped (about ¾ cup)

¾ cup toasted pine nuts

1 clove garlic, finely chopped

¼ cup chopped fresh mint leaves

pinch of cayenne pepper

¼ teaspoon salt

¾ cup sour cream

⅓ cup mayonnaise

Blanch the peas in boiling water for 4 to 5 minutes. Rinse under cold water and drain. Place in bowl with the chopped jicama and the toasted pine nuts.

In food processor bowl place garlic, mint leaves, cayenne pepper, salt, sour cream and mayonnaise. Pulse on and off until ingredients are well blended. Add dressing to vegetables and toss. Serve on lettuce leaves.

Author's note: Jicama is a root vegetable with white crisp meat resembling a potato. It is found in the produce department of the grocery store. If unavailable, canned whole water chestnuts may be substituted. Chop them and use as directed. If more color is desired in the salad, add ¼ cup chopped red bell pepper.

Serve with Sauvignon Blanc

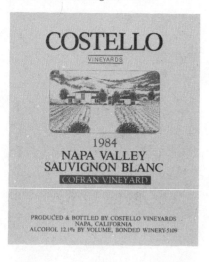

Huzarensla

Serves 6

(Soldier's Salad)

Recipe contributed by Mieke Costello; Costello Vineyards, Napa

This is a favorite luncheon dish in Holland where Mieke Costello was born and raised. She serves this often to her family and guests.

½ lb. baked ham, cubed*

2 tart apples, peeled and cubed

8 medium potatoes, boiled, peeled and cubed

12 small pickled cocktail onions, chopped

6 sweet gherkins, chopped

12 stuffed green olives, sliced

¾ cup mayonnaise, seasoned to taste with lemon juice, salt and cayenne

2 hard-boiled eggs, sliced

1 small can whole pickled beets

In a large bowl combine ham, apples, potatoes, onions, gherkins and olives. Fold in mayonnaise to moisten, adding more if necessary. Mound on platter lined with lettuce leaves. Put sliced eggs on top and decorate with beets around the mounded salad.

*1 lb. slab bacon, cut into ½ inch dice, fried and drained, may be substituted for the ham.

Southwest Pepper and Fusilli Salad

Serves 6 to 8

Recipe contributed by Susan Meyer, Rustridge Vineyards, St. Helena,

Serve with Johannisberg Riesling

Susan Meyer suggests this cold but spicy-hot salad be served at picnics or buffet lunches. Fusilli are corkscrew-shaped noodles, often used in pasta salads.

½ lb. egg fusilli

1 tablespoon virgin olive oil

1½ teaspoons chopped cilantro leaves

1 tablespoon chopped fresh jalapeño pepper

2 tablespoons chopped fresh chile pepper

2 medium-sized tomatoes

1 small green bell pepper, julienned

½ lb. Monterey Jack cheese, cut into ½-inch cubes

cilantro

DRESSING

1 tablespoon white wine vinegar

3 tablespoons virgin olive oil

1 to 2 tablespoons grated Romano cheese

2 cloves garlic, finely chopped

½ teaspoon cayenne pepper

Cook the fusilli in boiling water until al dente. Rinse in cold water and drain. Transfer to a serving bowl. Toss with the olive oil. Add the cilantro, jalapeño and green chile peppers. Score, then blanch the tomatoes in boiling water for 30 seconds to loosen the skins. Peel, halve and seed the tomatoes under running water. Pat dry and chop into bite-sized pieces. Add to salad. Add the bell pepper and cheese cubes to the salad and mix well.

Make the dressing by whisking the olive oil into the vinegar in a small bowl. Blend in the cheese, garlic and pepper. Toss the dressing with the salad. Garnish the salad with sprigs of cilantro.

Coriander Duck Salad

Serves 4

Recipe created by Shirley Sarvis for Sanford Winery, Buellton

Serve with Pinot Noir - Vin Gris

Shirley Sarvis is a West Coast free-lance food writer who has designed a number of hors d'oeuvres to pair with Sanford wines. One of these recipes has been modified for a first course salad.

8 oz. lean roasted duck breast, julienned

1 cup fresh coriander leaves

¼ teaspoon salt

¼ teaspoon black pepper

⅓ cup light olive oil

1 teaspoon sesame oil

Boston lettuce, small inside leaves

Place duck and coriander leaves in a medium-sized bowl. In another bowl mix salt, pepper, olive oil and sesame oil. Pour over duck and coriander, coating the duck mixture well. Add more oil if necessary.

On four salad plates, make lettuce cups from Boston lettuce leaves, combining two or more leaves if necessary. Pile ¼ of the duck mixture into each lettuce cup. Serve.

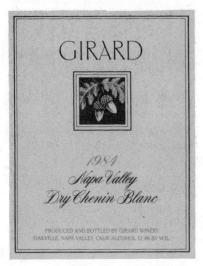

Shrimp Salad with Mushrooms

Recipe contributed by Carol Girard; Girard Winery, Oakville

This salad is an elegant start for any dinner party. The flavors blend especially well with a dry, crispy Chenin Blanc. Crabmeat (1 to 1½ pounds) may be substituted for the shrimp.

20 large shrimp, shelled and deveined (tails intact)

6 to 8 cups court bouillon (see note below)

½ cup snow peas

20 small white mushrooms, cleaned and left whole

½ cup chopped water chestnuts

3 tablespoons finely minced red onion

8 lettuce leaves

VINAIGRETTE

2 tablespoons Dijon mustard

¼ cup lime juice, or more

2 tablespoons chopped fresh dill or 2 teaspoons dried dill weed

½ cup olive oil

½ cup vegetable oil

salt and freshly ground pepper to taste

Poach shrimp in gently simmering court bouillon until pink, about 3 to 5 minutes. Transfer shrimp to a bowl using slotted spoon. Reserve bouillon for another use. Let shrimp cool to room temperature, then refrigerate.

Carefully slice 8 largest shrimp in half lengthwise down through the tails. Reserve for garnish. Slice remaining shrimp in medallions, crosswise, discarding tails. Blanch snow peas in boiling water for 2 to 3 minutes. Drain well and pat dry with paper towels. Cut each pod diagonally into 3 pieces.

Make vinaigrette. Combine mustard and lime juice in a small bowl and mix well. Add dill. Add oils, 1 tablespoon at a time, whisking well after each addition. Add more lime juice if desired. Season to taste with salt and pepper.

Combine shrimp, snow peas, mushrooms, water chestnuts and onion in a large bowl. Add vinaigrette to taste and toss gently. Arrange lettuce leaves on individual plates. Mound salad in center. Garnish each serving with 2 reserved shrimp halves. Pass remaining dressing separately.

Author's note: A court bouillon is a seasoned liquid. Add 2 or 3 teaspoons salt and 2 to 3 tablespoons vinegar or wine to the poaching liquid. You may also add such aromatic vegetables as onions, parsley or carrots, or any herbs and spices you like.

Marinated Prawns

Recipe contributed by Marcia Winters; Obester Winery, Half Moon Bay

This recipe was created by Marcia Winters for the Obester Winery. The chilled prawns may be served as a first course or as a summer luncheon dish. Serve with sourdough bread.

1 shallot, chopped fine

2 tablespoons unsalted butter

½ cup Johannisberg Riesling

6 jumbo prawns or ½ lb. medium prawns, shelled and deveined

MARINADE

¼ cup extra virgin olive oil

¼ cup safflower oil

½ cup Johannisberg Riesling

1 tablespoon fresh lemon thyme

¼ cup finely chopped parsley

4 green onions, tops only, sliced

salt and pepper to taste

In a medium sauce pan sauté shallot in butter. Add wine and reduce to marmalade consistency (reduce until liquid is almost gone and syrupy). Add prawns and cook until pink on both sides. Remove to glass dish, including drippings.

Mix the oils, wine, thyme, parsley, green onions and salt and pepper together. Pour over prawns and refrigerate covered for at least 4 hours. Divide prawns in half and arrange on lettuce leaves on two plates.

Chinese Chicken Salad

Serves 6

Recipe contributed by Marilyn Mason; Lakespring Winery, Napa

There are numerous versions of Chinese Chicken Salad. This one has many of the authentic flavorings associated with this delectable dish. Measurements for seasoning the chicken are not given — let your own tastes dictate. As for the dressing, it is best to follow the recipe to get the right proportions.

3 chicken breast halves, skinned

dash of chili oil

dash of sesame oil

ground ginger

garlic powder

ground pepper

1 cup salted peanuts, soaked in ¼ cup soy sauce

2 heads red lettuce, chopped

1 red bell pepper, sliced

3 carrots, chopped

1 cup bean sprouts

1 cup oyster mushrooms (or white mushrooms) sliced

DRESSING

¼ cup soy sauce

4 tablespoons white wine vinegar

3 tablespoons Chenin Blanc

¼ cup sesame oil

½ tablespoon freshly ground ginger

¼ teaspoon freshly ground pepper

¼ teaspoon chopped garlic

Pour a dash each of chili oil and sesame oil over the chicken breasts and sprinkle with ginger, garlic and ground pepper. Place in a flat baking dish and bake in a preheated 375° oven for 30 minutes or microwave on high for 7 minutes. Let cool and shred into bite-sized pieces. Place chicken and remaining salad ingredients in a salad bowl.

Combine dressing ingredients and toss with salad.

Smoked Salmon and Caper Linguine Salad

Serves 6 to 8

Serve with Chardonnay

Recipe contributed by Susan Meyer; Rustridge Vineyards, St. Helena

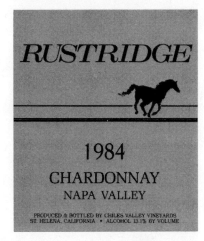

Susan Meyer's forte is pasta salads. She has recently written a book on the subject. Susan suggests this refreshing light salad be served as a luncheon dish or as an appetizer.

½ lb. spinach and egg linguine

1 tablespoon virgin olive oil

1 tablespoon chopped fresh dill

1 to 2 tablespoons chopped red onions

1 tablespoon capers

¼ lb. smoked salmon or lox, thinly sliced and cut into bite-sized pieces

12 asparagus spears, blanched and trimmed

LEMON VINAIGRETTE DRESSING

2 tablespoons lemon juice

1 teaspoon Dijon mustard

¼ teaspoon sugar

¼ cup olive oil

Cook the linguine in boiling water until al dente. Rinse in cold water and drain. Transfer to a serving bowl. Toss with the olive oil. Add the dill, onions, and capers and mix well. Add the smoked salmon and set aside.

In a small bowl make the dressing by combining the lemon juice with the mustard and sugar. Whisk in the olive oil. Toss the dressing with the salad. Garnish with asparagus spears.

· BEEF ·

Serve with Cabernet Sauvignon

Green Pepper Steak

Serves 4 to 6

Recipe contributed by Katherine Bartolucci; Mont St. John Cellars, Napa

This flavorful Green Pepper Steak is similar to an oriental stir-fried beef dish. The recipe, however, calls for pounding and simmering the meat strips. It makes them more tender and provides flavor for the gravy.

1 lb. lean beef round steak, cut ½ inch thick

1 tablespoon paprika

2 tablespoons butter

2 cloves garlic, crushed

1½ cups beef broth

1 cup sliced green onions, tops included

2 green peppers, cut in strips

2 tablespoons cornstarch

¼ cup water

¼ cup soy sauce (low-sodium)

2 large fresh tomatoes, cut in eighths

3 cups cooked rice

Pound steaks to ¼-inch thickness and cut into ¼-inch strips. Sprinkle the meat with paprika and allow to stand for a few minutes.

In a large skillet melt butter over medium-high heat and brown meat, stirring while browning. Add garlic and broth. Cover and simmer 30 minutes. Stir in onions and green peppers. Cover and cook 5 more minutes. In a small bowl blend cornstarch, water and soy sauce. Stir into meat mixture. Cook, stirring, until clear and thickened, about 2 minutes. Add tomatoes and stir gently. Heat just enough to warm the tomatoes. Serve over fluffy rice.

Serve with Cabernet Sauvignon

Steak Jake

Serves 4

Recipe contributed by Nancy Bundschu; Gundlach-Bundschu Winery, Vineburg

This is a quick, simple and different way to prepare a steak. The flamed tequila is a good flavor combination with the beef.

1 tablespoon olive oil

3 tablespoons chives, chopped

3 tablespoons green onions, chopped

3 tablespoons parsley, chopped

1 tablespoon Worcestershire sauce

4 filet steaks

salt and pepper to taste

2 to 3 tablespoons oil

3 oz. tequila

In a small frying pan heat 1 tablespoon olive oil and sauté chives, green onions and parsley for a few minutes. Add Worcestershire sauce and blend. Set aside and keep warm.

Sprinkle steaks with salt and pepper. Heat 2 to 3 tablespoons oil in a heavy skillet
til very hot. Add filets to the hot oil and fry 3 minutes on first side. Turn and
ead onion mixture on top. Fry 3 minutes on second side. Add tequila and flame.
hen flame dies down serve steaks. (If this is your first experience with flaming, use
ong match and stand back.)
The cooking time is approximate for medium steaks. Adjust cooking time
pending on the thickness and on desired doneness. Remember meat will contin-
cooking while it is being flamed.

ilets Cabernet

Serves 6

Serve with Cabernet Sauvignon

cipe contributed by Judy Groth, Groth Vineyards and Winery, Oakville

*is recipe is a Groth family favorite. It is easy to prepare and the basis of a
mpany meal.*

5 tablespoons butter	**1 tablespoon olive oil**
½ lb. mushrooms, quartered	**½ cup beef broth**
3 tablespoons minced green onions	**1 tablespoon tomato paste**
6 filet steaks	**¼ cup Cabernet Sauvignon**
6 slices bacon	**3 tablespoons cornstarch**
salt and freshly ground pepper to taste	**parsley for garnish, optional**

a small skillet heat 3 tablespoons butter and sauté mushrooms and onion. Set
ide. Wipe steaks dry. Wrap each steak with a slice of bacon and secure with
othpick. Season with salt and pepper. In a large skillet heat 2 tablespoons butter
d the olive oil. Sear the steaks. Reduce heat and sauté until done to taste — rare,
edium or well-done. Put steaks on platter, discard bacon, and set platter in a warm
en.
Add beef stock, tomato paste and Cabernet Sauvignon to skillet. Increase heat
d reduce liquid by half. Dissolve cornstarch in some water and add a little at a
ne to the sauce until desired consistency is attained. Add the mushroom mixture
d heat, stirring. Pour sauce over the filets and serve, garnished with parsley if
sired.

athor's note: Do not overcook the filets. They will continue to cook a little in
e warm oven.

*Serve with Domaine Elucia —
Proprietor's Reserve*

Peppered Beef Tenderloin

Serves 8

Recipe contributed by Lucy Shaw; Charles F. Shaw Vineyard and Winery, St. Helena

At dinner parties, Lucy Shaw likes to serve simple meat entrées such as this one to showcase the remainder of her meal. (See her sample menu, Saturday Night Company Dinner, page 208.) This entrée could hardly be simpler. Just time it to go in the oven 2 hours before serving time.

1 4-lb. beef tenderloin

oil

¼ cup freshly ground pepper

BÉARNAISE SAUCE

½ teaspoon tarragon

½ teaspoon chervil

1 teaspoon minced green onions

3 tablespoons tarragon vinegar

4 egg yolks at room temperature

1 cup hot melted butter, not browned

Preheat oven to 500°. Have meat at room temperature. Rub with oil and pat in pepper all over the meat. Place meat on rack in pan and place in oven for 12 minutes, then turn off the heat. DO NOT OPEN OVEN DOOR until 1 hour and 45 minutes later. The meat will have cooked a total of 1 hour and 57 minutes and should be rare and tender.

To make the sauce, boil herbs in vinegar until 2 teaspoons liquid remain. Blend yolks in blender. Add hot butter, drop by drop with blender running. When all butter is incorporated add herb mixture. Slice beef and serve with béarnaise sauce.

Serve with Cabernet Sauvignon

Marinated London Broil

Serves 4 to 6

Recipe contributed by Yvonne Kreck; Mill Creek Vineyards, Healdsburg

Sonoma County weather permitting, Yvonne Kreck and her husband, Bill, prefer to entertain with a barbecue on the patio rather than a formal dinner inside. Yvonne feels this creates a more relaxed atmosphere for their guests. With the London Broil she often serves Mill Creek Potatoes (see page 342).

2- to 3-lb. London broil, or other high quality meat

MARINADE

¼ cup salad oil

½ cup Cabernet Sauvignon

1 tablespoon Italian Seasoning

2 cloves garlic, crushed

½ teaspoon salt

¼ teaspoon pepper

several small sprigs fresh rosemary

Put meat in a large pan. Combine marinade ingredients and pour over meat. Marinate 8 to 10 hours, turning meat every 2 hours. Barbecue over hot coals to desired doneness.

Author's note: If fresh rosemary is not available, use ¾ teaspoon dried rosemary leaves. Italian seasonings may be made by combining oregano, marjoram, thyme, savory, basil, rosemary and sage in equal quantities.

Chile Marinated Flank Steak

Serves 6

Recipe contributed by Kathryn Kennedy; Kathryn Kennedy Winery, Saratoga

Serve with Cabernet Sauvignon

Kathryn Kennedy learned to make this dish back in the '50s when flank steak was one of the cheapest cuts of meat you could buy. She now prepares it often for guests and for her children, since it is one of their favorite meals.

- 1 large beef flank steak, lightly scored
- ⅔ cup garlic-flavored wine vinegar
- ⅔ cup olive oil
- 2½ teaspoons seasoning salt

- ½ teaspoon freshly ground black pepper
- 3 tablespoons finely chopped fresh or canned California chiles (seeds discarded)
- 3 tablespoons Cabernet Sauvignon
- 1 huge onion

Put the flank steak in a shallow nonmetal dish. Mix oil, vinegar, seasoning salt, pepper, chiles and wine. Pour over the steak. Thinly slice onion into rings and distribute over flank steak. Spoon marinade over onions and steak. Cover and refrigerate overnight (turning occasionally) or marinate at room temperature 4 to 5 hours, turning frequently. If meat has been chilled, bring to room temperature before cooking.

Barbecue on grill to desired doneness, about 4 minutes per side for medium. Baste frequently with marinade. Place onions in a tightly sealed aluminum foil package and place on grill to steam while the steak is cooking.

The flank steak may also be broiled in the oven. Cook to desired doneness, basting frequently with marinade. Spread onion on top of meat during the last minute or two of cooking so that they will brown.

To serve, slice meat thinly on the diagonal and serve with onion slices.

Flank Steak

Serves 4

Recipe contributed by Marcella McLester; McLester Winery, Inglewood

Serve with Cabernet Sauvignon

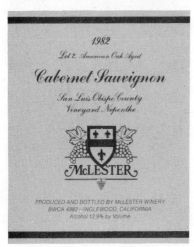

The orange juice, cloves and ginger give this flank steak recipe oriental flavor.

- 2 lb. flank steak

MARINADE

- 2 tablespoons oil
- ¼ teaspoon each sesame seeds, garlic powder and onion salt

- ⅛ teaspoon each powdered cloves and ginger
- 5 tablespoons each soy sauce, orange juice concentrate and brandy
- coarsely ground pepper, to taste

Score the flank steak on both sides and place in a shallow pan. In a small bowl combine the rest of the ingredients pour over steak and marinate at room temperature for several hours, turning occasionally. Broil 3 to 4 inches from heat, 5 minutes per side for medium. Slice thinly across the grain at a 45° angle.

Carbonades of Beef with Ripe Olives

Serves 4

Recipe contributed by Rosalie Hallock; Ballard Canyon Winery, Solvang

This easy-to-prepare hearty entrée is well suited to Rosalie Hallock's busy schedule of winery and family activities. The ripe olives and mushrooms add an interesting flavor component to the beef. Carbonades are thin slices of lean beef which have been stewed in a sauce.

4 tablespoons flour	2 large onions, sliced
½ teaspoon salt	1 cup mushrooms, sliced
5 tablespoons butter or margarine	½ cup white
8 small cube steaks, or thin slices of round steak	½ cup beef bouillon
	⅛ teaspoon thyme
	3 tablespoons light cream
	1 cup canned pitted ripe olives

Mix together flour and salt. Bread the steaks in 3 tablespoons of the flour mixture, working the flour into the steaks. Melt 4 tablespoons butter in a large skillet over medium-high heat. Add steaks and brown on both sides. Put steaks in a single layer in a medium-sized baking dish. Add onions to skillet and brown lightly. Spoon over meat. Melt remaining butter. Add mushrooms and brown lightly. Stir in remaining flour. Add wine, bouillon, thyme and cream to the mushrooms and cook, stirring constantly, until sauce boils and is slightly thickened. Drain olives and add to the sauce. Spoon sauce over the meat. Cover baking dish and bake in preheated 325° oven for 1½ hours or until meat is tender.

Beef Pot Roast

Serves 6 to 8

Recipe contributed by Linda Burgess; Burgess Cellars, St. Helena

Serve with mashed potatoes and green beans for a hearty, traditional fall or winter meal.

1 5- to 6-lb. boneless beef rump roast, trimmed of excess fat and rolled in flour	1 cup Cabernet Sauvignon
2 tablespoons salad oil	12 small white boiling onions, peeled
4 tablespoons butter	8 medium carrots, cut into 3-inch lengths
1 medium-large onion, sliced	3 to 4 tablespoons flour for gravy
1 bay leaf	1 cup water
1 teaspoon pepper	Worcestershire sauce
1½ teaspoons fresh thyme leaves	

Heat oil and 3 tablespoons butter in Dutch oven over medium heat. Add meat and brown well on all sides. (It is important to brown meat well for a good brown gravy.) While meat is browning, melt remaining butter in a skillet and add sliced onions and lightly brown. Add browned onions to roast along with bay leaf, pepper, thyme and wine. Additional wine and/or water may be added during cooking as needed. Cover and place in a preheated 325° oven for about 2 hours.

Add onions and carrots, and continue to cook, covered, until meat and vegetables are tender when pierced, about 1 more hour. Remove meat and vegetables to a platter and keep warm. In glass measuring cup, add water to flour and stir well until a very smooth liquid. Add flour mixture gradually to the liquid in the pan, stirring constantly until gravy thickens. May not need all of flour-water mixture. Add several shakes of Worcestershire sauce to gravy.

Beef Bourguignon

Serves 7 or 8

Recipe contributed by Alma Tudal; Tudal Winery, St. Helena

Serve with Cabernet Sauvignon

Alma Tudal suggests that this dish be prepared a day or two in advance so that the flavors can develop. She usually serves this over cooked noodles.

3 lbs. beef chuck, cut into 1½-inch pieces

½ cup flour

1 teaspoon salt

½ teaspoon pepper

¼ cup butter

¼ cup olive oil

¼ cup cognac

5 carrots, coarsely chopped

2 medium yellow onions, coarsely chopped

1 leek, coarsely chopped

5 sprigs parsley, chopped

4 cloves garlic, finely minced

⅓ lb. bacon, diced

1 teaspoon thyme

3 tablespoons tomato paste

1 cup dry red wine

2 cups beef broth

salt and freshly ground pepper to taste

20 small white pearl onions

¼ lb. butter

1 lb. fresh mushrooms, sliced

Dredge meat in flour, salt and pepper. In a large heavy pan brown meat on all sides in butter and oil over high heat. Do this in small batches adding butter and oil if necessary. As meat is browned, place it in a 5-quart casserole or deep roasting pan. Deglaze pan by pouring cognac into it and stirring to loosen particles. Pour gravy over meat.

To the same pan add carrots, onions, leek, parsley, garlic and bacon. Cook, stirring until vegetables and bacon are lightly browned. Skim off bacon fat. Add thyme and tomato paste to pan, stir and add to beef. Add wine and beef broth to barely cover meat and mix well. Taste for salt and pepper and add if necessary.

Cover casserole and bake for 1 hour in preheated 325° oven. Stir occasionally and add more beef broth if needed. Meanwhile, peel onions by dropping in boiling water for 1 minute and slipping off skins. Brown them in ¼ cup butter. Remove from pan and then sauté mushrooms. Add onions and mushrooms to beef casserole and bake 1 more hour.

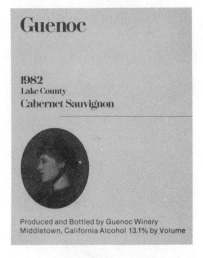

Filet Mignon with Confit and Red Wine Sauce

Serves 4

Recipe contributed by Margaret Clark, Guenoc Winery, Middletown

There are three steps to preparing this entrée, but the confit and the sauce may be prepared ahead of time and held warm while the filets are broiling or sautéing. A confit is a highly concentrated preserve or syrup, in this case an extract of pearl onions and garlic.

4 filet mignon steaks

CONFIT

16 pearl onions, peeled, trimmed and cut with an x at base

1 large head garlic, cloves peeled and cut, small center bulb removed

2 tablespoons butter

salt and freshly ground pepper to taste

pinch of sugar

⅓ cup unsalted beef stock

RED WINE SAUCE

2 shallots, finely chopped

2 tablespoons butter

1 cup red wine

1 tablespoon red wine vinegar

1½ cup double strength beef broth, unsalted

salt and pepper to taste

To make the confit, blanch onions and garlic in boiling water for 2 minutes and drain. Put all confit ingredients except the beef stock in a small heavy sauté pan. Cover and cook over lowest heat setting, shaking occasionally to prevent sticking. When onions and garlic are golden all over, add beef stock and cover again. Continue to braise until about 2 tablespoons of rich brown liquid remains.

To make the wine sauce, sauté shallots in a small, heavy saucepan in 1 tablespoon butter for 2 to 3 minutes over medium heat. Do not brown. Add red wine and vinegar and reduce until 3 to 4 tablespoons remain. Add beef broth, bring to a simmer and reduce again until sauce is shiny and becomes slightly thickened (about ½ cup in volume). Add salt and pepper to taste. Just before serving swirl in 1 tablespoon butter.

Broil or sauté filets to desired doneness. Top each steak with confit and red wine sauce and serve.

Author's note: Removing the center or bulb of the garlic clove is said to prevent garlic breath and aftertaste.

Estouffade de Boeuf

(Beef Stew)

Recipe contributed by Annamaria Roudon, Roudon-Smith Vineyards, Santa Cruz

Annamaria Roudon's Estouffade de Boeuf reflects her keen interest in international cuisine. This stew is a favorite of the Roudon family and emphasizes the robust flavor of the Zinfandel served with it.

MARINADE	STEW
2 lbs. beef round, cubed	4 slices bacon
1 medium-sized onion, sliced	3 medium-sized carrots, sliced
1 medium-sized carrot, sliced	3 medium-sized onions, sliced
½ teaspoon salt	1 calf knuckle
¼ teaspoon pepper	4 tomatoes, peeled and chopped
pinch of thyme	½ to 1 cup beef broth
4 cloves	30 green Greek olives, pitted
1 bay leaf	1 tablespoon arrowroot
6 cloves garlic	
1 to 2 cups Zinfandel	

In a medium-sized bowl combine beef, 1 sliced onion, 1 sliced carrot, salt, pepper, thyme, cloves, bay leaf, garlic and enough wine to cover mixture. Marinate in the refrigerator for 8 to 10 hours, stirring occasionally. Dry meat with paper towels and strain marinade.

In a large Dutch oven fry bacon for 5 minutes. Remove bacon and set aside. Add meat to the remaining bacon grease and brown well on all sides. Lower heat, cover and simmer for 20 minutes. (Meat at this point will have drawn a considerable amount of liquid.) Add calf knuckle, all sliced carrots and all sliced onions (including those from marinade), and tomatoes. Combine juice of marinade and beef broth in equal proportions for sufficient amount to just cover the mixture of meat and vegetables. Bring to a boil and simmer for 3 hours.

Meanwhile cook olives in boiling water for 5 minutes. (This removes some of the salt.) Drain olives.

When beef is done remove calf knuckle. Add olives. Combine arrowroot in a little water and add to beef to thicken gravy. Serve.

Author's note: If Greek olives are unavailable use either canned green or black olives. Rinse the olives to remove excess salt before adding to the stew. The stew may also be cooked in a preheated 300° oven for 2½ to 3 hours.

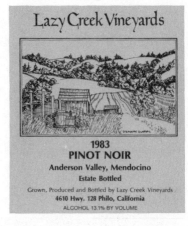

Beef Stroganoff á la Minute

Serves 4

Recipe contributed by Hans and Theresia Kobler; Lazy Creek Vineyards, Philo

The Kobler family finds much pleasure in picking wild mushrooms in the hills surrounding their vineyards. The black and yellow chanterelles are the most abundant. The Kobler's recipes are based on their years of working in the finest restaurants of the world.

2 tablespoons cooking oil

1½ lbs. beef filet, sliced ½ inch thick

2 tablespoons butter

¼ cup finely chopped shallots

1 oz. brandy

4 tablespoons paprika

2 cups mushrooms, quartered (white mushrooms, black or yellow chanterelles, or a mixture)

½ cup heavy cream

½ cup sour cream

salt and freshly ground pepper to taste

In a large heavy skillet heat the oil over high heat. Add meat and sear quickly. Meat should be medium-rare in the center. Remove meat to a warm platter.

In another skillet, heat the butter over medium-high heat and sauté shallots until they are soft. Add mushrooms and cook quickly for 3 to 4 minutes or until done. (The chanterelles will draw quite a bit of liquid which will be incorporated into the sauce.) Lower heat to medium. Add brandy and paprika and stir into mushrooms. Cook for 1 minute. Add heavy cream and sour cream and stir until heated. Do not allow mixture to boil. Return meat to sauce and heat, again do not allow sauce to boil. Season to taste with salt and pepper.

Author's note: The beef may also be cut into long thin strips, instead of ½-inch thick slices.

Top Sirloin Kebobs

Serves 4

Recipe contributed by Juelle Fisher; Fisher Vineyards, Santa Rosa

Juelle Fisher makes these kebobs for informal dinners at the winery. She prefers to grill the meat without vegetables on the skewers. The Fishers have a large barbecue with sufficient heat surface to permit Juelle to stir-fry vegetables in a wok while the meat is cooking on the grill. The Fishers put grape canes on top of the hot coals for additional flavor.

½ cup soy sauce

1 tablespoon grated fresh ginger

3 cloves garlic, minced

2 tablespoons olive oil

2 lbs. top sirloin, cut into 1-inch cubes

In a medium-sized bowl combine soy sauce, ginger, garlic and olive oil. Place beef cubes in the soy sauce mixture and marinate overnight or 8 to 10 hours. Place meat on metal skewers and set on grill 3 to 4 inches above a bed of hot coals. Turn and brush on marinade frequently to retain and develop all of the flavors. Grill to desired doneness.

Author's note: If there are vineyards near you, check in the early spring for the availability of grape canes. If preferred, pieces of vegetables such as green pepper, onions, mushrooms and cherry tomatoes may be threaded onto the skewers with the meat and grilled together.

Fajitas with Salsa

Serves 4 to 6

Serve with Johannisberg Riesling

Recipe contributed by Kevin Reed; Ballard Canyon Winery, Solvang

Fajitas are a creation of the "Tex-Mex" school of cooking. They are a do-it-yourself meal usually comprised of barbecued meat or fish, flour tortillas and a variety of hot sauces. Here is a California version.

1 cup soy sauce	**SALSA**
½ cup vinegar	4 to 6 jalapeño peppers
1 tablespoon ground cumin	7 firm tomatoes, diced
1 tablespoon brown sugar	2 bell peppers, diced
½ teaspoon pepper	2 medium-sized onions, diced
1½ lbs. lean top sirloin steak	2 bunches of cilantro, chopped
1 large bell pepper	
2 firm tomatoes	
1 large red onion	
olive oil	
1 dozen flour or corn tortillas	

In a medium-sized bowl combine the soy sauce, vinegar, brown sugar, cumin and pepper. Slice the steak very thin and place in the soy sauce marinade for 30 minutes to 1 hour. Cut bell pepper and tomatoes into large pieces. Dice the onion. Wrap tortillas in paper towels and warm in a microwave oven on low setting or in a warm oven. Drain meat. In a large frying pan heat a small amount of olive oil and stir fry the steak. When meat is half done add peppers, tomatoes and onions. Cook until meat and vegetables are done. Cover with lid if necessary, about 5 minutes. Spoon some of the meat mixture into each warmed tortilla. Roll up like a jelly roll and serve with refried beans, rice and salsa for a delicious Mexican-style meal.

To make salsa, stab the jalapeño peppers with a fork and blacken the skin over a gas flame (like roasting a marshmallow) or, for electric ovens, in the broiler. The purpose is to loosen the skin. Then, under running water, rub the black skins off. Do not touch the fingers to the face or eyes. The pepper really stings! (Disposable surgical gloves may be used.) Dice the peppers and combine with the rest of the ingredients. The salsa is better if allowed to sit for several hours to combine the flavors. It may be stored in the refrigerator for several weeks.

Author's note: Salsa may be purchased canned in various degrees of hotness and with or without tomatoes.

Serve with Zinfandel

Beef Stew and Polenta

Serves 6

Recipe contributed by Silvia Nerelli; Pesenti Winery, Templeton

The beef stew has some flavorings which are typical of California and Mexico. However, the polenta is Italian, as is the Nerelli heritage. This is an easy meal to prepare and is frequently served during crush time at the winery. Polenta is a coarsely ground corn meal; it is a staple dish in many areas of Northern Italy. If there are any leftovers, polenta is delicious fried.

BEEF STEW

3½ to 4 lbs. lean beef chuck, cut
   into cubes

3 tablespoons butter

1 8-oz. can tomato sauce

1 jar salsa

1 cup Zinfandel

beef broth

POLENTA

8 cups water

1 teaspoon salt

3½ cups polenta

In a large saucepan bring water and salt to a boil. Slowly add the polenta, stirring constantly to prevent lumping. Turn heat down to simmer and cook for 45 minutes to 1 hour. Stir frequently during cooking time to prevent sticking.

    In a Dutch oven melt butter over medium-high heat and add meat. Brown on all sides. Then add tomato sauce, salsa, red wine and enough beef broth to cover. Turn heat to simmer and continue cooking for about 3 hours or until meat is tender. Serve over individual servings of polenta.

Serve with Zinfandel

Rouladen

Serves 6 to 8

Recipe contributed by Toni Klein; Hidden Cellars Winery, Ukiah

Rouladen are thin strips of meat or fish rolled up around a filling. This particular recipe originated with Toni Klein's mother-in-law who is German. Her version of this classic German dish does not include the typical gherkin and is a much more flavorful one. You may need to pound the beef first to get it thin enough to roll up.

½ lb. bacon

1 medium-sized onion, chopped

¼ cup Dijon or German mustard

12 thinly sliced pieces of top
   round (sandwich steaks)

2 to 4 tablespoons oil

2 tablespoons flour

1 cup Zinfandel

1 to 2 cups beef broth

salt and pepper to taste

Cut bacon into ¼- to ½-inch square pieces, discarding the larger pieces of fat. Sauté with the onion in a heavy 12-inch frying pan until onion is tender, about 5 minutes. (Bacon will be only partially cooked.) Remove bacon and onion mixture to a small bowl using a slotted spoon, reserving drippings. Mix mustard with onion.

    Pat meat dry and spread an equal amount of bacon mixture on each slice. Roll up each piece and secure with a toothpick. Add 2 tablespoons oil to the reserved drippings and brown half the rouladen on all sides. Remove and brown the remaining rouladen, using additional oil if necessary. Remove from pan.

Stir flour into pan to make a roux. Cook until golden brown. Slowly add wine and 1 cup of beef broth and stir until smooth. Add salt and pepper to taste. Return rouladen to pan, cover and simmer, turning rouladen occasionally and adding more broth if necessary. Cook for about 1½ hours, or until tender. Arrange rouladen in a heated dish, remove toothpicks and keep warm. Strain liquid. If necessary, return liquid to pan and boil down to thicken gravy. Pour gravy over rouladen and serve with mashed potatoes.

Sarma (Cabbage Rolls)

Serves 6 to 8

Recipe contributed by Tatjana Grgich, Grgich Hills Cellar, Rutherford

Sarma is an old family recipe from Tatjana Grgich's native Yugoslavia. It is a different preparation of cabbage rolls since it also includes sauerkraut. The dish is even better when reheated the next day. Tatjana grinds and chops the meats in her food processor. She prefers to use finely chopped meat, instead of "store-ground."

Serve with Cabernet Sauvignon

1 large head cabbage

2 tablespoons vinegar

FILLING

1¼ lbs. ground lean beef

½ lb. finely chopped pork (use food processor)

6 oz. bacon, finely chopped (use food processor)

2 onions, minced

1 teaspoon grated lemon rind

2 whole cloves, smashed

pinch of nutmeg

pinch of cinnamon

salt and pepper to taste

4 cloves garlic, minced

1 tablespoon lard

1 onion, chopped

1 quart sauerkraut, in glass jar

2 smoked ham hocks, ham bone or piece of smoked ham for flavor

In a medium-sized bowl combine all filling ingredients, mixing well to blend. Set aside while blanching cabbage.

In a large kettle combine water and vinegar. Heat to boiling and add cabbage. Blanch cabbage for 2 to 3 minutes, so that leaves will be pliable. Remove from water and drain. Separate all the leaves and cut away hard core. Place 1 tablespoon filling on short end of each leaf. Starting rolling, tucking sides in, until end of leaf is reached. Repeat for all leaves (about 16).

Melt lard in Dutch oven over medium heat and sauté chopped onions until light brown. Spread onions evenly over bottom of pot. Place half of the sauerkraut on top of onions. Arrange cabbage rolls on top. Cover with remaining sauerkraut. Add smoked pork or ham. Pour in enough water to cover contents of pan (may use half water and half beef broth for extra flavor). Bring slowly to a boil over medium heat. Then cover and simmer for 2 to 3 hours, shaking pan occasionally to prevent sticking.

Serve with Cabernet Sauvignon

Special Burgers with Gorgonzola

Serves 4

Recipe contributed by Stephanie and Larry Rosenbloom; Creston Manor Vineyards and Winery, Creston

The Rosenblooms enjoy experimenting with foods. Here, the addition of mushrooms and blue cheese plus the last minute "fireworks" turn a simple hamburger into something special.

1½ lbs. lean ground beef	½ teaspoon minced garlic
¼ lb. Gorgonzola cheese	2 tablespoons cognac
salt and pepper to taste	2 tablespoons finely chopped parsley
2 tablespoons butter	
1 cup thinly sliced mushrooms	

In a medium-sized bowl combine the beef, cheese, salt and pepper. Blend well and shape into 4 patties. Heat a cast iron skillet. When hot, add patties and cook over moderate heat 3 to 4 minutes or until well browned on one side. Turn and cook 1½ to 2½ minutes.

Meanwhile, heat butter in a separate medium-sized skillet and add mushrooms and garlic. Cook about 2 minutes or until golden brown.

Add the cognac to the patties and ignite, cooking until flame dies down. Spoon mushrooms over the patties and add chopped parsley. Serve.

Serve with Zinfandel

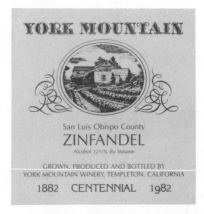

Marinated Hamburgers

Serves 6

Recipe contributed by Suzanne Goldman Semones; York Mountain Winery, Templeton

This hamburger recipe has been used in the Goldman family for many years. Suzanne Semones recalls her mother marinating huge beef patties and her father grilling them on the barbecue, using the sauce for basting. "It was always a taste treat!" she recalls. Suzanne recommends that fresh herbs be used. The marinade can be used on other cuts of meat, too. (See below.)

2½ to 3 lbs. lean ground beef	2 whole bay leaves
	1 tablespoon each freshly chopped oregano, sweet basil and rosemary
MARINADE	
1 cup olive oil	4 cloves garlic, minced
1 cup Zinfandel	salt and pepper to taste
5 tablespoons chopped fresh parsley	

In a bowl combine marinade ingredients. Shape meat into 6 large hamburgers, making sure they are tightly formed. Place hamburgers in a flat dish and pour marinade over them. Marinate at room temperature for 1 hour, turning meat after 30 minutes. Barbecue to desired doneness, using marinade as a basting sauce.

For barbecued roast: Marinate a 4- to 5-lb. pot roast in the same mixture for 8 hours in the refrigerator. About an hour before cooking remove roast from refrigerator to bring it up to room temperature. Broil on grill to desired doneness, basting with the marinade, 25 to 40 minutes, depending on thickness of roast.

Author's note: If fresh herbs are not available, substitute ¾ teaspoon dried herbs for each of the herbs called for.

London Broil Salad

Serves 6 to 8

Recipe contributed by Lisa Buehler; Buehler Vineyards, St. Helena

Serve with Zinfandel

Lisa Buehler serves this main dish salad surrounded with her Tomato Couscous, see page 345. The salad is at its best made a day previous to serving and keeps refrigerated for several days. The recipe is also an excellent way to use leftover beef from roasts or barbecued steaks.

2 lbs. London broil

MARINADE

½ cup Zinfandel

½ cup olive oil

1 clove garlic, pressed

DRESSING

¼ cup Grey Poupon mustard

1 tablespoon lemon juice

1 cup olive oil

SALAD

4 cups thinly sliced pale celery

1 cup finely minced fresh basil

½ cup finely sliced green onions, optional

25 tiny nicoise olives, pitted and sliced

4½-inch slices feta cheese, cut in ½-inch cubes

In a glass baking dish about the same size as the meat, marinate the London broil for 6 hours in the refrigerator. Cover with plastic wrap. Turn meat after the first 3 hours.

Pour marinade into a pot, along with enough boiling water to cover the meat. Cut the meat in half, add to pot and simmer for 20 minutes. Remove and cool.

Make the dressing by whisking together the mustard and lemon juice. Slowly, in a very thin stream, whisk in the oil.

Slice meat on the diagonal in ¼-inch slices, then stack three together and slice again into ¼-inch, or a little wider, ribbons. Put meat into a very large bowl and toss with the dressing. Add the celery, basil, green onions and olives. Toss. Last of all gently fold in the cheese, using a spatula. Serve on lettuce surrounded by Tomato Couscous.

Author's note: The meat for this dish may be broiled rather than boiled. The crust of the broiled meat will change the flavor somewhat.

Serve with Gewurztraminer

Meatball Chowder

Serves 8 to 10

Recipe contributed by Jeri Mosby; Vega Vineyards, Buellton

This chowder is a Mosby family favorite, particularly at harvest time. Jeri Mosby also serves this often as an informal Friday night supper. Any leftovers are excellent reheated.

2 lbs. ground lean beef	6 cups tomato juice
2 teaspoons seasoned salt	4 beef bouillon cubes
⅛ teaspoon pepper	3 cups sliced carrots
2 eggs, lightly beaten	3 cups sliced celery
¼ cup chopped parsley	2½ cups diced potatoes
⅓ cup cracker crumbs	¼ cup long grain rice
2 tablespoons milk	1 tablespoon sugar
3 tablespoons flour	1 teaspoon oregano
1 tablespoon salad oil	1 teaspoon basil
4 to 6 onions, cut into eighths	2 bay leaves, crumbled
6 cups red wine (or wine and water mixed)	1 12-oz. can "Mexi-corn"

Combine the first 7 ingredients and shape into 40 meatballs about the size of walnuts. Dip the meatballs in flour. Heat oil in an 8- to 10-quart Dutch oven and brown the meatballs. Add all of the rest of the ingredients except the Mexi-corn to the kettle. Bring to a boil, cover and reduce heat to medium-low. Simmer for 20 minutes; add the Mexi-corn and simmer 10 minutes more. Serve in soup bowls.

Serve with Pinot Noir

Gourmet Sauerkraut with Meats

Serves 4

Recipe contributed by Robert Stemmler; Robert Stemmler Winery, Healdsburg

This dish typifies the food served in the section of Germany where Robert Stemmler grew up and learned winemaking. He recommends serving this dish with mashed potatoes seasoned with nutmeg.

2 lbs. canned sauerkraut	4 lamb shanks
1½ cups sweet Sauvignon Blanc	4 smoked veal sausages, optional
1 lb. pork spareribs	salt and pepper to taste
1 lb. beef ribs	juniper berries

Rinse the sauerkraut under running water until all salt and canned flavor is removed. Place drained sauerkraut in a bowl and pour the sweet Sauvignon Blanc over it. Leave at room temperature for 30 minutes to let sauerkraut soak up the wine.

Season pork ribs, beef ribs and lamb shanks with salt and pepper. Place meats on rack on broiler pan and broil the meats for 7 minutes. Then turn and broil another 5 to 7 minutes until browned and most of the fat is rendered. If veal sausages are used broil them alone for 4 minutes after the other meats have been broiled. Split them in half. Discard all the fat saving the browned drippings.

In a flat casserole dish place the sauerkraut and sprinkle with juniper berries. Pour any of the remaining wine over the sauerkraut. Add meat drippings. Place the broiled meats on top. Cover and bake in a 350° oven for about 1½ hours or until the meats are cooked. If using sausages add them in the last 15 minutes of cooking.

Bagna Cauda

Serves 6 garlic lovers

Recipe contributed by Richard and Paulé Crescini; Crescini Wines, Soquel

Serve with Cabernet Sauvignon

Bagna cauda is similar to a fondue — raw vegetables are dipped, but not cooked, in a hot olive oil-butter sauce. No vintner's cookbook would be complete without a recipe for this traditional Italian dish. This particular recipe came from Richard Crescini's family who came from the Piemonte region of Italy. It is customary to serve bagna cauda on Christmas Eve, but the Crescinis prefer to have their feast on Saturday night of the three-day Washington's birthday weekend. This is an excellent dish for a cold winter day.

SAUCE

2 cups thinly sliced or diced garlic (red garlic preferably)

5 whole anchovies

1 cup butter

½ onion, finely chopped

2 cups olive oil

vegetables (cabbage, carrots, cauliflower, green beans, mushrooms, cherry tomatoes, bell peppers, radishes, turnips, squash, etc.)

lean beef (optional)

shrimp (optional)

French bread

Place the sauce ingredients in a pot and cook slowly until anchovies and garlic dissolve, about 30 minutes. Serve hot and keep hot at the table with a table warmer. Provide skewers or fondue forks. Chunks of French bread are used to dip in the sauce. Thin pieces of raw beef steak and shrimp can be cooked in the sauce, too.

Since the dish is loaded with garlic, a word of caution. Garlic does penetrate the entire system and close encounters with people who have not participated in the bagna cauda are not advised for a minimum of 24 hours after the event.

⸙ LAMB ⸙

Serve with Cabernet Sauvignon

Butterflied Leg of Lamb

Serves 6 to 8

Recipe contributed by Julie Garvey; Flora Springs Wine Co., St. Helena

This is a real favorite in the Komes-Garvey families when they are entertaining in the summer. It is a "never fail" and "oh so easy" recipe. The key is to have your butcher trim and butterfly the lamb. Julie Garvey usually does a little more trimming after she gets home and makes an additional cut or two to assure that the meat "opens up" to more equal thickness to insure even cooking.

1 butterflied leg of lamb

MARINADE

4 tablespoons olive oil

2 tablespoons soy sauce

juice of ½ lemon

good pinch of rosemary (if dried, rub it in the palm of your hand to "revive" it)

2 cloves garlic, chopped very fine

A day in advance of the cooking combine marinade ingredients and rub into the lamb. Place lamb in a large plastic bag and refrigerate until ready to cook. Barbecue for 45 minutes to 1 hour depending on the desired doneness. When done allow the meat to sit for 10 minutes, then slice it in fairly thin slices as you would a flank steak.

Serve with Zinfandel

Lamb Shish Kebobs

Serves 6

Recipe contributed by Jo Anne Strobl; Hop Kiln Winery, Healdsburg

These Lamb Shish Kebobs have become the traditional Easter dinner for wine-maker Steve Strobl's family.

3 lbs. lamb, boneless, free of fat and gristle

½ lb. onions, thinly sliced

⅓ cup dry sherry

2 tablespoons olive oil

1½ teaspoons salt

1 teaspoon oregano

½ teaspoon black pepper

12 cherry tomatoes

12 pearl onions

12 mushrooms

1 green bell pepper, cut into 1-inch chunks

Cut lamb into 1-inch cubes. In a large bowl combine sliced onions, sherry, olive oil, salt, oregano and pepper. Add meat and marinate for several hours (preferably overnight) turning occasionally.

Thread the lamb onto skewers alternately with cherry tomatoes, pearl onions, mushrooms and green pepper. Broil over charcoal or in a broiler until brown on all sides. Do not overcook. Serve on a bed of rice.

Cassoulet

Serves 8   *Serve with Cabernet Sauvignon*

Recipe contributed by Courtney Turman; Girard Winery, Oakville

This cassoulet would make a hearty, cool weather entrée. It is easy to prepare and can be made ahead and reheated.

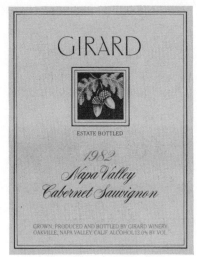

2 lbs. small white beans	1 tablespoon tarragon
½ lb. Italian sausage, sliced thick	1 tablespoon paprika
8 cloves garlic, minced	2 large tomatoes, chopped
3 onions, chopped	¼ cup wine vinegar
1 tablespoon dried Bouquet Garni	1 lb. lamb sausage, sliced thick, or ground lamb formed into 1½-inch patties

Soak beans at least 12 hours, preferably 24 hours, changing water several times.

In a Dutch oven sauté Italian sausage, garlic and onions until cooked. Add beans, herbs, tomatoes and vinegar. Lay lamb sausage pieces or lamb patties on top. Cover tightly and simmer slowly for 1½ to 2 hours until beans are tender, or, if desired, bake in preheated 325° oven for same amount of time. The cassoulet may be frozen and reheated.

Rack of Lamb with Mustard Marinade

Serves 6 to 8   *Serve with Cabernet Sauvignon*

Recipe contributed by Marta Johnson; Johnson Turnbull Vineyards, Oakville

Marta Johnson enjoys preparing dishes that have a lot of flavor appeal and that pair well with Cabernet Sauvignon. The spices in this marinade help fulfill both aims. Serve it with Brown Rice with Onions and Red Peppers (page 347).

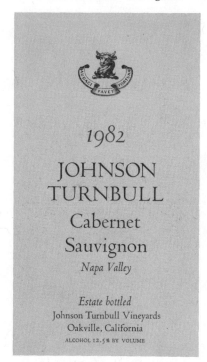

2 to 3 racks of lamb*	1 teaspoon lemon juice
	2 teaspoons minced garlic
MARINADE	½ teaspoon powdered ginger
1 tablespoon olive oil	pepper to taste
¼ cup Cabernet Sauvignon	1 tablespoon fresh chopped rosemary
⅓ cup Dijon mustard	

Trim racks of lamb completely of fat and membrane. Combine remaining ingredients in a bowl and stir to blend. Coat racks of lamb thoroughly with the marinade and allow to sit 1 to 2 hours at room temperature, or in the refrigerator if the day is hot.

Preheat oven to 500°. Line a shallow baking pan with aluminum foil and place racks of lamb in the pan. Bake for 20 minutes. Large chops will be medium rare and the smaller ones well done. (If rarer meat is desired, cut baking time to 15 to 18 minutes.) Cut into single chops and serve 2 to 3 per person.

* *Racks of lamb are sold in either 6- or 8-rib racks. If you purchase the 6-rib rack, ask for the first 6 ribs. These are larger chops and have less fat. Have butcher crack the ribs for easier slicing.*

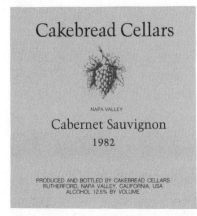

Grilled Rack of Lamb with Persillade

Recipe contributed by Dolores Cakebread; Cakebread Cellars, Rutherford

Dolores Cakebread has used her culinary expertise in combining a California inspired marinade of pomegranate juice with a French persillade, a seasoned bread crumb coating. The result is a piquant rack of lamb.

3 racks of lamb, trimmed well to remove layers of fat

MARINADE

1 cup pomegranate juice

1 cup Cabernet Sauvignon

½ cup olive oil

3 tablespoons fresh rosemary

2 tablespoons fresh thyme

4 cloves garlic, slivered

1 teaspoon black peppercorn

PERSILLADE

½ cup finely chopped parsley

¼ cup fine dried bread crumbs

2 cloves garlic, finely minced

Combine marinade ingredients and rub into trimmed lamb. Let marinate for 2 to 3 hours. Combine persillade ingredients in a small bowl.

On a Weber-type covered barbecue, light enough charcoal briquets to cover one layer of grill. When white ash forms, about 30, minutes, put on racks of lamb. Sear briefly on each side, then put on lid. About every 5 minutes turn lamb over. After 15 minutes, put on persillade, using the back of a spoon to make it adhere to the lamb. Do not turn lamb again and continue cooking for another 5 to 13 minutes. Total cooking time 20 to 28 minutes for medium rare. (Time will vary with thickness of meat and type of barbecue used.) Use a meat thermometer. Final temperature should be about 125° for rare, 160° for medium rare.

Remove from grill to a hot pan and cover with foil until ready for use. The lamb should sit for 10 minutes before serving.

Crown Roast of Lamb

Recipe contributed by Wade Mills; Acacia Winery, Napa

Wade Mills has created an unusual crown roast of lamb. The piquant flavor is due to the mustard and yogurt glaze and the dark beer.

1 4- to 5-lb. crown roast of lamb, tied to form a crown (allow 1 lb. per person; if necessary use 2 crowns and tie together to form 1 large roast.)

½ cup sweet mustard

½ cup yogurt

green peppercorns

1 large onion

4 cloves garlic

12 oz. dark beer (preferably Guinness Stout)

In a small bowl mix the yogurt and mustard. Mash in enough green peppercorns to turn the mixture a light green. Spread this mixture on inside and outside of the crown roast of lamb. (It will not look very pretty, but as it cooks the sugars caramelize and form a delicious brown crust.)

Place roast in a shallow Dutch oven or shallow baking pan. Chop half of the onion and cut the other half in large pieces. Place the pieces inside the crown roast. On outside of roast place chopped onions and garlic. Pour half of the beer (or all of the beer, depending on size of roast) around the roast. Place pan in a preheated 325° oven and bake 15 minutes per pound for a pink appearance to the meat. As the roast bakes, occasionally add more beer. Remove roast and thicken gravy if desired.

Small partially cooked whole new potatoes may be placed in the center of the roast and baked along with the meat.

Lamb and Vegetable Stew

Serves 4

Serve with Merlot

Recipe contributed by William H. Davidge; Santa Ynez Valley Winery, Santa Ynez

This lamb stew is a meal in itself. Serve it with rice or French bread for those with hefty appetites. Follow directions and cook starting components of stew separately for maximum flavor.

2½ lb. boneless lamb shoulder, cut into bite-sized pieces	beef stock
flour	salt and freshly ground pepper to taste
butter	12 small white onions, peeled and left whole
2 yellow onions, chopped	4 carrots, diced
3 fresh tomatoes, peeled, cut into segments, or their equivalent in canned tomato pulp	6 small potatoes, cubed
1 bay leaf	1 medium turnip, halved and sliced
1 cup Cabernet Sauvignon	1½ cups shelled green peas
	minced parsley

Start with 3 saucepans and a good big ovenproof casserole with closely fitted cover. Dredge lamb in flour. Heat 2 tablespoons butter in pan #1 over medium-high heat and sauté lamb until browned. Transfer to casserole. In pan #2 over medium-high heat brown the onions in 1 tablespoon butter. Transfer onions to casserole. In pan #3 heat the tomato segments with bay leaf. When tomato cooks remove bay leaf, and transfer tomatoes to casserole.

Add wine and enough stock to barely cover lamb mixture in casserole. Cover and simmer for 1 hour and 45 minutes, or until meat is tender. Add peeled onions, carrots, potatoes and turnip. Cover closely and bake in preheated 350° oven for 45 minutes.

In the meantime, cook the peas until just tender. Drain and set aside. When stew is done, add peas, minced parsley and adjust seasonings. Gently stir to blend. Thicken gravy with flour and water if desired. Serve.

Lamb Chops en Croûte with Sauce

Serves 6

Recipe contributed by Lisille B. Matheson; Mount Veeder Winery, Napa

Lisille Matheson says this elegant recipe is very simple to prepare and makes a lovely presentation. Ask your butcher to prepare the boned double lamb chops you need for this dish.

12 French-cut lamb chops

2 pkgs. frozen patty shells, defrosted

12 oz. pâtè (any smooth kind)

egg wash (1 egg plus 1 tablespoon water, mixed)

SAUCE

3 tablespoons butter

1 tablespoon flour

1 cup beef broth

½ cup Madeira

Trim fat from chops. Top each chop with 1 oz. of pâtè. With a rolling pin, roll out patty shells and encase each lamb chop. Place on baking sheet and brush with egg wash. Bake in a preheated 400° oven for 30 minutes.

About 10 minutes before the chops are done make the sauce. In a small saucepan over medium heat melt the butter and cook it to a light nutty color. Be careful not to make it too dark. Add flour and cook a few seconds. Add the beef broth and Madeira wine and simmer briefly. Lightly spoon sauce over chops just before serving.

Author's note: If a slightly thicker sauce is desired use 1½ tablespoons flour.

Pot-to-Table Lamb Stew

Serves 6

Recipe contributed by Audrey Sterling; Iron Horse Vineyards, Sebastopol

Audrey Sterling usually serves this stew on cold, rainy days. It is very easy to prepare (Audrey suggests using your food processor for the slicing) and tastes even better when reheated the next day. This stew is similar to a French Ragout D'Agneau and is a favorite of the Sterlings, who live part of the time in southern France

3 lbs. potatoes, peeled and thinly sliced

salt and freshly ground pepper to taste

1 lb. onions, thinly sliced

3 lbs. stewing lamb (with bones) cut into cubes

5 cups water

½ cup pearl barley

chopped parsley for garnish

Line the bottom of an enameled cast-iron casserole with half the sliced potatoes. Season with salt and pepper. Add a layer of half the onions and season, then add the layer of lamb and season. Continue layering with the rest of the onions and then finish with a layer of potatoes and season again. Pour in the water and bring rapidly to a boil. Skim the surface of the stew of any scum that forms, then lower heat, cover and simmer until meat is tender, about 2 hours.

Add pearl barley for the last 30 minutes of cooking time. To serve, sprinkle stew with fresh chopped parsley and ladle into large soup plates.

Author's note: For additional flavor add some thyme, bay leaf or rosemary when adding salt and pepper to the layers of stew. Sliced carrots may also be added for additional flavor and color.

Mother's Lamb Stew

Serves 4

Serve with Merlot

Recipe contributed by Joel Peterson; Ravenswood Winery, Sonoma

This recipe was formulated by Mrs. Frances Garbelland, Joel Peterson's mother, to complement the Ravenswood Merlot wine. The stew is usually served with brown rice and a green salad.

2 lbs. lamb stew meat, carefully trimmed

2 to 3 tablespoons olive oil

½ cup diced onions

½ cup diced carrots

2 cloves garlic, minced

1 wedge unpeeled orange

1 large strip lemon peel

1 cup Merlot

1 cup tomato juice

6 whole cloves

1 stick cinnamon

1 teaspoon powdered coriander

In a medium-sized Dutch oven, brown lamb lightly in hot olive oil. Add onions, carrots and garlic and sauté briefly. Add rest of the ingredients. Cover and bring to a simmer on top of the stove. Place in a preheated 325° oven and bake until tender, about 1½ to 2 hours. Check occasionally. If more liquid is needed add equal parts Merlot and tomato juice. Degrease and thicken sauce with flour and water if necessary.

Author's note: The orange, lemon, cinnamon and cloves are a wonderful flavor complement for the lamb. The wedge of orange may be cut into two or three pieces. You may substitute ½ teaspoon ground cinnamon and ½ teaspoon ground cloves for the whole spices.

Roast Leg of Spring Lamb

Recipe contributed by Linda Burgess; Burgess Cellars, St. Helena

Linda Burgess's recipe for roast leg of lamb is a traditional one, including roasted potatoes. Steamed, buttered asparagus is a nice accompaniment.

slivers of garlic

5 to 6 lb. boned, rolled and tied spring leg of lamb

butter, softened

Italian herb seasoning

salt and pepper to taste

1 large onion, peeled and quartered

water, as needed

10 small potatoes, peeled and cut in half

2¼ cups water

2 tablespoons cornstarch

Make a small gash in lamb surface and insert a garlic sliver. Make more gashes about 3 inches apart, inserting a garlic sliver in each gash. Rub soft butter over surface of lamb on one side, turn and rub other side with butter. Sprinkle lamb with Italian herb seasoning, salt and pepper. Insert meat thermometer into thickest portion of lamb. Place in shallow roasting pan, and roast uncovered in a preheated 325° oven for about 3 hours or until thermometer registers 175° for well done, 160° for medium rare, 140° for rare. (Roast 30 minutes per pound for well done.)

About 1 hour after placing roast in oven, add onion and potatoes placing them around the roast. Baste occasionally with pan drippings. Additional water may be added if needed.

When roast is done, remove to a platter and keep warm. Leave onion in pan. Put potatoes in a dish in oven to keep warm. For more browned and crusty potatoes drizzle some of the fat drippings over the potatoes and place in hot oven for 5 to 10 minutes to crisp and brown the potatoes.

Skim fat from pan drippings. Add 2 cups water to pan and scrape browned particles free from pan. Combine cornstarch and ¼ cup water and stir in drippings. Add additional seasonings if necessary and cook until smooth.

♥ PORK ♥

Sweet and Sour Ribs

Serves 6

Serve with Ruby Cabernet

Recipe contributed by Marcia Gerwer; Gerwer Winery, Somerset

This recipe was developed by Marcia and Vernon Gerwer when their four girls were young. It is still a family favorite and is now being requested by a new generation of youngsters — the grandchildren.

2 slabs pork ribs

salt and pepper to taste

2 10½-oz. cans tomato soup

1 8-oz can tomato sauce

1 20-oz. can pineapple chunks, juice reserved

½ cup brown sugar

½ cup vinegar

1 tablespoon mustard

1 onion, thinly sliced

2 green bell peppers, cut into chunks

1 tablespoon Worcestershire sauce

Have butcher cut ribs into two rib sections. Salt and pepper them and place fat-side up in a large baking pan. Bake 1 hour at 250° to render the fat. Pour off fat.

Combine remaining ingredients and pour over the ribs. Bake an additional 1½ hours at 350°, basting occasionally with sauce.

If using as an appetizer, have butcher cut ribs into finger-sized pieces. Ingredients may be cut in half for appetizer use. In that case use an 8-oz. can of pineapple chunks. Beef ribs may be substituted for the pork.

Barbecued Ribs and Chicken Breasts

Serves 8

Serve with Cabernet Sauvignon

Recipe contributed by Roger Cook; R. & J. Cook, Clarksburg

Roger Cook cooks all the meat, poultry and fish while his wife, Joanne, prepares the rest of the meal. Roger particularly likes to grill meats on his gas barbecue. He never measures anything, as he prefers to cook by taste — but has given us some approximate measures here for his barbecue sauce. This sauce has been a standard of his whether he's cooking for 2 or for large winery functions of 400.

1 side of lean pork spareribs, 3 to 3½ lbs.

4 whole chicken breasts, split

BARBECUE SAUCE

1 cup catsup

⅓ red wine

1 teaspoon Worcestershire sauce

cayenne pepper, to taste

Tabasco sauce, to taste

1 or 2 cloves garlic, pressed

Combine barbecue sauce ingredients and brush onto spareribs and chicken. Grill over medium-high heat, brushing with additional sauce as needed. Cook for 1 hour or longer, testing occasionally for doneness.

Serve with Cabernet Sauvignon

Estate Bottled
1982 CABERNET SAUVIGNON
El Dorado
SIERRA VISTA

Pork Scallopini

Serves 4

Recipe contributed by Barbara MacCready; Sierra Vista Winery, Placerville

El Dorado County produces wonderful vegetables and fruit and excellent lamb and lean pork. The latter inspired Barbara MacCready to create this recipe. It makes an excellent substitute for the traditional veal scallopini. According to Barbara, the key to successful substitution of pork for veal is to use lean pork.

1 lb. mushrooms, sliced	2 cloves garlic, minced
⅓ cup olive oil	1 cup Marsala
2 lbs. lean pork tenderloin, sliced 3/8 inch thick	1 cup Fumé Blanc
1 teaspoon salt	2 tablespoons arrowroot
⅓ cup flour	¼ cup freshly grated Parmesan cheese
1 cup finely chopped onions	

In a large skillet, heat 2 tablespoons olive oil; add mushrooms and sauté briefly. Remove mushrooms and set aside. Combine salt and flour and roll meat slices in the flour. Add ¼ cup olive oil to the skillet and heat. When oil is fragrant, brown pork slices until no more red juices exude from the meat. If necessary, do this in two batches. Remove meat to a warm platter and keep warm while preparing the sauce.

In the same skillet, sauté onion and garlic until onion is transparent, adding a small amount of olive oil if necessary. Add Marsala and Fumé Blanc and blend well with the pan drippings. Reduce liquid slightly. If sauce is too thin, mix 2 tablespoons arrowroot with some water and add to sauce. Add meat, mushrooms and Parmesan cheese. Stir, heat thoroughly and serve.

Author's note: Adding grated Parmesan cheese will also thicken the sauce.

Serve with Gewurztraminer

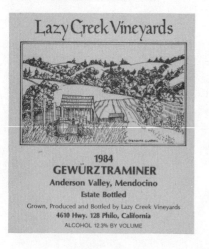

Lazy Creek Vineyards

1984
GEWÜRZTRAMINER
Anderson Valley, Mendocino
Estate Bottled
Grown, Produced and Bottled by Lazy Creek Vineyards
4610 Hwy. 128 Philo, California
ALCOHOL 12.3% BY VOLUME

Lazy Creek Pork Chops

Serves 2

Recipe contributed by Hans Kobler; Lazy Creek Vineyards, Philo

When Hans Kobler prepares this dinner dish, his wife, Theresia, usually makes Spaetzle to accompany it (see page 326 for recipe). Hans learned this recipe when he worked in some of the outstanding restaurants of Switzerland.

2 small carrots, finely julienned	1 teaspoon flour
1 tablespoon oil	⅓ cup Gewurztraminer
2 thick center-cut pork chops, well trimmed	¼ cup beef broth
¼ cup finely chopped shallots	⅓ cup heavy cream
1 small clove garlic, minced	2 teaspoons Dijon mustard
	salt and freshly ground pepper, to taste

Cook carrots until crisp tender and set aside. Heat oil in heavy skillet over medium-high heat and brown pork chops on each side. Lower heat to medium and cook until pork is done, 12 to 15 minutes. Do not overcook. Remove meat and keep in warm place while sauce is being prepared.

In the same pan, sauté shallots and garlic until lightly golden. Sprinkle flour over the shallots. Stir well and cook for 1 minute. Remove from heat. Pour the wine and beef broth over the mixture, stirring well. Return the pan to heat and continue cooking, stirring to blend until mixture is thick, 3 to 5 minutes. Add cream and mustard. Stir well and reduce heat. Continue cooking until heated and smooth, but do not boil. Stir in the carrots and return the chops and any accumulated juices to the sauce. Warm the chops, but do not boil. Season to taste with salt and pepper. Serve.

Pork Chops and Sausages with Cabbage

Serves 4

Recipe contributed by Stephanie and Larry Rosenbloom; Creston Manor Vineyards and Winery, Creston

Serve with November New Petit d'Noir or Pinot Noir

The Rosenblooms particularly like to serve this stew at crush time when work at the winery is at a peak. The stew can be made well in advance, even a day or two, and reheated. The spices used are a perfect combination for the recommended wines. Do not use any more than the prescribed amount of seasonings in order to retain a good balance with the wine, especially the November wine.

2 lbs. white cabbage

1 tablespoon butter

4 loin pork chops, about ½ lb. each

salt and pepper to taste

1 cup finely chopped onion

1 tablespoon finely minced garlic

½ cup dry white wine

½ teaspoon ground cumin

1 bay leaf, crumbled

½ teaspoon dried thyme

2 whole cloves

½ cup water

1 lb. Kielbasa (Polish sausage)

Cut away the core of the cabbage and cut cabbage lengthwise into eighths. Cut each piece crosswise into ½-inch pieces. There should be about 12 cups of shredded cabbage.

Heat butter in a 3-quart stovetop-to-oven casserole or Dutch oven with a tight fitting lid. Sprinkle the chops with salt and pepper and add to casserole. Cook over medium-high heat about 2 minutes on each side or until lightly browned. Scatter onions and garlic over the chops and cook, stirring, until wilted. Add wine and stir. Add cabbage, cumin, bay leaf, thyme, cloves and water. Cover tightly and cook for 30 minutes. Add pieces of sausage, cover and continue cooking for 15 more minutes. Serve with boiled potatoes.

Harvest Pork Roast

Recipe contributed by Brigit Poole; Mount Palomar Winery, Temecula

The stuffing made with wine-soaked apricots and raisins makes the roast juicy and adds an interesting flavor component to this dish. The apricots and raisins need to soak at least 4 hours, and allow 3 hours for the roast.

6-oz. dried apricots, cut into pieces	1 6-lb boneless pork loin, opened and flattened
1 cup golden raisins	salt and pepper to taste
1 bottle Johannisberg Riesling	1 clove garlic
5 to 6 large carrots, julienned	flour
oil	2 tablespoons butter
fresh sprigs of rosemary	3 Pippin apples, peeled and sliced
	½ lb. fresh green grapes

In a covered glass dish, soak apricots and raisins in 1 cup Johannisberg Riesling for 4 hours or overnight.

Place carrots in bottom of Dutch oven which has been lightly oiled. Scatter rosemary leaves over carrots. Set aside. Put pork roast, opened up with flat side down, on a large piece of cheesecloth. Season with salt and pepper to taste. Smash clove of garlic with flat side of a knife and rub over meat. Drain apricot and raisins and spread down center of meat. Fold meat closed and wrap in cheesecloth; tie with string to form a roll.

Lightly pat roast with flour. Melt butter in a large frying pan and brown meat evenly on all sides. Place roast on carrots in Dutch oven and put sliced apples on one side. Deglaze frying pan with ½ cup Riesling, stirring pan to loosen all particles and blend them into a sauce. Pour the liquid over the roast. Cover and place in preheated 350° oven.

Roast for ½ hour, uncover and pour ½ cup Riesling over meat. Cover and return to oven. Baste with pan juices every half hour until meat thermometer register 170° (about 3 hours). Remove roast and carrots from pan and keep warm.

Put cooked apples and pan juices in a saucepan. Deglaze Dutch oven with ½ cup Riesling and pour into apple mixture. Skim off fat. Place on low heat and add a little more wine to thin sauce. Add grapes. Cover and cook over low heat for 15 minutes. Thicken gravy if desired. Carefully remove cheesecloth from roast. Serve with apple-grape sauce.

Spicy Sausage Stew with Polenta

Serves 4 to 6

Serve with Cabernet Sauvignon

Recipe contributed by Valerie E. Ahlgren; Ahlgren Vineyard, Boulder Creek

Valerie Ahlgren usually prepares this sausage stew during crush time and lets it simmer on low so that it can be served whenever the work is finished. Actually, the stew used to be used as a pasta sauce, but the cheese and polenta give it a "stick-to-the-ribs" heartiness of a full meal.

6 to 10 cloves garlic, minced

2 medium yellow onions, diced

1 bay leaf, crumbled

3 tablespoons olive oil

1 lb. linguica

1 lb. mild Italian sausage

½ lb. hot Italian sausage, optional

½ lb. mushrooms, quartered

2 28-oz. cans Italian-style whole tomatoes

¼ teaspoon each black pepper, white pepper and Tabasco sauce

½ teaspoon salt

1½ cups Cabernet Sauvignon

4 to 6 slices Teleme cheese, ¼ inch thick

Polenta (see recipe on page 260)

In a medium-sized Dutch oven sauté garlic, onions and bay leaf in olive oil until onions are soft. Slice linguica and add to pan. Skin the Italian sausages and add. Use a fork to break up meat as it browns. When sausage is completely browned, add mushrooms, chopped canned tomatoes and their liquid, pepper, Tabasco sauce, salt and 1 cup Cabernet Sauvignon. Cover and simmer about 45 minutes over low heat, stirring occasionally. Remove lid, stir well and adjust seasonings if necessary. Simmer uncovered until well thickened and reduced (up to several hours if desired), stirring occasionally. Ten minutes before serving add ½ cup wine and simmer to blend flavors.

To serve, place one slice of cheese on each plate. Spoon enough polenta over each to just cover the cheese. Wait a few minutes to let the polenta set up, then top with a generous helping of stew.

Author's note: If linguica or Italian sausage are not available, consult your butcher as to the availability of local spicy sausages since they vary with the section of the country. The stew may be made a day ahead up to the point of adding the ½ cup Cabernet Sauvignon. After refrigerating the stew, remove hardened fat and reheat.

❦ GAME ❦

Serve with Cabernet Sauvignon

Grilled Wild Boar

Serves 6

Recipe contributed by A. Crawford Cooley; Hacienda Wine Cellars, Sonoma

Wild boar are frequently hunted on Crawford Cooley's ranch in northern Sonoma County, and served at the Hacienda Ranch dinners. Domestic pork may be used in this recipe with good result.

1 3-lb. boneless tenderloin of wild boar or domestic pork

MARINADE

¼ cup olive oil

2 cloves garlic, finely chopped

2 teaspoons dried rosemary, crumbled

1 teaspoon salt

½ teaspoon freshly ground pepper

1 cup dry white wine

Place roast in pan small enough so that marinade will cover roast. Combine marinade ingredients and pour over roast. Marinate for several hours, or overnight. Grill over hot mesquite coals for 40 minutes to 1 hour.

Serve with Chardonnay

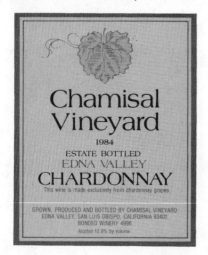

Rabbit in Chardonnay

Serves 6

Recipe contributed by Carolyn Goss; Chamisal Vineyard, San Luis Obispo

Carolyn Goss serves this rabbit dish with dumplings, small whole carrots and green peas.

1 6-lb. rabbit, cut into 6 pieces (4 legs and the saddle cut crosswise in 2)

salt and pepper to taste

1 tablespoon butter

1 tablespoon olive oil

1 large onion, sliced

1 clove garlic, pressed

1 tablespoon Worcestershire sauce

2 tablespoons chopped parsley

1 bay leaf

⅛ teaspoon each rosemary, thyme and oregano

pinch of tarragon

1 cup chicken broth

⅔ cup Chardonnay

Salt and pepper the rabbit pieces. In a Dutch oven or ovenproof casserole heat butter and oil over medium-high heat. Brown pieces of rabbit well on all sides. Add the remaining ingredients. Bring to a slow boil. Cover and cook on low heat for 1 hour, turning pieces twice during cooking. Add more salt and pepper before serving, if necessary. Thicken gravy if desired.

Grilled Marinated Rabbit

Serves 6

Recipe contributed by Jamie Davies; Schramsberg Vineyards and Cellars, Calistoga

Serve with Cuvée de Pinot Champagne

Cuvée de Pinot, which is full of fruit and spice, is a light, dry complement to the grilled rabbit. For best results, barbecue the rabbit over mesquite charcoal in a covered barbecue.

2 rabbits, about 3 lbs. each

MARINADE

¾ cup olive oil

½ cup champagne or dry white wine

1 clove garlic, chopped

½ lemon, thinly sliced

1 teaspoon fresh thyme, or ½ teaspoon dry thyme

1 teaspoon fresh rosemary, or ½ teaspoon dry rosemary

1 small bay leaf

Cut rabbits in serving pieces and place in large bowl. Combine marinade ingredients and pour over rabbit. Marinate for several hours.

Build charcoal fire and push coals to the side when they are ash gray. Arrange rabbit pieces down center of grill. Cover. Turn rabbit after 10 minutes. Brush with marinade and cook 10 minutes. Turn and grill for 10 minutes more.

Venison Parmigiana

Serves 4

Recipe contributed by James P. "Bo" Barrett; Chateau Montelena Winery, Calistoga

Serve with Cabernet Sauvignon

Bo Barrett credits Diane Vella, wife of the vineyard manager at Chateau Montelena Winery, for teaching him how to cook this venison dish. Bo tries to use as much bread crumbs as the meat will hold and also uses lots of cheese for the topping. He suggests that no salt be used in the preparation of the meat since salt draws out moisture from the meat as it cooks. Canned marinara sauce may be used, but Bo prefers homemade sauce.

4 venison round steaks (or venison sirloin)

1 egg

¼ cup milk

2 cups seasoned bread crumbs

olive oil

1½ cups marinara sauce

2 cups grated Parmesan, Romano or Fontina cheese (or a mixture of all, which is best)

Moderately pound steaks with a tenderizing hammer. Mix egg and milk together. Dip steaks in egg mixture then dredge thoroughly in bread crumbs. Lightly pound in the bread crumbs with the back of a spoon. Repeat until all the bread crumbs are absorbed.

In a large skillet (preferably ovenproof) heat enough olive oil to cover the skillet bottom. Fry steaks slightly on each side. Pink juice should still be running out of the meat. Remove steaks and drain oil if using an ovenproof skillet. Otherwise, place steaks in an ovenproof baking dish. Evenly pour marinara sauce over steaks. Sprinkle grated cheese over the top. Broil until cheese is melted and sauce is hot. Serve with brown and wild rice and steamed broccoli.

Chile Verde
á la Sea Ridge

Recipe contributed by Tim Schmidt; Sea Ridge Winery, Cazadero

This is a hearty stew that borrows heavily from the cuisine of Mexico. The spices blend surprisingly well with the venison and would work just as favorably with wild boar or domestic pork.

2 lbs. venison, cut into ¾-inch cubes (less desirable cuts such as shoulder may be used)

flour

½ cup olive oil

1 large onion, sliced

1 bunch fresh cilantro, chopped

¼ cup fresh oregano, chopped

4 cloves garlic, finely diced

1 7-oz. can green chiles, diced (seeds may be removed)

2 teaspoons cumin

1 pint tomatillos, canned or fresh (if using fresh remove husks and simmer in water 15 or 20 minutes until tender)

½ cup Zinfandel

½ cup beef broth

chile powder to taste (optional)

Dredge venison cubes in flour. Heat oil in large cast iron skillet and brown meat on all sides. Remove meat and add onion to remaining oil, cooking about 5 minutes over medium heat, stirring frequently. Add cilantro, oregano and garlic. Sauté a few more minutes until onion starts to become transparent. Return venison to the skillet and add chiles, cumin, tomatillos, wine and beef broth. If desired, add chile powder to taste. Cover and simmer on stovetop or in a preheated 300° oven for 2 to 3 hours, or until venison is very tender. Serve with warmed flour tortillas.

Author's note: Tomatillos, also called Mexican green tomatoes, are about the size of a walnut and have a parchment-like gray-brown covering which is easily peeled off. They are available fresh in the produce section or canned in the special foods section of most grocery stores.

Venison Sauté

Serves 6   *Serve with Cabernet Sauvignon*

Recipe contributed by Aurora Pepi; Robert Pepi Winery, Oakville

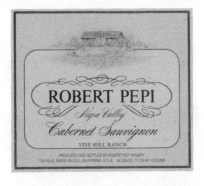

Aurora Pepi likes to serve this dish with rice, mashed potatoes or polenta. If you do not like a "hot" dish leave out the dried red pepper. The Pepis usually grow the little red peppers in their garden.

4 tablespoons olive oil

3 lbs. venison, cut into 1-inch cubes

1 shallot, minced

1 tablespoon minced fresh rosemary

1 tablespoon minced fresh thyme

1 clove garlic, minced

1 small dried red pepper, minced (optional)

½ cup Cabernet Sauvignon

½ cup chicken stock

1 cup canned tomatoes, chopped

½ lb. fresh mushrooms, sliced

In a Dutch oven heat the olive oil and brown the venison over high heat, turning pieces as they brown. Lower heat to medium, add shallots and sauté a few minutes. Add minced herbs, garlic and optional red pepper. Sauté a few minutes more, then add the Cabernet and chicken stock. Turn heat to high, cook a few minutes and add tomatoes. Bring to a boil, cover and simmer until almost tender, about 1 hour. Add mushrooms and simmer until mushrooms are done, about 10 minutes. Serve over rice, mashed potatoes or polenta.

Author's note: If fresh herbs are not available ½ teaspoon dried rosemary and ½ teaspoon dried thyme may be substituted.

▾ VEAL ▾

Serve with Chardonnay

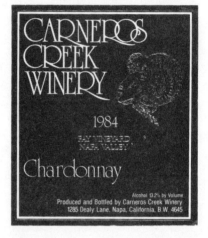

Veal with Chardonnay

Serves 4

Recipe contributed by Julie Morrison; Carneros Creek Winery, Napa

The tartness of the capers in this recipe is a good balance for the almonds. Serve with sautéed asparagus.

10 tablespoons butter	1 teaspoon capers
1 lb. veal, sliced thin and pounded	¼ cup blanched almonds, sliced
¼ cup flour	lemon slices and parsley for garnish
½ cup Chardonnay	
¼ lb. mushrooms, sliced	

In a large heavy skillet melt 4 tablespoons butter of medium-high heat. Flour veal and sauté until lightly browned on both sides. Add butter as needed. Remove veal from pan and keep warm. Add 4 more tablespoons butter and the Chardonnay. Scrape pan, reduce head to medium-low and let liquid simmer and reduce. Add mushrooms and simmer for 10 minutes. Return veal to pan. Cover and cook over low heat for 15 minutes. Place veal on serving platter. Add almonds to liquid, stir and pour over the meat. Garnish platter with lemon slices and parsley

Serve with Pinot Noir

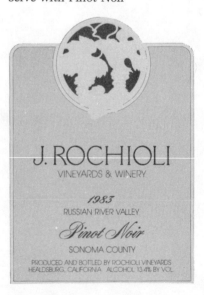

Veal con Vino

Serves 3 to 4

Recipe contributed by Theresa Rochioli; J. Rochioli Vineyards and Winery, Healdsburg

Theresa Rochioli prefers to cook without salt and says the only product with salt she uses is Worcestershire sauce. She feels that the use of herbs and lemon juice in cooking is a better complement to the wines used in her recipes as well as to the wines she serves with the dishes.

1 lb. veal cutlets, pounded to ¼-inch thickness	1 teaspoon basil
flour	1 teaspoon rosemary
4 tablespoons butter	1 teaspoon pepper
Parmesan cheese, grated	1 tablespoon Worcestershire sauce
3 medium shallots, thinly sliced	⅓ cup Pinot Noir
3 cloves garlic, minced	½ bouillon cube dissolved in ⅓ cup water
1 lb. mushrooms, sliced	juice of ½ lemon

Cut veal into bite-sized chunks and roll in flour. Shake off excess. Melt 2 tablespoons butter in skillet over medium-high heat. Brown veal pieces and sprinkle with Parmesan cheese as they brown. Remove veal to covered casserole. Preheat oven to 350°.

Reduce heat to medium on skillet and add 2 tablespoons butter. Sauté shallots and garlic until tender. Add mushrooms and sauté until tender. Add herbs, pepper, Worcestershire sauce, wine, bouillon and lemon juice. To thicken, add 1 teaspoon flour to small amount of water and stir to a smooth paste. Add to mushroom mixture and stir until smooth. Pour over veal and cover dish. Bake in 350° oven for 15 minutes. Sprinkle with additional Parmesan cheese and serve over rice.

Stuffed Breast of Veal

Serves 6 to 8

Serve with Pinot Noir Blanc

Recipe contributed by Joan Ellis, Mark West Vineyards, Forestville

This dish features a marinated breast of veal rolled up around a spinach and ground veal stuffing. It takes a little extra time and effort to prepare this, but the results are well worth it — not only is it delicious, it looks most attractive when served.

3 to 4 lb. breast of veal, boned	1 lb. ground veal
1½ cups Pinot Noir Blanc	1 egg
1 clove garlic	½ cup cream
¼ cup vegetable oil	1 tablespoon chopped parsley
1 10-oz. pkg. frozen chopped spinach	½ teaspoon allspice
2 slices bread	salt and pepper to taste
milk or water	arrowroot

Place breast of veal in large flat pan. Mix together Pinot Noir Blanc, garlic and vegetable oil and pour over the veal. Refrigerate for 24 hours, turning several times. Remove from refrigerator and reserve marinade.

Defrost the chopped spinach and squeeze dry. Soften the bread slices in milk or water. Combine with ground veal, spinach, egg, cream, parsley, allspice and salt and pepper. Spread mixture over breast of veal and roll from small end. Tie with string. Place stuffed veal roll on a rack in a roasting pan. Preheat oven to 350° and roast for approximately 2 hours or until meat is done (175° internal temperature). Baste often with reserved marinade.

When roast is done, make sauce from pan juices, seasoning to taste and thickening with arrowroot for a clear sauce. Allow meat to stand for about 15 minutes before slicing. Carve carefully so as not to disturb the pinwheel pattern made by the stuffing.

Author's note: Substitute 1½ cup chopped fresh spinach for the frozen spinach if desired.

DAVIS BYNUM
1984

Sonoma County
CHARDONNAY
RESERVE BOTTLING

ALCOHOL CONTENT 12.9% BY VOLUME
Produced and bottled by the Davis Bynum Winery
Healdsburg, CA, USA

Westside Road by Dorothy Bynum

Sautéed Veal Kidney Chops

Recipe contributed by Dorothy and Davis Bynum; Davis Bynum Winery, Healdsburg

This is one of the Bynums' favorite main dishes. It is served with noodles and a green salad.

4 veal kidney chops	**½ cup dry vermouth**
flour	**½ cup dry white wine**
1 tablespoon butter	**salt to taste**
1 tablespoon olive oil	**2 tablespoons chopped parsley**
2 shallots, chopped	**a touch of lemon zest**
1 clove garlic, minced	**dash of Worcestershire sauce**
paprika	

Lightly dust veal chops with flour. In an ovenproof skillet with a cover, heat butter and oil over medium-high heat. Add chops, turn heat to medium and sauté until golden brown on one side. Turn chops and add shallots and garlic. Sprinkle chops with paprika and continue cooking until other side is brown. Increase heat slightly and pour vermouth over chops, letting it bubble in the pan. Baste the chops and let liquid swirl for a couple of minutes. Add white wine, a bit more paprika and salt to taste. Cover pan, leaving lid slightly cracked, place in a preheated 325° oven and cook until chops are tender, 25 to 30 minutes. Baste once or twice during cooking time, adding parsley, lemon zest and Worcestershire sauce during last basting. The liquid will reduce to a thick stock.

Serve with noodles that have been cooked al dente and tossed with some Parmesan cheese and a little olive oil.

Wine Country Veal Scallopini

Serves 4

Serve with Chardonnay

Recipe contributed by Linda Burgess; Burgess Cellars, St. Helena

Linda Burgess serves this dish with pasta or rice and a tossed green salad

¾ to 1 lb. veal scallopini (6 slices)

flour

2 cloves garlic, minced

½ cup Chardonnay

2 medium tomatoes, peeled and chopped

salt and freshly ground pepper to taste

2 tablespoons olive oil

½ lb. fresh mushrooms, sliced

chopped parsley for garnish

Pound veal lightly. Dredge in flour. Combine garlic, wine, tomatoes, salt and pepper and set aside. (Tomatoes are easily peeled if immersed in boiling water for a few seconds.)

Heat oil in skillet, add veal and brown quickly on both sides. Remove meat from pan. (Do not crowd meat in pan. Do in two batches if necessary.) Add mushrooms to pan and cook, stirring often, for 2 to 3 minutes. Return veal to pan, arrange mushrooms on top of meat and spoon around them the reserved tomato-wine mixture. Simmer 5 to 10 minutes. Serve sprinkled with fresh parsley.

Veal Medallions in Fresh Tomato Sauce

Serves 6

Serve with Chardonnay

Recipe contributed by Robin Gainey; The Gainey Vineyard, Santa Ynez

Robin Gainey likes to serve these veal medallions with blanched snow peas and lightly buttered baby carrots. Since Robin is a frequent visitor to France, she is greatly influenced by the culinary arts of that country. In this dish she uses Meaux Mustard made by Pommeroy. If you cannot find it, any sweet French honey mustard will do.

6 veal medallions, approx. 6 oz. each

6 tablespoons unsalted butter

4 tablespoons shallots, minced

⅓ cup brandy

1 cup heavy cream

2 tablespoons sweet French honey mustard

1 cup ripe tomatoes, peeled, seeded and chopped

4 tablespoons minced parsley

In a large skillet over moderate heat, sauté the veal in 2 tablespoons butter no more than 2 to 3 minutes on each side, until golden. Remove veal to warm platter and keep warm. Add shallots to the pan and deglaze the pan with brandy. Reduce liquid by half. Add cream and reduce to thicken slightly. Add mustard and whisk in remaining butter a bit at a time. Reduce heat and add the chopped tomatoes and parsley, blending well. Place a medallion on each plate and top with sauce.

Serve with Chardonnay

Chicken Coins in Tarragon Cream Sauce

Serves 6

Recipe contributed by Dr. Alan Steen; Whitehall Lane Winery, St. Helena

Dr. Steen, who owns Whitehall Lane Winery with his brother, gave up his medical practice to devote full time as Director of Marketing for the winery. He enjoys cooking as a hobby, and particularly likes creating menus to go with Whitehall Lane wines.

3 large chicken breasts, boned, skinned and halved

salt and freshly ground white pepper to taste

2 medium carrots, peeled and finely julienned

1 medium leek, trimmed to white and tender green portion, finely julienned

4 cups chicken stock

TARRAGON CREAM SAUCE

1 tablespoon butter

2 tablespoons finely chopped shallot

1 cup Chardonnay

2 cups homemade chicken stock

2 cups whipping cream

1 tablespoon chopped fresh tarragon

freshly ground white pepper to taste

4 tablespoons unsalted butter

Pound chicken breasts between wax paper to ¼ to ½ inch thickness. Season chicken lightly with salt and pepper. Divide carrots and leeks evenly, placing them on one end of each piece of chicken. Roll up like a jelly roll. Place each roll on a piece of plastic wrap wide enough to leave 2-inch margins on each end. Roll up tightly in plastic wrap, carefully twisting ends to totally enclose the chicken. Bring stock to a simmer in a large saucepan. Add chicken packages and simmer 16 minutes.

Meanwhile make sauce. Melt butter in heavy wide-based saucepan over medium heat. Add shallot and stir 2 minutes, or until soft. Add wine, increase heat to high and boil until reduced to a glaze — about 2 tablespoons. Stir in stock and boil until reduced to ½ cup. Add cream and tarragon; boil until sauce is thickened to coat spoon. Season with white pepper.

Remove chicken packages from stock with a slotted spoon. Unwrap immediately to prevent overcooking. Slice each chicken breast diagonally into 6 to 8 coins. Arrange on plate. Just before serving, bring sauce to a boil, remove from heat and whisk in remaining butter, a tablespoon at a time. Spoon sauce over chicken and serve immediately. Pass remaining sauce.

Chicken in Cabernet Sauvignon

Serves 4

Serve with Cabernet Sauvignon

Recipe contributed by Nancy Hart; Hart Winery, Temecula

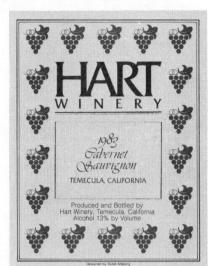

Nancy Hart's version of the traditional Coq au Vin is simple to prepare. The Dijon mustard adds another complexity to the dish.

½ lb. pork shoulder steak, or ¼ lb. salt pork, cut into small cubes

3- to 4-lb. fryer, cut up

1 lb. boiling onions, skinned

½ lb. small mushrooms

1 14½-oz. can beef broth

1 cup Cabernet Sauvignon

2 tablespoons Dijon mustard

1 tablespoon cornstarch

1 tablespoon water

In a Dutch oven over medium-high heat, cook pork in its own fat until very crisp. Remove from pan and set aside. Add chicken and onion to the pork fat and cook until browned, about 20 minutes. Remove chicken and onions from pan. Add mushrooms and brown. Then remove from pan.

Pour the beef bouillon into the pan and boil until liquid is reduced to 1 cup. Stir in the wine and mustard. Blend well. Add chicken, pork, mushrooms and onions. Cook covered on medium-low heat for 30 to 40 minutes or until chicken is done. Remove chicken, pork and vegetables to a serving dish and keep warm. Degrease pan if necessary. Blend cornstarch and water, and add to sauce, stirring until thickened. Pour over all and serve.

Chicken á la Mark West

Serves 4

Serve with Gewurztraminer

Recipe contributed by Joan Ellis; Mark West Vineyards, Forestville

Joan Ellis's easy yet elegant chicken dish blends the flavors of onions and artichokes with chicken — a delightful taste combination.

1 3- to 3½-lb. chicken, cut up

4 tablespoons butter

1 tablespoon vegetable oil

12 small white boiling onions, skinned

1 10-oz. pkg. frozen artichoke hearts, defrosted and drained

1 teaspoon lemon juice

½ cup Gewurztraminer

½ cup chicken stock

salt and pepper to taste

2 bay leaves

Heat butter and oil in a 10- to 12-inch skillet over medium-high heat and brown chicken pieces. Remove chicken pieces from skillet and place in a 13 × 9-inch glass baking dish. In the same skillet, brown onions until golden. Place onions in baking dish with chicken. Using the same skillet, add lemon juice and sauté artichoke hearts slightly. Arrange in baking dish with chicken and onions. Combine wine, chicken stock, salt and pepper and bay leaves. Pour over chicken. Bake uncovered at 350° 50 minutes to 1 hour, or until chicken is done.

Serve with Zinfandel

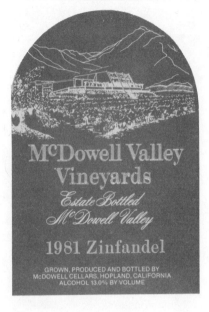

Chicken with Rosemary Wine Sauce

Serves 8

Recipe contributed by Karen Keehn; McDowell Valley Vineyards, Hopland

The original recipe for this dish was given to Karen Keehn by an Italian friend many years ago. Over the years it has taken on a character of its own with the revision of ingredients and the addition of McDowell wines. Karen prepares it when she doesn't want to be tied down to a particular serving time — the longer and more slowly this dish cooks, the more delicious the sauce.

½ cup virgin olive oil	3 tablespoons fresh rosemary, minced
2 cloves garlic, minced	3 cups rich chicken broth
1 large onion chopped	1 cup sliced mushrooms
2 chickens, quartered	3 cups Fumé Blanc
2 cups Zinfandel	
1 2-oz. can anchovies	

In a large skillet, heat oil and sauté garlic and onions until translucent. Lift out and set aside. Add chicken pieces to the oil and sear on both sides. Do not burn. When chicken is browned, pour in Zinfandel. Add onion mixture, anchovies (no salt is needed in this dish) and rosemary and simmer uncovered for 20 minutes. Add chicken broth and mushrooms and continue to simmer uncovered for another 45 minutes.

Add Fumé Blanc and continue to simmer uncovered for another 30 to 40 minutes. Chicken should be so tender it nearly falls off the bone. Simmering uncovered will reduce the liquid and make a nice rich sauce. Serve in soup plates with French bread to soak up the gravy.

Author's note: If a thicker gravy is desired, remove chicken and keep warm while reducing sauce further, or add some cooked puréed vegetable for thickening

Serve with Chardonnay

Rolled Chicken Breasts

Serves 6

Recipe contributed by Barbara Shilo; Domaine Laurier, Forestville

Barbara Shilo usually serves Chardonnay with this dish, but it is also excellent with Pinot Noir. The walnut stuffing is rather substantial.

3 whole chicken breasts, skinned, boned and split	1 combined tablespoon salt, pepper and chopped parsley
1 tablespoon chopped garlic	1 cup cornflake crumbs
1 tablespoon chopped scallions	½ teaspoon dried basil
1 tablespoon chopped walnuts	½ teaspoon curry powder
1 tablespoon chopped mushrooms	⅓ cup melted butter

Pound the chicken breasts thin and cut into 4 × 4-inch squares. Mix garlic, scallions, walnuts, mushrooms, salt, pepper and parsley together well and set aside. Combine crumbs with basil and curry. Put about 1 tablespoon of walnut mixture on each chicken piece and roll up. Roll in melted butter, then in the crumb mixture. Place chicken rolls in baking dish, one next to another. Bake in preheated 375° oven for 30 minutes or until golden.

This dish can be prepared in advance, refrigerated and baked when needed.

Chicken Cacciatore

Serves 6

Serve with Cabernet Sauvignon

Recipe contributed by Alma Tudal; Tudal Winery, St. Helena

This recipe has been in Alma Tudal's family for almost 70 years. It is always served with mashed potatoes to make good use of the sauce. Although white wine is generally served with chicken, the Cabernet Sauvignon complements the richness of this sauce. Sautéed zucchini is a good accompaniment

3 whole chicken breasts, skinned and halved

¼ cup olive oil

2 tablespoons butter

½ cup fresh parsley, chopped

1 large yellow onion, chopped

4 cloves garlic, chopped

1 2-inch sprig fresh rosemary

4 4-inch sprigs each fresh thyme and fresh marjoram

¼ cup Cabernet Sauvignon

2 8-oz. cans tomato sauce

½ cup hot water

salt and freshly ground pepper to taste

1 6-oz. can pitted olives, drained

¼ lb. mushrooms, sliced

In a medium-sized Dutch oven heat oil and butter and sauté chicken breasts until golden brown. Remove breasts and sauté chopped parsley, onion and herb mixture for a few minutes. Add more oil and butter if necessary. Add wine and simmer a few minutes more. Add tomato sauce, water, salt and pepper to taste. Stir well, replace breasts and cook covered over low heat for about 30 minutes. Add olives and mushrooms and simmer for 15 minutes more.

Author's note: Alma Tudal has a large herb garden, so she has fresh herbs available year round. If you cannot get fresh herbs, dried ones may be substituted — ¼ teaspoon rosemary, ½ teaspoon thyme, and ¼ teaspoon marjoram. Taste sauce and add more herbs if desired.

Serve with Chardonnay

Boneless Barbecued Chicken Breasts

Serves 6 to 8

Recipe contributed by Dr. Thomas Fogarty; Thomas Fogarty Winery, Portola Valley

The marinade for this chicken gives it a distinctly oriental flavor. This dish would go well with rice and stir-fried vegetables.

6 whole chicken breasts, skinned, boned and halved

1½ cups teriyaki sauce

juice of 3 lemons

1 teaspoon garlic salt

1 teaspoon black pepper

½ cup white wine

2 teaspoons fresh ground ginger

olive oil

In a large bowl combine teriyaki sauce, lemon juice, garlic salt, pepper, wine and ginger. Add the chicken breasts and marinate overnight in the refrigerator. Before broiling remove chicken breasts from marinade and dip in olive oil. Place on hot barbecue and grill 3 to 4 minutes on each side. Before placing second side on grill, again dip the chicken breasts in olive oil. The chicken may also be broiled in an oven following the same procedures.

Serve with Chardonnay

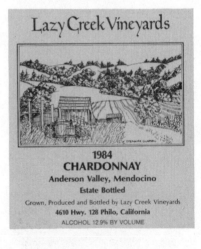

Chicken Flambé

Serves 4

Recipe contributed by Hans and Theresia Kobler; Lazy Creek Vineyards, Philo

This chicken recipe is an old Swiss one that has been passed down through the years in Theresia Kobler's family. It is quickly prepared and can easily be done at the table for a little showmanship. Serve with a rice pilaf and green beans or broccoli.

2 whole chicken breasts, boned, skinned and halved

2 tablespoons butter

2 to 3 shallots, finely chopped

1 clove garlic, minced

3 to 4 tablespoons flour seasoned with salt and pepper

½ lb. mushrooms, sliced

3 oz. Scotch whiskey

¾ cup heavy cream

⅛ teaspoon Worcestershire sauce

salt and pepper to taste

chopped parsley for garnish

Cut chicken into ¼-inch thick slices and dust with seasoned flour. In a large frying pan, heat butter over medium heat. Add chopped shallots and garlic. Sauté, stirring, until golden. Add the chicken and sauté, stirring until chicken is golden. Add sliced mushrooms and cook for 1 minute. Pour Scotch over the chicken and flame it. (If this is a first experience with flambé, take care to use a long match and keep your head back.)

When the flame begins to die down, stir in the cream, slowly at first, being careful to mix all ingredients well into the sauce as it forms. Add Worcestershire sauce and season to taste with salt and pepper. Place portions on heated plates and sprinkle lightly with parsley.

Hungarian Chicken Paprikash

Serves 4   *Serve with Zinfandel*

Recipe contributed by Etza Tomka; Soda Rock Winery, Healdsburg

When the Tomka family fled Hungary in 1956, they brought not only winemaking expertise with them, but many old family recipes. This chicken recipe is one of them. It is served with homemade Egg Drop Noodles (Spaetzle). See page 326 for recipe.

- 1 large onion, finely chopped
- 3 tablespoons butter
- 3 lbs. chicken parts
- 2 tablespoons sweet red ground Hungarian paprika (not hot paprika)
- 1 cup water
- 1 medium-sized tomato, chopped
- 2 tablespoons chopped green pepper
- salt to taste
- 1 cup sour cream

In a large skillet or Dutch oven, heat butter over medium-high heat and sauté onions until golden, but not brown. Sprinkle chicken with salt, add to skillet and brown lightly on both sides. Sprinkle chicken with paprika and add water to barely cover chicken. (Chicken will create its own juice as it cooks. Do not add too much water.) Add tomato, green pepper and salt to taste. Cover and simmer 30 to 35 minutes or until chicken is tender. Gently fold in sour cream, heat thoroughly, but do not boil. Serve over Egg Drop Noodles (see page 326).

Author's note: Chicken broth may be used instead of water. If doing so omit salt.

Italian Chicken

Serves 4   *Serve with Barbera*

Recipe contributed by Bev Borra; Borra's Cellar, Lodi

This simple chicken recipe has been in the Borra family for several generations. Bev, who leads a busy life, serves this often since it is easy to prepare. Buttered noodles or rice and a green vegetable complete the dinner.

- 2 tablespoons olive oil
- 1 3- to 3½-lb. frying chicken, cut up
- 1 tablespoon minced parsley
- ½ stalk celery, chopped
- ½ clove garlic, crushed
- ½ teaspoon salt
- ¼ teaspoon pepper
- 2 bay leaves
- ½ cup dry white wine
- 2 tablespoons water

In a large skillet heat oil and brown chicken on all sides. Add parsley, celery and garlic, and brown lightly. Sprinkle with salt and pepper and add the remaining ingredients except the water. Simmer, uncovered, until wine is almost evaporated. Add the water, cover and cook slowly for about 30 minutes, or until chicken is tender. Remove bay leaves. Place chicken on a heated platter and pour any of the juices over the chicken.

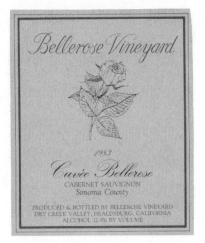

Mediterranean Sautéed Chicken

Serves 4

Recipe contributed by Charles Richard; Bellerose Vineyards, Healdsburg

This is Charles Richard's version of a classic Mediterranean dish which he has encountered in his many travels. He usually serves this dish with rice and buttered green beans. Mr. Richard says that the chicken is better slightly overcooked than undercooked.

1 3- to 3½ lb. chicken
¼ cup olive oil
salt and pepper to taste
garlic powder to taste

Herbes de Provence — ¼ teaspoon each of thyme, rosemary and sage
paprika
½ cup Sauvignon Blanc, room temperature

Cut chicken into desired pieces. Rub chicken pieces on both sides with olive oil. Season with salt pepper, garlic powder and herbs and dust with paprika. Place chicken pieces in shallow roasting pan or a 13 × 9-inch glass baking dish that has been coated with a very light film of olive oil. Bake in preheated 400° oven for 30 minutes, turning pieces so that chicken begins to brown and becomes crispy.

Reduce heat to 350° and "splash" the wine over the chicken. Return to oven for another 30 to 40 minutes, basting with pan juices occasionally.

Author's note: If a less crispy chicken is desired, do not turn the chicken pieces. The pan juices may be removed and reduced for a sauce while the chicken is kept warm.

Chicken Breast Picante

Serves 2

Recipe contributed by Annamaria Roudon; Roudon-Smith Vineyards, Santa Cruz

Annamaria Roudon likes to experiment with various types of international cooking. This chicken recipe with a hint of Mexican flavors is excellent served with steamed rice and a green vegetable.

2 slices bacon, cut into small bits
1 whole chicken breast, boned and halved
salt and pepper
½ cup Chardonnay

1 12-oz. can chile salsa
4 tablespoons grated Parmesan cheese
2 teaspoons dried oregano, finely crumbled

In a medium-sized heavy iron skillet, fry the bacon bits until crisp and set aside. Pour off all but 2 tablespoons fat. Lightly sprinkle chicken with salt and pepper. Brown chicken breasts on both sides in the remaining fat. Pour wine and chile salsa around the chicken, then top the breasts with Parmesan cheese, oregano and bacon bits. Cover and simmer for 20 minutes.

Three Pepper Chicken with Pineapple

Serves 4 to 6   Serve with Chardonnay

Recipe contributed by Steve White; The Daumé Winery, Camarillo

Steve White was given a wok by a Chinese friend 15 years ago and has been addicted to wok cooking ever since. He is constantly amazed by the simplicity of this utensil and with the inventiveness it evokes. He serves this stir-fried chicken with rice and corn on the cob (see below). The corn is an amazingly pleasing complement to the Chardonnay.

MARINADE

2 tablespoons soy sauce (low sodium preferred)

2 tablespoons Chardonnay

1 tablespoon cornstarch

FINISHING SAUCE

2 tablespoons each soy sauce, Chardonnay and pineapple juice

1 tablespoon cornstarch

1 teaspoon sesame oil

1 teaspoon sugar

½ teaspoon salt, optional

1½ to 2 lbs. chicken breast meat, cut in 1-inch pieces

2 green and 2 red peppers, cut into long strips

1 yellow pepper, cut into long strips

½ cup canned diced pineapple (save juice)

3 cloves garlic, minced

2 cups grape seed or corn oil

Combine marinade ingredients in a medium-sized bowl. Add chicken pieces, turning them to coat with marinade. Let stand 1 hour, stirring pieces occasionally.

In a small bowl prepare finishing sauce and set aside. Heat wok or a large frying pan until very hot. Add oil and stir-fry chicken 45 to 60 seconds, stirring to sauté evenly. Remove chicken with slotted spoon. Discard all but 2 tablespoons of oil. Sauté garlic until fragrant but not brown (about 10 seconds). Add the peppers and pineapple and stir-fry 30 seconds. Add chicken. Add the finishing sauce and mix everything well, stirring until sauce thickens.

Serve over hot rice. Season a large bowl of fresh steamed corn on the cob with a lemon pepper butter and pass separately.

Apricot Chicken

Serves 6 to 8

Recipe contributed by Richard N. Sherwin; Lytton Springs Winery, Healdsburg

This elegant recipe for chicken breasts features a savory stuffing and a fruity sauce. Only a red wine, like Zinfandel, would complement this dish. Richard sometimes makes this recipe using breaded flattened chicken breasts without the stuffing. Brown the chicken pieces first in a little hot oil and then proceed with the sauce.

6 8-oz. chicken breasts, halved and boned, skin left intact

STUFFING

2 cups chopped mushrooms

1 cup chopped onion

1 cup chopped celery

2 tablespoons butter

2 cups chopped apples

1 cup bread crumbs

SAUCE

1 16-oz. can halved apricots

1 cup orange marmalade

¾ cup Zinfandel

½ cup orange juice

¾ cup apricot juice (from can)

2 tablespoons red currant jelly

2 tablespoons brown sugar

2 tablespoons cornstarch dissolved in ¼ cup cold water

For filling: In a medium-sized skillet sauté mushrooms, onion and celery in 2 tablespoons butter until tender. Stir in apples and bread crumbs. Carefully lift skin up from each breast and place stuffing into pocket. Seal each chicken breast with your hands and place in a single layer in a baking dish.

Purée half of the can of apricots, leaving the rest for garnish. Reserve juice for the sauce. In a medium-sized sauce pan combine the puréed apricots with the orange marmalade, wine, orange juice, apricot juice, jelly and brown sugar. Simmer gently over low heat, stirring frequently until well blended. Slowly add cornstarch mixture, stirring constantly. Simmer until thickened, about 5 minutes. Pour sauce over chicken breasts and cover dish with aluminum foil. Bake in preheated 350° oven for 1 hour. To serve, garnish each chicken piece with an apricot half and pour extra sauce on top.

Orange Minted Chicken

Serves 4

Recipe contributed by Marcia Gerwer; Gerwer Winery, Somerset

Serve with White Zinfandel

This recipe was given to Marcia Gerwer by a family member from Colorado. It is a great way to cook with White Zinfandel.

1 frying chicken, cut up

2 oranges

salad oil

seasoned flour (may be seasoned
   with seasoned salt)

½ cup chicken broth

½ cup White Zinfandel

fresh mint leaves, chopped, or 2
   teaspoons dried mint

Thinly slice (with rind on) 1 orange and set aside. Grate the rind of the other orange and squeeze the juice over the chicken pieces (or roll chicken pieces in the juice). Roll the chicken pieces in seasoned flour. Put enough salad oil in a heavy skillet to cover the bottom and heat to medium. Add chicken and brown on both sides. Remove pieces to a 13 × 9-inch glass baking dish. Sprinkle chicken with the grated orange rind and chopped mint leaves. Mix chicken broth and wine together and pour around the chicken in the dish. Top with orange slices. Bake uncovered at 375° for 50 minutes, or until chicken is tender.

Author's note: For a more pungent orange flavor, marinate chicken pieces in the orange juice for 1 hour, then roll in flour

Chicken and Sausages in Champagne

Serves 6

Recipe contributed by Martha M. Culbertson; John Culbertson Winery, Fallbrook

Serve with Champagne Brut

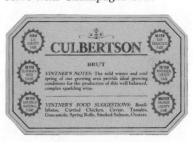

The spiciness of the sausages combine well with the mild flavor of the chicken. Martha Culbertson accompanies this dish with carrots, green beans and new potatoes.

3 chicken breasts, halved

18 1-inch slices of sausage,
   preferably a spicy type

3 tablespoons butter

3 shallots, minced

1 cup champagne, brut

¾ cup chicken stock

¾ cup heavy cream

salt and pepper to taste

Brown chicken breasts and sausage slices in 2 tablespoons butter in a large heavy skillet. When brown on both sides, add shallots, champagne and chicken stock. Simmer uncovered for about 20 minutes.

Remove chicken and sausage and keep warm. Reduce cooking liquid until ½ cup remains in the skillet. Add cream and cook for 3 to 4 minutes over low heat, stirring constantly. Add the remaining butter and whisk to mix. Season with salt and pepper to taste. Put the chicken and sausage pieces back into the sauce to warm. Serve.

Chicken Supreme

Serves 4

Recipe contributed by Silvia Nerelli; Pesenti Winery, Templeton

This version of the classic dish uses some typical California ingredients — artichoke hearts and ripe olives. Serve this quick-to-prepare dish with rice or fettuccine.

3 whole chicken breasts, skinned, boned and split	**1 cup heavy cream**
salt and pepper to taste	**1 10-oz. pkg. frozen artichoke hearts, cooked and drained**
flour	**½ lb. mushrooms**
¾ cup butter	**1 cup pitted ripe olives, halved or sliced**
½ cup dry white wine	**lemon wedges, optional**

Pound chicken breasts between wax paper to ¼ inch thickness. Cut each into 2 or 3 pieces. Sprinkle with salt and pepper and coat lightly with flour. Melt 4 tablespoons butter in a large heavy skillet over medium-high heat and add chicken pieces. Sauté quickly, turning once, until golden brown. (Add more butter if necessary.) Remove chicken to platter and keep warm. Sauté mushrooms, adding more butter if needed, and cook until lightly browned. Add wine and cream to skillet. Simmer until sauce thickens. Stir in artichokes and olives. Heat through. Top chicken with sauce and garnish with lemon wedges, if desired.

Author's note: Chicken pieces may be returned to the skillet to heat through, however they will lose some of their crispness.

Chicken and Mushrooms in Wine

Serves 8

Recipe contributed by Lynne Russell; Granite Springs Winery, Somerset

Lynne Russell serves this dish with a mound of rice and a green vegetable.

8 whole chicken breasts, split lengthwise	**salt and freshly ground pepper to taste**
½ cup butter	**½ teaspoon thyme, crumbled**
2 tablespoons olive oil	**1 cup Sauvignon Blanc**
2 large green onions, minced	**½ teaspoon thyme (optional)**
1½ lbs. mushrooms, sliced	

Heat 2 tablespoons butter and oil in heavy-bottomed skillet. Add onions and mushrooms. Sauté over medium-high heat for several minutes until mushrooms are lightly browned. Stir occasionally. Season with salt, pepper and thyme. Set aside.

Melt remaining 6 tablespoons butter in shallow casserole large enough to hold chicken breasts in a single layer. Pour in white wine. Turn chicken breasts in butter-wine mixture and arrange skin-side up in casserole. Season with salt and pepper and additional thyme if desired. Bake in a preheated 400° oven for 20 minutes, adding sautéed mushrooms and onions after 10 minutes. To serve, arrange chicken and mushrooms around a mound of rice on a heated platter.

Author's note: A cut up 3½ lb. fryer may be substituted for the chicken breasts. Use only 4 tablespoons butter and ¾ cup wine. Sauté ¾ lb. mushrooms and 2 green onions in 1 tablespoon each butter and oil. Bake chicken for 50 to 60 minutes, adding mushroom mixture last 10 minutes. Strain juices into a saucepan and thicken with a little flour and water for a gravy, if desired.

Mozzarella Chicken

Serves 4 *Serve with Chardonnay*

Recipe contributed by Theresa Rochioli, J. Rochioli Vineyards and Winery, Healdsburg

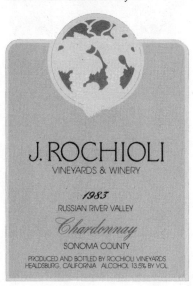

Theresa Rochioli's Mozzarella Chicken may be served with steamed rice, parboiled broccoli (flavored with a fresh squeezed lemon) and a salad.

½ cup butter, room temperature	¼ cup flour
4 large mushrooms, chopped	1 egg, beaten
2 whole chicken breasts, boned, skinned and halved	⅔ cup dry bread crumbs
pepper	2 cloves garlic, finely chopped
¼ teaspoon thyme	⅓ cup Chardonnay
4 ¼-inch slices Mozzarella cheese	sesame seeds
	fresh chopped parsley

In a small skillet melt 1 tablespoon butter and sauté the chopped mushrooms. Set aside.

Pound chicken breasts between 2 pieces of waxed paper to ¼ inch thickness. Spread each piece with 1 teaspoon butter. Season with pepper and a pinch of thyme. Top each chicken breast with a slice of Mozzarella cheese and ¼ of the sautéed mushrooms. Fold chicken over to enclose cheese and mushrooms and secure with toothpicks. Roll in flour, then dip in beaten egg, and roll in bread crumbs. Put chicken, seam-side down in an 8-inch square baking dish. Repeat with remaining chicken.

Preheat oven to 350°. Melt remaining butter with chopped garlic in small saucepan over low heat. Add wine. Pour over chicken and bake until golden brown, 35 to 40 minutes. Sprinkle with sesame seeds just before removing from oven. Then sprinkle with chopped parsley and serve.

Serve with Sonoma Riesling

Bobs-Kebobs

Serves 8

Recipe contributed by Nancy Bundschu; Gundlach-Bundschu Winery, Vineburg

Nancy Bundschu's kebobs recipe is unusual since it uses turkey and an oriental type of marinade. Serve with rice or Barley Pilaf (see page 346).

1 4-lb. turkey breast, skinned, boned and cut into 2-inch cubes	**MARINADE**
	½ cup Late Harvest Riesling
2 large zucchini, cut into ½-inch slices	¼ cup brown sugar
	½ cup oil
8 to 12 cherry tomatoes	⅔ cup soy sauce
1 leek, sliced crosswise in ¼-inch pieces	1 tablespoon fresh grated ginger, or 1 teaspoon ground ginger
chopped parsley	1 clove garlic, minced
	1 teaspoon grated lemon rind
	1 teaspoon paprika
	4 green onions, minced

Place turkey cubes in a large shallow pan. Combine marinade ingredients and pour over turkey. Leave at room temperature about 4 hours, stirring occasionally.

Prepare the vegetables for skewering. In boiling salted water, cook the sliced leek for 2 minutes and the sliced zucchini for 1 minute. Drain and immediately run vegetables under cold water and pat dry.

Thread eight 10-inch skewers with the marinated turkey cubes and the vegetables. Arrange kebobs on rack of broiler pan and brush with marinade. Broil about 4 inches from heat for 4 minutes. Turn and baste again. Broil another 4 to 5 minutes or until turkey is firm. Transfer to heated platter or individual plates. Sprinkle with chopped parsley.

Serve with Chardonnay

Herisah

Serves 4 to 6

Recipe contributed by Lila Burford; Adler Fels, Santa Rosa

Herisah is a longtime favorite of Lila Burford's Armenian family. At one time it was served only to the family, but now it is served to guests, too, because it is so unusual. Lila usually serves a green salad and French or Armenian bread with it. "The salad dressing should be made with lemon instead of vinegar so it will not conflict with the Chardonnay," she adds.

1 whole frying chicken, 3 to 4 lbs.	2 chicken bouillon cubes
2 cups whole grain, skinless wheat (available in most gourmet shops)	salt and freshly ground pepper to taste
	paprika
	4 oz. butter, melted

Bring 2 quarts of water to a boil in a heavy saucepan or casserole with a lid and add the chicken. Boil over moderate heat until the chicken is extremely tender and is falling off the bone. Cool the chicken enough so that the bones and skin can be removed easily. Add 2 chicken bouillon cubes to the water and return the chicken meat to the pot. Add the wheat and stir. Simmer over low heat, stirring occasionally, until the chicken actually melts into the cereal. (The herisah can cook all day.) Add more water if necessary during cooking. Season with salt and pepper to taste. Spoon into heated soup bowls, drizzle melted butter over all, dust with paprika and serve. May also be served as an appetizer.

Author's note: This old dish, also known as *keshkeg*, was served to pilgrims in early Armenian monasteries. Usually the herisah is beaten to the consistency of a thin porridge. Two cups of coarse bulgur, soaked overnight, may be substituted for the wheat.

Moroccan Stew with Couscous

Serves 8

Serve with Pinot Noir

Recipe contributed by Daniel Davis; Bonny Doon Vineyard, Santa Cruz

Daniel davis often uses his mother's Moroccan Stew recipe. Daniel's mother grew up in Morocco, immigrated to Israel as a young woman, and came to the United States in the 1970s. She has an international repertoire of recipes — this one is a family favorite.

1 3-lb. chicken, cut up	3 small turnips
1 onion, diced	3 small potatoes
2 tablespoons olive oil	4 carrots
1 teaspoon grated lemon rind	1 cup chicken broth
2 tablespoons chopped cilantro	2 crookneck squash
1 teaspoon cumin	4 small zucchini
1 teaspoon salt	1 cup raisins
½ teaspoon pepper	1 cup cooked chick-peas
2 lbs. lean, boneless lamb, cut into small cubes	1 tablespoon sweet paprika
2 tomatoes, chopped	1 cup couscous

In a large Dutch oven over medium-high heat sauté onion in oil until golden. Add chicken and brown on all sides. Add just enough water to cover the chicken. Add lemon peel, cilantro, cumin, salt and pepper. Bring to a boil, cover and turn heat to low. Simmer until chicken is barely tender, about 35 to 40 minutes. Remove chicken from broth.

Prepare the vegetables by cutting into large cubes. Add the lamb, tomatoes, turnips, potatoes, carrots and chicken broth to the pot. Bring to a boil, cover and cook over low heat for 30 minutes. Add all remaining ingredients except couscous and cook for another 15 minutes, until lamb is barely tender. Return chicken to the pot; bring stew to a boil. Put couscous into a colander on top of stew. Lower heat and cover pot. Steam couscous for 20 minutes over the stew or until it is tender. If couscous is cooked separately, cook stew another 20 minutes.

Author's note: Couscous may be purchased in the gourmet section of most groceries or in food stores specializing in Middle Eastern products.

Serve with Gewurztraminer

Green Chile Enchiladas

Serves 12

Recipe contributed by Katrina Staten; Field Stone Winery, Healdsburg

This recipe is of Southwestern origin. John Staten is a native of El Paso, Texas, and the recipe is from his mother's file. Katrina Staten serves these enchiladas as the main dish for a Mexican feast along with frijoles, a guacamole salad, fresh sliced mangoes and Mexican Wedding Cookies.

1 large bunch green onions, chopped	1 28-oz. can tomatoes, mashed
1 7-oz. can whole green chiles, coarsely chopped	5 cups grated Monterey Jack and/or Cheddar cheese
3 tablespoons butter	4 cups sour cream
3 cups cooked chicken or turkey meat, shredded	shortening or bacon fat
	1½ dozen corn tortillas

Reserve ½ cup chopped onion stems (the green part). Sauté the remaining green onions and chiles in butter in a large skillet. Add mashed canned tomatoes and simmer 10 minutes. Stir in 3 cups cheese and the sour cream and set aside.

In another skillet, heat shortening. Dip tortillas one at a time into hot fat, then drain on paper towels. Butter a large casserole dish and spoon in a thin layer of the tomato sauce. Spread each tortilla with a spoonful of sauce, 1 heaping tablespoon of chicken or turkey, a sprinkling of cheese and onion greens. Carefully roll the tortillas up and nestle them gently in the casserole seam-side down. Spoon remaining sauce over the enchiladas and sprinkle a handful of cheese across the top. Bake in pre-heated 350° oven until cheese melts and edges are bubbly — 30 to 45 minutes.

May be prepared a day or two ahead, refrigerated and then heated for about 1 hour. Preparing the dish ahead enhances the flavors even more.

Serve with Zinfandel

Tomato Chicken Fricassee

Serves 6

Recipe contributed by Patrice Martin; Martin Brothers Winery, Paso Robles

Patrice Martin serves this Italian inspired chicken dish with fried polenta and a tossed green salad. This dish, which uses only one spice, is a good complement to Zinfandel.

3½ to 4 lbs. chicken thighs	2 medium-sized onions, chopped
2 tablespoons olive oil	2 tablespoons marjoram
2 lbs. fresh plum tomatoes, chopped (3 cups canned plus the juices may be substituted)	1 cup Zinfandel
	salt and pepper to taste

Wash the chicken pieces and pat dry. In a large skillet heat the oil and quickly brown the chicken pieces. Add the remaining ingredients, adjust heat to a slow simmer, cover and cook. After 10 minutes, remove the cover and cook until the chicken is very well done and the sauce has thickened, about 25 minutes. Add more wine if needed. Serve with freshly grated Parmesan cheese on the side.

Carol's Chicken Supreme

Serves 4   *Serve with Chardonnay*

Recipe contributed by Carol Anderson; S. Anderson Wine Cellars, Napa

The trick to making this flavorful sauce is to boil down each additional liquid to keep it smooth. Serve with Savory Rice (page 345).

2 whole chicken breasts, boned, skinned and halved	¾ cup chicken stock
white pepper to taste	½ cup port
2 tablespoons butter	¾ cup heavy cream
juice of 2 oranges	minced parsley

Flatten chicken breasts slightly and season with white pepper. Heat butter in a heavy frying pan over medium-high heat until butter is bubbly. Add chicken breasts and sauté for 3 minutes on one side. Turn and sauté for 2 more minutes. Chicken should be golden brown and springy to the touch. Remove chicken to heated platter and keep warm in very low oven.

To the same frying pan add orange juice and cook down over medium heat until it is thick and bubbly. Add chicken stock and again boil until thick and bubbly, stirring occasionally. Add the port and repeat the process. Finally add the cream and reduce again, stirring, until sauce coats the spoon heavily. Return chicken breasts to pan, turning pieces to cover them with sauce. Serve chicken with sauce spooned over and sprinkled with a little minced parsley.

Author's note: Do not cook chicken any longer than specified. It will continue to cook in the oven.

Chicken Jack Sandwiches

Serves 4   *Serve with Sauvignon Blanc*

Recipe contributed by Alan Berris; Santa Ynez Valley Winery, Santa Ynez

This recipe makes four hefty sandwiches, each one a meal in itself. For variety, try using chopped turkey or pork, and with Chardonnay to bring out the stronger flavors of those meats.

12 oz. cooked chicken, chopped	1 clove garlic, minced
4 tablespoons butter	¼ cup Sauvignon Blanc
1 onion chopped	sour cream
1 cup mushrooms, sliced	1 medium avocado, thinly sliced
¼ teaspoon white pepper	4 slices Monterey Jack cheese
¼ teaspoon celery seed	8 thick slices sourdough bread

In a large frying pan sauté chicken, onion and mushrooms in 1 tablespoon butter over medium-high heat. Add seasonings and wine and continue sautéing for a few minutes. Set aside.

To make sandwiches, spread sour cream on 4 slices of sourdough bread, put on a layer of sliced avocado, a layer of chicken mixture and a layer of cheese. Spread sour cream on the remaining bread and close up the sandwiches. Heat remaining butter in frying pan and grill sandwiches.

Oriental Duck with Plum Sauce

Serves 4

Recipe contributed by Alexandra Casey; St. Clement Vineyards, St. Helena

Alexandra Casey uses a smoker with hickory chips to prepare the duck. Preparation instructions are given both for the smoker and for oven roasting.

1 5-lb. duckling	**PLUM SAUCE**
6 green onions	1 1-lb. can purple plums
5 sprigs parsley	¼ teaspoon grated orange peel
1 clove garlic, minced	3 tablespoons orange juice
⅓ cup soy sauce	2 tablespoons sugar
2 tablespoons lemon juice	¼ teaspoon cinnamon
2 tablespoons honey	½ teaspoon Worcestershire sauce

Rinse the duck with cold water and pat dry. Stuff cavity with green onions, parsley and garlic. Close cavity with trussing needles. Truss duckling. Make glaze: combine soy sauce, lemon juice and honey in a small saucepan and heat to combine ingredients. Smoke for 5 to 6 hours, basting occasionally with the glaze.

To oven roast, proceed as above. Instead of placing duck in smoker, put it in a flat ovenproof dish and baste with the glaze. Roast in a preheated 325° oven for about 3 hours or until done. Occasionally remove fat and the juices from the pan. Baste 3 or 4 times during baking.

To make the plum sauce, drain plums and reserve ¼ cup of the syrup. Force the plums through a sieve. Combine the plum purée with the reserved syrup and the remaining ingredients. Simmer in a small saucepan for 15 minutes. Serve over duck.

Wild Rice Stuffing

Makes 5 cups

Recipe from Katherine Bartolucci; Mont St. John Cellars, Napa

This light stuffing is a change from the traditional ones used to stuff the holiday bird. It can also be used with wild or domestic duck or goose. With any of these, Katherine serves a full-bodied Chardonnay.

⅓ cup chopped onions	¼ lb. sausage meat
4 tablespoons butter	3 cups cooked wild rice
1 cup chopped fresh mushrooms	1 teaspoon salt

In a medium-sized skillet over medium-high heat, melt 2 tablespoons of butter and sauté onions until lightly browned, about 5 minutes. Remove onions to a medium-sized bowl. Sauté mushrooms in remaining butter for 5 minutes. Add mushrooms to the bowl. In the same skillet, fry sausage meat until lightly browned, stirring constantly. Remove skillet from heat and stir in onions and mushrooms. Using the same bowl, gently stir together the wild rice and salt, and the sausage mixture.

This makes a very light stuffing, enough for a 10-lb. turkey.

Baked Cornish Game Hens

Serves 3

Serve with Zinfandel

Recipe contributed by Joel Peterson; Ravenswood Winery, Sonoma

Baked games hens can be the basis for a fall or winter dinner menu when served with polenta or buttered noodles. A vegetable such as peas or snow peas complete the meal.

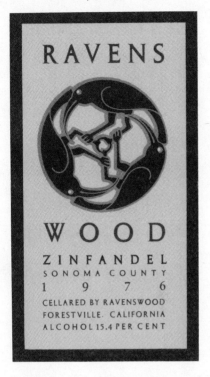

3 Cornish game hens	4 cloves garlic, peeled
2 to 3 tablespoons olive oil	6 sprigs fresh rosemary
1 teaspoon powdered cumin	1 cup Zinfandel
salt and ground pepper to taste	

Preheat oven to 350°. Sprinkle game hens with cumin, salt and pepper. Heat oil in an 8-quart Dutch oven. Add games hens and garlic, and brown over moderate heat for approximately 10 minutes. When birds are nicely browned, add rosemary. Cover the pot and place in oven for 45 minutes to 1 hour, or until birds are done.

Remove game hens and keep warm. Discard the rosemary. Skim fat from the juices in the pot. Mash the soft garlic cloves and deglaze the juices with Zinfandel. Increase heat and reduce liquid to about ⅔ the original volume. To serve, place each hen on an individual plate and spoon some sauce over it.

Author's note: This method of cooking produces a very moist and flavorful dish. The amount of garlic may be increased or decreased to your preference

Fred's Game Hens with Gravy

Serves 4

Serve with White Riesling

Recipe contributed by Fred Scherrer; Greenwood Ridge Vineyards, Philo

In this recipe, the game hens derive an interesting additional flavor from the apples and onions, and the gravy is given an added "zing" by the White Riesling.

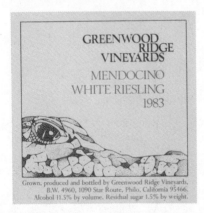

4 Cornish game hens	½ cup White Riesling
poultry seasoning to taste	2 tablespoons cornstarch
1 or 2 Pippin apples	2 tablespoons flour
1 red onion	¾ cup water
4 tablespoons soft butter	salt to taste

Preheat oven to 375°. Rinse hens and pat with poultry seasoning. Slice apples and onion and stuff the hens with them. Place hens in small roasting pan and place in oven. After 15 minutes, remove hens from oven and smear with butter. Roast another 15 minutes, then add wine to the pan. Bake 30 minutes more, basting 3 or 4 times to get flavors from hens into the liquid. Remove hens to a warm platter and keep warm while making gravy.

In a jar combine cornstarch and flour with ½ cup water. Shake well to blend. Add ¼ cup water to drippings in pan. Cook over medium heat for a few minutes to blend, scraping the sides to pick up any brown residue. Add salt to taste. Gradually add just enough of the flour mixture to thicken gravy to desired consistency, stirring constantly to blend. Serve with game hens.

Paella Sonoma

Serves 8

Created by Students of the San Francisco Culinary Academy for Landmark Vineyards, Windsor

1984

LANDMARK

CHARDONNAY
SONOMA COUNTY

PRODUCED AND BOTTLED BY LANDMARK VINEYARDS
WINDSOR, CA • BW 4731 • ALCOHOL 13.4% BY VOLUME

Paella Sonoma was the main course served at the October, 1985 luncheon created by students chefs of the San Francisco Culinary Academy for Landmark Vineyards. See page 209 for the full menu of that notable meal. For directions on peeling peppers refer to Two Bell Pepper Soup, page 236.

1 large onion, diced

2 cups rice

2 red and 2 green bell peppers, roasted, peeled and diced

4 cloves garlic, minced

olive oil

2 ducks, disjointed, cut into 8 pieces each

6 small sausages, hot and mild

8 each mussels and clams, scrubbed

2 cups Chardonnay

2 cups chicken stock

3 tomatoes, peeled, seeded and diced

1 teaspoon saffron threads

salt, pepper and cayenne to taste

8 baby zucchini, blanched

8 medium prawns, shelled and deveined

In a medium-sized skillet sauté onion, rice, peppers and garlic in olive oil. Grill duck and sausage over wood in a barbecue until crispy and rare (15 to 20 minutes — less time for sausages). Combine rice mixture, duck and sausages in a large baking pan.

Steam mussels and clams in Chardonnay about 2 minutes. (They will not be cooked through.) Reduce cooking liquid to 1 cup and strain. Combine cooking liquid, chicken stock and tomatoes.

Add saffron to rice-duck mixture. Add stock combination and season with salt, pepper and cayenne. Cover with foil and bake in preheateed 375° oven for 20 minutes. Add clams, mussels and zucchini on top and recover with foil. Bake 10 more minutes. Meanwhile, in a medium-sized skillet sauté prawns in olive oil until they just turn pink. Serve Paella Sonoma on large plates, making certain each serving has one of each shellfish, a zucchini and pieces of duck and sausage. Top each serving with a prawn.

Stuffed Trout with Asparagus

Recipe contributed by Bill Anderson; Chateau Julien, Carmel

Serves 2   *Serve with Sauvignon Blanc*

Bill Anderson is an expert at pairing food and wine and has created this most unusual recipe for trout. The spices and stuffing of the trout are a perfect complement to the sauce and the asparagus.

3 celery stalks, finely chopped	4 strips medium cooked bacon, chopped
1 cup small mushrooms, finely chopped	2 boned trout
¼ cup blanched almonds, finely chopped	4 tablespoons butter
1 cup canned baby clams, chopped	1 tablespoon reserved bacon drippings
pinch tarragon	3 tablespoons flour
pinch sweet basil	½ cup clam juice
2 cloves garlic, finely chopped	½ cup Sauvignon Blanc
	¾ lb. fresh asparagus

In a medium-sized bowl mix together chopped celery, mushrooms and almonds. Fold in clams, tarragon, basil, garlic and chopped bacon bits. Stuff trout with the mixture and seal fish with small skewers or toothpicks.

In an 8×14-inch glass baking dish place 2 tablespoons butter. Put dish in preheated 350° oven until butter is melted. Remove pan from oven and gently place the stuffed trout in the baking dish. Cover dish with aluminum foil with one corner folded back slightly. Bake trout in 350° oven for 20 to 25 minutes.

While trout is baking, place 2 tablespoons butter in medium-sized frying pan with the bacon drippings. Heat to slightly bubbling. Stir in flour and continue to stir while thickening, lower heat. Slowly stir in clam juice and Sauvignon Blanc. Add more liquid if sauce is too thick.

Steam asparagus until tender. When trout is cooked, place it and the asparagus on a platter. Pour sauce over both. Serve.

Serve with Chardonnay

Fish with White Wine Sauce

Serves 4

Recipe contributed by Nancy Hart; Hart Winery, Temecula

Nancy Hart serves this fish entrée with rice and steamed broccoli. The recipe may also be served as a first course for 8.

1½ lbs. fillets of sole or red snapper	½ teaspoon brown mustard
6 tablespoons butter	½ teaspoon Worcestershire sauce
4 tablespoons flour	dash each salt, pepper and thyme
½ cup milk	1 tablespoon chopped parsley
¾ cup cream	1 tablespoon chopped green onion
½ cup Chardonnay	½ cup freshly grated Parmesan cheese
2 tablespoons mayonnaise	paprika
2 tablespoons dry sherry	
1 teaspoon lemon juice	

Place fillets in a buttered 9 × 11-inch baking dish or individual casseroles.

In a small saucepan melt the butter, stir in flour and add milk, cream and wine, whisking mixture until it comes to a boil and thickens. Add all other ingredients except Parmesan cheese and paprika, and stir to combine. Spoon sauce over fish. Sprinkle with Parmesan cheese and paprika. Bake in preheated 400° oven for about 15 minutes or until fish flakes easily and is done.

Serve with Chardonnay

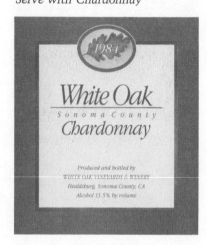

Red Salmon with Chardonnay

Serves 4

Recipe contributed by Bill Myers; White Oak Vineyards and Winery, Healdsburg

Bill Myers's recipe for salmon steaks is one which he has prepared often on his own Alaskan fishing boats and back home in the Sonoma wine country.

½ cup teriyaki sauce	½ cup butter
2 cups Chardonnay	juice of ½ lemon
4 salmon steaks, 1¼ inch thick	2 cups cooked short grain rice

In a small bowl combine teriyaki sauce and 1 cup Chardonnay. Place salmon steaks in an 8 × 8-inch baking dish. Dot salmon evenly with butter. Pour marinade over the salmon and let stand 1 hour. Just before cooking sprinkle the fish with lemon juice.

Broil 6 inches from heat for about 15 minutes, basting with some of the marinade every 2 to 3 minutes, so that fish will develop a slight crust. Do not overcook fish. Place the cooked rice on a heated platter and top with the salmon steaks. Keep warm. Drain juices into a small saucepan and add 1 cup of Chardonnay. Heat and boil down for a few minutes. Serve on the salmon.

Author's note: Short-grained, or calrose rice, is dense and moist when cooked enabling sauces to adhere to it easily.

Trout El Dorado

Serves 4

Serve with Semillon or Chenin Blanc

Recipe contributed by Greg Boeger; Boeger Winery, Placerville

Greg Boeger had been trout fishing in the mountain streams of El Dorado County for years before he ever thought of building a winery in that county. Susan Boeger's traditional "opening day of trout season" dinner also includes tagliarini with a light pesto sauce and fresh homegrown "horse beans" (fava beans). A tossed salad is served after the main course so that the vinegar does not spoil the taste of the wine.

4 to 6 trout	**oregano leaves**
salt and pepper	**powdered sage**
butter	**thyme leaves**
4 to 6 sprigs fresh mint	**1 lemon**
chopped fresh parsley	**dry white wine**

Salt and pepper body cavity of each trout and arrange in buttered baking dish. Place one sprig of mint inside each fish. Sprinkle the fish lightly with chopped parsley, oregano, sage, thyme, and squeeze lemon juices over all. Add wine to a depth of ¼ inch and cover dish with foil. Bake in a preheated 350° oven for approximately 20 minutes, or until done.

Fish with Herb Wine Sauce

Serves 2

Serve with Chenin Blanc

Recipe contributed by Echo Freestone; Britton Cellars, Temecula

Echo Freestone recently started this new wineryand became very involved in the marketing of its wines, so she likes to prepare entrées that are not time consuming. Her Fish with Herb Wine Sauce has interesting flavor combinations which go well with a Chenin Blanc.

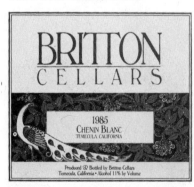

1 lb. fish fillets — sole, cod or red snapper	**½ cup dry sherry**
½ cup milk	**½ teaspoon dry dill**
½ teaspoon salt	**½ teaspoon tarragon**
½ to ¾ cup flour	**2 tablespoons capers**
¼ cup olive oil	**¼ cup slivered almonds**
	parsley sprigs for garnish

Soak fish in milk in the refrigerator for 2 hours. Mix flour and salt together. Remove fish from milk, shaking off any excess liquid. Coat fish with flour mixture. Heat olive oil in skillet and sauté fish until golden brown on both sides. Do not overcook. Remove fish to heated platter and place in oven to keep warm. Add wine, dill and tarragon to pan drippings and simmer until liquid reduces slightly. Add capers and almonds and pour over fish on heated platter. Serve garnished with parsley sprigs.

Pesce con Pesto

(Fish with Pesto Sauce)

Recipe contributed by Theresa Rochioli; J. Rochioli Vineyards and Winery, Healdsburg

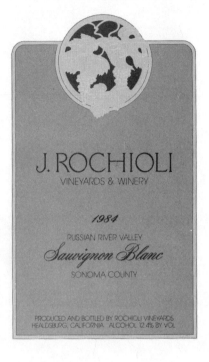

Although Theresa Rochioli is of Irish decent she does like to prepare many of her Italian husband's family recipes. She usually serves strips of sautéed zucchini, warm French bread and a simple salad of butter lettuce with this fish dish.

1 lb. fish fillets	¼ cup olive oil
butter, room temperature	¼ cup fresh grated Parmesan cheese
lemon slices	2 tablespoons fresh parsley
PESTO	¼ teaspoon pepper
2 cups basil leaves	
4 to 5 cloves garlic	

Pesto: Put basil leaves and garlic in food processor and chop until very fine. Add oil, cheese and parsley and continue to process until well mixed. Add pepper and mix again.

Preheat broiler. Line broiler pan with aluminum foil and spread fish fillets on foil. Spread small amount of butter on one side of fish and broil for 2 to 3 minutes. Turn fish over and spread with butter and pesto mixture. Broil for 2 to 3 more minutes or until fish flakes easily with fork. Serve with lemon slices.

Author's note: If fish fillets are very thin, lower broiler rack so as not to overcook and burn the fish. Extra pesto will store in the refrigerator for 3 to 4 weeks or it may be frozen. Also good with pasta.

Poached Halibut with Cucumber

Recipe contributed by Ben Zeitman; Amador Foothill Winery, Plymouth

Ben Zeitman says this is an easy dish to prepare. He likes to serve it with boiled small red potatoes and steamed broccoli.

2 halibut fillets	4 oz. heavy cream
2 oz. Fumé Blanc or dry Sauvignon Blanc	1 tablespoon lemon juice
1 oz. clam juice, optional	salt and pepper to taste
2 tablespoons cucumber, peeled, seeded and diced	2 tablespoons cold butter, cut into pieces
	¼ cup fresh chopped dill

Place the halibut steaks in a nonstick pan. Surround with cucumber; add the wine and the clam juice. Cover tightly, bring to a gentle simmer and continue simmering until fish is done, 4 to 5 minutes. Test for doneness. If not done simmer 1 to 2 minutes longer. Carefully remove fillets to warm plates. Reduce poaching liquid if necessary, then add cream and reduce until sauce begins to thicken. Add lemon juice and salt and pepper to taste. Add the butter and swirl to incorporate. Sprinkle with dill, then pour over fish.

Author's note: The degree of doneness varies with individual taste. If a soft fish is desired start checking doneness after 3 minutes of cooking time.

Barbecued Fillet of Red Snapper

Serves 4

Serve with Fumé Blanc

Recipe contributed by Keith and Marian Lamb; Chateau De Leu, Suisun City

Keith barbecues the fish while Marian prepares the sauce. This joint effort results in an easy and delicious way to prepare Pacific red snapper. Brushing the fish with mayonnaise keeps it from sticking to the grill. Steamed Brussels sprouts and steamed small red potatoes complete the entrée.

2 lbs. red snapper fillets or any firm fish

mayonnaise

½ cup Japanese soy sauce

¼ cup Fumé Blanc

SAUCE

⅓ cup butter

⅓ cup margarine

3 green onions, chopped

4 tablespoons slivered blanched almonds

4 teaspoons fresh chopped parsley

¼ cup Fumé Blanc

Light charcoal briquets and let them become white hot. (This takes about 15 to 20 minutes) Grill should be about 5 inches above the coals.

Brush the fillets with mayonnaise on both sides. Pour a little of the soy sauce over the fish. Do not saturate it. Peek under the fish gently to check the progress of the browning. Handle fish gently. After 5 minutes turn the fish and baste with additional soy sauce. A minute or two before total cooking time spoon the Fumé Blanc over the fish and let the fillets absorb the wine. The total cooking time for the fish is about 10 minutes. Fish should still be firm, but flake easily when a fork is inserted into thickest part.

While fish is cooking or just before cooking prepare sauce by melting the butter and margarine in a small saucepan. Add green onions, almonds, parsley and ¼ cup Fumé Blanc. Reheat until warmed through, but do not boil. Serve fish on individual plates and spoon some sauce over each serving.

Barbecued Fresh Salmon

Serves 6 to 8

Recipe contributed by Polly Mullen; Woodside Vineyards, Woodside

Polly Mullen has used this recipe for barbecued salmon for over thirty years. She usually serves her Green Pea Salad with the fresh fish (see page 244). The accompanying sauce may also be served with any other fish.

6 to 8 lb. whole salmon	**SAUCE**
bacon drippings	2 cups sour cream
fresh lemon juice	¼ cup mayonnaise
black pepper	¼ cup catsup
dill weed	1 tablespoon horseradish
	1 tablespoon Dijon mustard
	⅓ cup capers, drained

Have seafood vendor "back-fillet" the fish, removing only the center bone, but leaving the fish whole. Spread bacon drippings over the outside of the salmon very thickly. Squeeze lemon juice over entire fish and sprinkle with pepper and dill weed. Place on heavy aluminum foil, lifting edges to prevent fire from flaming. Place over medium fire on the grill. Cover and cook for 15 to 20 minutes, checking after 15 minutes for doneness. Do not overcook.

To make the sauce blend together the sour cream, mayonnaise and catsup in a medium-sized bowl. Add the horseradish, mustard and capers. Blend well. Serve with fish.

Author's note: If you like, add ¼ cup chopped fresh dill or 1 tablespoon dried dill to the sauce.

Prawns and Vermouth

Serves 4

Recipe contributed by Joel Peterson; Ravenswood Winery, Sonoma

Joel Peterson loves to experiment with different food tastes to determine which ones are complementary. He likes to serve this prawn dish with pasta or Japanese noodles. A dandelion or chicory and radicchio salad is the perfect accompaniment.

2 tablespoons butter	1 cup vermouth
2 shallots, chopped	1 lb. prawns, shelled, deveined
2 cloves garlic, minced	and butterflied
⅓ cup sun-dried tomatoes	½ cup cream
small pinch red pepper flakes	¼ cup chopped parsley

In a large skillet melt butter over medium heat and sauté shallots, garlic and sun-dried tomatoes until soft. Add red pepper flakes, vermouth and prawns. Cook over medium heat for 3 to 5 minutes or until prawns are just done. Do not overcook. Remove prawns to a warm plate. Add cream and reduce sauce by half. Return prawns to pan along with chopped parsley and warm briefly. Serve at once. Excellent with fresh pasta or Japanese noodles.

Author's note: Use red pepper flakes sparingly. If sun-dried tomatoes are unavailable, substitute ⅓ cup chopped fresh tomatoes and add along with the parsley.

Saffron Mussels with Semillon

Serves 4   *Serve with Semillon*

Recipe contributed by Terry Tenopir for Ahlgren Vineyard, Boulder Creek

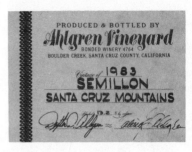

This mussel recipe may be served as an appetizer for 6 accompanied by French bread. As a main course it may be served with fresh pasta and a tossed salad.

1 clove garlic, crushed	small pinch of saffron
2 tablespoons butter	1½ lbs. mussels
2 tablespoons minced shallots	2 oz. heavy cream
1¼ cup Semillon	2 tablespoons each finely chopped
freshly ground pepper	parsley and minced chives

Over low heat, in a large heavy stainless steel or enamel skillet, cook garlic in butter until it turns color. Discard garlic. Add shallots to butter and sauté lightly. Add wine and 3 to 4 grinds from the pepper mill. Bring mixture to a boil and over high heat reduce by half. Add saffron and mussels. Cover pan. Shake pan lightly over the heat for 1 to 2 minutes until shells open. Add cream and cook for 1 to 2 minutes. Add parsley and chives and cook for an additional 30 seconds.

With a slotted spoon, remove mussels to serving bowls. Keep warm. Continue boiling sauce until it is reduced to a nice, rich consistency. Pour over mussels and serve.

Shrimp Creole

Serves 6   *Serve with Cabernet Sauvignon*

Recipe contributed by Gary Eberle; Eberle Winery, Paso Robles

Gary, who loves to cook, especially enjoys the cuisine of Louisiana where he lived for some time. This dish is a good example of that style of cooking.

6 tablespoons butter	½ teaspoon Tabasco sauce
2 medium-sized onions, chopped	1 bay leaf, crumbled
1 cup chopped celery	½ teaspoon powdered thyme
1 green pepper, chopped	¾ teaspoon basil
3 cloves garlic, minced	1 16-oz. can whole tomatoes
1 teaspoon salt	1 4-oz. can tomato sauce
¼ teaspoon black pepper	1 cup red wine
½ teaspoon cayenne	2 lbs. medium to large shrimp, shelled and deveined

In a large saucepan melt the butter over medium heat. Add onions, celery, green pepper and garlic and sauté until the onions are soft. Then add the remaining ingredients except the shrimp. Simmer sauce for 45 minutes. Add shrimp, turn heat up to medium and cook for about 7 minutes or until shrimp turn pink. Do not overcook the shrimp. Serve over individual portions of steamed rice.

Zinfandel Seafood Stew

Serves 8 to 10

Recipe contributed by Kathy Collins; Conn Creek Winery, St. Helena

Kathy Collins often serves this seafood stew to V.I.P. visitors to the winery. The seasonings do not vary, but the seafood depends on the availability of fresh fish at the moment.

SAUCE

2 yellow onions, chopped

2 leeks, coarsely chopped

2 red and 2 green peppers, seeded and chopped

2 fennel bulbs, chopped

2 stalks celery, chopped

2 cloves garlic, minced

¼ cup olive oil

4 tablespoons butter

1 bottle Zinfandel

3 cups clam juice

7 tomatoes, seeded and chopped

1 cup tomato sauce

1 bay leaf

1 tablespoon each fresh basil, oregano and thyme

¼ teaspoon Tabasco sauce

salt and pepper to taste

juice of 1 large lemon

STEW

2 lbs. shrimp, shelled and deveined

2 lbs. red snapper, sea bass, or lingcod, cut in bite-sized pieces

1 lb. scallops

2 or 3 clams per person

2 or 3 mussels per person

1 crab leg per person

fennel seeds

chopped parsley

¼ fresh lemon per person

In a large kettle sauté first seven ingredients in oil and butter over medium heat until tender. Add wine, clam juice, tomatoes, tomato sauce and seasonings. Heat to a gentle boil, reduce heat and simmer uncovered for about 1 hour. (This sauce can be made a day in advance.)

Before adding seafood, remove bay leaf, check seasonings, add lemon juice and additional wine to taste. To simmering sauce add clams and firm white-fleshed fish stirring gently for about 5 minutes. Then add remaining seafood and cook over low heat until shrimp turn pink. Be careful not to overcook the seafood.

Serve in warm soup bowls; garnish with several fennel seeds, parsley and lemon. Serve with French bread.

Chardonnay Seafood Casserole

Serves 6 to 8

Serve with Chardonnay

Recipe contributed by Tim Siemsen; Chateau Julien, Carmel

Tim Siemsen has created this California seafood dish to pair with California Chardonnay.

¼ cup olive oil

1½ cups chopped onions

1 cup julienned green bell pepper

1½ cups potatoes, peeled and diced

1 teaspoon salt

½ teaspoon pepper

1 clove garlic, minced

2 teaspoons chopped bay leaves

2 cups Chardonnay

4 teaspoons tomato paste

1 lb. fillet of sole, cut into bite-sized pieces

1 lb. raw shrimp, shelled and deveined

½ lb. cooked crabmeat

2 teaspoons minced parsley

sautéed French bread for garnish

Heat oil in a "stovetop-to-table" casserole and sauté onions over low heat for 10 minutes. Add green pepper and potatoes and cook for 5 minutes. Add salt, pepper, garlic, bay leaves, wine and tomato paste. Cover and cook over low heat for 20 minutes. Add filet of Sole and cook for five minutes. Mix in shrimp and cook covered for an additional 7 minutes or until shrimp turn pink. Do not overcook the fish. Add cooked crabmeat and cook just to heat through. Sprinkle with parsley. Arrange sautéed French bread slices as a garnish around the edges of the casserole. Serve.

Stuffed Mussels á la Sea Ridge

Serves 6 to 8 as entrée

Serve with Sauvignon Blanc

Recipe contributed by Tim Schmidt and Dan Wickham; Sea Ridge Winery, Cazadero

This recipe is influenced by Tim Schmidt's and Dan Wickham's interest in marine biology. It is a unique method of preparing mussels and may be served as an entrée or as hors d'oeuvres, in which case figure on 2 or 3 stuffed shells per person.

2 dozen live mussels (will yield approx. 2 cups chopped meat)

1 cup Sauvignon Blanc

2 cloves garlic, minced

½ cup chopped green onions

¼ cup chopped parsley

½ cup sour cream

½ cup Parmesan cheese

¼ cup bread crumbs

salt and pepper to taste

In a large saucepan steam the mussels in the wine for about 5 minutes. Remove mussels and remove meat from shells, saving the shells. Chop the meat and place in a bowl. Add the rest of the ingredients, mixing thoroughly. Fill the half shells of the mussels and place on cookie sheet. Bake in preheated 375° oven for 10 to 15 minutes until bubbling and browned on top. Garnish with a little more chopped parsley and serve either as an entrée or as an hors d'oeuvre.

California Cold Seafood Platter

Serves 8

Recipe contributed by Elinor Travers; Mayacamas Vineyards, Napa

Elinor Travers serves this seafood platter either as a luncheon or supper entrée on a warm summer day. The three dressings are good complements to the wine. Prepare the seafood early so it has time to chill.

8 salmon steaks	**1 fresh cooked Dungeness crab**
2 dozen mussels	**lettuce leaves and lemon slices for garnish**

Poach salmon steaks and refrigerate. Steam mussels and refrigerate. Clean and crack crab. Prepare the sauces. Sauce #1: Purée 1 cup basil leaves with ¼ cup olive oil. Add mayonnaise to taste. Sauce #2: Combine prepared sweet mustard and sour cream, to taste. Sauce #3. Fresh or canned mild tomato salsa.

When ready to serve, arrange seafood on lettuce leaves on a large platter. Garnish with lemon slices. Serve with bowls of the different sauces and let everyone mix and match the various tastes.

Author's note: If Dungeness crab is not available, substitute cold poached lobster or cold cooked prawns.

Asparagus in Crabmeat Sauce

Serves 4

Recipe contributed by Deborah Cahn; Navarro Vineyards, Philo

Deborah Cahn likes to serve Gewurztraminer with Chinese dishes. The spicy quality of the wine is a perfect companion to the many flavor components of oriental dishes. This dish takes just a few minutes to cook. So have everything else ready (rice, for instance) first.

4 cups water	**¼ teaspoon sugar**
3 tablespoons oil	**2 tablespoons peanut oil**
1½ lbs. asparagus, cleaned	**2 teaspoons Gewurztraminer**
1 cup homemade chicken stock	**6 oz. fresh cooked crabmeat**
1 tablespoon cornstarch	**2 egg whites**
¼ teaspoon salt	

In a large saucepan bring the water and 3 tablespoons oil to a boil. Add the asparagus. Bring to a boil and cook over medium heat for 2 minutes. Turn off heat and let asparagus remain in water while preparing the sauce.

Mix the chicken broth with cornstarch, salt and sugar. Heat wok, add the peanut oil. Add chicken stock mixture. Lower heat and stir sauce constantly until it is clear. Stir in the wine. Add the crabmeat. Quickly beat egg whites with a pinch of salt until frothy and add to sauce. Stir gently over low heat until sauce thickens.

Serve asparagus over steamed rice and top with the crabmeat sauce.

Author's note: If using canned broth, eliminate the salt.

Seafood Gumbo

Serves 6 *Serve with Merlot*

Recipe contributed by Sandra P. MacIver; Matanzas Creek Winery, Santa Rosa

Having been brought up in New Orleans, Sandra MacIver enjoys cooking gumbo and other New Orleans specialities. Warm French bread with sweet butter and a green salad emphasizing fresh herbs complete the main course.

STOCK

3 quarts water

shrimp shells and/or top shells of crabs (see below)

3 carrots, cut in large pieces

3 stalks celery, cut in large pieces

2 bay leaves

several sprigs of parsley

GUMBO

½ stick butter

1 large onion, chopped

2 cups chopped green onions

2 cups sliced okra

1 cup finely chopped green peppers

3 tablespoons butter

3 tablespoons flour

1 16-oz. can whole tomatoes

1 tablespoon filé powder (optional)

2 quarts stock (above)

1 California Dungeness crab or 3 Gulf of Mexico crabs, broken into eighths or quarters, top shell reserved for stock

2 to 3 cups peeled shrimp, shells reserved for stock

2 to 3 cups raw shelled oysters

salt, pepper and cayenne to taste

3 cups cooked rice

In a large saucepan combine the stock ingredients and simmer over low heat until boiled down to 2 quarts. Strain and set aside.

Melt the butter in a large pot over medium heat and sauté onion, green onions, okra and green peppers until soft. In a separate large frying pan make a roux of the 3 tablespoons butter and flour, cooking slowly and stirring constantly until brown. Add tomatoes and optional filé powder and cook to a paste. Add some stock to the roux, then add roux to sautéed onion mixture followed by remaining stock, stirring constantly. Bring to a simmer and add crab, shrimp and oysters. Add salt, pepper and cayenne to taste (should be spicy). Simmer very gently for 1½ hours. Serve in large soup bowls over rice.

Shrimp Curry

Serves 4

Recipe contributed by Christine DeLoach; DeLoach Vineyards, Santa Rosa

This simple to prepare shrimp curry is a favorite of the DeLoaches. Curried dishes go particularly well with Gewurztraminer — after all, the German word "gewurz" means spice.

1 stalk celery, finely chopped	**1 lb. shrimp, shelled and deveined**
1 onion, finely chopped	**1 cup chicken broth**
½ green pepper, chopped	**½ cup milk**
½ cup butter	**1 tablespoon flour**
2 tablespoons curry powder, or more to taste	

In a large skillet sauté celery, onions and green pepper in melted butter until onion is golden in color. Add curry powder and sauté a few minutes to blend. Add shrimp and cook until they just turn pink, approximately 5 to 6 minutes depending on size. Remove shrimp mixture to a warm platter. Add chicken stock and simmer for 5 minutes to blend flavors. Combine milk and flour to a smooth consistency. Add a little at a time to the liquid in the pan, stirring continuously until sauce reaches desired consistency. Pour sauce over shrimp.

Serve with steamed rice, passing condiments such as chutney, coconut, peanuts and raisins.

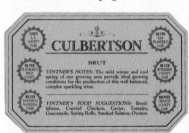

Shrimps in Mustard Sauce

Serves 4

Recipe contributed by Martha M. Culbertson; John Culbertson Winery, Fallbrook

Martha Culbertson, who studied with Julia Child, Jacques Pepin and Simone Beck, enjoys serving food with champagne. She has been quite instrumental in acquainting the public with the various ways champagne may be served other than as an apéritif. Shrimps in Mustard Sauce may be served as an entrée or the recipe will serve 8 as a first course. Martha Culbertson is also the owner of the Fallbrook Grocery, one of the leading restaurants of the San Diego area.

24 large fresh shrimps, shelled and deveined	**1 cup unsalted butter, diced**
2 tablespoons oil	**2 tablespoons Dijon mustard**
2 shallots, minced	**salt and pepper to taste**
½ cup champagne brut	**lemon juice to taste**
½ cup heavy cream	**green onions for garnish**

In a large skillet in hot oil stir-fry shrimp for about 1 minute. Remove to a plate and keep warm. The shrimp will be underdone. Sauté shallots for a minute. Pour in the champagne and cream. Cook over medium heat until slightly thickened. Whisk in butter, bit by bit, and whisk in mustard. DO NOT BOIL, or mustard will separate. Add salt and pepper and lemon juice to taste. Return shrimps to the sauce just to warm them. Serve on warmed plates garnished with onion brushes.

Seafood Casserole

Serves 8

Serve with Chardonnay

Recipe contributed by Audrey Cilurzo; Cilurzo Vineyard and Winery, Temecula

Serve this seafood "stew" with a green salad and sourdough French bread.

2 cups cooked rice

½ cup finely chopped green pepper

1 cup finely chopped onion

½ cup finely chopped celery

1 4½-oz. can water chestnuts, sliced

1 cup mayonnaise

1 cup tomato juice

½ teaspoon salt

⅛ teaspoon pepper

½ lb. fresh shrimp, peeled and deveined

½ lb. fresh cooked crabmeat

½ lb. bay scallops (or large scallops diced)

garlic powder to taste

basil to taste

chopped parsley

¼ cup sliced almonds

1 cup shredded Cheddar cheese

paprika

In a buttered 2-quart casserole combine rice, green pepper, onion, celery and water chestnuts. Combine mayonnaise, tomato juice, salt and pepper and pour half over the mixture in casserole. Arrange shrimp, crabmeat and scallops around the edge of the casserole. Leave the center free. Pour remaining tomato juice mixture over the seafood. Sprinkle with garlic powder, basil and parsley. Combine nuts and cheese and arrange in center of casserole. Sprinkle lightly with paprika. Bake, uncovered, in preheated 350° oven for 25 to 30 minutes, or until cheese melts and casserole is bubbly.

Author's note: a 7½-oz. can of crabmeat, well drained, may be substituted for the fresh crab.

Scallops St. Clement

Serves 6

Serve with Sauvignon Blanc

Recipe contributed by Alexandra Casey; St. Clement Vineyards, St. Helena

The trick to this dish is not to overcook the scallops. Have the rest of the meal ready and cook the scallops at the last minute.

1½ lbs. bay scallops

salt and pepper

flour

3 tablespoons butter

3 cloves garlic, finely minced

1½ teaspoons chopped parsley

1½ teaspoons Worcestershire sauce

3 teaspoons lemon juice

1½ teaspoons brandy

Salt and pepper the scallops and roll them in flour. In a large skillet over medium-high heat, melt the butter and sauté the scallops until they are golden. Add the garlic, parsley, Worcestershire sauce and lemon juice. Quickly blend these ingredients in the pan. Add brandy quickly. Heat and flame. Serve over rice.

Gemello Cioppino

Recipe contributed by Sandra Obester; Obester Winery, Half Moon Bay

This delectable fish stew is an Obester-Gemello family favorite. It is a typical Italian recipe passed down through the winemaking Gemello family to granddaughter, Sandra Obester. Crusty French bread and a salad complete the main course.

2 crabs
½ dozen clams or mussels
½ dozen medium or large shrimp
½ lb. scallops
1 or 2 firm fish fillets

SAUCE

½ cup celery
1½ cups chopped onions
¾ cup chopped bell peppers
3 cloves garlic, minced
¼ cup olive oil

1 1-lb. can tomatoes
2 cups Zinfandel
½ cup tomato sauce
3 teaspoons tomato paste
1 teaspoon salt
½ teaspoon oregano
½ teaspoon basil
¼ teaspoon pepper
pinch of cayenne
1 cup chicken broth, as needed
½ cup minced parsley

In a large Dutch oven sauté celery, onions, bell pepper and garlic in olive oil until soft; do not brown. Add remaining sauce ingredients and simmer covered for at least 2 hours.

Clean and remove legs and claws from crabs and divide body into quarters. Clean clams, wash shrimp. DO NOT remove shells from shellfish. Add all the seafood except the scallops to the sauce and simmer covered for about 10 minutes until shrimp turns pink and clam shells open wide. Do not overcook. Add scallops 5 minutes before finished cooking time. Sprinkle with some minced parsley. Serve in soup bowls.

♥ PASTA ♥

Imogene's Fettuccine

Serves 4

Serve with Cabernet Sauvignon

Recipe contributed by Imogene Prager; Prager Winery and Port Works, St. Helena

This dish combines the spices of the pesto sauce and the Italian sausages into a pleasing combination. Hot Garlic bread is the perfect accompaniment. (See Pesce con Pesto for a recipe for pesto sauce.)

16 oz. good quality fettuccine

1½ cups pesto sauce

4 mild Italian sausages

1 green pepper, sliced in 1-inch strips

1 red pepper, sliced in 1-inch strips

1 yellow pepper, sliced in 1-inch strips

2 fresh tomatoes, coarsely chopped

1 onion, sliced thin

6 fresh mushrooms, stems removed and buttons sliced thinly

Cook noodles in salted water until al dente. Drain and toss with pesto sauce on a warm platter. Keep warm while finishing topping.

Remove sausage from casing. Sauté in frying pan until completely cooked, but not dry. Discard all but 1 tablespoon of oil. Add peppers, tomatoes, onion and mushrooms to cooked sausage and cook for 2 minutes or until vegetables are crisp and tender. Spoon vegetables mixture over the noodles and toss lightly.

Pasta with Fresh Tomatoes and Basil

Serves 4

Serve with Chardonnay

Recipe contributed by Aurora Pepi; Robert Pepi Winery, Oakville

Aurora Pepi says that this sauce is excellent when made with garden fresh tomatoes. The basil must be added at the last minute to bring out its full flavor.

7 cloves garlic, finely minced

½ cup olive oil

1½ quarts fresh tomatoes, peeled, seeded and chopped

1 red pepper, seeded and finely chopped

½ cup freshly chopped basil

salt and pepper

1 lb. pasta, cooked al dente

In a large saucepan heat olive oil and sauté the garlic until it begins to color. Then add the tomatoes and red pepper. Sauté over medium-high heat until tomatoes lose the raw look. Simmer slowly for 15 to 20 minutes. Meanwhile cook the pasta al dente. Add salt and pepper to taste and the fresh basil. Immediately toss with the cooked drained pasta. Serve.

A pinch of oregano and chicken bouillon cube may be added at the same time as the tomatoes.

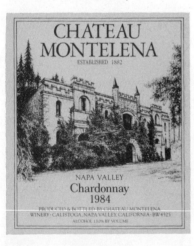

Goat Cheese and Walnuts with Pasta

Serves 2

Recipe contributed by John and Joni Trumbull; Chateau Montelena Winery, Calistoga

The Trumbulls serve this dish for dinner with a salad and French bread. It may also be used as a first course for 6. Homemade noodles are best for this dish. Dry fettuccine or shell pasta may also be used. While the pasta is boiling the sauce can be made since it is quick and simple.

1 lb. pasta	¾ cup walnuts, roughly chopped
⅓ cup olive oil	2 cloves garlic, minced
2 tablespoons butter	¾ cup mild goat cheese

In a large kettle boil water with a little olive oil. Cook pasta to al dente firmness.

Meanwhile, make the sauce by heating olive oil and butter in a medium-sized skillet over medium heat. When warm, add walnuts and garlic. Heat but do not brown the nuts. Oil mixture should be hot enough to melt cheese when combined with pasta and cheese.

Cut cheese into small chunks. When pasta is cooked, drain and put in a heated bowl. Add cheese. Then pour the warm oil mixture over the pasta. Toss. The warm oil will melt the cheese and form a creamy sauce. Serve.

Fettuccine Formaggio e Pomodoro

Serves 4

(Fettuccine with Cheese and Tomato)

Recipe contributed by James P. "Bo" Barrett; Chateau Montelena Winery, Calistoga

Sun-dried tomatoes add a tangy spiciness to this pasta dish. Bo Barrett developed this recipe using his homegrown sun-dried tomatoes which are less salty than the Italian ones. He stresses that it is important to use fresh semolina pasta, with homemade being the best, and to use freshly grated cheese. For variety he may add Italian spices and garlic as the mood strikes him.

3 tablespoons unsalted butter	2 cups freshly grated Parmesan cheese
2 medium shallots, minced	
2 pints heavy cream	½ cup sun-dried tomatoes, drained of olive oil and sliced
2 lbs. fresh semolina fettuccine	salt and white pepper, to taste

In a large kettle boil water, with a splash of olive oil, to cook pasta. Boil the pasta just until al dente and drain and put in heated bowl or warmed plates.

In a heavy medium-sized saucepan melt butter. Add shallots and sauté until translucent. Whisk 1 pint of the cream into the butter. Turn heat to high and when cream is mixed well add the other pint of cream. Keep heat on high to begin rapid reduction of sauce, whisking occasionally.

While cream is reducing, heat the tomato slices in a small frying pan on lowest heat possible. Avoid cooking the tomatoes. When sauce is reduced enough to coat the back of a spoon fairly thickly, whisk in the cheese. Keep heat high to completely melt the cheese. When the sauce is smooth again, not granular, reduce heat to medium-low, to keep sauce warm. Add sun-dried tomatoes to the sauce, mixing them nicely. If some oil is mixed into sauce, just blend it in. Serve sauce over fettuccine.

Fettuccine Alfredo con Prosciutto

Serves 4   *Serve with Chardonnay*

Recipe contributed by Gary Eberle; Eberle Winery, Paso Robles

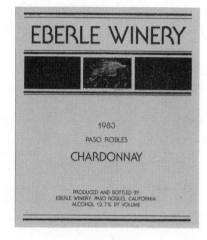

Gary Eberle is extremely fond of pasta. This is his version of the popular Fettuccine Alfredo. The recipe is really like making two sauces and then combining them. One sauce is the classic butter-cream-Parmesan combination; the second contains prosciutto, Italian sausage and mushrooms. The chopped cilantro gives the dish an added zest.

½ lb. butter

4 teaspoons olive oil

½ lb. prosciutto, diced

½ lb. mild Italian sausage, removed from casing

1 cup sliced mushrooms

2 cloves garlic, minced

1 pint heavy cream

1 lb. fettuccine

1 cup freshly grated Parmesan cheese

¼ cup chopped cilantro

In a medium-sized skillet over medium-high heat melt together 1 tablespoon butter and 4 teaspoons olive oil. Lower heat to medium and add prosciutto and sausage. Sauté until sausage is cooked, about 5 minutes. Drain fat. Add mushrooms and garlic and continue cooking for another 5 minutes until mushrooms have wilted.

At the same time, in a medium-sized saucepan melt the remaining butter until just frothy. Slowly add the cream and heat thoroughly, combining the two ingredients well. Continue cooking over medium heat until sauce is reduced slightly and coats the back of a spoon.

Cook fettuccine in boiling salted water with 1 teaspoon of oil added until pasta is al dente. Drain and place pasta in a heated bowl. Add cream sauce and toss. Add sausage mixture and toss again. Add about ½ the Parmesan cheese and the cilantro and toss again. Add more cheese if necessary or pass remainder at the table. Serve.

Author's note: Cream sauce may be cooked in a large enough saucepan so that the pasta, sausage, cheese and cilantro may all be tossed in the same pan and stay hot longer. When tossing the pasta remove pan from heat so as not to boil the ingredients.

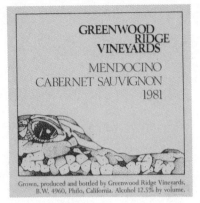

Serve with Cabernet Sauvignon

Ridge-Top Pasta

Serves 3

Recipe contributed by Ellen Saxe; Greenwood Ridge Vineyards, Philo

Ellen Saxe has created this pasta dish to feature the various vegetables grown in her garden. As vegetables ripen, the pasta changes. In the fall, Ellen uses red bell peppers and miniature eggplant instead of peas and squash. Pitted Greek olives are a good substitute for the pumate *(sun-dried tomatoes). Cabernet Sauvignon was chosen to complement the saltiness of the* pumate *or olives and the full flavors of the vegetables.*

½ lb. pasta, fresh if possible, any shape

2 to 3 tablespoons olive oil

1 small onion, finely sliced, or several scallions, sliced

1 clove garlic, minced

¼ lb. mushrooms, sliced

freshly grated Parmesan cheese

8 baby squash — zucchini, scallops, and/or crooknecks, cut lengthwise

1 cup shelled peas or sliced edible-podded peas

4 *pumate* (sun-dried tomatoes) slivered

1 or 2 grates of nutmeg

freshly ground pepper

While cooking pasta al dente in salted water, heat olive oil in large skillet and sauté vegetables in order given. Sauté the vegetables for 3 to 4 minutes. They should still be a little crisp.

Drain pasta and place in heated bowl. Add cooked vegetables and toss, adding a grate or two of nutmeg and some freshly ground pepper. Serve with Parmesan cheese.

Author's note: If using other vegetables, start sautéing those that require the longest cooking first.

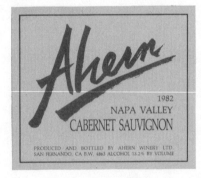

Serve with Cabernet Sauvignon

Hearty Macaroni and Tomatoes

Serves 6 to 8

Recipe contributed by Joyce Ahern; Ahern Winery, San Fernando

Joyce Ahern's recipe includes spinach and carrots which add a different flavor to the usual Italian tomato sauce.

1½ lbs. ground beef

1 large onion

2 stalks celery, chopped

2 small carrots, grated

1 2 lb. 3-oz. can Italian tomatoes

1 12-oz. can tomato sauce

1 teaspoon salt

¾ teaspoon oregano

½ teaspoon pepper

½ teaspoon garlic powder

¾ lb. sea shell or elbow macaroni

1 10-oz. pkg. frozen spinach, partially thawed

1 cup grated Parmesan cheese

In a large saucepan, brown the ground beef. Pour off fat. Add onion, celery and carrots. Cook over medium heat for 5 minutes. Stir in tomatoes and tomato sauce. Season with salt, oregano, pepper and garlic powder. Bring to a boil and simmer, uncovered, for 1 hour (or longer).

Cook the macaroni until al dente. Drain and add to finished sauce. Add the spinach and mix well. Pour into a 13 × 9-inch casserole. Sprinkle top with the Parmesan cheese. Bake in preheated 350° oven for about 30 minutes or until bubbly.

Author's note: Two cups chopped fresh spinach may be substituted for the frozen spinach. Cook sauce and macaroni for 1 to 2 minutes on medium heat to wilt the spinach before placing in baking dish.

Scallop Pasta

Serves 4

Serve with Chardonnay

Recipe contributed by Pam Wilder, Green and Red Vineyard, St. Helena

This dish is a perfect complement to Chardonnay. The light touches of garlic and pepper usually bring out the complex flavors of the wine. The bread crumbs serve the same purpose as using grated cheese with a pasta dish. The bread crumbs, however, are more compatible in flavor with the scallops. Pam uses them with any seafood pasta dish.

½ cup olive oil

2 cloves garlic, peeled

2 tablespoons butter

1 lb. bay scallops

lemon juice

2 sprigs fresh thyme, chopped (or ½ teaspoon dried thyme)

chopped parsley

½ cup dry white wine

3 green onions, sliced

1 red bell pepper, roasted, peeled and cut into strips

1 lb. fettuccine

2 cups fresh bread crumbs, toasted in the oven, then tossed in melted butter and olive oil

Heat olive oil in a large pan over medium-high heat and sauté garlic cloves until they just start to turn color. Remove from pan and discard garlic. Add butter to hot garlic oil and as soon as it melts, add the scallops which have been rinsed and patted dry. Sauté scallops only until they begin to lose their transparency, stirring constantly. Do not overcook. When barely cooked, remove from pan with a slotted spoon and sprinkle with lemon juice, thyme and parsley.

Deglaze the pan with the wine. Boil it down until slightly reduced, then add the green onions and red pepper strips. Sauté vegetables until tender but firm.

Meanwhile cook the pasta until al dente, drain and place in a large warm bowl. Add the scallops to the vegetables and heat through — do not cook — and pour the mixture over the pasta. Mix thoroughly. Serve in individual bowls garnished with bread crumbs. Place rest of bread crumbs in a bowl and pass at the table as you would grated cheese.

Raviolis

Recipe contributed by Dick and Leslie Bush; Madroña Vineyards, Camino

This traditional Italian recipe is made in three steps — well worth the effort. The longer the sauce simmers, the better it is.

TOMATO SAUCE

2 tablespoons olive oil

1 onion chopped fine

2 cloves garlic, minced

4 15-oz. cans tomato sauce

2 6-oz. cans tomato paste

3 cups water

1 cup minced parsley

2 3½-oz. cans mushrooms and juice

salt, pepper, rosemary, marjoram and thyme to taste

FILLING

2 lbs. sausage, or Italian sausage with casing removed

2 10-oz. pkgs. frozen spinach, cooked, drained and chopped fine

½ onion, minced very fine

1½ cloves garlic, minced very fine

¼ cup parsley, chopped fine

½ cup grated Parmesan cheese

2 or 3 eggs

pinch each of thyme and marjoram

PASTA

4 cups flour

2 eggs

½ teaspoon salt

lukewarm water

Step 1. Make sauce. In a large saucepan heat oil and add onion and garlic and cook until lightly browned. Add rest of the sauce ingredients and cook slowly for 4 hours or longer.

Step 2. Make filling. Mix all filling ingredients except the eggs. Add 2 or 3 eggs and combine. It should be a good spreading consistency. Add a speck of thyme and marjoram. Refrigerate until ready to use.

Step 3. Make raviolis. Mix flour, eggs and salt. Add enough lukewarm water to make a firm but elastic dough. Knead on floured board for about 5 minutes. Let dough rest 10 minutes. Break dough into 2 or 3 rounds. Roll each round very thin. Spread some filling over half of each round. Fold the other half over the filling. Roll with ravioli rolling pin and cut apart. Put on floured pan in a single layer, sift a little flour on top and let dry for 1 hour. Cook in boiling salted water for 20 minutes and serve with hot tomato sauce.

Vineyard Pasta

Serves 6   *Serve with Merlot*

Recipe contributed by Fran Replogle; Fenestra Winery, Livermore

Kathy Holland, Fran's sister, developed this interesting way to serve pasta. The inclusion of shitake mushrooms, pancetta (Italian bacon) and grape leaves sets this fettuccine dish apart from the ordinary.

1 whole chicken breast

2 cups chicken broth, canned or homemade

16 oz. fettuccine

2 tablespoons butter

¼ lb. pancetta, cubed

¼ lb. shitake mushrooms (or white mushrooms), sliced

¼ cup pine nuts

¾ cup whipping cream

¼ cup grape leaves (canned), rinsed, drained and shredded

4 tablespoons Parmesan cheese, freshly grated

salt and pepper to taste

Place chicken breast and chicken broth in a medium-sized pan. Bring to a boil and cook over low heat for 20 minutes. Remove chicken and cool. (Save broth for a later use.) Bone, remove skin and shred meat. Set aside.

Bring 4 quarts of lightly salted water to a boil. Drop fettuccine into water and cook for about 8 minutes or until al dente. Drain well.

While noodles are cooking prepare sauce. Melt butter in large skillet and sauté cubed pancetta lightly. Remove pancetta. In remaining butter, sauté mushrooms and pine nuts until lightly browned. Remove mushrooms and pine nuts and set aside. To pan juices add whipping cream and cook until slightly reduced.

Add noodles to reduced cream. Toss in shredded chicken, grape leaves, pancetta, mushrooms and pine nuts. Gently fold in cheese. Salt and pepper to taste. Serve immediately.

Linguine with Clam Sauce

Serves 4 to 6   *Serve with Chardonnay*

Recipe contributed by Mary Kaye Parks; Sycamore Creek Vineyards, Morgan Hill

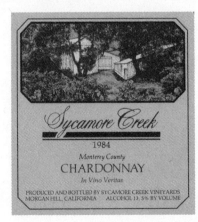

The Parks frequently prepare this pasta dish on Sunday night after the tasting room closes. It may be served just to family, but often friends who are visiting are included in this quick and easy, but delicious entrée. Mary Kaye adds a tossed salad and serves the meal with a bottle of Chardonnay for a relaxing evening.

¾ cup olive oil

10 cloves fresh garlic, pressed

4 6½-oz. cans minced clams

½ teaspoon lemon pepper

¼ teaspoon thyme

¼ cup chopped parsley

¼ lb. chopped mushrooms

1 lb. linguine, fresh if possible

Heat oil in a medium-sized saucepan. Add clam juice from cans, lemon pepper and thyme. Let simmer slowly.

In the meantime cook linguine in boiling salted water until al dente. Five minutes before linguine has finished cooking, add clams, parsley and mushrooms to the sauce. Simmer sauce to heat through and serve over cooked linguine.

Serve with Blanc de Noir Champagne

Serve with Zinfandel, or the dinner wine

Champagne Oysters on Tagliarini

Serves 6

Recipe contributed by Jamie Davies; Schramsberg Vineyards and Cellars, Calistoga

Jamie Davies's recipe successfully combines the complementary tastes of oysters and spinach. The sauce is light and goes well with the accompanying champagne.

2 tablespoons butter	salt and pepper to taste
4 shallots, chopped	2 cups spinach leaves, packed tightly
2 cups champagne	grated nutmeg
24 medium oysters, removed from shell	10 oz. fresh tagliarini, cooked al dente
½ cup whipping cream	

Melt butter in large skillet. Sauté shallots until just wilted, about 1 to 2 minutes. Pour in champagne and bring to simmer. Add oysters and poach gently until edges curl, about 1 minute. With a slotted spoon remove oysters to a plate and keep warm.

Turn heat to high and reduce champagne to half. Mix in whipping cream and continue cooking over high heat another 2 to 3 minutes. Season with salt and pepper. Add spinach leaves and stir 1 minute. Return oysters to the sauce. Serve at once over freshly cooked, hot tagliarini. Dust top with freshly grated nutmeg.

Egg Drop Noodles
(Spaetzle)

Serves 4

Recipe contributed by Etza Tomka; Soda Rock Winery, Healdsburg

These noodles go well with any entrée that has a sauce or gravy. It is especially good with Hungarian Chicken Paprikash (see page 291). This is a traditional Hungarian recipe of the Tomka family.

2 cups sifted all-purpose flour	½ teaspoon salt
2 eggs	⅔ to 1 cup water

In a medium-sized bowl place flour and make a hole in the center. Drop in the eggs and beat with a spoon, adding enough water to make a batter of medium consistency.

Bring a large saucepan of salted water to a rolling boil. Spoon about ⅓ of the batter onto a dampened cutting board. Using a table knife dipped in boiling water, scrape off small amounts of about ½-inch widths and let drop into boiling salted water. When noodles rise to the surface they are cooked, about 2 minutes. Remove from water with slotted spoon. Drain in colander and keep warm. Continue until all batter is used. Serve piping hot.

Seafood Pasta

Serves 5 to 6

Serve with Chardonnay

Recipe contributed by Linda Burgess; Burgess Cellars, St. Helena

A tossed salad and French bread complete this easy-to-prepare pasta dish. With a heartier meal, Linda Burgess suggests serving Cabernet Sauvignon. If a stronger garlic flavor is desired more garlic may be used. Linda usually uses 8 to 10 cloves. Parmesan cheese sprinkled over the finished dish acts as a thickening agent.

½ cup butter

¼ cup olive oil

4 cloves garlic, minced

¾ cup Chardonnay

1 teaspoon oregano

1 teaspoon dried basil, or 1 tablespoon fresh chopped basil

¼ teaspoon crushed red pepper

1½ cups chopped parsley

¾ cup broccoli, chopped

¾ cup mushrooms, sliced

1 6½-oz. can chopped clams

1 8-oz. can shrimp or fresh, cooked bay shrimp

1 lb. fettuccine, dry or fresh

1 cup grated Parmesan cheese

In a 3-quart pan over medium-low heat, melt butter in olive oil. Add garlic and cook until golden. Add wine, oregano, basil, red pepper and parsley. Simmer 3 to 4 minutes. Add broccoli and mushrooms. Simmer another 2 to 3 minutes. Add clams and shrimp and heat through.

Meanwhile, cook the fettuccine according to package directions until al dente, then drain. Toss sauce with fettuccine. Add cheese, toss and serve.

Author's note: One-fourth cup chopped red bell pepper may be added for additional color and flavor.

Gnocchi

Serves 6 to 8

Serve with Zinfandel

Recipe contributed by Johanna Rafanelli; A. Rafanelli Winery, Healdsburg

Gnocchi (pronounced nyok-kee*) are small dumplings made with flour, farina or potatoes. This is a traditional Italian family recipe using potatoes and flour. The gnocchi may be made ahead and frozen uncooked until ready for use. Serve it as a main dish, first course, or side dish.*

4 cups boiled, mashed potatoes

pinch of salt

4 eggs

¾ cup butter

4 cups flour, or more as needed

Mix all ingredients together into a fairly elastic dough, and roll out on floured board. Cut into cylinders about 1 inch long. Then dip a fork into flour and press and roll the cylinder off the fork. This should form a shell like pasta. Drop into boiling salted water. After gnocchi rises to the top of the water, cook for 2 to 3 minutes. Test for doneness. Remove with a slotted spoon and serve with spaghetti sauce, pesto sauce or just grated Parmesan cheese and butter.

If gnocchi have been frozen cook them about 10 minutes.

Gnocchi Palmieri

Serves 6 as a side dish

Recipe contributed by Susan Boeger; Boeger Winery, Placerville

These gnocchi differ from the traditional ones in that they are not made from potatoes. They are therefore much easier to make, yet very few people can tell the difference. Susan Boeger got this recipe from a friend who, in turn, had gotten it from an aunt from Italy.

1 lb. ricotta cheese	**RED SAUCE**
1 egg beaten	2 tablespoons butter
¼ teaspoon salt	¾ cup chopped onions
1¾ cups flour	1 clove garlic, minced
1 tablespoon oil	1 beef bouillon cube
grated Parmesan cheese	1 8-oz. can tomato sauce
	¼ teaspoon each dried parsley, sage, rosemary and thyme
	1 1-lb. can of tomatoes, undrained

In a medium-sized saucepan heat butter and sauté onions and garlic until soft. Add remaining sauce ingredients and simmer uncovered, stirring occasionally, for 30 minutes.

Mix together the ricotta cheese, egg, salt, flour and oil to make a dough. Cut off small pieces and roll with hands on a floured board until the size of a bread stick. Cut into 1-inch pieces and curl by rolling with your thumb, a spoon or a fork. (Using a fork seems to be the easiest.) Place on a floured sheet of wax paper and refrigerate until ready to cook.

Drop into boiling salted water and cook until the gnocchi surface, 3 to 5 minutes. Remove with a skimmer and drain.

Serve with Red Sauce and grated Parmesan cheese.

Spaghetti alla Carbonara

Serves 4   *Serve with Chardonnay*

Recipe contributed by Leon Santoro; Quail Ridge Cellars and Vineyards, Napa

This is a family adaptation of an old recipe. It has special significance to Leon Santoro, who is from Abruzzi, Italy — the region from which the recipe originated. The story goes that the woodsmen (known as carbonari*) would go up into the hills to chop wood and burn it slowly to make soft coal. They would eat off the land, or make simple hearty meals from easy to carry supplies — salt pork, cheese, pasta. Dairy products were usually available from local farms.*

8 slices of bacon, diced

½ cup chopped onions

1 teaspoon dried red pepper flakes (optional)

½ to 1 cup cream

6 to 8 quarts water

1 lb. spaghetti

4 tablespoons soft butter

2 whole eggs plus 2 egg yolks, well beaten

1 cup freshly grated Parmesan cheese

salt and freshly ground pepper to taste

Fry the bacon in a skillet until crisp. Add the onions and cook until soft. Pour off half the bacon drippings. Add the optional red pepper and cream to the frying pan and simmer very gently until the spaghetti is cooked.

While the bacon is cooking bring a pot of salted water to a rolling boil. Add the spaghetti, stir and cook over high heat for 7 to 12 minutes or until the spaghetti is tender. Drain the spaghetti thoroughly and transfer it to a large bowl.

Very quickly stir in the softened butter and the cream mixture, mixing them well with the spaghetti. Finally, add the beaten eggs and half of the cheese and toss rapidly, allowing the heat from the spaghetti to cook the eggs. Season to taste with salt and black pepper and serve at once. Pass the remaining cheese at the table.

Author's note: This dish will serve 6 to 8 when used as a first course.

CHEESE & EGGS

Serve with Chenin Blanc

Crustless Artichoke Quiche

Serves 4

Recipe contributed by Lynne Russell; Granite Springs Winery and Vineyards, Somerset

This is an easy and elegant dish for a luncheon or light dinner.

2 6-oz. jars marinated artichoke hearts, sliced in half lengthwise, reserve oil

3 green onions, chopped

6 eggs beaten

⅔ cups biscuit mix

½ lb. sharp Cheddar cheese, grated

1 clove garlic, minced

1 tablespoon chopped parsley

salt and freshly ground pepper to taste

Sauté green onions in oil reserved from artichokes. Add artichoke hearts and remaining ingredients, beating with fork to combine well. Pour into 9-inch oven-proof quiche dish, or 8-inch square pan. Bake in preheated 325° oven for 35 minutes or until knife inserted in center comes out clean. Serve hot or cold.

Serve with Sauvignon Blanc

Cheese Soufflé

Serves 4 to 6

Recipe contributed by Barbara Shilo; Domaine Laurier, Forestville

Barbara Shilo recommends using this recipe as a first course for 6 people or as a luncheon entrée for 4.

3 tablespoons butter or margarine

3 tablespoons flour

1 cup milk

dash of cayenne pepper

¼ teaspoon dry mustard

½ teaspoon salt

1 cup shredded Cheddar cheese

4 to 5 eggs (depending on size), separated

In a saucepan melt butter and stir in flour. Blend in milk, cayenne pepper, dry mustard and salt. Cook, stirring until thick. Add cheese and continue stirring until cheese is melted. Remove from heat and beat in egg yolks.

Beat egg whites until they have short but distinct peaks. Fold about half the whites into the sauce quite thoroughly. Fold in remaining whites as thoroughly as you wish. Less stirring produces a lighter fluffier soufflé; more stirring makes it denser and smoother.

Pour into buttered 1½ quart soufflé dish or 4 to 6 individual 1-cup ramekins. Draw a circle on surface, an inch from the rim with the tip of a knife or spoon. Bake in a preheated 375° oven for 35 minutes. Individual cups take 20 minutes.

Author's note: Omit the salt if less salty food is desired. The cheese usually has enough salt.

Roquefort Soufflé

Serves 4

Recipe contributed by Donna Hicks; Sarah's Vineyard, Gilroy

This elegant soufflé makes a wonderful luncheon entrée. Serve it with a salad and perhaps some French bread or rolls. Donna Hicks also serves this soufflé as a before-dinner appetizer.

Serve with Chardonnay

4 tablespoons butter	**4 oz. Roquefort cheese, crumbled**
parchment or butcher's paper	**½ teaspoon salt**
¼ cup flour	**⅛ teaspoon pepper**
¾ cup milk	**dash of nutmeg, freshly ground**
¼ cup Chardonnay	**3 egg yolks, lightly beaten**
	6 egg whites

Butter a 1½-quart soufflé dish using 1½ tablespoons butter. Extend the height of the dish by making a collar with a piece of parchment or butcher's paper that has been well buttered with ½ tablespoon butter.

Melt 2 tablespoons butter in a saucepan and stir in flour. Gradually add milk and wine, stirring over medium heat until the sauce thickens. Add cheese, salt, pepper and nutmeg. Remove from heat and stir in egg yolks. Set aside. Beat egg whites until stiff but not dry and gently fold into cheese mixture. Pour into prepared soufflé dish and bake in preheated 350° oven for 25 to 30 minutes. Serve immediately. Soufflé may sit assembled prior to baking for 45 minutes if covered with a large bowl.

Brunch Loaf

Serves 8

Recipe contributed by Judy Tijsseling; Tijsseling Vineyards, Ukiah

This brunch loaf is wonderful for Sunday morning since it may be prepared the night before and refrigerated then baked in the morning. Additional ingredients may vary as the appetite dictates. The Tijsselings serve Brunch Loaf with fresh fruit, fresh baked muffins and a glass of champagne.

Serve with Brut Champagne

6 to 7 slices white bread, crusts removed	**10 slices bacon, cooked crisp**
10 to 12 eggs	**optional: 1 cup chopped tomatoes, sautéed mushrooms, sautéed onions or blanched broccoli flowerets, or any of the above combined**
1 cup milk or half-and-half	
¾ cup shredded Cheddar cheese	

Cut bread into cubes and line a 9½ × 11-inch pan with them. Combine eggs with milk and beat well. Chop bacon into small pieces. Pour ½ of egg mixture over bread cubes. Layer crumbled bacon on top and top with 1 cup of vegetables, if being used. Then add rest of egg mixture and top with remaining cheese. Refrigerate overnight if desired.

Bake casserole in preheated 325° oven for 50 to 55 minutes. The loaf will puff up and be lightly browned.

Serve with Sparkling Johannisberg Riesling

Sunday Morning Omelette

Serves 4

Recipe contributed by Joyce Welch; Hop Kiln Winery, Healdsburg

Joyce Welch created this omelette recipe for Dr. Griffin's Sunday brunches. Dr. Griffin, the owner of Hop Kiln Winery, is very fond of cuisine that includes fresh vegetables from his garden. This recipe makes a large omelette that can easily serve 4 people.

3 tablespoons butter

1 clove garlic

1 tablespoon fresh basil, chopped

2 tablespoons chives, chopped

2 green onions, chopped

1 tomato, chopped

1 stalk celery, chopped

salt and pepper to taste

8 eggs

2 tablespoons plain yogurt

2 large ripe avocados, peeled and sliced

¾ cup grated Monterey Jack cheese

½ cup plain yogurt or sour cream

paprika

parsley for garnish

In 2 tablespoons butter, lightly sauté the garlic, basil, chives, onions, tomato and celery. Add salt and pepper to taste. Set aside.

In a bowl lightly beat the eggs with 2 tablespoons yogurt. Over medium heat, melt 1 tablespoon butter in a 12-inch Teflon frying pan. Lower heat and add eggs. Cook slowly until eggs begin to firm. Add sliced avocados in an even row; cover with sautéed vegetables and Jack cheese. When eggs are fairly firm, fold over to melt cheese and warm avocado. Spread top with yogurt or sour cream and sprinkle with paprika. Serve on platter garnished with parsley.

Serve with Chardonnay

Herb Goat Cheese Soufflé

Serves 4 to 6

Recipe contributed by Sandra P. MacIver; Mantanzas Creek Winery, Santa Rosa

This cheese soufflé is very good with a full-bodied Chardonnay, but it also stands up to reds. Serve it as a first course or as a luncheon entrée.

4 tablespoons butter

4 tablespoons flour

1 cup whipping cream

8 oz. goat cheese, crumbled

5 egg yolks, beaten

salt, pepper, nutmeg, and cayenne, to taste

1 teaspoon thyme

1 tablespoon chopped fresh chives

5 to 7 egg whites (depending on how fluffy a soufflé you like)

In a medium-sized saucepan over medium heat make a roux by melting the butter and slowly stirring in the flour. Continue to cook over low heat until flour is cooked, but not browned. Turn down heat and gradually stir in whipping cream and half the goat cheese. Remove from heat and slowly add the beaten egg yolks, stirring after each small addition. Add the remaining goat cheese, salt, pepper, nutmeg, and cayenne to taste. Add thyme and chives.

Beat egg whites until stiff. Add ¼ of the egg whites to the cheese mixture, and stir to lighten mixture. Add the rest of the egg whites at one time and fold into the cheese mixture, being careful not to deflate the egg whites.

Pour into a buttered 1½-quart soufflé dish and bake in a preheated 350° oven for 30 to 40 minutes until puffed and golden. Soufflé should be almost gooey inside.

Serve with a light tomato sauce spooned over each portion.

Gloria's Pizza

Makes 3 pizzas

Recipe contributed by Gloria Piconi; John Piconi Winery, Temecula

Gloria Piconi learned to make bread and pizza dough from her Italian mother-in-law. Over the years she has perfected this recipe and has taught pizza-making classes. The trick to the pizza is not to use excessive topping. A light topping will result in a crisp and chewy pizza.

Serve with Cabernet Sauvignon

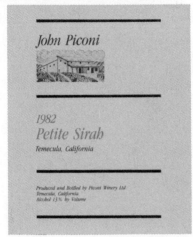

olive oil

Mozzarella cheese, sliced

Monterey Jack cheese, shredded

pepperoni, sliced thin

Italian sausage, casing removed,
    meat crumbled and precooked

chopped green pepper

grated Parmesan cheese

oregano

Pizza dough, see Cacci Nanza
    Bread recipe, page 357.

SAUCE

2 tablespoons olive oil

1 large onion, chopped

2 cloves garlic, minced

1 quart canned tomatoes, lightly
    chopped (home-canned, if
    available)

1 12-oz. can tomato paste

1 teaspoon oregano

salt and pepper to taste

Heat olive oil in medium-sized saucepan and sauté onion and garlic until wilted. Add rest of sauce ingredients and simmer for 30 minutes.

Cover dough with a light layer of olive oil. Lightly spoon on sauce, dotting it over the pizza and then spreading it with the back of the spoon. Avoid too much sauce. Add pepperoni slices, cooked sausage and green pepper. Sprinkle with oregano and Parmesan cheese. Bake in 375° oven for 20 minutes. Pizza dough should be firm enough to slide a spatula under it. If not, bake for a few more minutes. When dough is firm, slide a spatula under pizza and place it directly on the oven rack. Bake for 5 more minutes. Watch so that it does not burn.

Serve with French Colombard

Sour Cream Enchiladas

Serves 6 to 8

Recipe contributed by Karen Van Spanje; Greenstone Winery, Ione

This version of enchiladas with a white sauce is a favorite of Karen Van Spanje because it is simple to prepare and can be frozen to be baked later. A nice addition to the recipe is to include chicken in the filling.

12 corn tortillas	1 4-oz. can diced green chiles
¼ cup salad oil	2 cups grated cheddar cheese
1 10¾-oz. can cream of chicken soup	1 bunch green onions, chopped
1 cup sour cream	2 cups diced cooked chicken, optional

Heat oil in a frying pan over medium-high heat. When hot dip each tortilla in oil to soften. Drain on paper towels.

Mix together soup, sour cream and chiles. Spread a small amount of the mixture in the bottom of a 9 × 13-inch glass pan. Place 1 tablespoon of the soup mixture in each tortilla, add 1 heaping tablespoon cheese, some green onions, and 1 tablespoon chicken, if used. Roll up and place seam side down in the pan. Top with remaining soup mixture, cheese and onions.

Bake in preheated 350° oven for 35 minutes, or until casserole is bubbly and cheese has melted. If previously frozen, bake for 55 minutes to 1 hour.

Serve with Cabernet Sauvignon

Chile Rellenos

Serves 6 to 8

Recipe contributed by Judy Donatoni; Donatoni Winery, Inglewood

Judy Donatoni's Chile Rellenos is the perfect dish for a Mexican buffet dinner. The casserole may be assembled in the morning and stored in the refrigerator. Add the topping and bake an hour before serving.

1 1-lb. can green chiles (or 2 7-oz. cans)	**TOPPING**
2 7-oz. cans green salsa sauce	4 eggs, separated
¾ lb. Monterey Jack cheese, in one piece	2 tablespoons milk
¾ lb. mild Cheddar cheese, grated	4 tablespoons flour
½ onion, diced fine	½ teaspoon salt

Slit chiles lengthwise and remove seeds. Cut Jack cheese into ¼ × 3-inch strips. Insert sliced cheese into each pepper. Layer bottom of a 2-inch high flat baking dish with stuffed peppers. Pour salsa sauce over peppers. Sprinkle grated Cheddar cheese and onions over the top. To make topping, blend yolks with milk, flour and salt; whip egg whites until stiff and fold into egg yolk mixture. Lightly spread over the casserole. Bake in preheated 325° oven for 1 hour.

Onion Gruyère Tart

Serves 8 to 10

Recipe contributed by Richard Alexei, Culinary Director, Monticello Cellars, Napa

This dish was served at a special buffet in celebration of the 243rd anniversary of Thomas Jefferson's birthday held at the Monticello Cellars on April 13th, 1986. (See page 210 for the full menu.)

Serve with Gewurz Traminer (sic)

TART PASTRY

½ cup unsalted butter, chilled or frozen

1½ cups all-purpose flour

pinch of salt

3 to 4 tablespoons Gewurz Traminer

FILLING

2 lbs. yellow onions, peeled and sliced ¼ inch thick

4 tablespoons butter

½ cup heavy cream

1 teaspoon salad oil

pinch of sugar

½ cup Gewurz Traminer

1 teaspoon salt

dash of nutmeg

1 egg

¾ lb. Gruyère, coarsely grated

Make tart shell. Cut butter into small pieces. Process with flour and salt in food processor with steel blade until butter is cut into tiny flakes and mixture is mealy. With processor running, add 3 tablespoons of wine. Squeeze a little dough with fingertips. It should hold together and be moist. If dry and crumbly add more wine as necessary. Turn dough onto a board and compress into a ball. Flatten slightly to make a round flat patty. Chill for at least ½ hour. Roll out on a lightly floured board and fit into a 10- or 11-inch false-bottom tart tin. Trim off excess dough and prick bottom all over with a fork. Chill another ½ hour.

To make filling, heat butter and oil in a large heavy skillet. Add onions and cook covered over medium heat for about 10 minutes, or until onions are limp and begin to render liquid. Add a pinch of sugar and cook uncovered over medium-high heat 30 to 45 minutes. Stir frequently, using a wooden spoon or spatula to scrape up brownings in pan until onions are deep brown and reduced to a small mass. Watch carefully to prevent scorching and to insure even browning. Transfer onions to a medium-sized bowl. Add wine to skillet and boil, scraping up pan brownings. Reduce liquid to a thick glaze. Add glaze to onions along with remaining ingredients except the cheese. Stir until well blended.

Sprinkle half the cheese in the tart shell. Top with onion mixture and then the remaining cheese. Bake in preheated 375° oven for 40 to 45 minutes. If top browns too much, reduce heat slightly towards the end.

French Toast

Recipe contributed by Cecil McLester; McLester Winery, Inglewood

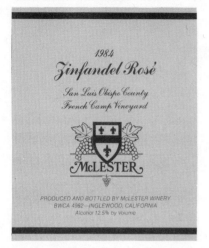

Cecil McLester often prepares French toast for Sunday breakfasts using his Suite 13, a California Muscat dessert wine, as part of the ingredients. The flavor is wonderful and no syrup is needed (syrup would only compete with the orange essence of the Suite 13). Wine is not always served with this, but for special occasions it may be.

3 eggs
⅓ cup milk
⅓ cup Suite 13, Muscat dessert wine

6 slices bread
1½ tablespoons butter

In a shallow bowl combine the eggs, milk and wine. Beat lightly to blend the mixture. In a large skillet over medium heat melt the butter. Dip slices of bread into the egg mixture, immersing them to coat the slices well. Place in skillet, not touching each other. Drizzle any leftover egg mixture on top until all liquid is absorbed. Cook about 4 minutes on each side or until nicely browned. May be served with powdered sugar.

VEGETABLES AND SIDE DISHES

Classic French Beans

Serves 8

Recipe contributed by Dolores Cakebread; Cakebread Cellars, Rutherford

Dolores Cakebread serves this classic white bean dish with grilled lamb.

1 lb. Great Northern beans	**2 cloves**
1 ham hock	**1 teaspoon bouquet garni**
4 cloves garlic	**salt and white pepper to taste**
2 carrots, minced	**2 tomatoes, seeded and chopped**
2 large onions, coarsely chopped	

Soak beans overnight. Drain and rinse. Place in a medium-sized Dutch oven with the ham hock. Cover with water and boil gently for 5 minutes. Drain again and rinse the beans and ham hock. Place ham hock and beans back in same Dutch oven. Add garlic, carrots, onions, and cloves. Cover with hot water and simmer slowly for 1¾ to 2 hours, or until tender. Skim off fat. Add salt and pepper to taste. Drain any excess liquid, keeping enough to keep beans moist. Stir in tomatoes and cook on low heat just to heat the tomatoes through.

Author's note: A traditional bouquet garni consists of herbs such as parsley, thyme and bay leaves tied in a bit of cloth. You can make your own, buy ready-made ones, or use commercial herb mixtures sold in jars.

Serve with Cabernet Sauvignon or the dinner wine

Cakebread Cellars

NAPA VALLEY

Cabernet Sauvignon
1982

PRODUCED AND BOTTLED BY CAKEBREAD CELLARS
RUTHERFORD, NAPA VALLEY, CALIFORNIA, USA
ALCOHOL 12.5% BY VOLUME

Honey-Glazed Carrots

Serves 4

Recipe contributed by Ken Burnap; Santa Cruz Mountain Vineyard, Santa Cruz

Ken Burnap serves this carrot dish with barbecued rack of lamb. Since he has an herb garden, he usually chops some herbs and rubs them on the lamb before putting it on the grill. The mint in the carrots goes well with the tanginess of the lamb.

6 medium-sized carrots, peeled and julienned	**2 tablespoons melted butter**
⅓ cup whole fresh mint leaves	**1½ tablespoons honey**

In a medium-sized saucepan, cook carrots with mint leaves over medium heat until tender, about 15 minutes. Drain and discard the mint leaves. Keep carrots warm. Combine melted butter and honey. Pour over carrots, toss and serve.

Serve with Pinot Noir, or the dinner wine

Santa Cruz Mountain Vineyard
Santa Cruz Mountains
Estate Bottled *Pinot Noir* 1981 Vintage

Produced and bottled by Santa Cruz Mountain Vineyard   Alcohol
2300 Jarvis Rd, Santa Cruz, Ca 95065, K.D. BURNAP, Proprietor   13½% by Vol.

Serve with Fumé Blanc

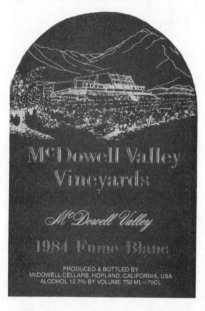

Asparagus with Red Pepper Sauce

Serves 8

Recipe contributed by Karen Keehn; McDowell Valley Vineyards, Hopland

After many years of experimenting Karen Keehn has found that the oxalic acids of asparagus can be "unfriendly" to wine flavors. Karen has also found that rich cream or cheese sauces or sweeter spices and butter sauces will counteract this effect. Red Pepper Sauce may also be used with poached fish or chicken breasts.

2 tablespoons sugar

2 lbs. fresh asparagus, washed and trimmed

salt and pepper

2 to 3 tablespoons butter

1 fresh fennel bulb, sliced

RED PEPPER SAUCE

4 tablespoons minced shallots

½ cup Fumé Blanc

2 tablespoons lemon juice

2 red bell peppers, chopped

2 tablespoons fresh parsley

½ cup unsalted butter, softened

Make Red Pepper Sauce. In a small saucepan simmer shallots, wine and lemon juice for 10 minutes to reduce liquid by half. Put chopped red pepper and parsley in a blender and purée. Add the shallot mixture and blend. Return to saucepan and whisk in butter, 1 tablespoon at a time. Blend thoroughly. Keep warm over warm water until ready to serve.

In a heavy skillet place two tablespoons sugar. Place asparagus on top of sugar. Add salt and pepper and barely cover with boiling water. Cook for 6 to 9 minutes or until asparagus is done, but still retains its fresh color.

While asparagus is cooking, melt butter in a sauté pan and sauté fennel slices until almost translucent. Arrange asparagus spears on a plate with sautéed fennel and spoon Red Pepper Sauce over both.

Serve with Gewurztraminer or the dinner wine

Zesty Carrots

Serves 2

Recipe contributed by Dorothy and Davis Bynum; Davis Bynum Winery, Healdsburg

The Bynums love to garden and enjoy fresh vegetables from their garden year round.

4 carrots, sliced or julienned

2 tablespoons butter

1 teaspoon port

1 teaspoon cider vinegar

2 tablespoons chopped parsley

Steam carrots until barely tender. In a small saucepan heat butter until hot. Add port, vinegar and carrots, mixing gently to coat carrots with sauce. Heat until all ingredients are piping hot. Sprinkle with chopped parsley and serve.

Uncle Owen's Red Cabbage

Serves 8

Serve with Cabernet Sauvignon

Recipe contributed by Rolayne Stortz; Sunrise Winery, Cupertino

This recipe was originated by "Uncle Owen," a family friend of the Stortzes. The friend was taught to cook by his Scandinavian mother, and his love for and expertise in cooking won him a place as a finalist in the Pillsbury Bake-Off one year. Rolayne serves this dish with roasts, turkey, goose or duck. She says that either Cabernet Sauvignon or Sauvignon Blanc may be served with it depending on the choice of meats.

1 large red cabbage	2 whole cloves
2 cups boiling chicken broth	1 tablespoon sugar
4 tablespoons butter	½ stick cinnamon
2 tablespoons vinegar	pinch of nutmeg
2 Pippin apples, peeled, cored and cut into wedges	salt and pepper to taste
	⅓ cup Cabernet Sauvignon

Remove any wilted outer leaves from the cabbage. Cut in quarters and remove center core. Shred cabbage and place in a Dutch oven or large iron skillet. Pour boiling chicken broth over cabbage. Add butter. Cook covered on low heat for 1 hour.

Add vinegar, apples, cloves, sugar, cinnamon, nutmeg and salt and pepper and continue to cook over low heat for another ½ hour. Ten minutes before serving add the Cabernet Sauvignon and simmer for 10 minutes.

Author's note: The use of cloves, cinnamon and nutmeg gives this red cabbage dish an extremely subtle flavor and aids in blending all of the ingredients into a most pleasing dish. If a stronger flavor is preferred red wine may be substituted for the chicken broth.

Honey-Glazed Chestnuts

Serves 6

Serve with Chardonnay or the dinner wine

Recipe contributed by A. Crawford Cooley; Hacienda Wine Cellars, Sonoma

Glazed Chestnuts may be served as a side dish with any grilled fowl or grilled pork. Crawford Cooley usually serves them with grilled wild boar.

3 teaspoons honey	1 lb. canned chestnuts, "natural," not sweetened

In a medium-sized saucepan heat honey and add chestnuts, stirring until heated and well coated.

Serve with White Zinfandel, or the dinner wine

Broccoli Casserole

Serves 6

Recipe contributed by Tamara Lucas; The Lucas Winery, Lodi

Tamara serves this casserole with baked chicken and a tomato salad. This is an old tried-and-true recipe that is also an easy one to prepare.

2 10-oz. pkgs. frozen broccoli

2 eggs beaten

1 onion, chopped fine

1 10¾-oz. can cream of mushroom soup

½ cup mayonnaise

1 cup grated Cheddar cheese

1 pkg. herbed stuffing mix

¼ cup melted butter

Cook broccoli according to package directions until barely tender. Drain and cut into 1½-inch pieces. In a bowl combine eggs, onion, soup and mayonnaise. In a 2-quart casserole place a layer of broccoli. Add a layer of cheese, and then a layer of the sauce. Repeat layers. Top with stuffing mix. Sprinkle butter on top. Bake in a preheated 350° oven for 30 minutes.

Author's note: Fresh broccoli may be used instead of frozen. You need about 1½ bunches. Cut off the flowerets and also use part of the peeled stems. Discard the bottom parts of the stems or save for soup. Blanch broccoli in boiling water for 5 minutes until barely tender. Then proceed with the recipe.

Serve with Pinot Noir or the dinner wine

Cabbage and Cauliflower with Wine

Serves 4

Recipe contributed by Joan Ellis; Mark West Vineyards, Forestville

Joan Ellis's vegetable dish is an excellent complement to any roast.

1 small head cauliflower

2 cups Chardonnay

1 small head red cabbage, thinly sliced

½ cup garlic-flavored vinegar

3 tablespoons olive oil

1 teaspoon Dijon mustard

½ teaspoon prepared horseradish

1 cup bacon, cooked and crumbled

cracked black pepper

Rinse, core and roughly chop cauliflower. Place cauliflower and Chardonnay in a medium-sized saucepan. Cover, bring to a boil over high heat. Reduce heat to medium and simmer 15 minutes, Drain cauliflower and reserve cooking liquid. Keep liquid hot. Whisk together red wine, vinegar, oil, mustard and horseradish in another medium-sized pan. Add cabbage. Cover, and bring to a boil, reduce heat to medium and cook until cabbage is wilted, about 10 minutes. Drain cabbage. Combine cauliflower, cabbage and bacon in a large bowl. Add half of the reserved cooking liquid, black pepper to taste and toss. Serve warm.

Stuffed Chiles and Tomato Sauce

Recipe contributed by Pam Wilder; Green and Red Vineyard, St. Helena

Serves 4   *Serve with Zinfandel*

Pam serves this dish as a first course or as a side dish with grilled meat. This is a typical Mexican-Californian dish.

10 medium-sized ripe tomatoes

½ cup olive oil

1 medium-sized onion, chopped

1 large clove garlic, chopped

2 tablespoons unsalted butter

salt and pepper to taste

6 chili peppers (poblano or Italian long)

Monterey Jack cheese

Cheddar cheese

1 jalapeño pepper, optional

Peel the tomatoes, quarter them and remove seeds. In a large skillet heat the olive oil over medium-high heat, add onion and sauté until soft. Add tomatoes. When the tomatoes start to juice, add the garlic and butter. Season with salt and pepper to taste. Simmer, uncovered for about 30 minutes or until the tomatoes reach a sauce consistency.

Put chiles in a 350° oven until skin is slightly scorched, then peel. Make a slit down one side and remove the seeds being careful to leave the rest intact. Cut the cheeses into strips to fit the chiles. Place a piece of Monterey Jack and a piece of Cheddar inside each chili. Put in a baking dish in one layer and bake in a preheated 350° oven until the cheese has melted and the chiles are tender, about 10 minutes. Watch so that cheese does not run. Serve with a small amount of tomato sauce on top.

The chili pepper used in this recipe are just a little on the hot side. If a hotter sauce is desired, add some jalapeño pepper to the sauce as it cooks.

Tomato Pie

Recipe contributed by Audrey Cilurzo; Cilurzo Vineyard and Winery, Temecula

Serves 8   *Serve with Petite Sirah*

Audrey Cilurzo serves this dish at outdoor barbecues at many winery functions. It can also be used as a luncheon dish.

1 9-inch pie crust

3 large ripe tomatoes, sliced

½ cup chopped onion

oregano

basil

garlic powder

1 cup grated Cheddar cheese

1 cup mayonnaise

Bake pie crust in preheated 400° oven for 7 minutes. Remove from oven. Layer sliced tomatoes and chopped onions in the pie shell. Sprinkle with oregano, basil and garlic powder. Mix Cheddar cheese and mayonnaise until blended. Spread on top of pie. Bake 30 minutes in a preheated 350° oven.

Serve with Zinfandel

Eve's Italian Eggplant

Serves 6

Recipe contributed by Eve Pagor; Rolling Hills Vineyards, Camarillo

Eve Pagor serves this eggplant dish as an entrée with a green salad and crusty French bread. This is an excellent meatless dish.

2 to 3 tablespoons olive oil	1 quart homemade marinara sauce
1 medium-sized eggplant, cut into ¼-inch slices	8-oz. Mozzarella cheese, sliced ¼ inch thick
flour	½ cup grated Parmesan cheese
2 eggs, beaten	
1½ cups seasoned bread crumbs	

In a large skillet heat the olive oil. Dip each eggplant slice in flour, then in egg and then into bread crumbs. Over medium heat fry eggplant about 5 minutes per side or until golden brown. After frying, place on paper towels to remove excess oil. Continue this process until all eggplant is sautéed. (More oil may be necessary.)

Place a layer of sauce in the bottom of an 8 × 12-inch ovenproof dish. Put a layer of eggplant on top. Place a slice of Mozzarella on each eggplant slice. Top with more sauce and sprinkle Parmesan on top. Place another layer of eggplant on top. Garnish each slice with a slice of Mozzarella. Top with sauce and sprinkle with Parmesan cheese. Bake in a preheated 350° oven for 30 to 40 minutes.

Serve with Cabernet Sauvignon for beef, Gamay Beaujolais for ham

Mill Creek Potatoes

Serves 4 to 6

Recipe contributed by Yvonne Kreck; Mill Creek Vineyards, Healdsburg

Yvonne Kreck serves this potato dish with either steak or ham. Cook in a stovetop-to-table dish for easy serving.

5 strips bacon	1 or 2 green peppers, cored and sliced into rings
1 large onion, chopped	1 teaspoon Italian seasoning
5 large potatoes, unpeeled and sliced ⅛ inch thick	3 tomatoes, sliced
salt and pepper to taste	¼ to ½ cup sugar

Cut bacon into ½-inch pieces and in a medium-sized skillet fry until crisp. Add onion; sauté until lightly browned. Reserve the entire mixture. Place sliced potatoes in a 3-quart saucepan. Sprinkle with salt and pepper. Add green pepper rings and top with the onion-bacon mixture. Sprinkle on Italian seasoning. Cover entire top with sliced tomatoes, and sprinkle sugar over top of tomatoes. Cover pan and simmer 30 to 40 minutes.

Author's note: The amount of sugar needed depends on the tartness of the tomatoes and individual preference.

Vegetable Marinade

Serves 6

Serve with Sauvignon Blanc

Recipe contributed by Joyce Ahern; Ahern Winery, San Fernando

Joyce Ahern uses the marinade with a great variety of vegetables — whatever is in season or will complement the remainder of her meal. The cold vegetables may be served on lettuce as a salad or as an accompaniment to a broiled meat entrée. The marinade goes well with wine since it does not contain vinegar.

MARINADE

⅔ **cup salad oil**

½ **teaspoon grated lemon rind**

⅓ **cup fresh lemon juice**

¼ **cup sweet pickle relish**

2 **tablespoons each finely chopped green onion and green pepper**

2 **tablespoons each chopped pimiento and parsley**

1 **teaspoon each sugar and salt**

VEGETABLE SUGGESTIONS

1 **1-lb. can cut green beans, drained**

1 **1-lb. can cut yellow beans, drained**

½ **cup sliced fresh mushrooms**

1 **cup blanched cauliflower flowerets**

12 **cherry tomatoes**

Combine all marinade ingredients, mixing well. In a bowl combine the beans, mushrooms and cauliflower and toss with the marinade. Marinate at least 1 hour.

Drain. Serve in individual bowls as an accompaniment to broiled meats, or place on lettuce leaves and serve as a salad. Garnish with cherry tomatoes.

Any cooked vegetables may be used and arranged with lettuce leaves on a platter for buffet service. Place marinade in a separate bowl for self-service.

Company Potatoes

Serves 10 to 12

Serve with Chardonnay, or the dinner wine

Recipe contributed by Imogene Prager; Prager Winery and Port Works, St. Helena

Imogene's potato casserole is a wonderful complement to all meat and fish dishes. It also travels well to potluck suppers and picnics.

6 **medium-large russet potatoes**

2 **10¾-oz. cans cream of chicken soup**

¼ **cup butter**

2 **cups sour cream**

6 **green onions, sliced**

crushed cornflakes

grated sharp Cheddar cheese

Boil potatoes and peel. Chill well. Slice potatoes into a 3-quart baking dish. Warm soup and butter together until the butter melts. Mix sour cream into warm soup mixture. Sprinkle green onions over sliced potatoes. Evenly spread the soup mixture on top. Then top soup mixture with crushed cornflakes. Cover entirely and generously with grated Cheddar cheese. Bake in preheated 350° oven for 20 minutes or until bubbly around edges.

This casserole may be prepared in advance and refrigerated unbaked. Prior to serving, bake at 350° for 30 minutes or until hot and bubbly.

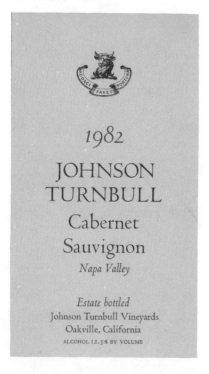

Fusilli with Vegetables

Serves 4

Recipe contributed by Marta Johnson; Johnson Turnbull Vineyards, Oakville

This dish may be served warm or at room temperature. For the latter it may be prepared ahead of serving time. Marta Johnson serves this vegetable-pasta combination with grilled meats but it would do nicely as a luncheon entrée. Since it does not contain any vinegar it does not conflict with the wine. Fusilli are a corkscrew-shaped pasta.

4 to 6 tablespoons olive oil	2 bunches baby carrots, (18 to 24)
1 small onion, minced	4 cups broccoli flowerets
2 large cloves garlic, minced	1 red bell pepper
1 teaspoon salt	½ lb. fusilli
pepper	½ cup freshly grated Parmesan cheese
¼ cup chicken stock	⅓ cup sliced black olives

Heat 2 to 3 tablespoons olive oil in a sauté pan; add minced onion and cook over low heat for 5 minutes to soften the onion. Stir in garlic, salt, pepper and chicken broth. Cover and simmer for 5 minutes. Transfer to a small bowl and set aside.

Steam baby carrots for 3 minutes. Cool and refrigerate. Steam broccoli flowerets for 2 minutes in boiling water. Rinse; cool and refrigerate. Cut red bell pepper in half and blanch for 2 minutes. Cool and cut into inch-long julienne strips. Refrigerate.

To serve: Add 1 to 2 teaspoons salt to rapidly boiling water and cook fusilli until al dente. At the same time, add 2 to 3 tablespoons olive oil to onion mixture. Place mixture in large sauté pan and cook over low heat so that it will be hot by the time the pasta is cooked. When pasta is almost done add carrots, broccoli and red pepper to the onion mixture. Cook another 30 seconds. Drain fusilli thoroughly and place in warm serving dish. Add vegetables and black olives. Toss and serve with grated Parmesan cheese.

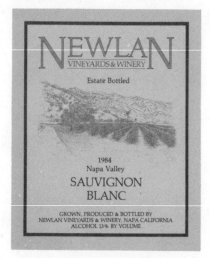

Zucchini Patties

Serves 4 to 6

Recipe contributed by Jonette Newlan; Newlan Vineyards and Winery, Napa

This recipe was devised to persuade the four Newlan sons to eat zucchini. The cheese and garlic adds to the flavor of the zucchini. Jonette Newlan also found the recipe of great help when their garden produced an abundance of zucchini.

2 large zucchini, grated	1 teaspoon garlic powder
2 cups grated Cheddar cheese	1 teaspoon garlic salt
3 eggs	10 to 12 soda crackers, crushed
1 tablespoon grated onion	

In a medium-sized bowl mix all ingredients well. Drop by spoonfuls onto a hot griddle and fry like pancakes. The mixture can also be put into a greased 8 × 11-inch casserole dish and baked in a preheated 350° oven for 25 to 30 minutes.

Savory Rice

Serves 4

Recipe contributed by Carol Anderson; S. Anderson Wine Cellars, Napa

Serve with Chardonnay, or the dinner wine

This flavorful rice may be served with chicken or veal.

1 cup uncooked white rice	1 tablespoon minced parsley
1 small onion, minced	½ teaspoon summer savory
2 tablespoons olive oil	½ cup dry sherry
1 teaspoon paprika	1¼ cups beef broth

In a medium-sized saucepan sauté rice and onion in olive oil over medium heat until golden brown, stirring often to be sure that the mixture does not burn. Remove from heat. Add herbs, sherry and beef broth. Bring to a boil, then lower heat to low, cover and cook until liquid is absorbed, about 20 minutes.

Popovers

Makes 9

Recipe contributed by Alan Steen; Whitehall Lane Winery, St. Helena

Serve with Chardonnay

These popovers may be served with chicken, veal or as an accompaniment to a luncheon salad. Dr. Steen enjoys all aspects of cooking and baking.

1 cup milk	¼ teaspoon salt
1 tablespoon melted butter	2 eggs
1 cup all-purpose flour	

Have all ingredients at room temperature. Preheat oven to 450°.

Butter a heavy popover or muffin tin. Beat milk, melted butter, flour and salt until smooth. Beat in one egg at a time, but do not overbeat. The batter should be no heavier than whipping cream. Fill buttered tins ¾ full. Bake immediately. After 15 minutes reduce heat to 350° without opening oven. Continue baking 20 minutes longer. When done, popovers should be easy to remove from tins and the sides firm. If not cooked long enough, popovers will collapse. Serve immediately.

Tomato Couscous

Serves 6 to 8

Recipe contributed by Lisa Buehler; Buehler Vineyards, St. Helena

Serve with White Zinfandel or Pinot Blanc

This side dish was created by Lisa Buehler to accompany her London Broil Salad, see page 263. Its mild taste and beautiful color make it versatile enough to serve with either chicken or shellfish.

1 cup chicken broth	3 tablespoons olive oil
1 cup tomato juice	1 cup cooked couscous

Bring chicken broth, tomato juice and olive oil to a boil. Stir in couscous. Remove from heat and cover. In 5 minutes fluff with a fork and serve.

Serve with Chardonnay

Barley Pilaf

Serves 6

Recipe contributed by Jeri Mosby; Vega Vineyards Winery, Buellton

Barley Pilaf is part of the traditional Thanksgiving meal at the Mosby house. Depending on the rest of the meal, Jeri Mosby varies the amount of mushrooms in the pilaf. She sometimes adds chopped pimiento to the casserole just before serving. For a Mediterranean meal she uses half barley and half wheat bulgur.

½ **cup butter**	**1 cup dry white wine**
1 12-oz. pkg. pearl barley	**1 cup chicken broth**
½ **lb. fresh mushrooms, sliced**	⅛ **teaspoon pepper**
2 medium onions, thinly sliced	**1 bay leaf, crumbled**

In a frying pan melt butter over medium heat. Add barley, mushrooms and onions and sauté, stirring constantly, until onions are limp and clear. Reduce heat if necessary to prevent barley from burning. Transfer mixture to a 2½-quart casserole. Pour in the liquid and stir in pepper and bay leaf. Cover the casserole and bake in a preheated 325° oven for 1 hour or until there is no free-flowing liquid and barley is tender.

Author's note: ¼ cup chopped red bell pepper and ¼ cup chopped parsley may be added.

Serve with Sauvignon Blanc, or the dinner wine

Zucchini with Wine

Serves 6

Recipe contributed by Jo Anne Strobl; Hop Kiln Winery, Healdsburg

The vegetable casserole would go well with a lamb or beef roast.

2 lbs. zucchini	**1 10¾-oz. can cream of mushroom soup**
3 tablespoons butter or margarine	½ **cup Sauvignon Blanc**
1 small onion, diced	½ **cup grated Parmesan or Romano cheese**
2 tablespoons flour	

Wash and trim ends of zucchini, then cut into 1-inch chunks. Cook in boiling water until barely tender, 5 to 8 minutes. Drain well and place in a greased baking dish. Melt butter, add onion and cook until tender. Stir in flour, then soup and wine. Cook and stir until smooth, about 5 minutes. Pour over zucchini and sprinkle with cheese. Bake in a preheated 375° oven for 20 to 25 minutes.

Brown Rice with Onion and Red Bell Pepper

Serves 6 to 8

Recipe contributed by Marta Johnson; Johnson Turnbull Vineyards, Oakville

Serve with Cabernet Sauvignon, or the dinner wine

Marta Johnson likes to serve this dish because it is most attractive, and is high in nutritional value. It goes particularly well with lamb.

3 cups water	1 tablespoon olive oil
½ teaspoon salt	1 onion, minced
2 cups brown rice	½ red bell pepper

In a medium-sized saucepan bring water to a boil. Add salt. Wash rice and add to the pot. Return to a boil. Cover and reduce heat and simmer for 40 minutes. Remove from heat and with the cover still on, allow the rice to sit for 20 minutes to swell and dry. Keep rice warm.

Meanwhile, heat olive oil in a sauté pan. Add onion and cook 5 minutes over low heat to soften the onions; reserve. Blanch red bell pepper, then dice into ¼-inch pieces. Reserve.

At serving time add red pepper to onion and heat, covered, until warmed through. Spoon over individual servings of rice just before serving.

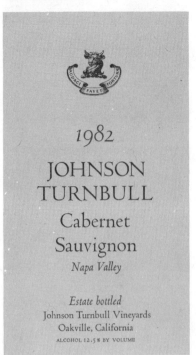

1982

JOHNSON TURNBULL

Cabernet Sauvignon

Napa Valley

Estate bottled
Johnson Turnbull Vineyards
Oakville, California

ALCOHOL 12.5 % BY VOLUME

Southwestern Wild Rice

Serves 6 to 8

Recipe contributed by Lucy Shaw; Charles F. Shaw Vineyards and Winery, St. Helena

Serve with Domaine Elucia — Proprietor's Reserve

This recipe is one which Lucy Shaw added to her culinary repertoire while living in Houston, Texas. Lucy, who is interested in regional as well as international cooking, is always on the lookout for interesting flavors. While the Shaws were living in Paris, Lucy attended the Cordon Bleu.

1½ cups uncooked wild rice	5 chicken livers, chopped
3 cups bouillon	½ cup butter
1 cup water	1 cup heavy cream
⅓ cup chopped scallions	grated Parmesan cheese
½ cup diced red pepper	
1½ cups fresh mushrooms, chopped	

In a medium-sized saucepan combine rice, water and bouillon. Bring to a boil and cook over low heat until tender, 20 to 25 minutes. Drain. In a medium-sized frying pan over medium-high heat sauté scallions, red pepper, mushrooms and chicken livers for about 5 minutes. Combine rice and sautéed items. Spoon into a 2-quart casserole. Pour in cream. Sprinkle with Parmesan cheese. Bake in preheated 350° oven for 40 minutes.

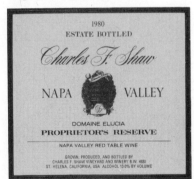

1980
ESTATE BOTTLED

Charles F. Shaw

NAPA VALLEY

DOMAINE ELUCIA
PROPRIETOR'S RESERVE

NAPA VALLEY RED TABLE WINE

GROWN, PRODUCED, AND BOTTLED BY
CHARLES F. SHAW VINEYARD AND WINERY B.W. 4930
ST. HELENA, CALIFORNIA, USA ALCOHOL 13.0% BY VOLUME

Lentils with Red Pepper Sauce

Recipe contributed by Susan Preston; Preston Vineyards and Winery, Healdsburg

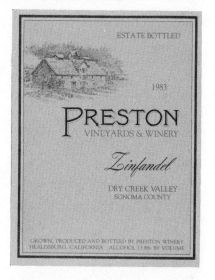

Susan Preston serves this dish hot in the winter and cool in the summer. It is an excellent luncheon dish, or can be served hot as an accompaniment to broiled meats.

¾ cup lentils, rinsed (use orange lentils if available)

3 cups water

1 teaspoon salt

1 teaspoon cumin seeds

few grinds of black pepper

2 bay leaves, crumbled

SAUCE

2 tablespoons olive oil

1 clove garlic, minced

2 red bell peppers, skinned and chopped

¼ cup chopped parsley

3 green onions, chopped

1 tablespoon chopped cilantro

In a medium-sized saucepan combine the lentils with the water, salt and herbs. Bring to a boil and cook, covered, over medium heat 15 to 25 minutes. Keep testing for doneness. In the meantime prepare the sauce.

Heat olive oil in a medium-sized skillet and sauté garlic until soft, but not browned. Add chopped red peppers and cook on low heat for ½ hour. Near end of cooking time add the rest of the ingredients and continue cooking over low heat for 5 minutes to combine ingredients. Pour sauce over lentils and mix to combine.

For summer serving as a salad add 2 to 3 tablespoons of vinaigrette to the red pepper sauce and serve at room temperature.

· DESSERTS ·

Champagne Sorbet

Makes 2 quarts

Recipe contributed by Robin Gainey; The Gainey Vineyard, Santa Ynez

Robin Gainey likes to serve this refreshing sorbet at the end of a meal on a hot summer's evening.

- 7 oranges
- 2 tablespoons superfine sugar
- 3 tablespoons water
- 1 bottle dry champagne

- juice of 1½ lemons
- 2 tablespoons Curaçao liqueur
- 3 pieces candied Clementines (candied orange peel) finely chopped

Peel the zest of 1 orange and mince. Cook the zest in 2 tablespoons sugar and 3 tablespoons water until zest is tender, being careful not to brown the mixture. Squeeze all the oranges and strain the juice. Mix juice with all the ingredients, including zest mixture. Taste, adding more sugar if desired. Freeze in an ice cream freezer and serve in chilled liqueur or champagne glasses.

Serve with Johannisberg Riesling

Ice Cream Pecan Balls with Fudge Sauce

Serves 8

Recipe contributed by Lucy Shaw; Charles Shaw Vineyard and Winery, St. Helena

This fabulous dessert is a special treat for dinner guests at the Shaw house. The rich sauce is perfect with the pecans and ice cream.

- rich vanilla ice cream (enough for 8 generous servings)
- 3 cups pecans, broken
- fresh raspberries
- mint leaves

FUDGE SAUCE

- ½ cup sugar
- 1 beaten egg yolk
- 6 tablespoons heavy cream
- 2 oz. unsweetened chocolate
- ½ teaspoon vanilla extract
- ½ teaspoon almond extract

Serve with Gamay Blanc or coffee

Roll 8 scoops of ice cream in pecans, covering completely. Freeze on a cookie sheet until ready to use. To make fudge sauce, place all ingredients in the top of a double boiler and cook over hot water until thick.

To serve, place an ice cream ball on each plate, ladle on fudge sauce, and place a mint leaf and a few raspberries on top.

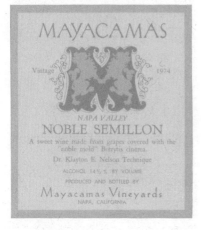

Kumquat-Ginger Mousse

Serves 12

Recipe contributed by Elinor Travers; Mayacamas Vineyards, Napa

Elinor Travers serves this dessert at special occasion dinners. The tartness of the kumquats are a good balance for the slight sharpness of the ginger.

9 eggs, separated

1 cup sugar

2 tablespoons gelatin

¼ cup cold water

4½ oz. orange juice concentrate

1 oz. brandy

4 cups whipping cream

¾ cup fresh kumquats, finely chopped

½ cup crystallized ginger, finely chopped

3 dozen lady fingers

In a large bowl, cream egg yolks and sugar. Dissolve gelatin in water and melt over hot water. In a small saucepan, warm the orange juice and brandy. Mix in melted gelatin and cool to room temperature. Slowly add to egg yolk mixture. Beat egg whites until soft peaks form and gently fold into egg yolk mixture. Whip 1 cup of cream and fold it in. When partially set, add kumquats and ginger.

Grease a spring form pan. Line bottom and sides with lady fingers. Whip the remaining cream. Pour ½ the egg yolk-orange mixture into the pan, then ½ the whipped cream. Add a layer of lady fingers. Top with remaining whipped cream, and finally the remaining egg yolk mixture. Refrigerate overnight. To serve, remove sides of spring form pan. Decorate top with additional crystallized ginger and whipped cream, if desired.

Gewurztraminer Crème

Serves 8

Recipe contributed by Joan Ellis; Mark West Vineyards, Forestville.

This dessert is excellent with summer fruits. Joan Ellis says that it can also be used to make a trifle or as a topping for chocolate squares. Make it a day ahead for best results.

8 egg yolks

½ cup sugar

¾ cup Gewurztraminer

¼ cup Grand Marnier, Cointreau or Triple Sec

1 cup whipping cream

In the top of a double boiler combine egg yolks, sugar, wine and liqueur of your choice. Set over boiling water and whisk continuously for about 5 minutes, or until it has thickened. Remove from heat and whisk occasionally until cool. Cover and refrigerate overnight.

To serve, fold in 1 cup stiffly beaten whipping cream. Pour into a serving bowl and serve with whole strawberries or other fresh berries in season.

Crème Chardonnay

Serves 6

Recipe contributed by Carolyn Goss; Chamisal Vineyard, San Luis Obispo

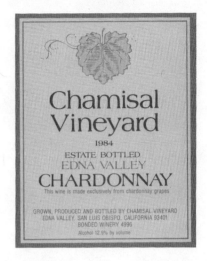

Serve with Chardonnay

Carolyn Goss serves this pretty fluffy pink dessert with cookies or a slice of plain pound cake.

1½ cups Chardonnay

3 oz. cream cheese

½ cup whipping cream

2½ cups powdered sugar

2 cups fresh strawberries, sliced thin

¼ teaspoon vanilla

pinch of salt

fresh mint leaves

In a small saucepan bring Chardonnay to a boil and continue boiling until reduced to ¾ cup. Cool completely. Place Chardonnay, and all remaining ingredients except mint leaves in a blender or food processor and blend at low speed until thoroughly mixed. Refrigerate 1 hour or longer. Serve in parfait glasses, garnished with a sprig of mint.

Baked Apples

Serves 6

Recipe contributed by Johanna Rafanelli; A. Rafanelli Winery, Healdsburg

Serve with Gamay Beaujolais

This is a simple fall dessert. It can be baked in the same oven along with another dish.

6 medium-sized apples — Golden Delicious or whatever is in season

⅓ cup raisins

2 tablespoons sugar

1 teaspoon cinnamon

1 cup Gamay Beaujolais

Core the apples. Mix together raisins, sugar and cinnamon and fill the apples with the mixture. Place in a baking dish and pour Gamay Beaujolais over the apples. Bake in preheated 350° oven for 1 hour, or until tender.

Zabaglione di Andrea

Serves 1

Recipe contributed by Robert Pecota; Robert Pecota Winery, Calistoga

Serve with Muscato di Andrea

Robert Pecota says this recipe was invented at one of his favorite restaurants one day when the owner was making zabaglione with Marsala wine. Robert suggested he use Muscato di Andrea instead, and a new dessert was born. Muscato di Andrea (and now the dessert) are named after Robert's daughter.

2 egg yolks

½ teaspoon sugar

1 oz. Muscato di Andrea

Place all ingredients in a copper bowl or double boiler. Beat with a whisk over heat, or mix with electric hand mixer over boiling water. Keep beating until mixture is thick and creamy, but not so thick that it holds peaks. Pour over fresh fruit — pineapple, banana, kiwi, sliced peaches.

Author's note: This recipe can be doubled, tripled or quadrupled. Simply adjust the quantities accordingly.

Serve with Merlot

Bing Cherries Stag's Leap

Serves 6

Recipe contributed by Barbara Winiarski; Stag's Leap Wine Cellars, Napa

Many of Barbara Winiarski's menus are made up as she grocery shops. Especially fresh seasonal items may suggest a method of serving or cooking. This recipe for Bing Cherries was inspired by the beautiful cherries at the market, and also by the fact that she had already planned to serve fish and white wine. She had no way to showcase Stag's Leap's red wines except with dessert. Thus the following recipe.

½ cup sugar

1 stick cinnamon

1 strip lemon zest

dash of Triple Sec

1¼ cups Merlot

3 cups Bing Cherries, pitted and halved

crème fraîche or whipped cream

Place sugar, cinnamon, lemon zest and Merlot in a medium-sized saucepan. Bring to a boil and simmer for 20 minutes. Cool. One-half hour before serving, stir in the cherries and steep. Serve in stemmed glasses with layers of crème fraîche or lightly whipped cream.

Serve with Crement Champagne

Filbert Roll with Ginger Cream

Serves 6 to 8

Recipe contributed by Jamie Davis; Schramsberg Vineyards and Cellars, Calistoga

This is Jamie Davis's variation of the classic dessert roll. The filbert and ginger combination complements the delicate sweetness of the Crement Champagne.

7 eggs, separated

¾ cup sugar

1½ cups toasted finely ground filberts

1 teaspoon baking powder

¼ teaspoon vanilla

2 cups whipping cream

3 tablespoons finely chopped preserved ginger

confectioners' sugar

Line a jelly roll pan (about 11 × 16 × ½ inch) with wax paper. Lightly oil paper. Beat egg yolks with ¾ cup sugar until mixture forms ribbons and is pale in color. Beat egg whites until stiff but not dry. Add ground nuts, baking powder and vanilla to yolks and blend. Fold in egg whites. Spread batter evenly in pan. Bake about 10 minutes, or until cake springs back when lightly pressed. Cool 2 to 3 minutes and turn cake onto slightly damp tea towel. Using towel to help, roll cake carefully, starting at long side.

At serving time, whip the cream until stiff and fold in the ginger. Unroll cake and spread on cream. Gently roll back. Dust with confectioners' sugar.

Strawberries 'n' Chocolate Cream

Serves 6 to 8

Recipe contributed by Marta Johnson; Johnson Turnbull Vineyards, Oakville

Marta Johnson likes to serve this simple-to-prepare dessert after a heavy meal. It is light and refreshing.

1 quart strawberries
¼ cup superfine sugar
1 cup whipping cream

⅓ cup grated semi-sweet
  chocolate
1 tablespoon strawberry liqueur

Slice strawberries into a bowl and sprinkle with sugar. Stir gently to mix. Place in refrigerator for 1 hour or more. Just before serving, whip cream until stiff and fold in the chocolate. Gently blend in the liqueur. Place strawberries in individual serving bowls and spoon cream over the berries.

Author's note: For a variation, use raspberries and raspberry liqueur.

Serve with Cabernet Sauvignon

1982

JOHNSON
TURNBULL
Cabernet
Sauvignon
Napa Valley

Estate bottled
Johnson Turnbull Vineyards
Oakville, California
ALCOHOL 12.5% BY VOLUME

Pears á la Hidden Cellars

Serves 6

Recipe contributed by Toni Klein; Hidden Cellars Winery, Ukiah

Although the sauce has to be prepared at the last minute, the end result is well worth the effort. The pears themselves can be prepared days in advance.

Serve with Late Harvest Johannisberg Riesling

POACHED PEARS

1 cup water
1 cup Johannisberg Riesling
2 tablespoons sugar
¼ teaspoon almond extract
3 to 4 medium pears, peeled,
  cored and sliced

ZABAGLIONE SAUCE

6 egg yolks
6 tablespoons sugar
½ cup Late Harvest Johannisberg
  Riesling
sliced toasted almonds for garnish

In a saucepan combine water, wine, 2 tablespoons sugar and almond extract. Cook over medium heat until sugar dissolves. Add pears and simmer 10 minutes, or until pears are tender. Remove from heat and cool pears in the liquid. Refrigerate pears in poaching liquid, covered, overnight or up to 3 days.

To make the sauce, put egg yolks in a ceramic bowl or stainless steel double boiler top. Beat or whisk egg yolks until frothy. Continuing to beat, add sugar, 1 tablespoon at a time, then gradually add the wine. Place the container over hot but not boiling water and continue to beat until thickened, about 5 to 8 minutes. Do not let the mixture boil or the eggs will curdle.

To serve, drain pear slices and arrange in parfait glasses. Pour warm sauce over the pears and garnish with toasted almond slices.

Chocolate Mousse

Serves 4

Recipe contributed by Mary Caparone; Caparone Winery, Paso Robles

This chocolate mousse is light and fluffy since beaten egg whites are included in the ingredients.

6 oz. chocolate chips

1 cup heavy cream, scalded and cooled to room temperature

2 eggs, separated

1 tablespoon chocolate- or orange-flavored liqueur

Place chocolate chips in double boiler over hot water and melt chocolate. Remove from heat and beat in 1 egg yolk at a time. Add liqueur and scalded cream. Blend well. Whip egg whites until stiff peaks form. Gently fold egg whites into chocolate mixture. Pour into individual *pots-de-crème* and chill in refrigerator for at least 4 hours.

Pashka with Raspberry Sauce

Serves 8

Recipe contributed by Shirley Sobon; Shenandoah Vineyards, Plymouth

This is Shirley Sobon's version of an old Russian dessert that is traditionally served at Easter time. In Russia, the pashka was also decorated with chopped pistachio nuts.

PASHKA

¾ cups dates or dried apricots, cut in small pieces

½ cup Black Muscat

12 oz. cream cheese, room temperature

⅔ cup sifted powdered sugar

1 teaspoon vanilla

½ teaspoon almond extract

1½ cups unsalted butter, room temperature

⅔ cup sour cream

whipped cream

RASPBERRY SAUCE

1 10-oz. pkg. frozen raspberries, thawed

½ cup superfine sugar

2 tablespoons reserved marinade from dates

1 tablespoon lemon juice

Place dates or apricots in a small bowl and cover with Black Muscat. Let stand at room temperature for several hours.

Lightly oil an 8-inch spring form pan. Combine cream cheese, powdered sugar, vanilla and almond extract in small bowl of electric mixer or food processor and blend well. Add butter, 1 stick at a time, beating constantly until smooth. Beat in sour cream. Drain dates well, reserving 2 tablespoons of marinade. Fold dates into cream cheese mixture. Turn into pan and smooth top. Chill until firm, several hours or overnight.

To make sauce, purée raspberries in blender or food processor. Strain through a fine sieve to remove seeds, if desired. Add sugar, marinade and lemon juice. Refrigerate until ready to use.

To serve, remove sides of spring form pan. Slice pashka into thin wedges. Serve with raspberry sauce and a dollop of whipped cream.

Chocolate Raspberry Trifle

Serves 8 to 10

Recipe contributed by Shirley Sobon; Shenandoah Vineyards, Plymouth

Serve with Zinfandel or Black Muscat

It takes a little work to prepare this extra-fancy dessert. The trick is to have everything ready and on hand before putting it together. Make the custard filling last.

1 3-layer sponge cake (see page 365)

crème de cacao

Black Muscat

1 quart raspberries

⅔ cup heavy cream, whipped stiff

2 cups raspberry jam

CUSTARD

2 boxes French vanilla instant pudding

2 cups sour cream

2 cups half-and-half

HOT FUDGE SAUCE

5 tablespoons unsalted butter

¼ cup cocoa

2 squares unsweetened chocolate

½ cup evaporated milk

¾ cup granulated sugar

1 teaspoon vanilla

Make the fudge sauce. In a small saucepan, melt butter. Remove from heat, add cocoa and whisk until smooth. Stir in chocolate, sugar and evaporated milk. Bring to a boil over medium heat, stirring constantly. Remove from heat and cool briefly. Add vanilla.

To make the custard, mix all ingredients together.

Place one sponge cake layer in the bottom of a clear glass bowl. Drizzle crème de cacao and Black Muscat over the cake. Spread a layer of raspberry jam over the cake and ⅓ of the fudge sauce. Add another layer of cake; drizzle it with liqueur and wine. Top with half the raspberries and half the custard. Add the last layer of cake, drizzle with liqueur and wine, raspberry jam, remaining custard, remaining raspberries, and remaining fudge sauce. Top with whipped cream.

Serve with Late Harvest Gewürztraminer

Holiday Persimmon Pudding

Serves 8

Recipe contributed by Mieke Costello; Costello Vineyards, Napa

If persimmons are not ripe, Mieke Costello suggests placing the fruit in the freezer overnight or longer. Thaw at room temperature and use.

1 cup sugar	½ cup milk
1 cup flour	juice of ½ lemon
2 teaspoons baking soda	1 teaspoon vanilla
½ teaspoon cinnamon	1 tablespoon melted butter
1 teaspoon salt	1 cup dates or raisins (or both mixed)
1 cup very ripe persimmons, mashed	1 cup walnuts, chopped

Mix dry ingredients, except dates and nuts. In another bowl, place mashed persimmons and add milk, lemon juice and vanilla, and mix. Combine the two mixtures. When well blended add the butter, dates and nuts. Mix to distribute, but do not overmix. Pour batter into a buttered 8 × 8 × 2-inch cake pan. Bake in preheated 325° oven 50 to 60 minutes, or until toothpick inserted in center comes out clean. The edges should be rather crusty. If desired, serve with sweetened whipped cream to which some vanilla extract has been added.

Serve with Chardonnay or French roasted coffee

Russian Cheesecake

Serves 8

Recipe created by Students of the San Francisco Culinary Academy for Landmark Vineyards, Windsor

This dessert was the finale of the October, 1985 luncheon created by students Nancy Thorne, Paul Weakland, Larry Bhe and Jan-Marz Baker for Landmark Vineyards. This cheesecake is made in flower pots. Small pots can be used for individual servings or larger pots can be used and cheesecake sliced into smaller pieces. Serve with any fruit sauce and fresh fruit of the season. At the October luncheon, a pumpkin sauce and fresh figs were served.

2 lbs. cream cheese	1½ teaspoons vanilla
1 lb. unsalted butter	¾ cup chopped unsalted pistachios
3 egg yolks	¾ cup mixed chopped dried apricots and dried pears.
1½ cups powdered sugar	

Cream together the cream cheese and butter. Slowly mix in egg yolks. Mix in powdered sugar, blending well. Fold in vanilla, nuts and fruit, mixing evenly. Line ceramic flower pots with cheesecloth. Fold mixture into pots. Refrigerate overnight (or longer). Decorate after unmolding and slicing. Serve with a fruit sauce and fresh fruit of the season.

Author's note: A strawberry or raspberry sauce may be prepared with jam or fruit pulp (strained of seeds) and diluted with syrup and flavored liqueurs.

Cacci Nanza Bread

Makes 3 loaves   *Serve with Fumé Blanc*

Recipe contributed by Gloria Piconi; John Piconi Winery, Temecula

Gloria Piconi learned to make bread from her mother-in-law who is of Italian origin and was a professional caterer. Serve Cacci Nanza with cheese and a glass of Fumé Blanc for dessert. The bread is fairly flat and the dough can be used for pizza (see below).

3 cups lukewarm water

1½ pkgs. yeast

3 teaspoons salt

3 tablespoons sugar

1 tablespoon olive oil

4 to 6 cups flour (may be ⅓ whole wheat and ⅔ unbleached)

olive oil

salt

rosemary

3 garlic cloves, halved

In a large mixing bowl combine water, yeast, salt sugar and 1 tablespoon olive oil. Gradually add flour to make a smooth dough. Turn dough onto floured board and knead 15 minutes, or until dough is smooth and elastic. Place in a large greased bowl, cover with a dampened cloth and let rise in a warm place until double in size, about 1½ hours.

Punch down dough and place on floured board. Divide into 3 parts. Oil 3 flat cake pans and lightly pat each dough ball into the pans. With fingers, make light indentations in the dough about 1 inch apart. Brush with additional olive oil and lightly sprinkle with salt and dried rosemary. Cover lightly (make a tent so as not to let cloth touch the dough) and let rise 45 minutes. Bake in preheated 375° oven 40 minutes, or until brown. After 30 minutes of baking and when bread is lightly browned, remove from oven and quickly rub cut garlic clove across the top of the bread. Garlic will melt into bread. Finish baking. Serve warm or cold with cheese for dessert.

For pizza dough: Use 4 cups of water and proceed as above through first rising. Divide dough into 3 balls and pat each onto an oiled pizza pan. No second rising needed — proceed with pizza toppings. (See Gloria's Pizza, page 333.)

CAKES & PASTRY

Serve with Muscat Canelli

Devlin Wine Cellars
1984 Central Coast
Muscat Canelli

Devlin Apple Pie

Serves 6 to 8

Recipe contributed by Cheryl Devlin; Devlin Wine Cellars, Soquel

Cheryl Devlin's apple pie is very juicy and flavorful. Prebaking the bottom crust prevents it from becoming soggy.

Pastry for 2-crust 9-inch pie	**1 tablespoon tapioca**
5 large Pippin apples, peeled and cored	**1 teaspoon vanilla extract**
½ cup water	**½ cup Chardonnay**
½ cup sugar	**sugar**
	cinnamon

Roll out half of pastry dough. Line a 9-inch pie pan with the dough. Prick dough with fork, then line it with buttered foil weighted with dry beans to keep it flat. Bake in preheated 400° oven for about 10 minutes. Remove foil and bean; let cool.

Cut apples into eighths. In saucepan combine water, sugar, tapioca, vanilla and Chardonnay. Add apples, bring to a boil and then cook gently for about 10 minutes until apples are almost tender. Turn apple mixture into baked pie shell.

Roll out remainder of pastry. Cut into ½-inch wide strips. Arrange lattice over the top and seal edges. Sprinkle with sugar and cinnamon. Bake in preheated 350° oven for 15 minutes or until lattice is brown.

Serve with Late Harvest Sauvignon Blanc

1985
SONOMA COUNTY
SAUVIGNON BLANC LATE HARVEST
Produced and Bottled by
ROBERT STEMMLER WINERY
HEALDSBURG, CALIFORNIA
Alcohol 11.0% by Volume
Residual Sugar: 9.7g/100ml

Sauvignon Blanc Lemon Pie

Serves 6

Recipe contributed by Robert Stemmler; Robert Stemmler Winery, Healdsburg

This is lemon pie with a twist. The technique uses the entire lemon and the Sauvignon Blanc softens the lemon flavor.

1 unbaked 9-inch pie shell	**½ cup Sauvignon Blanc**
6 lemons	**⅞ cup butter or margarine, room temperature**
1¼ cups sugar	
5 whole eggs	

Using pie weights, or pie beans, on wax paper to keep the bottom of the pie flat. Bake pie shell in preheated 400° oven for 10 minutes.

Slice lemons and remove the seeds. Place the slices in a food processor and chop to a pulp. Pour the chopped lemons into a mixing bowl. Add sugar, eggs, wine and the softened butter. Beat well to combine. Pour the lemon filling into the pie crust and bake in a preheated 300 degree oven for 40 minutes. The filling should be nicely browned when done and a knife inserted in the center should come out clean. Remove from oven and allow to cool before serving. Serve the pie cold and garnish with whipped cream if desired.

Apricot Almond Tart

Serves 6

Recipe created by Jim Stacy of Tarts Bakery, San Francisco for Quady Winery, Madera

Serve with Essensia (Orange Muscat dessert wine)

This apricot almond tart is simple to prepare and is excellent served in combination with Andrew Quady's Essensia dessert wine.

¾ cup apricot preserves	¼ teaspoon almond extract
4 oz. unsalted butter, softened	1 tablespoon lemon juice
3/8 cup sugar	1 tablespoon dark rum
2 eggs	¼ teaspoon grated lemon rind
1 cup blanched almonds, ground	1 baked 8-inch tart shell

Heat apricot preserves to melt. Cool. Cream butter and sugar. Beat in eggs. Fold in remaining ingredients. Glaze the tart shell with the melted preserves. Pour the filling on top. Bake in a preheated 375° oven until set, 30 to 35 minutes. Cool tart and brush with melted apricot preserves.

Author's note: For tart shell recipe, see Almond Tart, page 362 or Butter Tarts page 363.

Coconut Cream Pie

Serves 6

Recipe contributed by Susan Boeger, Boeger Winery, Placerville

This recipe came from Susan Boeger's grandmother, Grace McGinnis, who supported herself and four children by selling pies.

Serve with White Cabernet Sauvignon

3 egg yolks	1 cup shredded coconut
½ cup sugar	1 9-inch baked pie shell
2 tablespoons cornstarch	3 egg whites
2 cups milk	¼ teaspoon cream of tartar
⅛ teaspoon salt	6 tablespoons sugar
1 teaspoon vanilla	

Beat egg yolks. Then add the ½ cup sugar mixed with the cornstarch. Stir in milk and salt. Cook in saucepan, over medium heat, stirring constantly, until thick and smooth. Remove from heat, stir in vanilla and ¾ cup shredded coconut. Pour into pie shell.

Beat egg whites with cream of tartar until foamy. Beat in the 6 tablespoons of sugar, a little at a time, beating well after each addition. Beat until stiff and glossy. Spoon meringue over hot pie filling, being careful to seal the edges of crust. Sprinkle with remaining shredded coconut. Bake in preheated 350° oven for 12 to 15 minutes until lightly browned.

Variation: Top with bananas, fresh berries, or strawberries in a light glaze and garnish with whipped cream. In that case omit the meringue.

Rich Nectarine Tart

Serves 6 to 8

Recipe contributed by Alan Steen; Whitehall Lane Winery, St. Helena

This tart has a light baked cream cheese base topped with fresh nectarines. Alan Steen loves to cook and experiment with food and wine. This recipe uses some traditional cheesecake methods and pairs nicely with Late Harvest Johannisberg Riesling.

PASTRY DOUGH

- 1¼ cups all-purpose flour
- 6 tablespoons cold unsalted butter, cut into pieces
- 2 tablespoons cold vegetable shortening
- ¼ teaspoon salt
- 3 tablespoons ice water

FILLING

- 12 oz. cream cheese, softened
- ½ cup sugar
- 2 large eggs
- ¼ teaspoon freshly grated nutmeg
- 6 nectarines, blanched, peeled and sliced thin
- 3 tablespoons apricot preserves
- 1 tablespoon Late Harvest Johannisberg Riesling
- 1 teaspoon fresh lemon juice

In a large bowl with pastry cutter blend flour, butter, shortening and salt until the mixture resembles cornmeal. Add 3 tablespoons ice water, tossing mixture until the water is incorporated. Form into a ball and knead dough lightly against a smooth surface for about 1 minute. Reform into a ball, wrap in wax paper and chill for 1 hour.

Roll dough into a round ⅛ inch thick on a lightly floured surface, fit into a 10-inch ceramic quiche pan, and trim edge. Prick shell with fork and chill 30 minutes. Line shell with wax paper and pie weights or rice. Bake in lower third of preheated 425° oven for 15 minutes. Remove paper and weights. Bake shell 10 minutes more or until golden brown. Cool.

Make filling. In a bowl beat together the cream cheese and sugar; add the eggs one at a time and the nutmeg, beating the mixture until just smooth. Pour filling into the cooled shell and bake in middle of a preheated 350° oven for 30 minutes. Let tart cool on rack.

Arrange nectarine slices overlapping, in concentric circles on the tart. In a small saucepan melt preserves with the wine and lemon juice. Force the mixture through a fine sieve. Brush nectarines with the glaze. Chill tart for at least 1 hour.

Chocolate Chestnut Cake

Serves 6 to 8

Recipe contributed by Margaret Clark; Guenoc Winery, Middletown

This cake is light and delicate and brings out the flavor components of Petite Sirah.

8 oz. semi-sweet chocolate, chopped

¼ cup butter, room temperature

1 8¾-oz. can Crème de Marons (chestnut paste)

⅓ cup cream, room temperature

⅓ cup sugar

¼ cup brandy

3 eggs, slightly beaten

2 tablespoons flour

Grease sides of an 8-inch round cake pan and cover bottom of pan with a circle of parchment or wax paper.

Melt chocolate very slowly over hot water, stirring occasionally. With electric mixer, beat together butter, chestnut purée and cream. When chocolate is melted and cooled lukewarm to the touch, add it slowly to the chestnut mixture, blending well. Add sugar and brandy to mixture. Last stir in eggs and flour. As soon as mixture is blended well, pour into prepared pan and bake in preheated 325° oven until just set in the center, about 45 to 50 minutes. Cool completely in pan.

When ready to serve, turn out carefully onto a plate and peel off paper. Serve topped with a chocolate sauce (if you dare!). Decorate with candied violets.

Lillie's Baking Powder Bundt

Serves 12

Recipe contributed by Deborah Cahn; Navarro Vineyards, Philo

This recipe is Deborah Cahn's favorite to serve with a sweeter wine for dessert. The cake was originally made by her grandmother. "It is simple but elegant and does not compete with the complex flavors of a Late Harvest Riesling," says Deborah.

1 cup butter

2 cups sugar

4 eggs

1 teaspoon vanilla

3 cups flour

3 teaspoons baking powder

1 cup milk

1 cup walnuts or pecans, chopped

Grease and flour the bottom of a Bundt pan.

Cream butter and sugar. Add whole eggs, one at a time, and beat well after each addition. Add vanilla. Combine flour and baking powder. Then add flour and milk alternately, starting and ending with flour. Beat well after each addition. Then fold in the nuts. Bake 50 to 60 minutes in preheated 375° oven.

Author's note: This cake is also a good accompaniment to fresh fruit.

Rolling Hills Vineyards
1983
Santa Maria Valley
Chardonnay

PRODUCED AND BOTTLED BY ROLLING HILLS VINEYARDS,
CAMARILLO, CA BW-CA-5040 ALCOHOL 13.5% BY VOLUME

Kahlua Chocolate Pie

Serves 6 to 8

Recipe contributed by Eve Pagor; Rolling Hills Vineyards, Camarillo

Eve Pagor's Kahlua Pie is easy to prepare and provides a cool chocolate-vanilla dessert.

1 pint vanilla ice cream
½ pint whipping cream
⅓ cup Kahlua

1 chocolate cookie crumb pie shell
6 oz. mini chocolate chips
1 oz. unsweetened chocolate

Soften ice cream in a bowl. Whip whipping cream in a medium-sized bowl. Add softened ice cream and Kahlua to whipped cream. Pour ½ of the mixture into the prebaked pie shell. Spread mini chocolate chips over the ice cream mixture. Pour rest of cream on top. Garnish with shaved curls made from unsweetened chocolate. Put in freezer until just about ready to serve. Ten minutes before serving remove from freezer for easier cutting.

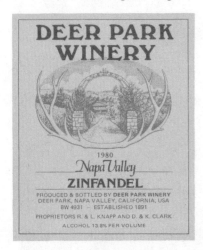

DEER PARK WINERY

1980
Napa Valley
ZINFANDEL

PRODUCED & BOTTLED BY DEER PARK WINERY
DEER PARK, NAPA VALLEY, CALIFORNIA, USA
BW 4931 – ESTABLISHED 1891
PROPRIETORS R. & L. KNAPP AND D. & K. CLARK
ALCOHOL 13.8% PER VOLUME

Almond Tart

Serves 8

Recipe contributed by Kinta Clark; Deer Park Winery, Deer Park

Kinta Clark's easy dessert may be made a day in advance. However, she recommends that the whipped cream and the shaved chocolate be put on top shortly before serving.

TART SHELL

1 cup flour
1 tablespoon sugar
½ cup very cold butter, cut into pieces
1 tablespoon water
1 tablespoon vanilla

FILLING

¾ cup sugar
½ cup heavy cream
1 teaspoon finely grated orange peel
1 teaspoon vanilla
¼ teaspoon almond extract
1 cup sliced almonds
whipped cream
shaved chocolate for topping

Place flour, sugar, butter, water and vanilla in food processor bowl. Process by pulsing on and off until mixture forms a ball. Press into a 9-inch tart pan, being careful not to have any holes. Chill. Line tart shell with aluminum foil and fill with pie weights, rice or beans. Bake on lowest shelf in preheated 400° oven for 8 minutes. Remove weights and foil and bake 3 to 4 minutes or until pastry is set. Cool.

Combine sugar, cream, orange peel, vanilla and almond extract. Stir in almonds. Let stand for 15 minutes. Pour into cooled pir shell. Bake in the middle of a preheated 400° oven for 25 to 30 minutes, or until golden. Cool. Before serving top with whipped cream and cover entire top with shaved chocolate.

Butter Tarts

Serves 6

*Serve with Late Harvest
Johannisberg Riesling*

Recipe contributed by Audrey Cilurzo; Cilurzo Vineyard and Winery, Temecula

This is an old Canadian recipe which Audrey Cilurzo learned to make when she was growing up in British Columbia.

TART PASTRY	BUTTER FILLING
1½ cups sifted flour	½ cup butter
1 teaspoon salt	½ cup brown sugar
¼ cup shortening	1 egg beaten
¼ cup butter	½ cup currants
3 to 4 tablespoons cold water	2 tablespoons cream
	1 teaspoon vanilla extract

To make the pastry, mix flour and salt in a medium-sized bowl. With a pastry cutter cut in the shortening and butter until the particles are the size of small peas. Sprinkle the water over the mixture 1 tablespoon at a time and mix with a fork until the dough starts to form a ball. Finishing shaping by hand. Roll dough out into 6 circles to fit individual tart pans. Place in pans, fluting the edges.

Make the filling. Melt butter and put in a medium-sized bowl. Add brown sugar and mix well. Mix in the beaten egg. Add currants, cream and vanilla and blend well. Pour into tart shells. Bake in preheated 350° oven for about 20 minutes or until brown.

Goat Cheese-Blackberry Tart

Serves 6

Serve with Nebbiolo

Recipe contributed by Patrice Martin; Martin Brothers Winery, Paso Robles

This unusual tart is very simple to prepare. It may be made with any berry that is in season. The Nebbiolo wine made from an Italian grape little known in America is a perfect flavor complement for the cheese and berries. Serve this red wine lightly chilled to accompany the dessert.

1 8-inch baked and cooled sweet tart shell made with unsalted butter	4 to 6 cups blackberries, cleaned and dry
8 oz. fresh, unflavored goat cheese	1 tablespoon heavy cream
	2 tablespoons sugar

In a medium-sized bowl, mash the goat cheese until it is very smooth. Soften with the heavy cream and sweeten with half of the sugar. Spread evenly on the tart shell, filling it halfway. Arrange as many berries as needed to entirely cover the tart. Purée the remaining berries and force through a sieve to remove all seeds. Sweeten the puréed berries with the remaining sugar and serve on the side with the tart.

Author's note: More sugar may be needed depending on the variety and sweetness of the berries used. For a tart shell recipe, see Almond Tart, page 362.

Serve with Cabernet Sauvignon

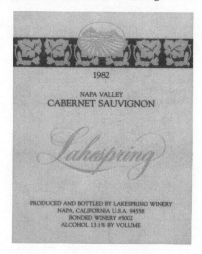

Lee's Chocolate Cake

Serves 12

Recipe contributed by Lee Battat; Lakespring Winery, Napa

Lee Battat's Chocolate Cake shows that red wine can be served with a dessert. The chocolate flavor enhances the complexities of Cabernet Sauvignon.

½ cup cocoa

½ cup butter

¾ cup boiling water

2 cups sugar

3 eggs

½ pint sour cream

½ teaspoon baking soda

2 cups cake flour

1 teaspoon vanilla extract

1 pint whipped cream

FROSTING

4 tablespoons cocoa

4 tablespoons melted butter

4 tablespoons hot milk

½ teaspoon vanilla extract

1 to 1½ cups powdered sugar

Grease sides and bottom of two 9-inch round cake pans and lightly flour the bottoms.

Mix cocoa with boiling water and allow to cool. In a medium-sized mixing bowl, cream butter and sugar until light and fluffy. Add eggs, sour cream, baking soda and the prepared chocolate mixture. Mix in the flour and the vanilla. Divide batter evenly between the two pans and bake in preheated 325° oven for 30 to 35 minutes. Cool before frosting.

To make frosting combine cocoa, butter, milk and vanilla. Add enough powdered sugar to make frosting spreadable. Put layers together with freshly whipped cream. Frost top and sides of cake.

Author's note: For an extra treat fresh raspberries, washed and drained dry, may be placed on top of whipping cream before adding top layer.

Serve with Chardonnay

Pear Tart

Serves 8

Recipe contributed by Susan Robbins; Spring Mountain Vineyards, St. Helena

This pear tart is easy to prepare. Top it with whipped cream or vanilla ice cream for extra richness.

5 ripe, unbruised pears (Comice or Bosc)

½ cup sugar

½ cup melted unsalted butter

1 tablespoon cream

pastry for a 10-inch pie

Peel and core pears. Cut in half and place in a large bowl with ¼ cup sugar.

Pour half of the melted butter into a glass pie plate or tart pan. Sprinkle on the remaining sugar. Arrange pears, cut side up on butter-sugar mixture. Cover with round of pie crust, tucking the edges down and around the edge of the pears. Cut 4 or 5 slits in pastry as vents for steam. Brush top of pastry with the cream. Bake 35 to 40 minutes in preheated 450° oven, until crust is golden. Sugar will caramelize around the pears and turn them golden.

Chocolate Sponge Cake

Serves 12

Serve with Black Muscat

Recipe contributed by Shirley Sobon; Shenandoah Vineyards, Plymouth

This cake can be baked in a 10-inch tube pan or in three 9-inch round cake pans. Use it, baked in layers, to make the Chocolate Raspberry Trifle, page 355. The cake is very light — perfect with fresh fruits such as berries or pears.

1 cup sifted all-purpose flour

⅔ cup cocoa

¼ teaspoon salt

7 eggs

2 egg yolks

1 cup sugar

1 teaspoon vanilla

3 tablespoons unsalted butter, melted

Preheat oven to 350°. Butter and flour three 9-inch cake pans or 1 10-inch tube pan.

Sift together the flour, cocoa and salt. Place eggs, extra yolks, sugar and vanilla in bowl of an electric mixer, and place in a pan of hot water over low heat. Stir until the eggs are just warm and the sugar has melted. Place bowl on the mixer and beat at medium speed for 9 minutes. The mixture should be very thick and quadruple in size. Fold the flour mixture into the eggs in 3 portions. Rapidly fold in the butter. Pour into pan(s). Bake at 350° — 30 to 40 minutes for layers, 40 to 45 minutes for tube cake. Cakes are done when a toothpick inserted in center comes out clean. Remove from oven and cool. Remove cake from pan.

Wine Cake

Serves 12

Serve with White Barbera

Recipe contributed by Bev Borra; Borra's Cellar, Lodi

Bev Borra serves this cake as dessert accompanied by fresh fruit.

1 pkg. yellow cake mix

1 pkg. lemon instant pudding

4 eggs

¾ cup oil

¾ cup cream sherry

pinch of salt

ICING

12 teaspoons cream sherry

7 tablespoons powdered sugar

Place cake mix, pudding, eggs, oil, ¾ cup sherry and the salt in a large mixing bowl. Beat at low speed for 1 minute; then at high speed until all ingredients are well blended. Pour into greased Bundt pan or 10-inch tube pan and bake in a preheated 350° oven for 45 minutes. Remove from oven and let cake sit for 5 minutes. To prepare icing, combine the 12 teaspoons of sherry with the powdered sugar. The mixture will be thin. Remove cake from pan and pour the icing mixture over the cake while the cake is still warm. If desired pierce holes in cake with a fork so icing will flow into cake.

Nagadoches Cake

Serves 12

Recipe contributed by Jane Fowler; Greenstone Winery, Ione

This is an old Texas recipe which Jane Fowler likes to serve not only with White Zinfandel, but also with Red Zinfandel or sherry.

2 cups flour	**FROSTING**
2 cups sugar	**½ cup margarine**
¼ lb. margarine	**4 tablespoons cocoa**
½ cup Crisco	**6 tablespoons milk**
4 tablespoons cocoa	**1 lb. powdered sugar**
1 cup water	**1 cup chopped nuts**
½ cup buttermilk	**½ teaspoon vanilla**
1 teaspoon baking soda	
2 eggs	

Grease a 13 × 9-inch cake pan.

Sift together the flour and sugar. In a small saucepan mix together the margarine, Crisco, cocoa and water and bring to a boil. Pour hot mixture over the sugar and flour and mix. Add the buttermilk, baking soda and eggs and mix well. Pour into prepared pan and bake in preheated 350° oven for 35 minutes.

Make frosting five minutes before cake is done. Put margarine, cocoa and milk in a saucepan and bring to a boil. Remove from heat and add powdered sugar. Beat with mixer until well blended. Then add nuts and vanilla. Spread on hot cake.

Quick Cake

Serves 8

Recipe contributed by Jonette Newlan; Newlan Vineyards and Winery, Napa

This basic recipe for this simple to prepare cake came from a relative — but adding the wine flavoring was Jonette's idea. Served with fresh fruit and Late Harvest Johannisberg Riesling it makes a most satisfying dessert.

½ cup milk	**1 cup flour**
1 tablespoon shortening	**2 teaspoons baking powder**
2 eggs	**1 tablespoon Late Harvest**
1 cup sugar	**Johannisberg Riesling**

Heat milk and shortening together. Do not boil. In a medium-sized bowl beat eggs until very light. Add sugar, alittle at a time, beating constantly. Fold in flour and baking powder. Add heated milk and shortening. Then add wine, blending well.

Pour batter into a 9-inch greased cake pan. Bake in preheated 350° oven for 25 minutes or until toothpick inserted in center comes out clean.

For a 13 × 9 × 2-inch cake double the ingredients and bake 10 minutes longer.

Orange Chiffon Cake

Serves 12 slices

Serve with Semi-Dry Chenin Blanc

Recipe contributed by Joanne Cook; R. & J. Cook, Clarksburg

Joanne Cook's speciality is desserts. She enjoys baking everything from scratch, since she was taught to do so by her mother. To Joanne that type of baking is a way of life—from biscuits and muffins to pies, cakes and cookies. No mixes of any kind are used. This cake may also be made with lemon rind and lemon juice. It will be a little more on the tart side. Joanne uses whichever fruit is ripe in her garden at the time.

CAKE

2¼ cups cake flour

1½ cups sugar

3 teaspoons baking powder

1 teaspoon salt

½ cup salad oil

12 eggs, separated

¾ cup cold water

4 tablespoons grated orange peel

¾ teaspoon cream of tartar

ORANGE FROSTING

3 cups powdered sugar, ¾ of a 1 lb. box

¾ tablespoons grated orange peel

2 tablespoons melted butter or margarine

3 tablespoons orange juice

1 teaspoon vanilla

In a medium-sized mixing bowl stir together flour, sugar, baking powder and salt. Make a "well" and add in the following order: oil, egg yolks, water and orange peel. Stir until very smooth.

In a large mixing bowl beat egg whites and cream of tartar until stiff peaks form. Gradually pour egg yolk mixture over beaten egg whites, gently folding until just blended. Pour into ungreased 10-inch tube pan. Bake in preheated 325° oven for 75 minutes or until top springs back when lightly touched. Invert tube pan and leave in that position until cake is cooled.

To make frosting, combine all frosting ingredients and beat until fluffy. Frost cake.

Author's note: If cake flour is unavailable, use 2 cups all purpose flour and sift it twice. For more flavor use ¼ cup strained orange juice and ½ cup water, instead of all water.

Apricot Bars

Makes 20

Recipe contributed by Jeanne Jensen; Calera Wine Company, Hollister

Not only are these Apricot Bars a good dessert, they also make a wonderful snack for the four Jensen children.

BOTTOM LAYER

⅓ cup softened butter

½ cup packed brown sugar

1 cup unbleached flour

TOP LAYER

1 cup dried apricots

1 teaspoon grated lemon peel

⅔ cup sugar

2 teaspoons cornstarch

½ cup chopped walnuts

Bottom Layer: In a food processor, combine sugar and butter until fluffy. Add flour and process until combined. Press dough into a lightly greased 8-inch square pan. Bake in preheated 350° oven for 10 to 12 minutes. Let cool completely.

Top layer: Place apricots in a small saucepan with enough water to cover apricots. Bring to a boil. Reduce heat and simmer covered for 15 minutes. Drain, reserving liquid. Chop apricots finely. In the saucepan, combine apricots with a half cup of reserved liquid, lemon peel, sugar and cornstarch. Bring to a boil, stirring and boil for 1 minute. Let topping cool 10 minutes. Spread evenly over bottom crust. Sprinkle with walnuts. Bake in preheated 350° oven for 20 minutes. Cool on rack. Cut into squares.

Persimmon Bread

Serves 12

Recipe contributed by Paulé Crescini; Crescini Wines, Soquel

This is an excellent way to use persimmons, a popular and plentiful fruit in California. Serve this bread with a glass of wine and some fruit as a dessert.

2 eggs

¾ cup sugar

½ cup oil

1 cup persimmon pulp (see note below)

1 teaspoon baking soda

1½ cups flour, sifted

1 teaspoon cinnamon

½ teaspoon salt

½ cup chopped walnuts

½ cup raisins, optional

Grease and flour bottom and sides of a 3×4×9-inch loaf pan.

In a medium-sized bowl, blend eggs, sugar and oil together. Mix baking soda with pulp. Add to sugar mixture, blending well. Mix together flour, cinnamon and salt. Add chopped nuts (and raisins) to dry ingredients and fold into persimmon mixture. Pour into prepared pan and bake in preheated 325° oven for about 75 minutes or until toothpick inserted in center comes out clean.

Author's note: Use only soft ripe fruit with a transparent skin. Unripe fruit has an acid taste and puckers the mouth. To get pulp, peel fruit and put through a colander, or mash, removing seeds. If not used at once, add a little lemon juice to prevent discoloration.

Orange Tea Cookies

Makes 4 dozen cookies

Recipe contributed by Richard Alexei; Monticello Cellars, Napa

Serve with Gewurztraminer

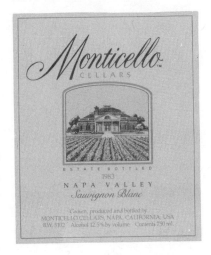

At Monticello Cellars these cookies are served with fresh fruit and a glass of wine.

1 orange	1 teaspoon vanilla
1 lemon	½ teaspoon salt
⅔ cup sugar	2 cups flour
1 cup unsalted butter, softened	1 cup finely ground walnuts
2 eggs, separated	

Remove peel from orange and lemon using a vegetable peeler and avoiding the white pith. Chop peel coarsely, then pulverize in food processor with sugar. In a medium-sized bowl with an electric mixer beat butter until light and fluffy. Add lemon-orange sugar mixture and gradually beat at high speed for several minutes. Add egg yolks, vanilla and salt and combine thoroughly. Gently fold in flour until incorporated, taking care to beat no more than necessary.

Chill dough slightly to firm it up; then roll into logs about ½ inch in diameter. Beat the egg whites until slightly frothy and paint the logs of dough with the egg whites. Roll in ground walnuts, pressing nuts into dough. Wrap logs in plastic wrap and chill thoroughly. (Can be prepared several days in advance.)

Slice logs into discs about ⅛ inch thick. Bake on lightly greased cookie sheets in a preheated 350° oven about 10 minutes or until very lightly browned.

Author's note: Since ovens vary in temperature, check cookies after 8 minutes of baking. Do not let them get too brown.

Challa (Egg Bread)

Makes 1 loaf

Recipe contributed by Deborah Cahn; Navarro Vineyards, Philo

Serve with Chardonnay

One often overlooks the beauty of serving a glass of fine wine, homemade bread and cheese for dessert. This is a favorite recipe of Deborah Cahn's for just such a treat. The recipe was given to her by a friend 15 years ago and has been in Deborah's culinary repertoire ever since.

2 teaspoons yeast	1 cup wheat germ
½ cup honey	about 6½ cups white flour
2½ cups lukewarm water	1 cup safflower oil
3 eggs, beaten (save a little egg)	2 teaspoons salt

In a large bowl, stir together the yeast, honey and water. Let stand 5 minutes. Add the eggs, wheat germ and 2½ cups flour. Beat well. Cover and let rise in a warm place until doubled in size (1 to 1½ hours).

Punch the dough down and add the oil, salt and about 4 more cups flour. Knead until smooth, cover and let rise until doubled, about 1 hour. Divide dough into 3 or 4 pieces. Roll out with hands into large ropes and braid. Place on greased baking sheet, tucking the ends under. Cover and let rise again, about 45 minutes. Brush with leftover egg. Bake in preheated 350° oven for 1 hour or until well browned.

Serve with White Riesling

Port Wine Turnovers

Makes 2 dozen

Recipe contributed by Fran Replogle; Fenestra Winery, Livermore

After a fancy dinner, Fran Replogle serves these turnovers with fruit and cheese. They are also a great "melt in the mouth" finale for a lovely picnic.

1½ cups flour

⅔ cup soft butter

1 small glass of port (amount varies)

raspberry jam

Sift the flour. With a pastry blender, work in the soft butter until the butter is the size of small peas. Then with a fork, work in the wine a tablespoon at a time until the consistency of pie pastry is reached. On a floured board roll out the dough and cut into rounds with a wine glass or round biscuit cutter. Put a spoonful of jam on one side of each round, wet edges with cold water, fold over, press closed and prick top. Place on lightly greased baking sheet and bake in preheated 350° oven until golden brown, 5 to 7 minutes. Remove from oven and roll in granulated sugar.

Author's note: These turnovers bake fast so keep an eye on them to prevent them from becoming too brown.

Serve with Johannisberg Riesling or Petite Sirah

Prune Spice Cake with Sherry Icing

Serves 12

Recipe contributed by Katrina Staten; Field Stone Winery, Healdsburg

This cake is served on special occasions at the Staten household. It is a wonderful birthday cake.

1 cup butter

1⅔ cups sugar

3 eggs

1½ cups mashed, stewed prunes

2¼ cups sifted cake flour

2¼ teaspoons soda

1½ teaspoons cinnamon

1 teaspoon ground cloves

¾ teaspoon salt

¾ cup buttermilk or sour milk

¾ cup broken walnuts

SHERRY ICING

½ cup butter, softened

1½ lbs. powdered sugar

pinch of salt

½ cup sherry (or Late Harvest Gewurztraminer)

1 tablespoon finely grated orange rind

Grease and line with wax paper 3 9-inch round cake pans.

Cream butter until fluffy, adding sugar gradually and beating until light. Add eggs one at a time, beating well after each addition. Stir in mashed prune pulp. Sift dry ingredients together and stir in alternately with the buttermilk, beginning and ending with the flour. Stir in nuts. Divide batter between the 3 pans and bake in preheated 375° oven for 25 to 30 minutes or until top springs back when lightly touched. Cool 10 minutes in the pans, then gently turn onto racks and finish cooling. Frost with Sherry Icing.

Make the icing. Cream butter and powdered sugar, plus salt, lightly. Gradually add sherry until frosting becomes of spreading consistency. Beat until very light. Spread on cake layers, top and sides. Sprinkle orange rind on top. If desired only layers and top may be frosted leaving sides bare.

Mendocino County Cookies

Makes 4 dozen cookies

Serve with French Colombard

Recipe contributed by Marguerite Frey, Frey Vineyards, Redwood Valley

Marguerite Frey leads a busy life as a physician and as a mother of 12 children. She often makes these chewy cookies because they are quick to prepare. The recipe originally came from an aunt who lives in Iowa. These cookies won first prize at the Mendocino County Fair in 1978.

1 cup butter or vegetable shortening, melted	1 teaspoon baking powder
1 cup light brown sugar	1 teaspoon baking soda
¼ cup granulated sugar	1 cup shredded coconut
2 eggs, beaten	½ cup chopped nuts or sunflower seeds
1 teaspoon vanilla	2 cups old fashioned oatmeal
2 cups flour	

In a large bowl combine the melted butter and the sugar. Beat until light and fluffy. Add eggs and vanilla and mix to combine well. Combine flour, baking powder and baking soda. Slowly add to butter mixture, mixing well. Stir in coconut, nuts and oatmeal, mixing well. Batter will be stiff.

Drop by tablespoonsful 2 to 3 inches apart on a greased baking sheet. Use the bottom of a moistened glass to flatten the cookies. Cookies should be about 4 inches in diameter. Bake in preheated 350° oven for 8 to 10 minutes, or until nicely browned.

Author's note: These cookies are large. Make them smaller, if you wish, and adjust baking time accordingly.

Bonded winery. Refers to the fact that the winery is licensed by the federal government. A bond of revenue is put up to guarantee the taxes levied on the wine. Each winery is given a number by the government.

Botrytis cinerea. Also known as the "noble rot." In the fall and under favorable weather conditions of warm weather and high humidity, a mold gathers on the skin of the grapes, but does not rot them. The skins shrink and the grapes become raisin-like. The juice becomes concentrated and high in sugar content. See Greenwood Ridge Winery, p. 22.

Brix. Scale used in the United States to determine the degree of sugar content in grapes.

Budding over. Otherwise known as grafting. In this method a vine is spliced and grafted onto a root stock of another type or varietal. Many times it is used to graft onto a disease resistant root, but may also be used to change varieties.

Cap. The mass of grape skin, pulp, seeds and sometimes stems which floats on top of fermenting grape juice. "Pushing down the cap" means mixing the cap with the fermenting juice. This method is used only for red wines in order to extract color from the skins.

Dry farmed. Vineyards growing without the use of irrigation, often on hillside property.

Fermentation. The process of converting sugar to alcohol and carbon dioxide in grape juice with the addition of yeast.

Filtering. The process of passing the wine through a filter for clarification. The filter is usually constructed of several porous layers held together as a unit in a frame.

Fining. The addition of an agent to a wine in order to remove small, suspended particles from the wine. When a fining agent, such as egg white, is added, the small particles cling to it and settle to the bottom of the barrel. After the settling, the clarified wine can then be transferred to another container. See William Wheeler Winery, p. 59.

Generic. A wine which is blended and labeled with a general category, such as red table wine, or with European geographical names such as Burgundy or Chablis.

Late harvest. Refers to wine made from grapes picked especially late in the season with a high sugar content. It also refers to grapes which have been subjected to botrytis. The latter is more common.

Lees. The residue or sediment thrown off by the wine soon after fermentation. This usually happens when the wines are aging in wooden barrels or casks. After the sediment settles to the bottom, the clear wine is siphoned off into another container. This latter process is called racking.

Maceration carbonique. Method of fermentation commonly used in the Beaujolais region of France. The process uses whole berry fermentation instead of crushing the grapes. See Creston Manor Winery, p. 167.

Malolactic fermentation. A secondary fermentation where the malic acid is converted into lactic acid through the induced action of Lactobacillus bacteria. The process helps to smooth out the harshness of wines and also stabilizes it.

Methode Champenoise. The original method of making sparkling wine (champagne) in the Champagne region of France. The second fermentation of the wine takes place in the bottle. See John Culbertson Winery, p. 186.

Must. The crushed grapes as they come out of the crusher and go into the fermentation tanks.

Phylloxera. A vine disease which is caused by a tiny underground burrowing louse that eats European rootstock. The parasite originally was a native to the eastern part of the United States. It was accidentally introduced into Europe in the 1880s and did extensive damage. Today European vines are grafted onto immune American root stock. See p. 14.

Racking. The siphoning off of wine above the settlement. This process is done several times during the aging process, particularly for red wines.

Stressed grapes. Usually grapes grown without irrigation on hillside property or in gravelly soil. The vines have to fight for life and nourishment, producing a fruit which is intense in flavor.

Sur lie. Refers to white wines which are allowed to remain in contact with the yeast and sediment in the oak barrels without racking. Usually produces a wine that is fuller in flavor.

Varietal. Term used in the United States to define a wine according to 75% of the grape variety which constitutes the wine.

Vin gris. A white or blush type of wine made from red grapes.

Index of
Wineries

Index of
Recipes

For the convenience of the reader, the appropriate wine to be served with each recipe is given and, following that, in parentheses, is the wine type (red, white, blush, dessert or champagne). Where no wine is listed, such as for a vegetable, the wine is determined by the accompanying entrée. Following is a listing of the wines types and their abbreviations:

White Wines (W)   Red Wines (R)   Dessert Wines (D)   Blush Wines (B)